Custom Textbook prepared for
DEPARTMENT OF INDUSTRIAL ENGINEERING
AND OPERATIONS RESEARCH
Columbia University

Includes Materials from:
Professor Soulaymane Kachani
for
IEOR E4003 & IEOR E4403
Columbia University

FINANCIAL ACCOUNTING: A Valuation Emphasis
Huges – Ayres – Hoskin

ADVANCED ENGINEERING ECONOMICS
Park – Sharp – Bette

and

VALUATION: Measuring and Managing the Value of Companies
McKinsey & Company – Koller – Goedhart – Wessels

This custom textbook includes materials submitted by the Author for publication by John Wiley & Sons, Inc. The material has not been edited by Wiley and the Author is solely responsible for its content.

To order books or for customer service, please call 1(800)-CALL-WILEY (225-5945).

ISBN   978-0-470-43619-6

10 9 8 7 6 5 4 3 2

Preface

New York, July 25th, 2008

This book is intended for students in my Industrial Economics (IEOR E4003) and my Advanced Engineering & Corporate Economics (IEOR E4403) courses at Columbia University.

The third edition of this custom book better covers the broad range of topics discussed in these courses using four different sources: "Financial Accounting, A Valuation Emphasis" by Hughes, Ayres and Hoskin; "Advanced Engineering Economics" by Park and Sharp-Bette; "Valuation: Measuring and Managing the Value of Companies" by McKinsey & Company, Koller, Goedhart and Wessels; and finally a subset of the lecture slides that I developed here at Columbia University, and that leverage my experience at McKinsey.

I would like to thank Alan Most at Wiley for his continued assistance in the publishing process. I would also like to thank my former students for their feedback.

Thanks to Ali Sadighian, this edition includes an improved index of important concepts and is free of many typos from the various books.

I look forward to your suggestions as, together, we continue to improve these courses and this custom book.

Sincerely,

Soulaymane Kachani
Department of Industrial Engineering & Operations Research

Table of Contents

Outline

Part I: Interpreting Financial Statements

- Lecture slides on financial analysis

- Chapters 1, 2, 3, 4, 5 and 6 of "Financial Accounting, A Valuation Emphasis" by Hughes, Ayres and Hoskin

The Big Picture

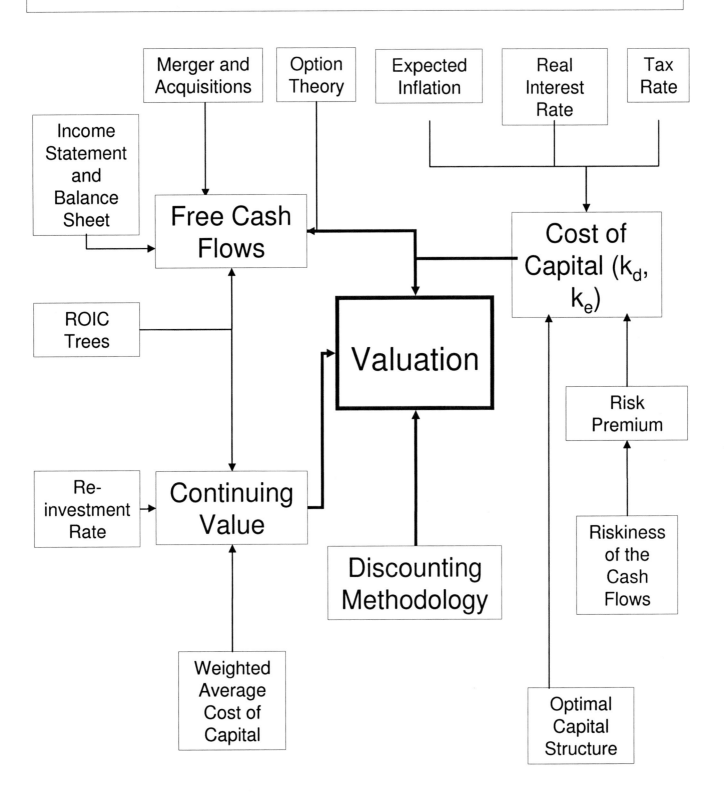

Interpreting Financial Statements

➢ **Cash Flow Cycle**

➢ **Balance Sheet**

➢ **Income Statement**

➢ **Sources and Uses Statement**

➢ **Cash Flow Statement**

➢ **Free Cash Flow**

➢ **Financial Statements and the Value Problem**

➢ **Balance Sheet Decomposition**

➢ **Sustainable Growth**

➢ **Financial Statement Footnotes**

Interpreting Financial Statements

1. Understand the difference between financial accounting (governed by generally accepted accounting principles) and management accounting (governed by the needs of a particular company)

- **GAAP: U.S.**

- **German accounting system**

- **IAS (International Accounting System)**

Interpreting Financial Statements

➢ Financial accounting:

- ✓ **Not for managerial decision making**
- ✓ **Invented by bankers in Spain some 400 years ago**
- ✓ **External accounting**

➢ Management/Cost accounting:

- ✓ **For managerial decision making (sunk cost, opportunity cost)**
- ✓ **Internal accounting**
- ✓ **Company decides cost accounting systems**
- ✓ **Management information systems**

Interpreting Financial Statements

2. The financial accounting rules differ from a country to another. We will concentrate on major principles that are similar across all countries

3. We have to understand the difference between financial reporting (straight line) and tax reporting (accelerated)

4. Purpose of doing all of this: understand how to determine expected cash flows for business units and company valuation

Interpreting Financial Statements

1. Realization principle / Accrual accounting

> When is a sales revenue recognized in accounting?

1. Order received
2. Service delivered ⌐
3. Invoice sent
4. Payment received

> Can we estimate the market value of a company from financial statements?

Interpreting Financial Statements

2. Matching principle

➤ **Cost must be recognized when we have recognized the corresponding revenue**

➤ **Problems with depreciation and future costs of guarantees**

3. Principle of prudence

➤ **Do not overestimate your profits (you are allowed to underestimate your profits)**

✓ R&D cost goes to the income statement: because you are not sure you are getting these benefits in the following years

Interpreting Financial Statements

➤ **Close interplay between company operations and finances**

➤ **Property 1:** *Financial statements are an important reflection of reality*

➤ **Property 2:** *Profits do not equal cash*

> ➤ **Financial snapshot, at a point in time, of all the assets a company owns and all the claims against these assets**

Assets = Liabilities + Shareholders' equity

Question: If a company is short in cash, can it spend some of its shareholders' equity? Why?

Interpreting Financial Statements

Assets

➤ Liquid assets

➤ Accounts receivable

➤ Inventories

➤ Net Fixed assets

➤ Other assets

Liabilities+S.E.

➤ Short term borrowing

➤ Accounts payable

➤ Net accruals

➤ Long-term debt

➤ Owners equity
  ➤ Paid-in capital
  ➤ Retained earnings

Interpreting Financial Statements

Assets

➤**Liquid assets**

- Cash, Market securities
- Belongs to shareholders
- Companies need to justify why they are holding to high levels of liquids assets

➤**Accounts receivable**

- FIFO, LIFO
- Financed by LTD

➤**Inventories**

- Financed by AP and STB

➤**Net Fixed assets**

- Financed from OE

➤**Other assets**

Intangible assets:

- Patents
- Trademarks
- Human capital
- Goodwill

Financing

➤**Short term borrowing**

➤**Accounts payable**

- Unpaid raw materials

➤**Net accruals**

- Unpaid energy bills and admin bills

➤**Long-term debt**

➤**Owners equity**

- How much owners have invested in the company
- Book value: may not include a lot of important value: e.g. trademark value (e.g. Coca Cola), human capital

➤ **Paid-in capital**

- Paid for by owner: investment

➤ **Retained earnings**

- Invested by owners instead of taking them in their pocket

Interpreting Financial Statements

➤ A record of flow of resources *over time* commonly divided into two parts:

- Operating segments

- Non-operating segments

➤ At least 5 issues associated with Earnings (Net Income) reported in an income statement:

- Accrual accounting

- Inventory methods: FIFO, LIFO, Average method

- Depreciation methods: Straight-line vs. Accelerated depreciation

- Taxes

- Research and Marketing, creation of trademarks and patents in the balance sheet

Interpreting Financial Statements

Net Sales

Gross Profit

Operating Profit

Earnings Before Interest & Taxes (EBIT)

Earnings Before Taxes (EBT)

Earnings After Taxes (EAT) or Net Income

Interpreting Financial Statements

Net Sales

- Cost of Good Sold (COGS)

Gross Profit

- Administrative & Selling Expenses (SG&A)

- Depreciation

Operating Profit

+/- Extraordinary Gain/Loss

+ Other Income

Earnings Before Interest & Taxes (EBIT)

- Interest Expenses

Earnings Before Taxes (EBT)

- Provision for Income Taxes

Earnings After Taxes (EAT) or Net Income

Interpreting Financial Statements

➤ **Answers two questions:**

- **Where does a company get its cash?**

- **How does a company spend its cash?**

➤ **Two-step approach:**

- **Place two balance sheets for different dates and note all the changes in accounts**

- **Segregate the changes in those that generate cash** *(reduce an asset or increase a liability)* **and those that consume cash** *(increase an asset account or reduce a liability account)*

Sources = Uses

➤ **Question:** *Is "Increase in cash" a source or a use of cash? Why?*

Interpreting Financial Statements

Statement of Cash Flows

> ➤ **Expands the Sources and Uses Statement, placing each source and use into 1 of 3 *(4)* categories**

- **Cash flows from operating activities**

- **Cash flows from investing activities**

- **Cash flows from financing activities**

- **Effect of exchange rate changes on cash**

Interpreting Financial Statements

Statement of Cash Flows

Net Income

Adjustment to net income:

1. + Depreciation
2. Changes in Working Capital
    1. **- Increase in Accounts receivable**
    2. **- Increase in Inventory**
    3. **+ Increase in Accounts Payable**
    4. **+ Increase in Accrued Liabilities**
3. Cash flow from investing
    1. **- Capital Expenditures**
    2. **- Increase in Other Assets**

Total Cash Flow from Operations and Investing

1. - Dividends and Stock Repurchases
2. + Increase in Short Term Debt
3. - Increase in Marketable Securities
4. + Increase in Long Term Debt

Total Cash Flow from Financing

Increase in Cash

Interpreting Financial Statements

➤ **Practically speaking, all large companies own other companies. To fully understand the impact of these ownership structures on companies' financial health, companies are required to publish consolidated financial statements. Typically, we divide the companies into three groups with respect to ownership levels:**

- **Ownership > 50% (control the other company): these companies are fully consolidated and are called subsidiaries**

- **50% ≥ Ownership ≥ 20% (include joint ventures): these companies are often called equity affiliates and they are accounted for by the equity method**

- **Ownership < 20%: these companies are treated as financial investments**

Interpreting Financial Statements

> ➤ **Fundamental determinant of the value of a business**

Free Cash Flow = **Total cash available for distribution to owners and creditors after funding all worthwhile investment activities**

= EBIT (1 –Tax rate) + Depreciation – Capital Expenditures - Increases in Working Capital

21

Interpreting Financial Statements

EBIT.(1-Tax Rate)

Adjustment to EBIT.(1- Tax Rate):

1. + Depreciation

2. Changes in Working Capital

    1. **- Increase in Accounts receivable**

    2. **- Increase in Inventory**

    3. **+ Increase in Accounts Payable**

    4. **+ Increase in Accrued Liabilities**

3. Cash flow from investing

    1. **- Capital Expenditures**

    2. **- Increase in Other Assets**

Free Cash Flow

Interpreting Financial Statements

The Value Problem

> ➢ **Issues in using accounting data for financial decision making:**

- **Market Value vs. Book Value**

  - ✓ Original costs vs. current values

    - Relevant & subjective vs. irrelevant & objective

  - ✓ Forward-looking vs. backward-looking

    - Exception: Goodwill

- **Economic Income vs. Accounting Income**

  - ✓ Realized vs. unrealized income

  - ✓ Cost of equity

Interpreting Financial Statements

➤ **This tool starts by dividing both investments and financing methods of a company into two parts**

- **Investments**

  - ✓ Investments in fixed assets

  - ✓ Investments in the operating cycle = Working Capital Requirement

- **Financing**

  - ✓ Short-term financing

  - ✓ Long-term financing

Interpreting Financial Statements

➤ **Using the four elements we identified, we can divide the balance sheet into 3 separate blocks which affect each other**

- **Net Long-term Financing (NLF)**

  - ✓ Long-term Financing – Fixed Assets

  - ✓ Should be positive (cushion)

  - ✓ Bigger NLF: more conservative financing strategy (low risk) but more expensive

- **Working Capital Requirement (WCR)**

  - ✓ Accounts Receivable + Inventories – Accounts Payable – Net Accruals

  - ✓ Money needed to run the company day to day

- **Net Short-term Borrowing (NSB)**

  - ✓ Short-term Financing – Liquid Assets

$$WCR = NLF + NSB$$

Interpreting Financial Statements

Balance Sheet Structure

Liquid Assets

Short-term Financing

NSB

Receivables

Inventories

Payables

Net Accruals

WCR

Fixed Assets

Long-term Financing

NLF

Interpreting Financial Statements

Concept of
Sustainable Growth

➢ **What is the maximum growth rate, if no external financing sources exist?**

➢ **More precisely, sustainable growth computes the maximum growth rate a company can sustain without financial difficulties assuming that:**

- **The company cannot raise new equity financing**

  ✓ Most applicable to small and medium size companies as well as government-owned companies

- **The company (or the banker) does not want to increase the financial risk of the company**

  ✓ D/E ratio is constant

- **The operational efficiency of the company is constant**

  ✓ Sales/Assets ratio is constant

Interpreting Financial Statements

➤ **Financial statements are not complete without footnotes which typically explain at least 3 different types of information**

- **Explanations how the company has interpreted different financial accounting principles**

- **More detailed information of income statement and balance sheet numbers**

- **Off-balance sheet items which do not show up in the balance sheet such as:**
  - ✓ Operating leases
  - ✓ Pending lawsuits
  - ✓ Executive stock options
  - ✓ Financial instruments

Outline

Part I: Interpreting Financial Statements

- Lecture slides on financial analysis

- Chapters 1, 2, 3, 4, 5 and 6 of "Financial Accounting, A Valuation Emphasis" by Hughes, Ayres and Hoskin

Financial Reporting: The Institutional Setting

LEARNING OBJECTIVES

After reading this chapter you should be able to:

1 Identify the types of business activities of publicly traded corporations reflected in financial accounting reports.

2 Explain the process governing the regulation of financial reporting and setting of Generally Accepted Accounting Principles (GAAP).

3 Describe the role of independent audits in monitoring compliance of financial reports with GAAP.

4 Recognize the economic consequences of accounting choices, and the link between owners' and managers' wealth and financial statement information.

5 Understand that a potential relationship exists between the value of a firm's stock and the information contained in financial reports, particularly the firm's statement of earnings.

During the day of August 25, 2000, the stock price of Emulex, a computer technology company, drastically dropped (see Exhibit 1.1) following an Internet story that it was under investigation by the Securities and Exchange Commission (SEC). The story also indicated that Emulex would restate its earnings downward as a result of the investigation. The stock quickly rebounded later that same day when investors learned that the story had been a hoax.

This event suggests that both earnings *per se*, and the credibility of that number are relevant to the stock market's assessment of a firm's value. Several questions come to mind: What are earnings? How are earnings linked to the market value of a company's stock? What role do the SEC and other institutions play in determining the reliability of reported earnings? These and many other questions pertaining to the construction of financial accounting information, and how that information relates to the value of the firm and the expectations of investors, lay at the heart of this text.

Exhibit 1.1

THE REAL WORLD

Emulex

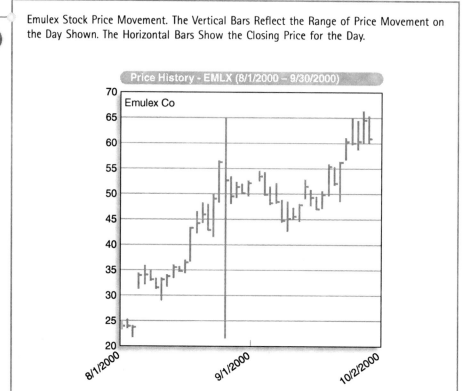

Emulex Stock Price Movement. The Vertical Bars Reflect the Range of Price Movement on the Day Shown. The Horizontal Bars Show the Closing Price for the Day.

Price History - EMLX (8/1/2000 – 9/30/2000)

Emulex Co

In this book, we focus on the presentation of accounting information for business entities (firms) and its interpretation by external decision makers, such as investors, financial analysts, and government regulators. Firms prepare periodic reports that are made available to such external parties. A key component of these reports consists of financial information generated from the firm's accounting system. This information is summarized in a set of financial statements and related notes. The false report on Emulex referred to one of these statements, the Earnings Statement.

The **earnings statement** for a firm reports its revenues and expenses for a given period of time. **Revenues** are the amounts collected, or relatively certain to be collected, from customers in return for providing goods or services. **Expenses** are the amounts paid, or expected to be paid, to vendors in return for resources that go into the production and marketing of goods or services (such as materials, salaries, and utilities). You may also see earnings referred to as *profits* or *net income*.

EARNINGS = REVENUE – EXPENSES

Although all types of business entities prepare financial statements, we will focus on corporations in this text. **Corporations** are distinguished from other business types (we provide a more complete description of various business types in Chapter 2) by the issuance of shares of **stock,** which represent ownership in the company. When companies initially form, investors (owners) exchange cash for shares of stock in the company. As an example, when Jeff Bezos formed Amazon.com, Inc. in the state of Washington on July 5, 1994, he invested $10,000 in exchange for 1,700,000 shares. Owners then profit from their investment by increases in the value of their shares or by receiving dividends from the company. **Dividends** can typically only be paid if the company has positive earnings on a cumulative basis and may be viewed as returning part of the earnings of the company to the owners. In Amazon.com's case, the company has not produced a profit yet and therefore has paid no dividends. The value of the shares has, however, fluctuated considerably over the life of the company consistent with changes in investors' expectations of the future earnings of Amazon. At the time of this writing Amazon's share price was $40.21 a share. As of April 4, 2003, Jeff Bezos owned almost 108 million shares of Amazon.

Because of their significance in our economy, we specifically focus on **publicly traded corporations,** which are those corporations whose shares trade in a public stock exchange, such as the New York Stock Exchange. Emulex is one example of a publicly traded corporation. Some other more recognizable publicly traded corporations include Starbucks, Nike, and Coca Cola. For publicly traded corporations, financial analysts make buy-and-sell recommendations to investors wishing to purchase or sell shares of stock. These buy-and-sell recommendations may influence investors' purchases and sales, and indirectly, the price of stock. For example, the incorrect Emulex story prompted some analysts to recommend that investors sell their stock. The increase in investors wishing to sell their stock, along with the decrease in those willing to buy the shares, led to price declines. Upon learning of the false report, the situation reversed, causing the price to adjust upward.

As evidenced by investors and analysts' reaction to the news that Emulex would have to restate its earnings, information about a company's earnings plays a key role in assessing a firm's value. For this reason, companies periodically make announcements (typically on a quarterly basis) about their most recent performance. See the announcement of Pepsico in Exhibit 1.2. Further, analysts routinely report their forecasts of earnings and ratios related to earnings, such as the *price-to-earnings ratio (P/E ratio),* which factor significantly into their assessment of the firm's value. For example, in July 2003, the P/E ratio for Pepsico was approximately 21:1, based on the current estimate for the following

> Because the return on investment to a firm's owners (stockholders) comes from future dividends and changes in share value and estimates of both are often based on earnings, earnings are of considerable importance to investors as they make decisions about whether to buy or sell shares of stock.

PEPSICO Q1 EARNINGS PER SHARE INCREASES 17 PERCENT TO 45 CENTS

Worldwide volume grew 3 percent
Division net revenues grew 5 percent, and 6 percent on a currency neutral basis
Division operating profits grew 7 percent, and 8 percent on a currency neutral basis, following 14 percent growth in Q1 2002
Total net income grew 13 percent

Note the prominence of earnings in this disclosure. Also note that because Pepsico has worldwide operations, many of its accounting numbers are influenced by currency differences around the world. Therefore, the company includes data both as reported and after some adjustment for currency differences.

Exhibit 1.2
First Quarter 2003
Performance Announcement
by Pepsico

THE REAL WORLD

Pepsico

year's earnings and the current stock price at the time. The P/E ratio can be viewed as the amount investors are willing to pay for each dollar of forecasted earnings. When the earnings in the ratio are the forecasted earnings, the ratio is more specifically known as the *forward* P/E ratio. If, instead, the calculation is based on the last reported earnings (i.e., the actual earnings) then the ratio is called the *trailing* P/E. We will discuss the interpretation of the P/E ratio later in the book.

As will become clearer as you progress through the book, earnings provides a measure of the value added to the owners' wealth as a result of the firm's activities. We describe next those firm activities captured by the accounting process.

REPORTING ON THE ACTIVITIES OF THE FIRM

When assessing a firm's value, most analysts begin by reviewing the economic activities of the firm. All business firms engage in three basic kinds of activities: financing, investing, and operating. **Financing activities** are those activities directed at raising funds for the firm. Firms raise funds (sometimes called **capital**) from two basic sources: owners (*equity capital*) and lenders (*debt capital*). To raise funds from owners, corporations issue shares of stock. To raise funds from lenders, firms typically issue to the lenders a written promise indicating how the money will be repaid as well as the interest rate associated with the loan. There are many types of lenders, but one common lender would be a bank. For example, Skechers USA, Inc. was incorporated in 1992 and by the end of 2001 had $18,498,000 in loans payable to two banks.

A firm generally uses the funds obtained from its financing activities to engage in investing and operating activities. **Investing activities** typically consist of the firm's purchase of property and equipment to enable the company to make products or provide services. Firms may also purchase shares of stock of other companies. These purchases are also considered investing activities. **Operating activities** include those relatively short-term activities that the firm engages in to make and sell products and services. Representative of these activities are the collection of sales dollars from customers, the payment of salaries to employees, and the payment of utility costs.

The accounting process captures the financial effects of these activities. Individual economic events that affect the accounting system are called *transactions*. Financial statements are then constructed from the combined results of the transactions that occur during a particular period of time (e.g., a month, a quarter, a year). These statements reflect the transactions that have been recorded to date and, as such, form a historical record of the firm's activities. The challenge for analysts and investors is to utilize this historical record to assist in forecasting the future economic events that will, in turn, affect the firm's future earnings and hence its value.

Financial statement users make many significant decisions based on the information included in these reports. As a result, the information needs to be as accurate and comprehensive as possible. To ensure this, firms need to follow specific regulations when reporting their main activities. In the next section, we discuss the institutional environment in which accounting regulations are formulated and the key characteristics that are considered in setting accounting standards.

REGULATION OF FINANCIAL REPORTING

Many financial statement users lack the influence to force a company to release information that they might need to make effective decisions. For instance, in the United States, large publicly traded corporations are owned by numerous individuals. The shareholders in these large companies typically do not work for the company and thus have little firsthand information about its day-to-day activities. They therefore rely upon the periodic financial statements issued by the company's management to obtain knowledge about the firm's activities. To ensure that owners or potential owners of public companies get relevant, reliable, and timely information regarding those companies, laws and regulations dictate much of the content of these reports.

The ultimate authority for regulating financial reports of publicly traded companies in the United States rests with the **Securities and Exchange Commission (SEC).** Prompted by the 1929 stock market crash, the U.S. Congress established the SEC to administer the 1933 Securities Act and 1934 Securities and Exchange Act. That is, Congress empowered the SEC with the legal authority to set disclosure and accounting standards that all publicly traded firms are obliged to follow.

To provide adequate disclosure, the SEC created a reporting structure (SEC's Regulation S-X and S-K) that all public companies must follow. For example, the regulations require an annual report (10K), quarterly reports (10Q), and a report of significant events (8K). The 8K report is often used to disclose earning announcements or public meeting with analysts. For instance, on August 6, 2003, American Express issued an 8K report that contained the Chief Executive Officer's presentation to the financial community regarding the company's second quarter results. All of the reports filed with the SEC are available electronically via the electronic filing site of the SEC known as EDGAR.

Although the SEC retains its authority over the disclosures of publicly traded firms, it delegates the primary responsibility for creating accounting standards to the **Financial Accounting Standards Board (FASB).** The FASB consists of individuals from the private sector, principally professional accountants. Since its inception in 1973, the FASB has generated several *Statements of Financial Accounting Concepts (SFACs),* putting forth broad objectives for financial reports (known as the FASB's *conceptual framework*), and many **Statements of Financial Accounting Standards (SFASs)** that address specific valuation and income measurement issues.

On occasion, the SEC intervenes in setting standards, through two series of publications: *Financial Reporting Releases (FRRs)* and *Accounting and Auditing Enforcement Releases (AAERs).* In addition, SEC staff issue a series of bulletins, known as *Staff Accounting Bulletins (SABs),* that reflect their opinion and interpretation of other releases. Congress may also become involved when it deems necessary. Collectively, the body of accounting concepts, standards, guidelines, and conventions governing the construction of financial statements and related disclosures are referred to as **Generally Accepted Accounting Principles (GAAP).**

International Accounting Standards

The development of accounting standards has, in general, been a country-specific process. Each country has developed its own standards, which reflect its political, social, and economic environment. With the development of world markets for both products and capital, however, countries need a greater consensus with regard to financial reporting. To meet this need, the International Accounting Standards Committee (IASC) has been actively formulating international accounting standards.

The IASC is an independent, private-sector body that is funded by donations from accounting organizations around the world. Effective March 2001, a new organization emerged from the IASC, the International Accounting Standards Board (IASB). The IASB now establishes international accounting standards; as of 2002, the IASC/IASB issued 41 International Accounting Standards (IAS). The IASB will issue new standards known as International Financial Reporting Standards (IFRS). To promote the development of international accounting standards, the IASB developed relationships with the primary standard-setting bodies in numerous countries, including the FASB within the United States. In late 2002 the FASB and the IASB agreed to make their standards compatible with one another by January 1, 2005.

DETERMINING GENERALLY ACCEPTED ACCOUNTING PRINCIPLES

Recognizing that it cannot set accounting standards for every economic event that might occur, the FASB developed the conceptual framework (FASB, SFAC No. 2, 1980) that serves as a guide for both standard setting and practice. The conceptual framework seeks to define the desirable characteristics of accounting information. Qualitatively, a number of characteristics shape the financial statement disclosures required under GAAP. Some of the key characteristics are:

- **Relevance**   The information is capable of making a difference in a decision. Relevant information may derive value from its role in predicting future performance (*predictive value*) or in assessing past performance (*feedback value*).

- **Reliability**   The information faithfully represents the economic events it is intended to portray. Reliable information is accurate, neutral (unbiased), and verifiable (see *Verifiability*).

- **Verifiability**   Independent measurers using the same methods reach the same results. Verifiable information allows independent observers to agree on what a reported amount represents.

- **Neutrality**   The information conforms to standards that are independent of the interests of any particular constituency. Neutral information is not withheld or modified to serve the company's or users' objectives.

- **Comparability**   The information can be compared across firms in a meaningful manner. Comparable information does not distort similarities or differences as a consequence of how the company uses accounting methods.

- **Consistency**   The information is determined under the same accounting methods from one period to the next. Consistent information is free of the effects of changing methods in its determination.

Exhibit 1.3
Qualitative Characteristics of Accounting Information

PRIMARY QUALITIES	
Relevance	Reliability
Understandability	Decision Usefulness
Predictive Value	Verifiability
Feedback Value	Neutrality
Timeliness	Representational Faithfulness

SECONDARY QUALITIES	
Comparability	Consistency

Trade-offs exist when applying these qualities to a particular economic event. Two of the primary qualities highlighted in Exhibit 1.3, relevance and reliability, are often the focus of these trade-offs. For example, the most relevant information about a company that sells a product in high demand but limited supply may be the number of backorders of the product. This information may be very *relevant* to assessing current firm value as a forecast of future sales, but may not be a very *reliable* measure of future sales. For example, a competitor may be able to supply the same or similar product in a more timely manner which would result in the backorder being cancelled. As a case in point, in mid-2002, Palm, Inc. was having difficulties providing sufficient quantities of a very popular color model of its handheld product. The major distributors (those who had the backorders) found that their customers would not wait and sought alternative distribution channels to get the model. One distributor was quoted in a press release saying "if we can't support our customers in a timely manner, the customer goes and finds the product online." As a result of these trade-offs, in determining specific accounting standards, such as when to recognize backorder sales of a product, the FASB must consider all of the qualities of the information and seek to determine an acceptable solution. In general, backorders are not recognized as sales under GAAP because they generally fail to meet the reliability criteria. However, backorders are still a very relevant piece of information and are often disclosed by firms in their press releases.

An ill-defined concept that also influences the content of financial statements is **materiality.** Materiality means that firms can use a flexible accounting approach for insignificant amounts. For example, firms should account for the purchase of an electric stapler, office equipment, as a long-term asset. However, most firms simply treat the stapler as an expense rather than as an asset. GAAP allows this simpler accounting treatment because treating the stapler cost as an expense would not (materially) affect our view of the firm's assets or expenses.

Financial statement users need to monitor how firms handle the materiality concept when assessing a firm's value and compliance with GAAP. In recent years, the SEC has been concerned that some firms misuse the concept of materiality by deciding that as long as an item is less than a certain percentage of income or assets that it is immaterial (5 percent is often quoted as a rule of thumb). In response, the SEC issued SAB 99 (in 1999), which states that misstatements are not considered immaterial simply because they fall beneath a certain threshold. Firms must consider many other aspects of the misstatement in determining whether to correct it or not. For instance, in SAB 99 two other factors that must be considered are (1) whether the misstatement has the effect of increasing management's compensation say, by satisfying requirements for the award of bonuses or other forms of incentive compensation (see our discussion concerning economic consequences later in this chapter for more information about this factor) and (2) whether the misstatement involves concealment of an unlawful transaction.

Finally, although not a quality explicitly sought under GAAP, financial statements tend to reflect conservatism. **Conservatism** indicates a firm's tendency to anticipate losses, but not gains; carry assets at values that are often low by comparison with current market prices or appraisal values; recognize liabilities in anticipation of obligations that may or may not arise; and delay recognition of revenues until uncertainties have been resolved. For example, under current GAAP, many construction companies recognize the profits from a long-term construction project over the period of construction. However, if they anticipate that there will be a loss on the overall contract at the end of the construction period, they recognize the loss immediately. To illustrate, Foster Wheeler LTD (a construction company specializing in petroleum processing facilities) reported this type of policy in their annual report:

> The Company has numerous contracts that are in various stages of completion. Such contracts require estimates to determine the appropriate cost and revenue recognition. However, current estimates may be revised as additional information becomes available. If estimates of costs to complete long-term contracts indicate a loss, provision is made currently for the total loss anticipated.

Note, however, that the conceptual framework explicitly states that firms must avoid misusing conservatism to understate assets or overstate liabilities.

At times, however, the conceptual framework fails to provide enough guidance. The FASB then moves to adopt a more specific standard for a particular economic event. To do this, the FASB follows a very public process of determining a new standard, encompassing three main stages:

1. The FASB analyzes the issue using the conceptual framework and other relevant existing standards. It then prepares a Discussion Memorandum laying out the alternatives with their pros and cons. The FASB elicits feedback of the Discussion Memorandum from interested parties such as investors, financial analysts, government regulators, corporate executives, and professional accountants.

2. After assessing the responses to this document, the FASB deliberates on the alternatives and issues an Exposure Draft of its proposed pronouncement. The FASB makes the Exposure Draft available for further public comment.

3. In the last step, the FASB incorporates any additional comments and then issues its pronouncement in the form of a Statement of Financial Accounting Standards (SFAS).

The process the FASB uses to set accounting standards is essentially political and subject to override by the SEC or the U.S. Congress. For example, during the oil crisis in the 1970s, the FASB issued SFAS 19 that eliminated certain accounting practices used by oil and gas producers. The new standard would have resulted in more volatile reported earnings for smaller companies engaged in significant exploration activities. Some opponents of the new standard argued that with more volatile earnings, smaller producers might be unable to raise capital to continue exploration, inconsistent with the national interest in encouraging exploration. The political pressures subsequently brought to bear resulted in the FASB rescinding the pronouncement it had originally issued (SFAS 52).

GAAP provides the framework and the specific rules for how the various activities of the firm should be recorded in their accounting system. However, if the firm does not follow these rules or they apply them inappropriately, investors and other readers of the financial statements could be misled about the performance of the firm. For this reason all publicly traded firms are required to present audited statements in their reports. The auditors provide the reassurance that the firm has appropriately applied GAAP. In the next section, we discuss the nature of the audit.

INDEPENDENT AUDITS OF FINANCIAL STATEMENTS

All publicly traded companies must provide a report by independent auditors (see the report for Hasbro, Inc. in Exhibit 1.4). This report attests to the fairness of presentation (that the statements fairly represent the results of the

Exhibit 1.4
Hasbro, Inc. Auditors' Report

THE REAL WORLD

Hasbro, Inc.

The Board of Directors and Shareholders
Hasbro, Inc.:

We have audited the accompanying consolidated balance sheets of Hasbro, Inc. and subsidiaries as of December 29, 2002 and December 30, 2001 and the related consolidated statements of operations, shareholders' equity and cash flows for each of the fiscal years in the three-year period ended December 29, 2002. These consolidated financial statements are the responsibility of the Company's management. Our responsibility is to express an opinion on these consolidated financial statements based on our audits.

We conducted our audits in accordance with auditing standards generally accepted in the United States of America. Those standards require that we plan and perform the audit to obtain reasonable assurance about whether the financial statements are free of material misstatement. An audit includes examining, on a test basis, evidence supporting the amounts and disclosures in the financial statements. An audit also includes assessing the accounting principles used and significant estimates made by management, as well as evaluating the overall financial statement presentation. We believe that our audits provide a reasonable basis for our opinion.

In our opinion, the consolidated financial statements referred to above present fairly, in all material respects, the financial position of Hasbro, Inc. and subsidiaries as of December 29, 2002 and December 30, 2001 and the results of their operations and their cash flows for each of the fiscal years in the three-year period ended December 29, 2002 in conformity with accounting principles generally accepted in the United States of America.

As discussed in note 1 to the consolidated financial statements, effective December 31, 2001, the first day of the Company's 2002 fiscal year, the Company adopted the provisions of Statement of Financial Accounting Standards No. 142, "Goodwill and Other Intangibles."

/s/ KPMG LLP

Providence, Rhode Island
February 12, 2003

economic events that have affected the firm) and compliance of those statements with GAAP. **Auditors** are professional accountants who meet certification requirements set by states (i.e., Certified Public Accountants, or **CPA**s for short). Auditors must also follow procedures under the oversight of the American Institute of Certified Public Accountants (AICPA). The AICPA sets Generally Accepted Auditing Standards (GAAS) that define the auditor's responsibilities.

> The auditor's opinion is important when using valuation techniques as it provides at least some level of assurance that the data being used to forecast future results are comparably prepared by companies.

In addition to assessing compliance with GAAP, auditors also examine the firm's internal controls, verify its principal assets, review for unusual changes in its financial statements, inquire with outside parties concerning the firm's exposure to losses, and determine the firm's ability to continue as a going concern. The term **going concern** means that the auditor expects that the firm will continue to operate into the foreseeable future; in other words, they do not expect the company to go out of business or file for bankruptcy. Investors and others might view the value of a company quite differently if they assumed it would soon quit operating. Auditors also consider the existence or prospect of fraud, though the firm's management has primary responsibility for its detection.

Auditors also apply the concept of materiality in their work. They typically limit their responsibility to material items when they state in their audit opinions that financial statements "present fairly, *in all material respects,* the financial position, results of operations, and cash flows" of a client firm.

Finally, auditors issue one of several types of reports. In an *unqualified opinion* the auditor expresses no reservations concerning the fairness of the financial statements and conformance with GAAP. A *qualified opinion* includes an exception to the conclusion of fairness or conformance with GAAP. Exceptions commonly relate to a deviation from GAAP or a limitation in the scope of the auditor's procedures under GAAS. An *adverse opinion* states that the financial statements do not fairly present the company's financial position and results of operations in conformity with GAAP. Under a *disclaimer,* the auditor does not express an opinion on the financial statements.

Firms appoint auditors and pay their fees. As a result, controversy exists on the independence of auditors whose fees are paid by the client. To help resolve these concerns, the accounting profession devised the *AICPA Code of Conduct* and a *peer review* process to monitor compliance with performance standards. In 2002, the U.S. Congress passed the Sarbanes-Oxley Act (SOX) to address these and other concerns about the auditing profession, partly in response to the Enron failure and the subsequent demise of Arthur Andersen (see Exhibit 1.5). The SOX created a Public Company Accounting Oversight Board that monitors auditing, quality control, and independence standards, and rules. For example, oversight of the public accountant must be done through the firm's audit committee, which must be composed of members who are independent of the company.

Independent audits help to ensure that the financial statements reflect those qualities of accounting information we discussed earlier. Owners, lenders, and managers face economic incentives in their interaction with a firm that may influence accounting decisions. In the next section, we discuss the economic consequences to owners, lenders, and managers from the accounting choices made by the firm. As illustrated by the Enron example, these consequences can be very significant.

Exhibit 1.5

In October, 2001 the SEC requested information from Enron Corporation regarding a set of transactions with several related parties. The transactions had the approval of Enron's auditors, Arthur Andersen. By the end of the month, the inquiry had turned into a formal SEC investigation. In an 8K filing (recall that 8K filings detail the occurrence of any material events or corporate changes that should be reported to investors or security holders) with the SEC on November 8, 2001, Enron agreed to restate its financial statements for 1997 through 2001 to record the effects of the related party transactions. The net effect: Enron reduced its owners' equity section by $1.2 billion. On December 2, 2001, Enron filed for protection from its creditors under Chapter 11 of the U.S. bankruptcy laws. In its continuing investigation the SEC requested audit working papers from Arthur Andersen (AA). The SEC then discovered that several individuals at AA had shredded documents related to the Enron audit. The government eventually filed an indictment for obstruction of justice against AA, and the company suffered the loss of numerous clients. AA was ultimately found guilty of obstructing justice and agreed not to audit publicly traded companies.

The loss in credibility of Enron's reported earnings, both past and present, along with the revelation of losses and exposure of business risks led investors to conclude that the stock was overvalued. As a result, Enron suffered such severe declines in its stock price and future prospects that the company was forced to declare bankruptcy.

THE REAL WORLD

Enron

ECONOMIC CONSEQUENCES OF ACCOUNTING PRACTICES

Although GAAP places restrictions on accounting choices, firms still enjoy considerable flexibility in their selection and application of accounting methods. As a result, managers can and do affect the amounts reported in the financial statements. Allowing flexibility is a two-edged sword. On one hand, it makes it possible for financial statements to better reflect economic reality in the sense that one size does not fit all. On the other hand, it may provide the opportunity for firm owners or managers to manipulate information.

For example, lenders closely monitor a firm's activities to ensure that they will be repaid. One common way for owners to provide assurances to lenders and for lenders to protect themselves is to put restrictions into their lending contracts. These restrictions, called *covenants*, typically set minimums for certain accounting numbers or ratios that the firm must meet. The agreements typically state that the lender can make the loan immediately due if the firm violates these covenants. If a company found itself in danger of violating a covenant, there might be enough incentive to either change accounting methods or misreport transactions to avoid the violation. A mitigating factor on this behavior is that lenders often find it in their best interests to work with firms to restructure debt when violations occur (see Exhibit 1.6 regarding Cogent Communications Group).

As another example, compensation arrangements for a firm's management often include bonuses based on achieving a targeted amount of earnings. Under GAAP, managers commonly have sufficient discretion over accounting policies to significantly influence the recognition of revenues and expenses. In order to meet bonus targets, therefore, managers may advance the recognition of revenues or delay expenses as a means of reporting higher earnings. Other forms of discretion might include relaxing credit requirements customers must satisfy

Exhibit 1.6
Cogent Communications
Group, Inc.—10K Report, April,
2003

THE REAL WORLD

**Cogent
Communications
Group**

Breach of Cisco Credit Facility Covenant. We have breached the minimum revenue covenant contained in our credit facility from Cisco Systems Capital. This breach permits Cisco Capital, if it wishes, to accelerate and require us to pay approximately $262.7 million we owed to Cisco Capital as of March 28, 2003. Should Cisco Capital accelerate the due date of our indebtedness, we would be unable to repay it. If it accelerates the indebtedness, Cisco Capital could make use of its rights as a secured lender to take possession of all of our assets. In such event, we may be forced to file for bankruptcy protection. We are currently in active discussions with Cisco Capital to restructure the Company's debt.

Note that violation of the covenant in this lending agreement had the potential to impose significant economic consequences to Cogent. You can imagine the pressure that this situation might exert on management to misstate revenues to be in compliance with the covenant. By June, however, Cogent had restructured its debt.

(to produce more revenues), postponing repairs and maintenance on equipment (to reduce expenses), and selling assets or retiring debt on which gains will be recorded (to increase income). These types of actions may actually reduce the firm's value. Although managers benefit by receiving a higher bonus, they do so at the expense of stockholders (lower firm value).

In compensation arrangements, firms try to design contracts that align the economic interests of managers with those of stockholders. One example is to provide some amount of a manager's compensation in the form of stock in the company. The idea is that managers will behave more like owners when managers' compensation includes stock. Stock could be awarded to managers directly. More frequently managers are given the option to buy shares of stock at a fixed price under what are called *stock option plans,* discussed later in the book. Often management compensation arrangements provide a combination of incentives, some based on earnings and some on stock price. For example, Intel compensates its executive managers with a combination of a base salary, a cash bonus tied to meeting an individual earnings performance target, a cash bonus tied to overall company earnings, and a stock option plan.

Other incentives to manipulate earnings may relate to lawsuits, labor negotiations, compliance with bank or insurance company regulations, and trade disputes with foreign rivals. For example, a firm facing litigation might prefer to ignore the likelihood of losing a lawsuit (by not recording a liability in advance of a settlement), thereby giving a false impression of the firm's value.

Many opportunities and incentives therefore exist for manipulating financial reports. One reason for allowing these opportunities to exist is that it may be too costly both to incorporate the level of detail required to set more stringent standards and to monitor compliance with those details. Another reason may be that allowing managers to select from a menu of accounting policies may provide an efficient means of communicating (*signaling*) information about the firm's future prospects when the economic consequences of a given policy depend on those prospects. For example, suppose that there are two companies in the same industry with similar debt agreements (including a restriction in their debt agreement that earnings must remain above $100,000). One firm has very good future sales prospects, and the other firm has very poor future sales prospects. If they both were faced with a decision about voluntarily (i.e., it was not a mandated change) adopting a new accounting policy that would reduce reported earnings in the future, the firm with good prospects would have little

problem in adopting this policy as it expects to have good future earnings which would not force the company to violate its debt restrictions (even though it would reduce their future reported earnings due to the policy change). However, the firm with bad prospects would likely not adopt the new policy as it already is in a position to potentially violate the debt restriction (due to its poor future sales prospects) and the change in policy will make it even more likely. Therefore, by observing their decisions about the choice of accounting policy lenders might be able to infer the future prospects of companies and set the interest rates that they require accordingly.

Another economic consideration that managers face in the determination of accounting methods is the effect of the decision on the taxes paid by the company. All corporations pay taxes to the federal government (*Internal Revenue Service* or *IRS*) based on their earnings. The accounting rules for reporting earnings to the IRS are determined by the tax code and in some cases differ from GAAP. The company's objective in choosing its accounting policies for tax purposes is usually to minimize or delay its tax payments. In contrast, the company's objective in choosing its accounting policies for financial reporting purposes is to comply with GAAP. Although the norm is for firms to use different accounting methods for tax and financial reporting purposes, there is at least one case (LIFO inventory accounting) in which the method chosen for tax purposes is only permitted if that same method is used for reporting purposes. Accordingly, there may be a tax incentive that influences an accounting choice.

FINANCIAL REPORTING AND VALUATION

As the discussion in this chapter suggests, financial accounting disclosures, especially earnings, provide information upon which financial analysts and investors at large may project a firm's future cash flows that, in turn, determine firm value. The central role of earnings as an important factor in determining firm value is evidenced by the prominence of earnings forecasts by financial analysts in the financial press and a vast empirical literature by academics that documents stock price reactions to information conveyed by changes in those forecasts, earnings announcements *per se,* and other related disclosures.

In the chapters that follow, we will seek to further an appreciation of the role that financial statements play in arriving at estimates of firm value. Our efforts in this regard culminate in Chapter 14 with the presentation of two principal approaches for mapping information contained in what are called *pro-forma financial statements* (statements based on forecasts of future operating, investing, and financing activities) into value estimates; specifically, *discounted cash flow (DCF)* analysis and *residual income (RI)* analysis. At this point, it is sufficient for you to begin to think of a firm's financial accounting disclosures as a starting point in assessing its future cash flow prospects.

SUMMARY AND TRANSITION

As should be clear by now, accounting information, particularly earnings, plays a key role with investors in guiding their decisions to buy or sell stock. Analysts who advise investors also make significant use of accounting information in estimating the value of a share of stock as a basis for their buy or sell recommendations to investors. The reliability and relevance of accounting information are enhanced by a standard setting process involving both public (SEC) and private (FASB) sector bodies. Auditors provide additional assurance to investors that the accounting information is prepared in compliance with those standards.

Within the framework of generally accepted accounting principles, managers have considerable discretion over accounting policies adopted by the firm. Often managers' choices have economic consequences for themselves, their stockholders, and lenders. The nature of the consequences is driven by the contracts written between managers, stockholders, and lenders.

In the remainder of the book we will continue to visit valuation issues and to examine economic consequences issues as they arise. The next few chapters explain the construction of the financial statements contained in financial accounting reports and describe the major concepts underlying this construction. Considerable attention is given to the principal concepts used in the determination of earnings. These chapters are followed by an initial exposure to the techniques of financial analysis with a focus on the use of financial statements in assessing past performance and forecasting future performance. Later chapters consider a comprehensive set of valuation and income measurement issues in depth. The final chapter of the text provides basic introduction to the forecasting of financial statements and the two major approaches for valuing the firm based on components from those statements.

END OF CHAPTER MATERIAL

KEY TERMS

Auditors	Financial Accounting Standards Board (FASB)
Capital	Financing Activities
Conservatism	Generally Accepted Accounting Principles (GAAP)
Corporation	Going Concern
Dividends	Investing Activities
Earnings Statement	Materiality
Expenses	Operating Activities

Publicly Traded Corporations
Revenue
Securities and Exchange Commission (SEC)

Statement of Financial Accounting Standards (SFAS)
Stock

ASSIGNMENT MATERIAL

REVIEW QUESTIONS

1. Describe and illustrate the three major types of activities that firms engage in.
2. Discuss the meaning of Generally Accepted Accounting Principles, and describe the organizations that establish these principles.
3. What is the purpose of an auditor's opinion, and what types of opinions can auditors render?
4. Identify at least three major users of corporate financial statements, and briefly state how they might use the information from those statements.
5. List and briefly describe the major qualitative characteristics that accounting information should possess, according to the FASB concepts statements.
6. Discuss how materiality is used in the choice of accounting methods.
7. Describe what is meant by economic consequences of accounting practices and provide an example of how accounting choices can affect the welfare of parties with an interest in the firm.
8. How might differences in accounting standards across countries affect the analysis done by an analyst in predicting stock prices?
9. Describe what conservatism means in the construction of the financial statements of the firm.

APPLYING YOUR KNOWLEDGE

10. For a manufacturing company, list two examples of transactions that you would classify as financing, investing, and operating.
11. The AMAX Company purchased land several years ago for $60,000 as a potential site for a new building. No building has yet been constructed. A comparable lot near the site was recently sold for $95,000.
    a. At what value should AMAX carry the land on its balance sheet? Support your answer with consideration for the relevance and reliability of the information that would result.
    b. If AMAX wanted to borrow money from a bank, what information about the land would the bank want to know?
12. You are the accounting manager for a U.S. company that has just been acquired by a German company. Helmut, the CEO of the German company, has just paid you a visit and is puzzled why American companies report on two different bases, one for reporting to their stockholders and another to the taxing authority, because in Germany these are one and the same. Draft a memo explaining to Helmut why there are two different bases

and a brief explanation for why they might involve different accounting rules.

13. Harmonization of accounting standards has been proposed on a global basis. As a CEO of an American company, what would you see as advantages and disadvantages of having the same set of standards across countries?

14. Suppose that the FASB proposed that inventory be accounted for at its current market price (i.e., what you could sell it for) rather than its historical cost. Provide an argument that supports or opposes this change on the basis of relevance and reliability.

15. Suppose that you started your own company that assembles and sells laptop computers. You do not manufacture any of the parts yourself. The computers are sold through mail order. Make a list of the information that you consider relevant to assessing your firm's performance. When you are through, discuss how you would reliably measure that performance.

16. Suppose that you own and operate your own private company. You need to raise money to expand your operations, so you approach a bank for a loan. The bank loan officer has asked for financial statements prepared according to GAAP. Why would the loan officer make such a request and, assuming that your statements were prepared according to GAAP, how could you convince the banker that this was so?

17. In order for a company's stock to be listed (i.e., traded) on most stock exchanges, the company's financial statements are required to be audited by a CPA firm. Why?

18. As a manager, suppose that you are responsible for establishing prices for the products your division sells. Under GAAP your firm uses a method of inventory costing called LIFO that means that the costs of the last units purchased are the first ones that are reported in the statement of earnings. Consequently, the costs that remain in inventory are those associated with the first purchases. Because inventory can build up over the years, some of these costs may be very old. How relevant would these old costs attached to ending inventory be to you as you decide how to price inventory in the coming year? If they are not relevant, what piece of information would be more relevant to you?

19. From time to time there have been calls from the user community for management to disclose their own forecasts of future results such as net income. As an external user of the financial statements, discuss the relevance and the reliability of this type of information.

20. Suppose a company decides to change accounting methods such that it reports its revenues sooner than it previously did. Discuss how this might effect investors' evaluation of the company's stock.

USING REAL DATA

21. Amazon.com, Inc. has operated at a net loss since its formation, yet its stock has a positive value. Explain why investors would value the shares of Amazon at a positive value.

22. In early February 2001 Emulex Corporation revised its quarterly sales estimates downward. Prior to the revision Emulex had been expecting a 28 percent sales increase over the previous year and had shown 40 percent increases in sales annually for the last five years. Upon hearing this news, investors drove the price of Emulex down from $77.50 per share on a Friday to $40.25 on the following Monday. Explain why the valuation of Emulex dropped given this announcement.

23. In early February 2001 CISCO announced that it was missing its first quarter sales estimates. This was the first time since July 1994 that it had come in under its sales estimates, and it was the first time in more than three years that it had failed to beat its sales estimates. As an investor, how might you react to this news and how might this announcement affect the valuation of the company's shares?

BEYOND THE BOOK

The Beyond the Book problems are designed to force you to find and utilize resources found outside the book.

24. Familiarize yourself with the resources that are available at your university to acquire information about corporations. Most universities have an electronic database that contains financial statement information. The following is a short list of resources that may be available:

   LEXIS/NEXIS Database This is an incredibly large database that contains all sorts of news and financial information about companies. It contains all of the SEC filings including the 10-K, 20-F (foreign registrants), and Proxy Statements. The financial information is in full text form.

   CD-Disclosure This database contains full text financial footnote information for thousands of companies but does not contain full text of the major financial statements.

   EDGAR Filings The EDGAR filings are electronic forms of the SEC filings that are included in the Lexis/Nexis database but are also accessible through the internet (www.sec.gov).

   ABI Inform (UMI, Inc.) This database contains full text information from numerous business periodicals.

25. Go to the FASB's website (www.fasb.org), locate the project activities section, and list the titles of the projects on its projects update list.

26. For a publicly traded company of your choosing, answer the following questions:

   a. What are the products (or product lines) and/or services that your company sells? Please be as specific as possible.

   b. Who are the customers of your company? Please be as specific as possible.

   c. In what markets, domestic and global, does your company sell its products and/or services?

   d. Who are the major competitors of your company?

   e. What are the major inputs your company needs to manufacture its products? Who are the suppliers of these inputs?

    f. Are any of the items listed in the questions above changing substantially? Use a two-year time span as a window to address this question.

    g. What has happened to the stock price of your company over the last two years?

To answer these questions it will be useful to collect a series of articles concerning your company over the most recent two-year period. Try to find at least five reasonably sized articles. Use these as references to write a two- to three-page background paper about your company.

CHAPTER 2

Financial Statements: An Overview

LEARNING OBJECTIVES

After reading this chapter you should be able to:

1. Understand the differences in the major forms of business organization, as well as some of the relative pros and cons for choosing a particular form of business.

2. Identify the nature of information contained in the main general-purpose financial statements: Statement of Financial Position, Statement of Earnings, Statement of Cash Flows, and Statement of Changes in Stockholders' Equity.

3. Explain the connection between statements of financial position at points in time and changes in financial position over time.

4. Describe the types of supplemental disclosures accompanying financial statements in a firm's annual report.

On October 12, 2001, Polaroid Corporation filed for protection from creditors under Chapter 11 of the U.S. bankruptcy laws. This action resulted from the financial difficulties that Polaroid faced when its sales declined significantly, starting in the fourth quarter of 2000. As Exhibit 2.1 shows, the value of the company's stock began its downward slide late in the first quarter of 2000. Note that the S&P 500 (Standard and Poor's) is an index of how the stock market performed overall during this same period. This correspondence between declining quarterly sales and relative stock price suggests that investors rely on information contained in financial statements. In this chapter, we begin to explore this relationship by describing the contents of those statements.

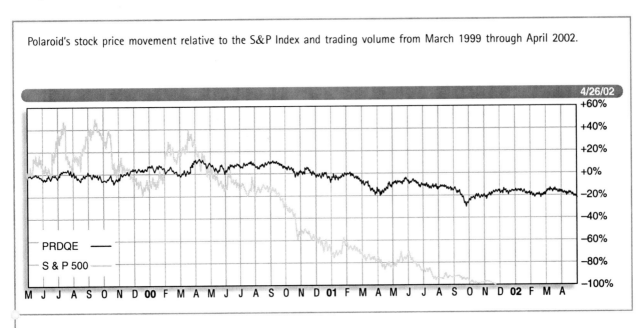

Polaroid's stock price movement relative to the S&P Index and trading volume from March 1999 through April 2002.

Exhibit 2.1

THE REAL WORLD

Polaroid

The changes in company value are very evident for a publicly traded corporation such as Polaroid since its stock price is published daily. This is not true for all forms of business. While we intend to focus on publicly traded corporations we would like to spend a little bit of time describing other forms of business so that you understand why the corporate form of business is the dominant one in the U.S. economy.

FORMS OF BUSINESS ORGANIZATION

The corporate form of business is by far the most popular for large publicly traded firms. This popularity stems from three principal features:

- Limited liability for its capital suppliers
- Ease of transferring ownership
- Ease of access to additional ownership funds

Limited liability means that investors in the firm's equity securities generally cannot lose more than the amounts that they invest, should the firm perform poorly. This feature can be compared to the unlimited liability of owners of **sole proprietorships** (single owners) and **partnerships** (multiple owners). If a sole proprietorship or partnership cannot meet its obligations to creditors, then creditors may seek satisfaction of their claims from the owner's or partners' personal assets, respectively. As a result, hybrid forms of organization have emerged, such as *limited liability companies (LLCs)* and *limited liability partnerships (LLPs)*, which, as their name suggests, include the limited liability feature of corporations. Many public accounting firms are organized as LLPs, such as PricewaterhouseCoopers, LLP and KPMG, LLP. Some relatively well known businesses are also organized as LLCs, such as Orbitz, LLC (the web-based travel service) and BMW of North America, LLC (an importer of BMW products in North America).

Corporations, particularly large ones, are typically owned by a vast number of individuals. This ownership structure spreads the limited risk of ownership over many investors. In the case of a sole proprietorship, the single owner bears all the unlimited risk, whereas in partnerships, the partners share that risk. This difference in the distribution of risks appears to have played an important role in the rise of corporations as the preferred type of business organization.

Transfers of ownership in publicly traded corporations can be easily accomplished through the purchase and sale of investors' equity securities, in other words, the trading of stock. To trade stock, a corporation lists its stock on major stock exchanges, such as the *New York Stock Exchange* or *NASDAQ*. These exchanges attract large numbers of investors, as they can easily and quickly acquire or sell securities as needed to maximize their economic welfare. From the firm's perspective, stock exchanges provide relatively easy access to one type of capital needed to fund its investment and operating needs. In contrast, ownership of sole proprietorships is more difficult to transfer, as it requires finding buyers without benefit of stock exchange services. Transferring ownership of partnerships is also more difficult. If an existing partner leaves or a new partner enters the business, the existing partnership must first be dissolved and a new one then created.

The corporate form of business also allows the firm to increase its equity capital by offering additional shares for sale. In a publicly traded corporation, this means that many individual investors, other then the present owners, might become owners in the firm. The larger set of investors in the public stock markets allows the company access to a considerable amount of resources as it grows. Sole proprietorships, in comparison, have limited access to additional funds as they are constrained by the owner's wealth and ability to borrow. Partnerships also are at a disadvantage, as they usually only raise ownership funds through additional contributions of the partners or by admitting new partners to the business.

The corporate form does possess a potentially significant negative consideration: taxes. Corporations are subject to corporate income taxation, whereas sole-proprietorship and partnership income is taxed only at the individual level. Because individual investors are taxed on the income they receive from corporations (in the form of dividends and capital gains), the net result is that corporate income is taxed twice, once at the corporate level and a second time at the individual level. This tax structure may influence who chooses to invest in corporations and how corporations' securities are priced relative to holdings in other forms of business entities.

> The tax status of an entity has significant valuation implications, as taxes reduce cash flows.

Exhibit 2.2 summarizes some of the pros and cons of the main forms of business organization. Because of their dominance in the market, we focus on the reporting of publicly traded corporations in the remainder of the book. In the next section, we expand an understanding of corporations by discussing the nature of their financial statements.

Exhibit 2.2
Pros and Cons of Forms of
Business Organization

Form of Organization	Pros	Cons
Proprietorship	Income taxed once	Unlimited liability Ownership transfer difficult No sharing of risk Limited access to additional ownership funds
Partnership	Income taxed once Some sharing of risk Some access to additional ownership funds	Unlimited liability Ownership transfer difficult
Corporation	Limited liability Ease of transfer of ownership Relatively easy access to additional ownership funds	Double taxation

FINANCIAL ACCOUNTING REPORTS

As we discussed in Chapter 1, to conduct business, publicly traded corporations raise long-term funds from individuals and institutions through both lending agreements and the issuance of stock. Both lending agreements and stock represent claims on the resources (assets) that the corporation controls. Corporations also obtain short-term funds from other creditors; for example, suppliers often sell inventory to companies on credit. Such credit purchases are, in effect, short-term loans from the suppliers. Exhibit 2.3 shows the *balanced* relationship between the firm's resources on the one side, and claims to those resources on the other.

Financial statements provide information about the firm's resources and claims to resources at periodic points in time, and also about the changes to those resources and claims to resources from the firm's activities between those points in time. The major financial statements include the:

- Statement of Financial Position
- Statement of Earnings

Exhibit 2.3
Resources and Claims against
Resources

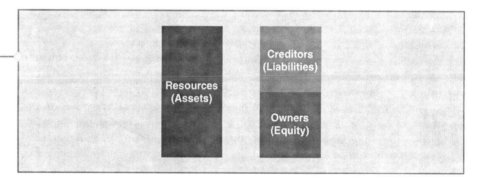

- Statement of Cash Flows
- Statement of Changes in Stockholders' Equity

Below we discuss each statement, as well as provide descriptions of many terms that each statement includes. In this chapter, we simply want to offer you a general sense of what each statement contains. We will provide more detailed explanations of the content in later chapters, so you need not try to fully understand them here.

STATEMENT OF FINANCIAL POSITION

The Statement of Financial Position describes the firm's resources and claims to those resources as seen in Exhibit 2.3. Accounting expressions for resources, creditors, and owners are, respectively, **assets, liabilities,** and **stockholders' equity** (or **common stockholders' equity** or simply **owners' equity**).

ASSETS

In simple terms assets are those resources owned by the company or those that the company has the right to use. From the accountant's point of view, assets are resources that have *probable future value* to the firm and are recognized under GAAP. Assets typically include *cash; accounts receivable* (amounts due from the firm's customers); *inventories* (for use in production or for sale); *plant, property, and equipment* (used to make products or provide services); and various *property rights* (the rights to use an economic resource such as a patent).

Accountants, however, do not consider some economic resources as assets because they fail to meet measurement criteria, such as the general criterion of reliability discussed in Chapter 1. For example, a brand image (e.g., the Coca Cola logo) created through advertising and customer satisfaction cannot be reliably valued and are not, therefore, recognized in the financial statements. Furthermore, the amounts at which resources are reflected as assets often differ from their current economic value. For example, the market or appraisal value of land some years after its acquisition might be greater than its recorded value (sometimes called the *carrying value*), as accounting standards stipulate that land be carried at its historical cost.

LIABILITIES

In simple terms, liabilities represent the amounts owed to others. From the accountant's point of view they represent *probable future sacrifices* of resources. Liabilities may include bank borrowings (*notes payable* or *mortgages payable*), borrowings that are done through publicly traded securities known as bonds (*bonds payable*), amounts due to suppliers (*accounts payable*), and amounts due to others providing goods or services to the company during production, such as utility companies and employees (*utilities payable* and *salaries payable,* respectively). Sometimes the word **accrued** appears with the liability titles (e.g., *accrued warranty liability, accrued expenses*), implying that the amounts have been estimated. Customers may also have some claim on resources if they have prepaid for goods and services that the company must deliver in the future. These types of claims, typically called *deferred revenue, unearned revenues,* or simply *deposits,* reflect items such as prepaid magazine subscriptions.

Similar to assets, accountants also do not consider all economic obligations as liabilities. For example, if a company contracts with another company to purchase goods that will be delivered at a future date at a fixed price, current accounting standards do not require the company to recognize the obligation to pay the supplier when the contract is signed. As neither company has satisfied its part of the contract, neither company recognizes the contract in its accounting records. In accounting jargon, this kind of contract is known as a *mutually unexecuted contract.* Also, some liabilities are so uncertain that they may not meet the criteria for recognition. For instance, potential legal liabilities associated with lawsuits are often excluded from liabilities because it is very uncertain as to whether the company will actually have to pay a settlement.

> As analysts try to predict the future cash flows of the firm, unrecorded liabilities may pose one of the more significant estimation challenges.

STOCKHOLDERS' EQUITY

Unlike creditor and customer claims that a firm settles within some specified time frame, equity claims have no specified time period for payment. Stockholders of a corporation are not assured a specific set of payments. Instead, they usually only receive cash payments when the company declares a *cash dividend* (when the firm generates positive earnings) or when stockholders elect to sell their shares. As a result, stockholders' equity is sometimes referred to as a **residual claim,** because owners can only claim what is left over after all creditor claims have been met. It can also be thought of as the residual claim on assets after deducting liabilities. In other words, owners can claim the difference between what the company owns and what it owes. **Net assets** (also referred to as **net book value**) can be calculated through the accounting equation that we discuss next.

THE ACCOUNTING EQUATION

As mentioned previously, the statement of financial position (often called a **balance sheet**) reports a firm's assets, liabilities, and stockholders' equity at a particular point in time. Further, a characteristic of a balance sheet is that the sum of assets equals the sum of liabilities and stockholders' equity (hence the word "balance"). This characteristic of the balance sheet is commonly referred to as the **accounting equation** (recall that Exhibit 2.3 illustrates this).

$$\text{Assets} = \text{Liabilities} + \text{Stockholders' Equity}$$

It follows from this equation that stockholders' equity equals assets less liabilities. That is:

$$\text{Stockholders' Equity} = \text{Assets} - \text{Liabilities}$$

Stockholders' equity is also called *net assets* or *net book value*. To illustrate a statement of financial position, based on the accounting equation, let's next look at a real company, Ross Stores.

STATEMENT OF FINANCIAL POSITION: ROSS STORES

Exhibit 2.4, Ross' 10K report, describes the company's business and operating goals. Reviewing this information first helps to provide insight into the information included in the financial statements.

Exhibit 2.5 shows Ross' Statement of Financial Position for the year ended February 1, 2003. Note that Ross presents two columns of data, one at the beginning of the year (2/2/2002) and the other at the end of the year (2/1/2003). The SEC requires two years of balance sheet data for annual reports. Further, the SEC requires firms to report the balance sheet data as of the end of their **fiscal** (financial) **year.** The fiscal year often ends on the same date as the calendar year, December 31. However, as with Ross, this need not be the case. Due to the seasonal nature of their business, many retail firms use year-ends other than December 31, for example, Tommy Hilfiger Corp (March 31), Wal-Mart (January 31), American Greetings (February 28), and Starbucks (September 30). Finally, note that the accounting equation is satisfied at both points in time. In fact, the accounting equation needs to be satisfied at all points in time in an accounting system.

Ross presents what is known as a **classified balance sheet.** This type of balance sheet lists assets in order of how quickly they can be converted into cash, sometimes referred to as **liquidity order.** In addition, a classified balance sheet also segregates assets into **current** and **noncurrent** categories. **Current assets** are cash and assets that are expected to be converted into cash or expire within one year or one operating cycle of the business, whichever is longer. For a manufacturing firm, the *operating cycle* is the time between the initial acquisition of raw materials and the collection on the sale of the inventory that is sold. Inventory is a current asset because it will be sold and converted into cash during the firm's current operating cycle, which, for most firms, is less than one year. Note that for certain kinds of inventory (e.g., any long-term construction project such as submarines and aircraft) the operating cycle could be longer than a year. This type of inventory would still meet the definition of a current asset as the inventory is sold within an operating cycle.

Ross Stores, Inc. ("Ross" or "the Company") operates a chain of off-price retail apparel and home accessories stores, which target value-conscious men and women between the ages of 25 and 54 primarily in middle-income households. The decisions of the Company, from merchandising, purchasing, and pricing, to the location of its stores, are aimed at this customer base. The Company offers brand-name and designer merchandise at low everyday prices, generally 20 percent to 60 percent below regular prices of most department and specialty stores. The Company believes it derives a competitive advantage by offering a wide assortment of quality brand-name merchandise within each of its merchandise categories in an attractive easy-to-shop environment.

Exhibit 2.4
Ross Stores Business
(from 10K)

THE REAL WORLD

Ross Stores

Exhibit 2.5
Ross Stores—Statement of
Financial Position
(in thousands)

THE REAL WORLD

Ross Stores

	2/1/2003	2/2/2002
ASSETS		
CURRENT ASSETS		
Cash and cash equivalents (includes $10,000 of restricted cash)	$ 150,649	$ 40,351
Accounts receivable	18,349	20,540
Merchandise inventory	716,518	623,390
Prepaid expenses and other	36,904	30,710
Total Current Assets	922,420	714,991
PROPERTY AND EQUIPMENT		
Land and buildings	54,772	54,432
Fixtures and equipment	412,496	351,288
Leasehold improvements	232,388	209,086
Construction-in-progress	61,720	24,109
	761,376	638,915
Less accumulated depreciation and amortization	358,693	307,365
	402,683	331,550
Other long-term assets	36,242	36,184
Total Assets	$1,361,345	$1,082,725
LIABILITIES AND STOCKHOLDERS' EQUITY		
CURRENT LIABILITIES		
Accounts payable	$ 397,193	$ 314,530
Accrued expenses and other	114,586	92,760
Accrued payroll and benefits	99,115	70,413
Income taxes payable	15,790	11,885
Total Current Liabilities	626,684	489,588
Long-term debt	25,000	—
Deferred income taxes and other long-term liabilities	66,473	48,682
STOCKHOLDERS' EQUITY		
Common stock, par value $.01 per share Authorized 300,000,000 shares Issued and outstanding 77,491,000 and 78,960,000 shares	775	790
Additional paid-in capital	341,041	289,734
Retained earnings	301,372	253,931
	643,188	544,455
Total Liabilities and Stockholders' Equity	$1,361,345	$1,082,725

Consistent with the nature of its business, Ross' assets include cash; accounts receivable, representing amounts due from its customers; merchandise inventories, representing costs of goods waiting to be sold; and property and equipment, representing the long-term investments in property and equipment that are necessary to its merchandising activities. In each case, these assets reflect an expected future benefit. For accounts receivable, it is the cash Ross expects to collect from customers. For merchandise inventories, it is the cash or receivables that Ross expects to arise from sales. For property and equipment, it is the sales that Ross expects to generate from their stores.

As with the asset section, the balance sheet classifies liabilities into a current and noncurrent section. Similar to current assets, **current liabilities** are liabilities that become due, or expected to be settled, within one year. Ross' liabilities are consistent with the nature of its business. They include accounts payable, principally representing amounts due to vendors of merchandise that it sells; accrued payroll, representing amounts owed to employees; accrued expenses, representing amounts owed to others for providing certain services, for example, utilities; and income taxes payable, representing amounts owed to the taxing authorities. Ross' liabilities also include long-term debt, representing amounts borrowed to finance its investment and operating activities.

As noted above, stockholders' equity represents the residual claim after liabilities have been met. **Common stock** and **additional paid-in capital** combined represent the amount contributed by stockholders when they purchased shares from the company. The remaining portion of stockholders' equity, **retained earnings,** represents the accumulated amount of net income less dividends distributed to stockholders since the company formed.

As explained earlier, not all resources that Ross controls may be reported as assets on its balance sheet. GAAP restricts what items can appear on the balance sheet, as well as the values assigned to those items that do appear. For example, Ross' slogan "Dress for Less" may have value for its company recognition. However, difficulties in how to measure the economic benefits of slogans or brand names generally prevent their recognition as assets in an accounting sense. Going back to the example of Polaroid that started this chapter, Polaroid states that patents and trademarks are valued at $1 on its financial statements. This treatment recognizes that these assets have value, but by only recognizing them at $1 there is no material effect on the interpretation of the financial statements. Polaroid therefore indicates to its financial statement readers that these items have value even though the company cannot report them under GAAP.

Recall that the accounting values for assets and liabilities may not reflect their current market values. Because stockholders' equity must equal assets less liabilities, it therefore follows that the book value of stockholders' equity does not necessarily equal its market value. For example, if we divide stockholders' equity from Ross' balance sheet ($643,188) by the number of shares of Ross' common stock outstanding (77,491), we obtain a **book value per share** of $8.35 at February 1, 2003. However, Ross' stock price during the year ended February 1, 2003 ranged from $32.76 to $46.88 a share.

> The amount in the common stock accounts represents a par value assigned to the shares at issuance and has little economic significance. Par value should not be confused with market value of the firm's stock. Market value takes into account the entire equity of stockholders and is not limited to the portion of initial contribution labeled as par value.

> Market values are not used to value owners' equity in the financial statements as it would be circular logic to value stockholders' equity at market prices that, in principle, depend on the information contained in financial reports.

FLOW STATEMENTS—CHANGES IN FINANCIAL POSITION

Changes in the firm's financial position from one point in time to another can be broadly classified into those related to *operating, investing,* and *financing activities.* Three statements describe these changes in the financial position of the firm: the Statement of Earnings, the Statement of Cash Flows, and the Statement

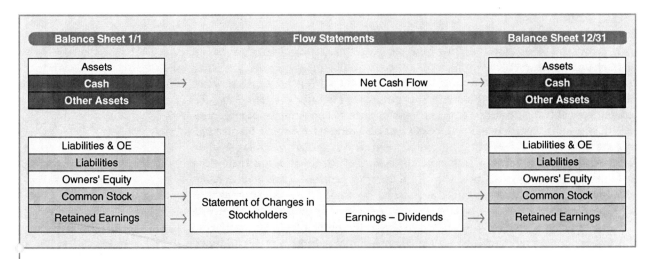

Exhibit 2.6
Financial Statement
Connections

of Changes in Stockholders' Equity. Exhibit 2.6 shows the relationships of the three flow statements to the balance sheet at the beginning and end of the period.

STATEMENT OF EARNINGS

The Statement of Earnings (sometimes called the *Statement of Income,* or *Income Statement*) explains changes in stockholders' equity arising from the firm's operating activities. It reports *revenues* from sales of goods and services to customers and the *expenses* of generating those revenues. Revenues are generally recognized at the point at which the company transfers the risks and benefits of ownership of the goods or services to the buyer. For most product firms, this happens at the date the product is delivered to the customer. Expenses are often classified into costs directly related to the goods sold **(cost of goods sold),** other operating expenses (including selling and administrative costs), financing costs (e.g., interest), and income taxes.

At the time revenues are recognized, the firm records the increase in assets that it has received in exchange for its goods or services. These assets are typically either cash or, if the customer is granted credit, accounts receivable. In some cases, a customer may pay for a product or service in advance of its receipt (e.g., school tuition). When this occurs, the firm cannot recognize the revenue from the sale until the product or service is delivered (as we will discuss in Chapter 4). Therefore, the receipt of cash results in the creation of a liability that represents this deferred revenue (the obligation of the firm to deliver the product or service in the future). Later, when revenue is recognized on the income statement, this liability account is reduced.

When expenses are recognized, they may be associated with decreases in assets (such as the decrease in inventory when cost of goods sold is recognized) or increases in liabilities (such as when salary expense is recognized before salaries are paid to employees).

Net income (loss) (also referred to as *net earnings*), then, is the excess of revenues (expenses) over expenses (revenues):

$$\text{Net Income} = \text{Revenues} - \text{Expenses}$$

Net income (loss) increases (decreases) owners' equity because it is added to the balance in retained earnings. Note that earnings can either be positive (income) or negative (loss).

Accounting recognition of the revenues and expenses that go into the determination of net income are governed by the **accrual concept** of accounting. As explained more fully in Chapter 4, under this concept, revenues are recorded as *earned,* not necessarily when cash is received, and expenses are recorded as *incurred,* not necessarily when cash is paid.

> The accrual concept is very important to fully understand because analysts often use earnings as a starting point to forecast future cash flows of the firm.

Let's look at the Statement of Earnings for Ross for three fiscal years (Exhibit 2.7). Ross prepares what is known as a single-step income statement. This type of income statement combines all revenues in one section and all expenses except income taxes in a second section. *Sales* are amounts charged to customers for merchandise. *Costs and Expenses* include *costs of goods sold, general and administrative costs,* and *interest expense.* As is the case for most retailers, costs of goods sold include costs associated with buying and distributing merchandise and building occupancy costs. General and administrative costs include salaries, wages, employee benefits, and other expense of managing the firm's activities. Interest expense pertains to the debt that appears on Ross' balance sheet and is therefore considered a nonoperating item. *Earnings before taxes* is then computed (subtracting all expenses from sales). The tax on this income is shown just prior to *Net earnings,* often referred to as the *bottom line.*

Net earnings summarizes the effect of Ross' operating activities on stockholders' equity. It is added to the balance of retained earnings at the end of the previous year in arriving at the balance at February 1, 2003. Because stockholders' equity equals net assets (assets less liabilities), net assets must also

For the years ended (in thousands)	2/1/2003	2/2/2002	2/3/2001
SALES	$3,531,349	$2,986,596	$2,709,039
COSTS AND EXPENSES			
Cost of goods sold, including related buying, distribution, and occupancy costs	2,628,412	2,243,384	2,017,923
General, selling, and administrative	572,316	485,455	438,464
Interest expense, net	279	3,168	3,466
	3,201,007	2,732,007	2,459,853
Earnings before taxes	330,342	254,589	249,186
Provision for taxes on earnings	129,164	99,544	97,432
Net earnings	$ 201,178	$ 155,045	$ 151,754

Exhibit 2.7
Ross Stores—Statement of Earnings

THE REAL WORLD

Ross Stores

reflect the results of operations. Intuitively, we can see that sales prices charged to customers not only increase net income (and hence owners' equity) in the form of revenues, but also increase assets by increasing either cash or accounts receivable. Likewise, salaries and wages of employees not only decrease net income (owners' equity) in the form of operating expenses, but either decrease assets by decreasing cash or increase liabilities by increasing accrued payroll. This two-sided effect of revenues or expenses is essential to preserve the relationship in the accounting equation. (This concept is discussed in detail in Chapters 3 and 4 so do not be concerned if it seems difficult to grasp at this point.)

STATEMENT OF CASH FLOWS

The Statement of Cash Flows also describes changes in financial position, specifically the changes in cash. This statement shows how investing, financing, and operating activities affect cash. Investment activities relate to the acquisition or disposal of long-term assets such as property and equipment. Financing activities relate to the issuance and repayment or repurchase of debt and equity. The operating activities section reports the cash inflows and outflows associated with the sales of goods and services to customers.

Under current accounting standards, the operating section of the statement can be presented in one of two forms: a **direct method,** under which the direct cash inflows and outflows are shown, or an **indirect method** (by far the most common), under which net income under the accrual concept is adjusted to its cash flow equivalent. Exhibit 2.8 illustrates the direct method of the Statement of Cash Flows for Rowe Companies (a group of companies that provides home furnishings). In contrast, Exhibit 2.9 shows the indirect method of the Statement of Cash Flows for Ross. Chapter 5 provides a more complete discussion of the differences in these two methods.

Looking at Exhibit 2.9, note how the operating section differs from the one presented in Exhibit 2.8. For the Ross Statement of Cash Flows, the operating section starts with net earnings, which is then adjusted to its cash flow equivalent (net cash provided by operating activities). Further note how the net earnings and the net cash provided by operating activities differ in each year. For instance, in 2003, net income was $201,178 (000s), whereas cash flow from operations was $332,445 (000s).

The investing section contains additions to property and equipment made during the year. Though not in Ross' case, this section may also include amounts invested in temporary investments or costs of acquiring the net assets of another firm. The financing section shows the proceeds and payments on long-term debt, the cash payments of dividends, the proceeds from the issuance of stock for employee stock plans (recall that we mentioned these in Chapter 1 as a common way to compensate certain managers), and repurchases of Ross' own shares.

Now that we have completed a look at three of the major financial statements for Ross, it is useful to revisit the diagram in Exhibit 2.6 that showed the connections among the balance sheet, income statement, and cash flow statement.

Exhibits 2.8
Statement of Cash Flows:
Direct Method

THE REAL WORLD

Rowe Companies

The Rowe Companies Annual Report 2003
CONSOLIDATED STATEMENTS OF CASH FLOWS

Year Ended (in thousands)	11/30/2003	12/1/2002	12/2/2001
Increase (Decrease) in Cash			
Cash flows from operating activities:			
Cash received from customers	$300,299	$336,853	$329,558
Cash paid to suppliers and employees	(287,266)	(317,217)	(331,014)
Income taxes received (paid), net	1,352	2,839	585
Interest paid	(5,225)	(4,028)	(2,397)
Interest received	225	347	480
Other receipts—net	942	1,340	1,109
Net cash and cash equivalents provided by (used in) operating activities	10,327	20,134	(1,679)
Cash flows from investing activities:			
Payments received on notes receivable	100	125	125
Increase in cash surrender value	(121)	(150)	(179)
Proceeds from sale of Mitchell Gold	39,573	—	—
Proceeds from sale of property and equipment	—	—	1,056
Capital expenditures	(3,995)	(3,323)	(3,317)
Payments under earn-out and related obligations (Note 2)	(15,759)	—	—
Net cash provided by (used in) investing activities	19,798	(3,348)	(2,315)
Cash flows from financing activities:			
Restricted cash released from (deposited to) collateral for letters of credit	264	(1,938)	—
Net borrowings (repayments) under line of credit	—	(9,368)	5,368
Draws under revolving loans	12,570	3,994	6,865
Proceeds from issuance of long-term debt	—	39,442	—
Repayments under revolving loans	(20,751)	(10,244)	(3,821)
Payments to reduce long-term debt	(18,759)	(47,874)	—
Payments to reduce loans on cash surrender value	(16)	—	—
Proceeds from loans against life insurance policies	—	—	3,014
Proceeds from issuance of common stock	3	38	27
Dividends paid	—	—	(1,379)
Purchase of treasury stock	(2)	(19)	(16)
Net cash provided by (used in) financing activities	(26,691)	(25,969)	10,058
Net increase (decrease) in cash and cash equivalents	3,434	(9,183)	6,064
Cash at beginning of year	274	9,457	3,393
Cash at end of year	$ 3,708	$ 274	$ 9,457

Exhibit 2.9
Ross Stores—Statement of
Cash Flows

THE REAL WORLD

Ross Stores

For the years ended (in thousands)	2/1/2003	2/2/2002	2/3/2001
CASH FLOWS FROM OPERATING ACTIVITIES			
Net earnings	$201,178	$155,045	$151,754
Adjustments to reconcile net earnings to			
net cash provided by operating activities:			
Depreciation and amortization of			
property and equipment	53,329	49,896	44,377
Other amortization	12,847	12,725	10,686
Deferred income taxes	17,375	12,633	10,015
Change in assets and liabilities:			
Merchandise inventory	(93,128)	(63,824)	(59,071)
Other current assets net	(4,003)	(16,901)	(980)
Accounts payable	81,958	54,064	5,751
Other current liabilities	54,541	34,384	(26,836)
Other	8,348	4,867	7,653
Net cash provided by operating activities	332,445	242,889	143,349
CASH FLOWS USED IN INVESTING ACTIVITIES			
Additions to property and equipment	(133,166)	(86,002)	(82,114)
Net cash used in investing activities	(133,166)	(86,002)	(82,114)
CASH FLOWS USED IN FINANCING ACTIVITIES			
Borrowings (repayments) under lines of credit	0	(64,000)	64,000
Proceeds from long-term debt	25,000	0	0
Issuance of common stock related			
to stock plans	50,863	54,581	14,303
Repurchase of common stock	(149,997)	(130,676)	(169,324)
Dividends paid	(14,847)	(13,595)	(12,389)
Net cash used in financing activities	(88,981)	(153,690)	(103,410)
Net increase (decrease) in cash and			
cash equivalents	110,298	3,197	(42,175)
Cash and cash equivalents:			
Beginning of year	40,351	37,154	79,329
End of year	$150,649	$ 40,351	$ 37,154
SUPPLEMENTAL CASH FLOW DISCLOSURES			
Interest paid	$ 409	$ 3,332	$ 3,352
Income taxes paid	$ 91,875	$ 61,433	$100,359

ARTICULATION OF THE FINANCIAL STATEMENTS

Exhibit 2.10 presents an update of Exhibit 2.6; we have now included the dollar amounts for the key components of these connections. Note how earnings and dividends affect the balance in retained earnings. However, in Ross' case, retained earnings is also affected by the repurchase of shares of its own stock. (We will discuss this type of transaction in Chapter 12.) Ross' Statement of

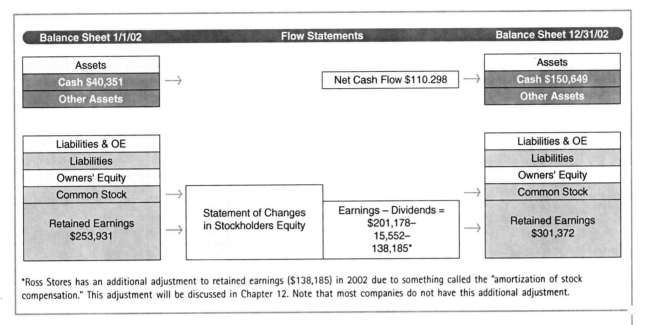

*Ross Stores has an additional adjustment to retained earnings ($138,185) in 2002 due to something called the "amortization of stock compensation." This adjustment will be discussed in Chapter 12. Note that most companies do not have this additional adjustment.

Exhibit 2.10
Financial Statement
Connections—Ross

Changes in Stockholders' Equity, discussed next, provides these same direct connections between the beginning and ending balances in the accounts, as well as changes in those accounts.

THE REAL WORLD

Ross Stores

STATEMENT OF CHANGES IN STOCKHOLDERS' EQUITY

The Statement of Changes in Stockholders' Equity provides details about all of the transactions that affect stockholders' equity, including such items as stock issuance, stock repurchases, net income, and dividends. Exhibit 2.11 shows Ross' Statement of Changes in Stockholders' Equity. Each column represents a particular account within stockholders' equity. The rows represent the balance and the transactions that have occurred over the most recent three years. Recall that retained earnings are increased by net income and decreased by dividends declared to stockholders (except for the adjustment for the repurchase of stock that we have already mentioned).

OTHER STATEMENT DISCLOSURES

A company's annual report to shareholders contains more than the financial statements themselves (see Exhibit 2.12). For example, footnotes describe significant accounting policies employed by the firm (see Exhibit 2.13), as well as elaborate on items that appear in the statements. The report of the firm's auditors attests to the fairness of the financial statements and their conformance

	Common Shares	Stock Amount	Additional Paid-In Capital	Retained Earnings	Total
BALANCE AT JANUARY 29, 2000	88,774	$888	$234,635	$237,908	$473,431
Common stock issued under stock plans, including tax benefit	1,854	18	14,285		14,303
Amortization of stock compensation			9,894		9,894
Common stock repurchased	(10,101)	(101)	(22,690)	(146,533)	(169,324)
Net earnings				151,754	151,754
Dividends declared				(12,511)	(12,511)
BALANCE AT FEBRUARY 3, 2001	80,527	805	236,124	230,618	467,547
Common stock issued under stock plans, including tax benefit	3,378	34	54,547		54,581
Amortization of stock compensation			11,881		11,881
Common stock repurchased	(4,945)	(49)	(12,818)	(117,809)	(130,676)
Net earnings				155,045	155,045
Dividends declared				(13,923)	(13,923)
BALANCE AT FEBRUARY 2, 2002	78,960	790	289,734	253,931	544,455
Common stock issued under stock plans, including tax benefit	2,341	23	50,840		50,863
Amortization of stock compensation			12,241		12,241
Common stock repurchased	(3,810)	(38)	(11,774)	(138,185)	(149,997)
Net earnings				201,178	201,178
Dividends declared				(15,552)	(15,552)
BALANCE AT FEBRUARY 1, 2003	77,491	$775	$341,041	$301,372	$643,188

Exhibit 2.11
Ross Stores—Statement of Changes in Stockholders' Equity (in thousands)

THE REAL WORLD

Ross Stores

with regulatory guidelines. Further, although not formally part of the company's financial statements, management provides its own assessment of the past year's operating results, liquidity, and capital expenditures, as well as financing strategies. Management provides this information through the management's discussion and analysis section of the annual report, commonly known as the *MD&A section*.

Exhibit 2.12
Typical Contents of an Annual Report

Message from Chief Executive Officer
Description of Principal Products or Services
Financial Highlights
Management's Discussion and Analysis
Statement of Financial Position
Statement of Earnings
Statement of Cash Flows
Statement of Changes in Stockholders' Equity
Notes to Financial Statements
Statement of Management's Responsibilities
Auditor's Report
Other Corporate Information

Exhibits 2.13
Ross Stores Footnotes:
Summary of Significant
Accounting Policies

THE REAL WORLD

Ross Stores

Merchandise Inventory. Merchandise inventory is stated at the lower of cost (determined using a weighted average basis) or net realizable value. The Company purchases manufacturer overruns and canceled orders both during and at the end of a season which are referred to as packaway inventory. Packaway inventory is purchased with the intent that it will be stored in the Company's warehouses until a later date, which may even be the beginning of the same selling season in the following year. Packaway inventory accounted for approximately 44 percent and 43 percent of total inventories as of February 1, 2003 and February 2, 2002, respectively.

Cost of Goods Sold. In addition to the product cost of merchandise sold, the Company includes its buying and distribution expenses as well as occupancy costs related to the Company's retail stores, buying, and distribution facilities in its cost of goods sold. Buying expenses include costs to procure merchandise inventories. Distribution expenses include the cost of operating the Company's distribution centers and freight expenses related to transporting merchandise.

Property and Equipment. Property and equipment are stated at cost. Depreciation is calculated using the straight-line method over the estimated useful life of the asset, typically ranging from five to 12 years for equipment and 20 to 40 years for real property. The cost of leasehold improvements is amortized over the useful life of the asset or the applicable lease term, whichever is less. Computer hardware and software costs are included in fixtures and equipment and are amortized over their estimated useful life generally ranging from five to seven years. Reviews for impairment are performed whenever events or circumstances indicate the carrying value of an asset may not be recoverable.

Analysts must understand the accounting choices that firms make in order to interpret their financial statements and to make fair comparisons across firms. The summary of significant accounting policies footnote is very important in conveying this information about the choices the firm has made.

Beyond the annual report, additional financial information is made publicly available through filings with the SEC. These filings include prospectuses accompanying new stock issues, annual 10K reports (such as Exhibit 2.4), and 10Q reports (a 10Q reports contains quarterly financial statement information). These reports typically offer greater detail than the annual report. For example, these filings might include information on competition and risks associated with the firm's principal business, holdings of major stockholders, compensation of top executives, and announcements of various events.

THE INFLUENCE OF FINANCIAL STATEMENTS

Financial statements embody the standards by which other information is often constructed. For example, professional security analysts project revenues and estimate research and development spending. Given that such forecasts and projections pertain to information that will ultimately surface in financial statements (see the report for Archer Daniels in Exhibit 2.14), these reports are likely to reflect the same accounting principles. In other words, the influence of financial reports extends well beyond their contents

Exhibit 2.14
Archer Daniels Midland
Operating Earnings Up

THE REAL WORLD

Archer Daniels

January 19, 2001

DECATUR, Ill. Jan 14 (Reuters)—Archer Daniels Midland Co., the largest U.S. grain producer, said on Friday its fiscal second-quarter operating earnings rose 22 percent, beating forecasts, as sales in ethanol, feed, and cocoa products boosted results.

This type of additional disclosure may potentially affect the company's stock valuation as it indicates changes in the expectations of future results ("beating forecasts"). How much the valuation changes depends, in part, on whether the increase in earnings is sustainable in the future. Although no obvious price reaction resulted on the day after this announcement, the price of ADMs stock rose from around $8 a share to $15 a share between October 2000 and February 2001. This clearly indicates the increased prospects of the company.

as such. There is a confirmation aspect to reports provided by the firm that becomes apparent as you look closely at financial information from other sources.

We opened the chapter relating how Polaroid suffered a drop off in sales, starting in the fourth quarter of 2000. Exhibit 2.15 shows the quarterly sales figures for Polaroid (taken from Polaroid's 10Q reports) over the period from the first quarter of 1998 through the second quarter of 2001. Notice the seasonal pattern of Polaroid's sales. That is, in a given year, Polaroid always realizes its highest sales in the fourth quarter, typically significantly up from the third quarter. However, in 2000, fourth-quarter sales are only slightly higher than those in the third quarter. This departure from the previous trend would be important to investors and analysts as they assessed the value of Polaroid's shares in the fourth quarter of 2001 and beyond. Note that sales then dramatically fell in the first and second quarters of 2001, leading up to Polaroid's declaration of bankruptcy in the third quarter of 2001. Sales are just one of the items that analysts would look at to understand earnings and the market value of Polaroid, but in this case perhaps, the most significant one.

Exhibit 2.15
Polaroid's Sales by Quarter

THE REAL WORLD

Polaroid

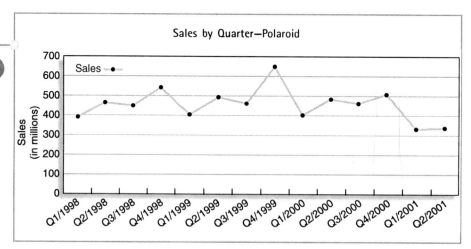

SUMMARY AND TRANSITION

In this chapter, we provided an overview of the corporate form of business and the major financial statements prepared under GAAP as a way to set the stage for examining the construction and use of financial accounting reports in the chapters that follow. As we described, corporations have become the dominant form of business entity due to such features as limited liability and the ease with which ownership can be transferred and capital can be raised.

The main general-purpose financial statements considered include a Statement of Financial Position, which describes the financial position in terms of its assets, liabilities, and stockholders' equity of the firm at a point in time; a Statement of Earnings, which describes the results of the firm's operations in terms of its revenues and expenses from one point in time to another; a Statement of Cash Flows, which describes the firm's investment, financing, and operating activities in terms of their effects on cash; and a Statement of Changes in Stockholders' Equity, which describes transactions affecting contributed capital and retained earnings in further detail.

Our description of these financial statements provides a first glimpse of the typical items comprising the resources that a firm may control (assets) and the claims to those resources held by creditors and owners (liabilities and stockholders' equity, respectively). We identified changes in assets and liabilities arising from the operating activities of the firm as composed of revenues and expenses, leading to the bottom-line number, net income or earnings. Other changes pertained to investment and financing activities. We also reviewed further details of changes in stockholders' equity. In Chapter 3, we describe the mechanics of the accounting system and how to analyze the effects of a particular transaction on these financial statements of the firm. Chapter 4 provides further detail on the measurement and reporting of revenues and expenses. Our coverage of the construction of financial statements then concludes with methods for distinguishing operating, investing, and financing cash flows.

END OF CHAPTER MATERIAL

KEY TERMS

Accounting Equation	Current Assets
Accrual Concept	Current Liabilities
Accrued	Direct Method
Additional Paid-in Capital	Fiscal Year
Assets	Indirect Method
Balance Sheet	Liabilities
Book Value per Share	Limited Liability
Classified Balance Sheet	Liquidity Order
Common Stock	Net Asset
Common Stockholders' Equity	Net Book Value
Cost of Goods Sold	Net income

Noncurrent Assets

Owners' Equity

Partnership

Residual Claim

Retained Earnings

Sole Proprietorship

Statement of Cash Flows

Statement of Changes in Stockholders' Equity

Statement of Earnings

Statement of Financial Position

Stockholders' Equity

ASSIGNMENT MATERIAL

REVIEW QUESTIONS

1. Describe the pros and cons for organizing a business as a corporation rather than a partnership.
2. Describe and illustrate the three major categories of items that appear in a typical statement of financial position.
3. Describe the purpose of the four main financial statements that are contained in all annual reports.
4. What is the meaning of the term net assets?
5. Why might certain economic resources not be considered assets by accountants? Provide an example.
6. What is the accounting equation?
7. What is meant by a classified balance sheet?
8. How do accountants distinguish between current and noncurrent assets and liabilities?
9. Explain the meaning of retained earnings.
10. Why might the book value of a company be different from the market value of the company?
11. What is net income?
12. What are the two methods for reporting cash flow from operations that are allowed under GAAP?
13. What is comprehensive income?
14. How is other comprehensive income reported in the financial statements?

APPLYING YOUR KNOWLEDGE

15. Compare and contrast the statement of earnings and the cash flow statement.

Use the following abbreviations to respond to question 16:

CA—Current Assets

NCA—Noncurrent Assets

CL—Current Liabilities

NCL—Noncurrent Liabilities

CS—Capital Stock

RE—Retained Earnings

NI—Income statement item

CF—Cash flow statement item

16. Classify the following items according to where the item would appear in the financial statements:

    a. Inventory

    b. Taxes Payable

    c. Interest Expense

    d. Dividends

    e. Sales to customers

    f. Manufacturing Equipment

    g. New issuance of common stock

    h. Cash

    i. Bonds Payable (debt due in ten years)

    j. Employee's Wages

Use the following abbreviations to respond to question number 17:

O—Operating Item

F—Financing Item

I—Investing Item

17. Classify each of the following transactions as to whether they are operating, financing, or investing activities:

    a. Cash collected from customers

    b. Repayment of debt

    c. Payment of dividends

    d. Purchase of a truck (by a manufacturing company)

    e. Purchase of a truck (by a truck dealer)

    f. Purchase of shares of stock of another company

    g. Sale of a plant

    h. Utility expenses are incurred

18. Compute the missing balance sheet amounts in each of the following independent situations:

	A	B	C	D
Current Assets	?	$650,000	$230,000	$40,000
Noncurrent Assets	250,000	?	400,000	?
Total Assets	?	1,050,000	?	190,000
Current Liabilities	50,000	500,000	300,000	25,000
Noncurrent Liabilities	?	90,000	?	10,000
Owners' Equity	225,000	?	80,000	?
Total Liabilities and Owners' Equity	350,000	?	?	?

19. Compute the missing amounts in the reconciliation of retained earnings in each of the following independent situations:

	A	B	C	D
Retained Earnings Dec. 31, Year 1	$20,000	$100,000	?	$40,000
Net Income	15,000	?	400,000	22,000
Dividends Declared and Paid	6,000	35,000	250,000	?
Retained Earnings Dec. 31, Year 2	?	115,000	300,000	52,000

20. For each of the following companies, list at least two types of assets and one type of liability that you would expect to find on their balance sheet (try to include at least one item in your list that is unique to that business):

   a. The Washington Post Company—This is a company that is primarily in the newspaper business but also has operations in television stations, cable systems, *Newsweek* magazine, as well as some other smaller operations.

   b. International Paper—This is a company that is primarily in the forest products business, selling both paper and wood products.

   c. SBC—This is a telecommunications company.

   d. Hartford Financial Services Group—This is a multiline insurance company.

   e. Philip Morris Companies, Inc.—This is a company that is primarily in the tobacco business but has also diversified into foods, beer, financial services, and real estate.

   f. Citibank—This is a major commercial bank.

   g. Delta—This is a major airline.

21. For each of the companies listed in question number 20 list at least two line items that you would expect to find on their income statement (try to include at least one item in your list that is unique to that business).

22. For each of the companies listed in question number 20 list at least two line items that you would expect to find on their cash flow statement (try to include at least one item in your list that is unique to that business).

23. Suppose that your best friend wanted to start a new business providing desktop publishing services to customers. Your friend has some savings to start the business but not enough to buy all of the equipment that she thinks she needs. She has asked you for some advice about how to raise additional funds. Give her at least two alternatives and provide the pros and cons for each alternative.

24. Suppose that you and a friend form a partnership in which you both contribute the same amount of cash and you agree to share in profits on a 50–50 basis. Further suppose that you are responsible for running the day-to-day operations of the firm but your friend is a silent partner in the sense that he doesn't work in the business (he has another job). Because you have no other job, the partnership agrees to pay you $1,500 per month. How should the partnership treat this payment, as a distribution of profits or as an expense of doing business? What difference would it make to the distribution to you and your partner?

USING REAL DATA

Base your answer to problems 25–28 on the data from Polaroid provided here.

POLAROID CORP. Balance Sheet	12/31/1999	12/31/2000
Assets		
Current Assets		
Cash and cash equivalents	$ 92,000,000	$ 97,200,000
Receivables, less allowances of $23.9 in 1999 and $23.8 in 2000 (Note 6)	489,700,000	435,400,000
Inventories (Notes 5 and 6)	395,600,000	482,500,000
Prepaid expenses and other assets (Note 4)	130,800,000	103,500,000
Total Current Assets	1,108,100,000	1,118,600,000
Property, Plant, and Equipment:		
Land	14,700,000	6,900,000
Buildings	322,700,000	313,500,000
Machinery and equipment	1,620,100,000	1,597,500,000
Construction in progress	65,500,000	49,600,000
Total property, plant and equipment	2,023,000,000	1,967,500,000
Less accumulated depreciation	1,423,800,000	1,398,300,000
Net Property, Plant, and Equipment	599,200,000	569,200,000
Deferred Tax Assets (Note 4)	243,700,000	279,500,000
Other Assets	89,000,000	75,700,000
Total Assets	$2,040,000,000	$2,043,000,000
Liabilities and Stockholders' Equity		
Current Liabilities		
Short-term debt (Note 6)	$ 259,400,000	$ 363,700,000
Payables and accruals (Note 7)	338,000,000	334,100,000
Compensation and benefits (Notes 10 and 11)	138,100,000	76,700,000
Federal, state and foreign income taxes (Note 4)	14,700,000	18,800,000
Total Current Liabilities	750,200,000	793,300,000
Long-term debt (Note 8)	573,000,000	573,500,000
Accrued postretirement benefits (Note 11)	234,800,000	222,700,000
Other long-term liabilities	111,500,000	78,300,000
Total Liabilities	1,669,500,000	1,667,800,000
Preferred stock, Series A and D, $1 par value, authorized 20,000,000 shares; all shares unissued	—	—
Common stockholders' equity (Note 9)		
Common stock, $1 par value, authorized 150,000,000 shares (75,427,550 shares issued in 1999 and 2000)	75,400,000	75,400,000
Additional paid-in capital	395,200,000	363,100,000
Retained earnings	1,208,800,000	1,219,500,000
Accumulated other comprehensive income	(48,900,000)	(68,900,000)
Less: Treasury stock, at cost (30,811,263 and 29,895,578 shares in 1999 and 2000, respectively)	1,259,700,000	1,213,800,000
Deferred compensation	300,000	100,000
Total common stockholders' equity	370,500,000	375,200,000
Total Liabilities and Common Stockholders' Equity	$2,040,000,000	$2,043,000,000

POLAROID CORP. Income Statement	12/31/1998	12/31/1999	12/31/2000
Net Sales	$1,845,900,000	$1,978,600,000	$1,855,600,000
Cost of goods sold	1,108,400,000	1,170,500,000	1,055,900,000
Marketing, research, engineering, and adminis- trative expenses (Note 2)	736,500,000	700,500,000	696,400,000
Restructuring charges/(credits) (Note 2)	50,000,000	–	(5,800,000)
Total Costs	1,894,900,000	1,871,000,000	1,746,500,000
Profit/(Loss) from Operations	(49,000,000)	107,600,000	109,100,000
Other income/(expense):			
Interest income	2,900,000	2,700,000	5,500,000
Other	64,800,000	(19,500,000)	28,600,000
Total other income/(expense)	67,700,000	(16,800,000)	34,100,000
Interest expense	57,600,000	77,400,000	85,300,000
Earnings/(Loss) before Income Tax Expense	(38,900,000)	13,400,000	57,900,000
Federal, state and foreign income tax expense (Note 4)	12,100,000	4,700,000	20,200,000
Net Earnings/(Loss)	($51,000,000)	$8,700,000	$37,700,000

POLAROID CORP. Cash Flow	12/31/1998	12/31/1999	12/31/2000
Cash Flows from Operating Activities			
Net earnings/(loss)	$ (51,000,000)	$ 8,700,000	$ 37,700,000
Depreciation of property, plant, and equipment	90,700,000	105,900,000	113,900,000
Gain on the sale of real estate	(68,200,000)	(11,700,000)	(21,800,000)
Other noncash items	62,200,000	73,800,000	22,900,000
Decrease/(increase) in receivables	79,000,000	(52,700,000)	41,800,000
Decrease/(increase) in inventories	(28,400,000)	88,000,000	(100,600,000)
Decrease in prepaids and other assets	39,000,000	62,400,000	32,900,000
Increase/(decrease) in payables and accruals	25,300,000	(16,500,000)	9,200,000
Decrease in compensation and benefits	(21,000,000)	(72,500,000)	(105,000,000)
Decrease in federal, state, and foreign income taxes payable	(29,900,000)	(54,000,000)	(31,500,000)
Net cash provided/(used) by operating activities	97,700,000	131,400,000	(500,000)
Cash Flows from Investing Activities			
Decrease/(increase) in other assets	(25,400,000)	16,500,000	4,500,000
Additions to property, plant, and equipment	(191,100,000)	(170,500,000)	(129,200,000)

	12/31/1998	12/31/1999	12/31/2000
Proceeds from the sale of property, plant, and equipment	150,500,000	36,600,000	56,600,000
Acquisitions, net of cash acquired	(18,800,000)	–	–
Net cash used by investing activities	(84,800,000)	(117,400,000)	(68,100,000)
Cash Flows from Financing Activities			
Net increase/(decrease) in short-term debt (maturities of 90 days or less)	131,200,000	(86,200,000)	108,200,000
Short-term debt (maturities of more than 90 days)			
Proceeds	73,000,000	41,800,000	–
Payments	(117,200,000)	(24,900,000)	–
Proceeds from issuance of long-term debt	–	268,200,000	–
Repayment of long-term debt	–	(200,000,000)	–
Cash dividends paid	(26,500,000)	(26,600,000)	(27,000,000)
Purchase of treasury stock	(45,500,000)	–	–
Proceeds from issuance of shares in connection with stock incentive plan	6,000,000	300,000	100,000
Net cash provided/(used) by financing activities	21,000,000	(27,400,000)	81,300,000
Effect of exchange rate changes on cash	3,100,000	400,000	(7,500,000)
Net increase/(decrease) in cash and cash equivalents	37,000,000	(13,000,000)	5,200,000
Cash and cash equivalents at beginning of year	68,000,000	105,000,000	92,000,000
Cash and cash equivalents at end of year	$105,000,000	$92,000,000	$ 97,200,000

25. Find the following amounts in the statements of Polaroid:

    a. Net sales in 2000

    b. Marketing, research, engineering, and administrative expenses incurred in 2000

    c. Interest expense in 2000

    d. Income tax expense in 1999

    e. Net income in 1999

    f. Inventories at the end of 2000

    g. Payables and accruals at the beginning of 2000

    h. Retained earnings at the end of 2000

    i. Accumulated other comprehensive income at the end of 2000

    j. Long-term borrowings at the beginning of 2000

    k. Cash produced from operating activities in 2000

l. Cash payments to acquire property, plant, and equipment in 2000

m. Dividends paid in 2000

n. Cash proceeds from new borrowings in 2000

o. Cash produced or used for investing activities in 2000

p. Amount of other comprehensive income in 2000

26. What is the trend in net income for the three years presented?

27. What is the trend in cash flow from operations for the three years presented?

28. What is the trend in net sales for the three years presented?

Base your answers to problems 29–35 on the data for Werner Enterprises provided here.

WERNER ENTERPRISES, INC.
CONSOLIDATED BALANCE SHEET
(In thousands, except share amounts)

	2000/12/31	1999/12/31
ASSETS		
Current assets:		
Cash and cash equivalents	$ 25,485	$ 15,368
Accounts receivable, trade, less allowance		
of $3,994 and $3,236, respectively	123,518	127,211
Receivable from unconsolidated affiliate	5,332	–
Other receivables	10,257	11,217
Inventories and supplies	7,329	5,296
Prepaid taxes, licenses, and permits	12,396	12,423
Current deferred income taxes	11,552	8,500
Other	10,908	8,812
Total current assets	206,777	188,827
Property and equipment, at cost		
Land	19,157	14,522
Buildings and improvements	72,631	65,152
Revenue equipment	829,549	800,613
Service equipment and other	100,342	90,322
Total property and equipment	1,021,679	970,609
Less accumulated depreciation	313,881	262,557
Property and equipment, net	707,798	708,052
Notes receivable	4,420	–
Investment in unconsolidated affiliate	5,324	–
Other noncurrent assets	2,888	–
	$ 927,207	$896,879
LIABILITIES AND STOCKHOLDERS' EQUITY		
Current liabilities:		
Accounts payable	$ 30,710	$ 35,686
Short-term debt	–	25,000
Insurance and claims accruals	36,057	32,993
Accrued payroll	12,746	11,846
Income taxes payable	7,157	926
Other current liabilities	14,749	14,755
Total current liabilities	101.419	121.206

	2000/12/31	1999/12/31
Long-term debt	105,000	120,000
Deferred income taxes	152,403	130,600
Insurance, claims, and other long-term accruals	32,301	30,301
Commitments and contingencies		
Stockholders' equity Common stock, $.01 par value, 200,000,000 shares authorized; 48,320,835 shares issued; 47,039,290 and 47,205,236 shares outstanding, respectively	483	483
Paid-in capital	105,844	105,884
Retained earnings	447,943	404,625
Accumulated other comprehensive loss	(34)	—
Treasury stock, at cost; 1,281,545 and 1,115,599 shares, respectively	(18,152)	(16,220)
Total stockholders' equity	536,084	494,772
	$ 927,207	$896,879

WERNER ENTERPRISES, INC.
CONSOLIDATED STATEMENTS OF INCOME
(In thousands, except per share amounts)

	2000/12/31	1999/12/31	1998/12/31
Operating revenues	$1,214,628	$1,052,333	$863,417
Operating expenses:			
Salaries, wages, and benefits	429,825	382,824	325,659
Fuel	137,620	79,029	56,786
Supplies and maintenance	102,784	87,600	72,273
Taxes and licenses	89,126	82,089	67,907
Insurance and claims	34,147	31,728	23,875
Depreciation	109,107	99,955	82,549
Rent and purchased transportation	216,917	185,129	139,026
Communications and utilities	14,454	13,444	10,796
Other	(2,173)	(11,666)	(11,065)
Total operating expenses	1,131,807	950,132	767,806
Operating income	82,821	102,201	95,611
Other expense (income):			
Interest expense	8,169	6,565	4,889
Interest income	(2,650)	(1,407)	(1,724)
Other	(154)	245	114
Total other expense	5,365	5,403	3,279
Income before income taxes	77,456	96,798	92,332
Income taxes	29,433	36,787	35,086
Net income	$ 48,023	$ 60,011	$ 57,246
Average common shares outstanding	47,061	47,406	47,667
Basic earnings per share	$ 1.02	$ 1.27	$ 1.20
Diluted shares outstanding	47,257	47,631	47,910
Diluted earnings per share	$ 1.02	$ 1.26	$ 1.19

WERNER ENTERPRISES, INC.
CONSOLIDATED STATEMENTS OF CASH FLOWS
(In thousands)

	2000/12/31	1999/12/31	1998/12/31
Cash flows from operating activities:			
Net income	$ 48,023	$ 60,011	$ 57,246
Adjustments to reconcile net income to net cash provided by operating activities:			
Depreciation	109,107	99,955	82,549
Deferred income taxes	18,751	22,200	14,700
Gain on disposal of operating equipment	(5,055)	(13,047)	(12,251)
Equity in income of unconsolidated affiliate	(324)	–	–
Tax benefit from exercise of stock options	130	663	389
Other long-term assets	(2,888)	–	–
Insurance, claims, and other long-term accruals	2,000	(500)	1,472
Changes in certain working capital items:			
Accounts receivable, net	3,693	(32,882)	(868)
Prepaid expenses and other current assets	(8,474)	(8,725)	(5,186)
Accounts payable	(4,976)	(12,460)	3,979
Accrued and other current liabilities	10,160	16,762	(4,090)
Net cash provided by operating activities	170,147	131,977	137,940
Cash flows from investing activities:			
Additions to property and equipment	(169,113)	(255,326)	(258,643)
Retirements of property and equipment	60,608	84,297	86,260
Investment in unconsolidated affiliate	(5,000)	–	–
Proceeds from collection of notes receivable	287	–	–
Net cash used in investing activities	(113,218)	(171,029)	(172,383)
Cash flows from financing activities:			
Proceeds from issuance of long-term debt	10,000	30,000	40,000
Repayments of long-term debt	(25,000)	–	–
Proceeds from issuance of short-term debt	–	30,000	20,000
Repayments of short-term debt	(25,000)	(15,000)	(20,000)
Dividends on common stock	(4,710)	(4,740)	(4,201)
Repurchases of common stock	(2,759)	(3,941)	(9,072)
Stock options exercised	657	2,188	1,335
Net cash provided by (used in) financing activities	(46,812)	38,507	28,062
Net increase (decrease) in cash and cash equivalents	10,117	(545)	(6,381)
Cash and cash equivalents, beginning of year	15,368	15,913	22,294
Cash and cash equivalents, end of year	$ 25,485	$ 15,368	$ 15,913
Supplemental disclosures of cash flow information:			
Cash paid during year for:			
Interest	$ 7,876	$ 7,329	$ 4,800
Income taxes	3,916	13,275	26,100
Supplemental disclosures of noncash investing activities:			
Notes receivable from sale of revenue equipment	$ 4,707	$ –	$ –

WERNER ENTERPRISES, INC.
CONSOLIDATED STATEMENTS OF STOCKHOLDERS' EQUITY
(In thousands, except share amounts)

	Common Stock	Paid-in Capital	Retained Earnings	Accumulated Other Comprehensive Loss	Treasury Stock	Total Stockholders' Equity
BALANCE, December 31, 1997	$387	$104,764	$296,533	$ —	($6,566)	$395,118
Purchases of 592,600 shares of common stock	—	—	—	—	(9,072)	(9,072)
Dividends on common stock ($.09 per share)	—	—	(4,428)	—	—	(4,428)
Five-for-four stock split	96	(96)	—	—	—	—
Exercise of stock options, 119,391 shares	—	670	—	—	1,054	1,724
Comprehensive income: Net income	—	—	57,426	—	—	57,246
BALANCE, December 31, 1998	483	105,338	349,351	—	(14,584)	440,588
Purchases of 302,600 shares of common stock	—	—	—	—	(3,941)	(3,941)
Dividends on common stock ($.10 per share)	—	—	(4,737)	—	—	(4,737)
Exercise of stock options, 198,526 shares	—	546	—	—	2,305	2,851
Comprehensive income: Net income	—	—	60,011	—	—	60,011
BALANCE, December 31, 1999	483	105,884	404,625	—	(16,220)	494,772
Purchases of 225,201 shares of common stock	—	—	—	—	(2,759)	(2,759)
Dividends on common stock ($.10 per share)	—	—	(4,705)	—	—	(4,705)
Exercise of stock options, 59,255 shares	—	(40)	—	—	827	787
Comprehensive income (loss): Net income	—	—	48,023	—	—	48,023
Foreign currency translation adjustments	—	—	—	(34)	—	(34)
Total comprehensive income	—	—	48,023	(34)	—	47,989
BALANCE, December 31, 2000	$483	$105,844	$447,943	($34)	($18,152)	$536,084

29. Verify that total assets equal total liabilities and owners' equity for Werner in 2000.

30. Find the following amounts in the statements of Werner:

   a. Revenues in 2000

   b. Salaries, wages, and benefits incurred in 2000

   c. Interest expense in 2000

   d. Income tax expense in 1999

  e. Net income in 1999

  f. Inventories at the end of 2000

  g. Accounts payable at the beginning of 2000

  h. Retained earnings at the end of 2000

  i. Long-term borrowings at the beginning of 2000

  j. Cash produced from operating activities in 2000

  k. Cash payments to acquire property, plant, and equipment in 2000

  l. Dividends paid in 2000

  m. Cash proceeds from new borrowings in 2000

  n. Cash produced or used for investing activities in 2000

31. Does Werner finance the firm mainly from creditors (total liabilities) or from owners (owners' equity) in 2000? Support your answer with appropriate data.

32. List the two largest sources of cash and the two largest uses of cash in 2000. (Consider operations to be a single source or use of cash.)

33. Suggest some reasons why income was $48,023 (000) in 2000, yet cash flow from operations was $170,147 (000).

34. What is the comprehensive net income for Werner in 2000?

35. On December 31, 2000, find the price of Werner's stock (use the library or the web) and compute the total market value of the company's stock that is outstanding based on the number of shares that were outstanding as of that date. Compare this value with the book value of owner's equity on Werner's balance sheet as of that date. If these numbers are different, offer an explanation for this discrepancy.

Base your answers to problems 36–42 on the data for Emulex Corporation provided here.

EMULEX CORP.: Balance Sheet	2001/07/01	2000/07/01
Assets		
Current assets:		
Cash and cash equivalents	$ 36,471,000	$ 23,471,000
Investments	148,204,000	128,234,000
Accounts and other receivables, less allowance for doubtful accounts of 1,298 in 2001 and 844 in 2000	40,239,000	24,332,000
Inventories, net	38,616,000	12,635,000
Prepaid expenses	2,527,000	1,021,000
Deferred income taxes	1,579,000	453,000
Total current assets	267,636,000	190,146,000
Property and equipment, net	18,379,000	6,927,000
Long-term investments	38,805,000	29,293,000
Goodwill and other intangibles, net	590,316,000	0
Deferred income taxes and other assets	2,878,000	3,629,000
Total Assets	$918,014,000	$229,995,000

	2001/07/01	2000/07/01
Liabilities and Stockholders' Equity		
Current liabilities:		
Accounts payable	$ 29,253,000	$ 17,869,000
Accrued liabilities	11,749,000	6,355,000
Income taxes payable and other current liabilities	300,000	320,000
Total current liabilities	41,302,000	24,544,000
Deferred income taxes and other liabilities	26,000	0
	41,328,000	24,544,000
Commitments and contingencies (note 9)		
Stockholders' equity:		
Preferred stock, $0.01 par value; 1,000,000 shares authorized (150,000 shares designated as Series A Junior Participating Preferred Stock); none issued and outstanding	0	0
Common stock, $0.10 par value; 120,000,000 shares authorized; 81,799,322 and 72,466,848 issued and outstanding in 2001 and 2000, respectively	8,180,000	7,247,000
Additional paid-in capital	861,461,000	155,190,000
Deferred compensation	(12,366,000)	0
Retained earnings	19,411,000	43,014,000
Total stockholders' equity	876,686,000	205,451,000
Total liabilities and stockholders' equity	$918,014,000	$229,995,000

EMULEX CORP.: Income Statement

	2001/07/01	2000/07/01	1999/07/01
Net revenues	$245,307,000	$139,772,000	$68,485,000
Cost of sales	120,812,000	73,346,000	40,138,000
Cost of sales—inventory charges related to consolidation	0	0	1,304,000
Total cost of sales	120,812,000	73,346,000	41,442,000
Gross profit	124,495,000	66,426,000	27,043,000
Operating expenses:			
Engineering and development	27,002,000	14,727,000	11,766,000
Selling and marketing	16,734,000	10,077,000	6,953,000
General and administrative	12,111,000	6,923,000	4,279,000
Amortization of goodwill and other intangibles	52,085,000	0	0
In-process research and development	22,280,000	0	0
Consolidation charges, net	0	0	(987,000)
Total operating expenses	130,212,000	31,727,000	22,011,000
Operating income (loss)	(5,717,000)	34,699,000	5,032,000
Nonoperating income	14,301,000	9,131,000	480,000
Income before income taxes	8,584,000	43,830,000	5,512,000
Income tax provision	32,187,000	11,016,000	247,000
Net income (loss)	($23,603,000)	$32,814,000	$5,265,000

EMULEX CORP.: Cash Flow

	2001/07/01	2000/07/01	1999/07/01
Cash flows from operating activities:			
Net income (loss)	($23,603,000)	$32,814,000	$5,265,000
Adjustments to reconcile net income (loss) to net cash provided by operating activities:			
Depreciation and amortization	4,801,000	1,814,000	1,648,000
Gain on sale of strategic investment	(1,884,000)	0	0
Stock-based compensation	1,756,000	0	0
Amortization of goodwill and other intangibles	52,085,000	0	0
In-process research and development	22,280,000	0	0
Loss (gain) on disposal of property, plant, and equipment	400,000	112,000	(750,000)
Deferred income taxes	(536,000)	(5,643,000)	0
Tax benefit from exercise of stock options	32,188,000	16,661,000	0
Impairment of intangibles	0	175,000	125,000
Provision for doubtful accounts	435,000	435,000	86,000
Changes in assets and liabilities:			
Accounts receivable	(15,714,000)	(7,679,000)	(5,033,000)
Inventories	(25,007,000)	(1,552,000)	(1,177,000)
Prepaid expenses and other assets	(111,000)	(701,000)	18,000
Accounts payable	5,882,000	6,474,000	4,486,000
Accrued liabilities	4,006,000	2,064,000	(2,987,000)
Income taxes payable	(37,000)	(32,000)	215,000
Net cash provided by operating activities	56,941,000	44,942,000	1,896,000
Cash flows from investing activities:			
Net proceeds from sale of property, plant, and equipment	0	30,000	2,999,000
Additions to property and equipment	(11,657,000)	(5,703,000)	(1,953,000)
Payment for purchase of Giganet, Inc., net of cash acquired	(15,530,000)	0	0
Purchases of investments	(524,091,000)	(637,892,000)	(115,380,000)
Maturity of investments	491,009,000	595,745,000	0
Proceeds from sale of strategic investment	5,484,000	0	0
Net cash used in investing activities	(54,785,000)	(47,820,000)	(114,334,000)
Cash flows from financing activities:			
Principal payments under capital leases	(12,000)	(18,000)	(76,000)
Net proceeds from issuance of common stock under stock option plans	9,742,000	4,083,000	184,000
Proceeds from note receivable issued in exchange for restricted stock	1,114,000	0	0
Net proceeds from stock offering	0	0	132,838,000
Net cash provided by financing activities	10,844,000	4,065,000	132,946,000
Net increase in cash and cash equivalents	13,000,000	1,187,000	20,508,000
Cash and cash equivalents at beginning of year	23,471,000	22,284,000	1,776,000
Cash and cash equivalents at end of year	$36,471,000	$23,471,000	$22,284,000

	2001/07/01	2000/07/01	1999/07/01
Supplemental disclosures:			
Noncash investing and financing activities			
Fair value of assets acquired	$ 7,832,000		
Fair value of liabilities assumed	8,136,000	$ 0	$ 0
Common stock issued and options			
assumed for acquired business	661,678,000	0	0
Cash paid during the year for:			
Interest	$ 352,000	$ 21,000	$ 60,000
Income taxes	221,000	32,000	53,000

36. What is Emulex's fiscal year-end date?

37. Find the following amounts in the statements of Emulex:

  a. Net sales in 2001

  b. Cost of sales in 2001

  c. Interest expense in 2001

  d. Income tax expense in 2001

  e. Amortization of goodwill in 2001 and in 2000

  f. Net income in 2001

  g. Inventories at the end of 2001

  h. Goodwill at the end of 2001

  i. Additional paid-in capital at the end of 2001

  j. Cash from operating activities for 2001

  k. Cash from investing activities for 2001

  l. Cash from financing activities for 2001

38. Does Emulex finance its business primarily from creditors or from owners? Support your answer with appropriate data.

39. In 2001 Emulex purchased a new business. How did Emulex pay for this acquisition?

40. What is the trend in sales and net income over the last three years, and can you provide an explanation for why there is a loss in 2001?

41. Does Emulex pay dividends on its stock?

42. On July 1, 2001 find the stock price of Emulex's stock (use the library or the web) and compute the total market value of the company's stock that is outstanding, based on the number of shares that were outstanding as of that date. Compare this value with the book value of owner's equity on Emulex's balance sheet as of that date. If these numbers are different, offer an explanation for this discrepancy.

BEYOND THE BOOK

43. For a company of your choosing, answer the following questions:

  a. What are the major sections included in your annual report?

  b. What are the three most important points made in the letter to the shareholders?

c. What are the titles to the major financial statements included in the report?

d. What are the total assets, total liabilities, and total stockholders' equity of the firm? What percent of the company's total assets are financed through liabilities?

e. What were the net sales in the most recent year? Is this up or down from the prior year (answer in both dollar and percentage amounts)?

f. What is the net income and earnings per share in the most recent year? Is this up or down from the prior year (answer in both dollar and percentage amounts)?

g. Are any of the following items reported in the income statement: discontinued operations, extraordinary items, accounting method changes? If so, which ones?

h. What is the net cash provided (used) by operating, financing, and investing activities for the most recent year?

i. What is the last day of your company's fiscal year end?

j. Who are the independent auditors, and what type of opinion did they give the company?

44. Refer to the footnotes that accompany the company you chose in 43.

a. In the section "Summary of Significant Accounting Policies," what key policies are discussed?

b. Does your company have long-term debt? If so, what is the interest rate?

c. If your company has inventory, what do the footnotes tell you about the inventory?

d. From the footnotes, does it appear that there are any obligations that the company may have that do not appear to be reflected as liabilities on the balance sheet? If so, what are they?

CHAPTER 3

The Accounting Process

After reading this chapter you should be able to:

① Recognize common business transactions and understand their impact on general-purpose financial statements.

② Understand the dual nature of accounting transactions as reflected in the accounting equation.

③ Explain the basic construction of the Statement of Financial Position, the Statement of Earnings, and the Statement of Cash Flows.

④ Distinguish between economic events that are commonly recognized in accounting as transactions and those that are not.

⑤ Apply the concept of nominal or temporary accounts to record revenues and expenses, and identify their relationship to the Statement of Earnings and Statement of Financial Position.

⑥ Describe the accounting cycle and recognize the timing issues inherent in reporting financial results.

On March 2, 2001, investors reacted very favorably to an initial public offering (an Initial Public Offering or IPO is the first time a private company decides to issue shares to the public) from AFC Enterprises, Inc. The company operates and franchises quick-service restaurants, bakeries, and cafés (3618 in the United States and 27 in foreign countries) under the names Popeye's Chicken & Biscuits, Church's Chicken, Cinnabon, Seattle's Best Coffee, and Torrefazione Italia. The company also sells specialty coffees at wholesale and retail under the Seattle Coffee brand name. Sales totaled about $2.4 billion in 2000.

Although originally issued at $17, AFC shares opened at $19.50, climbed as high as $20.75, and ended the day at $20.38 on the Nasdaq Stock Market. The company had originally expected the shares to be offered at between $15 and $17. After the IPO, AFC had 29.5 million shares outstanding. You can see that with almost 30 million shares issued, AFC raised a substantial amount of money to fund its operations.

Investors and analysts use financial statements to guide their predictions and investment decisions. For example, when a company such as AFC Enterprises decides to issue stock to the public, it files information (in a document called a *prospectus*) containing past and projected financial performance. Investors, potential investors, managers, and other stakeholders rely on this financial statement information to help determine the company's value. As a result, these users must understand the process and assumptions underlying the construction of financial statements in order to make sound decisions based (in part) on these statements.

In the following pages, we present the fundamental aspects of the *double-entry accounting system* for constructing financial statements. The mechanical aspects of recording transactions are sometimes referred to as *bookkeeping*. You may well question why you should be concerned with this bookkeeping aspect of accounting, especially in light of today's computerized technology. The answer: You need to understand what the preparers are doing so that you can better interpret the output of their work, the financial statements. Let's start first with the balance sheet accounts, which underlie the financial statements.

BALANCE SHEET ACCOUNTS

Most of the balance sheet accounts are categorized as assets, liabilities, or stockholders' equity. Before examining specific transactions, let's review these in more detail.

ASSETS

The Financial Accounting Standards Board (FASB) Concepts Statement Number 6 (CON 6) defines an asset as follows (FASB, SFAC No. 6, 1985):

> Assets are probable future economic benefits obtained or controlled by a particular entity as a result of past transactions or events.

Probable future economic benefits means that a firm expects either future cash inflows or smaller cash outflows to result from the asset. For example, a prepaid expense, such as the premium on an insurance policy, is considered to be an asset because the coverage that the policy provides benefits future periods. However, as we noted in Chapter 2, some items have economic value but are not recognized as assets. For instance, if a firm faces uncertainty about future realization of cash flows, an item might not be recognized as an asset (e.g., research and development expenditures). Pepsico spends a significant amount of money each year for marketing its products. While this may create value for the business (brand recognition), they expense their advertising costs as they are incurred. Or, an item may be valuable to an entity but not owned or controlled by that entity, such as skilled employees.

Most assets originate as the result of a transaction with a party outside of the firm. A firm generally recognizes assets at the price it paid to acquire the assets. Exhibit 3.1 lists assets commonly found on a balance sheet:

Exhibit 3.1
Common Assets

Cash The amount of money that the firm has, including the amounts in checking and savings accounts.

Marketable Securities Short-term investments, such as stocks and bonds, in the securities of other companies.

Accounts Receivable Amounts owed to the firm that result from credit sales to customers.

Inventory Goods held for resale to customers.

Prepaid Expenses Expenses that have been paid for, but have not been used, such as rent paid in advance and insurance premiums.

Property, Plant, and Equipment (PP&E) Buildings, land, and equipment to be used for business operations over several years.

Intangible Assets Assets that have value, but do not have a physical presence, such as patents, trademarks, and goodwill.

Deferred Tax Assets Amounts of expected future tax savings.

LIABILITIES

In contrast to assets, liabilities are amounts recognized in accounting that result in expected future outflows of cash or delivery of goods or services. Exhibit 3.2 lists some of the more common balance sheet liabilities. Similar to assets, liability recognition also usually involves a transaction with an external party. FASB Con 6 defines liabilities as follows (FASB, SFAC No. 6, 1985):

Liabilities are probable future sacrifices of economic benefits arising from present obligations of a particular entity to transfer assets or provide services to other entities in the future as a result of past transactions or events.

Exhibit 3.2
Common Liabilities

Accounts Payable Amounts owed to suppliers from the purchase of goods on credit.

Notes Payable Amounts owed to a creditor (bank or supplier) that are represented by a formal agreement called a note. Notes payable can be either short-term (due in less than one year) or long-term (due more than one year in the future).

Accrued Liabilities Amounts that are owed to others relating to expenses that the company has incurred, but are not paid in cash as of the balance sheet date, such as interest payable or a warranty liability.

Taxes Payable Amounts currently owed to taxing authorities.

Deferred Taxes Amounts that the company expects to pay to taxing authorities in the future.

Bonds Payable Amounts owed to a creditor that are paid out over longer periods; they generally involve fixed interest payments as well as a large payment at the end of some specified period. Some bonds payable can be traded on exchanges in the same way as stock is traded. Bonds payable are generally long-term in nature, meaning that they are payable in a period more than one year from the date of issuance.

STOCKHOLDERS' EQUITY

We would not expect a company to accumulate large amounts of cash, even if the company is very profitable. This is because cash as an asset does not generate high rates of return. Thus, management, seeking to maximize shareholders' wealth, generally keeps only as much cash as it requires to meet its operating needs and to make the repayment of its debt. Additional amounts may be held in anticipation of further investments.

Owners' or stockholders' equity is the last main category on the balance sheet. Stockholders' equity consists of two major components: contributed capital and retained earnings. **Contributed capital** reflects the amount of capital that a firm's owners have invested in the business. This amount is typically the sum of the **par** or **stated value** of stock issued, plus the amounts in excess of par, **additional paid-in-capital.** The sum of common stock plus additional paid-in-capital represents the total investment by shareholders at the time the company issued the stock.

Retained earnings is the total amount of earnings (revenues minus expenses) recorded in the accounting system to date, but not yet distributed to shareholders as dividends. Dividends are distributions of earnings to shareholders and are not considered an expense to the company. Remember that retained earnings are not cash. A company may have substantial earnings yet have no cash for at least two reasons. First, accounting rules require that earnings be recognized on an accrual basis. For example, firms sometimes recognize revenues before receiving cash (as in sales on account), and sometimes recognize expenses before paying cash out (as in wages owed to employees). Second, a company may use its cash to invest in noncash assets (e.g., a new computer system or repay debt).

NOMINAL ACCOUNTS

Balance sheet accounts (sometimes called **real** or **permanent accounts**) include a number of assets, liabilities, and stockholders' equity accounts such as those discussed in the previous sections. **Nominal accounts** (or **temporary accounts**) are accounts that a firm uses to determine its earnings. These accounts consist of revenue and expense accounts such as sales, cost of goods sold, wage and salary expenses, and selling and administrative expenses. Ultimately, these accounts affect a permanent account, namely retained earnings. (We'll discuss how this is accomplished later.) However, at this point, it is worth noting that the reason that revenue and expenses are considered to be temporary accounts is that the balances in these accounts are transferred (or *closed*) to retained earnings at the end of each accounting period. By closing revenue and expense accounts each period, the balances in these accounts reflect only the firm's operating performance for one period at a time. The retained earnings account contains cumulative earnings less dividends distributed to stockholders since the firm's inception.

Now that you have a good understanding of the types of accounts, let's see next how firms use them to record transactions.

ACCOUNTING FOR TRANSACTIONS

The starting point in constructing financial statements is the accounting recognition of **transactions,** or economic events. Most, but not all, transactions are triggered by an exchange between the firm and another party. Accounting recognition of these transactions take the form of an **entry,** which indicates the financial effects of that event on accounts that appear on the firm's financial statements.

Recall from Chapter 2 that the accounting equation states that

$$\text{Assets } = \text{ Liabilities } + \text{ Stockholders' Equity}$$

When firms record transactions in the accounting system, this equality must always be maintained.

To analyze transactions, you can use two approaches. The first approach is based on the accounting equation. Each transaction is analyzed in terms of how it affects assets, liabilities, and stockholders' equity (we'll illustrate this approach later in this chapter). The equation approach is only useful when first learning accounting, so you can more easily see how transactions affect the accounting equation and financial statements. However, this approach quickly becomes unwieldy and inefficient when dealing with a large number of transactions and accounts. As a result, most firms use the second approach, the double-entry accounting system.

DOUBLE-ENTRY ACCOUNTING SYSTEM

The **double-entry accounting system** expresses account balances and changes in account balances using terms called **debits** and **credits.** Although it requires some investment of your time and effort to be able to use debits and credits, having this skill is extremely useful. Once you understand the double-entry accounting system, you can efficiently assess the effects of a variety of types of transactions on a company's financial statements, as well as address valuation and income measurement issues.

The system of using debit and credits serves as the basis of virtually every accounting system worldwide. Further, the Sarbane's Oxley Act requires that top management certify to the fundamental accuracy of their company's financial statements. Such certification requires that management possess a basic understanding of the accounting process, in order to be able to communicate with the preparers of financial statements. Understanding the process of generating financial statements is an essential component of financial literacy.

T-ACCOUNTS

A debit means simply an entry or balance on the left-hand side of an account, and a credit is an entry or balance on the right-hand side of an account. Increases and decreases in specific accounts can be expressed by debit and credit entries following set conventions. The conventions that dictate the rules for debits and credits are structured so that all accounting transactions will maintain the equality of the accounting equation at all times. The basic form of an account can be represented using a so-called **T-account** of the following form (note that we have represented the balance on the debit side of the account but also recognize that the balance could appear on either side of the account):

Account Title	
Balance	
Debit	Credit
Balance	

A T-account shows the beginning and ending balance in an account, as well as the debit and credit entries for transactions affecting the account during a particular period of time. Whether an account is increased or decreased by a debit or credit depends on whether the account represents an asset, liability, or stockholders' equity, in other words, has a debit or a credit balance. As Exhibit 3.3 shows, assets are increased by debit entries and decreased by credit entries. Liabilities and stockholders' equity accounts (capital stock, additional paid in capital, and retained earnings) are increased by credits and decreased by debits.

As shown in Exhibit 3.3, we normally expect asset accounts to carry a debit balance, while liability and stockholders' equity accounts normally carry a credit balance. One way to think about these results is that the accounting equation shows assets on the left side (debit) and liabilities and stockholders' equity on the right (credit). An exception is retained earnings. A profitable company will have a credit balance in this account, but it can have a debit balance if it incurs a cumulative net loss. Finally, remember that to maintain the accounting equation, the sum of all debit account balances must equal the sum of all credit account balances.

JOURNAL ENTRIES

In a double-entry accounting system, firms typically track transactions as they occur in a chronological listing known as a **journal.** Each entry in the journal, known as a **journal entry,** summarizes both sides of a transaction (debit and

Exhibit 3.3
T-Accounts

T-Accounts for Assets, Liabilities, and Stockholders' Equity			
Assets		**Liabilities**	
Beginning balance Debits increase	Credits decrease	Debits decrease	Beginning balance Credits increase
Ending balance			Ending balance
Capital Stock (common stock + paid-in-capital)		**Retained Earnings**	
Debits decrease	Beginning balance Credits increase	Debits decrease	Beginning balance Credits increase
	Ending balance		Ending balance

credit). By convention, in a journal entry, the debit portion of the entry is shown first, followed by the credit portion. (See the sample journal entries that follow.) The credit entry is slightly indented from the debit to make the entry clear. The total debits for a transaction must equal the total credits for that transaction.

| Title of Account Debited | Amount Debited |
| Title of Account Credited | Amount Credited |

For example, the journal entry to record the purchase of $100 of inventory for cash would appear as follows:

| Inventory | 100 |
| Cash | | 100 |

We will explain this transaction later, but for now just recognize the form of the journal entry.

After recording journal entries, they are then posted to the T-accounts. Posting simply means transferring the information in the journal entry to the appropriate T-accounts. (In this text, we will often simplify this two-step approach by recording the transaction directly to the T-account, bypassing the journal entry step.) The set of T-accounts that a company uses is collectively referred to as the **ledger.**

To illustrate the application of the accounting equation, journal entries, and T-accounts, assume that a company borrows $50,000,000 cash from a bank and signs a promissory note. This note specifies an interest rate and when the amount borrowed must be repaid. Using the accounting equation approach, we view this transaction as shown here (shown in millions of dollars):

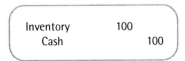

Assets = Liabilities + Stockholders' Equity
            Notes
Cash   Payable
+50 = +50

Notice that the asset (Cash) is increased, and the liability (Notes Payable) is also increased. Observe also that we maintain the equality of the accounting equation. The journal entry for this transaction would appear as follows:

| Cash | 50 |
| Notes Payable | | 50 |

The debit to the Cash account means that cash (an asset) has increased by $50 and the credit to Notes Payable (a liability) means that account is increased as well. Posting this journal entry to the appropriate T-accounts, the transaction would be recorded as:

Cash		Notes Payable	
50			50

Observe that both the T-account and the journal entry maintain the equality of total debits and total credits. Note also that dollar signs ($) are generally omitted from journal entries and T-accounts. Journal entries are a useful way to represent individual transactions, while T-accounts illustrate the effect of a series of transactions on the accounts that comprise a company's financial statements.

COMPUTERIZED ACCOUNTING

The basic accounting process, still used today, has existed for centuries. Before computers, firms literally recorded accounting entries in paper journals, and then posted the individual components of those entries to paper ledger accounts. You can easily imagine the large amount of paperwork involved in a manual accounting system, even for a modestly sized business. Although today's accounting systems are computerized, they continue follow the same basic process. Transactions still give rise to entries in some form (a journal), from which summaries (ledger) by account can be created, which then serve as a foundation for the construction of financial statements.

Modern accounting systems are structured much differently than in the past and may be simply one part of a company's software system. These sophisticated systems provide a wide variety of management tools. For example, some systems may instantly determine the impact of a revenue or expense transaction on a company's income statement and balance sheet. There are several companies that provide very sophisticated systems, and Oracle is one of those companies. Exhibit 3.4 provides a description of Oracle's business.

Even though computers have eased the paperwork requirements of accounting systems, you still need to know how they work. Let's look at an example that illustrates the accounting process and the preparation of financial statements.

Exhibit 3.4
Oracle Corporation: Description of Business (Oracle 10-K, 2003)

Oracle Corporation

We are the world's largest enterprise software company. We develop, manufacture, market, and distribute computer software that helps our customers manage and grow their businesses and operations. Our offerings include new software licenses, software license updates, and product support and services, which include consulting, advanced product services, and education. We also offer an integrated suite of business applications software and other business software infrastructure, including application server, collaborative software, and development tools.

AN ILLUSTRATION OF TRANSACTION ANALYSIS

Biohealth, Inc., is a hypothetical, wholesale health-products distributor (similar to an actual company in the health supply industry). As is often true for publicly traded companies, Biohealth is denoted by its *ticker symbol,* in this case BHT, used on the stock exchanges where the company's stock trades. BHT distributes (not manufactures) a wide variety of healthcare products and prescription medicines to hospitals, retail chains, and other health-related outlets. It also provides software solutions to a variety of businesses in the healthcare sector for managing their ordering and inventory. BHT was incorporated on December 20, 20X0 and began operations the following January.

The following economic events/transactions occurred in December prior to the start of BHT's operations:

1. BHT issued 250 million shares of common stock with a par value of $1 per share for $6.50 per share.

2. BHT acquired fixtures for $540 million. BHT estimates that the fixtures will be used for nine years.

3. The purchase of fixtures was partially financed with a $400 million note due in five years. The loan carries an interest rate of 7 percent.[1]

These transactions reflect BHT's start-up financing and investing activities. Let's look at them more closely.

ANALYSIS OF FINANCING AND INVESTING ACTIVITIES

Exhibit 3.5 summarizes the impact of these initial three transactions on the accounting equation. Notice how the accounts to the left of the equal (=) sign are added together, as well as the accounts to the right of the equal sign, to

| #–Type | Assets | | = | Liabilities | | | |
	Cash	Fixtures	=	Notes payable	Common Stock	Paid–in Capital	Retained Earnings
Bal. 12/20/20X0	0	0	=	0	0	0	0
1–Financing	1,625		=		250	1,375	
2–Investing	(540)	540	=				
3–Financing	400		=	400			
Bal. 12/31/20X0	1,485	540	=	400	250	1,375	0

Exhibit 3.5
Impact of BHT's Financing and Investing Activities on the Accounting Equation (in millions of dollars)

[1] A note is a loan accompanied by a written promise to repay the amount owed. Interest on notes is always expressed in terms of an annual rate even if the note is for a period longer or shorter than one year. For example, the total interest on a six-month $1,000 note with an interest rate of 5 percent would be $1,000 × .05 × 6/12 = $25.

determine the ending balance. On each line of the exhibit, from individual transactions to ending balances, the accounting equation holds. Negative amounts, as shown in Exhibit 3.5, are enclosed in parentheses.

Issuing Stock (Transaction 1)

The first transaction increases Cash by $1,625 million (250 million shares × $6.50/share), increases Common Stock by $250 million (250 million shares × $1/share), and increases Additional Paid-In Capital by $1,375 million (the difference between cash and par value). We classify this transaction as a financing activity because it relates to how the company funds its operating and investing activities. Note that dollar figures are reported in millions, a common practice in financial statements.

Purchasing Fixtures (Transaction 2)

The second transaction increases assets (Fixtures) by $540 million, and decreases Cash by $540 million. This transaction is an investing activity. Investing activities involve purchase and sale of assets that are used over multiple periods such as property, plant, and equipment. Note that later in the chapter we classify fixtures under property, plant, and equipment (PPE).

Borrowing Funds (Transaction 3)

Although the third transaction relates to the investing activity in Transaction 2, it, by itself, is a financing activity. Here, the company borrows funds to finance its purchase of fixtures. Note that interest is not recognized yet on the loan as it is a charge that the firm incurs with the passage of time. Investing and financing activities often occur simultaneously. For example, America Online (AOL) acquired all of Time-Warner's common stock in January 2000. We classify AOL's stock acquisition of Time Warner as an investing activity because America Online now controls the assets of Time Warner. However, we also classify this as a financing activity, as AOL funded this transaction by issuing additional shares of AOL stock.

Using Journal Entries and T-Accounts to Record Transactions

We show the journal entries and T-accounts for the first three BHT transactions in Exhibits 3.6 and 3.7, respectively. The journal entry for Transaction 1 summarizes

Exhibit 3.6
Journal Entries for BHT's Financing and Investing Transactions (in millions of dollars)

Transaction #1		
Cash	1,625	
Common Stock		250
Additional Paid-in Capital		1,375
Transaction #2		
Fixtures	540	
Cash		540
Transaction #3		
Cash	400	
Notes Payable		400

Exhibit 3.7
T-Accounts for BHT's Financing and Investing Transactions (in millions of dollars)

Cash		
Bal.	0	
(1)	1,625	540 (2)
(3)	400	
Bal.	1,485	

Fixtures		
Bal.	0	
(2)	540	
Bal.	540	

Notes Payable	
	Bal. 0
	400 (3)
	Bal. 400

Common Stock	
	Bal. 0
	250 (1)
	Bal. 250

Additional Paid-In Capital	
	Bal. 0
	1,375 (1)
	Bal. 1,375

BHT's issuance of stock by showing an increase in BHT's Cash (debit to Cash) and increases in both Common Stock and Additional Paid-in Capital (credits to those accounts). The journal entry for Transaction 2 reflects an increase in assets (Fixtures) by a debit to Fixtures and a decrease in Cash by a credit to Cash. Finally, the journal entry for Transaction 3 shows an increase in Cash and an increase in Notes Payable by a debit to Cash and a credit to Notes Payable, respectively.

As Exhibit 3.7 shows, each T-account includes the sum of all transactions affecting the account to date. The beginning balances in the accounts are zero as the company just started business at the beginning of this period. Finally, note that the sum of the debit balances equals the sum of the credit balances.

Observe that the three investing and financing transactions had no effect on the retained earnings account because none of them involved the generation of revenues or concurrent expenses. Earlier in the chapter, we mentioned the notion of permanent and nominal accounts. However, no nominal accounts have been affected by transactions thus far.

Now that we've recorded the journal entries and posted them to the ledger (T-accounts), we can use this information to construct the financial statements.

CONSTRUCTING THE FINANCIAL STATEMENTS

Exhibit 3.8 shows BHT's Balance Sheet as of 12/31/20X0, summarizing the financial statement position of the firm. The balance sheet omits the beginning of the period, because the balances are all zero. Further, we don't need to prepare an income statement, as none of the initial three transactions produced revenue or expenses.

Exhibit 3.9 shows BHT's Statement of Cash Flows for the month ended 12/31/20X0. The statement indicates that the firm has not yet produced any cash flows from operating activities. Also, note that the total change in cash equals

Exhibit 3.8

Biohealth, Inc. (BHT) Balance Sheet (in millions) as of 12/31/20X0

Assets	
Current Assets:	
Cash	$1,485
Property, Plant, and Equipment:	
Fixtures	540
Total Assets	$2,025
Liabilities and Stockholder's Equity	
Liabilities:	
Notes Payable	$ 400
Total Liabilities	400
Stockholders' Equity	
Common Stock	250
Additional Paid in Capital	1,375
Retained Earnings	0
Total Stockholders' Equity	$1,625
Total Liabilities and Stockholders' Equity	$2,025

Exhibit 3.9

Biohealth, Inc. (BHT) Statement of Cash Flows (in millions) for the Month Ending 12/31/20X0

Cash Flow from Investing Activities	
Purchase Fixtures	($540)
Cash Flow from Financing Activities	
Proceeds from Issuance of Common Stock	1,625
Proceeds from Loan	400
Total Cash from Financing Activities	2,025
Net Change in Cash	$1,485
Cash Balance 12/20/20X0	0
Cash Balance 12/31/20X0	$1,485

the cash balance at the end of 12/31/20X0, because the company started with no cash on hand. Finally, the beginning cash balance is as of 12/20/20X0, the date the company formed. Normally, in a month-ending statement, the date would have been 12/1/20X0.

ANALYSIS OF OPERATING ACTIVITIES

Now that we've examined BHT's initial financing and investing activities, let's next look at a series of transactions occurring in BHT's first year of operation, starting on 1/1/20X1. The following events occurred during 20X1 (all figures are in millions of dollars).

4. BHT purchased inventory costing $34,340 on account.

5. BHT sold goods for $35,724 on account.

6. The cost of the inventory sold was $30,420.

7. BHT received $33,260 in customer payments on accounts receivable.

8. BHT paid $29,200 on its accounts payable.

9. BHT paid $4,800 to lease warehouse space for inventory storage for the year and for other miscellaneous selling and administrative costs.

10. Depreciation expense on the fixtures was $60 ($540/9 years).

11. BHT paid interest on the note payable of $28.

12. BHT declared and paid dividends of $150.

Most of these transactions are operating transactions because they relate to BHT's profit-generating activities. Operating transactions can involve revenue and expense accounts (nominal accounts), but they may also involve only asset or liability accounts. For example, Inventory and Accounts Payable accounts are affected when a company buys inventory on credit. While this acquisition of inventory might be viewed as an investing activity, accounting standards classify it as operating because the company holds the inventory for resale in the short term. We classify assets such as Accounts Receivable, Inventory, and Prepaid Expenses as operating assets in part because they are short-term or current in nature, and in part because they relate to the operating cycle of the business. In contrast, we do not regard marketable securities as operating assets.

Recall from Chapter 2 that classification as a current asset generally means that we expect the asset to be converted into cash or consumed within one year or within one operating cycle of the business, whichever is longer. Similarly, obligations such as accounts payable and other short-term payables are considered operating liabilities in part because they will be paid in less than one year (current liabilities) and in part because they relate to operating activities. However, debt may also be classified as current if it is to be repaid within a year. Thus, some but not all changes in various current assets and current liabilities are considered to be operating transactions.

Before examining how we recognize these operating transactions in the accounting system, we need to first discuss revenues and expenses in more detail.

Revenues and Expenses

Revenues reflect the sales value of goods or services sold by an enterprise. *Expenses* are the costs related to generating revenue, such as the cost of inventory sold and employee wages. Recall that net income is the difference between revenues and expenses. The cumulative amount of net income, minus dividends paid to shareholders over all accounting periods to date, appears on the balance sheet in the form of retained earnings. Exhibit 3.10 shows the changes of Retained Earnings in the balance sheet.

While we could immediately proceed to talk about the nominal accounts (revenue and expense accounts) and how to incorporate them into our entries,

Exhibit 3.10
Retained Earnings Flow
through the Balance Sheet

Summary Impact of Operating Activities on the Accounting Equation

Transaction #– explanation	Assets					=	Liabilities		CS	PIC	Retained Earnings
	Cash	AR	Inventory	PPE	(AD)	=	AP	NP	CS	PIC	Revenue – Expenses
Balance 12/31/20X0	1,485			540		=		400	250	1,375	
4. Purchase inventory			34,340			=	34,340				
5. Sales revenue		35,724				=					35,724
6. Cost of sales			(30,420)			=					(30,420)
7. Cash collection	33,260	(33,260)				=					
8. Payment for inventory	(29,200)					=	(29,200)				
9. S&A expenses	(4,800)					=					(4,800)
10. Depreciation expense					(60)	=					(60)
11. Interest expense	(28)					=					(28)
12. Dividend paid	(150)					=					(150)
Balance 12/31/20X1	567	2,464	3,920	540	(60)	=	5,140	400	250	1,375	266

Exhibit 3.11
Impact of BHT's Operating
Transactions on the Balance
Sheet

we take a two-step approach to analyzing operating transactions. In the section that follows, we will focus our attention on the permanent accounts as portrayed in the accounting equation to examine BHT's operating transactions. We will, therefore, portray revenue and expense events in terms of their (ultimate) impact on the Retained Earnings account (a permanent account) on the balance sheet. Accordingly, we treat revenues as direct increases (credits) to retained earnings and expenses as direct decreases (debits) to retained earnings as shown in Exhibit 3.11. It is important that you understand the ultimate effects on the permanent accounts, and it is often easier to focus on this effect first before we look more closely at nominal accounts. Following the accounting equation analysis of the transactions, we will present a more in-depth discussion of the nominal accounts and then illustrate the same transactions using journal entries and T-accounts, including the nominal accounts. If you prefer to consider the balance sheet equation effects and the journal entries simultaneously, then prior to reading about the transactions that follow, skip ahead to the section called "Nominal Accounts Revisited" and read about nominal accounts. You can then simultaneously follow the accounting equation effects in Exhibit 3.11 as well as the journal entry effects in Exhibit 3.15.

Using the Accounting Equation to Analyze Operating Activities

Exhibit 3.11 summarizes the effects of Transactions 4 through 12 using the accounting equation. We use the following abbreviations for the balance sheet accounts: AR, Accounts Receivable; PPE, Property, Plant, and Equipment; AD, Accumulated Depreciation; AP, Accounts Payable; NP, Notes Payable; CS, Common Stock; PIC, Paid-In Capital; and RE, Retained Earnings.

Purchasing Inventory on Account (Transaction 4)

Transaction 4 involves the credit (on account) purchase of inventory for resale. We consider this an operating activity because BHT expects to sell the inventory during the upcoming year for a price that exceeds its cost, generating profit for the company. The purchase is "on account," meaning that BHT pays for the inventory after its purchase. The result is that BHT has a liability, Accounts Payable, for the cost of the inventory purchased. The impact on the accounting equation is as follows:

4. Purchase of inventory on account

		Assets			=	Liabilities		Stockholders' Equity		
Cash	AR	Inventory	PPE	(AD)	=	AP	NP	CS	PIC	RE
		34,340			=	34,340				

Purchasing inventory does not constitute an expense. The inventory holds future value and is owned by the firm. Therefore, it should be recorded as an asset. The cost of purchasing inventory eventually becomes an expense (cost of goods sold) at the time that BHT sells the inventory to a customer, that is, at the point when the firm no longer owns it (see Transactions 5 and 6).

Selling Inventory on Account (Transaction 5)

Transaction 5 involves the sale of inventory on account. "On account," in this context means that BHT did not collect cash at the time of the sale but expects to do so at some future date. The amount owed to BHT, accounts receivable, represents an asset. This new asset for BHT stockholders results in an increase in stockholders' equity. Further, BHT sells its inventory for more than its cost. We refer to the gross sales value of inventory sold as **sales revenue.** At the same time, the stockholders lost an existing asset (inventory). The cost of inventory sold is accounted for separately as an expense called **cost of goods sold** (see Transaction 6, which follows). The difference between the gross sales value of the inventory (sales revenue) and its cost (cost of goods sold) is **gross profit** to BHT. The gross profit amount affects BHT's stockholders' equity in the form of an increase in retained earnings. The impact of the sales revenue itself on the accounting equation is as follows:

5. Recognize sales revenue for sales on account

	Assets				=	Liabilities		Stockholders' Equity		
Cash	AR	Inventory	PPE	(AD)	=	AP	NP	CS	PIC	RE
	35,724				=					35,724

The recognition of revenues can often be a source of confusion and, potentially, manipulation. In some cases companies improperly recognize revenues and the SEC can force them to restate their earnings. Such an example is that of Lucent Technologies, as illustrated in Exhibit 3.12.

Recognizing Cost of Goods Sold (Transaction 6)

As previously mentioned, cost of goods sold is an expense related to generating the revenues recorded in Transaction 5. By accounting convention, a firm reports this expense in the same period as the related revenue. In this way, cost of goods sold is matched with the related revenue. An asset (inventory) was given up, so stockholders' equity also decreases. Specifically, this transaction decreases retained earnings. The impact on the accounting equation is shown as follows:

6. Recognize cost of goods sold

	Assets				=	Liabilities		Stockholders' Equity		
Cash	AR	Inventory	PPE	(AD)	=	AP	NP	CS	PIC	RE
		(30,420)			=					(30,420)

Exhibit 3.12

THE REAL WORLD

Lucent Technologies

In February 2001, Lucent Technologies, Inc. announced its cooperation with the SEC in a probe of the company's accounting practices. On November 21, 2000, Lucent had indicated that $125 million in improperly booked sales could reduce its results for the fourth quarter ended September 30, 2000. The announcement resulted in a 16 percent drop in the company's stock value. After an internal review, Lucent announced on December 21, 2000, that it was reducing previously reported fourth-quarter revenues by $679 million to $8.7 billion.

The fact that firms generally recognize revenues at the time of sale, rather than at the time of collection, could have important implications for the valuation of companies. Some companies may erroneously or fraudulently recognize sales by an accounting entry even when no legitimate sale has taken place. To minimize this type of opportunistic behavior, a firm's financial records are subject to examination by external auditors, internal control systems, and oversight by external members of a firm's board of directors. Further, legal sanctions apply to those firms that are found to have engaged in such behavior. However, as the Lucent example illustrates, none of these mechanisms is perfect.

Observe that neither the revenue or expense recognition for these transactions affected cash, due to accrual accounting. As we explain fully in Chapter 4, under this concept, a firm recognizes revenues when they have been earned. In this case, revenue recognition occurs when the inventory is delivered to the buyer and the firm can reasonably expect to collect cash in the future, not necessarily when BHT receives the cash. Similarly, a firm recognizes expenses not when it pays out cash, but when the cost (expenditure) can be matched to revenues (implying there is no future benefit to be received). Thus, a firm records inventory as assets upon purchase, and then records the cost of inventory sold as an expense when revenue is earned.

While some firms can calculate the cost of goods sold at the time of sale, many firms determine the cost of goods sold at the end of the period through the following calculation:

Cost of Goods Sold Calculation:

Cost of Goods Sold = Cost of Beginning Inventory + Purchases
− Cost of Ending Inventory

Collecting Receivables (Transaction 7)

Transaction 7 indicates the collection of cash for sales on account. This transaction involves an exchange of one type of an asset (accounts receivable) for another (cash), and therefore has no effect on retained earnings. BHT already recognized the revenue from the sale when the sale took place.

7. Recognize collection of cash from past sales

		Assets			=	Liabilities			Stockholders' Equity	
Cash	AR	Inventory	PPE	(AD)	=	AP	NP	CS	PIC	RE
33,260	(33,260)				=					

Paying Accounts Payable (Transaction 8)

Transaction 8 records the payment for the inventory and other items that BHT purchased on account during the year.

8. Record payments on account

		Assets			=	Liabilities			Stockholders' Equity	
Cash	AR	Inventory	PPE	(AD)	=	AP	NP	CS	PIC	RE
(29,200)					=	(29,200)				

Paying Selling and Administrative Costs (Transaction 9)

Transaction 9 involves the payment of cash for rent and other selling and administrative expenses that BHT incurred during the year. Because these cash expenditures do not result in assets with future value, these costs immediately become expenses. These expenses affect the accounting equation as follows:

9. Payment of cash for rent
and selling and
administrative expenses

| | | | | | | | | Stockholders' | |
| Assets | | | | = | Liabilities | | | Equity | |
Cash	AR	Inventory	PPE	(AD)	=	AP	NP	CS	PIC	RE
(4,800)					=					(4,800)

Depreciating Fixtures (Transaction 10)

When a firm purchases plant and equipment, it records these items as assets because they provide future benefits to the firm. Plant and equipment contribute to the production of products or services that can be sold in later periods. This productive capacity of plant and equipment, however, diminishes over time. As a result, for accounting purposes, the costs incurred in acquiring the plant and equipment should be expensed over the life of the plant and equipment. Specifically, accounting standards require that the costs incurred should be allocated to expense over the *useful life* of the asset using a rational and systematic method. We call these methods **depreciation methods,** and the expense that results **depreciation expense.** GAAP allows several depreciation methods, which we'll discuss in more detail in Chapter 9. These methods require several estimates. Exhibit 3.13 illustrates the disclosure made by Hasbro, Inc. regarding the use of estimates.

For example, the *straight-line depreciation* method assumes an equal amount of the cost of the asset is to be used up each year of its useful life. The method also factors in the possibility that the asset has some remaining estimated value

Exhibit 3.13
Hasbro, Inc. and Subsidiaries

THE REAL WORLD

Hasbro, Inc.

Notes to Consolidated Financial Statements

(1) Summary of Significant Accounting Policies

Preparation of Financial Statements

The preparation of financial statements in conformity with generally accepted accounting principles requires management to make estimates and assumptions that affect the amounts reported in the financial statements and notes thereto. Actual results could differ from those estimates.

Within GAAP, managers must make some significant estimates, such as the useful life and salvage value of a firm's property, plant, and equipment. Hasbro's disclosure reminds its financial statement readers of the estimates that management makes and the impact of these estimates on those statements.

at the end of its useful life, referred to as *salvage value*. A firm using this method therefore calculates depreciation expense dividing the original cost, less the salvage value, by the number of years of useful life. If BHT uses the straight-line method, with fixtures having a useful life of 9 years and a zero salvage value, its depreciation expense for the fixtures is [(Original Cost − Salvage)/Useful Life = ($540 − 0)/9 years = $60 million/year].

A firm records depreciation by an entry to Depreciation Expense (for the moment, retained earnings) and an entry to an account called Accumulated Depreciation. Accumulated Depreciation is a contra-asset account. **Contra-asset accounts** have credit balances and are an offset to a related asset account. In this case, the original cost of the fixtures is shown in the PP&E account. The entry shows Accumulated Depreciation as a direct reduction of this account. BHT reports the contra-asset on the balance sheet as a subtraction from the related asset account. The impact of recording depreciation on the accounting equation is shown as follows:

> The use of the accumulated depreciation account is helpful for analysis because it allows the financial statement user to observe the original cost of an asset from the asset account and then, using the information in the accumulated depreciation account, infer such information as the age of plant and equipment and how long before they may need to be replaced.

10. Recognition of depreciation expense

		Assets			=	Liabilities			Stockholders' Equity	
Cash	AR	Inventory	PPE	(AD)	=	AP	NP	CS	PIC	RE
				(60)	=					(60)

We show the Accumulated Depreciation account as a negative amount. On the balance sheet, after the first year's depreciation is recorded, the asset and related accumulated depreciation accounts for fixtures would appear on the balance sheet as follows:

Fixtures	$540
Less	
Accumulated depreciation	(60)
Net fixtures	$480

At the end of the second year, the accumulated depreciation account would show that two years of depreciation had been recognized, and fixtures and related accumulated depreciation on the balance sheet would appear as:

Fixtures	$540
Less	
Accumulated depreciation	(120)
Net Fixtures	$420

By keeping the accumulated depreciation separate from the original cost of the fixtures, the financial statement reader can estimate both how close assets are to being fully depreciated and the years remaining in the asset's estimated useful life. This information may be helpful predict when a firm will need to replace or upgrade equipment. For example, suppose a company discloses that its depreciation expense is $60 million, the asset is being depreciated using the straight-line method over nine years, and its accumulated depreciation is $300. We can then estimate that the asset's remaining useful life is 4 years (9 − (300/60) = 4). If a company does not list accumulated depreciation on the balance sheet, but instead shows property, plant, and equipment net of accumulated depreciation, a breakdown between the asset and related accumulated depreciation accounts is often provided in the firm's footnotes to the financial statements.

Paying Interest (Transaction 11)

When a firm borrows funds, it must pay for the use of the funds in the form of interest payments. In this case, we assume that the loan has simple interest at a rate of 7 percent per annum and is paid in cash. Thus, the interest on the loan is $28 million ($400 × .07) and affects the accounting equation as follows:

11. Payment of interest expense

		Assets			=	Liabilities		Stockholders' Equity		
Cash	AR	Inventory	PPE	(AD)	=	AP	NP	CS	PIC	RE
(28)					=					(28)

While we treat interest as an operating activity, others argue that interest expense should be considered a financing activity because it relates to borrowing funds. In fact, we employ this view in Chapter 14 when we consider valuing a firm. However, the FASB states that interest should be classified as an operating activity for cash flow purposes.

Dividends (Transaction 12)

Dividends return a certain amount of the profits to owners in the form of cash. A company's Board of Directors frequently declares dividends on a quarterly basis. However, a firm usually does not pay dividends at the date they are declared. Instead, a firm often pays them within the month following declaration. To deal with this delay, a firm creates a new liability, Dividends Payable. Dividends are not an expense of doing business and are not reported on the income statement. However, they do directly reduce retained earnings, as the owners are withdrawing a part of their profits from the firm. We will discuss dividends in more detail later in the text. Here, however, for simplicity, we assume that BHT pays dividends immediately in cash.

12. Declaration of dividends

		Assets			=	Liabilities		Stockholders' Equity		
Cash	AR	Inventory	PPE	(AD)	=	AP	NP	CS	PIC	RE
(150)					=					(150)

Now that we've examined how BHT's operating transactions affected the accounting equation, we're ready to look at the respective journal entries and T-accounting. However, before we can do that we need to provide more detail of the accounts used to record the firm's profit-measurement activities. In other words, we need to discuss nominal accounts.

Nominal Accounts Revisited

Recall that stockholders' equity consists of contributed capital and retained earnings. To record changes in retained earnings that result from a firm's operating activities, a firm uses *nominal accounts,* separate revenue and expense accounts, whose balances are transferred to retained earnings at the end of the accounting period. As mentioned earlier, the idea is to measure operating performance one period at a time, as retained earnings reflects *cumulative* revenues and expenses over all accounting periods. By using these nominal accounts, a firm can better analyze the inflows and outflows pertaining to the operating activities of the company for the accounting period just completed.

A firm uses separate accounts for each category of revenue and expense. A firm can then more easily determine the amounts to be included in the various line items on its income statement. Consistent with the usual effects of revenues increasing retained earnings and expenses decreasing retained earnings, revenues are increased by credits, while expenses are increased by debits. Accordingly, revenue accounts will normally have a credit balance, and expense accounts will normally have a debit balance. T-accounts for revenues and expenses are shown below:

T-Accounts for Revenues and Expenses

Revenues		Expenses	
Debits Decrease	Credits Increase	Debits Increase	Credits Decrease

Exhibit 3.14 summarizes the normal balance in each type of account and indicates how the account is affected by debit (left) and credit (right) entries.

With this improved understanding of nominal accounts, we're ready to resume analyzing BHT's operating transactions, now by using journal entries and T-accounts.

Exhibit 3.14
Normal Account Balances and
Debit and Credit Effects on
Accounts

Account Type	Normal Balance	Debit Entries	Credit Entries
Asset	Debit	Increase	Decrease
Liability	Credit	Decrease	Increase
Common Stock	Credit	Decrease	Increase
Paid-in-Capital	Credit	Decrease	Increase
Retained Earnings	Credit	Decrease	Increase
Revenue	Credit	Decrease	Increase
Expense	Debit	Increase	Decrease

Using Journal Entries and T-Accounts to Record Transactions

We show the journal entries and T-accounts for Transactions 4 through 12 in Exhibits 3.15 and 3.16, respectively. Note in Exhibit 3.16 that the beginning balances at the start of 20X1 carry forward from the end of the previous year (20X0). Further, note that the retained earnings account does not include entries other than the dividends declared at this point. This is because the nominal accounts, revenue and expense, have not yet been closed. These accounts will be closed and their balances moved to retained earnings after preparing the income statement. (We'll provide more details on the closing process in the next section.)

Exhibit 3.15
Journal Entries for Operating
Transactions

Transaction #4		
Inventory	34,340	
Accounts Payable		34,340
Transaction #5		
Accounts Receivable	35,724	
Sales		35,724
Transaction #6		
Cost of Sales	30,420	
Inventory		30,420
Transaction #7		
Cash	33,260	
Accounts Receivable		33,260
Transaction #8		
Accounts Payable	29,200	
Cash		29,200
Transaction #9		
S&A Expenses	4,800	
Cash		4,800
Transaction #10		
Depreciation Expense	60	
Accumulated Depreciation		60
Transaction #11		
Interest Expense	28	
Cash		28
Transaction #12		
Retained Earnings	150	
Cash		150

104

Exhibit 3.16
Added Operating Transactions to BHT's T-Accounts

Cash			Account Receivable			Inventory		
Bal. 1,485			Bal. 0			Bal. 0		
	29,200 (8)		(5) 35,724			(4) 34,340	30,420 (6)	
(7) 33,260	4,800 (9)			33,260 (7)				
	28 (11)							
	150 (12)							
Bal. 567			Bal. 2,464			Bal. 3,920		

Fixtures		Accumulated Depreciation Fixtures		Note Payable	
Bal. 540			Bal. 0		Bal. 400
			60 (10)		
			Bal. 60		

Account Payable		Capital Stock		Paid-in Capital	
	Bal. 0		Bal. 250		Bal. 1,375
(8) 29,200	34,340 (4)				
	Bal. 5,140				

Retained Earnings		Sales Revenue		Cost of Sales	
	Bal. 0		Bal. 0	Bal. 0	
(12) 150			35,724 (5)	(6) 30,420	
			Bal. 35,724	Bal. 30,420	

S&A Expense		Depreciation Expense		Interest Expense	
Bal. 0		Bal. 0		Bal. 0	
(9) 4,800		(10) 60		(11) 28	
Bal. 4,800		Bal. 60		Bal. 28	

Note: Beginning account balances include the financing and investing activities prior to the start of 20X1.

CONSTRUCTING THE FINANCIAL STATEMENTS

Exhibit 3.17 shows a balance sheet for 12/31/20X1 compared to 12/31/20X0. Although total assets have dramatically increased, cash has decreased. Note also that the ending balance in retained earnings is determined using the closing entries discussed in the next section. An income statement and statement of cash flows follow in Exhibits 3.18 and 3.19, respectively. BHT provides an income statement only for the year ending 12/31/20X1, as the firm did not begin operations during 20X0. BHT provides cash flow statements for 20X0 and 20X1 for comparative purposes. As briefly discussed in Chapter 2, BHT, like most firms, prepares the cash flow statement using the *indirect approach* (we'll cover this in more depth in Chapter 5). That is, BHT determines its cash from operations

Exhibit 3.17
Balance Sheet for Biohealth,
Inc. (BHT)

	As of 12/31/20X1	As of 12/31/20X0
Assets		
Current Assets:		
Cash	$ 567	$1,485
Accounts Receivable	2,464	0
Inventory	3,920	0
Total Current Assets	6,951	1,485
Property, Plant, and Equipment (Fixtures)	540	540
Less: Accumulated Depreciation	(60)	0
Net Property Plant and Equipment	480	540
Total Assets	$7,431	$2,025
Liabilities and Stockholders' Equity		
Liabilities:		
Current Liabilities:		
Accounts Payable	$5,140	$ 0
Long-Term Debt:		
Notes Payable	400	400
Total Liabilities	5,540	400
Stockholders' Equity		
Common Stock	250	250
Additional Paid-In Capital	1,375	1,375
Retained Earnings	266	0
Total Stockholders' Equity	1,891	1,625
Total Liabilities and Stockholders' Equity	$7,431	$2,025

Exhibit 3.18
Income Statement for
Biohealth, Inc. (BHT)

	Year Ending 12/31/20X1
Sales Revenue	$35,724
Less: Cost of Goods Sold	(30,420)
Gross Profit	5,304
Selling and Administrative Expenses	(4,800)
Depreciation Expense	(60)
Interest Expense	(28)
Net Income	$ 416
Earnings per Share[2]	$ 1.66

[2]Earnings per share is the amount of earnings per share of common stock outstanding. There are some specific requirements regarding how this is computed that will be discussed later. However, in this case it is simply net income/shares of common stock outstanding, or $416,000,000/250,000,000.

	Year Ending 12/31/20X1	Year Ending 12/31/20X0
Cash from Operations:		
Net Income	$416	$ 0
Add: Noncash Expenses		
Depreciation	60	0
Less: Changes in Current Assets and Current Liabilities:		
Increase in Accounts Receivable	(2,464)	0
Increase in Inventory	(3,920)	0
Increase in Accounts Payable	5,140	0
Total Cash from Operations	(768)	0
Cash from Investing		
Purchase Fixtures	0	(540)
Total Cash from Investing	0	(540)
Cash from Financing		
Borrow on Long-Term Note	0	400
Dividend Payments	(150)	
Issue Stock	0	1,625
Total Cash from Financing	(150)	2,025
Total Change in Cash	($918)	$1,485

Exhibit 3.19
Statement of Cash Flows for the Years Ending 20X1 and 20X0 Biohealth, Inc. (BHT)

starting with net income and then adjusting for noncash operating transactions. Note that the activities in 20X0 were limited to financing and investing activities, as no BHT operations occurred during this start-up period.

The cash flow statement for 20X1 illustrates why cash decreased even though the company earned a profit. Although dividends somewhat reduced cash during the period, operations proved to be the primary driver of the decline in cash, as it had a negative cash flow of $768. This decrease was caused primarily by the increase in accounts receivable and inventory. Increasing inventory requires cash to buy or make the inventory, and the increase in accounts receivable reflects uncollected revenues, resulting in less cash. Offsetting this was the positive effect of the increase in accounts payable during the period. When a company buys things on credit (thereby increasing accounts payable), it conserves cash. Finally, depreciation also produced a minor effect. Depreciation expense is added back to net income. Although it is an expense and it decreases net income, it does not use cash.

CLOSING ENTRIES

After preparing the income statement, the balances in the temporary revenue and expense accounts must be transferred to the retained earnings account (a permanent account). This will reset the balance in each temporary account to zero, to start the next accounting period. For example, the accounting period for BHT was from 1/1/20X1 through 12/31/20X1. The entries that accomplish the transfer of balances from the revenue and expense accounts to retained earnings are called **closing entries.** We'll distinguish closing entries in this text by lettering the entries rather than numbering them.

Sometimes companies use a single temporary account, the **income summary account,** to accumulate balances from all the income statement accounts. Firms often find it useful to summarize the net of the revenues and expenses during the closing process to calculate taxes. Firms use the income summary account only during the closing process; it carries a zero balance at all other times. The balances from all the individual revenue and expense accounts are closed to this summary account. The balance in the income summary account is then closed to retained earnings. Exhibit 3.20 shows the journal entries and T-accounts to close the revenue and expense accounts for BHT. After making these closing entries, the balances in the revenues, expenses, and income summary accounts return to zero.

Exhibit 3.20
Closing Entries for BHT Revenue and Expense Accounts Period Ended 12/31/20X1

Journal Entries

Account Titles	Debit	Credit
a. Sales Revenue	35,724	
Income Summary		35,724
b. Income Summary	35,308	
Cost of Sales		30,420
S&A Expenses		4,800
Depreciation Expense		60
Interest Expense		28
c. Income Summary	416	
Retained Earnings		416

Closing Entries T-Accounts

Sales Revenue		Cost of Sales		S&A Expenses	
	Bal. 35,724	Bal. 30,420		Bal. 4,800	
(a) 35, 724			30,420 (b)		4,800 (b)
	Bal. 0	Bal. 0		Bal. 0	

Depreciation Expense		Interest Expense		Retained Earnings	
Bal. 60		Bal. 28			Bal. 0
	60 (b)		(28) (b)	(12) 150	416 (c)
Bal. 0		Bal. 0			Bal. 266

Income Summary	
	Bal. 0
(b) 35,308	35,724 (a)
(c) 416	
	Bal. 0

Finally, just prior to making closing entries, a firm typically makes **adjusting entries.** Adjusting entries improve the accuracy of firm's financial statements, by enabling it to meet the accrual concept. For example, BHT's recording of depreciation is one type of adjusting entry. Other adjusting entries include the recognition of interest expense that has not been paid and wages that have been incurred but not paid. We'll discuss adjusting entries again in Chapter 4 and Appendix A covers adjusting entries in more detail.

THE ACCOUNTING CYCLE

The accounting cycle refers to the series of steps in the accounting process, which a firm repeats each time it prepares financial statements. While accounting systems may differ from very simple systems in a sole proprietorship, to multibillion-dollar systems in large companies, the process remains essentially the same:

1. *Identify transactions.* As we indicated earlier, some economic events are not recognized in accounting as transactions. For example, if Dell signed a contract with another company to furnish a large number of computers to the company over a period of time, this would be an event of economic consequence to Dell, but it would not be recorded as an accounting transaction.

2. *Journalize transactions.* A journal entry provides a summary of a particular event's impact on assets, liabilities, and stockholders' equity.

3. *Post journal entries to ledger accounts.* In this book, we use T-accounts to represent ledgers. In real accounting systems, ledger accounts can take many forms, but the key to thinking about the ledger is to realize that it carries forward all of the transactions that affect a particular account. In the case of permanent accounts as seen on the balance sheet (assets, liabilities, and various stockholders' equity accounts), the balances carry-forward over accounting periods. For example, the balance in accounts receivable at the end of 20X0 is the same as the balance at the beginning of 20X1. In contrast, the nominal or temporary accounts (revenues and expenses) will start each accounting period with a zero balance.

4. *Prepare period-end adjusting entries and then post them to ledger accounts.* An example would be recording depreciation.

5. *Prepare the income statement.*

6. *Close nominal accounts to retained earnings.*

7. *Prepare the balance sheet and cash flow statement.*

One final issue with regard to the accounting cycle is the frequency with which financial statements should be prepared. On one hand, a firm should prepare financial statements as often as necessary to provide timely information to management, stockholders, creditors, and others with an interest in the firm. On the other hand, a firm must balance the benefits of having up-to-date information with the cost of preparing the statements. In some businesses, management may need up-to-date information, in which case daily reports may be necessary. This is becoming more common as the cost of compiling timely information continues to decrease. In other businesses, a monthly statement may be sufficient.

Regardless of what time period a firm selects, firms will follow the same procedures as outlined in this chapter.

Companies whose stock is traded on a public exchange and who fall under the authority of the SEC are required to file financial statements quarterly, as well as on an annual basis. The frequency with which a firm prepares its financial statements is sometimes expressed in terms of how often the firm closes its books. If it closes its books monthly, the accounting cycle for the firm is one month, and the nominal (temporary) accounts are reset on a monthly basis. However, although a company may close its books more frequently than at year-end, annual financial statements require that revenues and expenses be accumulated over the entire year. Thus, firms do interim closings only for purposes of preparing interim statements.

ANALYZING FINANCIAL STATEMENTS

Understanding the accounting cycle will help you to use the information in the financial statements more effectively. To illustrate, as an investor or potential investor, you can obtain financial statements, but not information about the individual transactions that gave rise to those statements. However, by understanding the accounting process, you may be able to deduce some of the major transactions by analyzing the financial statements.

Say you looked at Exhibits 3.17, 3.18, and 3.19 without knowing BHT's transactions. By understanding the accounting process, you would be able to observe the following:

- Cash has declined for the year despite the fact that BHT reported a profit.
- The balance sheet shows an increase in Accounts Receivable, suggesting that cash collection from sales was less than the revenue recognized.
- The balance sheet shows an increase in Inventory, indicating that the company is purchasing more inventory than it is selling.
- Accounts Payable increased during the year, suggesting that the company is purchasing more inventory than it is paying to suppliers.

As BHT formed in 20X0, we would not be surprised by these findings, as they are typical of a new business. However, in an established company, significant changes in balance sheet accounts may signal information about the company's future cash flows. For example, if a company records large amounts of sales on account, and accounts receivable increases more rapidly than the sales, the company may not be collecting its accounts receivable on a timely basis or it may have relaxed its credit policies. This may signal future cash flow problems (defaults by customers). Similarly, increasing inventory coupled with decreasing (or less rapidly) increasing sales may signal that a company is having difficulty selling its inventory. In Chapter 6, we continue to consider how to assess past performance based on the information contained in financial statements, as well as to predict future performance.

As you progress through this text, you will appreciate more fully the power of the information conveyed about a company in its financial statements and the value to you of understanding the concepts underlying financial statement construction. Of particular importance is predicting transactions' impact on each of the major financial statements. For example, as a manager, you might consider generating additional sales by providing a more liberal credit policy (e.g., allowing customers with weaker credit to purchase goods on account). With a good knowledge of accounting, you could anticipate the effects of such a change in credit policies on the financial statements. In this particular case, you would likely see increased sales on the income statement, coupled with increased accounts receivable because weaker credit customers might pay more slowly or not at all. You might also see cash flows decline even if sales increased. This could occur due to a combination of two factors, slower sales collections and a need to purchase and pay for more inventory to sell to customers who have not yet paid. Thus, this business decision would impact all of the major financial statements.

SUMMARY AND TRANSITION

This chapter provided an overview of the accounting process used to generate financial statements. Understanding the framework of accounting allows you to readily determine the impact of economic events on the financial statements. This knowledge will allow you as a manager or investor to make sound decisions using information generated from the accounting process.

The accounting process contains two basic concepts: duality and the nominal (temporary) account. The concept of duality portrays accounting events in terms of the dual effects on the resources of the firm (its assets), the claims of creditors (its liabilities), and the owners' wealth (stockholders' equity). The duality concept is apparent in the accounting equation and the requirements that debits equal credits in the accounting representation of each transaction. Nominal accounts are used to describe changes in stockholders' equity that result from operating activities, principally revenues and expenses.

Understanding the accounting process is necessary to understanding the information conveyed in the financial statements that are the final product of that process. However, apart from the accounting process itself, there are many accounting choices and judgments that affect the implementation of that process and, thereby, shape the content of those statements. Chief among these are the recognition criteria which determine when an economic event should get recognized in the accounting system (such as the timing of recognizing revenues and expenses) and the valuation principles that determine the values of the assets and liabilities of the firm that meet the recognition criteria. These choices and judgments are addressed in the chapters that follow.

END OF CHAPTER MATERIAL

KEY TERMS

Additional Paid-In Capital
Adjusting Entries
Closing Entries

Contra-Asset Account
Contributed Capital
Cost of Goods Sold

Credits

Debits

Depreciation Expense

Depreciation Methods

Double-Entry Accounting System

Entry

Journal

Journal Entry

Ledger

Nominal Accounts

Par Value

Permanent Accounts

Retained Earnings

Sales Revenue

Stated Value

Summary Account

T-Account

Temporary Accounts

Transactions

ASSIGNMENT MATERIAL

REVIEW QUESTIONS

1. Explain what double-entry accounting means and provide an example.
2. Define an asset, according to GAAP.
3. Define a liability, according to GAAP.
4. Describe what owners' equity represents.
5. Discuss how retained earnings changes over time.
6. What is a permanent account?
7. What is a nominal or temporary account?
8. What is the proper form for a journal entry?
9. What is a ledger?
10. What is depreciation?
11. How is straight-line depreciation calculated?
12. What is a contra-asset account and how is it used in the context of depreciation?
13. "Expense accounts have debit balances, and debit entries increase these accounts." Reconcile this statement with the normal effects of entries on owners' equity accounts and the resulting balances.
14. Describe the closing process.
15. Discuss why one firm might close their books monthly and another might close them weekly.

APPLYING YOUR KNOWLEDGE

15. Explain why you agree or disagree with the following statement: "Retained earnings are like money in the bank; you can always use them to pay your bills if you get into trouble."
16. Respond to each of the following statements with a true or false answer:
    a. Debits increase liability accounts.
    b. Revenues are credit entries to owners' equity.

112

c. Cash receipts from customers are debited to accounts receivable.

d. Dividends declared decrease cash at the date of declaration.

e. Dividends are an expense of doing business and should appear on the income statement.

f. Selling goods on account results in a credit to accounts receivable.

g. Making a payment on an account payable results in a debit to accounts payable.

17. For each of the transactions below, indicate which accounts are affected and whether they increase or decrease.

a. Issue common stock for cash.

b. Buy equipment from a supplier on credit (short term).

c. Buy inventory from a supplier partly with cash and partly on account.

d. Sell a unit of inventory to a customer on account.

e. Receive a payment from a customer on his or her account.

f. Borrow money from the bank.

g. Declare a dividend (to be paid later).

h. Pay a dividend (that was previously declared).

18. For each of the following transactions, indicate how income and cash flow are affected (increase, decrease, no effect) and by how much:

a. Issue common stock for $1,000.

b. Sell, on account, a unit of inventory for $150 that cost $115. The unit is already in inventory.

c. Purchase equipment for $500 in cash.

d. Depreciate plant and equipment by $300.

e. Purchase a unit of inventory, on account, for $100.

f. Make a payment on accounts payable for $200.

g. Receive a payment from a customer for $75 on his or her account.

h. Declare a dividend for $400.

i. Pay a dividend for $400.

19. Show how each of the following transactions affects the balance sheet equation:

a. Borrow $1,500 from the bank.

b. Buy land for $20,000 in cash.

c. Issue common stock for $5,000. The par value of the stock is $1,500.

d. Buy inventory costing $3,000 on account.

e. Sell inventory costing $2,500 to customers, on account, for $3,500.

f. Make a payment of $250 to the electric company for power used during the current period.

g. Declare a dividend of $350.

h. Depreciate equipment by $500.

20. Show how each of the following transactions affects the balance sheet equation:

a. Issue common stock for $10,000. The stock has no par value attached to it.

b. Receive a payment from a customer on his or her account in the amount of $325.

c. Make a payment to the bank of $850. Of this amount, $750 represents interest and the rest is a repayment of principal.

d. Return a unit of inventory costing $200 that was damaged in shipment. You have already paid for the unit and have requested a refund from the supplier.

e. Dividends of $175 that were previously declared are paid.

f. Purchase equipment costing $1,800. You pay $600 in cash and give the supplier a note for the balance of the purchase price.

g. Sales on account of $15,000 are reported for the period.

h. A count of physical inventory at the end of the period indicates an ending balance of $575. The beginning balance was $485, and the purchases for the period were $11,500. Record the cost of goods sold.

21. For each of the following transactions, indicate how each immediately affects the balance sheet equation and what other effects there will be in the future as a result of the transaction:

a. Purchase equipment.

b. Borrow money from the bank.

c. Purchase inventory on account.

d. Sell inventory on account to customers.

e. Buy a patent for a new production process.

22. Indicate the effects of the following transactions on the balance sheet equation developed in the chapter. Assume that the fiscal year end of the firm is December 31.

a. Borrow $2,500 from the bank on 1/1/X1.

b. Pay interest on the bank loan on 12/31/X1. The interest rate is 10 percent.

c. Buy equipment on 1/1/X1 for $2,000. The equipment has an estimated useful life of five years and an estimated salvage value at the end of five years of $500.

d. Record the depreciation for the equipment as of 12/31/X1, assuming the firm uses the straight-line method.

e. Sales for the period totaled $5,500, of which $3,500 were on account. The cost of the products sold was $3,600.

f. Collections from customers on account totaled $2,800.

g. Purchases of inventory on account during 20X1 totaled $2,700.

h. Payments to suppliers totaled $2,900 during 20X1.

i. Dividends were declared and paid in the amount of $100.

23. Indicate the effects of the following transactions on the balance sheet equation developed in the chapter. Assume that the fiscal year end of the firm is December 31.

a. Issue common stock for $25,000, with a par value of $8,000.

b. Sales recorded for the period totaled $60,000, of which $25,000 were cash sales.

c. Cash collections on customer accounts totaled $37,000.

d. Sign a contract to purchase a piece of equipment that costs $1,200, and put a downpayment of $100 on the purchase.

e. Dividends of $1,300 are declared.

f. Dividends of $1,150 that had previously been declared are paid.

g. Depreciation of $3,300 was taken on the property, plant, and equipment.

h. Purchase $31,350 of inventory on account.

i. Inventory costing $35,795 was sold.

24. Indicate whether each of the following accounts normally has a debit or a credit balance:

a. Accounts Receivable

b. Accounts Payable

c. Sales Revenue

d. Dividends Declared

e. Dividends Payable

f. Depreciation Expense

g. Common Stock (par value)

h. Cost of Goods Sold

i. Loan Payable

25. For each of the following accounts indicate whether the account would normally have a debit or a credit balance:

a. Cash

b. Accounts Payable

c. Common Stock

d. Sales Revenues

e. Inventory

f. Cost of Goods Sold

g. Paid-In Capital

h. Retained Earnings

i. Accumulated Depreciation

26. For each of the following transactions construct a journal entry:

a. Inventory costing $1,500 is purchased on account.

b. Inventory costing $1,200 is sold on account for $1,800.

c. Accounts receivable of $800 are collected.

d. The firm borrows $10,000 from the bank.

e. The firm issues common stock for $2,500 and $1,500 is considered par value.

f. New equipment costing $3,500 is purchased with cash.

27. The T. George Company started business on 1/1/X2. Listed below are the transactions that occurred during 20X2.

Required:

a. Construct the journal entries to record the transactions of the T. George Company for 20X2.

b. Post the journal entries to the appropriate T-accounts.

c. Prepare a balance sheet and income statement for 20X2.

d. Prepare the closing entries for 20X2.

Transactions:

1. On 1/1/X2, the company issued 10,000 shares of common stock for $175,000. The par value of the stock is $10 per share.

2. On 1/1/X2, the company borrowed $125,000 from the bank.

3. On 1/2/X2, the company purchased (for cash) land and a building costing $200,000. The building was recently appraised at $140,000.

4. Inventory costing $100,000 was purchased on account.

5. An investment was made in Calhoun Company stock in the amount of $75,000.

6. Sales to customers totaled $190,000 in 20X2. Of these, $30,000 were cash sales.

7. Collections on accounts receivable totaled $135,000.

8. Payments to suppliers totaled $92,000 in 20X2.

9. Salaries paid to employees totaled $44,000. There were no unpaid salaries at year end.

10. A count of inventories at year end revealed $10,000 worth of inventory.

11. The building was estimated to have a useful life of 20 years and a salvage value of $20,000. The company uses straight-line depreciation.

12. The interest on the bank loan is recognized each month and is paid on the first day of the succeeding month; that is, January's interest is recognized in January and paid on February 1. The interest rate is 12 percent.

13. The investment in Calhoun Company paid dividends of $5,000 in 20X2. All of it had been received by year end.

14. Dividends of $15,000 were declared on 12/15/X2 and were scheduled to be paid on 1/10/X3.

28. The Hughes Tool Company started business on 10/1/X3. Its fiscal year runs through September 30 of the following year. Following are the transactions that occurred during fiscal year 19X4 (the year starting 10/1/X3 and ending 9/30/X4).

Required:

a. Construct the journal entries to record the transactions of the The Hughes Tool Company for fiscal year 20X4.

b. Post the journal entries to the appropriate T-accounts.

c. Prepare a balance sheet and income statement for fiscal year 20X4.

d. Prepare the closing entries for fiscal year 20X4.

Transactions:

1. On 10/1/X3, J. Hughes contributed $100,000 to start the business. Hughes is the sole proprietor of the business.

2. On 10/2/X3, Hughes borrowed $300,000 from a venture capitalist (a lender who specializes in start-up companies). The interest rate on

the loan is 11 percent. Interest is paid twice a year on March 31 and September 30.

3. On 10/3/X3, Hughes rented a building. The rental agreement was a two-year contract that called for quarterly rental payments of $20,000, payable in advance on January 1, April 1, July 1, and October 1. The first payment was made on 10/3/X3 and covers the period from October 1 to December 31.

4. On 10/3/X3, Hughes purchased equipment costing $250,000. The equipment had an estimated useful life of seven years and a salvage value of $40,000.

5. On 10/3/X3, Hughes purchased initial inventory with a cash payment of $100,000.

6. Sales during the year totaled $800,000, of which $720,000 were credit sales.

7. Collections from customers on account totaled $640,000.

8. Additional purchases of inventory during the year totaled $550,000, all on account.

9. Payments to suppliers totaled $495,000.

10. Inventory on hand at year end amounted to $115,000.

11. J. Hughes withdrew a total of $40,000 for personal expenses during the year.

12. Interest on the loan from the venture capitalist was paid at year-end, as well as $20,000 of the principal.

13. Other selling and administrative expenses totaled $90,000 for the year. Of these, $20,000 were unpaid as of year end.

29. The A.J. Smith Company started business on 1/1/X4. The company's fiscal year ends on December 31. Following are the transactions that occurred during 20X4.

Required:

a. Construct the journal entries to record the transactions of the The A.J. Smith Company for fiscal year 20X4.

b. Post the journal entries to the appropriate T-accounts.

c. Prepare a balance sheet and income statement for fiscal year 20X4.

d. Prepare the closing entries for fiscal year 20X4.

Transactions:

1. On 1/1/X4, the company issued 25,000 shares of common stock at $15 per share. The par value of each share of common stock is $10.

2. On 1/1/X4, the company purchased land and buildings from another company in exchange for $50,000 in cash and 25,000 shares of common stock. The land's value is approximately one-fifth of the total value of the transaction.

3. Equipment worth $100,000 was purchased on 7/1/X4, in exchange for $50,000 in cash and a one-year, 10 percent note, principal amount $50,000. The note pays semiannual interest, and interest was unpaid on 12/31/X4.

4. The equipment is depreciated using the straight-line method, with an estimated useful life of 10 years and an estimated salvage value of $0.

5. The buildings purchased in transaction 2 are depreciated using the straight-line method, with an estimated useful life of 30 years and an estimated salvage value of $40,000.

6. During the year, inventory costing $200,000 was purchased, all on account.

7. Sales during the year were $215,000, of which credit sales were $175,000.

8. Inventory costing $160,000 was sold during the year.

9. Payments to suppliers totaled $175,000.

10. At the end of the year, accounts receivable had a positive balance of $10,000.

11. On March 31, 20X4, the company rented out a portion of its building to Fantek Corporation. Fantek is required to make quarterly payments of $5,000 each. The payments are due on April 1, July 1, October 1, and January 1 of each year, with the first payment on 4/1/X4. All scheduled payments were made during 20X4.

12. Selling and distribution expenses amounted to $30,000, all paid in cash.

13. During the year, inventory worth $10,000 was destroyed by fire. The inventory was not insured.

14. The company calculates taxes at a rate of 30 percent. During the year, $3,000 was paid to the taxing authority.

15. Dividends of $4,000 were declared during the year, and $1,000 remained unpaid at year end.

30. The accounting system closing process takes some amount of time at the end of the accounting period in order to check for errors, make adjusting entries, and prepare the financial statements. In recent years there has been a real push to speed up this process for most firms. Discuss the incentives that companies might have to implement in order to make this a faster process.

31. During the year-end audit process, the auditing firm may find errors and omissions in the recording of transactions and will then ask management to make an adjusting entry to correct for these errors. In light of the purpose of the audit opinion, discuss plausible arguments that management might give to convince the auditor to waive making these suggested adjustments.

32. Suppose that a company has a bonus plan in which managers can earn a bonus if they meet certain net income targets. If the management team has discretion as to which depreciation method they might use, with the straight-line reporting the least amount of depreciation in the early years of the life of the asset, discuss the incentives that management would have in choosing a depreciation method. Also discuss how owners might protect themselves from any self-serving behavior on the part of management.

33. Discuss how creditors might protect their interests (relative to owners) when they negotiate their lending agreement with the firm.

USING REAL DATA

34. Base your answers to the following questions on the financial statements of Russ Berrie.

RUSS BERRIE & Co., Inc.:
Income Statement

	12/31/2001	12/31/2000	12/31/1999
Net sales	$294,291,000	$300,801,000	$287,011,000
Cost of sales	132,611,000	132,908,000	123,216,000
Gross profit	161,680,000	167,893,000	163,795,000
Selling, general and administrative expense	112,570,000	106,991,000	108,023,000
Information system write-off	0	0	10,392,000
Investment and other income net	(8,560,000)	(10,202,000)	(8,587,000)
Income before taxes	57,670,000	71,104,000	53,967,000
Provision for income taxes	17,496,000	23,163,000	17,531,000
Net income	$ 40,174,000	$ 47,941,000	$ 36,436,000

RUSS BERRIE & Co., Inc.:
Balance Sheet

	12/31/2001	12/31/2000
Assets		
Current assets		
Cash and cash equivalents	$148,872,000	$ 77,794,000
Marketable securities	94,181,000	141,032,000
Accounts receivable, trade, less allowance of $3,454 in 2001 and $3,460 in 2000	63,481,000	58,673,000
Inventories, net	37,374,000	47,430,000
Prepaid expenses and other current assets	4,550,000	5,508,000
Deferred income taxes	6,705,000	6,003,000
Total current assets	355,163,000	336,440,000
Property, plant, and equipment, net	24,623,000	26,745,000
Inventories—long-term, net	2,284,000	0
Other assets	4,574,000	3,824,000
Total assets	$386,644,000	$367,009,000
Liabilities and Shareholders' Equity		
Current liabilities		
Accounts payable	5,376,000	4,913,000
Accrued expenses	20,003,000	20,313,000
Accrued income taxes	6,848,000	7,192,000
Total current liabilities	32,227,000	32,418,000

	12/31/2001	12/31/2000
Commitments and contingencies		
Shareholders' equity		
Common stock: $0.10 stated value; authorized 50,000,000 shares; issued 2001, 25,682,364 shares; 2000, 25,413,626 shares	2,587,000	2,541,000
Additional paid-in-capital	73,794,000	63,103,000
Retained earnings	392,272,000	381,479,000
Accumulated other comprehensive loss	(4,165,000)	(4,310,000)
Unearned compensation	(75,000)	(149,000)
Treasury stock, at cost (5,632,014 shares at December 31, 2001 and 5,557,514 shares at December 31, 2000)	(109,996,000)	(108,073,000)
Total shareholders equity	354,417,000	334,591,000
Total liabilities and shareholders' equity	$386,644,000	$367,009,000

RUSS BERRIE & Co., Inc.:
Cash Flow

	12/31/2001	12/31/2000	12/31/1999
Cash flows from operating activities:			
Net income	$ 40,174,000	$47,941,000	$36,436,000
Adjustments to reconcile net income to net cash provided by operating activities:			
Depreciation and amortization	4,021,000	3,998,000	5,008,000
Information system write-off	0	0	10,392,000
Provision for accounts receivable reserves	1,828,000	2,298,000	2,534,000
Income from contingency reserve reversal	0	(2,544,000)	0
Other	415,000	390,000	(456,000)
Changes in assets and liabilities:			
Accounts receivable	(6,636,000)	414,000	(9,058,000)
Inventories, net	7,772,000	(3,123,000)	894,000
Prepaid expenses and other current assets	958,000	3,995,000	(197,000)
Other assets	(166,000)	78,000	(1,460,000)
Accounts payable	463,000	(1,315,000)	1,979,000
Accrued expenses	(310,000)	(631,000)	421,000
Accrued income taxes	(344,000)	1,086,000	(1,099,000)
Total adjustments	8,001,000	4,646,000	8,958,000
Net cash provided by operating activities	48,175,000	52,587,000	45,394,000
Cash flows from investing activities:			
Purchase of marketable securities	(97,335,000)	(48,959,000)	(46,365,000)
Proceeds from sale of marketable securities	144,331,000	45,567,000	60,017,000

	12/31/2001	12/31/2000	12/31/1999
Proceeds from sale of property, plant, and equipment	89,000	79,000	116,000
Capital expenditures	(2,405,000)	(4,087,000)	(8,435,000)
Net cash provided by (used in) investing activities	44,680,000	(7,400,000)	5,333,000
Cash flows from financing activities:			
Proceeds from issuance of common stock	10,737,000	2,155,000	2,416,000
Dividends paid to shareholders	(29,381,000)	(17,764,000)	(16,861,000)
Purchase of treasury stock	(1,923,000)	(15,619,000)	(44,292,000)
Net cash (used in) financing activities	(20,567,000)	(31,228,000)	(58,737,000)
Effect of exchange rate changes on cash and cash equivalents	(1,210,000)	(1,073,000)	(146,000)
Net increase (decrease) in cash and cash equivalents	71,078,000	12,886,000	(8,156,000)
Cash and cash equivalents at beginning of year	77,794,000	64,908,000	73,064,000
Cash and cash equivalents at end of year	$148,872,000	$77,794,000	$64,908,000
Cash paid during the year for:			
Interest	$ 196,000	$ 127,000	$ 118,000
Income taxes	17,841,000	22,077,000	18,630,000

a. Determine the amount of dividends declared during fiscal 2001.

b. Determine the amount of dividends paid during fiscal 2001.

c. Assuming that all sales were on account, determine the amount of cash collected from customers.

d. Assuming that the only transactions that flow through the accounts payable to suppliers and others are purchases of inventory and assuming that all additions to inventory were purchases of inventory, determine the cash payments to suppliers.

e. The other comprehensive income account reflects the translation of Russ Berrie's foreign subsidiaries. What has been the experience with these subsidiaries over time—have they resulted in net gains or net losses from translation?

f. In 1999, the company wrote off the cost of some of its information systems. How significant was this write-off (express your answer as a percent of income before the write-off)? How might an analyst factor this loss into his or her evaluation of the company's stock?

g. How does the company finance its business (use data to support your answer)?

h. How healthy is the company from a cash flow perspective?

35. Use the data from the financial statements of the GAP to answer the following questions:

a. Determine the amount of dividends declared during the year ended 2/2/2002.

b. Determine the amount of dividends paid during the year ended 2/2/2002.

c. The GAP reports the ratio of each expense line item relative to net sales on its income statement. Use these data to discuss how profitable GAP has been over the last three years in selling its products.

d. What has been the trend in revenues and earnings over the last three years (use data to support your answer)?

e. How does the company finance its business (use data to support your answer)?

f. How healthy is the company from a cash flow perspective?

g. If you were an analyst, how might you react to the trends you see in income, debt, and cash flows over the years presented?

GAP, Inc. Income Statement
($ in thousands except share and per share amounts)

	52 Weeks Ended		53 Weeks Ended		52 Weeks Ended	
	Feb. 2, 2002	% to Sales	Feb. 3, 2001	% to Sales	Jan. 29, 2000	% to Sales
Net sales	$13,847,873	100.00%	$13,673,460	100.00%	$11,635,398	100.00%
Costs and expenses						
Cost of goods sold and occupancy expenses	9,704,389	70.1	8,599,442	62.9	6,775,262	58.2
Operating expenses	3,805,968	27.5	3,629,257	26.5	3,043,432	26.2
Interest expense	109,190	0.8	74,891	0.5	44,966	0.4
Interest income	(13,315)	(0.1)	(12,015)	(0.0)	(13,211)	(0.1)
Earnings before income taxes	241,641	1.7	1,381,885	10.1	1,784,949	15.3
Income taxes	249,405	1.8	504,388	3.7	657,884	5.6
Net earnings (loss)	($7,764)	(0.1%)	$877,497	6.4%	$1,127,065	9.7%

GAP, Inc. Balance Sheet

	Feb. 2, 2002	Feb. 3, 2001
Assets		
Current assets:		
Cash and equivalents	$1,035,749,000	$408,794,000
Merchandise inventory	1,677,116,000	1,904,153,000
Other current assets	331,685,000	335,103,000
Total current assets:	3,044,550,000	2,648,050,000
Property and equipment		
Leasehold improvements	2,127,966,000	1,899,820,000

	Feb. 2, 2002	Feb. 3, 2001
Furniture and equipment	3,327,819,000	2,826,863,000
Land and buildings	917,055,000	558,832,000
Construction-in-progress	246,691,000	615,722,000
	6,619,531,000	5,901,237,000
Accumulated depreciation and amortization	(2,458,241,000)	(1,893,552,000)
Property and equipment, net	4,161,290,000	4,007,685,000
Lease rights and other assets	385,486,000	357,173,000
Total assets	$7,591,326,000	$7,012,908,000
Liabilities and shareholders' equity:		
Current liabilities		
Notes payable	$ 41,889,000	$ 779,904,000
Current maturities of long-term debt	0	250,000,000
Accounts payable	1,105,117,000	1,067,207,000
Accrued expenses and other current liabilities	909,227,000	702,033,000
Total current liabilities	2,056,233,000	2,799,144,000
Long-term liabilities:		
Long-term debt	1,961,397,000	780,246,000
Deferred lease credits and other liabilities	564,115,000	505,279,000
Total long-term liabilities	2,525,512,000	1,285,525,000
Shareholders' equity:		
Common stock $.05 par value		
Authorized 2,300,000,000 shares; issued 948,597,949 and 939,222,871 shares; outstanding 865,726,890 and 853,996,984 shares	47,430,000	46,961,000
Additional paid-in capital	461,408,000	294,967,000
Retained earnings	4,890,375,000	4,974,773,000
Accumulated other comprehensive losses	(61,824,000)	(20,173,000)
Deferred compensation	(7,245,000)	(12,162,000)
Treasury stock, at cost	(2,320,563,000)	(2,356,127,000)
Total shareholders' equity	3,009,581,000	2,928,239,000
Total liabilities and shareholders' equity	$7,591,326,000	$7,012,908,000

GAP, Inc. Cash Flow	52 Weeks Ended	53 Weeks Ended	52 Weeks Ended
Cash Flows from Operating Activities	Feb. 2, 2002	Feb. 3, 2001	Jan. 29, 2000
Net earnings (loss)	($7,764,000)	$877,497,000	$1,127,065,000
Adjustments to reconcile net earnings (loss) to net cash provided by operating activities:			
Depreciation and amortization	810,486,000	590,365,000	436,184,000
Tax benefit from exercise of stock options and vesting of restricted stock	58,444,000	130,882,000	211,891,000
Deferred income taxes	(28,512,000)	(38,872,000)	2,444,000

	52 Weeks Ended Feb. 2, 2002	53 Weeks Ended Feb. 3, 2001	52 Weeks Ended Jan. 29, 2000
Change in operating assets and liabilities:			
Merchandise inventory	213,067,000	(454,595,000)	(404,211,000)
Prepaid expenses and other	(13,303,000)	(61,096,000)	(55,519,000)
Accounts payable	42,205,000	249,545,000	118,121,000
Accrued expenses	220,826,000	(56,541,000)	(5,822,000)
Deferred lease credits and other long-term liabilities	22,390,000	54,020,000	47,775,000
Net cash provided by operating activities	1,317,839,000	1,291,205,000	1,477,928,000
Cash flows from investing activities:			
Net purchase of property and equipment	(940,078,000)	(1,858,662,000)	(1,238,722,000)
Acquisition of lease rights and other assets	(10,549,000)	(16,252,000)	(39,839,000)
Net cash used for investing activities	(950,627,000)	(1,874,914,000)	(1,278,561,000)
Cash flows from financing activities:			
Net increase (decrease) in notes payable	(734,927,000)	621,420,000	84,778,000
Proceeds from issuance of long-term debt	1,194,265,000	250,000,000	311,839,000
Payments of long-term debt	(250,000,000)	0	0
Issuance of common stock	139,105,000	152,105,000	114,142,000
Net purchase of treasury stock	(785,000)	(392,558,000)	(745,056,000)
Cash dividends paid	(76,373,000)	(75,488,000)	(75,795,000)
Net cash provided by (used for) financing activities	271,285,000	555,479,000	(310,092,000)
Effect of exchange rate fluctuations on cash	(11,542,000)	(13,328,000)	(4,176,000)
Net increase (decrease) in cash and equivalents	$ 626,955,000	($41,558,000)	($114,901,000)
Cash and equivalents at beginning of year	408,794,000	450,352,000	565,253,000
Cash and equivalents at end of year	$1,035,749,000	$408,794,000	$ 450,352,000

36. Use the financial statements of Hasbro to answer the following questions:

a. Determine the amount of dividends declared during fiscal year 2001.

b. Determine the amount of dividends paid during fiscal year 2001.

c. Assuming that all sales were on account, determine the amount of cash collected from customers.

d. Assuming that the only transactions that flow through the accounts payable to suppliers and others are purchases of inventory, and assuming that all additions to inventory were purchases of inventory, determine the cash payments to suppliers.

e. What has been the trend in revenues and earnings over the last three years (use data to support your answer)?

f. How does the company finance its business (use data to support your answer)?

g. How healthy is the company from a cash flow perspective?

h. If you were an analyst, how might you react to the trends you see in income, debt, and cash flows over the years presented?

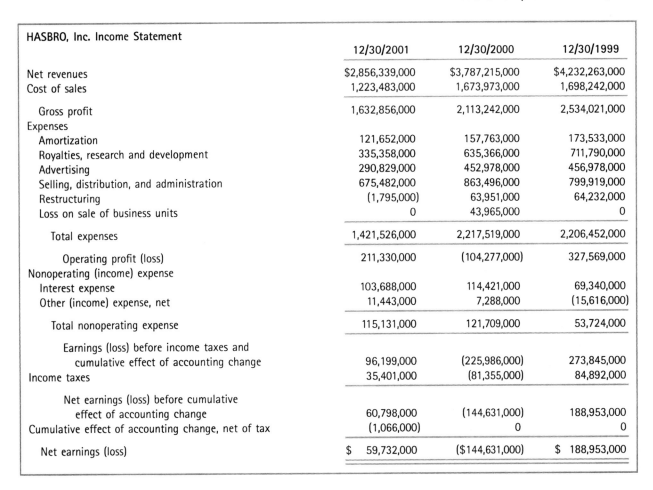

HASBRO, Inc. Income Statement

	12/30/2001	12/30/2000	12/30/1999
Net revenues	$2,856,339,000	$3,787,215,000	$4,232,263,000
Cost of sales	1,223,483,000	1,673,973,000	1,698,242,000
Gross profit	1,632,856,000	2,113,242,000	2,534,021,000
Expenses			
Amortization	121,652,000	157,763,000	173,533,000
Royalties, research and development	335,358,000	635,366,000	711,790,000
Advertising	290,829,000	452,978,000	456,978,000
Selling, distribution, and administration	675,482,000	863,496,000	799,919,000
Restructuring	(1,795,000)	63,951,000	64,232,000
Loss on sale of business units	0	43,965,000	0
Total expenses	1,421,526,000	2,217,519,000	2,206,452,000
Operating profit (loss)	211,330,000	(104,277,000)	327,569,000
Nonoperating (income) expense			
Interest expense	103,688,000	114,421,000	69,340,000
Other (income) expense, net	11,443,000	7,288,000	(15,616,000)
Total nonoperating expense	115,131,000	121,709,000	53,724,000
Earnings (loss) before income taxes and cumulative effect of accounting change	96,199,000	(225,986,000)	273,845,000
Income taxes	35,401,000	(81,355,000)	84,892,000
Net earnings (loss) before cumulative effect of accounting change	60,798,000	(144,631,000)	188,953,000
Cumulative effect of accounting change, net of tax	(1,066,000)	0	0
Net earnings (loss)	$ 59,732,000	($144,631,000)	$ 188,953,000

HASBRO, Inc. Balance Sheet

	12/30/2001	12/30/2000
Assets:		
Current assets		
Cash and cash equivalents	$ 233,095,000	$ 127,115,000
Accounts receivable, less allowance for doubtful accounts of $49,300 in 2001 and $55,000 in 2000	572,499,000	685,975,000
Inventories	217,479,000	335,493,000
Prepaid expenses and other current assets	345,545,000	431,630,000
Total current assets	1,368,618,000	1,580,213,000
Property, plant, and equipment, net	235,360,000	296,729,000
Other assets		
Goodwill, less accumulated amortization of $269,496 in 2001 and $225,770 in 2000	761,575,000	803,189,000
Other intangibles, less accumulated amortization of $398,183 in 2001 and $347,149 in 2000	805,027,000	902,893,000

	12/30/2001	12/30/2000
Other	198,399,000	245,435,000
Total other assets	1,765,001,000	1,951,517,000
Total assets	$3,368,979,000	$3,828,459,000

Liabilities and shareholders' equity:

Current liabilities

	12/30/2001	12/30/2000
Short-term borrowings	$ 34,024,000	$ 226,292,000
Current installments of long-term debt	2,304,000	1,793,000
Accounts payable	123,109,000	191,749,000
Accrued liabilities	599,154,000	819,978,000
Total current liabilities	758,591,000	1,239,812,000
Long-term debt	1,165,649,000	1,167,838,000
Deferred liabilities	91,875,000	93,403,000
Total liabilities	2,016,115,000	2,501,053,000

Shareholders' equity

	12/30/2001	12/30/2000
Preference stock of $2.50 par value. Authorized 5,000,000 shares; none issued	0	0
Common stock of $.50 par value. Authorized 600,000,000 shares; issued 209,694,630 shares in 2001 and 2000	104,847,000	104,847,000
Additional paid-in capital	457,544,000	464,084,000
Deferred compensation	(2,996,000)	(6,889,000)
Retained earnings	⇒1,622,402,000	1,583,394,000
Accumulated other comprehensive earnings	(68,398,000)	(44,718,000)
Treasury stock, at cost, 36,736,156 shares in 2001 and 37,253,164 shares in 2000	(760,535,000)	(773,312,000)
Total shareholders' equity	1,352,864,000	1,327,406,000
Total liabilities and shareholders' equity	$3,368,979,000	$3,828,459,000

HASBRO, Inc. Cash Flow

	12/30/2001	12/30/2000	12/30/1999
Cash flows from operating activities:			
Net earnings (loss)	$59,732,000	($144,631,000)	$188,953,000
Adjustments to reconcile net earnings (loss) to net cash provided by operating activities:			
Depreciation and amortization of plant and equipment	104,247,000	106,458,000	103,791,000
Other amortization	121,652,000	157,763,000	173,533,000
Deferred income taxes	38,697,000	(67,690,000)	(38,675,000)
Compensation earned under restricted stock program	2,532,000	2,754,000	0
Loss on sale of business units	0	43,965,000	0
Change in operating assets and liabilities (other than cash and cash equivalents):			
Decrease (increase) in accounts receivable	99,474,000	395,682,000	(11,248,000)
Decrease (increase) in inventories	109,002,000	69,657,000	(44,212,000)

	12/30/2001	12/30/2000	12/30/1999
Decrease (increase) in prepaid expenses and other current assets	45,936,000	(84,006,000)	(26,527,000)
(Decrease) increase in accounts payable and accrued liabilities	(194,525,000)	(292,313,000)	193,626,000
Other, including long-term advances	(14,272,000)	(25,083,000)	(147,729,000)
Net cash provided by operating activities	372,475,000	162,556,000	391,512,000
Cash flows from investing activities:			
Additions to property, plant, and equipment	(50,045,000)	(125,055,000)	(107,468,000)
Investments and acquisitions, net of cash acquired	0	(138,518,000)	(352,417,000)
Other	(7,734,000)	82,863,000	30,793,000
Net cash utilized by investing activities	(57,779,000)	(180,710,000)	(429,092,000)
Cash flows from financing activities:			
Proceeds from borrowings with original maturities of more than three months	250,000,000	912,979,000	460,333,000
Repayments of borrowings with original maturities of more than three months	(250,127,000)	(291,779,000)	(308,128,000)
Net (repayments) proceeds of other short-term borrowings	(190,216,000)	(341,522,000)	226,103,000
Purchase of common stock	0	(367,548,000)	(237,532,000)
Stock option and warrant transactions	8,391,000	2,523,000	50,358,000
Dividends paid	(20,709,000)	(42,494,000)	(45,526,000)
Net cash (utilized) provided by financing activities	(202,661,000)	(127,841,000)	145,608,000
Effect of exchange rate changes on cash	(6,055,000)	(7,049,000)	(5,617,000)
Increase (decrease) in cash and cash equivalents	105,980,000	(153,044,000)	102,411,000
Cash and cash equivalents at beginning of year	127,115,000	280,159,000	177,748,000
Cash and cash equivalents at end of year	$233,095,000	$127,115,000	$280,159,000
Supplemental information			
Interest paid	$103,437,000	$ 91,180,000	$ 64,861,000
Income taxes paid (received)	($34,813,000)	$ 95,975,000	$108,342,000

BEYOND THE BOOK

37. Find the 10-K, proxy statement, and annual report of a typical company in the manufacturing business. Answer the following questions:

a. From either the 10-K or annual report, discuss how important inventory is in relationship to other assets on the firm's balance sheet. Also address how important property, plant, and equipment is to the firm.

b. How does the company finance its business?

c. Compare the information provided in the 10-K and annual report and discuss at least five things that are in the 10-K that are not in the annual report. If you were a stockholder, would you want to know these things and why?

    d. From the proxy statement, what were the major issues (at least four) that were discussed at the annual meeting?

    e. What is the total compensation paid to the five highest-paid employees? Who was the highest paid? What percent of sales was the total paid? Does this seem reasonable and why?

    f. How many directors does the company have? How old are they and what percent of the board is female? How much do the directors get paid to attend meetings?

38. For the company you selected in problem 31, find at least three articles that discuss the nature of the markets for this company and the forecast of what the future may be for this sector of the economy. Write a one-page summary of your findings.

CHAPTER 4

Income Measurement and Reporting

LEARNING OBJECTIVES

After reading this chapter you should be able to:

1. Understand and apply the accrual basis of accounting and the related recognition and matching concepts.

2. Explain the operating cycle and its relation to accrual accounting.

3. Discuss revenue recognition methods and the reasons why revenue is recognized at different times for different economic events.

4. Identify links between accrual accounting and firm valuation.

5. Construct accrual entries for both revenue and expense transactions.

6. Explain how the income statement format reflects the concept of separating transitory items from operating earnings.

In late May 2001, ConAgra Foods announced that accounting and conduct matters at its United Agri Products Company (UAP) subsidiary would result in the restatement of its financial results. Certain accounting adjustments would also result in a restatement for fiscal 1998. The restatement reduced revenues and earnings for fiscal years 1998, 1999, and 2000, and increased revenues and earnings in fiscal year 2001. ConAgra restated its earnings due to accounting irregularities in its UAP subsidiary that related, in part, to its revenue recognition practices. In the days leading up to the announcement, ConAgra's stock price fell by approximately 6 percent. Clearly, as ConAgra's press release illustrates, investors and analysts pay close attention to the earnings reported by publicly traded companies.

To further your understanding of the earnings reported by companies, we examine the concepts of accrual-basis accounting in this chapter. Specifically, we examine the recognition criteria for revenues and expenses, and related implications for the recognition of assets and liabilities. We compare and contrast this accrual-basis recognition of revenues and expenses with the timing of the actual cash flows that result from these transactions.

You need to understand accrual accounting and how it differs from a cash basis for at least two reasons. First, investors and analysts often use forecasts of earnings to estimate future cash flows, which, in turn, affects their assessments of a firm's value. Second, owners often use earnings and stock prices (which may depend on earnings) to measure management performance. Accrual accounting, however, allows managers sufficient latitude to influence the performance measures upon which they are evaluated and paid. As a result, owners must understand this latitude in setting management compensation arrangements, and investors and analysts must do so in assessing firm value.

Let's begin with a discussion of the general concepts of accrual-based accounting.

ACCRUAL ACCOUNTING

In **accrual-basis accounting,** a firm recognizes revenues and expenses in the period in which they occur, rather than in the period in which the cash flows related to the revenues and expenses are realized. In contrast, **cash-basis accounting** recognizes revenues and expenses in the period in which the firm realizes the cash flow. For example, under the accrual basis, a firm that sells goods to customers on credit recognizes the sales revenue at the point of physical transfer of the goods. Under the cash basis, however, the firm waits to recognize the sale until it collects the cash. As the diagram in Exhibit 4.1 illustrates, this difference in timing of revenue recognition can have a significant impact on the period in which the revenues are reported if the date of delivery of the goods falls in a different accounting period than the collection of cash. Because the cash might be collected in an accounting period later than the period in which the goods were delivered, it is clear that the choice of when to recognize revenue may have a significant impact on the statement of earnings.

Firms use accrual-basis accounting because it provides information about future cash flows that is not available under the cash method. In our sales example, investors want to know the firm's sales, even if the cash has not been collected, in order to better predict the future cash flows upon which the value of the firm depends. Similarly, a company's expected future payments are also relevant information. However, accrual accounting, while more informative than the cash basis, also involves considerable judgment. As a result, accounting standard setters developed criteria to assure that firms use similar assumptions in

Exhibit 4.1
Revenue Recognition Timing

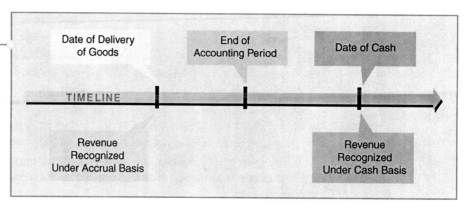

their judgments. In that way, the resulting revenue and expense numbers will be as consistent as possible with the qualitative characteristics of accounting information discussed in Chapter 1, such as neutrality, reliability, and verifiability.

The FASB's criteria are intended to guide all recognition decisions. These criteria detail what items should be recognized in the financial statements and when the items should be recognized. The following criteria apply to all financial statement components, including revenues, expenses, assets, liabilities, and stockholders' equity accounts:

> *Definition:* The item meets the definition of an element of financial statements.
>
> *Measurability:* The item has a relevant attribute measurable with sufficient reliability.
>
> *Relevance:* The information about the item is capable of making a difference in user decisions.
>
> *Reliability:* The information about the item is representationally faithful, verifiable, and neutral.

The above criteria include the concept of an attribute. *Attributes* are characteristics of financial statement items that we might choose to measure. For instance, inventory possesses several attributes. One of them is the cost the company incurs to either make or buy the inventory. A second attribute is the current selling price of the inventory. Whatever attribute we choose to measure, however, the recognition criteria require it to be "relevant." Often, accounting regulators must determine which attribute is the most relevant and reliable to report in the financial statements. We continue to address this issue as we progress through the text.

Recall in Chapter 3 that we defined assets, liabilities, and owners' equity. Later in this chapter we define revenues and expenses. All these definitions are based on the concepts of accrual accounting. Double-entry accounting links the recognition of revenues, expenses, assets, and liabilities. Let's look more closely at how revenue and expense recognition reflects these accrual-accounting concepts.

REVENUE RECOGNITION

Revenue recognition refers to the point in time at which revenue should be reported on the statement of earnings, a crucial element of accrual accounting. Typically, firms implement accrual accounting by first determining the revenues to be recognized and then matching the costs incurred in generating that revenue to determine expenses. It follows that the timing of revenue and expense recognition determines the earnings that are reported. Given that the information conveyed by earnings is a factor in estimating the value of the firm, revenue recognition is particularly important to analysts, investors, managers, and others with an interest in those estimates.

It is reasonable to imagine that these individuals desire earnings to be reported as early as possible in order to gain access to information upon which they can improve their estimates. However, this desire is likely to be tempered by an understanding that revenue recognized in advance of collecting the cash from customers implies some uncertainty that could be avoided if revenue recognition can be delayed until those collections are made. In other words, there is a trade-off between early access to information and the level of uncertainty contained in the revenue and related expenses reported on the statement of earnings. For example, an extreme view would argue that when a firm purchases inventory, it immediately adds value to the company because the goods can be sold later for a profit. Therefore, the firm should recognize the revenue (profit) upon inventory purchases, assuming that future sales will occur. The difficulty with this argument, of course, is the considerable uncertainty about both the timing and the amount of revenue that may be realized from future sales. For example, a company might purchase or manufacture inventory and be unable to sell it because of changing demand or excess supply.

Consider the electronic game industry in 2001. Three competitors, Microsoft, Sony, and Nintendo, sought industry dominance with the XBox, Playstation 2, and the Game-Cube, respectively. Manufacturers of these products needed to determine how many units to manufacture, set prices for the product, make arrangements with distributors (such as Toys Я Us, Wal-Mart, and Target), and ship the product in sufficient numbers to satisfy customers. Furthermore, the companies needed to consider the costs of product warranties and returns of unsold products. Finally, the three firms assumed that third-party software manufacturers would be able to offer a sufficient quality and variety of games on the different platforms to satisfy consumer demand. All of these factors worked to create substantial uncertainty about the profits from a particular product line. Thus, it would be difficult for any of these companies to argue that sales should have been recognized at the time they manufactured the products.

Because of the tension between the desire to recognize the value added by investment and production activities as early as possible, and the uncertainties involved in accurately portraying these results, accounting standard setters developed **revenue recognition criteria.** These criteria establish the requirements that must be met in order to recognize revenue on a company's books.

REVENUE RECOGNITION CRITERIA

At the time of this writing, the FASB is considering an approach for revenue recognition that is more closely linked to changes in assets and liabilities than the notions of realization and completion of the earnings process. Concerns with the present criteria for revenue realization are that they are sometimes in conflict with concepts of assets and liabilities, imprecisely defined, and difficult to consistently apply when the revenue generating process involves multiple steps.

GAAP requires that revenues be recognized at the earliest point in the firm's operating cycle, at which it meets the following criteria:

- Revenue is realized or realizable
- Revenue is earned by the enterprise

Realized or **realizable** means that an exchange of goods or services has taken place, the seller has either received cash or the right to receive cash, and collection is reasonably assured. **Earned** means that the goods or services have been delivered, and related obligations are substantially complete. In applying the earned criteria, a firm must apply judgment in determining whether the risks and rewards of ownership of the product have effectively been transferred to the buyer. That is, has there been substantial performance by both the seller and the buyer such that the earnings process is essentially complete? For instance, Werner Enterprises, a major trucking company, recognizes "operating revenues and related direct costs when the shipment is delivered." Because Werner is

Exhibit 4.2

THE REAL WORLD

Target Corporation

Target Corporation—Revenues

Revenue from retail sales is recognized at the time of sale. Leased department sales, net of related cost of sales, are included within sales and were $33 million in 2000, $31 million in 1999, and $29 million in 1998. Net credit revenues represent revenue from receivable-backed securities, which is comprised of finance charges and late fees on internal credit sales, net of the effect of publicly held receivable-backed securities. Internal credit sales were $5.5 billion, $5 billion, and $4.5 billion in 2000, 1999, and 1998, respectively.

responsible for transporting the goods of the customer, management judges that the earning process is only complete when the goods are ultimately delivered.

The revenue recognition criteria can be met at different points in a firm's operating cycle depending on the nature of the business. In the following sections, we illustrate some common points of revenue recognition used by various industries.

At Point of Delivery

A fairly common point of revenue recognition for manufacturing and retail firms is at the point when they deliver a product or service to a customer. As we noted previously, Werner, Inc. reports its revenue when the shipment is delivered. This is the point at which the customer accepts the risks and rewards of ownership of the asset, and at which point Werner ceases its obligation to the customer (the revenue has been earned). Further, the customer is now obligated to pay Werner for the delivery (the revenue is realizable).

Target's revenue recognition policy as shown in Exhibit 4.2 is more complex than that of Werner. Target derives its revenues not only from product sales but also from interest on credit sales to customers. However, for its product sales, the method of revenue recognition is at the time of delivery (which is also the time of sale). Target's 2000 income statement (shown later in Exhibit 4.11) reports sales of $36,362 million and net credit revenues of $541 million.

As Service Is Provided or Cost Incurred

For a firm that sells subscriptions, cash may be received in advance. The firm recognizes the revenue as it incurs costs in the fulfillment of those subscriptions. For example, Reader's Digest sells magazine subscriptions to individuals and newstands. In a footnote to its 2003 annual report, the company describes its revenue recognition methods as reported in Exhibit 4.3. As the footnote describes, Reader's Digest has three primary sources of revenue. It uses a

Exhibit 4.3

THE REAL WORLD

Readers Digest

Footnote on Revenue Recognition

Sales of our magazine subscriptions, less estimated cancellations, are deferred and recognized as revenues proportionately over the subscription period. Revenues from sales of magazines through the newsstand are recognized at the issue date, net of an allowance for returns. Advertising revenues are recorded as revenues at the time the advertisements are published, net of discounts and advertising agency commissions.

Because circulation numbers drive the rates that magazines charge to advertisers, magazine publishers sometimes overstate their sales. This practice of overestimating monthly sales has led advertisers to be unwilling to pay the full cost for ads that are published or to demand refunds when new figures reveal that the estimated sales figures were missed. A publisher would need to recognize this reduction in revenues through an estimate of refunds. For instance, the following is the revenue recognition policy for Primedia, Inc. and it indicates that revenues are stated less an amount (provisions) for rebates, adjustments, and so forth.

"Advertising revenues for all consumer magazines are recognized as income at the on-sale date, net of provisions for estimated rebates, adjustments and discounts."

different recognition method for each type of revenue. The company recognizes subscriptions over the subscription period, newsstand sales at the issue date, and advertising revenues upon advertisement publication. The collection of cash does not determine the timing of revenue recognition. In the case of subscriptions, the revenue is earned as the goods are furnished to the purchaser. In the case of newsstand sales, the shipments are determined on a standing order (based on past sales), and newsstands pay only for the magazines that they sell. Thus, recognizing revenues at the issue date means that accurate estimation of the number of magazines to issue and of returns is critical to accurate revenue recognition. Finally, advertising revenues are recognized when the magazine is published (which constitutes providing the service to those purchasing advertisements).

Based on Contractual Agreements

Firms sometimes retain a substantial financial interest in the product or service, even after the initial sale. For example, Krispy Kreme, a typical franchiser, provides a significant amount of service related to establishing the business between the time of signing the agreement and the opening of the business. The company typically provides financing to the purchaser, allowing franchise fees to be paid in installments. Krispy Kreme defers revenues from the initial franchise fee until the opening of the new store is complete (i.e., the revenue has been earned).

Retail land sales also pose unique accounting problems. Retail land sales involve the sale of undeveloped land. Sales contracts may offer buyers below-market interest rates and attractive financing terms, with the land serving as collateral for the sale (sometimes called a *collateralized sale*). Because of uncertainties regarding the future costs of developing the land as well as the collectibility of the receivable (particularly when there are low down payments), accounting regulators established criteria to determine the conditions under which revenue from a retail land sale could be recognized at the signing of a sales contract. For example, footnotes to Amrep Corporation's annual report (reported in Exhibit 4.4) illustrate a typical disclosure in the case of retail land sales.

At Time of Production

When both the value and the assurance of sale can be estimated at the time of production, such as in certain agricultural and mining operations, a firm recognizes revenue at that point. Often, the company has a supply contract with

Exhibit 4.4

THE REAL WORLD

Amrep Corporation

Revenue Recognition Footnote

Land sales are recognized when the parties are bound by the terms of the contract, all consideration (including adequate cash) has been exchanged, and title and other attributes of ownership have been conveyed to the buyer by means of a closing. Profit is recorded either in its entirety or on the installment method depending on, among other things, the ability to estimate the collectibility of the unpaid sales price. In the event the buyer defaults on the obligation, the property is taken back and recorded in inventory at the unpaid receivable balance, net of any deferred profit, but not in excess of fair market value less estimated cost to sell.

a buyer that establishes the price of the commodity to be delivered and a time schedule for its delivery. For example, Kinross Gold Corporation (Kinross Annual Report 2000) notes that "Gold and Silver in inventory, in transit and at refineries, are recorded at net realizable value and included in accounts receivable with the exception of Kubaka bullion. The estimated net realizable value of Kubaka bullion is included in inventory until it is sold."

As Cash Is Collected

In most cases, revenue recognition criteria are met prior to collection. Firms can reasonably estimate collections at the time of sale, and the revenue is thus realizable. However, for some circumstances, collection of the receivable is sufficiently in doubt that revenue cannot be recognized at the time of sale. Recognition prior to collection would therefore not reflect the underlying economic reality. In these cases firms can use two methods to recognize revenue and related expenses as cash is collected: the installment method and the cost recovery method.

With the **installment method,** a firm recognizes gross profits in proportion to cash payments received. With the **cost recovery method,** a firm defers gross profit recognition until enough cash is collected to recover the costs. For example, assume that Wilson Land Company sells a home site for $100,000 that cost Wilson $60,000. The purchaser agrees to pay Wilson for the land in three payments of $40,000, $30,000, and $30,000. Exhibit 4.5 shows the amount of gross profit recognized each year under the installment method and the cost recovery method.

Either method results in the same total gross profit over three years. How, then, to determine the appropriate method of revenue recognition in a particular case? Firms generally use the cost recovery method only when considerable uncertainty exists about ultimate collection of the total sales price (so no profit is recognized until the costs have been covered). The decision, then, becomes whether to recognize a real estate sale under the installment method or at the time of sale. As a rule, retail land sales should only be recognized at the time of sale if both collection is assured and the seller has no remaining obligations to the buyer.

During Construction

In the long-term construction industry, major projects can take years to complete. Thus the operating cycle in this industry is very long, requiring special income recognition methods: the completed contract method and the percentage completion method. Under the **completed contract method,** a firm waits to recognize revenues and expenses until the project is complete. Under the **percentage**

Exhibit 4.5
Installment Method versus Cost Recovery Method

Profit % = ($100,000 − 60,000)/$100,000 = 40%

Year	Installment method gross profit	Cost recovery method gross profit
1	40% × $40,000 = $16,000	$0 ($40,000 cost recovered)
2	40% × $30,000 = $12,000	$10,000 ($20,000 cost recovered)
3	40% × $30,000 = $12,000	$30,000
Total	$40,000	$40,000

Exhibit 4.6
Revenue Recognition Using
Percentage of Completion
Method (dollars in billions)

Year	Degree of Completion	Revenue Recognized	Expenses Recognized	Gross Profit Recognized
1	$8/$15 = 53.33%	.533 × $20 = $10.67	$8	$2.67
2	$4/$15 = 26.67%	.267 × $20 = $5.33	$4	$1.33
3	$3/$15 = 20.00%	.20 × $20 = $4.00	$3	$1.00
Total	100.00%	$20.00	$15	$5.00

of completion method, a firm recognizes revenues and expenses in proportion to the degree of completion of the project. Degree of completion is typically measured by the cost incurred to date relative to the total estimated cost. For example, assume that Horning Construction agrees to build a casino. The purchaser agrees to pay $20 billion to Horning for the project. Horning expects to spend three years building the casino and estimates the following costs: Year 1, $8 billion; Year 2, $4 billion; Year 3, $3 billion. Exhibit 4.6 shows the amount of revenue and expenses recognized each year under percentage of completion.

Under the completed contract method, Horning Construction would recognize all of the revenue and expense at the end of year 3, at contract completion. Typically, though, firms use the completed contract method for short construction periods. However, to use the percentage completion method, firms must be able to accurately estimate costs to obtain reliable profit forecasts. As a result, if there is a high degree of cost uncertainty, the completed contract method may be used even for long-term contracts.

Although the percentage of completion and completed contract methods are the more common, firms sometimes use other methods of accounting for long-term construction contracts, such as the installment and cost recovery methods described earlier. Firms will likely use the installment method when the uncertainty pertains largely to assurance of collection (buyer's performance) rather than the reliability of future cost estimates (seller's performance). The cost recovery method is especially conservative and appropriate in cases where considerable uncertainty exists about collection and future costs.

Now that we have reviewed several aspects of revenue recognition, let's turn to the related issue of expense recognition.

EXPENSE RECOGNITION

The **matching concept** requires that firms recognize both the revenue and the costs required to produce the revenue (expenses) at the same time. The implications of this are two-fold. First, it means that firms must defer some costs on the balance sheet until they can be matched with sales. In some cases, though, direct matching with sales is not practical. In these cases, firms often expense the deferred costs based on the passage of time. Second, firms will not incur some costs at the time of the sale (e.g., warranty costs). Firms will thus need to estimate these costs, and accrue an expense to give proper matching with the revenue reported.

Perhaps the best example of direct matching is when a retail or wholesale company recognizes revenue at the time of delivery. Here, a related expense, **cost of goods sold,** which represents the cost of inventory that the company had on its balance sheet as an asset prior to the sale, must also be recognized. Target provides an example of such a company. Its cost of goods sold can be seen in Exhibit 4.11 (later in the chapter).

Matching is applied differently depending on the type of cost. Some costs, such as costs of goods sold, can be matched directly with sales. However, other costs, such as executive salaries, insurance, and depreciation of various assets used in the business, can be more difficult to directly link to revenue. In this case, firms usually either charge the costs to income as incurred (e.g., salaries and various administrative costs) or allocate the costs systematically over time periods (e.g., depreciation, interest, insurance). Werner, Inc. (the trucking company mentioned earlier) provides a service to its customers, so it has no cost of goods sold. However, if you review the income statement for Werner, you would see sales-related expenses such as salaries, fuel costs, and depreciation on its trucks, which are related to the delivery service it provides to its customers.

With expense recognition, GAAP guidelines focus on whether or not a cost should be treated as an asset (a **deferred expense**) or as an expense. For example, Prepaid Legal Services pays its sales force an advance of up to three years' worth of commissions on new customer sales. In the years prior to 2001, Prepaid treated these prepayments as deferred expenses (assets) and then expensed these deferred expenses over time to match them with revenues from the provided legal services. However, in 2001 the SEC concluded that Prepaid's accounting methods were not in accordance with GAAP arguing that the future revenue from these sales was highly uncertain. Effective in its third quarter 10-Q filing with the SEC as shown in Exhibit 4.7, Prepaid changed its accounting

---

Exhibit 4.7

THE REAL WORLD

Prepaid Legal Services

In the November 14, 2001, 10-Q filing of Prepaid Legal Services, the following disclosure was made:

As previously reported, in January 2001 and May 2001, the staff of the Division of Corporation Finance of the Securities and Exchange Commission (SEC) reviewed the Company's 1999 and 2000 Forms 10-K, respectively. On May 11, 2001, the Company received a letter from the staff of the Division of Corporation Finance advising that, after reviewing the Company's Forms 10-K, it was the position of the Division that the Company's accounting for commission advance receivables was not in accordance with GAAP. The Company subsequently appealed this decision to the Chief Accountant of the SEC. On July 25, 2001, the Company announced that the Chief Accountant concurred with the prior staff opinion of the Division of Corporation Finance. The Company subsequently announced that it would not pursue any further appeals and that it would amend its previously filed SEC reports to restate the Company's financial statements to reflect the SEC's position that the Company's advance commission payments should be expensed when paid. As previously discussed, the change in accounting treatment reduced total assets from $247 million at December 31, 2000 to $93 million, reduced total liabilities from $100 million to $48 million (due to the elimination of deferred taxes related to the receivables) and therefore reduced stockholders' equity from $147 million to $45 million. The elimination of the receivables reduced 2000 net income from $43.6 million, or $1.92 per diluted share, to $20.5 million, or $.90 per diluted share. The Company expects to amend its 2000 Annual Report on Form 10-K in the near future to reflect the change in accounting for commission of advance receivables and restate all periods included in the 2000 Form 10-K. The financial statements and the explanation thereof contained in this Form 10-Q reflect the change in the accounting treatment for advance payments made to associates.

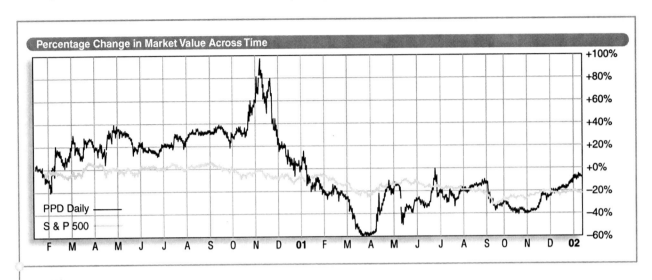

Exhibit 4.8
Prepaid Legal Services Inc.

methods to conform with the SEC ruling. The company now expenses the commissions in the period in which they were paid.

The concern over Prepaid's accounting methods stemmed back to December 2000, when a research report questioned the firm's economic viability. The graph in Exhibit 4.8 demonstrates the changes in value that took place between the issuance of this report and the change of policy in late 2001.

Now that we've discussed accrual-accounting concepts, let's next look at how firms put into practice these revenue and expense recognition criteria.

RECORDING ACCRUAL ENTRIES

In this section, we use four common types of economic events to illustrate how accrual accounting is applied and how the cash flow timing differs for each event. Exhibit 4.9 summarizes these revenue and expense events, and provides a simple example of each. Let's look more closely at each of these transactions.

REVENUES THAT ARE RECEIVED IN CASH BEFORE THEY ARE EARNED

In this situation the firm must record the cash received as an asset. However, as the firm cannot yet treat the transaction as earned revenue, it must postpone the recognition of revenue. The firm will, therefore, record a liability, **deferred revenue** (or *unearned revenue* or *customer deposits*), that represents an obligation to provide goods or services to the customer in the future. This obligation clearly meets the definition of a liability in that it most definitely represents a future sacrifice of resources to the firm. Recall our earlier illustration of Reader's Digest and its revenue recognition of subscriptions.

To illustrate the entries to be made for this type of transaction, let's return to our BHT example from Chapter 3. Suppose that BHT receives $20 million

Exhibit 4.9
Common Accrual Accounting
Events

Revenue Events	Example
Cash that is received in advance before the revenues are recognized as having been earned	Magazine subscriptions are usually paid in advance and earned when the publisher delivers the magazines.
Revenues that are recognized as having been earned before the revenues are received in cash	Sales on account, interest revenue on notes is earned with the passage of time and paid at regular intervals.

Expense Events	Example
Expenses that are paid in advance before they are recognized as having been incurred	Insurance is generally paid in advance to cover a future period. The expense is incurred with the passage of time as dictated by the policy.
Expenses that are recognized as having been incurred before they are paid in cash	Salary expense is incurred when the employees work, even though they may be paid later, such as once every two weeks.

in cash from customers for goods to be delivered in the future. BHT would make the following journal entry at the time cash is received:

```
Cash                    20
    Deferred Revenue         20
```

Later, when BHT earns the revenues (likely at delivery), the firm would make the following entry:

```
Deferred Revenue        20
    Revenue                  20
```

REVENUES THAT ARE EARNED BEFORE THEY ARE RECEIVED IN CASH

For most firms, revenue recognition criteria are most often met before the firms collect the cash. Here, the firm records revenues on its income statement and also an asset (accounts receivable). Accounts receivable meets the definition of an asset as the firm has probable future value in the right to receive cash from the customer at some point in the future. Recall in Chapter 3 that we showed you this type of transaction for BHT, as follows:

```
Accounts Receivable     35,724
    Sales                        35,724
```

As another example, consider interest accrued on a note receivable. A firm earns revenue (interest) on the note with the passage of time, periodically receiving cash. If the cash hasn't yet been received, the firm would record interest revenue and an asset (typically called interest receivable). To illustrate, suppose that BHT allows a customer to pay its bill over a longer period than normal by issuing a note receivable for the amount of the sale (say $100). Further, suppose that this note specifies that the customer pays 5 percent interest. At the end of the first year, the customer would owe an additional $5 for the interest ($100 × 5%). BHT records this earned revenue (assuming it hadn't been paid yet) as follows:

Interest Receivable	5	
Interest Revenue		5

When BHT collects the interest, it makes the following entry:

Cash	5	
Interest Receivable		5

EXPENSES THAT ARE PAID IN CASH BEFORE THEY ARE INCURRED

Cash payment often precedes the incurrence of an expense, such as with prepaid insurance. Insurance companies usually require payment of insurance policy premiums in advance of the coverage. If the firm has just paid its premium, then it should record the reduction in cash and the creation of an asset, typically called prepaid insurance. Prepaid insurance meets the definition of an asset: the insurance provides probable future value in terms of coverage (protection from risk) over the remaining period of the policy. The firm will then convert the prepaid insurance into an expense with the passage of time. For example, if BHT pays $150 for an insurance policy covering its plant, property, and equipment for the following year, it records the following entry at the date of payment:

Prepaid Insurance	150	
Cash		150

As time passes, the insurance is consumed as coverage expires. If six months have passed and half of the coverage, or $75 worth of the amount prepaid, has been consumed, BHT would make the following entry:

Insurance Expense	75	
Prepaid Insurance		75

EXPENSES THAT ARE INCURRED BEFORE THEY ARE PAID IN CASH

Salary expense is often incurred prior to it being paid, as most firms issue checks to employees after services have been received. If employees have worked for the firm, but haven't been paid, the firm should record an expense and a liability (salaries payable) indicating its obligation to pay the employees at a later date. To illustrate, if BHT employees earned $25 during the last week of December but will not be paid until the end of the first week in January, BHT would make the following entry on December 31:

Salaries Expense	25	
Salaries Payable		25

When BHT pays the employees, it would make the following entry:

Salaries payable	25	
Cash		25

Note that the initial entry in each of the previous four examples results in the creation of an asset or liability. These accrual-based assets and liabilities would not exist under the cash basis. In fact, most assets and liabilities that exist on a GAAP-prepared balance sheet, except cash, arise as a consequence of accrual-based accounting. These include receivables (revenue recognized before cash is received), inventories, prepaid expenses, property and equipment, intangible assets (cash paid before expense is recognized), payables and accrued liabilities (expense recognized before cash is paid), and deferred revenues (cash received before revenue is recognized).

Almost all of the transactions we have just discussed involve the use of an adjusting entry. Recall from our discussion in Chapter 3 that adjusting entries are made at the end of the period for transactions that do not involve an exchange with an external party. For example, when BHT recorded its deferred revenue, this entry was triggered by the receipt of cash. However, the later recognition of deferred revenue on the income statement was not accompanied by an exchange event and therefore was recorded via an adjusting entry. Similarly, the recording of prepaid insurance was triggered by the cash payment of the premium, while the recognition of insurance expense was recorded via an adjusting entry by the accountant after it was determined how much of the insurance coverage had expired. For a more detailed discussion of various adjusting entries refer to Appendix A.

> The flexibility within GAAP as it relates to accrual entries might allow management to understate discretionary or estimated expenses or overstate estimated revenues in order to meet analysts' forecasts or internal performance targets. Considerable attention has been given to the implications of management's discretion within GAAP on earnings forecasts, estimates of firm value, and management compensation.

VALUATION IMPLICATIONS OF INCOME RECOGNITION

Reported net income plays an important role in determining a company's value. Simply put, net income from an accrual-accounting is informative about future cash flows to the business that, in turn, implies future potential cash flows to investors. The stream of future cash flows to investors determines the value of a company (as we describe more fully in Chapter 14). A company must generate positive cash flows for investors either in the form of dividends or an increased stock price in order to remain a viable business.

Both revenue and expense recognition involve assumptions and estimation. Accounting standards seek to provide relevant and timely information about a company to assist in forecasting its future while at the same time assuring the reliability of the information in the face of estimation and uncertainty. The criteria for revenue and expense recognition seek to balance these desired attributes in providing guidelines for the determination of earnings. Nevertheless, the link between current income and future cash flows remains uncertain. To improve our understanding of the imprecise relation between current earnings and future cash flows, let's look at the income statement more closely.

INCOME STATEMENT FORMAT

Financial statements should provide information that helps current and potential investors, creditors, and other users to assess the amount, timing, and uncertainty of prospective net cash flows to the firm. The income statement reports on a company's financial performance and provides information about future expected cash flows.

GAAP does not specify the format of the income statement in detail. As a result, the degree to which specific line items are combined into the aggregate line items that appear on the statement (sometimes referred as the degree of aggregation), as well as the labels used for the aggregate items, vary widely across firms. Because this can make statement interpretation challenging for the novice financial statement user, let's take a closer look at the line items.

LINE ITEM DEFINITIONS

When looking at the income statement, you should first determine which items relate to the core operations of the business, or are *persistent,* and which are *transitory,* or unrelated to the company's core operations. Investors value persistent profits more highly than transitory ones as they are more likely to continue in the future. For example, a business might report a loss from a lawsuit that involves a substantial cash outlay. However, this one-time cost has different implications for the value of the firm than a loss caused by operations (e.g., when product's costs exceed its sales). Thus, proper classification of items as continuing/recurring or noncontinuing/nonrecurring provides investors and financial statement users with more accurate forecasts of future cash flow.

To this end, the FASB provides direction in its definition (FASB Concepts No. 6, "Elements of Financial Statements") of revenues and expenses (FASB, SFAC No. 6, 1985):

- *Revenues:* "inflows or other enhancements of assets of an entity or settlements of its liabilities (or a combination of both) from delivering or producing goods, rendering services, or other activities that constitute the entity's ongoing major or central operations."

- *Expenses:* "outflows or other using up of assets or incurrences of liabilities (or a combination of both) from delivering or producing goods, rendering services, or carrying out other activities that constitute the entity's ongoing major or central operations."

- *Gains:* "increases in equity (net assets) from peripheral or incidental transactions of an entity and other events and circumstances affecting the entity except those that result from revenues or investments by owners."

- *Losses:* "decreases in equity (net assets) from peripheral or incidental transactions of an entity and from all other transactions and other events and circumstances affecting the entity except those that result from expenses or distributions to owners."

INCOME STATEMENT LABELS

The degree of aggregation and labeling of income statement items varies widely across companies. For example, some companies will explicitly list items such as gross profit, income from continuing operations, and other subcategories, while others simply list all revenues and subtract all costs. Income statements that provide greater detail and breakdown of costs by category are referred to as **multiple step.** Those that simply list revenue and expenses in two broad categories are called **single step.** Because valuing companies requires the ability to estimate future cash flows to owners, financial disclosures that help users to discern which revenues and costs are related to core continuing activities are most useful to financial statement users.

In general, multiple-step income statements include the following categories:

- Gross Profit
- Income from Continuing Operations
- Nonrecurring Items
- Extraordinary Items
- Accounting Changes and Errors

Let's look at each of the categories in more detail.

Income from Continuing Operations

Income from continuing operations is the difference between a company's operating revenues and its operating expenses. It does not include revenues from nonoperating sources nor from operations that a company discontinues. For example, Exhibit 4.10 shows the income statement for Albertson's, Inc., a large national grocery store chain. Note the line "Operating Profit," which reflects income from continuing operations. However, while Albertson's expects most of the operating items to continue from period to period, the company also lists several items that might not be considered recurring: "Merger-Related and Exit Costs," "Litigation Settlement," and "Impairment Store Closures." Albertson's separately discloses these one-time or limited-term items to allow analysts to adjust these charges out of the operating profits before trying to use the historical data to forecast future operating profits.

Exhibit 4.11 shows an income statement for Target for 2000 including comparative results for 1999 and 1998. Note that a complete income statement also includes earnings per share information (described later in the chapter). Target

Exhibit 4.10
Albertson Corporation
Consolidated Statement of
Earnings (millions except per
share data)

THE REAL WORLD

Albertson Corporation

In millions except per share data	52 weeks 02/01/2001	52 weeks 02/01/2000	52 weeks 01/28/1999
Sales	$36,762	$37,478	$35,872
Cost of sales	26,336	27,164	26,156
Gross profit	10,426	10,314	9,716
Selling, general, and administrative expenses	8,740	8,641	7,846
Merger-related and exit costs	24	396	195
Litigation settlement		37	
Impairment-store closures			24
Operating profit	1,662	1,240	1,651
Other (expense) income:			
Interest, net	(385)	(353)	(337)
Other, net	(3)	12	24
Earnings before taxes and extraordinary items	1,274	899	1,338
Income taxes	509	472	537
Earnings before extraordinary items	765	427	801
Extraordinary loss on extinguishment of debt, net of tax benefit of $7		(23)	
Net earnings	$ 765	$ 404	$ 801

Exhibit 4.11
Target Corporation
Consolidated Results of
Operations (millions except
per share data)

THE REAL WORLD

Target Corporation

	2000	1999	1998
Sales	$36,362	$33,212	$30,203
Net credit revenues	541	490	459
Total revenues	36,903	33,702	30,662
Cost of sales	25,295	23,029	21,085
Selling, general, and administrative expenses	8,190	7,490	6,843
Depreciation and amortization	940	854	780
Interest expense	425	393	398
Earnings before income taxes and extraordinary charges	2,053	1,936	1,556
Provision for income taxes	789	751	594
Net earnings before extraordinary charges	1,264	1,185	962
Extraordinary charges from purchase and redemption of debt, net of tax	—	41	27
Net earnings	$ 1,264	$ 1,144	$ 935
Earnings before extraordinary charges	$ 1.40	$ 1.32	$ 1.07
Extraordinary charges	—	(.04)	(.03)
Basic earnings per share	$ 1.40	$ 1.28	$ 1.04
Earnings before extraordinary charges	$ 1.38	$ 1.27	$ 1.02
Extraordinary charges	0	(.04)	(.03)
Diluted earnings per share	$ 1.38	1.23	.99

reports cost of sales; selling, general, and administrative expenses; depreciation; and amortization and interest expense. These reflect typical categories for a retail or wholesale company that sells products. However, Target's income statement does not explicitly show operating earnings. Thus Target's income statement readers must determine from the account titles, placement on the financial statement, and the disclosures provided in Target's footnotes which items represent Target's operating income.

Note that Target shows "Net Credit Revenues" in its total revenue section. This is interest income that represents income from Target's financing operations. Financing is one of Target's core operations, so analysts would probably classify this as a part of operating revenues. If, however, firms report interest income primarily from investment activities, the revenue would be classified as nonoperating or other revenue.

Nonrecurring Items

In addition to separating operating from nonoperating items, investors also want to identify recurring versus nonrecurring items. Unusual or infrequent revenues and/or expenses should be highlighted to signal financial statement users that the items do not have the same kind of information about future cash flows as do normal recurring ones. Some firms simply label unusual items as such. In other cases, accounting standard setters provide specific guidelines for how to report such items.

GAAP requires three items to be shown after the computation of tax expense: **discontinued operations, extraordinary items,** and the **cumulative effect of changes in accounting principles.** Because these items appear below both operating and nonoperating items and after the computation of tax expense, they are often referred to as "below the line" items. Because they are shown after the tax computation, firms show these items on a net of tax basis. For example, Target reported an extraordinary charge of $41 million in 1999. This $41 million represents the net amount after subtracting the tax effect.

Discontinued Operations

Results from discontinued operations represent amounts related to a line of business, such as a product, that a company decides to discontinue. The income statement items related to discontinued operations include (1) any gain or loss from operations of the discontinued business after the decision is made to discontinue and prior to actual termination of operations, and (2) any gain or loss on disposal of the business. In December, 2002, H.J. Heinz decided to spin off its pet snacks, U.S. tuna, U.S. retail private label soup and private label gravy, College Inn broths, and its U.S. infant feeding businesses. The income statement for Heinz in Exhibit 4.12 reflects the discontinued operations.

> Note that analysts often consider certain items as nonrecurring beyond those specified for GAAP purposes when they are valuing the firm. For instance, if a firm recorded a restructuring charge during the period, it wouldn't earmark this item as extraordinary but it is nonrecurring. If an item is less than likely to recur, then an analyst would put less weight on this item when determining value.

Extraordinary Items

Extraordinary items are both unusual in nature and infrequent in occurrence. These gains and losses are not expected to recur, and hence are segregated from operations. Because management may have an incentive to classify all bad news as extraordinary, the FASB developed guidelines that specify when a firm may classify an item as extraordinary. For example, the "unusual" nature criteria guidelines specify that the item must be unusual within the existing context of

Exhibit 4.12
H.J. HEINZ Co. Income
Statement

THE REAL WORLD

H.J. Heinz

52 Weeks Ended (in 000s):	Apr-30-03	May-1-02	May-2-01
Sales	$8,236,836	$7,614,036	$6,987,698
Cost of products sold	5,304,362	4,858,087	4,407,267
Gross profit	2,932,474	2,755,949	2,580,431
Selling, general, and administrative expenses	1,758,658	1,456,077	1,591,472
Operating income	1,173,816	1,299,872	988,959
Interest income	31,083	26,197	22,597
Interest expense	223,532	230,611	262,488
Other expense/(income), net	112,636	44,938	(5,358)
Income from continuing operations before income taxes and cumulative effect of change in accounting principle	868,731	1,050,520	754,426
Provision for income taxes	313,372	375,339	190,495
Income from continuing operations before cumulative effect of change in accounting principle	555,359	675,181	563,931
Income/(loss) from discontinued operations, net of tax	88,738	158,708	(70,638)
Income before cumulative effect of change in accounting principle	644,097	833,889	493,293
Cumulative effect of change in accounting principle	(77,812)	–	(15,281)
Net income	$ 566,285	$ 833,889	$ 478,012

The issues surrounding extraordinary items highlight the difficulties involved in determining operating earnings or income from continuing operations. Management has an incentive to classify losses as extraordinary and to suggest that the losses will not persist into the future, and to move nonoperating and one-time gain items to revenues to make them appear as if they will recur. Accounting and auditing standards are intended to minimize these opportunities.

the business. Tornado damage in Oklahoma City, Oklahoma, would likely not be considered extraordinary because these storms frequently occur in Oklahoma. The possibility of tornado damage would therefore be considered a normal business risk of locating in Oklahoma. However, tornado damage in New Hampshire might meet these criteria.

GAAP also occasionally specifies extraordinary-item treatment for transactions that would not normally meet the criteria. For example, from 1975 through 2001, when companies retired debt early and incurred a book gain or loss, they reported these items as extraordinary. These gains and losses had no future cash flow implications. However, early retirements of debt have become so common that the FASB recently concluded that gains and losses on debt retirements should no longer be classified as extraordinary.

The FASB concluded that events related to the terrorist attack on the World Trade Center on September 11, 2001 were not extraordinary. The event would clearly be classified as unusual and infrequent, but the FASB was not convinced that the costs associated with this event were easily measurable. Further, the FASB was concerned that managers of poorly performing firms (particularly in the airline industry) would be tempted to classify all of their operating losses as extraordinary. Firms can still give significant footnote disclosure to explain any event that they believe significantly impacted their operations during the fiscal year. The obvious difficultly for analysts is to sort out which of the firm's results are expected to continue and which were related to this one-time event.

Accounting Changes and Errors

Accounting changes and errors comprise a third category of item that can result in separate disclosure. Accounting changes can occur from a change in accounting principle or from a change in estimate. Changes in accounting estimates do not require any restatements and may not even be disclosed. However, voluntary changes in accounting principle require firms to provide an adjustment for the effects of the change in prior years. In the year of the change, there will be a catch-up adjustment, known as the *cumulative effect* of the accounting principle change. Firms report this catch-up adjustment in a matter similar to that used for disposal of a segment of a business and extraordinary items. Accounting errors in prior period do require the restatement of prior periods through an adjustment to the beginning balance of the retained earnings account. These are called **prior period adjustments.**

PRO-FORMA EARNINGS

Recently, the SEC increased its focus on companies' misuse of accounting to mislead investors. One area of concern has been the presentation of pro forma earnings that represent a company in a more favorable light than actual earnings. **Pro forma earnings,** also called "as if" earnings, are earnings restated to reflect certain assumptions different from those in the actual earnings statement. For example, Waste Management, Inc. reported net income of $30 million for the third quarter of 2001. However, in its press release announcing its third quarter earnings, Waste Management reported pro forma earnings of $225 million. Items that the company eliminated from the pro forma earnings included consulting fees and truck painting.

In the November 2001 press release, Waste Management, Inc. announced financial results for its third quarter ended September 30, 2001. Revenues for the quarter were $2.90 billion as compared to $3.12 billion in the one-year-ago period. Included in the third quarter revenues was $203 million from operations which have since been sold. Net income reported for the quarter was $30 million, or $.05 per diluted share, for the third quarter 2000. On a pro forma basis, after adjusting for unusual costs and certain other items, including a charge related to the agreement to settle the class action lawsuit, third quarter 2001 net income was $225 million, or $.36 per diluted share as compared with $208 million or $33 per diluted share, in the one-year-ago period. Note that this disclosure offers significant information about which items are nonrecurring (e.g., sold operations and the lawsuit settlement). Also note that the company failed to include these items in its pro-forma disclosure.

EARNINGS PER SHARE

GAAP requires firms to disclose **earnings per share** in the income statement. (See the disclosure of Target in Exhibit 4.11.) There are two components of earnings per share, basic earnings per share and fully-diluted earnings per share. **Basic**

earnings per share is simply net income divided by the weighted average number of shares of common stock outstanding for a company. Hence, it measures the per share earnings accruing to shareholders. A company reports **fully-diluted earnings per share** when it has stock options and other instruments that are convertible into shares of common stock that could potentially reduce the common shareholder's proportionate share of earnings if the instruments were converted. For example, when a company provides an executive stock option plan, more shares outstanding will occur if and when the executives exercise their options. This will reduce the proportionate equity in earnings of current shareholders. The fully-diluted earnings per share figure provides an estimate of this type of dilution. It calculates how low earnings per share might become if everything is converted. We'll provide a more detailed discussion of earnings per share and its computation in Chapter 12.

> Analysts often focus on per share earnings when forecasting earnings and, as we discussed, the ability to meet earnings forecasts can significantly affect a company's share price.

COMPREHENSIVE INCOME

FASB Concepts Statement 6 (FASB, SFAC No. 6, 1985) defines **comprehensive income** as the change in equity of a firm due to transactions and other events and circumstances from nonowner sources. It includes all changes in equity except those resulting from investments by owners and distributions to owners. At first glance, this appears to be a definition of earnings. The difference is that accounting standards allow for some items that affect owners' equity to bypass the income statement and be recorded directly in stockholders' equity.

Primarily, these transactions relate to holding gains and losses on certain investments in equity securities and the balance sheet effects of foreign currency translations. Foreign currency translation gains and losses occur when a company has a subsidiary in another country whose accounting records are maintained in a currency other than the U.S. dollar. When the results of this subsidiary are combined to produce the consolidated financial statements of the company, they must be translated from the currency in which they are kept to U.S. dollars by applying various exchange rates. This translation produces gains and losses in dollar terms that must be accounted for and reported. In many circumstances, these gains and losses bypass the income statement and end up in comprehensive income. Accounting standards require that comprehensive income be reported separately from earnings, usually disclosed in the Statement of Shareholders' Equity.

SUMMARY AND TRANSITION

Understanding the basis for recognition of revenues and expenses, as well as how those are presented, is critical to analyzing and using financial statements for decision making. The income statement provides useful information about future cash flows, but that information must also be both timely and reliable. In some cases, the trade-offs for more timely information may reduce the certainty of the information presented. As we saw in this chapter, a firm might wait and recognize revenues on long-term construction contracts until it receives cash. However, months or even years may lapse between the time construction begins and the contract price is fully collected. This lag reduces the usefulness of the information. Financial accounting standards are not intended to eliminate uncertainty, but they are intended to balance the conflict between the goals of providing relevant and timely information with information that is reliable and accurate.

At a conceptual level, accrual accounting seeks to recognize revenues as earned, rather than as the cash is received, and expenses as incurred, rather than as the cash is paid. To implement this concept, those who set the standards have devised criteria for revenue and related expense recognition that identify where in the operating cycle recognition is appropriate.

The usefulness of earnings in valuing the firm is enhanced by separating continuing/recurring operating items from more transitory noncontinuing/nonrecurring ones, such as profits or losses from discontinued operations, restructuring charges, and extraordinary items. The effects of accounting changes should also be identified to improve estimates of future earnings numbers.

END OF CHAPTER MATERIAL

KEY TERMS

Accrual-Basis Accounting	Deferred Revenue
Cash-Basis Accounting	Multiple-Step Income Statement
Revenue Recognition	Single-Step Income Statement
Revenue Recognition Criteria	Income from Continuing Operations
Realized/Realizable	Discontinued Operations
Earned	Extraordinary Items
Installment Method	Cumulative Effect of Changes in Accounting Principles
Cost Recovery Method	Prior Period Adjustment
Completed Contract Method	Pro Forma Earnings
Percentage Completion Method	Earnings per Share
Matching Concept	Basic Earnings per Share
Cost of Goods Sold	Fully-Diluted Earnings per Share
Deferred Expense	Comprehensive Income

ASSIGNMENT MATERIAL

REVIEW QUESTIONS

1. What advantages and disadvantages do you see in using the cash basis of accounting rather than the accrual basis?
2. Respond to each of the following statements with a true or false answer:
   a. Dividends declared decrease cash immediately.
   b. The cash basis recognizes expenses when they are incurred.
   c. There is no such thing as a prepaid rent account on the cash basis.

d. Dividends are an expense of doing business and should appear on the income statement.

e. On the accrual basis, interest should only be recognized when it is paid.

3. Explain how a prepaid expense (such as rent) gets handled under accrual basis accounting.

4. Explain how an accrued expense (such as interest) gets handled under accrual basis accounting.

5. Suppose that a firm's accounting policy was to recognize warranty expense only when warranty service was provided. Discuss whether this meets the matching concept under accrual basis accounting and other ways that this transaction might be handled.

6. Diagram a typical operating cycle of a manufacturing firm and briefly explain what assets and liabilities are likely to be created as a result of this operating cycle.

7. List the two major revenue recognition criteria that exist under GAAP.

8. Describe the concept of revenue being "earned" and contrast it with the concept of revenue being "realized."

9. Explain the difference between the percentage completion method and the completed contracts method.

10. Explain the difference between the installment method and the cost recovery method.

11. Explain the meaning of the matching concept.

APPLYING YOUR KNOWLEDGE

12. Brickstone Construction Company signs a contract to build a building in four years for $40,000,000. The expected costs for each year are:

Year 1:	$ 9,750,000
Year 2:	12,025,000
Year 3:	6,500,000
Year 4:	4,225,000
Total	$32,500,000

The building is completed in year 4. Compute for each year, the total revenue, expenses, and profit under:

a. The Percentage of Completion Method

b. The Completed Contract Method

13. Sandra Carlson sold her house, which cost her $210,000, to Bob Fletcher for $300,000. Bob agreed to pay $60,000 per year for a period of five years. Compute the revenue, expense, and profit for each of the five years (ignoring interest):

a. The Installment Method

b. The Cost-Recovery Method

14. Imperial Corporation purchases a factory from Superior Manufacturing Company for $1,500,000. The cost of the factory on Superior's book is $975,000. The terms of agreement are that yearly installment payments of $705,000, $505,000, $455,000, and $255,000 will be made over the next four years. Each of these payments includes an interest payment of $105,000 per year. Compute the revenue, expense, and profit for each of the four years accruing to Superior Manufacturing Company as per:

    a. The Installment Method

    b. The Cost Recovery Method

15. Cruise Shipping, Inc. agreed to rebuild the *Santa Marice;* an old cargo ship owned by the Oceanic Shipping Company. Both parties signed the contract on November 28, Year 1, for $120 million which is to be paid as follows:

    $12 million at the signing of the contract
    $24 million on December 30, Year 2
    $36 million on June 1, Year 3
    $48 million at completion, on August 15 Year 4.

    The following cost were incurred by Cruise Shipping, Inc. (in millions):

Year 1:	$19.2
Year 2:	38.4
Year 3:	24.0
Year 4:	14.4
Total	$96.0

    a. Compute the revenue, expense, and profit for each of the four years (ignoring interest) for Cruise Shipping, Inc. as per:

    1. The Installment Method

    2. The Cost-Recovery Method

    3. The Percentage of Completion Method

    4. The Completed Contract Method

    b. Which method do you think should be employed by Cruise Shipping, Inc. to show the company's performance under the contract? Why?

16. Computronics Corporation received a contract on March 3, Year 1 for setting up a central communication and pricing center for a small university. The contract price was $1,000,000 which is to be paid as follows:

    $150,000   at the signing of the contract
    $ 60,000   on July 1, Year 1
    $ 30,000   on December 31, Year 1
    $ 80,000   on March 25, Year 2
    $100,000   on August 25, Year 2
    $180,000   on December 31, Year 2
    $400,000   on June 30, Year 3

The system was completed on June 30, Year 3.
Estimated and actual costs were:

$150,000   for the six months ending June 30, Year 1
$225,000   for the six months ending December 31, Year 1
$262,500   for the six months ending June 30, Year 2
$75,000   for the six months ending December 31, Year 2
$37,500   for the six months ending June 30, Year 3

Total $750,000

a. Compute the revenue, expense, and profit for each of the six months as per:

1. The Percentage of Completion Method

2. The Completed Contract Method

3. The Installment Method

4. The Cost-Recovery Method

b. Which method should be used by Computronics Corporation? Why?

17. Forte Builders, a construction company, recognizes revenue from its long-term contracts using the percentage completion method. On March 29, 20X3, the company signed a contract to construct a building for $500,000. The company estimated that it would take four years to complete the contract and would cost the company an estimated $325,000. The expected costs in each of the four years are as follows:

Year	Cost
20X3	$113,750
20X4	97,500
20X5	81,250
20X6	32,500
Total	$325,000

On December 31, 20X4, the date Forte closes its books, the company revised its estimates for the cost in 20X5 and 20X6. It estimated that the contract would cost $200,000 in 20X5 and $100,000 in 20X6 to complete the contract. Compute the revenue, expense, and profit/loss for each of the four years.

18. Samson Industries purchased furniture and appliances from the Metal and Wood Company for $75,000 under the following payment plan which called for semiannual payments over two years:

Payment	Amount
1	$33,600
2	16,800
3	22,400
4	11,200
Total	$84,000

Each payment contains interest (assume that the proportionate share of interest in each payment is the same as the proportion of that payment to the total payments). Assuming that the cost of the furniture and appliances is $60,000, compute the revenue, expense, and profit that Metal and Wood Company would report for each of the installment payments under:

a. The Installment Method

b. The Cost-Recovery Method

19. On June 21, 20X1, Tristar Electric Company signed a contract with Denton Power, Incorporated to construct a small hydroelectric generating plant. The contract price was $10,000,000, and it was estimated that the project would cost Tristar $7,850,000 to complete over a three-year period. On June 21, 20X1, Denton paid Tristar $1,000,000 as a default-deposit. In the event that Denton backed out of the contract, Tristar could keep this deposit. Otherwise the default-deposit would apply as the final payment on the contract (assume for accounting purposes that this is treated as a deposit until completion of the contract). The other contractual payments are as follows:

Date	Amount
10/15/X1	$3,150,000
4/15/X2	1,350,000
12/15/X2	1,800,000
3/15/X3	1,755,000
8/10/X3	945,000
Total	$9,000,000

Estimated costs of construction were as follows:

Year	Amount
1	$3,532,500
2	2,747,500
3	1,570,000

The contract was completed on January 10, 20X4. Tristar closes its books on December 31 each year. Compute the revenue, expense, and profit to be recognized in each year using:

a. The Installment Method

b. The Cost-Recovery Method

c. The Percentage Completion Method

d. The Completed Contracts Method

20. Financial analysts frequently refer to the quality of a firm's earnings. Discuss how the quality of two firms' earnings might differ depending on the revenue recognition method that the two firms use.

21. Suppose that a firm is currently private but is thinking of going public (i.e., issuing shares in a publicly traded market). Discuss the incentives that the

firm might have to misstate its income statement via its revenue recognition policies.

22. Suppose that you are the sales manager of a firm with an incentive plan that provides a bonus based on meeting a certain sales target. Explain how meeting your sales target is influenced by the revenue recognition principles of the firm.

23. Suppose that you are a sales manager of a U.S.-based firm that sells products in Israel, which has traditionally had a high inflation rate. This means that the exchange rate of shekels per dollar typically increases dramatically from year to year. If your compensation is a function of sales as measured in dollars, what risks do you face in meeting your targets and how might you mitigate the risks that you face in meeting those targets?

24. Explain the incentives that a firm has in choosing its revenue recognition method for both financial reporting and tax purposes.

25. In the toy industry it is common to allow customers to return unsold toys within a certain specified period of time. Suppose that a toy manufacturer's year end is December 31 and that the majority of its products are shipped to customers during the last quarter of the year in anticipation of the Christmas holiday. Is it appropriate for the company to recognize revenue upon shipment of the product? Support your answer citing references to revenue recognition criteria.

26. Suppose that an importer in Seattle buys goods from a supplier in Hong Kong. The goods are shipped by cargo vessel. For goods that are in transit at year end, what recognition should the Seattle importer make of these goods in its financial statements? Support your answer based on revenue recognition criteria.

27. Suppose that a company recognizes revenues at the time that title passes to its inventory and that it ships its inventory FOB (free on board) shipping point (i.e., title passes at the shipping point). Suppose at year end that it has loaded a shipment of goods on a truck that is parked on the grounds of the company based on a firm purchase order from a customer. How should the firm treat this inventory in its financial statements at year end?

28. Firms often sell their accounts receivable to raise cash to support their operations. Suppose that a firm sells its accounts receivable with recourse. Recourse means that the buyer can return the account receivable to the selling company if it cannot collect on the receivable. How should this transaction be treated in the financial statements of the selling company?

29. Suppose that ESPN (the sports channel) sells $10,000,000 in advertising slots to be aired during the games that it broadcasts during the NCAA basketball tournament. Suppose further that these slots are contracted for during the month of September with a downpayment of $2,000,000. The ads will be aired in March. If the fiscal year end of ESPN is December 31, how should ESPN recognize this revenue in its financial statements?

30. Suppose that The GAP (a clothing retailer) sells gift certificates for merchandise. During the Christmas holiday period, suppose that it issues $500,000 in gifts certificates. If the firm's fiscal year end is December 31, how should it recognize the issuance of these gift certificates in its financial statements at year end?

31. Suppose that the XYZ Software company produces an inventory tracking software that it sells to manufacturing companies. Further suppose that the software sells for $100,000 each and it requires the company to provide customization to the buyers' operations, which can take several months. If the fiscal year end is September 30 and the company sells ten units of the product in August, how should it recognize these "sales" in the financial statements at year end?

32. Suppose that you are the auditor of ABC Manufacturing Company and during your audit of the firm's inventory you observe a significant amount of inventory that appears to be extremely old. How would you recommend that the firm deal with this inventory and how will it affect the revenues and expenses recognized during the period? Explain the incentives that the management of the firm might have for keeping the inventory in its warehouse.

33. Assume that a company is discontinuing a line of products due to lack of profitability. It is not sure whether this discontinuance meets the criteria for separate recognition as a discontinued line of business. The alternatives are to incorporate the losses from this line within normal operations or report them as a separate line item called "discontinued operations." As a stock analyst, discuss how the alternatives might affect your analysis of the company's stock.

USING REAL DATA

34. Zale Corporation sells fine jewelry and giftware in a chain of stores nationwide. The following footnotes appeared in the 2001 annual report along with the income statement below:

Revenue Recognition

The Company recognizes revenue in accordance with the Securities and Exchange Commissions Staff Accounting Bulletin No. 101, Revenue Recognition in Financial Statements (SAB 101). Revenue related to merchandise sales is recognized at the time of the sale, reduced by a provision for returns. The provision for sales returns is based on historical evidence of the Company s return rate. Repair revenues are recognized when the service is complete and the merchandise is delivered to the customers. Net Sales include amortized extended service agreements (ESA) which are amortized over the two-year service agreement period. ESA revenue and related expenses were previously netted in selling, general, and administrative expenses. Prior periods sales and cost of sales have been restated to reflect ESA revenue. The amortized ESA revenues were $25.0 million, $20.8 million, and $16.8 million for the years ended July 31, 2001, 2000, and 1999, respectively, and related ESA costs were $12.5 million, $10.8 million, and $9.5 million for the years ended July 31, 2001, 2000, and 1999, respectively.

Advertising Expenses are charged against operations when incurred and are a component of selling, general, and administrative expenses in the consolidated income statements. Amounts charged against operations were $78.5 million, $66.4 million, and $49.0 million for the years ended July 31, 2001, 2000, and 1999, respectively, net of amounts contributed by vendors to the Company. The amounts of prepaid advertising at July 31, 2001 and 2000, are $6.0 million and $6.4 million, respectively, and are classified as components of other assets in the Consolidated Balance Sheet.

Unusual Charges—Executives

Effective September 6, 2000, Robert J. DiNicola retired as Chairman of the Board but remained as a nonemployee member of the Board. In connection with his severance arrangement, the Company agreed to pay certain benefits of approximately $1.9 million consisting principally of an amount equivalent to one year of salary and bonus and other severance-related benefits including the accelerated vesting of certain options held by Mr. DiNicola.

Additionally, the Board approved the provision to Mr. DiNicola by the Company of a full recourse, $2.2 million interest-bearing loan at 8.74 percent for the sole purpose of purchasing 125,000 stock options prior to their expiration. The Company also extended the exercise period on an additional 500,000 stock options set to expire on September 6, 2002 to the earlier of the original ten-year term (to expire July 9, 2007), the maximum term pursuant to the Company's stock option plan, or two years after Mr. DiNicola leaves the Board of Directors. Based on the intrinsic value of these stock options on the modification date, no compensation charge was recorded by the Company.

Effective February 12, 2001, Beryl B. Raff resigned as Chairman of the Board and Chief Executive Officer. In connection with her resignation, the Company agreed to pay certain benefits of approximately $2.5 million consisting principally of an amount equivalent to three years of salary and other severance-related benefits including accelerated vesting of certain options and restricted stock.

Robert J. DiNicola was reappointed as Chairman of the Board and Chief Executive Officer, effective February 21, 2001, under a three-year contract with terms substantially consistent with his previous contract when he held the same position. In August 2001, the Company entered into a five-year employment agreement with Mr. DiNicola effective upon Mr. DiNicola's reelection as Chairman of the Board and Chief Executive Officer, replacing the earlier employment agreement. In April 2001, the Company extended a $2.1 million, three-year interest bearing loan at 7.25 percent to Mr. DiNicola for the purpose of purchasing a home. In August 2001, the loan was modified and extended with the entire principal amount to be repaid in August 2006.

Nonrecurring Charge

Upon the return of Robert J. DiNicola as Chairman and Chief Executive Officer on February 21, 2001, the Company performed an in-depth review to determine the inventory that was not of a quality consistent with the strategic direction of the Company's brands. As a result of that review, the Company recorded a nonrecurring charge in Cost of Sales of $25.2 million to adjust the valuation of such inventory and provide for markdowns to liquidate or sell-through the inventory.

ZALE CORP.: Income Statement

	07/31/2001	07/31/2000	07/31/1999
Net sales	$2,068,242,000	$1,814,362,000	$1,445,634,000
Cost of sales	1,034,970,000	930,826,000	746,663,000
Nonrecurring charge	25,236,000	0	0
Gross margin	1,008,036,000	883,536,000	698,971,000
Selling, general, and administrative Expenses	804,780,000	630,687,000	509,570,000
Depreciation and amortization expense	58,290,000	42,431,000	29,478,000
Unusual item—executive transactions	4,713,000	0	0
Operating earnings	140,253,000	210,418,000	159,923,000
Interest expense, net	6,857,000	32,178,000	30,488,000
Earnings before income taxes	133,396,000	178,240,000	129,435,000
Income taxes	51,348,000	66,726,000	48,503,000
Net earnings	$ 82,048,000	$ 111,514,000	$ 80,932,000

a. Provide support for Zale's revenue recognition policy for its extended service agreements.

b. From an analyst's point of view, discuss why the change in reporting ESA's as part of revenue rather than as an offset to expenses would be important.

   c. From an analyst's point of view, discuss why the disclosure of advertising costs by year might be important.

   d. From an analyst's point of view, discuss how you might use the disclosures concerning the unusual and nonrecurring charges to assist you in predicting the stock price for Zale.

35. Lands' End, Incorporated is a direct merchant of clothing and other cloth products that are sold primarily through catalog mailings. The cost of catalog production and mailing is fairly substantial for a company such as Lands' End. Discuss how the costs associated with catalog production and mailing should be treated for accounting purposes. Frame your answer in terms of the revenue recognition criteria and the matching concept discussed in this chapter.

36. Many consumer electronics retailers have offered extended warranty contracts to their customers. These contracts typically provide warranty coverage beyond the manufacturer's warranty period, usually anywhere between 12 and 60 months from the date of purchase. The cost of these contracts is generally collected at the time of the purchase of the product. The following is the revenue recognition Disclosure for Best Buy, Inc.:

Revenue Recognition

We recognize revenues from the sale of merchandise at the time the merchandise is sold. We recognize service revenues at the time the service is provided, the sales price is fixed or determinable, and collectibility is reasonably assured.

   We sell extended service contracts, called Performance Service Plans, on behalf of an unrelated third party. In jurisdictions where we are not deemed to be the obligor on the contract at the time of sale, commissions are recognized in revenues at the time of sale. In jurisdictions where we are deemed to be the obligor on the contract at the time of sale, commissions are recognized in revenues ratably over the term of the service contract.

Discuss why Best Buy's revenue recognition policy, with regard to commissions on Performance Service Plans, is different in different jurisdictions. Base your defense on the nature of the transaction and the revenue recognition criteria found in GAAP. In jurisdictions in which they are the obligor, what might happen to them should the third party not be able to live up to this agreement?

37. In the early 1990s a new business emerged to help individuals deal with the financial burdens of terminal illnesses, such as AIDS. If a terminally ill person has a life insurance policy, an investor group of companies could buy the insurance policy from the individual for a lump sum settlement amount. The seller could then use the proceeds to pay their bills. The buyer agrees to continue to make the premium payments until the individual dies and then collects the proceeds of the insurance policy upon death. These types of agreements are called viatical settlements. Depending on the estimated life span of the individual and the creditworthiness of the insurance company, the buyer might offer somewhere between 25 to 80 percent of the face value of the policy.

   a. If you were an investor, how would you decide how much to pay for a given viatical agreement?

   b. Having agreed on a price, how would you recognize revenue from this agreement (assume for the purposes of this question that there is more than one year from the inception of the agreement to the death of the seller) over the life of the contract?

c. Given your revenue recognition method outlined in part b, how would you treat the payment of premiums over the life of the contract?

d. Discuss any ethical dilemmas that the buyers of viatical agreements might face in the conduct of their business.

BEYOND THE BOOK

38. Using an electronic database, search for a company that has changed its revenue recognition methods during the last three years. Answer the following questions:

a. Describe the method that was used before the change as well as the new method.

b. Does the company give a reason for the change? If so, describe the change; if not, speculate on why the change occurred.

c. How significant an effect did the change have on the firm's financial statements? As an investor, how would you view this change?

d. Did the auditor agree with the change? Do you agree and why?

Prepare a short two- to three-page paper to respond to these questions.

CHAPTER 5

Financial Statements: Measuring Cash Flow

After reading this chapter you should be able to:

1. Understand and interpret the information about operating, investing, and financing activities found in the cash flow statement.

2. Explain the relationship between the cash flow statement and changes in balance sheet accounts.

3. Construct a cash flow statement using the indirect method.

4. Define free cash flows and explain how they can be determined from the Statement of Cash Flows.

moody's Investor Service announced it was reviewing the debt rating for Georgia-Pacific (GP), citing concerns with Georgia-Pacific's weakening cash flow. Mark Gray, an analyst with Moody's said, "We looked at the company's position and we were concerned about the scope of the asset sales to Willamette and the weakening cash flow over the near term that would limit their debt reduction ability."

The announcement of Moody's review of Georgia-Pacific's debt rating highlights the importance of strong cash flows to a company's value. A downgrade in debt raises the cost of borrowing for Georgia-Pacific as well as lowers equity values. In this chapter we discuss the content and meaning of the information contained in the statement of cash flows.

Broadly speaking, the statement of cash flows reflects the operating, investing, and financing activities of the firm described in Chapter 1. As such, the statement of cash flows provides different information than the income statement that focuses on changes in stockholders' equity arising from operations. The cash flow statement explains changes in cash in terms of changes in noncash accounts appearing on successive balance sheets. These changes are not limited to those involving operations, but include those involving investing and financing.

Further, with respect to operating activities, the cash flow statement offers a different perspective than reflected on the income statement. As we discussed in Chapter 4, firms determine net income on an accrual basis by the application of revenue and expense recognition criteria. Recall that under the accrual basis of accounting, revenue may be earned and expenses incurred before or after the cash flows to which they relate. Net income, therefore, reflects the revenues earned and the expenses incurred by the firm as a result of its operating activities during the period, *not* the operating cash inflows and outflows. Operating cash flows may precede or follow the recognition of revenues or expenses on the income statement. Timing issues thus separate the recognition of income from the actual cash flows of the firm.

For example, if a firm's sales grow rapidly but a significant lag exists between the cash outflows to make the company's product and the inflows from the sales collections, the firm may experience a severe liquidity crisis. In other words, a firm may possess insufficient available cash to make the required payments for items such as salaries and accounts payable. This liquidity crisis may then spark the need to obtain additional financing to pay bills and to support the company's growth. If analysts focused on only the income statement, they would miss the liquidity crisis. Further, as the income statement does not report on the investing and financing activities of the firm, analysts would not see any attempts made by the firm to address the liquidity crisis (e.g., through additional financing or a slowdown in investing). The cash flow statement not only makes any liquidity crisis transparent, it also indicates how a firm addresses the crises. Because it contains such crucial data, let's take a closer look at the information a typical cash flow statement provides.

CASH FLOW STATEMENT COMPONENTS

SFAS 95 (FASB, SFAS No. 95, 1987) requires that all companies issue a cash flow statement and provides guidelines regarding its format. The Statement of Cash Flows provides information about changes in cash flows from all sources: operating, investing, and financing activities of an entity.

CASH FLOW FROM OPERATING ACTIVITIES

Cash flow from operations includes cash inflows from sales of goods and services to customers, and cash outflows from expenses related to the sales of goods and services to customers, such as cost of goods sold and selling and administrative expenses. In fact, cash from operations can be viewed as a measure of cash-basis

TECH DATA CORP.: Cash Flow	01/31/2002	01/31/2001	01/31/2000
Cash flows from operating activities:			
Cash received from customers	$17,511,511,000	$20,114,486,000	$16,788,960,000
Cash paid to suppliers and employees	(16,406,265,000)	(20,047,551,000)	(16,684,316,000)
Interest paid	(55,871,000)	(94,823,000)	(69,554,000)
Income taxes paid	(72,745,000)	(62,048,000)	(34,176,000)
Net cash provided by (used in) operating activities	976,630,000	(89,936,000)	914,000
Cash flows from investing activities:			
Acquisition of businesses, net of cash acquired	(183,000)	(19,198,000)	(42,898,000)
Expenditures for property and equipment	(28,466,000)	(38,079,000)	(59,038,000)
Software development costs	(20,719,000)	(22,705,000)	(18,381,000)
Net cash used in investing activities	(49,368,000)	(79,982,000)	(120,317,000)
Cash flows from financing activities:			
Proceeds from the issuance of common stock, net of related tax benefit	36,432,000	35,539,000	19,663,000
Net (repayments) borrowings on revolving credit loans	(1,118,167,000)	248,712,000	99,447,000
Proceeds from issuance of long-term debt, net of expense	284,200,000	0	0
Principal payments on long-term debt	(634,000)	(557,000)	(162,000)
Net cash (used in) provided by financing activities	(798,169,000)	283,694,000	118,948,000
Effect of change in year end of certain subsidiaries (Note 3)	0	0	23,626,000
Effect of exchange rate changes on cash	(10,091,000)	(6,637,000)	0
Net increase in cash and cash equivalents	119,002,000	107,139,000	23,171,000
Cash and cash equivalents at beginning of year	138,925,000	31,786,000	8,615,000
Cash and cash equivalents at end of year	$ 257,927,000	$ 138,925,000	$ 31,786,000

Exhibit 5.1
Direct Method Cash Flow Statement

THE REAL WORLD

Tech Data Corp.

earnings because it measures the cash inflows from sales in the period of collection and the cash outflows for expenses in the period of payment.

There are two approaches to presenting cash flow from operations, the **direct method** and the **indirect method.** Under the direct method, a firm first reports cash received from revenue-producing activities, and then subtracts its cash payments for expenses. Exhibit 5.1 illustrates this type of statement (see the shaded operating section). Notice that the company shown (Tech Data, a distributor of hardware and software products) combined its operating cash outflows to employees and suppliers into a single line item.

In contrast, the indirect method starts with net income and shows the adjustments necessary to arrive at cash flows from operations. Exhibit 5.2 shows this method in the statements of Tofutti Brands, Inc. (a producer of soy-based products).

FASB 95 allows the use of either method, as both methods produce identical results of cash from operations. However, most firms use the indirect approach. As a result, FASB 95 requires firms that report under the direct

Exhibit 5.2
Indirect Method Cash Flow
Statement

THE REAL WORLD

Tofutti Brands

TOFUTTI BRANDS, Inc.: Cash Flow

	12/29/2001	12/29/2000	12/30/1999
Cash flows from operating activities:			
Net income	$ 1,150,000	$ 956,000	$ 850,000
Adjustments to reconcile net income to net cash flows from operating activities:			
Provision for bad debts	40,000	60,000	60,000
Accrued interest on investments	0	(34,000)	(3,000)
Deferred taxes	(119,000)	(176,000)	332,000
Change in assets and liabilities:			
Accounts receivable	(625,000)	(105,000)	64,000
Inventories	92,000	(342,000)	17,000
Prepaid expenses	(1,000)	(1,000)	5,000
Accounts payable and accrued expenses	9,000	17,000	(51,000)
Accrued compensation	0	175,000	115,000
Income taxes payable	(144,000)	209,000	103,000
Net cash flows from operating activities	402,000	759,000	1,492,000
Cash flows from investing activities:			
Proceeds from redemption of investments	269,000	0	(250,000)
Other assets	(144,000)	(22,000)	(22,000)
Net cash flows from investing activities	125,000	(22,000)	(272,000)
Cash flows from financing activities:			
Notes payable	(8,000)	(22,000)	(18,000)
Issuance of common stock	35,000	50,000	84,000
Purchase of treasury stock	(436,000)	(247,000)	0
Net cash flows from financing activities	(409,000)	(219,000)	66,000
Net change in cash and equivalents	118,000	518,000	1,286,000
Cash and equivalents, at beginning of period	2,211,000	1,693,000	407,000
Cash and equivalents, at end of period	$ 2,329,000	$2,211,000	$1,693,000
Supplemental cash flow information:			
Interest paid		$ 2,000	$ 5,000
Income taxes paid	$ 750,000	$ 579,000	$ 151,000

method to also disclose the operating section data prepared under the indirect method (see Exhibit 5.3). Compare the net cash from operations in both Exhibits 5.1 and 5.3, and note how the amounts are identical. However, you can see that the indirect method disclosure (Exhibit 5.3) provides more information about investments in current operating assets net of operating liabilities than the direct method (Exhibit 5.1).

TECH DATA CORP.: Cash Flow	01/31/2002	01/31/2001	01/31/2000
Reconciliation of net income to net cash provided by (used in) operating activities:			
Net income	$ 110,777,000	$177,983,000	$127,501,000
Adjustments to reconcile net income to net cash provided by (used in) operating activities:			
Depreciation and amortization	63,488,000	63,922,000	57,842,000
Provision for losses on accounts receivable	40,764,000	41,447,000	40,877,000
Special charges (Note 13)	27,000,000	0	0
Deferred income taxes	(11,848,000)	(1,789,000)	1,306,000
Changes in assets and liabilities:			
Decrease (increase) in accounts receivable	314,000,000	(313,197,000)	(202,790,000)
Decrease (increase) in inventories	702,219,000	(146,093,000)	(220,585,000)
(Increase) in prepaid and other assets	(6,248,000)	(11,603,000)	(25,430,000)
(Decrease) increase in accounts payable	(264,722,000)	11,863,000	136,748,000
Increase in accrued expenses	1,200,000	87,531,000	85,445,000
Total adjustments	865,853,000	(267,919,000)	(126,587,000)
Net cash provided by (used in) operating activities	$976,630,000	($89,936,000)	$ 914,000

Exhibit 5.3
Indirect Method Disclosure under Direct Method

THE REAL WORLD

Tech Data

CASH FLOW FROM INVESTING ACTIVITIES

Investing activities involve the cash flow effect of transactions related to a company's long-term assets and investments. Examples include cash paid or received to purchase or sell property, plant, and equipment; investments in securities of other companies; and acquisitions of other companies. The investing activities section provides information about how a company uses its cash to generate future earnings. Investments represent opportunities for future earnings growth. For a growth company, we would normally expect cash from investing activities to be a net outflow, although this depends on the company's growth strategy.

For example, in Tech Data's cash flow statement (Exhibit 5.1), you see significant annual investments in property and equipment, and software development. Contrast this with Tofutti's cash flow statement (Exhibit 5.2), which includes little activity in the investing section. The company primarily leases its facilities (the cash flows from leasing would appear in the operating section) and therefore does not have significant investments in plant and equipment.

The investment section of the cash flow statement is where you would also see investments in other companies including acquisitions. You can see this kind of activity in Tech Data's statements. Note that in most acquisitions the investment cash flow occurs on the date of acquisition. Subsequent to the date of acquisition, the cash flows from operating the newly acquired company will start to appear in the operating section. At the date of acquisition, the firm reports new assets and liabilities from the acquisition (e.g., receivables, inventory, PP&E, accounts payable) that would appear in the firm's balance sheet as of the acquisition date. If a firm acquired a new company mid-year, then the net change in certain asset accounts (such as inventories) would include the changes due to operations and the changes due to the acquisition.

CASH FLOW FROM FINANCING ACTIVITIES

This section of the cash flow statement provides information about transactions with owners and creditors. Financing activities include issuance and repayment of debt such as loans, bank advances, and bonds payable, as well as issuances and repurchases of stock and payments of dividends.

Tofutti (Exhibit 5.2) shows relatively minor outflows of cash to repay notes payable. The remaining transactions relate to issuance of stock and repurchase of shares that are held in its treasury account. Tech Data's statements (Exhibit 5.1) show significantly more activity related to long-term debt.

Now that you can identify the components of the cash flow statement, how do you use its information? One of the best ways is by understanding the mechanics of preparing a cash flow statement. Going through the preparation process can shed light on how a firm generates and uses cash. Additionally, reconciling a firm's cash flow statement to its balance sheet and income statement can be a useful tool for financial statement analysis.

PREPARATION OF THE STATEMENT OF CASH FLOWS

In this section, we'll show how to prepare a cash flow statement (indirect method) using Biohealth, Inc. (BHT), the fictitious wholesale company we discussed in previous chapters. Exhibit 5.4 shows the balance sheets for BHT at 12/31/20X2 and 12/31/20X1. Exhibit 5.5 shows the income statement for BHT for the year ending 12/31/20X2.

We use a T-account worksheet to determine the net effects of the transactions for BHT for 20X2 on the cash account, as shown in Exhibit 5.6. Note that we use this worksheet only to assist in the construction of the cash flow statement. Do not confuse this worksheet with the firm's accounting system that contains the actual entries made to the system. In fact, you can also use a simple spreadsheet instead of a T-account worksheet.

The first step is to place the beginning and ending balances of all of the accounts from the balance sheet in the T-accounts, as shown in Exhibit 5.6. Then, we analyze the changes in the various accounts on the balance sheet and classify them into operating, investing, and financing activities. In order to do this, we rely on information from the income statement as well as any additional information provided about the company's operating, financing, and investing transactions. For example, the following additional information applies to the transactions of BHT for the year ending 12/31/20X2:

Exhibit 5.4
BHT Balance Sheet

Biohealth, Inc. (BHT)
Balance Sheet ($ in millions)

	As of 12/31/20X2	As of 12/31/20X1
Assets		
Current assets:		
Cash	$ 1,510	$ 567
Accounts receivable	3,650	2,464
Inventory	4,400	3,920
Prepaid expenses	360	0
Total current assets	9,920	7,101
Property, plant, and equipment (PPE)	950	540
Less: accumulated depreciation	(210)	(60)
Net property plant and equipment	740	480
	$10,660	$7,581
Liabilities and Stockholders' Equity		
Liabilities:		
Current liabilities:		
Accounts payable	$ 6,671	$5,140
Long-term debt:		
Notes payable	950	400
Total liabilities	7,621	5,540
Stockholders' equity		
Common stock	300	250
Additional paid-in capital	1,950	1,375
Retained earnings	789	266
Total stockholders' equity	3,039	2,041
	$10,660	$7,581

Exhibit 5.5
BHT Income Statement

Biohealth, Inc. (BHT)
Income Statement

	Year ending 12/31/20X2
Revenues	$43,850
Less: Cost of goods sold	(37,272)
Gross profit	6,578
Selling and administrative expenses	5,320
Depreciation expense	150
Interest expense	85
Net income	$1,023

Exhibit 5.6
BHT Cash Flow T-Account
Worksheet

BHT Cash Flow T-Account Worksheet Set Up

	Cash		Accumulated Depreciation—PPE	
Bal.	567		60	Bal.
Operating:				
Investing:			210	Bal.
			Accounts payable	
Financing:			5,140	Bal.
Bal.	1,510		6,671	Bal.
	Accounts receivable		**Notes payable**	
Bal.	2,464		400	Bal.
			950	Bal.
Bal.	3,650			
	Inventory		**Common Stock**	
Bal.	3,920		250	Bal.
Bal.	4,400		300	Bal.
	Prepaid Expenses		**Additional Paid-in capital**	
Bal.	0		1,375	Bal.
Bal.	360			
			1,950	Bal.
	PPE		**Retained Earnings**	
Bal.	540		266	Bal.
Bal.	950		789	Bal.

1. All inventory is purchased on credit from suppliers.
2. All sales to customers are for credit.
3. Borrowed $550 million during 20X2.
4. Issued 50 million shares of $1 par stock at $12.50 per share during 20X2.
5. Declared and paid $500 million in dividends to shareholders during 20X2.

Items 1 and 2 simply summarize common assumptions and need not correspond to the transactions that actually occurred. Items 3 through 5 provide information that you would find in the Statement of Stockholders' Equity and Notes to the Financial Statements.

We are now ready to create the worksheet entries for the cash flow statement. The basic approach is to examine each balance sheet account (other than cash) that changed and then assess its effect on cash. Next, we create a worksheet entry to show this effect on cash along with the corresponding change in the balance sheet account. Once we analyze all of the balance sheet accounts and complete the worksheet entries, we should have the basis of our cash flow statement. Let's start now with determining the worksheet entries for the operating section and then proceed through the investing and financing sections.

WORKSHEET ENTRIES FOR CASH FROM OPERATIONS

The starting point typically begins with analyzing the change in retained earnings. In the indirect approach, we record net income in the Cash account of the worksheet (as well as in the Retained Earnings account, to ensure that debits equal credits) as if it increased cash. We know, however, that not all revenues increase cash and not all expenses use cash. Therefore, subsequent entries will make adjustments to correct for the noncash components of earnings.

We obtain net income from the income statement in Exhibit 5.5, giving us the first entry:

(1)	Cash	1,023	
	Retained Earnings		1,023

We now need to correct our "mistake" of reporting net income as if it were all cash. We start with adjustments to correct the revenue portion of net income.

Adjusting Net Income

Changes in current assets and liabilities in the operating section serve to correct line items in the net income number to their cash flow equivalent. For revenues, these adjustments serve to undo the effects of recognizing revenues when earned rather than as the cash is received, and for expenses the effects of recognizing them when incurred rather than when paid. We can thus view increases in current operating assets as requiring cash (and decreases providing cash) and increases in current operating liabilities as providing cash (and decreases requiring cash). Exhibit 5.7 summarizes the effects of these changes. With this understanding of adjustments, let's return now to our BHT example.

Exhibit 5.7
Adjustments to Net Income
Using the Indirect Method

> **Positive adjustments to income to determine cash from operations result from:**
>
> Decreases in current operating assets (A/R, inventory, prepaid assets, etc.)
> Increases in current operating liabilities (A/P, Salaries Payable, etc.)*
>
> **Negative adjustments to income to determine cash from operations result from:**
>
> Increases in current operating assets other than cash
> Decreases in current operating liabilities
>
> *Notes Payable and the Current Portion of Long-Term Debt are typically not considered to be a part of operating liabilities even though they are generally classified as current liabilities. Also, there are instances where operating liabilities are classified as noncurrent and changes in those liabilities are included in the operating section of the cash flow statement.

Revenue Adjustments to Net Income

Because sales revenue is recorded on an accrual basis, not when cash is collected, we need to adjust income for the difference between sales revenue recognized and cash collected on accounts receivable (AR). This difference can be found in the change in the accounts receivable balance. In the case of BHT, accounts receivable increased, meaning that cash collections on account were less than the amount of sales recognized. Recall that we assume that all sales are on account. Therefore, we calculate cash collections on accounts receivable as follows:

$$\text{Cash Collections} = \text{Beginning AR} + \text{Sales} - \text{Ending AR}$$
$$= \text{Sales} - (\text{Ending AR} - \text{Beginning AR})$$
$$= \text{Sales} - \text{Change in AR}$$

For BHT, cash collections for 20X1 are therefore:

$$\text{Cash Collections} = \$2,464 + \$43,850 - \$3,650$$
$$\text{Cash Collections} = \$43,850 - (\$3,650 - \$2,464)$$
$$= \$43,850 - \$1,186 = \$42,664$$

Because cash collections are less than sales, when we reported net income in the cash account, we overstated the effect of sales on cash. As a result, we need to adjust by reducing cash for the increase in accounts receivable. A simpler alternative to the previous calculation would be to identify the change in the accounts receivable account. With a net debit to the accounts receivable account, by default, we would need to credit the Cash account for this difference, thereby reducing the amount reported in net income in the Cash account from Transaction 1. The entry to record this is:

> (2)   Accounts receivable   1,186
>   Cash   1,186

> Management could possibly report fraudulent earnings by reporting nonexistent sales and accounts receivable. Note however that the increase in sales that result from this behavior would be offset by the increase in receivables in the determination of operating cash flows; i.e., operating cash flows are unaffected by accruals per se. It would be far more difficult to implement fraud that affected cash flows.

This negative adjustment to cash matches the increase in the current operating asset, accounts receivable.

Cost of Goods Sold Adjustment to Net Income

After revenues, cost of goods sold is typically the first expense that appears on the income statement. Understanding the cash flow impact of the cost of inventory sales requires considering two separate timing relationships: (1) the relationship between the purchase of inventory (INV) and its recognition as a cost when sold, and (2) the relationship between the purchase of inventory and the payment for that inventory.

Recall from Chapter 3 the cost of goods sold equation:

$$\text{Cost of Goods Sold} = \text{Beginning Inventory} + \text{Purchases} - \text{Ending INV}$$
$$= \text{Purchases} - (\text{Ending INV} - \text{Beginning INV})$$
$$= \text{Purchases} - \text{Change in INV}$$

Because we assume that all inventory is purchased on accounts payable (AP), we therefore calculate cash paid for purchases as:

$$\text{Payments} = \text{Beginning AP} + \text{Purchases} - \text{Ending AP}$$
$$= \text{Purchases} - (\text{Ending AP} - \text{Beginning AP})$$
$$= \text{Purchases} - \text{Change in AP}$$

The difference between the expense (cost of goods sold) on the income statement and the cash paid to suppliers can be explained by the change in accounts payable less the change in inventory:

$$\text{Cost of Goods Sold} - \text{Payments}$$
$$= (\text{Purchases} - \text{Change in INV}) - (\text{Purchases} - \text{Change in AP})$$
$$= \text{Purchases} - \text{Purchases} - \text{Change in INV} + \text{Change in AP}$$
$$= \text{Change in AP} - \text{Change in INV}$$

The cost of goods sold for BHT was $37,272 during the current year. We can apply the above equations to calculate the purchases for the period as $37,752 (= CGS + Ending INV − Beginning INV = 37,272 + 4,400 − 3,920). Then we can use the purchases to calculate the payments for the period as $36,222 (= Purchases + Beginning AP − Ending AP = 37,752 + 5,140 − 6,671). The difference between the cost of goods sold reported in income and the payments is therefore $1,051 ($37,272 − 36,222). Notice that this amount equals the difference between the change in AP (1,531) and the change in INV (480).

Again, we can avoid calculations by recording an entry that explains the change in the balance of both inventory and accounts payable with the corresponding entry to the operating section of the cash account, as follows:

(3)	Inventory	480	
	Cash		480

169

The change in accounts payable is:

| (4) | Cash | 1,531 | |
| | Acct. Payable | | 1,531 |

Depreciation Adjustment to Net Income

Depreciation is a noncash expense that a firm recognizes for financial reporting. It represents the allocation of the cost of plant and equipment over its useful life. Because depreciation expense is noncash, the amount of expense is added back to earnings to arrive at cash from operations. Sometimes depreciation is mistakenly thought of as a source of cash. This is incorrect in that depreciation does not generate cash for a business. Rather, it is an expense that does not require the use of cash (beyond the amount previously reported as an investment activity on earlier cash flow statements).

For many companies, depreciation is a large expense. Hence, cash from operations may be considerably larger than net income. However, because BHT is a wholesaling company and it leases its warehouses, it does not have proportionately as much depreciation as companies with large amounts of plant and equipment (e.g., in Exhibit 5.3 you can see a fairly substantial adjustment for depreciation for Tech Data Corp.). The entry to add back the depreciation expense to net income is:

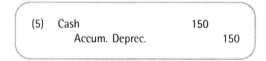

| (5) | Cash | 150 | |
| | Accum. Deprec. | | 150 |

Prepaid Expense Adjustment to Net Income

BHT also had an increase in its prepaid expenses account. While we could calculate the differences between expenses related to this prepayment and the actual cash flows as we did with inventory, we can again avoid this. Instead, we simply determine how the balance in this operating asset account changes and record the appropriate entry, as follows:

| (6) | Prepaid Expenses | 360 | |
| | Cash | | 360 |

This completes the adjustments for the operating activities for BHT, as there are no other operating asset or liability accounts to consider. Other companies might also have accrued expenses, such as salaries payable, that would require adjustment. Further, GAAP requires firms to recognize all interest and tax cash flows in the operating section, so we might also have to adjust for changes in accounts such interest payable, taxes payable, and deferred taxes.

WORKSHEET ENTRIES FOR CASH FROM INVESTING

Only one investing activity occurred for BHT for the year ending 20X2: the acquisition of property, plant, and equipment. The entry is:

(7)	Property, Plant, and Equipment	410	
	Cash		410

Analyzing the cash from investing, however, may be more complex for a company that acquires or disposes of multiple groups of assets during a period. When a company disposes of a long-term asset such as property, plant, and equipment, it may report a gain or loss in the income statement from that transaction. Notice that the cash inflow from this sale should appear in the investing section. However, the gain or loss will appear in net income (and therefore will have been included in the cash account as part of net income in Transaction 1). Should this occur, we would need to remove the gain or loss from the operating section as the cash flows associated with these transactions should appear in the investing section. To remove a gain, we would credit the cash account; to remove a loss, we would debit the cash account.

WORKSHEET ENTRIES FOR CASH FROM FINANCING

BHT had several financing transactions during 20X2, including payment of dividends of $500 million. Recall that dividends are a distribution to shareholders, and as such are not an expense to the company. Hence, dividends are considered a financing transaction. When the board of directors declares dividends, an entry is made debiting retained earnings and crediting dividends payable. Later, when the dividend is actually paid to stockholders, dividends payable is debited and cash is credited. Because there is no dividends payable account, we know that all declared dividends have also been paid. Thus, the aggregate entry to record this in the worksheet is:

(8)	Retained earnings	500	
	Cash		500

BHT also issued a note payable. This is also a financing activity that increases the amount of cash available to BHT to fund its operations. The entry is:

(9)	Cash	550	
	Note payable		550

		Cash			
Bal.		567			
Operating:					
Net Income	(1)	1,023	1,186	(2)	AR Increase
Increase in AP	(4)	1,531	480	(3)	Inventory Increase
Depreciation Expense	(5)	150	360	(6)	Increase in Prepaid Expenses
Investing:					
			410	(7)	Purchase PPE
Financing:					
Issue note payable	(9)	550			
Issue common stock	(10)	625	500	(8)	Pay Dividends
Bal.		1,510			

		Accounts Receivable	
Bal.		2,464	
	(2)	1,186	
Bal.		3,650	

		Inventory	
Bal.		3,920	
	(3)	480	
Bal.		4,400	

		Prepaid Expenses	
Bal.		0	
	(6)	360	
Bal.		360	

		PPE	
Bal.		540	
	(7)	410	
Bal.		950	

Accumulated Depreciation—PPE		
	60	Bal.
	150	(5)
	210	Bal.

Accounts Payable		
	5,140	Bal.
	1,531	(4)
	6,671	Bal.

Notes Payable		
	400	Bal.
	550	(9)
	950	Bal.

Common Stock		
	250	Bal.
	50	(10)
	300	Bal.

Additional Paid-In Capital		
	1,375	Bal.
	575	(10)
	1,950	Bal.

Retained Earnings			
		266	Bal.
(8)	500	1,023	(1)
		789	Bal.

Exhibit 5.8
T-Account Worksheet
Entries for BHT

	Year ending 12/31/20X2	Year ending 12/31/20X1
Cash from operations:		
Net income	$1,023	$416
Add: noncash expenses		
Depreciation	150	60
Changes in current assets and liabilities		
Increase in accounts receivable	(1,186)	(2,464)
Increase in inventory	(480)	(3,920)
Increase in prepaid expenses	(360)	
Increase in accounts payable	1,531	5,140
Total cash from operations	678	(768)
Cash from investing		
Purchase fixtures (PPE)	(410)	(0)
Total cash from investing	(410)	(0)
Cash from financing		
Issuance of long-term note	550	0
Issuance of common stock	625	
Dividends	(500)	(150)
Total cash from financing	675	(150)
Total change in cash	943	(918)
Cash balance 1/1/20X2	567	1,485
Cash balance 12/31/20X2	$1,510	$567

Exhibit 5.9
Statement of Cash Flows for the Years Ending 20X2 and 20X1 Biohealth, Inc (BHT)

The final financing transaction affecting cash is the issuance of common stock. We record this as follows:

(10)	Cash	625	
	Common Stock		50
	Additional Paid-In Capital		575

At this point, we have analyzed all of the changes in the balance sheet accounts other than cash and, therefore, also explained all of the changes in cash. Exhibit 5.8 shows our completed worksheet entries. We can now construct the cash flow statement from the information contained within the Cash account in Exhibit 5.8. Exhibit 5.9 shows our completed cash flow statement for 2002, along with the cash flow statement from the prior year (which we presented in Chapter 3).

SUMMARY OF CASH FLOW STATEMENT PREPARATION—INDIRECT METHOD

To summarize, the preparation of the cash flow statement involves the following steps:

Cash from operations:
  Net income
  Add:
            Depreciation and amortization
            Losses on sales of noncurrent assets and liabilities
            Decreases in current operating assets other than cash
            Increases in operating liabilities
  Deduct:
            Gains on sales of noncurrent assets and liabilities
            Increases in current operating assets other than cash
            Decreases in current operating liabilities
Cash from investing:
  Add:
            Proceeds from sales of noncurrent assets and nonoperating current assets
            Proceeds from sales of other companies
  Deduct:
            Purchases of noncurrent assets and nonoperating current assets
            Acquisitions of other companies
Cash from financing:
  Add:
            Issuance of debt (borrowings)
            Issuance of stock
  Deduct:
            Debt repayments
            Dividends
            Stock repurchases

ARTICULATION OF THE CASH FLOW STATEMENT

As we said earlier, reconciling a firm's cash flow statement to its balance sheet and income statement can be a useful analytical tool. In simple cases, such as for Tofutti, the adjustments for changes in the various assets and liabilities that appear on the cash flow statement **articulate** with (are the same as) the corresponding changes in the balance sheet of the company. Exhibit 5.10 shows the balance sheet of Tofutti and includes a column that shows the net changes in the assets and liabilities of the firm. The operating items are highlighted. To demonstrate the articulation, look at the net change in inventories, accounts payable, and accrued expenses, and compare these changes with the net adjustments on the cash flow statement in Exhibit 5.2. Note that both the decrease in inventory and the increase in accounts payable result in a positive adjustment to net income consistent with the information in Exhibit 5.10.

The one account that does not appear to articulate is accounts receivable, where you will observe a change on the balance sheet of $585,000 and a change

TOFUTTI BRANDS, Inc.:
Balance Sheet

	12/29/2001	12/29/2000	Net Change
Assets			
Current assets:			
Cash and equivalents	$2,329,000	$2,211,000	$ 118,000
Short-term investments	0	269,000	(269,000)
Accounts receivable, net of allowance for doubtful accounts of $325,000 and $270,000, respectively	1,461,000	876,000	585,000
Inventories	816,000	908,000	(92,000)
Prepaid expenses	10,000	9,000	1,000
Deferred income taxes	478,000	359,000	119,000
Total current assets	5,094,000	4,632,000	462,000
Other assets:			
Other assets	325,000	181,000	144,000
	$5,419,000	$4,813,000	$606,000
Liabilities and stockholders' equity			
Current liabilities:			
Notes payable	$ 0	$ 8,000	($8,000)
Accounts payable and accrued expenses	155,000	146,000	9,000
Accrued compensation	375,000	375,000	0
Income taxes payable	187,000	331,000	(144,000)
Total current liabilities	717,000	860,000	(143,000)
Commitments and contingencies			
Stockholders' equity:			
Preferred stock—par value $.01 per share; authorized 100,000 shares, none issued	0	0	0
Common stock—par value $.01 per share; authorized 15,000,000 shares, issued and outstanding 6,091,267 shares at December 29, 2001 and 6,354,567 shares at December 30, 2000	61,000	64,000	(3,000)
Less: Treasury stock, at cost (18,100 shares and 122,400 shares at December 29, 2001 and December 30, 2000, respectively)	(38,000)	(247,000)	209,000
Additional paid-in capital	3,156,000	3,763,000	(607,000)
Accumulated earnings	1,523,000	373,000	1,150,000
Total stockholders' equity	4,702,000	3,953,000	749,000
Total liabilities and stockholders' equity	$5,419,000	$4,813,000	$606,000

of ($625,000) on the cash flow statement. However, the adjustment for the provision for bad debts in the cash flow statement also affects the accounts receivable account, because accounts receivable is reported net of the effects of bad debts on the balance sheet. Therefore, if you net the $40,000 adjustment for bad debts on the cash flow statement with the change in accounts receivable of ($625,000), you get the same change in net accounts receivable of $585,000

THINKING GLOBALLY

Although not all countries require preparation of a cash flow statement, cash flows are increasingly important in international markets. Many companies voluntarily disclose cash flow statements. International accounting standards (IAS Number 7) state that the cash flow statement is a basic financial statement that explains the change in cash and cash equivalents during a period. In some countries, a funds flow statement is presented. The funds statement is similar to the cash flow statement, but it reconciles changes in total working capital rather than cash.

reported on the balance sheet. We will revisit the issue of accounting for bad-debts in Chapter 7. The cash statement will not always articulate with the balance sheet primarily due to acquisitions and foreign currency translation, both of which are beyond the scope of this book.

SUPPLEMENTAL DISCLOSURES TO THE CASH FLOW STATEMENT

Companies often report supplemental disclosures on the cash flow statement. For example, GAAP requires firms to report all interest cash flows in the operating section. However, because users might want to view these amounts as financing cash flows, GAAP requires that firms disclose the dollar amount of interest cash flows that exist in the operating section. Many firms (like Tofutti) do this by providing supplemental cash flow information at the bottom of the statement, as shown in Exhibit 5.2. Other firms provide this information in a footnote to the financial statements. GAAP also requires all tax cash flows to be reported in the operating section, even though you could argue that they apply to all three sections. As a result, GAAP requires supplemental disclosure of the tax cash flows (again, see Exhibit 5.2).

In addition, a firm may engage in transactions that do not directly affect cash. However, if a transaction is considered a significant noncash activity, GAAP requires the firm to disclose this type of transaction as supplemental information. For example, Polaroid disclosed that, in 2000, it recorded noncash items of $22.9 million in cash flow from operating activities that consisted primarily of $12.0 million for the issuance of shares relating to their Retirement Savings Plan.

INTERPRETING THE CASH FLOW STATEMENT

The cash flow statement provides both insights into the effectiveness with which a company manages its cash flows, as well as signals of the underlying quality of its earnings flows. Management of cash flows is an important activity in a business. If a company's operating cash inflows are insufficient to meet operating cash outflow demands, a company may be forced to engage in additional borrowing or issuance of stock, or sale of long-term assets to meet cash needs. If the firm cannot raise sufficient cash from these sources, it may be forced into bankruptcy. For example, Kmart Corporation filed Chapter 11 bankruptcy following a slow holiday season in 2001. One source of the company's problem was the inability to pay suppliers on a timely basis due to the declining sales.

In the case of Tofutti (Exhibit 5.2), you can see that net income increased each year over the most recent three-year period of time. However, you also can observe that cash from operating activities has declined over this same period. To understand why, look to the adjustments to net income. Observe that in 2000 the three largest negative adjustments were for inventories, deferred taxes, and accounts receivable.

Although we discuss deferred taxes in greater depth later in Chapter 10, the simple explanation for now is that federal tax laws often allow or require different accounting methods to be used in calculating taxable income than those methods used to report under GAAP. In the case of depreciation, for example, the tax code provides a benefit to businesses in the form of allowing for more rapid depreciation write-offs for tax purposes than firms use for financial reporting. As a result, tax payments are deferred because taxable income (i.e., income reported for tax purposes) is usually less than income before taxes reported for financial accounting purposes. Hence, tax payments are less than the tax expense reported on net income. The difference between the actual tax liability and the tax expense reported for financial reporting is reported as an account called "deferred taxes." Notice for Tofutti that the adjustment for deferred taxes goes in different directions in different years. Negative adjustments mean that there were net, noncash, income-improving effects during the year as a result of deferred taxes, and vice versa for positive adjustments.

While taxes are a difficult item to fully explain at this point, we can provide interpretation for the other two items. The negative adjustments for both the inventory and accounts receivable balance mean that they are increasing over the year. One explanation might be an increase in the firm's sales. Looking at the income statement for Tofutti (Exhibit 5.11), sales did significantly increase in 2000 over 1999. In fact, Tofutti's sales showed a growth of approximately

Exhibit 5.11
Income Statement

THE REAL WORLD

Tofutti Brands, Inc.

TOFUTTI BRANDS, Inc.:
Income Statement

	12/29/2001	12/29/2000	12/30/1999
Net sales	$16,254,000	$13,343,000	$11,912,000
Cost of sales	10,550,000	8,192,000	7,349,000
Gross profit	5,704,000	5,151,000	4,563,000
Operating expenses:			
Selling	1,896,000	1,724,000	1,521,000
Marketing	391,000	277,000	199,000
Research and development	483,000	397,000	376,000
General and administrative	1,381,000	1,288,000	1,043,000
	4,151,000	3,686,000	3,139,000
Operating income	1,553,000	1,465,000	1,424,000
Other income	268,000	103,000	12,000
Income before income tax	1,821,000	1,568,000	1,436,000
Income taxes	671,000	612,000	(586,000)
Net income	$1,150,000	$956,000	$850,000

12 percent. However, the net change in inventories of $342,000 (see the cash flow statement, Exhibit 5.2) to bring the balance in inventories to $908,000 (see the balance sheet, Exhibit 5.10) seems to be approximately a 60 percent increase in inventories. This seems out of line with the growth in sales. You would want to, therefore, seek a better explanation for what happened to inventories during 2000. Tofutti explains in its 10-K that part of this increase in inventory was the result of introducing new products (as well as an increase in sales).

In 2001 the largest single adjustment ($625,000) is in accounts receivable, while inventories actually show a decline. Again, looking at the income statement, you can see that sales grew substantially in 2001. This provides some explanation for the growth in accounts receivable, but the growth in accounts receivable is much higher (67 percent) than the annual sales growth (22 percent). If you read Tofutti's annual report, you will see that management indicates that sales increased significantly in the last quarter of the year that led to the high level of accounts receivable at year end. This is obviously good news in terms of future prospects as sales are going up significantly.

However, notice that in the current period this immense growth is starting to put a strain on cash from operations. This is not unusual for a rapid-growth company, but is something that the company must take into consideration in its planning to make sure that it does not end up in a cash crisis. Because Tofutti has a significant balance in its cash account (which has also been increasing over this period of time), it seems to be in no immediate danger of a cash crisis.

Interestingly, Tofutti reported a smaller amount of bad debt expense in 2001 than in 2000 despite a considerable increase in accounts receivable. Bad debt expense reported in 2001 was $40,000 compared to $60,000 in 2000 and 1999. In Tofutti's statement, the provision for bad debts (sometimes called bad debt expense) is a deduction in arriving at net income, for the company's estimate of the sales made during the period that it does not expect to collect (customers who never pay their bill). As such it is a noncash expense.

Further, as the balance sheet shows, although Tofutti's allowance for uncollectible accounts increased about 20 percent from 2000 to 2001, it did not increase proportionately to the increase in accounts receivable. This is a potential concern because a relationship usually exists between sales, accounts receivable, and the amount of estimated bad debt expense recognized (we discuss this in more depth in Chapter 7). If Tofutti underestimated its bad debt expense during 2001, the reported net accounts receivable may be too high, leading to overstated assets and earnings for Tofutti. The fact that a significant portion of Tofutti's increased earnings has not been collected may be a red flag, signaling to investors that future cash flows may not be as strong as the income statement alone suggests.

In summary, cash from operations can provide important information about a company's current and future prospects. GAAP guidelines for revenue and expense recognition are intended to result in earnings that, in part, reflect expected future cash flows, but both revenue and expense recognition rules, even if appropriately applied, involve significant estimation. Furthermore, managers may manage earnings to meet targeted earnings numbers or analyst's forecasts. As a result, careful study of cash from operations, together with the other financial statement information, may provide clues about a company's performance not evident from either statement alone. A company with increasing receivables, inventory, and payables may show positive earnings. However, if the company fails to generate cash and pay its creditors, the company may have financial distress regardless of the earnings reported.

VALUATION IMPLICATIONS OF THE CASH FLOW STATEMENT

Cash flows can have significant implications for the valuation of firms, and firms like Procter & Gamble often refer to cash flow in their announcements of performance as shown in Exhibit 5.12.

The cash flow statement provides information not directly available from either the income statement or the balance sheet. In order for a company to retain and grow in value, it must not only earn a profit, it must also generate cash that can be used to invest in growing the business or paying dividends to shareholders. The cash flow statement provides insights not only into the sources of a company's cash, but how it uses that cash. Analysts look at both sources of information to help determine the company's ultimate profit potential.

Many companies even report performance in terms of cash flows as well as earnings. Cemex reported the following information about its 2001 fourth-quarter results (the term EBITDA stands for Earnings Before Interest, Taxes, Depreciation, and Amortization): "Cash earnings increased 11% to US$446 million, compared to US$400.5 million in the fourth quarter of 2000; lower interest expense enabled cash earnings to outpace EBITDA growth." Note that the "cash earnings" referred to in the Cemex disclosure is close to the cash from operations a firm would report on its cash flow statement except that it is before taxes and there are no adjustments for the changes in the working capital accounts (i.e., accounts receivable, inventories, accounts payable).

Analysts' estimates of the market value of firm typically rely on projections of free cash flows to equity holders as the principal input. **Free cash flows** to equity holders are the cash flows from operating activities, less cash flows used for investing activities, plus cash flows from debt financing activities, and less the increase in cash needed to sustain operations. Equivalently, if the entire increase in cash is required by operations, then free cash flows to equity holders

---

CINCINNATI, January 31, 2002—The Procter & Gamble Company today reported that it exceeded consensus expectations for second quarter results. P&G delivered on the high end of its financial guidance for the October–December quarter, behind record quarter unit volume. For the quarter ended December 31, 2001, unit volume grew five percent versus the prior year led by double-digit growth in the health and beauty care businesses. Excluding acquisitions and divestitures, unit volume increased four percent. Net sales were $10.40 billion, up two percent versus one year ago. "We are seeing clear improvements in our results, and we're pleased to have met our commitments once again," said P&G President and Chief Executive A. G. Lafley. "We're continuing our unyielding focus on delivering better consumer value on our brands, building core categories, reducing the company's cost structure, and improving our cash flow."

Exhibit 5.12

THE REAL WORLD

Procter & Gamble

are cash distributions to stockholders (dividends and stock repurchases), net of cash proceeds from stock issues. The concept is that these are cash flows that would be available to stockholders each period to provide a return to them.

To illustrate the calculation of free cash flows, consider the calculation of the free cash flows for our BHT example (refer back to Exhibit 5.11 for the line items on the cash flow statement):

Cash from operations:	$678
Cash from investing:	(410)
Cash from borrowing:	550
Change in cash:	(943)
Total free cash flows to equity:	($125)

Observe that the total free cash flows to equity (stockholders) can also be determined by subtracting proceeds from the issuance of stock from dividends ($500 − $625 = −$125). Note that we are assuming the entire change in cash ($943) is needed to support operations.

SUMMARY AND TRANSITION

In order to help determine firm value, earnings must provide a signal of future cash flows. This means that earnings should be indicative of the firm's ability to generate future cash flows. This does not imply a one-to-one correlation between the pattern of operating cash flows and earnings, but it does suggest that revenues should reflect cash inflows in a systematic manner and that expenses should likewise reflect operating cash outflows. One way to think about earnings is as a smoothing of cash flows. The cash flow statement makes the association between earnings and operating cash flows more apparent than it might be otherwise.

Cash flows from investing activities are also important. In order to grow, companies must generally invest in long-term assets. The cash flow statement provides information about asset replacements as well as investments in new assets. The difference between operating cash flows and investing cash flows is a measure of the extent to which the company is able to finance its growth internally.

Cash flows from financing activities show amounts raised externally from creditors and stockholders, net of repayments and dividends. Careful analysis of this section provides indications of the company's debt commitments and dependency of stockholders in obtaining the cash necessary to sustain operating and investing activities.

We will return to an analysis of the information contained in the cash flow statement in the next chapter. As is probably evident from reading this chapter, full understanding of the cash flow statement can be daunting. While the cash flow statement can be complex, an investment in understanding its information is worth the time for anyone with a serious interest in interpreting and using financial statements. The cash flow statement can be a useful tool to help filter the information provided in the balance sheet and income statement in order to get a more complete view of a company's past and future expected performance.

END OF CHAPTER MATERIAL

KEY TERMS

Articulate

Direct Method

Free Cash Flows

Indirect Method

ASSIGNMENT MATERIAL

REVIEW QUESTIONS

1. Discuss why it is important for firms to prepare a cash flow statement in addition to an income statement.

2. Discuss how a firm's receivables, inventory, and payables policies affect cash flow relative to the income produced in a given period.

3. What is meant by a lead/lag relationship in terms of the cash flow statement?

4. For a firm with a cash flow problem, list at least three potential reasons for the problem, and suggest a possible solution for each of these reasons.

5. Describe the three major categories of cash flows that are required to be disclosed by SFAS 95.

6. Discuss the difference between the direct and indirect (reconciliation) methods for constructing the operation section of the cash flow statement.

7. Depreciation is a source of cash. Explain your reasons for agreeing or disagreeing with this statement.

APPLYING YOUR KNOWLEDGE

8. In what section of the cash flow statement (operating, investing, or financing) would each of the following items appear?

   a. Purchase of net plant, property, and equipment

   b. Proceeds from a bank loan

   c. Collections from customers

   d. Dividends to stockholders

   e. Proceeds from the sale of marketable securities (stocks and bonds)

   f. Retirements of debt

   g. Change in accounts receivable

   h. Net income

   i. Gain/loss from the sale of plant, property, and equipment

   j. Cash proceeds from the sale of plant, property, and equipment

9. Explain why a high sales growth rate can create significant cash flow problems for a company.

10. Explain the timing of the cash flows related to the purchase, use, and ultimately the sale of property, plant, and equipment.

11. Discuss the classification of interest cash flows in the statement of cash flows under SFAS No. 95 and discuss why you believe this is either appropriate or not.

12. For each of the transactions listed below,

  a. Indicate the effect on balance sheet categories in the following format:

Trans. #	Cash	Other Current Assets	Noncurrent Assets	Current Liabilities	Noncurrent Liabilities	Owners' Equity

  b. State, for the transactions affecting cash, whether they relate to an operating, investing, or financing activity.

  Transactions:

  1. Credit purchases, $10,000

  2. Cash paid to suppliers, $8,000

  3. Credit sales, $25,000

  4. Cost of goods sold, $15,000

  5. Cash payments received on accounts receivable, $18,000

  6. Salaries accrued, $1,500

  7. Salaries paid (previously accrued), $1,000

  8. Machine purchased for $800 in cash

  9. Depreciation expense, $200

  10. Borrowed (long-term) $5,000 to purchase plant

  11. Interest of $50 is accrued and paid on the amount borrowed for the purchase of the plant

  12. Debentures worth $1,000 are issued

  13. Equipment having book value of $700 is sold for $700 cash

  14. Dividends declared, $350

  15. Dividends paid, $200

  16. Insurance premium for the next year paid, $175

  17. 1000 shares of stock issued at $1 per share

  18. Rent received for building, $250

  19. Income taxes accrued and paid, $325

13. For each of the transactions listed below,

  a. Indicate the effect on balance sheet categories in the following format:

Trans. #	Cash	Other Current Assets	Noncurrent Assets	Current Liabilities	Noncurrent Liabilities	Owners' Equity

  b. State, for the transactions affecting cash, whether they relate to an operating, investing, or financing activity.

  Transactions:

  1. 5,000 shares of common stock are issued at $10 per share.

  2. Plant, property, and equipment worth $120,000 is purchased for $50,000 in cash and the balance in common stock.

3. Rent payments of $5,000 are received in advance.

4. Sales contracts for $100,000 are signed and a $25,000 deposit is received in cash.

5. Merchandise inventory worth $85,000 is purchased on account.

6. Goods worth $15,000 were found defective and returned to suppliers. These goods had been purchased on account.

7. Sales were $175,000 of which $100,000 was on account.

8. Cash is paid to suppliers in the amount of $60,000.

9. Equipment recorded at $10,000 was destroyed by fire.

10. The company purchased 500 shares of X Company stock at $5 per share for short-term investment purposes.

11. The company purchased 2,000 shares of Z Company at $8 per share in an effort to buy a controlling interest in the company (a supplier).

12. Interest expense for the year amounted to $2,500 and was paid in cash.

13. The sales contract in question 4 was cancelled. $10,000 of the deposit was returned and the rest was forfeited.

14. A bank loan for $75,000 was taken out and is due in five years.

15. Equipment with a cost of $50,000 was sold for $60,000. The $60,000 was in the form of a note.

16. During the year, warranty services costing $3,500 were provided to customers. A provision for warranty services was provided in a separate transaction.

17. Depreciation for the year totaled $20,000.

18. Dividends of $10,000 were declared and $5,000 remained unpaid at year end.

19. Patents on a new manufacturing process were purchased for $5,000.

20. Research and development expenses amounted to $15,000 and were charged to expense as incurred.

14. Compute the cash flow from operations in each of the following cases:

	I	II	III
Sales Revenues	$25,000	$35,000	$65,000
Depreciation Expense	3,000	5,000	20,000
Cost of Goods Sold	15,000	38,000	41,000
Other Expenses	1,500	700	1,200
Dividends Paid	3,000	–	1,000
Increase (Decrease) in:			
Inventories	5,000	(10,000)	15,000
Accounts Receivable	3,500	1,000	(2,000)
Prepayments	(500)	(1,000)	1,800
Salaries Payable	(10,000)	5,000	(15,000)
Interest Payable	(5,000)	(500)	5,000
Other Current Liabilities	8,000	(10,000)	800

15. Compute the cash flow from operations in each of the following cases:

	I	II	III
Sales Revenues	$175,000	$200,000	$225,000
Cost of Goods Sold	100,000	185,000	195,000
Depreciation	20,000	15,000	10,000
Interest Expense	5,000	25,000	15,000
Dividends Paid	8,000	–	5,000
Profit (Loss) on Sale of PP&E	–	(10,000)	25,000
Increase (Decrease) in:			
Common Stock	10,000	5,000	–
Bonds Payable	20,000	(30,000)	(15,000)
Interest Payable	(25,000)	(5,000)	10,000
Accounts Payable	(25,000)	10,000	15,000
Accounts Receivable	50,000	(40,000)	35,000
Inventories	(10,000)	(15,000)	25,000
PP&E	100,000	(50,000)	–

16. Financial statement data for Dennison Corporation for 20X8 is as follows:

Dennison Corporation Comparative Balance Sheets	12/31/X7	12/31/X8
Assets		
Cash	$25,500	$4,400
Accounts Receivable	59,000	35,000
Inventories	30,000	50,000
Total Current Assets	114,500	89,400
Property, Plant, and Equipment	165,000	180,000
Accumulated Depreciation	(61,900)	(80,400)
Total Noncurrent Assets	103,100	99,600
Total Assets	$217,600	$189,000
Liabilities and Owners' Equity		
Accounts Payable	$38,600	$28,500
Salaries Payable	24,000	12,000
Total Current Liabilities	62,600	40,500
Bank Loan	50,000	40,000
Total Liabilities	112,600	80,500
Common Stock	100,000	100,000
Retained Earnings	5,000	8,500
Total Liabilities and Owners' Equity	$217,600	$189,000
Income Statement		
Sales		$185,500
Expenses:		
Cost of Goods Sold	87,500	
Salaries Expense	48,000	
Depreciation Expense	23,500	
Interest Expense	8,000	
Loss on Sale of PP&E	5,000	
Total Expenses		172,000
Net Income		$13,500

Additional Information:

1. Equipment originally costing $35,000 was sold for $25,000.

2. Dividends declared and paid during the year were $10,000.

Required:

Prepare a statement of cash flows for Dennison Corporation for the year ended 12/31/X8, supported by a T-account worksheet. Use the indirect approach to prepare the operating section.

17. Financial statement data for Matrix, Incorporated is as follows:

Matrix, Incorporated
Balance Sheets

	12/31/X3
Assets	
Cash	15,500
Accounts Receivable	10,000
Trade Notes Receivable	5,000
Inventories	20,500
Total Current Assets	51,000
Property, Plant, and Equipment	160,000
Accumulated Depreciation	(35,500)
Total Noncurrent Assets	124,500
Total Assets	$175,500
Liabilities and Owners' Equity	
Accounts Payable	5,000
Salaries Payable	18,000
Total Current Liabilities	23,000
Bonds Payable	50,000
Total Liabilities	73,000
Common Stock	100,000
Retained Earnings	2,500
Total Liabilities and Owners' Equity	$175,500

Matrix, Incorporated
Trial Balance for the Year
Ended 12/31/X4

	Debits	Credits
Cash	$2,900	
Accounts Receivable	12,500	
Prepaid Rent	6,000	
Inventories	18,900	
Cost of Goods Sold	275,500	
Depreciation Expense	10,000	
Rent Expense	12,000	
Interest Expense	15,000	
Salaries Expense	24,000	
Property, Plant, and Equipment	160,000	
Accumulated Depreciation		$ 45,500
Accounts Payable		13,800

	Debits	Credits
Interest Payable		9,000
Salaries Payable		6,000
Bonds Payable		10,000
Common Stock		100,000
Retained Earnings		2,500
Sales		350,000
Totals	$536,800	$536,800

Required:

a. Prepare an income statement and a reconciliation of retained earnings for the year ended 12/31/X4.

b. Prepare a balance sheet for the year ended 12/31/X4.

c. Prepare a statement of cash flows for the year ended 12/31/X4 supported by a T-account worksheet. Use the indirect approach to prepare the operating section.

18. The financial statement data for Crescent Manufacturing Company is as follows:

Crescent Manufacturing Company Comparative Balance Sheets	12/31/X0	12/31/X1
Assets		
Cash	17,800	12,800
Marketable Securities	125,000	25,000
Accounts Receivable	38,600	69,600
Prepaid Insurance	6,000	—
Inventories	43,300	93,300
Total Current Assets	230,700	200,700
Property, Plant, and Equipment	225,000	300,000
Accumulated Depreciation	(36,300)	(86,300)
Total Noncurrent Assets	188,700	213,700
Total Assets	$419,400	$414,400
Liabilities and Owners' Equity		
Accounts Payable	12,600	15,000
Interest Payable	8,000	5,600
Dividends Payable	20,000	30,000
Total Current Liabilities	40,600	50,600
Mortgage Payable	100,000	75,000
Bonds Payable	75,000	75,000
Total Liabilities	215,600	200,600
Common Stock	250,000	250,000
Treasury Stock	(50,000)	(60,000)
Retained Earnings	3,800	23,800
Total Owners' Equity	203,800	213,800
Total Liabilities and Owners' Equity	$419,400	$414,400

	12/31/X0	12/31/X1
Income Statement		
Sales	$508,000	
Interest Revenue	12,500	
Gain on Sale of Marketable Securities	25,000	
Total Revenues		$545,500
Expenses:		
Cost of Goods Sold	330,000	
Depreciation Expense	50,000	
Insurance Expense	12,000	
Interest Expense	43,500	
Salaries Expense	60,000	
Total Expenses		495,500
Net Income		$ 50,000

Additional Information:

1. 10,000 shares of Sigma Company, which were purchased at a cost of $10 per share, were sold at a price of $12.50 per share.

2. Dividends declared during the year amounted to $30,000 and remained unpaid at year end.

Required:

Prepare a statement of cash flows for Crescent Manufacturing Company for the year ended 12/31/X1 supported by a T-account worksheet. Use the indirect method to prepare the operation section.

19. The Balance Sheet for Simco Corporation as of the beginning and the end of the 20X1 appears below. During the year, no dividends were declared or paid, there was no sale of PP&E and no debt repaid. Net Income for the period was $35,000 and included $25,000 in depreciation expenses. Prepare a statement of cash flows for Simco Corporation for the current year and also prepare a T-account worksheet supporting the cash flow statement. Use the cash reconciliation approach.

SIMCO CORPORATION
Balance Sheet

	12/31/X0	12/31/X1
Assets		
Current Assets		
Cash	$ 10,000	$ 8,000
Accounts Receivable	86,000	100,000
Inventories	102,000	112,000
Total Current Assets	198,000	220,000
Property, Plant, and Equipment	485,000	600,000
Less: Accumulated Depreciation	125,000	150,000
Total PP&E	360,000	450,000
Total Assets	$558,000	$670,000

	12/31/X0	12/31/X1
Liabilities and Owners' Equity		
Current Liabilities		
Accounts Payable	$ 78,000	$ 95,000
Wages Payable	30,000	40,000
Total Current Liabilities	108,000	135,000
Long-Term Debt		
Bonds Payable	100,000	125,000
Total Liabilities	208,000	260,000
Owners' Equity		
Common Stock	150,000	175,000
Retained Earnings	200,000	235,000
Total Liabilities and Owners' Equity	$558,000	$670,000

20. Comparative Balance Sheets of Marvel Cosmetics Company for 20X2 are as follows:

MARVEL COSMETICS COMPANY
Comparative Balance Sheet

	12/31/X1	12/31/X2
Assets		
Current Assets		
Cash	$ 188,000	$ 200,000
Accounts Receivable	133,000	120,000
Trade Notes Receivable	61,000	70,000
Inventory	326,000	439,000
Total Current Assets	708,000	829,000
Noncurrent Assets		
Land	500,000	525,000
Machinery	238,000	483,000
Accumulated Depreciation	(97,500)	(143,000)
Total Noncurrent Assets	640,500	865,000
Total Assets	$1,348,500	$1,694,000
Liabilities and Owners' Equity		
Current Liabilities		
Accounts Payable	$ 158,000	$ 145,000
Interest Payable	10,000	17,500
Total Current Liabilities	168,000	162,500
Noncurrent Liabilities		
Debentures	200,000	350,000
Total Liabilities	368,000	512,500
Owners' Equity		
Common Stock	550,000	650,000
Retained Earnings	430,500	531,500
Total Owners' Equity	980,500	1,180,500
Total Liabilities and Owners' Equity	$1,348,500	$1,694,000

Additional Information:

a. Net Income is $151,000 and includes depreciation expenses of $105,500.

b. Dividends declared and paid during the year were $50,000.

c. A machine costing $80,000 was sold at its book value of $20,000.

d. There was no Repayment of long-term debt.

Prepare a Statement of Cash Flows for Marvel Cosmetics Company for the year ended 12/31/X2, supported by a T-account worksheet.

21. The financial statement data for Pharmex Pharmaceutical Company for 20X5 is as follows:

PHARMEX PHARMACEUTICAL COMPANY		
	12/31/X4	12/31/X5
Comparative Data		
Debits		
Cash	80,000	50,000
Accounts Receivable	185,000	235,000
Inventories	296,000	325,000
Machinery	545,000	555,000
Total	1,106,000	1,165,000
Credits		
Accumulated Depreciation	122,500	172,500
Accounts Payable	97,500	82,500
Bonds Payable	150,000	175,000
Common Stock	350,000	400,000
Retained Earnings	386,000	335,000
Total	1,106,000	1,165,000
Income Statement Data		
Sales		1,052,000
Gain on Sale of PP&E		15,000
Cost of Goods Sold		878,000
Depreciation Expense		75,000
Interest Expenses		60,000
Rent Expense		85,000

Additional Information:

Acquisition cost of new machinery is $135,000. Old machinery having an original cost of $125,000 was sold at a gain of $15,000. Dividends of $20,000 were declared and paid.

a. Prepare an income statement including a reconciliation of retained earnings for the year ended 12/31/X5.

b. Prepare a statement of cash flows for Pharmex Pharmaceuticals Company for the year ended 12/31/X5 supported by a T-account work sheet.

22. From the perspective of a bank loan officer, discuss why the cash flow statement may or may not be more important in your analysis of a company that is applying for a loan.

23. From the perspective of a stock analyst, discuss why the cash flow statement may or may not be more important in your analysis of a company for which you must make a recommendation.

USING REAL DATA

24. Use the data in the cash flow statement for Amazon.Com, Inc. to answer the questions that follow.

Amazon.com, Inc. Consolidated Statements of Cash Flows (in thousands) Years Ended December 31,	2001	2000	1999
Cash and cash equivalents, beginning of period	$822,435	$ 133,309	$ 71,583
Net loss	(567,277)	(1,411,273)	(719,968)
Adjustments to reconcile net loss to net cash used in operating activities:			
Depreciation of fixed assets and other amortization	84,709	84,460	36,806
Stock-based compensation	4,637	24,797	30,618
Equity in losses of equity-method investees, net	30,327	304,596	76,769
Amortization of goodwill and other intangibles	181,033	321,772	214,694
Noncash restructuring-related and other	73,293	200,311	8,072
Loss (gain) on sale of marketable securities, net	(1,335)	(280)	8,688
Other losses (gains), net	2,141	142,639	–
Noncash interest expense and other	26,629	24,766	29,171
Cumulative effect of change in accounting principle	10,523	–	–
Changes in operating assets and liabilities:			
Inventories	30,628	46,083	(172,069)
Prepaid expenses and other current assets	20,732	(8,585)	(54,927)
Accounts payable	(44,438)	22,357	330,166
Accrued expenses and other current liabilities	50,031	93,967	95,839
Unearned revenue	114,738	97,818	6,225
Amortization of previously unearned revenue	(135,808)	(108,211)	(5,837)
Interest payable	(345)	34,341	24,878
Net cash used in operating activities	(119,782)	(130,442)	(90,875)
Investing Activities:			
Sales and maturities of marketable securities	370,377	545,724	2,064,101
Purchases of marketable securities	(567,152)	(184,455)	(2,359,398)
Purchases of fixed assets, including internal use software and web-site development	(50,321)	(134,758)	(287,055)

	2001	2000	1999
Investments in equity-method investees and other investments	(6,198)	(62,533)	(369,607)
Net cash provided by (used in) investing activities	(253,294)	163,978	(951,959)
Financing Activities:			
Proceeds from exercise of stock options and other	16,625	44,697	64,469
Proceeds from issuance of common stock, net of issuance costs	99,831	–	–
Proceeds from long-term debt and other	10,000	681,499	1,263,639
Repayment of long-term debt and other	(19,575)	(16,927)	(188,886)
Financing costs	–	(16,122)	(35,151)
Net cash provided by financing activities	106,881	693,147	1,104,071
Effect of exchange-rate changes on cash and cash equivalents	(15,958)	(37,557)	489
Net increase (decrease) in cash and cash equivalents	(282,153)	689,126	61,726
Cash and cash Equivalents, end of period	$540,282	$ 822,435	$ 133,309
Supplemental cash flow information:			
Fixed assets acquired under capital leases	$ 4,597	$ 4,459	$ 25,850
Fixed assets acquired under financing agreements	1,000	4,844	5,608
Equity securities received for commerical agreements	331	106,848	54,402
Stock issued in connection with business acquisitions and minority investments	5,000	32,130	774,409
Cash paid for interest	112,184	67,252	30,526

a. Why is net cash provided by operating activities less negative than net income for the three years presented?

b. What specific items contributed most to the greater net loss in 2000 than in the other two years?

c. How were investment activities in 1999 financed?

d. What trend do you observe for debt and related cash paid for interest over the three years presented?

e. What general concerns do you have about the future operating activities of the company based on your review of the cash flow statement for the three years presented?

25. Use the data in the cash flow statement for Barnes Group, Inc. to answer the questions that follow.

BARNES GROUP, Inc.: Cash Flow

	12/31/2001	12/31/2000	12/31/1999
Operating activities:			
Net income	$19,121,000	$35,665,000	$28,612,000
Adjustments to reconcile net income to net cash provided by operating activities:			
Depreciation and amortization	37,045,000	35,871,000	30,602,000
Loss (gain) on disposition of property, plant, and equipment	2,093,000	(1,960,000)	(857,000)
Changes in assets and liabilities:			
Accounts receivable	11,378,000	1,087,000	(1,731,000)
Inventories	(3,629,000)	(7,631,000)	1,980,000
Accounts payable	13,634,000	(5,415,000)	17,356,000
Accrued liabilities	(5,552,000)	1,026,000	(9,524,000)
Deferred income taxes	6,510,000	5,863,000	3,655,000
Other	(13,700,000)	(12,649,000)	(7,296,000)
Net cash provided by operating activities	66,900,000	51,857,000	62,797,000
Investing activities:			
Proceeds from disposition of property, plant, and equipment	1,093,000	2,744,000	1,929,000
Capital expenditures	(22,365,000)	(26,575,000)	(27,222,000)
Business acquisitions, net of cash acquired	(1,036,000)	(104,935,000)	(92,239,000)
Redemption of short-term investments	–	–	2,566,000
Other	(4,286,000)	(5,776,000)	(2,019,000)
Net cash used by investing activities	(26,594,000)	(134,542,000)	(116,985,000)
Financing activities:			
Net (decrease) increase in notes payable	(1,583,000)	(5,201,000)	5,249,000
Payments on long-term debt	(28,000,000)	(60,000,000)	(70,000,000)
Proceeds from the issuance of long-term debt	22,765,000	150,000,000	159,000,000
Proceeds from the issuance of common stock	2,845,000	3,920,000	1,486,000
Common stock repurchases	(8,798,000)	(9,197,000)	(22,351,000)
Dividends paid	(14,806,000)	(14,677,000)	(14,564,000)
Proceeds from the sale of debt swap	13,766,000	–	–
Net cash (used) provided by financing activities	(13,811,000)	64,845,000	58,820,000
Effect of exchange rate changes on cash flows	(930,000)	(2,489,000)	(1,206,000)
Increase (decrease) in cash and cash equivalents	25,565,000	(20,329,000)	3,426,000
Cash and cash equivalents at beginning of year	23,303,000	43,632,000	40,206,000
Cash and cash equivalents at end of year	$48,868,000	$23,303,000	$43,632,000

a. What changes in assets and liabilities contributed most to the increase in net cash provided by operating activities in 2001 over that in 2000?

b. How were business acquisitions financed in 1999 and 2000?

c. What changes in financing activities do you observe in 2001 by comparison to the two previous years?

d. What is your general assessment of the company's ability to finance its investing activities from operating cash flows beyond 2001?

26. Use the data in the cash flow statement for GAP, Inc. to answer the questions that follow.

GAP, Inc.: Cash Flow	52 Weeks Ended Feb. 2, 2002	53 Weeks Ended Feb. 3, 2001	52 Weeks Ended Jan. 29, 2000
Cash flows from operating activities:			
Net earnings (loss)	$ (7,764,000)	$877,497,000	$1,127,065,000
Adjustments to reconcile net earnings (loss) to net cash provided by operating activities:			
Depreciation and amortization	810,486,000	590,365,000	436,184,000
Tax benefit from exercise of stock options and vesting of restricted stock	58,444,000	130,882,000	211,891,000
Deferred income taxes	(28,512,000)	(38,872,000)	2,444,000
Change in operating assets and liabilities:			
Merchandise inventory	213,067,000	(454,595,000)	(404,211,000)
Prepaid expenses and other	(13,303,000)	(61,096,000)	(55,519,000)
Accounts payable	42,205,000	249,545,000	118,121,000
Accrued expenses	220,826,000	(56,541,000)	(5,822,000)
Deferred lease credits and other long-term liabilities	22,390,000	54,020,000	47,775,000
Net cash provided by operating activities	1,317,839,000	1,291,205,000	1,477,928,000
Cash flows from investing activities:			
Net purchase of property and equipment	(940,078,000)	(1,858,662,000)	(1,238,722,000)
Acquisition of lease rights and other assets	(10,549,000)	(16,252,000)	(39,839,000)
Net cash used for investing activities	(950,627,000)	(1,874,914,000)	(1,278,561,000)
Cash Flows from financing activities:			
Net increase (decrease) in notes payable	(734,927,000)	621,420,000	84,778,000
Proceeds from issuance of long-term debt	1,194,265,000	250,000,000	311,839,000
Payments of long-term debt	(250,000,000)	–	–
Issuance of common stock	139,105,000	152,105,000	114,142,000
Net purchase of treasury stock	(785,000)	(392,558,000)	(745,056,000)
Cash dividends paid	(76,373,000)	(75,488,000)	(75,795,000)
Net cash provided by (used for) financing activities	271,285,000	555,479,000	(310,092,000)
Effect of exchange rate fluctuations on cash	(11,542,000)	(13,328,000)	(4,176,000)
Net increase (decrease) in cash and equivalents	626,955,000	(41,558,000)	(114,901,000)
Cash and equivalents at beginning of year	408,794,000	450,352,000	565,253,000
Cash and equivalents at end of year	$1,035,749,000	$408,794,000	$ 450,352,000

a. What trend do you observe in net income for the three years presented?

b. Why does net cash provided by operating activities not display the same trend as noted in your answer to a.?

c. What other information from the cash flow statements can be used to explain the substantial increase in depreciation and amortization from 2001 to 2002?

d. How would you describe the events pertaining to debt that occurred in 2002?

27. Use the data in the cash flow statement for Polaroid Corporation to answer the questions that follow.

POLAROID CORP.: Cash Flow	12/31/1998	12/31/1999	12/31/2000
Cash flows from operating activities:			
Net earnings/(loss)	$ (51,000,000)	$ 8,700,000	$37,700,000
Depreciation of property, plant, and equipment	90,700,000	105,900,000	113,900,000
Gain on the sale of real estate	(68,200,000)	(11,700,000)	(21,800,000)
Other noncash items	62,200,000	73,800,000	22,900,000
Decrease/(increase) in receivables	79,000,000	(52,700,000)	41,800,000
Decrease/(increase) in inventories	(28,400,000)	88,000,000	(100,600,000)
Decrease in prepaids and other assets	39,000,000	62,400,000	32,900,000
Increase/(decrease) in payables and accruals	25,300,000	(16,500,000)	9,200,000
Decrease in compensation and benefits	(21,000,000)	(72,500,000)	(105,000,000)
Decrease in federal, state, and foreign income taxes payable	(29,900,000)	(54,000,000)	(31,500,000)
Net cash provided/(used) by operating activities	97,700,000	131,400,000	(500,000)
Cash flows from investing activities:			
Decrease/(increase) in other assets	(25,400,000)	16,500,000	4,500,000
Additions to property, plant, and equipment	(191,100,000)	(170,500,000)	(129,200,000)
Proceeds from the sale of property, plant, and equipment	150,500,000	36,600,000	56,600,000
Acquisitions, net of cash acquired	(18,800,000)	–	–
Net cash used by investing activities	(84,800,000)	(117,400,000)	(68,100,000)
Cash flows from financing activities:			
Net increase/(decrease) in short-term debt (maturities 90 days or less)	131,200,000	(86,200,000)	108,200,000
Short-term debt (maturities of more than 90 days)			
Proceeds	73,000,000	41,800,000	–
Payments	(117,200,000)	(24,900,000)	–
Proceeds from issuance of long-term debt	–	268,200,000	–
Repayment of long-term debt	–	(200,000,000)	–
Cash dividends paid	(26,500,000)	(26,600,000)	(27,000,000)
Purchase of treasury stock	(45,500,000)	–	–
Proceeds from issuance of shares in connection with stock incentive plan	6,000,000	300,000	100,000
Net cash provided/(used) by financing activities	21,000,000	(27,400,000)	81,300,000
Effect of exchange rate changes on cash	3,100,000	400,000	(7,500,000)
Net increase/(decrease) in cash and cash equivalents	37,000,000	(13,000,000)	5,200,000
Cash and cash equivalents at beginning of year	68,000,000	105,000,000	92,000,000
Cash and cash equivalents at end of year	$105,000,000	$92,000,000	$97,200,000

a. Why is the upward trend in net earnings/(loss) not reflected in net cash provided/(used) by operating activities for the three years presented?

b. How were net additions to property, plant, and equipment in 2000 principally financed?

c. What would be a reasonable estimate of the change in property, plant, and equipment during 2000?

d. What indications are there that the company will need to seek external financing in 2001?

28. Use the data in the cash flow statement for Tech Data Corporation to answer the questions that follow.

TECH DATA CORP.: Cash Flow

	01/31/2002	01/31/2001	01/31/2000
Cash flows from operating activities:			
Cash received from customers	$17,511,511,000	$20,114,486,000	$16,788,960,000
Cash paid to suppliers and employees	(16,406,265,000)	(20,047,551,000)	(16,684,316,000)
Interest paid	(55,871,000)	(94,823,000)	(69,554,000)
Income taxes paid	(72,745,000)	(62,048,000)	(34,176,000)
Net cash provided by (used in) operating activities	976,630,000	(89,936,000)	914,000
Cash flows from investing activities:			
Acquisition of businesses, net of cash acquired	(183,000)	(19,198,000)	(42,898,000)
Expenditures for property and equipment	(28,466,000)	(38,079,000)	(59,038,000)
Software development costs	(20,719,000)	(22,705,000)	(18,381,000)
Net cash used in investing activities	(49,368,000)	(79,982,000)	(120,317,000)
Cash flows from financing activities:			
Proceeds from the issuance of common stock, net of related tax benefit	36,432,000	35,539,000	19,663,000
Net (repayments) borrowings on revolving credit loans	(1,118,167,000)	248,712,000	99,447,000
Proceeds from issuance of long-term debt, net of expense	284,200,000	–	–
Principal payments on long-term debt	(634,000)	(557,000)	(162,000)
Net cash (used in) provided by financing activities	(798,169,000)	283,694,000	118,948,000
Effect of change in year end of certain subsidiaries (Note 3)	–	–	23,626,000
Effect of exchange rate changes on cash	(10,091,000)	(6,637,000)	–
Net increase in cash and cash equivalents	119,002,000	107,139,000	23,171,000
Cash and cash equivalents at beginning of year	138,925,000	31,786,000	8,615,000
Cash and cash equivalents at end of year	$ 257,927,000	$ 138,925,000	$ 31,786,000

TECH DATA CORP.: Cash Flow

	01/31/2002	01/31/2001	01/31/2000
Reconciliation of net income to net cash provided by (used in) operating activities:			
Net income	$ 110,777,000	$177,983,000	$127,501,000
Adjustments to reconcile net income to net cash provided by (used in) operating activities:			
Depreciation and amortization	63,488,000	63,922,000	57,842,000
Provision for losses on accounts receivable	40,764,000	41,447,000	40,877,000

	01/31/2002	01/31/2001	01/31/2000
Special charges (Note 13)	27,000,000	–	–
Deferred income taxes	(11,848,000)	(1,789,000)	1,306,000
Changes in assets and liabilities:			
Decrease (increase) in accounts receivable	314,000,000	(313,197,000)	(202,790,000)
Decrease (increase) in inventories	702,219,000	(146,093,000)	(220,585,000)
(Increase) in prepaid and other assets	(6,248,000)	(11,603,000)	(25,430,000)
(Decrease) increase in accounts payable	(264,722,000)	11,863,000	136,748,000
Increase in accrued expenses	1,200,000	87,531,000	85,445,000
Total adjustments	865,853,000	(267,919,000)	(126,587,000)
Net cash provided by (used in) operating activities	$976,630,000	$ (89,936,000)	$ 914,000

a. How does the format of the cash flow statements for this company differ from the format used by most companies?

b. What changes do you note in the reconciliation of net income to net cash provided by (used in) operating activities that most explain the dramatic increase in net cash provided by those activities?

c. How did the company finance its investing activities in 2000 and 2001?

d. Where were the funds obtained to repay borrowings on revolving credit loans in 2002?

e. What evidence is there that the company has reversed its growth during 2002 from what it was during the previous two years?

BEYOND THE BOOK

29. For a company of your own choosing, answer the following questions related to its cash flow statement:

a. What is the trend in net income for the three years presented?

b. What is the trend in cash from operations for the three years presented?

c. In the most recent year, explain why the cash from operations differs from net income.

d. What other cash needs did the firm have in the most recent time period outside of operations?

e. Where did the company get the cash to cover the needs identified in part (d)?

f. What concerns do you have about the financial health of the company from your analysis of the cash flow statement?

Financial Statement Analysis

After studying this chapter students should be able to:

1 Understand how to adjust financial statements to give effect to differences in accounting methods.

2 Be able to calculate and interpret common financial ratios.

3 Evaluate a firm's short-term and long-term debt repayment abilities and its profitability.

4 Have a basic understanding of methods of forecasting future revenues or earnings.

5 Understand the concept of present value and its application to valuing free cash flows and residual earnings.

In late 2001 Starbucks Corp. announced that it had beat analysts' expectations and reported a first quarter profit (for the quarter ended September 30, 2001) of 25 cents a share. The analysts' previous estimate was 23 cents a share. In the same announcement Starbucks also reported record revenues of $667 million, up 26 percent from $529 million in the same period a year ago. Earnings were $49 million, up 41% over the same period a year ago of $34.7 million. Starbucks also indicated that it had raised its own projections of the year's fiscal earnings by a penny per share.

Despite the very sizeable increase in revenues and earnings over the previous year for Starbucks, note that analysts' forecasts nearly matched Starbucks' reported amounts and thus we would expect very little adjustment to Starbucks' market value as a result of this disclosure. The prominence of revenues in this earnings release is consistent with analysts viewing changes in revenues as a measure of growth and, hence, as a key factor in forecasting future performance.

In virtually all cases, financial statement users are concerned with predicting future outcomes of a firm. However, these forecasts usually begin with an assessment of the firm's *past performance.* In this chapter, we'll show you how financial statement analysis provides this link from evaluating past performance to forecasting future expectations.

OVERVIEW OF FINANCIAL STATEMENT ANALYSIS

Financial statement analysis refers to a set of procedures for transforming past data from a firm's published financial statements into information useful for future decisions. Many different types of decisions are based on financial statement analysis, such as whether to extend credit, buy or sell securities, or reward managers for their performance.

Financial statement analysis typically involves making **inter-temporal** (across time) and **cross-sectional** (across firms) comparisons. Inter-temporal comparisons help to identify trends in past data as well as reveal areas of concern that may warrant special attention. Cross-sectional comparisons (of a firm with its main rivals) indicate relative performance that may have a bearing on future market share. One complication in making both types of comparisons using raw financial statement data is the effect of changes or differences in firm size. For instance, if we were analyzing the pizza business and wanted to compare Domino's, Sbarro, and Bertucci's, they are very different in size with revenues of $1,275 million, $360 million, and $162 million, respectively. Analysts commonly adjust for such differences by using financial ratios in making these comparisons.

Another complication is that accounting policies may vary across time or across firms. When this occurs, analysts may need to adjust for these variations by restating financial statements in order to place them on a common basis. Such restatements answer the question of what the firm's financial statements would look like "as if" they had been prepared under the same set of accounting policies.

Once analysts transform the data into ratios and understand the trends that may be present, they next assess future prospects by constructing **operating forecasts,** for example, the forecast of net income from operations. A formal approach to forecasting extrapolates past operating data through statistical models that take advantage of inter-temporal relationships present in that data (these models are often called *time-series models*). Less formal approaches rely more on analysts' subjective judgments of future trends. Regardless of the approach used, operating forecasts should factor in the outlook for the industry and the economy as a whole, the company's business plan, and the nature of competition.

	02/01/2003	02/01/2002	02/01/2001
Net sales	$1,380,966,000	$1,299,573,000	$1,232,776,000
Cost of sales	633,473,000	651,808,000	622,036,000
Gross margin	747,493,000	647,765,000	610,740,000
Selling, general, and administrative expenses	612,479,000	576,584,000	501,460,000
Amortization of goodwill	–	11,040,000	11,040,000
Operating income	135,014,000	60,141,000	98,240,000
Interest income	3,279,000	1,390,000	2,473,000
Interest expense	6,886,000	6,869,000	7,315,000
Income before income taxes	131,407,000	54,662,000	93,398,000
Income tax provision	51,249,000	25,557,000	41,035,000
Net income	$ 80,158,000	$ 29,105,000	$ 52,363,000

Exhibit 6.1
Consolidated Statements of Income

THE REAL WORLD

AnnTaylor Stores Corporation

We're now ready to take a closer look at financial statement analysis. We'll use the data from AnnTaylor Stores Corporation (see Exhibits 6.1 and 6.2) to illustrate the process of financial statement analysis. Our first step is to review the financial statements to determine if they need to be restated.

CREATING COMPARABLE DATA FOR FINANCIAL STATEMENT ANALYSIS

Analysts must often consider how a firm's financial statements would appear if it used a different accounting method. For example, analysts may seek to undo the effects of overly aggressive income recognition ("as if" restatements), assess the effects of an impending change in accounting policy, or compare the performance of firms that employ different accounting methods. These adjustments can be quite complex in some situations. A full understanding of restatements requires a level of understanding of accounting that is beyond the scope of this book. However, a basic knowledge of accounting is sufficient to understand the idea of restatements and how to make basic restatements. Here we provide examples of some common restatements. Let's review how analysts create comparable data for each of these situations.

"AS IF" RESTATEMENTS

A useful technique in restating revenues, expenses, or income is to determine first how balances of related accounts appearing on comparative balance sheets would be affected; then, adjust the item in question by the change in the difference between the beginning and ending balances. For example, suppose a company recognized revenue for sales of goods or services at the time of delivery, despite considerable uncertainty about future collections from customers. Analysts determine the effect on the company's revenues, if it

Exhibit 6.2
Consolidated Balance Sheets

THE REAL WORLD

AnnTaylor Stores Corporation

	02/01/2003	02/01/2002
Current assets:		
Cash and cash equivalents	$ 212,821,000	$ 30,037,000
Accounts receivable, net	10,367,000	65,598,000
Merchandise inventories	185,484,000	180,117,000
Prepaid expenses and other current assets	46,599,000	50,314,000
Total current assets	455,271,000	326,066,000
Property and equipment, net	247,115,000	250,735,000
Goodwill, net	286,579,000	286,579,000
Deferred financing costs, net	4,170,000	5,044,000
Other assets	17,691,000	14,742,000
Total assets	$1,010,826,000	$883,166,000
Liabilities and stockholders' equity:		
Current liabilities		
Accounts payable	$ 57,058,000	$ 52,011,000
Accrued salaries and bonus	27,567,000	12,121,000
Accrued tenancy	10,808,000	10,151,000
Gift certificates and merchandise credits redeemable	25,637,000	21,828,000
Accrued expenses	30,125,000	37,907,000
Current portion of long-term debt		1,250,000
Total current liabilities	151,195,000	135,268,000
Long-term debt, net	121,652,000	118,280,000
Deferred lease costs and other liabilities	23,561,000	17,489,000
Stockholders' equity common stock, $.0068 par value; 120,000,000 shares authorized; 48,932,860 and 48,275,957 shares issued, respectively	332,000	328,000
Additional paid-in capital	500,061,000	484,582,000
Retained earnings	296,113,000	218,600,000
Deferred compensation on restricted stock	(3,968,000)	(9,296,000)
	792,538,000	694,214,000
Treasury stock, 4,050,972 and 4,210,232 shares, respectively, at cost	(78,120,000)	(82,085,000)
Total stockholders' equity	714,418,000	612,129,000
Total liabilities and stockholders' equity	$1,010,826,000	$883,166,000

adopted the less-aggressive procedure of delaying recognition until cash was received, as follows:

Revenue (as if recognized at time of collection) =
Revenue (as Reported) + Decrease (−Increase) in Accounts Receivable

Consider the data from AnnTaylor. From Exhibit 6.1 we find reported revenues of $1,381.0 (all numbers in millions, rounded to the nearest hundred thousand). From Exhibit 6.2, we compute a decrease in accounts receivable of $55.2 ($10.4 − $65.6). Thus, if AnnTaylor recognized revenue as it collected cash from customers, revenues would equal $1,436.2 ($1,381.0 + $55.2).

Inventories provide another illustration. Different firms often value inventories under different methods, such as the "first-in, first-out" (FIFO) and "last-in, first-out" (LIFO) methods. For instance, Ford Motor Company uses LIFO, whereas Dell Computer uses FIFO. As discussed in more detail in Chapter 8, LIFO usually results in higher costs of goods sold and lower inventory levels on the balance sheet than FIFO. However, GAAP requires firms that apply the LIFO method to include a disclosure explaining the net difference in inventory values as a result of applying these two methods. Firms often report this difference, known as the LIFO reserve, in a footnote. Using these data, you can calculate what the cost of goods sold would have been under FIFO using the following calculation:

> Cost of goods sold (as if FIFO had been used) =
> Cost of goods sold (as reported, LIFO) + Decrease (−Increase) in LIFO Reserve

One last illustration of the adjustment process relates to a company's accounting treatment of warranty expenses. Most companies, for example Ford Motor Company, recognize warranty costs (on an estimated basis) as expenses at the time of sale rather than when paid. Suppose, however, that an analyst wants to determine a company's warranty settlement cost. In this case, we adjust the expense under the former treatment to determine the amount of claims settled as follows:

> Warranty Expense (as if recorded when settled) =
> Warranty Expense (as reported) + Decrease (−Increase) in Warranties Payable

THINKING GLOBALLY

International Accounting Issues

Because countries employ different accounting standards, analysts frequently need to make adjustments before conducting a cross-sectional analysis across countries. For example, Canadian companies selectively capitalize (record as assets) research and development (R&D) costs at the time these costs are incurred, while U.S. companies are required by GAAP to write off (record as expenses) those costs immediately.

If research and development (R&D) costs were initially recorded as an asset (as they might be under Canadian standards) and subsequently amortized as an expense, then one could calculate what R&D expense would be reported under the U.S. policy (which requires immediate recognition as an expense when the expenditures are made) as shown below:

> R&D Expense (U.S.) = R&D Amortization Expense (Canadian)
> + Increase (−Decrease) in Unamortized R&D Costs (Canadian)

Note that adjustments made to the income statement might also affect the calculation of income taxes, and therefore all as-if adjustments should also include adjustments for the tax effects.

Note that all of these adjustments focus on the income statement. In each case, however, to maintain the accounting equation, an impact also occurs on the balance sheet through an adjustment of an asset or a liability account. Further, because these adjustments affect net income, a change also occurs in retained earnings. For example, if a company begins accruing an expense that it previously recognized only when paid, then the balance in accrued liabilities increases, expenses on the income statement also increase, and the balance in retained earnings decreases by the reduction in net income.

Finally, note that some changes in the timing of revenue and expense recognition materially affect only the balance sheet. For example, as mentioned, Canadian companies are allowed to capitalize (record as an asset) some research and development (R&D) costs and then later amortize the costs to income. Suppose that a particular Canadian company capitalized costs in an amount equal to its amortization expense in the year you are analyzing. If you were to adjust the statements to conform to U.S. GAAP (where the firm must expense all R&D as incurred), the adjusted expense would be the same as the original expense and therefore there would be no effect of this adjustment on the income statement. However, the balance sheets would still differ as both assets and retained earnings would be lower if no R&D costs had ever been capitalized. In other words, balance sheet restatements reflect the cumulative effects (the effects of applying the new method in all prior years) of differences in accounting methods, whereas income statement restatements reflect only the current year effect.

MANDATED ACCOUNTING CHANGES

Accounting rule changes by the FASB and the SEC frequently occur. Accordingly, analysts need to be aware of the consequences of these changes on the financial statements. However, analysts are assisted with this task as follows:

- The FASB and the SEC typically specify how firms must handle these mandated changes within the financial statements.
- Firms usually document these changes in the footnotes of the financial statements in the period in which the change is made.
- The FASB and the SEC often require that firms also restate past financial statements to give effect to the mandated change in question.
- In some cases, these changes require that the cumulative effects on income of applying the new rules be shown as a separate line item in the income statement for the year in which the change is made.
- Auditors call attention to accounting rule changes in their report to stockholders.

Hence, a question seldom arises as to whether a change has occurred.

The greater challenge for analysts in dealing with mandated accounting changes is to evaluate the economic consequences of the change. For example, suppose a firm previously issued debt containing a covenant (a contractual restriction) that requires net worth (stockholders' equity) determined under GAAP to stay above a specified level. Now suppose that the FASB changes a rule governing revenue recognition, with the result of reducing the firm's net income to the point where it violates the covenant. To avoid this, the firm might have to cut its dividend. This might cause the value of the company's stock to fall due to an increase in risk, because of the reduction of cash flows (dividends) to shareholders.

Another consequence of a change to a more conservative method of revenue recognition might be to alter the incentives (often earnings-based bonuses) to managers provided by compensation contracts. For example, consider an executive who receives a bonus if reported income exceeds a certain level. If the accounting change makes it highly unlikely that this level will be reached in the year of change, no matter how much effort the executive applies, he or she may decide to postpone initiatives until the following year when it is more likely that he or she would receive the bonus. This reduced effort may negatively affect firm value.

DISCRETIONARY ACCOUNTING CHANGES

Within the GAAP framework, managers have considerable discretion in their choices of accounting treatments. Further, evidence suggests that managers make use of their discretion in responding to incentives and furthering the interests of shareholders (when their incentives are aligned). Beyond the consideration of the comparability of the data that result when the change occurs, the bigger issues for analysts are the motivation of the firm's management and the potential for significant economic consequences.

For example, consider firms in an industry that seeks trade relief. These firms must show they have been injured by the anticompetitive practices of foreign rivals. Managers in these companies would have an incentive to make accounting decisions that lower their reported income, in order to demonstrate such injury. Evidence (Lenway and Rayburn, *Contemporary Accounting Research,* 1992) does indicate that in the mid-1980s, U.S. semiconductor producers generally had higher negative accruals coincident with petitions alleging dumping by Japanese producers.

Accounting treatments may also influence real investment and financing decisions. For example, firms generally do not recognize changes in the market value of debt (sometimes referred to as unrealized holding gains and losses) that result when interest rates in the economy change. However, a company seeking to increase or decrease its reported income for reasons mentioned above might decide to retire its debt early, causing the recognition of the gain or loss.

Finally, note that accounting decisions might serve as signaling devices, whereby a firm may be able to persuade investors that it has more favorable future cash flow prospects. For example, as we will see in Chapter 8, if a firm uses the LIFO method of valuing inventories for tax purposes, it must also use this same method for reporting to its shareholders (in periods of rising prices, LIFO results in lower reported net income and therefore lower tax payments). Theorists suggest that firms choosing to forego the tax benefits of LIFO by using FIFO for reporting purposes (and hence for tax purposes) may be signaling that they have stronger cash flow prospects than comparable firms that use LIFO.

Once analysts complete reviewing a firm's financial statements, and restating as necessary, calculating ratios can lead to more meaningful information. In the next section, we'll see how to use ratios to analyze a firm's past performance, which is the next step in financial statement analysis.

> Firms using LIFO could mimic the firms with stronger cash flow prospects by also choosing FIFO. However, they may find the loss of tax benefits to outweigh the benefits of not having investors learn that they have weaker cash flow prospects.

USING FINANCIAL RATIOS TO ASSESS PAST PERFORMANCE

To assess a firm's past performance from periodic financial statements, analysts must first adjust the contents for inter-temporal changes or cross-sectional variations in firm size. For example, it does not mean much when assessing operating efficiency to compare income either over time for a firm that is changing in size or between small and large firms. Analysts remove effects of scale (size) by employing financial ratios. Financial ratios are often broadly organized into those that assess profitability and those that assess debt-repayment ability.

ASSESSING PROFITABILITY

From an investor's perspective, **rate of return on equity (ROE)** presents a comprehensive accounting measure of a firm's performance. For a company with only common stock outstanding (we consider other types of stock in Chapter 12), we determine ROE as follows:

$$\text{ROE} = \frac{\text{Net Income}}{\text{Average Stockholders' Equity}}$$

Because a firm earns net income over a period of time, the denominator of this ratio also reflects the level of stockholders' investment over this same period of time. Hence, it makes sense to calculate the average amount invested during the period in the denominator. Most analysts compute the average as simply the sum of the beginning and ending balances of stockholders' equity, divided by two. The implicit assumption in this computation is that the change in balances remained uniform over the period. If the change in balances varied over the period, analysts might then use more sophisticated averaging techniques.

ROE is an accounting measure of the profitability of the firm's past investments. We can compare this measure to the expected rate of return investors require in order to buy the firm's stock, called the cost of equity. Investors measure returns on the firm's stock from market data such as dividends and changes in market prices. The expected rate of return on the firm's stock depends on the risks that equity holders cannot eliminate through holding a well-diversified portfolio (in other words, a portfolio of a wide variety of stocks); something that we discuss further in Chapter 14. An ROE greater than the cost of equity suggests that the firm has been successful in finding projects to invest in whose returns exceed investors' expectations. However, a firm's ability to consistently find projects that result in an ROE in excess of its cost of equity is likely to be limited by competitors attracted to the same projects. Accordingly, in the long run we would anticipate that ROE would converge toward the cost of equity and that the ROE of firms in the same industry would converge to the industry average.

ROE can be decomposed into both a measure of the efficiency with which a firm uses its assets to generate income and of the capital structure of the firm.

$$\text{ROE} = \frac{\text{Net Income}}{\text{Average Assets}} \times \frac{\text{Average Assets}}{\text{Average Stockholders' Equity}}$$

The first component is commonly referred to as **rate of return on assets (ROA),** and the second component is commonly referred to as **financial leverage.** Thus, a shorthand expression for ROE is:

$$ROE = ROA \times Leverage$$

ROA can be further decomposed into profit margin and asset turnover:

$$ROA = \frac{Net\ Income}{Sales} \times \frac{Sales}{Average\ Assets}$$

or:

$$ROA = Profit\ Margin \times Total\ Asset\ Turnover$$

This decomposition allows us to distinguish between operating strategies that emphasize profit per dollar of sales (profit margin) versus sales per dollar of investment in assets (total asset turnover).

For AnnTaylor, we calculate ROE and ROA as follows:

$$ROE = \frac{80.2}{(714.4 + 612.1)/2} = 12.1\%$$

$$ROA = \frac{80.2}{1,381} \times \frac{1,381}{(1,010.8 + 883.2)/2} = 8.5\%$$

$$ROA = 5.8\% \times 1.46 = 8.5\%$$

ROA, as a measure of return on investment on assets, is complicated by employing a numerator (net income) that includes the return to debtholders in the form of interest expense. An alternative measure, more focused on the efficiency of assets employed in the firm's operating activities, is the **rate of return on capital (ROC).** Here, the numerator of ROC uses operating income. Operating income can be obtained by adding back interest expense, net of taxes, to net income. Because this ratio is an after-tax ratio, we must adjust for taxes related to interest expense. In the denominator, debt and stockholders' equity replace total assets, to represent the net assets contributed by the firm's capital suppliers (total assets less operating liabilities, i.e., liabilities other than debt).

$$ROC = \frac{Net\ Income + Interest\ Expense \times (1 - tax\ rate)}{Average\ Debt + Average\ Stockholders'\ Equity}$$

We calculate ROC for AnnTaylor as follows:

$$ROC = \frac{80.2 + 6.9 \times (1 - 51.2/131.4)}{((121.7 + 23.6 + 1.3 + 118.3 + 17.5)/2 + (714.4 + 612.1)/2)} = 10.3\%$$

We obtain the tax rate by comparing the tax expense reported by AnnTaylor ($51.2) with the income before tax ($131.4), resulting in a tax rate of 39 percent (51.2/131.4). We determine the total debt by adding together the long-term debt and the deferred lease cost and other liabilities on the balance sheet (including the current portion of long-term debt from the current liability section). We can then compare the above measure to the composite market return required by the suppliers of both debt and equity capital, commonly referred to as the company's **weighted average cost of capital (WACC).** However, this calculation is beyond the scope of this book. We will provide more discussion on estimating the cost of equity capital in Chapter 14.

Shareholders of a firm leverage their investment by borrowing additional funds from debtholders to invest in additional assets. **Trading on equity** refers to the use of leverage to generate a higher ROE for shareholders. Because ROC provides a measure of the return to investments in assets (before distributions to any capital suppliers), shareholders can generate higher returns to themselves (ROE) as long as ROC on assets financed through debt exceeds the after-tax interest rate charged by debtholders, in other words, the cost of debt capital. Whether stockholders will benefit from trading on equity in the long run depends on the trade-off between the added risk of their position and the added expected return. Note that AnnTaylor generated a ROE of 12.1 percent, versus a ROA of 8.5 percent and a ROC of 10.3 percent. This indicates that they have used leverage to their shareholders' advantage, as ROE is greater than either ROA or ROC.

Recall from the decomposition of ROA that we calculate profit margin by dividing net income by sales. To further explore factors that influence profit margin, we can prepare a common size income statement. A **common size income statement** expresses each component of net income as a percent of sales. Exhibit 6.3 presents common size income statements for AnnTaylor.

The advantage of a common size statement is that it allows analysts to identify factors responsible for changes in profit margin. For example, rising product costs that are not passed on to customers might be reflected in higher cost of sales, as a percent of sales, and lower gross profit margins. Similarly, holding unit costs constant, a change in pricing policy might be evident from a comparison of gross profit margins. Administrative and marketing efficiencies may

Exhibit 6.3
Common Size Income Statement

THE REAL WORLD

AnnTaylor Stores Corporation

	02/01/2003	02/01/2002	02/01/2001
Net sales	100.0%	100.0%	100.0%
Cost of sales	45.9%	50.2%	50.5%
Gross margin	54.1%	49.8%	49.5%
Selling, general, and administrative expenses	44.4%	44.4%	40.7%
Amortization of goodwill	0.0%	0.8%	0.9%
Operating income	9.8%	4.6%	8.0%
Interest income	0.2%	0.1%	0.2%
Interest expense	0.5%	0.5%	0.6%
Income before income taxes	9.5%	4.2%	7.6%
Income tax provision	3.7%	2.0%	3.3%
Net income	5.8%	2.2%	4.2%

also become more apparent when the direct effects of growth in sales are removed.

In Exhibit 6.3, Net Income (as a percent of sales in 2003) is 5.8 percent, the same amount we calculated in the Profit Margin Ratio component of ROA. Net Income in 2003 presents a significant improvement as indicated by the increase in profit margin to 5.8 percent from the 2.2 percent in 2002. Reviewing the common size income statement, we identify this change as a direct result of a significant improvement in the cost of sales relative to sales revenues (50.5 percent to 45.9 percent), as well as a decline in the amortization of goodwill (which disappeared in 2003).

As another example of how to interpret the common size income statement, in Exhibit 6.4 find the common size income statement for Amazon.com for the years 2000 through 2002. Note that Amazon was able to maintain its gross profit percentage at approximately 25 percent over the three years. However, it cut its total operating expenses from 55 percent of sales to 24 percent of sales over

Amazon.com, Inc.
Common Size Income Statement

	12/31/2002	12/31/2001	12/31/2000
Net sales	100%	100%	100%
Cost of sales	75%	74%	76%
Gross profit	25%	26%	24%
Operating expenses:	0%	0%	0%
Fulfillment	10%	12%	15%
Marketing	3%	4%	7%
Technology and content	5%	8%	10%
General and administrative	2%	3%	4%
Stock-based compensation	2%	0%	1%
Amortization of goodwill and other intangibles	0%	6%	12%
Restructuring-related and other	1%	6%	7%
Total operating expenses	24%	39%	55%
Loss from operations	2%	−13%	−31%
Interest income	1%	1%	1%
Interest expense	−4%	−4%	−5%
Other income (expense), net	0%	0%	0%
Other gains (losses), net	−2%	0%	−5%
Net interest expense and other	−5%	−4%	−9%
Loss before equity in losses of equity method investees	−4%	−17%	−40%
Equity in losses of equity-method investees, net	0%	−1%	−11%
Loss before change in accounting principle	−4%	−18%	−51%
Cumulative effect of change in accounting principle	0%	0%	0%
Net loss	−4%	−18%	−51%

Exhibit 6.4
Amazon.com, Inc. Common Size Income Statement

THE REAL WORLD

Amazon.Com, Inc.

this same period. Note further that this resulted in the conversion of an operating loss of 31 percent from operations in 2000 to a gain of 2 percent from operations in 2002. While Amazon has still shown a net loss, this analysis implies that it has demonstrated significant progress in trying to achieve profitability from its operations.

ASSESSING TURNOVER RATIOS

Total asset turnover, as depicted in the decomposition of ROA, equals sales divided by total assets. The concept of a turnover is that we invest in assets to sell goods and services. We then expect that our investment in assets will be converted (or turned over) into sales. For AnnTaylor this ratio is 1.46, indicating that the investment in total assets is converted or turned over into sales 1.46 times a year. This ratio reflects significant averaging, as property and equipment turns over much less than 1.46 times a year and merchandise inventories turn over much more frequently. As a result, analysts seeking a better understanding of the company's performance in managing its operating assets may find it useful to consider more specific asset turnover ratios, including accounts receivable and inventory turnovers.

We calculate accounts receivable turnover and inventory turnover as follows:

$$\text{Receivables Turnover} = \frac{\text{Sales}}{\text{Average Receivables}}$$

$$\text{Inventory Turnover} = \frac{\text{Cost of Goods Sold}}{\text{Average Inventories}}$$

This type of ratio provides a measure of how many times a firm converts a particular asset into a sale (inventory turnover) or how much a firm needs a particular type of asset to support a given level of sales (accounts receivable turnover). In effect, asset turnover ratios reflect the ability of the company to efficiently use its assets to generate sales.

Often, we convert turnover ratios into an alternative form to represent the number of days that a firm, in a sense, holds an asset, as follows:

$$\text{Days Receivables} = \frac{\text{Average Receivables}}{\text{Average Sales per day}}$$

or:

$$\text{Days Receivables} = \frac{365}{\text{Receivables Turnover}}$$

$$\text{Days Inventory} = \frac{\text{Average Inventories}}{\text{Average Cost of Goods Sold per day}}$$

or:

$$\text{Days Inventory} = \frac{365}{\text{Inventory Turnover}}$$

Decreases in receivables and inventory turnover ratios, or increases in days receivables and inventory, may indicate collection and sales problems, respectively.

Similarly, accounts payable turnover reflects the efficiency with which a firm manages its credit from its suppliers, or alternatively, how much credit the firm needs in support of its sales efforts. We calculate this ratio as follows:

$$\text{Payables Turnover} = \frac{\text{Cost of Goods Sold}}{\text{Average (Accounts) Payable}}$$

$$\text{Days Payables} = \frac{\text{Average (Accounts) Payable}}{\text{Average Cost of Goods Sold per day}}$$

or:

$$\text{Days Payables} = \frac{365}{\text{Payables Turnover}}$$

Other turnover ratios consider various asset groupings such as:

$$\text{Working Capital Turnover} = \frac{\text{Sales}}{\text{Average Current Assets} - \text{Average Current Liabilities}}$$

$$\text{Capital Assets Turnover} = \frac{\text{Sales}}{\text{Average Plant, Property, and Equipment}}$$

Here again, lower turnover ratios may indicate deterioration in operating efficiency. We calculate the applicable turnover ratios for AnnTaylor as follows:

$$\text{Receivables Turnover} = \frac{1{,}381}{(10.4 + 65.6)/2} = 36.3$$

$$\text{Days Receivables} = \frac{365}{36.3} = 10$$

$$\text{Inventory Turnover} = \frac{633.5}{(185.5 + 180.1)/2} = 3.4$$

$$\text{Days Inventory} = \frac{365}{3.4} = 107.3$$

$$\text{Payables Turnover} = \frac{633.5}{(57.1 + 52.0)/2} = 11.6$$

$$\text{Days Payables} = \frac{365}{11.6} = 31.4$$

$$\text{Working Capital Turnover} = \frac{1{,}381}{(455.3 + 326.1)/2 - (151.2 + 135.3)/2} = 5.6$$

$$\text{Capital Assets Turnover} = \frac{1{,}381}{(247.1 + 250.7)/2} = 5.5$$

Looking at these ratios, we can make several observations about AnnTaylor. The days in receivables seems to be relatively small. However, recognize that many of AnnTaylor's sales are for cash. Therefore, by including total sales in the numerator of the turnover ratio we have overstated the sales that result in receivables. This results in an understatement of the days to collect from credit sales. Further recognize that AnnTaylor's credit sales are typically via a nonproprietary credit card and those are immediately converted into cash. Inventory turns over more than three times a year. For a clothing retailer such as AnnTaylor, this makes sense as its product line changes from one season to the next. It also appears that AnnTaylor receives approximately 30 days of credit from their suppliers as the days of payables is slightly over 30 days.

In addition to turnover ratios, we can prepare a common size balance sheet to assess the investments being made in asset categories as well as the amounts and forms of financing. A **common size balance sheet** expresses each line item as a percent of total assets. Exhibit 6.5 presents common size balance sheets for AnnTaylor.

Exhibit 6.5
Common Size Balance Sheet

THE REAL WORLD

AnnTaylor Stores Corporation

	02/01/2003	02/01/2002
Current assets		
Cash and cash equivalents	21.1%	3.4%
Accounts receivable, net	1.0%	7.4%
Merchandise inventories	18.3%	20.4%
Prepaid expenses and other current assets	4.6%	5.7%
Total current assets	45.0%	36.9%
Property and equipment, net	24.4%	28.4%
Goodwill, net	28.4%	32.4%
Deferred financing costs, net	0.4%	0.6%
Other assets	1.8%	1.7%
Total assets	100.0%	100.0%
Liabilities and stockholders' equity:		
Current liabilities		
Accounts payable	5.6%	5.9%
Accrued salaries and bonus	2.7%	1.4%
Accrued tenancy	1.1%	1.1%
Gift certificates and merchandise credits redeemable	2.5%	2.5%
Accrued expenses	3.0%	4.3%
Current portion of long-term debt	0.0%	0.1%
Total current liabilities	15.0%	15.3%
Long-term debt, net	12.0%	13.4%
Deferred lease costs and other liabilities	2.3%	2.0%
Stockholders' equity common stock, $.0068 par value; 120,000,000 shares authorized; 48,932,860 and 48,275,957 shares issued, respectively	0.0%	0.0%
Additional paid-in capital	49.5%	54.9%
Retained earnings	29.3%	24.8%
Deferred compensation on restricted stock	−0.4%	−1.1%
	78.4%	78.6%
Treasury stock, 4,050,972 and 4,210,232 shares, respectively, at cost	−7.7%	−9.3%
Total stockholders' equity	70.7%	69.3%
Total liabilities and stockholders' equity	100.0%	100.0%

In looking at this common size balance sheet, a couple of questions arise. For example, why have accounts receivable and inventory declined? If production costs have declined as shown on the income statement, perhaps the carrying value of inventory has also declined. This, however, does not explain the change in accounts receivable. As sales have actually increased during the year, we would have to investigate further to understand this change. By reading the details of the 10-K report for AnnTaylor, we discover that the firm sold the receivables associated with its proprietary credit card in fiscal year 2003 (we will refer to the fiscal year as the year in which the fiscal year ended, e.g., AnnTaylor ended fiscal year 2003 on February 1, 2003). This resulted in the much lower level of receivables at the end of 2003.

> Analysts are often led to search other sources of information to answer the questions that are raised by financial statement analysis such as the changes in accounts receivable for AnnTaylor.

In terms of its financing, the common size balance sheet indicates that AnnTaylor finances its assets with approximately 12 percent long-term debt and 70 percent equity (relative to total assets). This leads us to the next section in which we focus on the ability of the company to pay its long-term debt.

ASSESSING DEBT REPAYMENT ABILITY

Analysts assessing a company's debt-paying ability often separate short-term and long-term debt-paying ability. While this distinction may be somewhat arbitrary, a qualitative difference exists in how we measure the ability of a firm to repay debt that either matures before cash flows are generated by future operations or concurrently with those flows.

SHORT-TERM DEBT

Measures of the firm's ability to meet current obligations from existing assets include:

$$\text{Current Ratio} = \frac{\text{Current Assets}}{\text{Current Liabilities}}$$

$$\text{Quick Ratio} = \frac{\text{Cash, Marketable Securities, and Receivables}}{\text{Current Liabilities}}$$

$$\text{Cash Ratio} = \frac{\text{Cash and Cash Equivalent Investments}}{\text{Current Liabilities}}$$

These ratios primarily differ by the ease and speed with which assets included in the numerator can be converted to cash. Inventories are the furthest removed, as sales of inventory often give rise to receivables before producing cash. Receivables are closer to being converted to cash but are less easily converted than marketable securities. Low ratios may suggest future problems in repaying short-term liabilities as they become due.

The following ratios reflect AnnTaylor's short-term debt-repayment ability:

$$\text{Current Ratio} = \frac{455.3}{151.2} = 3$$

$$\text{Quick Ratio} = \frac{212.8 + 10.4}{151.2} = 1.5$$

$$\text{Cash Ratio} = \frac{212.8}{151.2} = 1.4$$

Due to the significant changes in cash and receivables that we noted earlier, these ratios may differ somewhat in the current year. In fact, when we compute them for the prior year, the ratios are 2.4, 0.7, and 0.2, respectively.

LONG-TERM DEBT

In the long term, a firm's ability to meet obligations is closely related to its ability to generate cash flows from operations. Interest coverage ratios consider the ability of the firm either to earn sufficient income or produce sufficient cash to make interest payments on the long-term debt.

$$\text{Interest Coverage} = \frac{\text{Income before Interest and Tax Expenses}}{\text{Interest Expense}}$$

The interest coverage ratio is based on net income, a long-run predictor of cash from operations but is not a cash flow measure itself. Some analysts also compute the cash equivalent ratio as follows:

$$\text{Interest Coverage} = \frac{\text{Cash from Operations before Interest and Tax Payments}}{\text{Interest Payments}}$$

Why do we compute income or cash before taxes? Recall that a firm meets its interest requirements before taxes are assessed. Low interest coverage ratios imply a greater risk of being unable to service debt as a consequence of fluctuations in operating results.

A different perspective on repayment ability focuses on debt capacity as measured by balance sheet leverage ratios:

$$\text{Debt Equity Ratio} = \frac{\text{Short-term Debt + Long-term Debt}}{\text{Stockholders' Equity}}$$

The debt-equity ratio predominantly measures the financial risk when assessing the risk/expected return trade-off relevant to investors. The more debt a company has, the more interest payments the company will be obligated to pay before common stock investors can earn a return on their investment.

The following ratios reflect AnnTaylor's long-term debt repayment ability and financial risk:

$$\text{Interest Coverage} = \frac{151.4 + 6.9}{6.9} = 20$$

$$\text{Debt Equity Ratio} = \frac{121.6}{714.4} = .2$$

We calculate the cash flow measure of interest coverage from information contained in the cash flow statement (not included here). In the statement, we see that cash from operations equaled $155.5 in 2003. In the supplemental disclosure to the statement, we find interest payments of $1.3 and tax payments of $40.1 (all figures in millions). We therefore calculate the cash measure as 151.5 (($155.5 + 1.3 + 40.1)/1.3). This amount is primarily due to a large portion of the company's interest expense being noncash expenses.

We have reviewed many financial ratios and how to compute them. Exhibit 6.6 provides a summary listing. Next, let's review how we can use this information

Exhibit 6.6
Summary Table of Ratios

$$\text{ROE} = \frac{\text{Net Income}}{\text{Average Stockholders' Equity}}$$

$$\text{ROA} = \frac{\text{Net Income}}{\text{Sales}} \times \frac{\text{Sales}}{\text{Average Assets}}$$

$$\text{ROC} = \frac{\text{Net Income} + \text{Interest Expense} \times (1 - \text{tax rate})}{\text{Average Debt} + \text{Average Stockholders' Equity}}$$

$$\text{Receivables Turnover} = \frac{\text{Sales}}{\text{Average Receivables}}$$

$$\text{Days Receivables} = \frac{365}{\text{Receivables Turnover}}$$

$$\text{Inventory Turnover} = \frac{\text{Cost of Goods Sold}}{\text{Average Inventories}}$$

$$\text{Days Inventory} = \frac{365}{\text{Inventory Turnover}}$$

$$\text{Payables Turnover} = \frac{\text{Cost of Goods Sold}}{\text{Average (Accounts) Payable}}$$

$$\text{Days Payables} = \frac{365}{\text{Payables Turnover}}$$

$$\text{Working Capital Turnover} = \frac{\text{Sales}}{\text{Average Current Assets} - \text{Average Current Liabilities}}$$

$$\text{Capital Assets Turnover} = \frac{\text{Sales}}{\text{Average Plant, Property, and Equipment}}$$

$$\text{Current Ratio} = \frac{\text{Current Assets}}{\text{Current Liabilities}}$$

$$\text{Quick Ratio} = \frac{\text{Cash, Marketable Securities, and Receivables}}{\text{Current Liabilities}}$$

$$\text{Cash Ratio} = \frac{\text{Cash and Cash Equivalent Investments}}{\text{Current Liabilities}}$$

$$\text{Interest Coverage} = \frac{\text{Income Before Interest and Tax Expenses}}{\text{Interest Expense}}$$

$$\text{Debt/Equity Ratio} = \frac{\text{Short-term Debt} + \text{Long-term Debt}}{\text{Stockholders' Equity}}$$

to get a better understanding of a firm's past performance as well as make more accurate forecasts of the future.

USING FINANCIAL RATIOS TO ASSESS COMPARATIVE PERFORMANCE

Ratios can be used to assess comparative performance. To do so, the analyst typically would look for trends in the data both across time (*inter-temporal* comparisons) and across firms (*cross-sectional* comparisons).

INTER-TEMPORAL COMPARISONS

We use inter-temporal comparisons of financial ratios to help reveal changes in performance as well as identify causes for those changes. For example, AnnTaylor's ROE increased from 4.9 percent (29.1/(612.1 + 574)/2) in fiscal year 2002 to 12.1 percent in 2003. From the common-size income statements (Exhibit 6.3), we find that the major cause of this improvement results from the change in profit margins (from 2.2 percent to 5.8 percent). Further investigation points to a reduction in cost of sales as a percent of sales (from 50.2 percent to 45.9 percent). In turn, from management's discussion and analysis (not included here but available in the 10-K report), we note that the higher percent cost of sales in 2001 is a consequence of an inventory write-down (inventory values written down resulting in a loss) in that year.

Another significant change pertains to AnnTaylor's short-term debt-paying ability. The current ratio, quick ratio, and cash ratio all increased significantly during fiscal year 2003. Most of the change in these ratios relates to an increase in cash, as reflected in the cash ratio that went from 0.2 at the end of fiscal year 2002 to 1.4 at the end of fiscal year 2003. Offsetting some of the increase in the current and quick ratios due to cash is the decline in the accounts receivable. Again, management's discussion and analysis provide an explanation: the company sold its proprietary credit card receivables during fiscal year 2003. Further, we observe that the company's receivables turnover increased from 21 (1,299.6/(65.6 + 58)/2) to 36.3 during that year.

CROSS-SECTIONAL COMPARISONS

Another dimension in the use of financial ratios to evaluate performance lies in cross-sectional comparisons with other companies, especially those in the same industry. In order to illustrate, we calculated similar ratios from the Talbots' financial statements (Exhibits 6.7 and 6.8). Talbots, like AnnTaylor, is also a women's clothing retailer specializing in classic styles.

Exhibit 6.9 provides a comparison of the ratios for AnnTaylor and Talbots. Looking first at profitability:

	AnnTaylor	Talbots
ROE	12.1%	21.3%
ROA	8.5%	14.2%
ROC	10.3%	18.0%

Exhibit 6.7
Statement of Net Income

THE REAL WORLD

Talbots

	02/01/2003	02/01/2002	02/01/2001
Net sales	$1,595,325,000	$1,612,513,000	$1,594,996,000
Costs and expenses:			
Cost of sales, buying, and occupancy	963,501,000	967,163,000	936,009,000
Selling, general, and administrative	435,757,000	435,334,000	467,324,000
Operating income:	196,067,000	210,016,000	191,663,000
Interest			
Interest expense	3,262,000	6,102,000	7,706,000
Interest income	409,000	927,000	3,364,000
Interest expense, net	2,853,000	5,175,000	4,342,000
Income before taxes	193,214,000	204,841,000	187,321,000
Income taxes	72,455,000	77,840,000	72,119,000
Net Income	$120,759,000	$127,001,000	$115,202,000

	02/01/2003	02/01/2002	02/01/2001
Net sales	100.0%	100.0%	100.0%
Costs and expenses:			
Cost of sales, buying, and occupancy	60.4%	60.0%	58.7%
Selling, general, and administrative	27.3%	27.0%	29.3%
Operating income:	12.3%	13.0%	12.0%
Interest			
Interest expense	0.2%	0.4%	0.5%
Interest income	0.0%	0.1%	0.2%
Interest expense, net	0.2%	0.3%	0.3%
Income before taxes	12.1%	12.7%	11.7%
Income taxes	4.5%	4.8%	4.5%
Net Income	7.6%	7.9%	7.2%

Talbots surpasses AnnTaylor on all the above measures of profitability. We can trace a major cause of this higher performance to selling, general, and administrative expenses from a common size income statement (shown in Exhibit 6.7). These expenses are only 27.3 percent for Talbots as compared to 44.3 percent for AnnTaylor. Total asset turnover provides another contributing factor to the difference in these rates of return (1.9 for Talbots versus 1.5 for AnnTaylor). AnnTaylor does a better job of collecting on its receivables but is less efficient with regard to its inventory turnover.

From a debt-repayment point of view, Talbots also has an advantage in the long-run in that its interest coverage ratio is 60. However, it does have a slightly higher debt-to-equity ratio at 0.28 and its current, quick, and cash ratios are all less favorable than AnnTaylor's at 2.95, 1.4, and 0.17, respectively.

Exhibit 6.8
Balance Sheet

THE REAL WORLD

Talbots

Current assets:	02/01/2003	02/01/2002
Cash and cash equivalents	$ 25,566,000	$ 18,306,000
Customer accounts receivable, net	181,189,000	172,183,000
Merchandise inventories	175,289,000	183,803,000
Deferred catalog costs	5,877,000	8,341,000
Due from affiliates	8,793,000	9,618,000
Deferred income taxes	10,255,000	8,222,000
Prepaid and other current assets	28,929,000	29,089,000
Total current assets	435,898,000	429,562,000
Property and equipment, net	315,227,000	277,576,000
Goodwill, net	35,513,000	35,513,000
Trademarks, net	75,884,000	75,884,000
Deferred income taxes	0	3,595,000
Other assets	9,403,000	8,934,000
Total Assets	$871,925,000	$831,064,000
Current liabilities:		
Accounts payable	$ 48,365,000	$ 49,645,000
Accrued income taxes	11,590,000	1,019,000
Accrued liabilities	87,986,000	79,628,000
Total current liabilities	147,941,000	130,292,000
Long-term debt	100,000,000	100,000,000
Deferred rent under lease commitments	20,688,000	19,542,000
Deferred income taxes	2,921,000	0
Other liabilities	32,699,000	13,354,000
Commitments		
Stockholders equity:		
Common stock, $0.01 par value; 200,000,000 authorized; 75,270,013 shares and 74,935,856 share issued, respectively, and 57,505,802 shares and 60,382,406 shares outstanding, respectively	753,000	749,000
Additional paid-in capital	389,402,000	378,955,000
Retained earnings	572,741,000	472,594,000
Accumulated other comprehensive income (loss)	(15,437,000)	(5,508,000)
Restricted stock awards	(78,000)	(697,000)
Treasury stock, at cost:17,764,211 shares and 14,553,450 shares, respectively	(379,705,000)	(278,217,000)
Total stockholders' equity	567,676,000	567,876,000
Total liabilities and stockholders' equity	$871,925,000	$831,064,000

While the assessment of past performance is useful, analysts are primarily concerned with forecasting the future. To that end, analysts often use their analysis of past performance to assist them in the forecasting of the future results of the firm. We now turn to a discussion of forecasting.

Ratio	Ann Taylor	Talbots
ROE	12.1%	21.3%
ROA	8.5%	14.2%
Profit Margin	5.8%	7.6%
Total Asset Turnover	1.46	1.90
ROC	10.3%	18.0%
Receivables Turnover	36.3	9.0
Days of Receivables	10.0	40.4
Inventory Turnover	3.4	5.4
Days of Inventory	107.3	68.0
Accounts Payable Turnover	11.6	19.7
Days of Accounts Payable	31.4	18.6
Working Capital Turnover	5.6	5.4
Capital Asset Turnover	5.5	5.4
Current Ratio	3	2.95
Quick Ratio	1.5	1.4
Cash Ratio	1.4	0.17
Interest Coverage	20	60
Debt/Equity	0.2	0.28

Exhibit 6.9
Ratio Comparison of Ann Taylor and Talbots

THE REAL WORLD

Ann Taylor and Talbots

FORECASTING

The financial analyst's principal stock-in-trade lies in forming estimates of firm values based on forecasts of future earnings or cash flows. In developing forecasts, analysts may use their understanding of markets for the firm's products or services to model supply and demand, formal statistical methods to exploit past observations in characterizing time series behavior, experience and judgment to determine future trends, or some combination of these approaches. The value of a forecast ultimately is derived from improved decision making based on the estimates that the forecast produces.

Forecasting future operating performance usually begins with predicting sales. There are many ways in which to approach this task. An economist might form a set of equations that models industry supply and demand (called *structural* equations as they describe the structure of market supply and demand conditions faced by the firm). Economists may then use estimates of these equations to predict the future price of a firm's output, which, when combined with projected production, would lead to a forecast of sales. The data required by such a model might include wages of workers and income of consumers, implying the need to forecast these factors.

An alternative modeling approach looks for a functional relationship between sales and time. By examining past observations of sales, analysts may detect a systematic relationship between sales and the passage of time that can be reasonably portrayed by a mathematical equation. For example, sales might be growing at a fixed rate such as 2 percent a year or it might be growing at a certain percentage of another variable, such as population growth.

Evidence indicates that the market may react differentially to whether a firm meets or fails to meet analysts' forecasts, although the evidence is mixed as to the direction. See Skinner and Sloan, *Review of Accounting Studies* (2002) and Payne and Thomas, *The Accounting Review* (2003).

Less-formal approaches to forecasts rely on analysts' intuition and judgment. The simplest approach would be to predict that next period's sales would equal this period's sales. Another approach might be to portray future sales as a weighted average of current sales and the previous forecast. Last, but not least, rather than rely on economic or mathematical models or simply intuition, we can instead build a statistical model of time series behavior from an analysis of past observations based only on the data. In other words, an analyst might statistically examine the properties of the data themselves to specify a forecasting model. Let's look at this approach in more detail.

TIME SERIES ANALYSIS

Time series analysis basically estimates a model of the process generating the variable of interest (in our case, sales) from past observations. Typically, the initial step in identifying such a model is to estimate the *statistical correlations* (how one variable behaves relative to another) between lagged observations. For example, current sales might be correlated with sales of the previous period, sales of two periods ago, sales of three periods ago, and so on. These correlations allow analysts to determine a tentative model. For example, some firms display seasonal variations in quarterly sales such that, say, fourth quarter sales are more highly correlated with fourth quarter sales of the previous year than with third quarter sales of the current year (e.g., holiday-season sales for toy manufacturers). Accordingly, a suitable forecasting model of quarterly sales would likely take that correlation information into account.

Once we formulate a model, we then check how well the estimated model captures the time series behavior of the data. This might involve a measure of *forecast errors* (deviations between actual sales and sales predicted by the model). If necessary, we repeat the process until the measure used to check the model indicates that it fits the data sufficiently well.

However, analysts want to forecast earnings, so providing a sales forecast using time series analysis is only half the battle. Analysts must also forecast expenses for the firm, usually by relating them to sales. For example, analysts might employ common-size ratios under the assumption that expenses would remain a constant percentage of sales. Some expenses may also depend on planned investments in working capital and long-term assets, such as plant, property, and equipment. Thus, a comprehensive approach toward forecasting earnings or cash flows often involves projecting a full set of financial statements including successive balance sheets. These forecasted financial statements are called the **pro forma statements.**

PRO FORMA STATEMENTS

Firms sometimes prepare pro forma statements to depict the consequences of a future financing event. For example, an initial public offering (IPO) of stock for sale to the public requires the preparation of a *prospectus* (a document filed with the SEC) containing financial statements that reflect the disposition of the anticipated proceeds from the sale of stock and the pro forma changes to assets, liabilities, and stockholders' equity that would result.

Exhibit 6.10
Intel Corporation

The Real World

Intel Corporation

Pro forma information is required by SFAS No. 123 as if the company had accounted for its employee stock options (including shares issued under the Stock Participation Plan, collectively called "options") granted subsequent to December 31, 1994 under the fair value method of that statement.

For purposes of pro forma disclosures, the estimated fair value of the options is amortized to expense over the options' vesting periods. The company's pro forma information follows:

(In millions-except per share amounts)	2001	2000	1999
Net income	$254	$9,699	$6,860

To judge the significance of these adjustments, note that the reported net income for Intel was $1,291, $10,535, and $7,314 (in millions) for the years 2001, 2000, and 1999, respectively. Therefore, the effect of this adjustment was less than 10 percent of net income in 1999 and 2000 but was an 80 percent decline in income in 2001. This could have a significant influence on an analyst's forecast of the future income on the company.

Firms also use pro forma statements to depict the consequences of an alternative accounting treatment when more than one method is allowed. For example, accounting rules for employee stock options (considered in Chapter 12) allow firms to either recognize compensation expense associated with those options or not recognize compensation expense but disclose pro forma net income as if the compensation expense had been recorded. Exhibit 6.10 illustrates the disclosure for Intel.

Although our principal perspective in developing forecasts of operating data is at the firm level, analysts must also characterize the future prospects of the industry and economy at large. Business cycles and industry trends often factor prominently in forming predictions regarding the outlook for firms susceptible to the influence of those factors. In such cases, we might begin to build a forecast for the firm by first developing or obtaining forecasts at an industry- or economy-wide level. An integrated approach might involve joint analyses of firm, industry, and economy data with the objective of improving estimates at the firm level.

A risk to forecasting models that focus only on time series data is that analysts might be ignoring changes in competitive strategy and changes in organizational structure. For example, how would analysts handle a firm's merger with another company? This event might fundamentally alter the basic statistical properties of a the firm's sales or earnings. In this case, analysts can capture this change with a more encompassing model. Or, analysts might modify pre-merger operating data as if both firms had always been a single entity (an example of employing pro forma statements) and then apply one of the forecasting approaches described above.

TIME VALUE OF MONEY

Analysts utilize forecasts of future results to help them value the stock of a company today. Before we explain more fully how analysts incorporate their forecasts of future results to arrive at these value estimates, it is important to talk about the concepts of the time value of money, specifically the *present value* of money.

A standard question in an effort to convey the concept of time value of money is to ask whether you would prefer to receive a dollar today or a dollar tomorrow. Most people will respond by saying that they would prefer to receive the dollar today. When asked why, many observe that if they had the dollar today then they would be at least as well off as if they waited until tomorrow because they could always choose to hold the dollar rather than spend it. Moreover, they would have the option not to hold the dollar and spend it if they so chose, which implies more value. It often occurs to at least some that if they had the dollar today, then they could immediately deposit it in their bank and, given that their bank pays interest on a daily basis, they would have more than a dollar tomorrow. In other words, there is a time value to money.

There are many familiar examples of the time value of money. TV ads for automobiles often present prospective buyers with a low interest rate on funds borrowed to pay for a car or a lump sum reduction in the purchase price if they pay in cash. Bank statements may show interest earned on funds held on deposit, copies of information returns filed by insurance companies and brokerage houses also report interest earned, while similar filings by mortgage companies report interest paid. It is hard to escape some exposure to the notion of interest and a time value to money.

In virtually all of the situations where time value of money is relevant, the problem is to somehow compare a dollar amount today, known as **present value,** with an amount in the future, known as **future value.** The calculations that we often employ to compare values at different points in time are referred to as **time value of money** calculations and they all involve the time value of money being expressed as an **interest rate** or **discount rate.** Next we consider the process of converting a present value into a future value and vice versa.

FUTURE VALUE

A useful way to approach the concept of the present value of a future value (sometimes referred to as a **future sum**) is to turn the issue around and ask what an investment of cash today would yield in terms of cash in the future if, in the interim, that investment earned interest. Suppose that one could invest $1,000 in a bank savings account that pays interest at a rate of 5 percent for one year. At the end of the year, the account would contain $1,050, the initial investment of $1,000 plus interest of $50 ($1,000 × 0.05). Now, suppose that the $1,050 was left in the savings account for a second year and the interest was allowed to also earn interest (called **compounding of interest**). At the end of that year the account would contain $1,102.50 ($1,050 + $1,050 × 0.05 or $1,000 × (1 + 0.05)^2). Note that the $50 of interest earned in the first year then earned $2.50 of interest in the second year, reflecting the compounding of interest. Mathematically, the future value of C dollars at the end of two years at an interest rate of r, compounded annually, can be expressed as follows (where **FV** is referred to as a **future value factor**):

$$\text{Future Value(2)} = C + rC + r(C + rC) = C + 2rC + r^2C = C(1 + r)^2 = C \times \text{FV}_{2r}$$

Generalizing in the above to n years at rate r, we obtain

$$FV_{n,r} = (1 + r)^n$$
$$\text{Future Value}(n) = C \times FV_{n,r}$$

Note that many books, this one included, contain a table of such future value factors arranged by the number of periods (n) and the interest rate per period (r). Such tables are often referred to as **future value of \$1** tables. Functions that calculate these factors are also incorporated into handheld financial calculators and spreadsheet programs such as Microsoft Excel™.

PRESENT VALUE

The concept of present value reverses the exercise by posing the question: what is an amount to be received in the future worth now? Intuitively, one would expect present value to be less than the future amount because, if we had the cash now, then it could be invested, earn interest, and be worth more in the future.

In the numerical example above, the present value of \$1,050 to be received in one year given an interest rate (discount rate) of 5 percent and annual compounding would be \$1,050 ÷ 1.05 or \$1,000. Similarly, the present value of \$1,102.50 to be received two years hence would be \$1,102.50 ÷ $(1.05)^2$, or \$1,000 again. It should be fairly clear that mathematically, the present value of C dollars to be received in two years at a discount rate of r, compounded annually, can be expressed as follows (where **PV** is the **present value factor**):

$$\text{Present Value}(2) = \frac{C}{(1 + r)(1 + r)} = \frac{C}{(1 + r)^2} = C \times PV_{2,r}$$

Again, generalizing to n years, results in:

$$PV_{n,r} = \frac{1}{(1 + r)^n}$$
$$\text{Present Value}(n) = C \times PV_{n,r}$$

ADJUSTING FOR UNCERTAINTY

In applying time value of money concepts to an investor's decisions, the interest rate (discount rate) that the investor would use should reflect their own personal time preference for money. Typically this rate will be a function of the other opportunities available to the investor for return on investment and some adjustment for the risk or uncertainty associated with the investment opportunity. The issue of risk is that if one waits until tomorrow to receive the dollar, then something may happen between today and tomorrow such that tomorrow's dollar (or some portions of the dollar) might not materialize. All else held constant, the interest rate required by an investor when there is uncertainty about the outcome of the investment might be higher than the interest rate on a sure thing, depending on the risk preferences of the investor. If the investor is risk averse, then the discount rate employed by that investor would likely be higher to compensate for bearing the risk. By risk averse we mean that the individual strictly prefers a sure thing to a gamble for which the expected payoff is the same as the payoff on the sure thing. For example, risk averse individuals often buy insurance. They prefer to pay a certain premium to an insurance company for coverage of a possible loss when the expected loss is less than the premium.

MODELS FOR VALUING EQUITY

One application of both forecasting and the time value of money is to estimate the value of the equity of a firm. The two basic approaches used by analysts for estimating the value of equity are the **discounted cash flow (DCF)** and **residual income (RI)** models. Both approaches begin with forecasts of operating results. In the DCF approach, forecasting techniques are used to estimate future free cash flows to equity (discussed in Chapter 5); in the RI approach, a quantity known as *future abnormal earnings* is estimated rather than cash flows.

DCF APPROACH

Under the DCF approach, operating income is transformed into cash from operations by adding back noncash expenses including depreciation and amortization of operating assets, and subtracting changes in operating working capital. This is the same format used in the cash flow statement to produce cash from operations under GAAP. Cash from operations is then reduced by cash used in investment activities and increased by net borrowings (or reduced by net repayments of borrowings) to arrive at an amount known as **free cash flow** to equity holders (i.e., stockholders). Free cash flows must then be forecasted over the future life of the firm. Typically, DCF analysis also establishes a **time horizon** for the analysis, and the firm's value at the end of that time period (known as the **terminal value**) is estimated. This terminal value is then discounted along with the estimates of free cash flow, using the present value techniques described earlier, to obtain the estimate of the value for the firm's stock. The discount rate employed reflects the rate of return investors require in order to buy the firm's stock. This rate is sometimes called the firm's equity **cost of capital.**

To illustrate, let FCF_1, FCF_2, and FCF_n denote free cash flows received at the end of future periods 1, 2, and so forth, up to the end of the life of the firm in period n. The terminal period is n, and let TV_n be the estimated terminal value. We can calculate the present value of the firm and the estimated value of stockholders' equity as follows:

$$\text{Value of Stockholders' Equity} = \frac{FCF_1}{(1 + r)} + \frac{FCF_2}{(1 + r)^2} + \cdots + \frac{FCF_n}{(1 + r)^n} + \frac{TV_n}{(1 + r)^n}$$

Exhibit 6.11 provides condensed financial data for a hypothetical firm in the form of pro forma financial statements over an assumed remaining firm life (investment horizon) of four years. The initial balance sheet at time 0 reflects

Exhibit 6.11
Pro forma Financial
Statements Hypothetical Firm

Balance Sheet Period	0	1	2	3	4
Equipment, Net	1,000	750	500	250	0
Total Assets	1,000	750	500	250	0
Common Stock	1,000	1,000	1,000	1,000	0
Retained Earnings	0	−250	−500	−750	0
Total Liability and Owners' Equity	1,000	750	500	250	0

Income Statement Period		1	2	3	4
Revenue		500	500	500	500
Depreciation		−250	−250	−250	−250
Net Income		250	250	250	250

Cash Flow Statement Period		1	2	3	4
Net Income		250	250	250	250
Depreciation		250	250	250	250
Operating Cash Flow		500	500	500	500
Dividends		−500	−500	−500	−500
Change in Cash		0	0	0	0

equipment of $1,000 purchased from the proceeds of a common stock issue for that amount. The equipment will last four years, at which point it becomes valueless. To keep the calculation simple we will assume that the terminal value is zero at that point in time. Revenues are forecasted to be $500 per year. The only expense is depreciation, which we assume is $250 per year. All available cash each year is distributed in the form of a dividend to common stockholders. The cost of equity is assumed to be 10 percent.

In this example, free cash flows are equivalent to cash from operations on the cash flow statement as there are no investment or debt cash flows. Because free cash flow is the same in all four years, the present value of those cash flows, our estimate of equity value, can be calculated as follows:

Value of Stockholders' Equity

$$= 500 \times \left(\frac{1}{1 + .10} + \left(\frac{1}{1 + .10} \right)^2 + \left(\frac{1}{1 + .10} \right)^3 + \left(\frac{1}{1 + .10} \right)^4 \right)$$

$$= 500 \times \left(\frac{1 - (1 + .10)^{-4}}{.10} \right) = 1,585$$

where the last term contained in parentheses is a shorthand way of expressing the present value factor for a series of constant amounts received each year. This stream of cash flows (the four $500 payments) is called an **annuity,** and the factor in the last equation would be called a *present value of an annuity factor.* A more detailed description of present value and annuities, along with related tables of present value factors, is provided in Appendix B.

Observe that the value of stockholders' equity derived from the free cash flows of $1,585 is also the present value of the stream of future dividends. Thus, a value of stockholders' equity of $1,585 makes sense when one looks at firm value from an investor's perspective. The interpretation would be that if you purchased the stock in this company for $1,585 and received the four dividends of $500 each, you would have received a return of 10 percent on your investment, due to the fact that we used a discount rate of 10 percent to present value the cash flows.

RI APPROACH

Under the RI approach, a quantity known as **abnormal earnings** is calculated. Abnormal earnings are simply those earnings that are above or below the earnings currently expected by investors, given their investment in the firm and their required (expected) rate of return. Abnormal earnings are calculated by deducting a charge for the use of capital provided by stockholders from net income. This **capital charge** is determined by multiplying the book value of stockholders' equity at the start of the year by cost of equity capital (rate). The present value of abnormal earnings projected over the life of the firm is then added to the initial book value of stockholders' equity to arrive at an estimate of the value of stockholders' equity. To put this in simple terms, if the firm issued stock for $1,000 and invested the proceeds in operating assets and stockholders expected to earn 10 percent on their investment, then they would expect $100 in earnings every period. If earnings were above or below $100 then they would be viewed as abnormal earnings.

Let AE_1, AE_2 and AE_K denote abnormal earnings for future periods $1, 2, k$, and so on over the remaining life of the firm. The value of stockholders' equity is then:

$$\text{Value of Stockholder's Equity} = \text{Book Value of Stockholder's Equity} + \frac{AE_1}{(1 + r)} + \frac{AE_2}{(1 + r)^2} + \cdots\cdots + \frac{AE_k}{(1 + r)^k} + \cdots\cdots$$

Using the data from Exhibit 6.11, the cost of capital charge is calculated by multiplying stockholders' equity at the beginning of each period by the cost of capital (10 percent). Abnormal earnings are then calculated as the reported net income minus the capital charge:

Year 1: $150 = $250 − (10% × $1,000)
Year 2: $175 = $250 − (10% × $750)
Year 3: $200 = $250 − (10% × $500)
Year 4: $225 = $250 − (10% × $250)

The book value of stockholders' equity is the $1,000 of common stock at the start of the forecast horizon. Accordingly, the value of stockholders' equity can be determined from accounting numbers as follows:

$$
\text{Value of Stockholders' Equity} = 1{,}000 + 150 \times \left(\frac{1}{1.10}\right) + 175 \times \left(\frac{1}{1.10}\right)^2
$$

$$
+ \; 200 \times \left(\frac{1}{1.10}\right)^3 + 225 \times \left(\frac{1}{1.10}\right)^4 = 1{,}585
$$

Not surprisingly, the value of stockholders' equity is the same under both a DCF and an RI approach. It should also not be surprising that this asset is worth more than the $1,000 paid to acquire it given that the investor is expecting a 10 percent return. If you just consider the first year, the asset would be expected to return only $100 in income, yet it returns $250 or $150 more than expected. This is true in each of the four years of the asset's life, as shown in the calculation of abnormal earnings. Therefore, the $1,000 asset is worth more ($1,585) than its cost.

SUMMARY AND TRANSITION

Financial statement analysis encompasses many dimensions. Because companies often employ different methods of accounting, it may be necessary to transform financial statements to reflect common accounting practices when making cross-sectional comparisons. Fortunately, accounting reports often contain sufficient information, either in the statements themselves or in accompanying footnotes and supporting schedules, to make these transformations.

A further problem in working from data contained in financial statements for purposes of both time series and cross-sectional comparisons is adjusting for differences in size. To remedy this problem, analysts construct financial ratios that place accounting numbers on a common scale. Besides controlling for differences in size, financial ratios are useful in assessing operating performance. Two broad classes of financial ratios for use in this respect are ratios that measure profitability and ratios that measure debt-repayment ability.

One of the more common ratios for assessing profitability from the stockholders' perspective is rate of return on equity (ROE), determined by dividing net income by stockholders' equity. ROE can be usefully broken down into rate of return on assets (ROA) and leverage, as measured by the ratio of total assets-to-debt. In turn, ROA can be broken down into profit margin and asset turnover, measures of the company's efficiency in converting sales into profits and assets into sales, respectively. The company's ability to generate a higher return on stockholders' equity through the use of financial leverage can be determined by comparing ROE to the rate of return on capital (ROC), where capital is defined as debt plus stockholders' equity, and interest, net of taxes, is added to net income in the numerator of this ratio.

Indicators of a company's short-term debt repayment ability include liquidity ratios, such as the current ratio (current assets divided by current liabilities), quick ratio (current assets other than inventories and prepaid expenses divided by current liabilities), and cash ratio (cash divided by current liabilities). Common ratios for assessing long-term debt-repayment ability include interest coverage (income before interest expense and taxes divided by interest expense) and debt to total debt and equity.

Financial analysts are principally concerned with predicting future performance. This typically begins with a forecast of sales. Sales forecasts might be based on economic models of supply and demand facing the firm, mathematical models that relate sales to time, models based on subjective judgment, and statistical models that extrapolate past sales behavior. Projections of future operating expenses often involve common-size ratios and an assumption that costs will remain proportional to sales. Industry- and economy-wide data may also be useful in forming predictions concerning how the company will fare. The company's strategies in meeting its competition may be relevant as well.

Analysts may then use the forecasted data to provide an estimate of the market value of equity using time value of money techniques. Two basic models are used in this process: the discounted cash flow model and the residual income model.

At this point in the book, we have provided an overview of the basics of financial reporting and financial statement analysis. In the next several chapters, we will return to the balance sheet and focus on more detailed accounting issues related to each of the major types of assets, liabilities, and owners' equity accounts.

END OF CHAPTER MATERIAL

KEY TERMS

Abnormal Earnings	Interest Rate
Annuity	Inter-temporal
Capital Asset Turnover	Inventory Turnover
Capital Charge	Operating Forecasts
Cash Ratio	Present Value
Common Size Balance Sheet	Present Value Factor
Common Size Income Statement	Pro Forma Statements
Compounding of Interest	Profit Margin
Cost of Capital	Quick Ratio
Cross-sectional	Receivables Turnover
Current Ratio	Residual Income Model (RI)
Debt/Equity Ratio	Return on Assets (ROA)
Discount Rate	Return on Capital (ROC)
Discounted Cash Flow Model (DCF)	Return on Equity (ROE)
Financial Leverage	Terminal Value
Financial Statement Analysis	Time Horizon
Free Cash Flow	Time Value of Money
Future Sum	Total Asset Turnover
Future Value	Trading on Equity
Future Value Factor	Weighted Average Cost of Capital (WACC)
Interest Coverage	Working Capital Turnover

ASSIGNMENT MATERIAL

REVIEW QUESTIONS

1. Compare and contrast inter-temporal and cross-sectional analysis.
2. For each of the following ratios, reproduce the formula for their calculation:
   a. ROA
   b. ROC
   c. ROE
   d. Receivable Turnover
   e. Inventory Turnover
   f. Payables Turnover
   g. Current
   h. Quick
   i. Debt/Equity
   j. Interest Coverage
3. Describe leverage and explain how it is evidenced in the ROA, ROC, and ROE ratios.
4. Explain, using the profit margin and total asset turnover ratios, how two companies in the same industry can earn the same ROA, yet may have very different operating strategies.
5. What is the advantage of preparing common-size statements in financial statement analysis?
6. Explain why the current ratio is subject to manipulation as a measure of liquidity.
7. Explain how as-if restatements might be used in financial statement analysis.
8. Explain how mandated and discretionary accounting method changes can affect financial statement analysis.
9. What is the purpose of adjusting for scale?
10. Describe the discounted cash flow approach to estimating the value of stockholders' equity.
11. Describe how free cash flow would be calculated.
12. Describe the residual income approach to estimating the value of stockholders' equity.

APPLYING YOUR KNOWLEDGE

13. Discuss the implications that different country accounting standards have for the statement analysis of foreign competitor companies.
14. Suppose that you are analyzing two competitor companies, one a U.S. company and the other a company in the United Kingdom, whose statements are expressed in pounds. Discuss whether it is necessary to convert the statements of the UK company into U.S. dollars before computing ratios.

15. Auditors typically conduct a preliminary review of a firm's financial statements using analytical procedures, which include ratio analysis. As an auditor, why would ratio analysis be useful in auditing the financial statements?

16. Contracts with lenders, such as bonds, typically place restrictions on the financial statement ratios. Two commonly used ratios are the current ratio and the debt/equity ratio. Explain why these might appear as restrictions; in other words, do they protect the lender?

17. Management compensation plans typically specify performance criteria in terms of financial statement ratios. For instance, a plan might specify that management must achieve a certain level of return on investment (e.g., ROA). If management were trying to maximize their compensation, how could they manipulate the ROA ratio to achieve this maximization?

18. The financial data for Nova Electronics Company and Pulsar Electricals for the current year is as follows:

	Annual Sales	Accounts Receivable Jan 1	Accounts Receivable Dec 31
Nova Electronics	3,893,567	1,103,879	1,140,251
Pulsar Electricals	1,382,683	357,934	243,212

a. Compute the Accounts Receivable Turnover for each company.

b. Compute the average number of days required by each company to collect the receivables.

c. Which company is more efficient in terms of handling its accounts receivable policy?

19. Information regarding the activities of Polymer Plastics Corporation is as follows:

	Year 1	Year 2	Year 3	Year 4	Year 5
Cost of Goods Sold	363,827	411,125	493,350	579,686	608,670
Average Inventory	60,537	76,560	107,338	156,672	202,895

a. Do a time series analysis for the inventory turnover for each year and also compute the average number of days that inventories are held for the respective years.

b. Is Polymer Plastics Corporation efficiently managing its inventories?

20. The following financial information relates to Delocro Mechanical, Inc. (amounts in thousands):

	Year 1	Year 2	Year 3	Year 4
Sales	2,000	2,200	2,420	2,662
Average Total Assets	1,111	1,222	1,344	1,479
Average Owners' Equity	620	682	750	825
Net Income	200	230	264	304
Interest Expense	50	55	61	67
Tax Rate	40%	40%	40%	30%

For each year calculate:

a. Return on Owners' Equity (ROE)

b. ROI

    i. Profit Margin Ratio

    ii. Total Asset Turnover

c. Comment on the profitability of Delocro Mechanical, Inc.

21. Empire Company's balance sheet is as follows:

Total Assets	$500,000	Liabilities	$100,000
		Owner's Equity	400,000
	$500,000		$500,000

The interest rate on the liabilities is 10 percent, and the income tax rate is 30 percent.

a. If the ROE is equal to the ROI, compute the Net Income.

b. Compute the ROE, taking the Net Income determined in part a.

c. Compute the income before interest and taxes for the net income derived in part a.

d. Assume that total assets remain the same (i.e., at $500,000) and that loans increase to $300,000, while Owners' Equity decreases to $200,000. The interest rate is now 8 percent, and the income tax rate remains at 30 percent. What is the ROE if you require the same ROA as calculated in part b?

e. Compare the ROE in both situations and comment.

22. Spectrum Associates' financial data is as follows (amounts in thousands):

		Year 1	Year 2	Year 3	Year 4
Current Assets					
	Accounts Receivable	$ 700	$ 800	$ 600	$ 650
	Cash	200	100	200	150
	Other Current Assets	100	100	250	100
	Inventories	500	1,000	1,450	2,100
		$1,500	$2,000	$2,500	$3,000
Current Liabilities					
	Accounts Payable	$ 600	$ 700	$ 825	$ 800
	Accrued Salaries	300	400	495	400
	Other Current Liabilities	100	150	165	300
		$1,000	$1,250	$1,475	$1,500

a. Compute the current and quick ratios for years 1 through 4.

b. Comment on the short-term liquidity position of Spectrum Associates.

23. Artscan Enterprises' financial data is as follows:

	Year 1	Year 2	Year 3
Income before Interest and Taxes	$ 400	$ 600	$ 800
Interest	70	100	135
Current Liabilities	375	475	750
Noncurrent Liabilities	625	1,125	1,600
Owners' Equity	$1,000	$1,500	$2,000

   a. Compute the Debt/Equity and Times Interest Earned Ratio.

   b. Comment on the long-term liquidity position of Artscan Enterprises.

24. State the immediate effect (increase, decrease, no effect) of the following transactions on:

   a. Current Ratio

   b. Quick Ratio

   c. Working Capital

   d. ROE

   e. Debt/Equity Ratio

   Transaction:

   1. Inventory worth $25,000 is purchased on credit.

   2. Inventory worth $125,000 is sold on account for $158,000.

   3. Payments of $65,000 are made to suppliers.

   4. A machine costing $120,000 is purchased. $30,000 is paid in cash, and the balance will be paid in equal installments for the next three years.

   5. Shares of common stock worth $100,000 are issued.

   6. Equipment costing $80,000 with accumulated depreciation of $50,000 is sold for $40,000 in cash.

   7. Goods worth $35,000 were destroyed by fire. Salvage value of some of the partly burnt goods was $3,000, which is received in cash. The goods were not insured.

25. Calculate the present value of $10,000 to be received ten years from now at 12 percent assuming that interest is compounded:

   a. annually

   b. quarterly

   c. monthly

26. Calculate the present value of an annuity of $100 each year for the next ten years at 12 percent assuming that interest is compounded once a year.

27. Suppose that the free cash flows for a firm are estimated to be $500 per year in each of the next ten years and that the terminal value at the end of the ten years is expected to be $2,000. If your desired rate of return given the risk of this investment was 15 percent, using the DCF approach, what would be the maximum price you would be willing to pay for the entire firm?

28. Suppose that the abnormal earnings of the firm are estimated to be $200 a year for each of the next ten years and that it has a current book value of

$1,500. Using the residual income approach, what would be the maximum amount you would pay for the entire firm if your desired rate of return given the risk of this investment were 12 percent?

USING REAL DATA

29. Use the data from the financial statements of Dell and Gateway to answer the following questions.

DELL COMPUTER CORP. Balance Sheet	01/31/2003	01/31/2002
Current assets:		
Cash and cash equivalents	$ 4,232,000,000	$ 3,641,000,000
Short-term investments	406,000,000	273,000,000
Accounts receivable, net	2,586,000,000	2,269,000,000
Inventories	306,000,000	278,000,000
Other	1,394,000,000	1,416,000,000
Total current assets	8,924,000,000	7,877,000,000
Property, plant, and equipment, net	913,000,000	826,000,000
Investments	5,267,000,000	4,373,000,000
Other noncurrent assets	366,000,000	459,000,000
Total assets	$15,470,000,000	$13,535,000,000
Liabilities and stockholders' equity		
Current liabilities:		
Accounts payable	$ 5,989,000,000	$ 5,075,000,000
Accrued and other	2,944,000,000	2,444,000,000
Total current liabilities	8,933,000,000	7,519,000,000
Long-term debt	506,000,000	520,000,000
Other	1,158,000,000	802,000,000
Commitments and contingent liabilities (Note 6)		
Total liabilities	10,597,000,000	8,841,000,000
Stockholders' equity:		
Preferred stock and capital in excess of $.01 par value; shares issued and outstanding: none	–	–
Common stock and capital in excess of $.01 par value; shares authorized: 7,000; shares issued: 2,681 and 2,654, respectively	6,018,000,000	5,605,000,000
Treasury stock, at cost; 102 and 52 shares, respectively	(4,539,000,000)	(2,249,000,000)
Retained earnings	3,486,000,000	1,364,000,000
Other comprehensive income (loss)	(33,000,000)	38,000,000
Other	(59,000,000)	(64,000,000)
Total stockholders' equity	4,873,000,000	4,694,000,000
Total liabilities and stockholders' equity	$15,470,000,000	$13,535,000,000

DELL COMPUTER CORP. Income Statement

	01/31/2003	01/31/2002	01/31/2001
Net revenue	$35,404,000,000	$31,168,000,000	$31,888,000,000
Cost of revenue	29,055,000,000	25,661,000,000	25,445,000,000
Gross margin	6,349,000,000	5,507,000,000	6,443,000,000
Operating expenses:			
Selling, general, and administrative	3,050,000,000	2,784,000,000	3,193,000,000
Research, development, and engineering	455,000,000	452,000,000	482,000,000
Special charges	–	482,000,000	105,000,000
Total operating expenses	3,505,000,000	3,718,000,000	3,780,000,000
Operating income	2,844,000,000	1,789,000,000	2,663,000,000
Investment and other income (loss), net	183,000,000	(58,000,000)	531,000,000
Income before income taxes and cumulative effect of change in accounting principle	3,027,000,000	1,731,000,000	3,194,000,000
Provision for income taxes	905,000,000	485,000,000	958,000,000
Income before cumulative effect of change in accounting principle	2,122,000,000	1,246,000,000	2,236,000,000
Cumulative effect of change in accounting principle, net	–	–	59,000,000
Net income	$ 2,122,000,000	$ 1,246,000,000	$ 2,177,000,000

DELL COMPUTER CORP. Cash Flow Statement

	01/31/2003	01/31/2002	01/312/001
Cash flows from operating activities:			
Net income	$2,122,000,000	$1,246,000,000	$2,177,000,000
Adjustments to reconcile net income to net cash provided by operating activities:			
Depreciation and amortization	211,000,000	239,000,000	240,000,000
Tax benefits of employee stock plans	260,000,000	487,000,000	929,000,000
Special charges	–	742,000,000	105,000,000
(Gains)/losses on investments	(67,000,000)	17,000,000	(307,000,000)
Other, primarily effects of exchange rate changes on monetary assets and liabilities denominated in foreign currencies	(410,000,000)	178,000,000	135,000,000
Changes in:			
Operating working capital	1,210,000,000	826,000,000	642,000,000
Noncurrent assets and liabilities	212,000,000	62,000,000	274,000,000
Net cash provided by operating activities	3,538,000,000	3,797,000,000	4,195,000,000
Cash flows from investing activities:			
Investments:			
Purchases	(8,736,000,000)	(5,382,000,000)	(2,606,000,000)
Maturities and sales	7,660,000,000	3,425,000,000	2,331,000,000
Capital expenditures	(305,000,000)	(303,000,000)	(482,000,000)
Net cash used in investing activities	(1,381,000,000)	(2,260,000,000)	(757,000,000)

	01/31/2003	01/31/2002	01/312/001
Cash flows from financing activities:			
Purchase of common stock	(2,290,000,000)	(3,000,000,000)	(2,700,000,000)
Issuance of common stock under employee plans	265,000,000	298,000,000	395,000,000
Net cash used in financing activities	(2,025,000,000)	(2,702,000,000)	(2,305,000,000)
Effect of exchange rate changes on cash	459,000,000	(104,000,000)	(32,000,000)
Net increase (decrease) in cash	591,000,000	(1,269,000,000)	1,101,000,000
Cash and cash equivalents at beginning of period	3,641,000,000	4,910,000,000	3,809,000,000
Cash and cash equivalents at end of period	$4,232,000,000	$3,641,000,000	$4,910,000,000

GATEWAY, INC. Balance Sheet

	12/31/2003	12/31/2002
ASSETS		
Current assets:		
Cash and cash equivalents	$ 349,101,000	$ 465,603,000
Marketable securities	739,936,000	601,118,000
Accounts receivable, net	210,151,000	197,817,000
Inventory	114,136,000	88,761,000
Other, net	250,153,000	602,073,000
Total current assets	1,663,477,000	1,955,372,000
Property, plant, and equipment, net	330,913,000	481,011,000
Intangibles, net	13,983,000	23,292,000
Other assets, net	20,065,000	49,732,000
	$2,028,438,000	$2,509,407,000
Liabilities and equity		
Current liabilities:		
Accounts payable	$ 415,971,000	$ 278,609,000
Accrued liabilities	277,455,000	364,741,000
Accrued royalties	48,488,000	56,684,000
Other current liabilities	257,090,000	240,315,000
Total current liabilities	999,004,000	940,349,000
Other long-term liabilities	109,696,000	127,118,000
Total liabilities	1,108,700,000	1,067,467,000
Commitments and contingencies (Note 5)		
Series C redeemable convertible preferred stock, $.01 par value, $200,000 liquidation value, 50 shares authorized, issued and outstanding in 2003 and 2002	197,720,000	195,422,000
Stockholders' equity:		
Series A convertible preferred stock, $.01 par value, $200,000 liquidation value, 50 shares authorized, issued and outstanding in 2003 and 2002	200,000,000	200,000,000
Preferred stock, $.01 par value, 4,900 shares authorized; none issued and outstanding	–	–
Class A common stock, nonvoting, $.01 par value, 1,000 shares authorized; none issued and outstanding	–	–

	12/31/2003	12/31/2002
Common stock, $.01 par value, 1,000,000 shares authorized; 324,392 shares and 324,072 shares issued and outstanding in 2003 and 2002, respectively	3,244,000	3,240,000
Additional paid-in capital	734,550,000	732,760,000
Retained earnings (Accumulated deficit)	(218,571,000)	307,379,000
Accumulated other comprehensive income	2,795,000	3,139,000
Total stockholders' equity	722,018,000	1,246,518,000
	$2,028,438,000	$2,509,407,000

GATEWAY, INC. Income Statement

	12/31/2003	12/31/2002	12/31/2001
Net sales	$3,402,364,000	$4,171,325,000	$ 5,937,896,000
Cost of goods sold	2,938,800,000	3,605,120,000	5,099,704,000
Gross profit	463,564,000	566,205,000	838,192,000
Selling, general, and administrative expenses	974,139,000	1,077,447,000	2,022,122,000
Operating loss	(510,575,000)	(511,242,000)	(1,183,930,000)
Other income (loss), net	19,328,000	35,496,000	(94,964,000)
Loss before income taxes and cumulative effect of change in accounting principle	(491,247,000)	(475,746,000)	(1,278,894,000)
Provision (benefit) for income taxes	23,565,000	(178,028,000)	(271,683,000)
Loss before cumulative effect of change in accounting principle	(514,812,000)	(297,718,000)	(1,007,211,000)
Cumulative effect of change in accounting principle, net of tax	–	–	(23,851,000)
Net loss	(514,812,000)	(297,718,000)	(1,031,062,000)
Preferred stock dividends and accretion	(11,138,000)	(11,323,000)	–
Net loss attributable to common stockholders	$ (525,950,000)	$ (309,041,000)	$(1,031,062,000)

GATEWAY, INC. Cash Flow

	12/31/2003	12/31/2002	12/31/2001
Cash flows from operating activities:			
Net loss	$(514,812,000)	$(297,718,000)	$(1,031,062,000)
Adjustments to reconcile net loss to net cash provided by (used in) operating activities:			
Depreciation and amortization	163,973,000	159,458,000	199,976,000
Provision for uncollectible accounts receivable	11,297,000	11,139,000	23,151,000
Deferred income taxes	6,000,000	257,172,000	(27,282,000)
Loss on investments	808,000	30,272,000	186,745,000
Write-down of long-lived assets	66,397,000	52,975,000	418,304,000
Gain on settlement of acquisition liability	–	(13,782,000)	–
Loss on sale of property	6,052,000	–	–
Cumulative effect of change in accounting principle	–	–	23,851,000
Gain on extinguishment of debt	–	–	(6,890,000)
Other, net	1,941,000	(1,929,000)	(1,707,000)
Changes in operating assets and liabilities:			
Accounts receivable	(23,633,000)	11,020,000	301,630,000

	12/31/2003	12/31/2002	12/31/2001
Inventory	(25,375,000)	31,505,000	194,799,000
Other assets	306,258,000	(76,975,000)	21,729,000
Accounts payable	137,716,000	(59,856,000)	(442,312,000)
Accrued liabilities	(95,117,000)	(103,868,000)	(87,714,000)
Accrued royalties	(8,196,000)	(79,014,000)	(2,747,000)
Other liabilities	39,382,000	54,924,000	(40,810,000)
Net cash provided by (used in) operating activities	72,691,000	(24,677,000)	(270,339,000)
Cash flows from investing activities:			
Capital expenditures	(72,978,000)	(78,497,000)	(199,493,000)
Proceeds from sale of investment	–	11,100,000	–
Purchases of available-for-sale securities	(530,323,000)	(614,023,000)	(638,869,000)
Sales of available-for-sale securities	401,109,000	436,316,000	356,071,000
Proceeds from the sale of financing receivables	–	9,896,000	569,579,000
Purchase of financing receivables, net of repayments	–	–	(28,476,000)
Proceeds from notes receivable	20,045,000	–	50,000,000
Other, net	–	–	189,000
Net cash provided by (used in) investing activities	(182,147,000)	(235,208,000)	109,001,000
Cash flows from financing activities:			
Proceeds from issuance of notes payable	–	–	200,000,000
Principal payments on long-term obligations and notes payable	–	–	(3,984,000)
Proceeds from stock issuance	–	–	200,000,000
Payment of preferred dividends	(8,840,000)	(5,878,000)	–
Stock options exercised	1,794,000	367,000	9,431,000
Net cash provided by (used in) financing activities	(7,046,000)	(5,511,000)	405,447,000
Foreign exchange effect on cash and cash equivalents	–	–	2,893,000
Net increase (decrease) in cash and cash equivalents	(116,502,000)	(265,396,000)	247,002,000
Cash and cash equivalents, beginning of year	465,603,000	730,999,000	483,997,000
Cash and cash equivalents, end of year	$ 349,101,000	$ 465,603,000	$ 730,999,000

a. Calculate the following ratios:

ROE, ROC, ROA, Profit Margin, Total Asset Turnover, Receivable Turnover, Inventory Turnover, Payables Turnover Current, Quick, Debt/Equity

b. Calculate the common-size balance sheet and income statement.

c. Comment on the financial health of the two organizations from the point of view of a lender who has been asked to make a $200 million loan to each of the companies.

d. Estimate Dell's and Gateway's 2003 net sales if sales were recognized as cash is collected rather than on the accrual basis. Comment on the significance of the difference between your estimate and reported sales.

e. Suppose you are interested in forecasting future sales for Dell and Gateway. Describe methods that can be used. Forecast Dell's and Gateway's sales for 2006. Justify your answer.

30. Use the data from the financial statement of Home Depot and Lowes to answer the following questions.

HOME DEPOT, INC. Balance Sheet	02/01/2004	02/01/2003
Assets		
Current assets:		
Cash and cash equivalents	$ 2,826,000,000	$ 2,188,000,000
Short-term investments, including current maturities of long-term investments	26,000,000	65,000,000
Receivables, net	1,097,000,000	1,072,000,000
Merchandise inventories	9,076,000,000	8,338,000,000
Other current assets	303,000,000	254,000,000
Total current assets	13,328,000,000	11,917,000,000
Property and equipment, at cost:		
Land	6,397,000,000	5,560,000,000
Buildings	10,920,000,000	9,197,000,000
Furniture, fixtures, and equipment	5,163,000,000	4,074,000,000
Leasehold improvements	942,000,000	872,000,000
Construction in progress	820,000,000	724,000,000
Capital leases	352,000,000	306,000,000
	24,594,000,000	20,733,000,000
Less accumulated depreciation and amortization	4,531,000,000	3,565,000,000
Net property and equipment	20,063,000,000	17,168,000,000
Notes receivable	84,000,000	107,000,000
Cost in excess of the fair value of net assets acquired, net of accumulated amortization of $54 at February 1, 2004 and $50 at February 2, 2003	833,000,000	575,000,000
Other assets	129,000,000	244,000,000
Total assets	$34,437,000,000	$ 30,011,000,000
Liabilities and stockholders' equity		
Current liabilities:		
Accounts payable	$ 5,159,000,000	$ 4,560,000,000
Accrued salaries and related expenses	801,000,000	809,000,000
Sales taxes payable	419,000,000	307,000,000
Deferred revenue	1,281,000,000	998,000,000
Income taxes payable	175,000,000	227,000,000
Current installments of long-term debt	509,000,000	7,000,000
Other accrued expenses	1,210,000,000	1,127,000,000
Total current liabilities	9,554,000,000	8,035,000,000

	02/01/2004	02/01/2003
Long-term debt, excluding current installments	856,000,000	1,321,000,000
Other long-term liabilities	653,000,000	491,000,000
Deferred income taxes	967,000,000	362,000,000
Stockholders' equity		
Common stock, par value $0.05; authorized: 10,000 shares, issued and outstanding 2,373 shares at February 1, 2004 and 2,362 shares at February 2, 2003	119,000,000	118,000,000
Paid-in capital	6,184,000,000	5,858,000,000
Retained earnings	19,680,000,000	15,971,000,000
Accumulated other comprehensive income (loss)	90,000,000	(82,000,000)
Unearned compensation	(76,000,000)	(63,000,000)
Treasury stock, at cost, 116 shares at February 1, 2004 and 69 shares at February 2, 2003	(3,590,000,000)	(2,000,000,000)
Total stockholders' equity	22,407,000,000	19,802,000,000
Total liabilities and stockholders' equity	$34,437,000,000	$30,011,000,000

HOME DEPOT, INC. Income Statement

	02/01/2004	02/01/2003	02/01/2002
Net sales	$64,816,000,000	$58,247,000,000	$53,553,000,000
Cost of merchandise sold	44,236,000,000	40,139,000,000	37,406,000,000
Gross profit	20,580,000,000	18,108,000,000	16,147,000,000
Operating expenses:			
Selling and store operating	12,502,000,000	11,180,000,000	10,163,000,000
Pre-opening	86,000,000	96,000,000	117,000,000
General and administrative	1,146,000,000	1,002,000,000	935,000,000
Total operating expenses	13,734,000,000	12,278,000,000	11,215,000,000
Operating income	6,846,000,000	5,830,000,000	4,932,000,000
Interest income (expense):			
Interest and investment income	59,000,000	79,000,000	53,000,000
Interest expense	(62,000,000)	(37,000,000)	(28,000,000)
Interest, net	(3,000,000)	42,000,000	25,000,000
Earnings before provision for income taxes	6,843,000,000	5,872,000,000	4,957,000,000
Provision for income taxes	2,539,000,000	2,208,000,000	1,913,000,000
Net earnings	$ 4,304,000,000	$3,664,000,000	$3,044,000,000

HOME DEPOT, INC. Cash Flow	02/01/2004	02/01/2003	02/01/2002
Cash flows from operations:			
Net earnings	$4,304,000,000	$3,664,000,000	$3,044,000,000
Reconciliation of net earnings to net			
Cash provided by operations:			
Depreciation and amortization	1,076,000,000	903,000,000	764,000,000
Decrease (increase) in receivables, net	25,000,000	(38,000,000)	(119,000,000)
Increase in merchandise inventories	(693,000,000)	(1,592,000,000)	(166,000,000)
Increase in accounts payable and accrued liabilities	790,000,000	1,394,000,000	1,878,000,000
Increase in deferred revenue	279,000,000	147,000,000	200,000,000
(Decrease) increase in income taxes payable	(27,000,000)	83,000,000	272,000,000
Increase (decrease) in deferred income taxes	605,000,000	173,000,000	(6,000,000)
Other	186,000,000	68,000,000	96,000,000
Net cash provided by operations	6,545,000,000	4,802,000,000	5,963,000,000
Cash flows from investing activities:			
Capital expenditures, net of $47, $49, and $5 of noncash capital expenditures in fiscal 2003, 2002 and 2001, respectively	(3,508,000,000)	(2,749,000,000)	(3,393,000,000)
Purchase of assets from off-balance sheet financing arrangement	(598,000,000)	–	–
Payments for businesses acquired, net	(215,000,000)	(235,000,000)	(190,000,000)
Proceeds from sales of businesses, net	–	22,000,000	64,000,000
Proceeds from sales of property and equipment	265,000,000	105,000,000	126,000,000
Purchases of investments	(159,000,000)	(583,000,000)	(85,000,000)
Proceeds from maturities of investments	219,000,000	506,000,000	25,000,000
Other	0	0	(13,000,000)
Net cash used in investing activities	(3,996,000,000)	(2,934,000,000)	(3,466,000,000)
Cash flows from financing activities:			
Repayments of commercial paper obligations, net	–	–	(754,000,000)
Proceeds from long-term debt	–	1,000,000	532,000,000
Repayments of long-term debt	(9,000,000)	–	–
Repurchase of common stock	(1,554,000,000)	(2,000,000,000)	–
Proceeds from sale of common stock, net	227,000,000	326,000,000	445,000,000
Cash dividends paid to stockholders	(595,000,000)	(492,000,000)	(396,000,000)
Net cash used in financing activities	(1,931,000,000)	(2,165,000,000)	(173,000,000)
Effect of exchange rate changes on cash and cash equivalents	20,000,000	8,000,000	(14,000,000)
Increase (decrease) in cash and cash equivalents	638,000,000	(289,000,000)	2,310,000,000
Cash and cash equivalents at beginning of year	2,188,000,000	2,477,000,000	167,000,000
Cash and cash equivalents at end of year	2,826,000,000	2,188,000,000	2,477,000,000
Supplemental disclosure of cash payments made for:			
Interest, net of interest capitalized	70,000,000	50,000,000	18,000,000
Income taxes	$2,037,000,000	$1,951,000,000	$1,685,000,000

Lowe's Companies, Inc.
Consolidated Balance Sheets
(In Millions, Except Par Value Data)

	Jan-30-04	Jan-31-03
Assets		
Current assets:		
Cash and cash equivalents	$ 1,446,000,000	$ 853,000,000
Short-term investments (note 3)	178,000,000	273,000,000
Accounts receivable, net (note 1)	131,000,000	172,000,000
Merchandise inventory (note 1)	4,584,000,000	3,968,000,000
Deferred income taxes (note 13)	59,000,000	58,000,000
Other current assets	289,000,000	244,000,000
Total current assets	6,687,000,000	5,568,000,000
Property, less accumulated depreciation (notes 4 and 5)	11,945,000,000	10,352,000,000
Long-term investments (note 3)	169,000,000	29,000,000
Other assets (note 5)	241,000,000	160,000,000
Total assets	$19,042,000,000	$16,109,000,000
Liabilities and shareholders' equity		
Current liabilities:		
Short-term borrowings (note 6)	$ —	$ 50,000,000
Current maturities of long-term debt (note 7)	77,000,000	29,000,000
Accounts payable	2,366,000,000	1,943,000,000
Employee retirement plans (note 12)	74,000,000	88,000,000
Accrued salaries and wages	335,000,000	306,000,000
Other current liabilities (note 5)	1,516,000,000	1,162,000,000
Total current liabilities	4,368,000,000	3,578,000,000
Long-term debt, excluding current maturities (notes 7, 8, and 11)	3,678,000,000	3,736,000,000
Deferred income taxes (note 13)	657,000,000	478,000,000
Other long-term liabilities	30,000,000	15,000,000
Total liabilities	8,733,000,000	7,807,000,000
Shareholders' equity (note 10):		
Preferred stock $5 par value, none issued	—	—
Common stock −$.50 par value; shares issued and outstanding January 30, 2004 − 787 January 31, 2003 − 782	394,000,000	391,000,000
Capital in excess of par value	2,237,000,000	2,023,000,000
Retained earnings	7,677,000,000	5,887,000,000
Accumulated other comprehensive income	1,000,000	1,000,000
Total shareholders' equity	10,309,000,000	8,302,000,000
Total liabilities and shareholders' equity	$19,042,000,000	$16,109,000,000

Lowe's Companies, Inc. Consolidated Statements of Earnings Years Ended on	Jan-30-04	Jan-31-03	Feb-1-02
Net sales	$30,838,000,000	$26,112,000,000	$21,714,000,000
Cost of sales	21,231,000,000	18,164,000,000	15,427,000,000
Gross margin	9,607,000,000	7,948,000,000	6,287,000,000
Expenses:	–	–	–
Selling, general, and administrative (note 5)	5,543,000,000	4,676,000,000	3,857,000,000
Store opening costs	128,000,000	129,000,000	140,000,000
Depreciation	758,000,000	622,000,000	513,000,000
Interest (note 15)	180,000,000	182,000,000	174,000,000
Total expenses	6,609,000,000	5,609,000,000	4,684,000,000
Pre-tax earnings	2,998,000,000	2,339,000,000	1,603,000,000
Income tax provision (note 13)	1,136,000,000	880,000,000	593,000,000
Earnings from continuing operations	1,862,000,000	1,459,000,000	1,010,000,000
Earnings from discontinued operations, net of tax (note 2)	15,000,000	12,000,000	13,000,000
Net earnings	$ 877,000,000	$ 1,471,000,000	$ 1,023,000,000

LOWES COMPANIES, INC. Cash Flow

	01/30/2004	01/30/2003	01/30/2002
Cash Flows from operating activities:			
Net earnings	$1,877,000,000	$1,471,000,000	$1,023,000,000
Earnings from discontinued operations, net of tax	(15,000,000)	(12,000,000)	(13,000,000)
Earnings from continuing operations	1,862,000,000	1,459,000,000	1,010,000,000
Adjustments to reconcile net earnings to net cash provided by operating activities:			
Depreciation and amortization	781,000,000	641,000,000	530,000,000
Deferred income taxes	178,000,000	208,000,000	42,000,000
Loss on disposition/write-down of fixed and other assets	31,000,000	18,000,000	39,000,000
Stock-based compensation expense	41,000,000	–	–
Tax effect of stock options exercised	31,000,000	29,000,000	35,000,000
Changes in operating assets and liabilities:			
Accounts receivable, net	2,000,000	(9,000,000)	(5,000,000)
Merchandise inventory	(648,000,000)	(357,000,000)	(326,000,000)
Other operating assets	(45,000,000)	(41,000,000)	(37,000,000)
Accounts payable	423,000,000	228,000,000	1,000,000
Employee retirement plans	(14,000,000)	40,000,000	114,000,000
Other operating liabilities	399,000,000	461,000,000	193,000,000

	01/30/2004	01/30/2003	01/30/2002
Net cash provided by operating activities from continuing operations	3,041,000,000	2,677,000,000	1,596,000,000
Cash flows from investing activities:			
Decrease (increase) in investment assets:			
Short-term investments	139,000,000	(203,000,000)	(30,000,000)
Purchases of long-term investments	(381,000,000)	(24,000,000)	(1,000,000)
Proceeds from sale/maturity of long-term investments	193,000,000	–	3,000,000
Increase in other long-term assets	(95,000,000)	(33,000,000)	(14,000,000)
Fixed assets acquired	(2,444,000,000)	(2,359,000,000)	(2,196,000,000)
Proceeds from the sale of fixed and other long-term assets	45,000,000	44,000,000	42,000,000
Net cash used in investing activities from continuing operations	(2,543,000,000)	(2,575,000,000)	(2,196,000,000)
Cash flows from financing activities:			
Net decrease in short-term borrowings	(50,000,000)	(50,000,000)	(150,000,000)
Long-term debt borrowings	–	–	1,087,000,000
Repayment of long-term debt	(29,000,000)	(63,000,000)	(63,000,000)
Proceeds from employee stock purchase plan	52,000,000	50,000,000	38,000,000
Proceeds from stock options exercised	97,000,000	65,000,000	77,000,000
Cash dividend payments	(87,000,000)	(66,000,000)	(60,000,000)
Net cash provided by (used in) financing activities from continuing operations	(17,000,000)	(64,000,000)	929,000,000
Net cash provided by discontinued operations	112,000,000	16,000,000	14,000,000
Net increase (decrease) in cash and cash equivalents	593,000,000	54,000,000	343,000,000
Cash and cash equivalents, beginning of year	853,000,000	799,000,000	456,000,000
Cash and cash equivalents, end of year	$1,446,000,000	$ 853,000,000	$ 799,000,000

a. Calculate the following ratios:

ROE, ROC, ROA, Profit Margin, Total Asset Turnover, Receivable Turnover, Inventory Turnover, Payables Turnover Current, Quick, Debt/Equity

b. Calculate the common-size balance sheet and income statement.

c. Comment on the financial health of the two organizations from the point of view of a lender who has been asked to make a $200 million loan to each of the companies.

d. Estimate Lowe's and Home Depot's sales for the year ending February 1, 2004 if sales had been recorded as cash is collected rather than on the accrual basis. Comment on the significance of the difference between your estimate and reported sales.

Suppose you are interested in forecasting future sales for Lowes and Home Depot. Describe methods that can be used. Forecast Lowe's and Home Depot's sales for 2006. Justify your answer.

Assuming that the amount forecast for 2006 will continue indefinitely into the future, estimate the market value of Lowes and Home Depot using the free cash flow and residual income approaches. Assume a required rate of return of 10 percent. Hint: The present value of a stream of cash flows that continues into infinity is computed as the amount divided by the required rate of return. For example, the present value of $10 to be received annually forever is $10/.1 = \$100$ (assuming a 10 percent required rate of return).

BEYOND THE BOOK

31. Prepare a comparative ratio analysis of two competitor companies. At the direction of your instructor, pick either two domestic or one domestic and one foreign competitor. At a minimum, use the set of ratios discussed in the text and at least three years of data. Use any additional ratios that might be commonly used in the industry that you select (you may also need to drop some of the ratios discussed in the book if they are not relevant).

Required: Prepare a written report summarizing your comparative analysis. For the purpose of this report, assume some sort of decision perspective; for instance, you might assume that you are a bank loan officer evaluating the two competitors to decide which has the best lending risk profile.

Outline

Part II: Evaluating Economic Performance of Companies and Projects

- Lecture slides on ratio analysis, discounted cash flows and transform techniques

- Chapters 2 and 3 of "Advanced Engineering Economics" by Park and Sharp-Bette

- Lecture slides on figures of merit

- Chapters 6 and 7 of "Advanced Engineering Economics" by Park and Sharp-Bette

Evaluating Financial Performance

➢ **Return on Equity (ROE)** = Net income / Shareholders' Equity

➢ **Return on Assets (ROA)** = Net income / Assets

➢ **Return on Invested Capital (ROIC)** = EBIT (1- Tax rate) / (Interest-bearing debt + Shareholders' equity)

➢ **Profit Margin (PM)** = Net income / Sales

➢ **Gross Margin (GM)** = Gross profit / Sales

➢ **Price to Earnings (P/E ratio)** = Price per share / Earnings per share

Evaluating Financial Performance

ROE = Net income/ Shareholders' Equity

= **(Net income/Sales) x (Sales/Assets) x (Assets/Shareholders' Equity)**

= **Profit margin** x **Asset Turnover** x **Financial Leverage**

I.S. **Left B.S.** **Right B.S.**

➤ **ROE is not a reliable financial yardstick:**

- **Timing problem**
- **Risk problem**
- **Value problem**

246

Evaluating Financial Performance

➤ **Asset Turnover** = Sales / Assets

➤ **Fixed-Asset Turnover** = Sales / Net property, plant and equipment

➤ **Inventory Turnover** = Cost of goods sold / Ending inventory

➤ **Collection Period** = Accounts receivable / Credit sales per day

(Use sales if credit sales unavailable)

➤ **Days' Sales in Cash** = Cash and securities / Sales per day

➤ **Payables Period** = Accounts payable / Credit purchases per day

(Use COGS if credit purchases unavailable))

247

Evaluating Financial Performance

> **Assets to Equity** = Assets / Shareholders' equity

> **Debt to Assets** = Total liabilities / Assets

> **Debt to Equity** = Total liabilities / Shareholders' equity

> **Times Interest Earned** = EBIT / Interest expense

> **Current Ratio** = Current assets / Current liabilities

> **Acid Test** = (Current assets – Inventory) / Current liabilities

Compounding, Equivalence and Transform Techniques

➤ Payback period and accounting rate of return

➤ Time value of money

➤ Interest rates

➤ Useful formulas

➤ Discrete compounding

➤ Continuous compounding

➤ Equivalence of cash flows

➤ Effect of inflation on cash flow equivalence

➤ Z-transforms and discrete cash flows

➤ Laplace transforms and continuous cash flows

Compounding, Equivalence and Transform Techniques

➢ **Simple interest**

➢ $F_N = P + I = P(1 + Ni)$

➢ **Compound interest**

➢ $F_N = P + I = P(1 + i)^N$

➢ **Nominal and effective interest rates**

➢ Annual percentage rate (APR) vs. Effective annual rate (EAR)

✓ m: number of interest periods per year

✓ $EAR = (1 + APR/m)^m - 1$

Compounding, Equivalence and Transform Techniques

➢ **4 major types of discrete payments**

- **Single payment**

$$F_N = F \quad \text{and} \quad F_n = 0, \; \forall n \in \{1,..., N-1\}$$

- **Uniform series or equal-payment series**

$$F_n = A, \; \forall n \in \{1,..., N\}$$

- **Arithmetic gradient series**

$$F_n = (n-1)G, \; \forall n \in \{1,..., N\}$$

- **Geometric gradient series**

$$F_n = F_1(1+g)^{n-1}, \; \forall n \in \{1,..., N\}$$

Compounding, Equivalence and Transform Techniques

➢ **Compound amount:** $(F/A, i, N)$

$$F = A[\frac{(1+i)^N - 1}{i}]$$

➢ **Sinking fund:** $(A/F, i, N)$

$$A = F[\frac{i}{(1+i)^N - 1}]$$

➢ **Present worth:** $(P/A, i, N)$

$$P = \frac{A}{i}[1 - \frac{1}{(1+i)^N}]$$

➢ **Capital recovery:** $(A/P, i, N)$

$$A = P \frac{i}{1 - \frac{1}{(1+i)^N}}$$

Compounding, Equivalence and Transform Techniques

➤**Present worth:** $(P / G , i , N)$

$$P = G[\dfrac{1 - \dfrac{(1 + Ni)}{(1 + i)^N}}{i^2}]$$

➤**Uniform gradient series conversion factor:** $(A / G , i , N)$

$$A = G[\dfrac{1}{i} - \dfrac{N}{(1 + i)^N - 1}]$$

➤**Future worth equivalent of a gradient series:** $(F / G , i , N)$

$$(F / G, i, N) = \dfrac{G}{i}[(F / A, i, N) - N]$$

Compounding, Equivalence and Transform Techniques

➢**Present worth:**

$$P = F_1 \frac{1 - (\frac{1+g}{1+i})^N}{i - g}$$

Using $g' = \frac{1+i}{1+g} - 1$, we also obtain

$$P = \frac{F_1}{1+g}(P/A, g', N)$$

Compounding, Equivalence and Transform Techniques

Continuous Compounding

Discrete Payments

➢ **Continuous compounding at rate r**

▪ **The effective interest rate i is:**

✓ $i = e^r - 1$

▪ **Use the formulas of discrete compounding**

Compounding, Equivalence and Transform Techniques

Continuous Compounding

Continuous Cash Flows

➢ **Continuous compounding at rate r with flow rate at time t of F_t**

- **Present value**

$$P = \int_0^N F_t e^{-rt} \, dt$$

- **Future value**

$$F = \int_0^N F_t e^{r(N-t)} \, dt$$

Compounding, Equivalence and Transform Techniques

Continuous Compounding

Continuous Cash Flows

➤ **Special case:** $F_t = B$

- **Funds flow present worth factor**

$$P = B \int_0^N e^{-rt}\, dt = B\left(\frac{1 - e^{-rN}}{r}\right)$$

- **Funds flow compound amount factor**

$$F = B \int_0^N e^{rt}\, dt = B\left(\frac{e^{rN} - 1}{r}\right)$$

Compounding, Equivalence and Transform Techniques

➤ **Two cash flows are equivalent *at interest i* if we can convert one cash flow into the other using proper compound interest factors**

➤ **Cash flow equivalence is used a lot in the stock market and is the basis of the "absence of arbitrage" principle**

Compounding, Equivalence and Transform Techniques

Effect of Inflation on
Cash Flow
Equivalence

- **Measures of inflation:**

  - ➢ CPI (Consumer Price Index) based on market basket

  - ➢ GNPIPD (Gross National Product Implicit Price Deflator)

  - ➢ PPI (Producer Price Index)

- **These measures tend to overstate inflation as they do not take into account:**

  - ➢ Improvements in quality

  - ➢ Opportunities for substitution

Compounding, Equivalence and Transform Techniques

- **Explicit and implicit treatments of inflation in discounting**

  - ➤ Actual dollars (current dollars, future dollars, inflated dollars, nominal dollars)

  - ➤ Constant dollars (real dollars, deflated dollars, todays dollars)

  - ➤ Market interest rate i

  - ➤ Inflation-free interest rate i' (real interest rate, true interest rate, constant-dollar interest rate)

  - ➤ General inflation rate f

$$i' = \frac{i - f}{1 + f}$$

Compounding, Equivalence and Transform Techniques

- **Z- transform of an infinite cash flow $\{f(n)\}$ is:**

$$F(z) = Z\{f(n)\} \equiv \sum_{n=0}^{\infty} f(n) z^{-n}$$

$$F(1+i) = \sum_{n=0}^{\infty} f(n)(1+i)^{-n}$$

- **Properties:**
  - ➤ **There is a one to one mapping between an infinite cash flow and its Z-transform**
  - ➤ **Linear combinations of cash flows correspond to the same linear combinations of their Z-transforms**
- **Z-transforms have been pre-computed for a large number of cash flows**

261

Compounding, Equivalence and Transform Techniques

- **Laplace transform of an infinite continuous cash flow $\{f(t)\}$ is:**

$$PV(r) = F(z) \equiv \int_0^\infty f(t)e^{-rt}\,dt$$

- **Properties:**
  - ➢ **There is a one to one mapping between an infinite cash flow and its Laplace transform**
  - ➢ **Linear combinations of cash flows correspond to the same linear combinations of their Laplace transforms**
- **Laplace transforms have been pre-computed for a large number of cash flows**

Outline

Part II: Evaluating Economic Performance of Companies and Projects

- Lecture slides on ratio analysis, discounted cash flows and transform techniques

- Chapters 2 and 3 of "Advanced Engineering Economics" by Park and Sharp-Bette

- Lecture slides on figures of merit

- Chapters 6 and 7 of "Advanced Engineering Economics" by Park and Sharp-Bette

2
Interest
and Equivalence

2.1 INTRODUCTION

Engineering economic analysis is primarily concerned with the evaluation of economic investment alternatives. We often describe these investment alternatives by a cash flow diagram showing the amount and timing of estimated future receipts and disbursements that will result from each decision. Because the time value of money is related to the effect of time and interest on monetary amounts, we must consider both the timing and the magnitude of cash flow. When comparing investment alternatives, we must consider the expected receipts and disbursements of these investment alternatives on the same basis. This type of comparison requires understanding of the concepts of equivalence and the proper use of various interest formulas. In this chapter we will examine a number of mathematical operations that are based on the time value of money, with an emphasis on modeling cash flow profiles.

2.2. CASH FLOW PROFILE

An investment project can be described by the amount and timing of expected costs and benefits in the planning horizon. (We will use the terms *project* and *proposal* interchangeably throughout this book.) The terms *costs* and *benefits* represent *disbursements* and *receipts,* respectively. We will use the term *payment* (or *net cash flow*) to denote the receipts less the disbursements that occur at the same point in time. The stream of disbursements and receipts for an investment project over the planning horizon is said to be the *cash flow profile* of the project.

To facilitate the description of project cash flows, we classify them in two categories: (1) discrete-time cash flows and (2) continuous-time flows. The discrete-time cash flows are those in which cash flow occurs at the end of, at the start of, or within discrete time periods. The continuous flows are those in which money flows at a given rate and continuously throughout a given time period. The following notation will be adopted:

F_n = discrete payment occurring at period n,

F_t = continuous payment occurring at time t.

If $F_n < 0$, F_n represents a net disbursement (cash outflow). If $F_n > 0$, F_n represents a net receipt (cash inflow). We can say the same for F_t.

2.3 TIME PREFERENCE AND INTEREST

2.3.1 Time Preference

Cash flows that occur at different points in time have different values and cannot be compared directly with one another. This fact is often stated simply as "money has a time value." There are several reasons why we must assess cash flows in different periods in terms of time preference.

First, money has a potential *earning power*, because having a dollar now gives us an opportunity to invest this dollar in the near future. In other words, equal dollar amounts available at different points in time have different values based on the opportunity to profit from investment activity.

Second, money has a time value because a user may have a different utility of consumption of dollars (i.e., consider them more or less desirable to use) at different times. The preference for consumption in different periods is measured by the rate of time preference. For example, if we have a rate of time preference of i per time period, we are indifferent toward the prospect of either consuming P units now or consuming $P(1 + i)$ units at the end of the period. The rate of time preference is often called the *interest rate* (or *discount rate*) in economic analysis.

Third, money has time value because the *buying power* of a dollar changes through time. When there is inflation, the amount of goods that can be bought for a certain amount of money decreases as the time of purchase is further in the future. Although this change in the buying power of money is important, we limit our concept of time preference to the fact that money has an *earning power*, or utility of consumption. We will treat the effects of inflation explicitly in a later section, and any future reference to the time value of money will be restricted to the first two aspects. Before considering the actual effect of this time value, we will review the types of interest and how they are calculated.

2.3.2 Types of Interest

If an amount of money is deposited in a financial institution, interest accrues (accumulates) at regular time intervals. Each time interval represents an *interest period*. Then the interest earned on the original amount is calculated according to a specified interest rate at the end of the interest period. Two approaches are in use in calculating the earned interest: *simple interest* and *compound interest*.

The first approach considers that the interest earned in any present activity is a linear function of time. Consider the situation in which a present amount P is borrowed from the bank, to be repaid N periods hence by a future amount F. The difference, $F - P$, is simply the interest payment I owed to the bank for the

266

use of the principal P dollars. Because the interest earned is directly proportional to the principal, the interest i is called *simple interest* and is computed from

$$I = F - P$$
$$= (Pi)N$$
$$F = P + (Pi)N$$
$$= P(1 + iN) \qquad (2.1)$$

The second approach assumes that the earned interest is not withdrawn at the end of an interest period and is automatically redeposited with the original sum in the next interest period. The interest thus accumulated is called *compound interest.* For example, if we deposit $100 in a bank that pays 5% compounded annually and leave the interest in the account, we will have

after 1 year $100 (1.05) = $105.00
after 2 years $105.00 (1.05) = $110.25
after 3 years $110.25 (1.05) = $115.7625

The amount $115.7625 is greater than the original $100 plus the simple interest of $100(0.05)(3), which would be $115.00, because the interest earned during the first and second periods earns additional interest. Symbolically, we can represent a future amount F at time N in terms of a present amount P at time 0, assuming i% interest per period:

$$F_1 = P(1 + i) \qquad \text{after 1 year}$$
$$F_2 = F_1(1 + i) = P(1 + i)^2 \qquad \text{after 2 years}$$
$$\vdots$$
$$F_N = F_{N-1}(1 + i) = P(1 + i)^N \qquad \text{after } N \text{ years}$$

or

$$F = P[(1 + i)^N] \qquad (2.2)$$

From Eq. 2.2, the total interest earned over N periods with the compound interest is

$$I = F - P \doteq P[(1 + i)^N - 1] \qquad (2.3)$$

The additional interest earned with the compound interest is

$$\Delta I = P[(1 + i)^N - 1] - PiN$$
$$= P[(1 + i)^N - (1 + iN)] \qquad (2.4)$$

As either i or N becomes large, ΔI also becomes large, so the effect of compounding is further pronounced.

Example 2.1

Compare the interest earned by $1,000 for 10 years at 9% simple interest with that earned by the same amount for 10 years at 9% compounded annually.

$$\Delta I = 1000[(1 + 0.09)^{10} - (1 + 0.09(10))] = \$467.36$$

The difference in interest payments is $467.36. □

Unless stated otherwise, practically all financial transactions are based on compound interest; however, the length of the interest period for compounding and the interest rate per period must be specified for individual transactions. In the next section we discuss the conventions used in describing the interest period and the compounding period in business transactions.

2.3.3 Nominal and Effective Interest Rates

In engineering economic analysis, a year is usually used as the interest period, because investments in engineering projects are of long duration and a calendar year is a convenient period for accounting and tax computation. In financial transactions, however, the interest period may be of any duration—a month, a quarter, a year, and so on. For example, the interest charge for the purchase of a car on credit may be compounded monthly, whereas the interest accrued from a savings account in a credit union may be compounded quarterly. Consequently, we must introduce the terms nominal interest rate and effective interest rate to describe more precisely the nature of compounding schemes.

Nominal Interest.   If a financial institution uses more than one interest period per year in compounding the interest, it usually quotes the interest on an annual basis. For example, a year's interest at 1.5% compounded each month is typically quoted as "18% (1.5% × 12) compounded monthly." When the interest rate is stated in this fashion, the 18% interest is called a *nominal interest rate* or *annual percentage rate*. The nominal interest rate, while convenient for a financial institution to use in quoting interest rates on its transactions, does not explain the effect of any compounding during the year. We use the term effective interest rate to describe more precisely the compounding effect of any business transaction.

Effective Interest Rate.   The effective interest rate represents the actual interest earned or charged for a specified time period. In specifying such a time period, we may use the convention of either a year or a time period identical to the payment period. The effective interest rate based on a year is referred to as the *effective annual interest rate* i_a. The effective interest rate based on the payment period is called the *effective interest rate per payment period i.*

We will first look at the expression of the effective annual interest rate. Suppose a bank charges an interest rate of 12% compounded quarterly. This means that the interest rate per period is 3% (12%/4) for each of the 3-month periods during the year. Then interest for a sum of $1 accrued at the end of the year (see Eq. 2.3) is

$$\left(1 + \frac{0.12}{4}\right)^4 - 1 = 0.1255$$

Thus, the effective annual interest rate is 12.55%. Similarly, an interest rate of 12% compounded monthly means that the interest rate per period is 1% (12%/12) for each month during the year. Thus, the effective annual interest rate is

$$\left(1 + \frac{0.12}{12}\right)^{12} - 1 = 0.1268 = 12.68\%$$

Now we can generalize the result as

$$i_a = \left(1 + \frac{r}{M}\right)^M - 1 \tag{2.5}$$

where i_a = the effective annual interest rate,
  r = the nominal interest rate per year,
  M = the number of interest (compounding) periods per year,
  r/M = the interest rate per interest period.

For the special case where $M = 1$ (i.e., one interest period per year, or annual compounding) and $r/M = r$, Eq. 2.5 reduces to $i_a = r = i$. This simply means that with annual compounding we do not need to distinguish between the nominal and effective interest rates.

The result of Eq. 2.5 can be further generalized to compute the effective interest rate in *any payment period*. This results in

$$i = \left(1 + \frac{r}{M}\right)^C - 1$$

$$= \left(1 + \frac{r}{CK}\right)^C - 1 \tag{2.6}$$

where i = the effective interest rate per payment period,
  C = the number of interest periods per payment period,
  K = the number of payment periods per year,
  r/K = the nominal interest rate per payment period.

In deriving Eq. 2.6, we should note the relationships $M \geq C$ and $M = CK$. Obviously, when $K = 1$, C is equal to M, and therefore $i = i_a$. Figure 2.1 illustrates the relationship between the nominal and effective interest rates.

Some financial institutions offer a large number of interest periods per year, such as $M = 365$ (daily compounding). As the number of interest periods M becomes very large, the interest rate per interest period, r/M, becomes very small. If M approaches infinity and r/M approaches zero as a limit, the limiting

Situation: Interest is calculated on the basis of 12% compounded monthly. Payments are made quarterly.

$K = 4$, 4 quarterly payment periods per year
$C = 3$, 3 interest (compounding) periods per quarter
$r = 12\%$
$M = 12$, 12 monthly interest (compounding) periods per year
$r/M = 1\%$, the interest rate per month
$r/K = 3\%$, the nominal interest rate per quarter

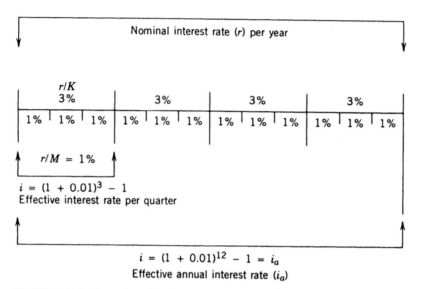

FIGURE 2.1 Functional relationships of r, i, and i_a for monthly compounding with quarterly payments.

condition is equivalent to continuous compounding. By taking limits on both sides of Eq. 2.6, we obtain

$$i = \lim_{M \to \infty} \left[\left(1 + \frac{r}{M} \right)^M - 1 \right]$$

$$= \lim_{CK \to \infty} \left[\left(1 + \frac{r}{CK} \right)^C - 1 \right]$$

$$= \lim_{CK \to \infty} \left(1 + \frac{r}{CK} \right)^C - 1$$

$$= \lim_{CK \to \infty} \left[\left(1 + \frac{r}{CK} \right)^{CK} \right]^{1/K} - 1$$

$$= (e^r)^{1/K} - 1$$

$$= e^{r/K} - 1 \tag{2.7}$$

270

For the effective annual interest rate for continuous compounding, we simply evaluate Eq. 2.7 by setting K to 1. This gives us

$$i_a = e^r - 1 \qquad (2.8)$$

Example 2.2

Find the effective interest rate per quarter at a nominal rate of 18% compounded (1) quarterly, (2) monthly, and (3) continuously.

1. Quarterly compounding

$$r = 18\%, \quad M = 4, \quad C = 1, \quad K = 4$$

$$i = \left(1 + \frac{0.18}{4}\right)^1 - 1 = 4.5\%$$

2. Monthly compounding

$$r = 18\%, \quad M = 12, \quad C = 3, \quad K = 4$$

$$i = \left(1 + \frac{0.18}{12}\right)^3 - 1 = 4.568\%$$

3. Continuous compounding

$$r = 18\%, \quad K = 4, \quad (M = \infty, C = \infty)$$

$$i = e^{0.18/4} - 1 = 4.603\%$$

If we deposit $1,000 in a bank for just one quarter at the interest rate and compounding frequencies specified, our balance at the end of the quarter will grow to $1,045, $1,045.68, and $1,046.03, respectively. □

In Example 2.2 we examined how our deposit balance would grow for a time period of one quarter, but these results can be generalized for deposits of any duration. In the sections ahead, we will develop interest formulas that facilitate the interest compounding associated with various types of cash flow and compounding frequencies. For this presentation, we will group the compound interest formulas into four categories by the type of compounding and type of cash flow. We will first consider discrete compounding in which compounding occurs at a discrete point in time: annual compounding, monthly compounding, and so forth.

2.4 DISCRETE COMPOUNDING

2.4.1 Comparable Payment and Compounding Periods

We first consider the situations for which the payment periods are identical to the compounding periods (annual payments with annual compounding, quarterly payments with quarterly compounding, monthly payments with monthly compounding, and so forth).

Single Sums. In the simplest situation we deposit a single sum of money P in a financial institution for N interest periods. To determine how much can be accumulated by the end of N periods, we may use the result developed in Eq. 2.2,

$$F = P(1 + i)^N \tag{2.9}$$

The factor $(1 + i)^N$ is called the *single-payment compound amount factor* and is available in tables indexed by i and N. It is represented symbolically by $(F/P, i, N)$. Note that where payment and compounding periods are identical, the effective interest rate is simply $i = r/M$. This transaction can be portrayed by the cash flow diagram shown in Figure 2.2. (Note the time scale convention: the first period begins at $n = 0$ and ends at $n = 1$.)

For example, consider a deposit of \$1,000 for 8 years in an individual retirement account (IRA) that earns an interest rate of 11% compounded annually. The balance of the account at the end of 8 years will be

$$F = \$1000(1 + 0.11)^8 = \$2,304.54$$

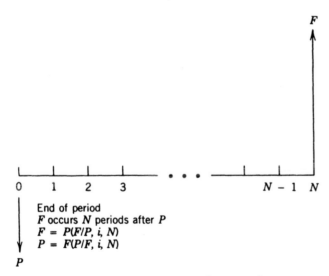

FIGURE 2.2 Cash flow diagram for a single payment.

If the account earns the interest at the rate of 11% compounded quarterly, the balance becomes

$$F = \$1000\left(1 + \frac{0.11}{4}\right)^{32} = \$2,382.42$$

If we wish to know what sum P we must deposit with a bank now, at $i\%$ compounded periodically, in order to have a future sum F in N periods, we can solve Eq. 2.9 for P.

$$P = F[(1 + i)^{-N}] \tag{2.10}$$

The bracketed term is called the *single-payment present-worth factor,* designated by $(P/F, i, N)$.

For example, we will have \$100 at the end of 3 years if we deposit \$86.38 in a 5% interest-bearing account:

$$P = \$100(\overset{P/F,5\%,3}{0.8638}) = \$86.38$$

Uniform Series. Most transactions with a financial institution involve more than two flows. If we have equal, periodic flows, we can develop formulas for determining beginning and ending balances. For example, an amount A deposited at the *end* of each compounding period in an account paying $i\%$ will grow to an amount after N periods of

$$A\sum_{n=1}^{N}(1 + i)^{N-n} = A\left[\frac{(1 + i)^{N} - 1}{i}\right] \tag{2.11}$$

The term in brackets is called the *uniform-series compound amount factor,* or *equal-series compound amount factor,* and is represented by $(F/A, i, N)$. The transaction can be portrayed by the cash flow diagram shown in Figure 2.3. In deriving the summation results in Eq. 2.11, we refer the reader to Table 2.1, which contains closed-form expressions for selected finite summations that are useful in developing interest formulas.

The inverse relationship to Eq. 2.11 yields the *uniform-series sinking-fund factor,* or *sinking-fund factor,*

$$A = F\left[\frac{i}{(1 + i)^{N} - 1}\right] \tag{2.12}$$

designated by $(A/F, i, N)$. The name derives from a historical practice of depositing a fixed sum at the end of each period into an interest-bearing account (a sinking fund) to provide for replacement moneys for fixed assets.

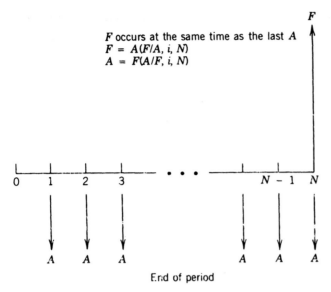

F occurs at the same time as the last A
$F = A(F/A, i, N)$
$A = F(A/F, i, N)$

FIGURE 2.3 Cash flow diagram of the relationship between A and F.

Table 2.1 *Summations Useful in Deriving Interest Formulas*

Geometric series

$$\sum_{n=0}^{N} x^n = 1 + x + x^2 + \cdots + x^N = \frac{1 - x^{N+1}}{1 - x}$$

where $x \neq 1$

If $-1 < x < 1$, then

$$\sum_{n=0}^{\infty} x^n = 1 + x + x^2 + x^3 + \cdots = \frac{1}{1 - x}$$

Arithmetic–geometric series

$$\sum_{n=0}^{N} nx^n = 0 + x + 2x^2 + \cdots + Nx^N = \frac{x[1 - (N + 1)x^N + Nx^{N+1}]}{(1 - x)^2}$$

where $x \neq 1$

If $-1 < x < 1$, then

$$\sum_{n=0}^{\infty} nx^n = 0 + x + 2x^2 + 3x^3 + \cdots = \frac{x}{(1 - x)^2}$$

Educational endowment funds can be constructed conveniently by using the sinking-fund factor: to build a $12,000 fund in 18 years at 5% compounded annually requires

$$A = \$12,000 \overset{A/F,5\%,18}{(0.0356)} = \$427.20 \quad \text{at the end of each year}$$

The relationships among P, F, and A can be manipulated to relate a series of equal, periodic flows (defined by A) to a present amount P. Substituting Eq. 2.11 into Eq. 2.9 yields

$$P = A\left[\frac{(1 + i)^N - 1}{i(1 + i)^N}\right] \tag{2.13}$$

and its inverse

$$A = P\left[\frac{i(1 + i)^N}{(1 + i)^N - 1}\right] \tag{2.14}$$

The bracketed term in Eq. 2.13 is the *uniform-series present worth factor*, designated by $(P/A, i, N)$. The term in Eq. 2.14 is the *uniform-series capital recovery factor*, or simply the *capital recovery factor*, represented by $(A/P, i, N)$. Figure 2.4 shows the cash flow transactions associated with these factors. The latter factor can be used to determine loan repayment schedules so that principal and interest are repaid over a given time period in equal end-of-period amounts.

To illustrate the use of A/P and P/A factors, consider a commercial mortgage at 8% over 20 years, with a loan principal of $1 million. If equal year-end payments are desired, each annual payment must be

$$\overset{A/P,8\%,20}{\$1,000,000(0.10185)} = \$101,850$$

The loan schedule can then be constructed as in Table 2.2. The interest due at n = 1 is 8% of the $1 million outstanding during the first year. The $21,850 left over is applied to the principal, reducing the amount outstanding in the second year to $978,150. The interest due in the second year is 8% of $978,150, or $78,252, leaving $23,598 for repayment of the principal. At n = 20, the last $101,850 payment is just sufficient to pay the interest on the outstanding loan principal and to repay the outstanding principal.

Such an equal-payments scheme is also common for home mortgages and automobile loans. In each period a decreasing amount of interest is paid, leaving a larger amount to reduce the principal. Each reduction of loan principal increases an owner's equity in the item by a corresponding amount.

The series present worth factor can be useful for determining the outstanding balance of a loan at any time, as portrayed in Table 2.2. At the end of the fifth year, for example, we still owe 15 payments of $101,850. The value of those

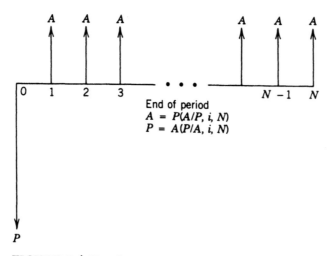

FIGURE 2.4 Equal-payment series and single present amount.

Table 2.2 *A Loan Repayment Schedule Showing Principal and Interest Payments*

Year	Beginning Loan Balance	Interest Payment	Principal Payment	Total Payment
1	1,000,000*	80,000	21,850	101,850
2	978,150	78,252	23,598	101,850
3	954,552	76,364	25,486	101,850
4	929,066	74,325	27,525	101,850
5	901,541	72,123	29,727	101,850
6	871,814	69,745	32,105	101,850
7	839,709	67,177	34,673	101,850
8	805,036	64,403	37,447	101,850
9	767,589	61,407	40,443	101,850
10	727,146	58,172	43,678	101,850
11	683,468	54,677	47,173	101,850
12	636,295	50,904	50,946	101,850
13	585,349	46,828	55,022	101,850
14	530,327	42,426	59,424	101,850
15	470,903	37,672	64,178	101,850
16	406,725	32,538	69,312	101,850
17	337,413	26,993	74,857	101,850
18	262,556	21,005	60,845	101,850
19	181,711	14,537	87,313	101,850
20	94,398	7,452	94,398	101,850

*All figures are rounded to nearest dollars.
NOTE: Loan Amount = $1,000,000
      Loan life = 20 years
      Loan interest = 8% compounded annually
      Equal annual payment size = $1,000,000(A/P, 8%, 20)
                                = $1,000,000(0.10185)
                                = $101,850

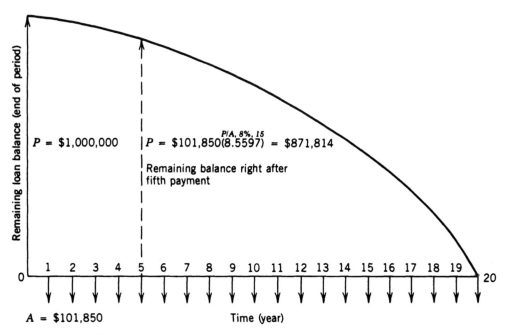

FIGURE 2.5 loan balance as a function of time (n).

payments at time 5 can be represented as in Figure 2.5 with the time scale shifted by 5 and is found from the equation to be

$$P = \$101,850(\overset{P/A,8\%,15}{8.5595}) = \$871,785$$

which is the same as the \$871,814 in Table 2.2.

Example 2.3

Suppose we are in the market for a medium-sized used car. We have surveyed the dealers' advertisements in the newspaper and have found a car that should fulfill our needs. The asking price of the car is \$7,500, and the dealer proposes that we make a \$500 down payment now and pay the rest of the balance in equal end-of-month payments of \$194.82 each over a 48-month period. Consider the following situations.

1. Instead of using the dealer's financing, we decide to make a down payment of \$500 and borrow the rest from a bank at 12% compounded monthly. What would be our monthly payment to pay off the loan in 4 years? To find A,

$$i = \frac{12\%}{12 \text{ periods}} = 1\% \text{ per month}$$

$$N = (4 \text{ years})(12 \text{ periods per year}) = 48 \text{ periods}$$

$$A = P(A/P,\ i,\ N) = (\$7,500 - \$500)(\overset{A/P,1\%,48}{0.0263}) = \$184.34$$

2. We are going to accept the dealer's offer but we want to know the effective rate of interest per month that the dealer is charging. To find i, let $P = \$7,000$, $A = \$194.82$, and $N = 48$.

$$\$194.82 = \$7,000(A/P, i, 48)$$

The satisfying value i can be found by trial and error from

$$(A/P, i, 48) = \frac{i(1 + i)^{48}}{(1 + i)^{48} - 1} = 0.0278$$

to be $i = 1.25\%$ per month. This value is used to find the nominal annual interest rate used by the dealer.

$$r = (i)(M) = (1.25\% \text{ per month})(12 \text{ months per year})$$

$$= 15\% \text{ per year}$$

Then the effective annual interest used by the dealer is simply

$$i_a = \left(1 + \frac{0.15}{12}\right)^{12} - 1 = 16.08\% \quad \square$$

Linear Gradient Series. Many engineering economy problems, particularly those related to equipment maintenance, involve cash flows that change by a constant amount (G) each period. We can use the gradient factors to convert such gradient series to present amounts and equal annual series. Consider the series

$$F_n = (n - 1)G, \qquad n = 1, 2, \ldots, N \tag{2.15}$$

As shown in Figure 2.6, the gradient G can be either positive or negative. If $G > 0$, we call the series an increasing gradient series. If $G < 0$, we have a decreasing gradient series. We can apply the single-payment present-worth factor to each term of the series and obtain the expression

$$P = \sum_{n=1}^{N} (n - 1)G(1 + i)^{-n} \tag{2.16}$$

Using the finite summation of a linear function in Table 2.1, we obtain

$$P = G\left[\frac{1 - (1 + Ni)(1 + i)^{-N}}{i^2}\right] \tag{2.17}$$

The resulting factor in brackets is called the *gradient series present-worth factor* and is designated $(P/G, i, N)$.

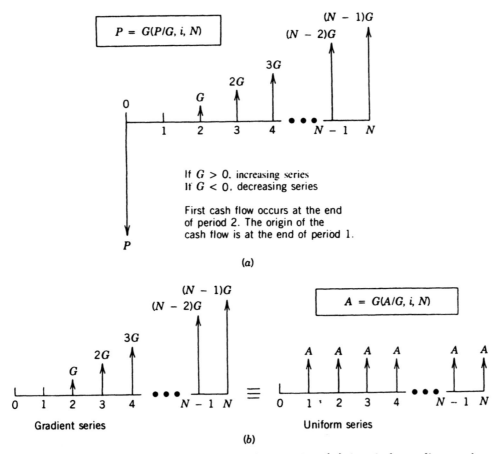

FIGURE 2.6 Cash flow diagram for a gradient series. (a) A strictly gradient series. (b) Conversion factor from a gradient series to a uniform series.

A uniform series equivalent to the gradient series can be obtained by substituting Eq. 2.17 into Eq. 2.14 for P,

$$A = G\left[\frac{1}{i} - \frac{N}{(1 + i)^N - 1}\right] \tag{2.18}$$

where the resulting factor in brackets is referred to as the *gradient-to-uniform-series conversion factor* and is designated $(A/G, i, N)$.

To obtain the future-worth equivalent of a gradient series, we substitute Eq. 2.18 into Eq. 2.14 for A

$$F = \frac{G}{i}\left[\frac{(1 + i)^N - 1}{i} - N\right]$$

$$= \frac{G}{i}\left[(F/A, i, N) - N\right] \tag{2.19}$$

Example 2.4

An example of the use of a gradient factor is to find the future amount of the following series with $i = 10\%$ per period.

n	0	1	2	3	4	5	6	7	8
F_n	0	100	106	112	118	124	130	136	142

The constant portion of 100 is separated from the gradient series of $0,0,6,12, \ldots, 42$.

n	0	1	2	3	4	5	6	7	8
F_n	0	100	100	100	100	100	100	100	100
	0	0	6	12	18	24	30	36	42

We can quickly verify that the portion of the strict gradient series will accumulate to $206.15.

$$F = 100 \overset{F/A,10\%,8}{(11.436)} + \frac{6}{0.1} [\overset{F/A,10\%,8}{(11.436)} - 8]$$

$$= 1{,}143.60 + 206.15$$

$$= 1{,}349.76 \quad \square$$

Geometric Series. In many situations periodic payments increase or decrease over time, not by a constant amount (gradient) but by a constant percentage (geometric growth). If we use g to designate the percentage change in the payment from one period to the next, the magnitude of the nth payment, F_n, is related to the first payment, F_1, by

$$F_n = F_1(1 + g)^{n-1}, \qquad n = 1, 2, \ldots, N \tag{2.20}$$

As illustrated in Figure 2.7, g can be either positive or negative, depending on the type of cash flow. If $g > 0$ the series will increase, and if $g < 0$ the series will decrease.

To find an expression for the present amount P, we apply the single-payment present-worth factor to each term of the series

$$P = \sum_{n=1}^{N} F_1(1 + g)^{n-1}(1 + i)^{-n} \tag{2.21}$$

Bringing the term $F_1(1 + g)^{-1}$ outside the summation yields

$$P = \frac{F_1}{1 + g} \sum_{n=1}^{N} \left(\frac{1 + g}{1 + i} \right)^n \tag{2.22}$$

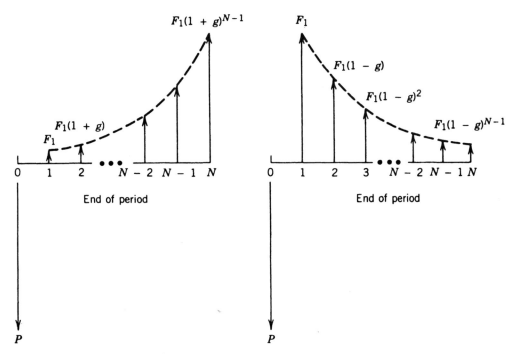

FIGURE 2.7 Cash flow diagram of the geometric series.

The summation in Eq. 2.22 represents the first N terms of a geometric series, and the closed-form expression for the partial geometric summation yields the following relationship.

$$P = \begin{cases} F_1\left[\dfrac{1 - (1 + g)^N(1 + i)^{-N}}{i - g}\right] & i \neq g \\ \\ \dfrac{NF_1}{1 + i} & i = g \end{cases} \tag{2.23}$$

This present-worth factor is designated $(P/A, g, i, N)$.

The future-worth equivalent of the geometric series is obtained by substituting Eq. 2.23 into Eq. 2.5 to find $(F/A, g, i, N)$.

$$F = \begin{cases} F_1\left[\dfrac{(1 + i)^N(1 + i)^{-N}}{i - g}\right] & i \neq g \\ \\ NF_1(1 + i)^{N-1} & i = g \end{cases} \tag{2.24}$$

We may use an alternative expression of Eq. 2.23 as shown in [4]. In Eq. 2.22 we may rewrite the term $(1 + g)/(1 + i)$ as

$$\frac{1 + g}{1 + i} = \frac{1}{1 + g'} \tag{2.25}$$

or

$$g' = \frac{1 + i}{1 + g} - 1$$

We then substitute Eq. 2.25 back into Eq. 2.22 to obtain

$$P = \frac{F_1}{1 + g} \sum_{n=1}^{N} (1 + g')^{-n} \tag{2.26}$$

The summation term constitutes the uniform-series present-worth factor for N periods. Therefore,

$$P = \frac{F_1}{1 + g}\left[\frac{g'(1 + g')^N}{(1+g') - 1}\right]$$

$$= \frac{F_1}{1 + g}(P/A, g', N), g \neq i \tag{2.27}$$

If $g < i$, then $g' > 0$, and we can use the $(P/A, g', N)$ factor to find P. If $g = i$, then $g' = 0$, and the value of $(P/A, g', N)$ will be N. The geometric-series factor thus reduces to $P = F_1 N/(1 + g)$. If $g > i$, then $g' < 0$. In this case, no table values can be used to evaluate the P/A factor, and it will have to be calculated directly from a formula. Table 2.3 summarizes the interest formulas developed in this section and the cash flow situations in which they should be used.

Example 2.5

A mining company is concerned about the increasing cost of diesel fuel for their mining operation. A special piece of mining equipment, a tractor-mounted ripper, is used to loosen the earth in open-pit mining operations. The company thinks that the diesel fuel consumption will escalate at the rate of 10% per year as the efficiency of the equipment decreases. The company's records indicate that the ripper averages 18 gallons per operational hour in year 1, with 2,000 hours of operation per year. What would the present worth of the cost of fuel for this ripper be for the next five years if the interest rate is 15% compounded annually?

Assuming that all the fuel costs occur at the end of each year, we determine the present equivalent fuel cost by calculating the fuel cost for the first year:

$$F_1 = (\$1.10/\text{gal})(18 \text{ gal/hr})(2{,}000 \text{ hr/year}) = \$39{,}600/\text{year}$$

$$(g = 0.10, N = 5, i = 0.15)$$

Then, using the appropriate factors in Eq. 2.23, we compute

$$P = \$39{,}600\left[\frac{1 - (1 + 0.10)^5(1 + 0.15)^{-5}}{0.15 - 0.10}\right] = \$157{,}839.18$$

Table 2.3 Summary of Discrete Compounding Formulas with Discrete Payments

Flow Type	Factor Notation	Formula	Cash Flow Diagram
Single	Compound amount $(F/P, i, N)$	$F = P(1 + i)^N$	
	Present worth $(P/F, i, N)$	$P = F(1 + i)^{-N}$	
Equal payment series	Compound amount $(F/A, i, N)$	$F = A\left[\dfrac{(1 + i)^N - 1}{i}\right]$	
	Sinking fund $(A/F, i, N)$	$A = F\left[\dfrac{i}{(1 + i)^N - 1}\right]$	
	Present worth $(P/A, i, N)$	$P = A\left[\dfrac{(1 + i)^N - 1}{i(1 + i)^N}\right]$	
	Capital recovery $(A/P, i, N)$	$A = P\left[\dfrac{i(1 + i)^N}{(1 + i)^N - 1}\right]$	
Gradient series	Uniform gradient Present worth $(P/G, i, N)$	$P = G\left[\dfrac{(1 + i)^N - iN - 1}{i^2(1 + i)^N}\right]$	
	Geometric gradient Present worth $(P/A, g, i, N)$ F_1	$P = \begin{cases} F_1\left[\dfrac{1 - (1 + g)^N(1 + i)^{-N}}{i - g}\right] \\ \dfrac{NF_1}{1 + i} \quad \text{(if } i = g) \end{cases}$	

Source: Park [3].

Using the alternative formula in Eq. 2.27, we first compute

$$g' = \frac{1.15}{1.10} - 1 = 0.04545$$

We then obtain

$$P = \frac{39{,}600}{1.10} \overset{P/A,\ 4.545\%,5}{(4.38442)} = 157{,}839.20$$

Although Eq. 2.27 looks more compact than Eq. 2.23, it does not provide any computational advantage in this example.   ☐

All the interest formulas developed in Table 2.3 are applicable only to situations in which the compounding period coincides with the payment period. In the next section we discuss situations in which we have noncomparable payment and compounding periods.

2.4.2 Noncomparable Payment and Compounding Periods

Whenever the payment period and the compounding period do not correspond, we approach the problem by finding the effective interest rate based on the payment period and then using this rate in the compounding interest formulas in Table 2.3.

The specific computational procedure for noncomparable compounding and payment periods is as follows.

1. Identify the number of compounding periods per year (M), the number of payment periods per year (K), and the number of interest periods per payment period (C).
2. Compute the effective interest rate per payment period, using Eq. 2.6.

$$i = \left(1 + \frac{r}{M}\right)^{C} - 1$$

3. Find the total number of payment periods.

$$N = K\,(\text{number of years})$$

4. Use i and N in the appropriate formula given in Table 2.3.

Example 2.6

What is the present worth of a series of equal quarterly payments of $1,000 that extends over a period of 5 years if the interest rate is 8% compounded monthly? The variables are

$K = 4$ payment periods per year

$M = 12$ compounding periods per year

$C = 3$ interest periods per payment period (quarter)

$r = 8\%$

$$i = \left(1 + \frac{r}{M}\right)^C - 1 = \left(1 + \frac{0.08}{12}\right)^3 - 1 = 2.0133\% \text{ per quarter}$$

$N = (5)(4) = 20$ payment periods

Then the present amount is

$$P = A(P/A, i, N)$$
$$= \$1000(P/A, 2.0133\%, 20) = \$16,330.37 \quad \square$$

In certain situations the compounding periods occur *less* frequently than the payment periods. Depending on the financial institution involved, no interest may be paid for funds deposited during an interest period. The accounting methods used by most firms record cash transactions at the end of the period in which they have occurred, and any cash transactions that occur within a compounding period are assumed to have occurred at the end of that period. Thus, when cash flows occur daily but the compounding period is monthly, we sum the cash flows within each month (ignoring interest) and place them at the end of each month. The modified cash flows become the basis for any calculations involving the interest factors.

In the extreme situation in which payment occurs more frequently than compounding, we might find that the cash flows continuously throughout the planning horizon on a somewhat uniform basis. If this happens, we can also apply the approach discussed earlier (integrating instead of summing all cash flows that occur during the compounding period and placing them at the end of each compounding period) to find the present worth of the cash flow series. In practice, we avoid this cumbersome approach by adopting the funds flow concept, which is discussed in the next section.

Example 2.7

Consider the cash flow diagram shown in Figure 2.8*a*, where the time scale is monthly. If interest is compounded quarterly, the cash flows can be relocated as shown in Figure 2.8*b*. The cash flow shown in Figure 2.8*b* is equivalent to the cash flow in Figure 2.8*a* for quarterly compounding. After the equivalent cash flow is determined, we can proceed as previously discussed for the situation in which the compounding periods and the payment periods coincide.

Let $i = 3\%$ per quarter. Then the present worth of cash flow given in Figure 2.8*a* is equivalent to the present worth of cash flow given in Figure 2.8*b*. Since $G = \$90$,

$$P = \$330 \overset{P/A,3\%,8}{(7.0197)} + \$90 \overset{P/G,3\%,8}{(23.4806)} = \$4,429.76 \quad \square$$

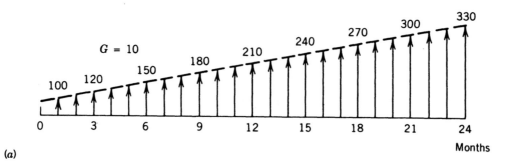

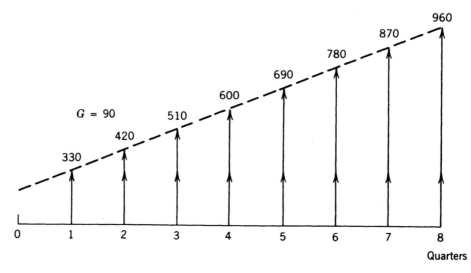

(a)

(b)

FIGURE 2.8 Example of cash flows where compounding is less frequent than payment. (*a*) Original cash flows. (*b*) Equivalent quarterly cash flows.

2.5 CONTINUOUS COMPOUNDING

2.5.1 Discrete Payments

When payments occur at discrete points in time but interest is permitted to compound an infinite number of times per year (that is, continuously in time), we have the special instance of more frequent compounding than payments discussed in Section 2.4.2. Therefore, we approach the problem in the following way.

1. Identify the payment periods per year (K).

2. Compute $i = e^{r/K} - 1$ by using Eq. 2.7.

3. Find the total number of payment periods.

$$N = K \quad \text{(number of years)}$$

4. Use i and N in the appropriate interest formulas given in Table 2.3.

We can derive a new family of interest factors under continuous compounding by substituting $e^{r} - 1$ for i when payments are annual and $e^{r/K} - 1$

Table 2.4 *Summary of Continuous Compounding Formulas with Annual Payments*

Flow Type	Factor Notation	Formula	Cash Flow Diagram
Single	Compound amount $(F/P, r, N)$ Present worth $(P/F, r, N)$	$F = P(e^{rN})$ $P = F(e^{-rN})$	
Equal payment series	Compound amount $(F/A, r, N)$ Sinking fund $(A/F, r, N)$	$F = A\left(\dfrac{e^{rN} - 1}{e^r - 1}\right)$ $A = F\left(\dfrac{e^r - 1}{e^{rN} - 1}\right)$	
Equal payment series	Present worth $(P/A, r, N)$ Capital recovery $(A/P, r, N)$	$P = A\left[\dfrac{e^{rN} - 1}{e^{rN}(e^r - 1)}\right]$ $A = P\left[\dfrac{e^{rN}(e^r - 1)}{e^{rN} - 1}\right]$	
Gradient series	Uniform gradient Present worth $(P/G, r, N)$	$P = G\left[\dfrac{e^{rN} - 1 - N(e^r - 1)}{e^{rN}(e^r - 1)^2}\right]$	
Gradient series	Geometric gradient Present worth $(P/A, g, r, N)$	$P = \begin{cases} F_1\left[\dfrac{1 - e^{(g-r)N}}{e^r - e^g}\right] \\[2ex] \dfrac{NF_1}{e^r} \quad (\text{if } g = e^r - 1) \end{cases}$	

Source: Park [3].

287

for i when payments are more frequent than annual. Table 2.4 summarizes the resulting compound interest factors for annual payments.

Example 2.8

What is the present worth of a uniform series of year-end payments of $500 each for 10 years if the interest rate is 8% compounded continuously?

Let $r = 0.08$

$i = e^r - 1 = 8.33\%$

$N = 10$

$A = \$500$

Then

$$P = A\left[\frac{e^{rN} - 1}{e^{rN}(e^r - 1)}\right] = \$500(6.6117) = \$3,305.85$$

Using the discrete compounding formula with $i = 8.33\%$, we also find that

$$P = A(\overset{P/A,8.33\%,10}{6.6117}) = \$3,305.85 \quad \square$$

Example 2.9

A series of equal quarterly payments of $1,000 extends over a period of 5 years. What is the present worth of this quarterly time series at 8% interest compounded continuously?

Since the payments are quarterly, the calculations must be quarterly. The required calculations are

$$\frac{r}{K} = \frac{8\%}{4 \text{ quarters}} = 2\% \text{ per quarter compounded continuously}$$

$$i = e^{r/K} - 1 = e^{0.02} - 1 = 0.0202 = 2.02\% \text{ per quarter}$$

$$N = (4 \text{ payment periods per year})(5 \text{ years}) = 20 \text{ periods}$$

$$P = A\left[\frac{e^{(r/K)N} - 1}{e^{(r/K)N}(e^{r/K} - 1)}\right] = \$1,000(15.3197) = \$16,319.70$$

Using the discrete compounding formula with $i = 2.02\%$, we also find that

$$P = A(\overset{P/A,2.02\%,20}{16.3197}) = \$16,319.70 \quad \square$$

2.5.2 Continuous Cash Flows

It is often appropriate to treat cash flows as though they were continuous rather than discrete. An advantage of the continuous flow representation is its

Table 2.5 Summary of Interest Factors for Continuous Cash Flows with Continuous Compounding

Type of Cash Flow	Cash Flow Function	Parameters		Algebraic Notation	Factor Notation
		To Find	Given		
Uniform (step)	$F_t = \bar{A}$	P	$\bar{A}$	$\bar{A}\left(\dfrac{e^{rN}-1}{re^{rN}}\right)$	$(P/\bar{A},\ r,\ N)$
		$\bar{A}$	P	$P\left(\dfrac{re^{rN}}{e^{rN}-1}\right)$	$(\bar{A}/P,\ r,\ N)$
		F	$\bar{A}$	$\bar{A}\left(\dfrac{e^{rN}-1}{r}\right)$	$(F/\bar{A},\ r,\ N)$
		$\bar{A}$	F	$F\left(\dfrac{r}{e^{rN}-1}\right)$	$(\bar{A}/P,\ r,\ N)$
Gradient (ramp)	$F_t = Gt$			$\dfrac{G}{r^2}(1-e^{-rN})$	
		P	G	$-\dfrac{G}{r}(Ne^{-rN})$	
Decay	$F_t = ce^{-jt}$ j = decay rate with time	P	c, j	$\dfrac{c}{r+j}(1-e^{-(r+j)N})$	
Exponential	$F_t = ce^{jt}$	P	c, j	$\dfrac{c}{r-j}(1-e^{-(r-j)N})$	
Growth	$F_t = c(1-e^{jt})$	P	c, j	$\dfrac{c}{r}(1-e^{-rN})$ $-\dfrac{c}{r+j}(1-e^{-(r+j)N})$	

flexibility for dealing with patterns other than the uniform and gradient ones. Some of the selected continuous cash flow functions are shown in Table 2.5.

To find the present worth of a continuous cash flow function under continuous compounding, we first recognize that the present-worth formula for a discrete series of cash flows with discrete compounding is

$$P = \sum_{n=0}^{N} F_n(1 + i)^{-n}$$

Since F_n becomes a continuous function F_t and the effective annual interest rate i for continuous compounding is $e^r - 1$, integration of the argument instead of summation yields

$$P = \int_0^N (F_t)e^{-rt}\, dt \tag{2.28}$$

[Note that $n \to t$, $F_n \to F_t$, $\sum_{n=0}^{N} \to \int_0^N$, and $(1 + i)^{-n} \to e^{-rt}$.] Then the future value equivalent of F_t over N periods is simply

$$F = \int_0^N F_t e^{r(N-t)}\, dt \tag{2.29}$$

To illustrate the continuous flow concept, consider F_t to be a uniform flow function when an amount flows at the rate $\bar{A}$ per period for N periods. (This cash flow function is presented in Table 2.5 and is expressed as $F_t = \bar{A}$, $0 \le t \le N$.) Then the present-worth equivalent is

$$P = \int_0^N \bar{A}e^{-rt}\, dt = \bar{A}\left(\frac{e^{rN} - 1}{re^{rN}}\right) = \bar{A}\left(\frac{1 - e^{-rN}}{r}\right) \tag{2.30}$$

The resulting factor in parenthesis in (2.30) is referred to as the *funds flow present-worth factor* and is designated $(P/\bar{A}, r, N)$. The future-worth equivalent is obtained from

$$F = \int_0^N \bar{A}e^{rt}\, dt = \bar{A}\left(\frac{e^{rN} - 1}{r}\right) \tag{2.31}$$

The resulting factor $(e^{rN} - 1)/r$ is called the *funds flow compound amount factor* and is designated $(F/\bar{A}, r, N)$. Since the relationships of $\bar{A}$ to P and F are given by Eqs. 2.30 and 2.31, we can easily solve for $\bar{A}$ if P or F is given. Table 2.5 summarizes all the funds flow factors necessary to find present-worth and future-worth equivalents for a variety of cash flow functions.

As a simple example, we compare the present-worth figures obtained in two situations. We deposit $10 each day for 18 months in a savings account that has an interest rate of 12% compounded daily. Assuming that there are 548 days in the 18-month period, we compute the present worth.

$$P = 10 \overset{P/A,0.032877\%,548}{(501.4211)} = \$5,014.21$$

Now we approximate this discrete cash flow series by a uniform continuous cash flow profile (assuming continuous compounding). In doing so, we may define $\bar{A}$ as

$$\bar{A} = 10(365) = \$3,650/\text{year}$$

Note that our time unit is a year. Thus, an 18-month period is 1.5 years. Substituting these values back into Eq. 2.30 yields

$$P = \int_0^{1.5} 3,650e^{-0.12t} = \frac{3,650}{0.12}\left(1 - e^{-0.18}\right)$$

$$= \$5,010.53$$

The discrepancy between the values obtained by the two methods is only $3.68.

Example 2.10

A county government is considering building a road from downtown to the airport to relieve congested traffic on the existing two-lane divided highway. Before allowing the sale of a bond to finance the road project, the court has requested an estimate of future toll revenues over the bond life. The toll revenues are directly proportional to the growth of traffic over the years, so the following growth cash flow function (with units in millions of dollars) is assumed to be reasonable.

$$F_t = 5(1 - e^{-0.10t})$$

Find the present worth of toll revenues at 6% interest compounded continuously over a 25-year period.

Expanding F_t gives us

$$F_t = 5 - 5e^{-0.10t}$$

If we let $f(t)_1 = 5$ and $f(t)_2 = -5e^{-0.10t}$, the present-worth equivalent for each function would be

$$P_1 = \int_0^{25} 5e^{-0.06t}\, dt = 5\left[\frac{e^{0.06(25)} - 1}{(0.06)e^{0.06(25)}}\right] = \$64.74$$

$$P_2 = \int_0^{25} -5e^{-(0.10 + 0.06)t}\, dt = -5\left[\frac{e^{0.16(25)} - 1}{(0.16)e^{0.16(25)}}\right] = -\$30.68$$

291

and

$$P = P_1 + P_2 = \$34.06$$

The present worth of toll revenues over a 25-year period amounts to $34.06 million. This figure could be used for bond validation. □

2.6 EQUIVALENCE OF CASH FLOWS

2.6.1 Concept of Equivalence

When we compare two cash flows, we must compare their characteristics on the same basis. By definition, two cash flows are equivalent if they have the same economic effect. More precisely, two cash flows are equivalent at interest i if we can convert one cash flow into the other by using the proper compound interest factors. For example, if we deposit $100 in a bank for 3 years at 8% interest compounded annually, we will accumulate $125.97. Here we may say that, at 8% interest, $100 at time 0 is equivalent to $125.97 at time 3.

Consider another example in which an individual has to choose between two options. Option I is to receive a lump sum of $1,000 now. Option II is to receive $600 at the end of each year for 2 years, which provides $1,200 over the 2-year period. Our question is what interest rate makes these two options equivalent. To answer the question, we need to establish a common base in time to convert the cash flows. Three common bases are the equivalent future value F, the equivalent present value P, and the equivalent annual value A. Future value is a measure of the cash flow relative to some "future planning horizon," considering the earning opportunities of the intermediate cash receipts. The present value represents a measure of future cash flow relative to the time point "now" with provisions that account for earning opportunities. The annual equivalent value determines the equal payments on an annual basis. The uniform cash flow equivalent might be the more appropriate term to use. The conceptual transformation from one type of cash flow to another is depicted in Figure 2.9.

For our example, we will use F as a base of reference value and set the planning horizon at the end of year 2. To find the future value of option I, we may use an $(F/P, i, A)$ factor.

$$F_I = 1000(F/P, i, 2) = 1000(1 + i)^2$$

For option II, we may use an $(F/A, i, n)$ factor.

$$F_{II} = 600(F/A, i, 2) = 600(1 + i) + 600$$

If we specify i, we can easily evaluate F_I and F_{II}. Table 2.6 summarizes these values at selected interest rates. We observe from the table that $F_I = F_{II} = \$1,278$ at $i = 13\%$. In other words, the two options are equivalent if the individual can earn a 13% interest from the investment activity. We also observe that at $i = 13\%$ $P_I = P_{II}$ and $A_I = A_{II}$. This is not surprising, because the present value amount is merely the future amount times a constant. The same can be said for the annual

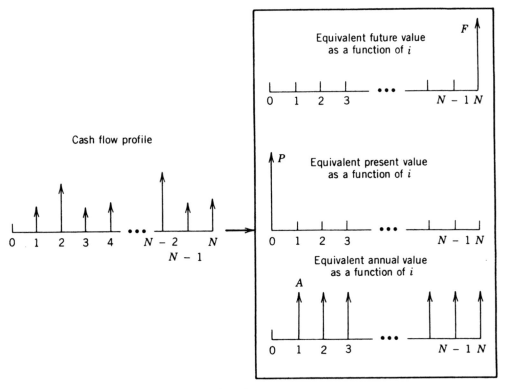

FIGURE 2.9 Conversion to equivalent bases.

Table 2.6 *Equivalence Calculations*

i (%)	Option I $F_{\mathrm{I}} = 1,000(1 + i)^2$	Option II $F_{\mathrm{II}} = 600(1 + i) + 600$	Equivalence
0	$1,000	$1,200	
5	1,103	1,230	
7	1,145	1,242	$F_{\mathrm{I}} < F_{\mathrm{II}}$
12	1,254	1,272	
13	1,277	1,277	$F_{\mathrm{I}} = F_{\mathrm{II}}$
15	1,323	1,290	$F_{\mathrm{I}} > F_{\mathrm{II}}$
20	1,440	1,320	

Option I

$1,000

0 1 2

Option II

$600 $600

0 1 2

equivalent value amount. Therefore, we should expect that any equivalent value that directly compares future value amounts could just as well compare present value amounts or annual equivalent amounts without affecting the selection outcome.

2.6.2 Equivalence Calculations with Several Interest Factors

Thus far we have used only single factors to perform equivalence calculations. In many situations, however, we must use several interest factors to obtain an equivalent value. To show this, we will take an example from home financing instruments offered by many banks. The particular financing method to be considered is called the graduated-payment method (GPM). This mortgage financing is designed for young people with low incomes but good earning prospects. (The term mortgage refers to a special loan for buying a piece of property such as a house.) The Department of Housing and Urban Development (HUD) initiated the GPM with a fixed interest rate for 30 years. During the first 5 or 10 years the monthly payments increase in stair-step fashion each year, allowing buyers to make a lower monthly payment in the beginning; the payments then level off at an amount higher than those of a comparable conventional fixed-rate mortgage. The monthly payment is applied to both principal and interest and can carry negative amortization. (The loan balance actually grows instead of decreasing under negative amortization when monthly payments are lower than monthly loan interests.) Our question is how the monthly payments are computed for a certain loan amount, interest rate, and life of the loan.

Let

P = loan amount,

A = monthly payment for the first year,

i = loan interest rate per month,

g = annual rate of increase in the monthly payment,

K = number of years the payment will increase,

N = number of months to maturity of the loan.

Figure 2.10*a* illustrates the cash flow transactions associated with the GPM. From the lender's view, lending the amount P now should be equivalent to a transaction in which the monthly payments are as shown in Figure 2.10*a*. To establish the equivalence relation between P and A with fixed values of i, g, K, and N, we convert each group of 12 equal monthly payments to a single present equivalent amount at the beginning of each year. Then the remaining $(N - 12K)$ equal payments are converted to a single present equivalent amount at $n = 12K$. The equivalent cash flow after this transformation should look like Figure 2.10*b*. To find the present equivalent value of this transformed cash flow, we simply calculate

$$P = A(P/A, i, 12) + A(1 + g)(P/A, i, 12)(P/F, i, 12)$$
$$+ A(1 + g)^2(P/A, i, 12)(P/F, i, 24) + \cdots$$

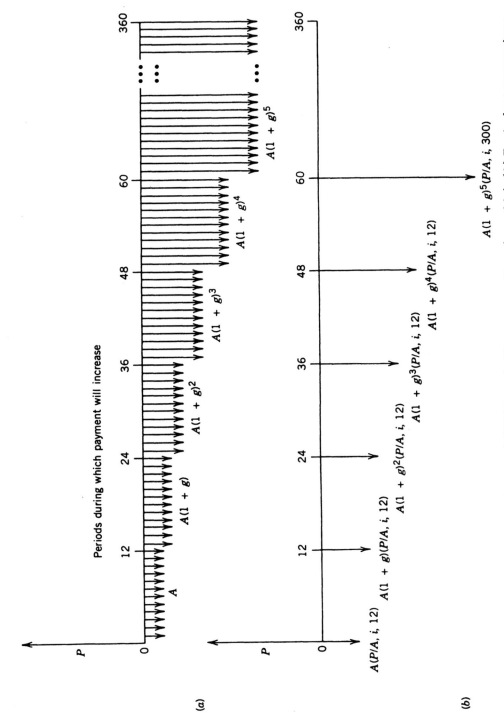

FIGURE 2.10 Cash flow diagram of a typical GPM loan. (*a*) Loan transactions (monthly). (*b*) Equivalent transactions.

$$+ A\{(1 + g)^{K-1} (P/A, i, 12)[P/F, i, 12(K - 1)]\}$$
$$+ A(1 + g)^K(P/A, i, N - 12K)(P/F, i, 12K) \qquad (2.32)$$

We multiply each term by $(1 + i)^{12}$ or $(F/P, i, 12)$.

$$P(1 + i)^{12} = A(P/A, i, 12)(1 + i)^{12} + A(1 + g)(P/A, i, 12)$$
$$+ A(1 + g)^2(P/A, i, 12)(1 + i)^{-12} + \cdots$$
$$+ A(1 + g)^{K-1}(P/A, i, 12)(1 + i)^{-12(K-2)}$$
$$+ A(1 + g)^K(P/A, i, N - 12K)(1 + i)^{-12(K+1)} \qquad (2.33)$$

We multiply each term in Eq. 2.32 by $1 + g$.

$$P(1 + g) = A(1 + g)(P/A, i, 12) + A(1 + g)^2(P/A, i, 12)(1 + i)^{-12}$$
$$+ A(1 + g)^3(P/A, i, 12)(1 + i)^{-24} + \cdots$$
$$+ A(1 + g)^K(P/A, i, 12)(1 + i)^{-12(K-1)}$$
$$+ A(1 + g)^{K+1}(P/A, i, N - 12K)(1 + i)^{-12K} \qquad (2.34)$$

Now we subtract Eq. 2.34 from Eq. 2.33 and solve for A to get

$$A = P[(1 + i)^{12} - (1 + g)]\{(1 + g)^K(1 + i)^{-12(K+1)}[(P/A, i, N - 12K)$$
$$- (P/A, i, 12)] + [(P/A, i, 12)(1 + i)^{12}$$
$$- (1 + g)^{K+1}(P/A, i, N - 12K)(1 + i)^{-12K}]\}^{-1} \qquad (2.35)$$

For an example of such an equivalence calculation, consider the following data:

$P = \$45,000,$

$i = \frac{3}{4}\%$ per month (9% compounded monthly),

$g = 5\%$ per year,

$K = 5$ years (no further increase in monthly payment after the sixth year),

$N = 360$ months (30 years).

Evaluating Eq. 2.35 with these figures yields

$$A = 45,000[0.04387]\{0.8916 [107.7267] + 12.5076 - 101.9927\}^{-1}$$
$$= \$300.18/\text{month}$$

Then the monthly payment will increase the second year to \$315.19, the third year to \$330.95, the fourth year to \$347.50, the fifth year to \$364.87, and for the remaining years to \$383.11.

Example 2.11

The following two cash flow transactions are said to be equivalent in terms of economic desirability at an interest rate of 10% compounded annually. Determine the unknown value A.

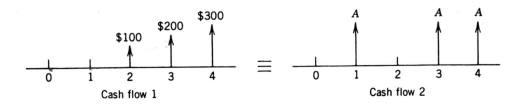

We will first use the present equivalent as the basis of comparison. Cash flow 1 represents a strict gradient series, whereas cash flow 2 can be viewed as an equivalent payment series with the second payment missing. Therefore, the equivalence would be expressed by

$$100 \overset{P/G,10\%,4}{(4.3781)} = A \left[\overset{P/F,10\%,1}{(0.9091)} + \overset{P/F,10\%,3}{(0.7513)} + \overset{P/F,10\%,4}{(0.6830)} \right]$$

Solving for A yields

$$A = \$186.83$$

If we use the annual equivalent as the basis of comparison, we compute

$$100 \overset{A/G,10\%,4}{(1.3812)} = A - A \overset{P/F,10\%,2}{(0.8264)} \overset{A/P,10\%,4}{(0.3155)}$$

Solving for A yields $A = \$186.83$ again. The second approach should be computationally more attractive because it takes advantage of the cash flow pattern and thus requires fewer interest factors in the computation. □

2.7 EFFECT OF INFLATION ON CASH FLOW EQUIVALENCE

Up to this point we have shown how we properly account for the time value of money in equivalence calculations in the absence of inflation. In this section we present methods that incorporate the effect of inflation in our equivalence calculations.

2.7.1 Measure of Inflation

Definition. Before discussing the effect of inflation on equivalence calculations, we need to discuss how we measure inflation. In simple terms, the results of investment activity are stated in dollars, but the dollar is an imperfect unit of measure because its value changes from time to time. Inflation is the term used to describe a decline in the value of the dollar. For example, if we deposit $1,000 in a one-year savings certificate and withdraw $1,090 a year later, we say that our rate of return has been 9%—and it has, as long as those dollars we withdraw at year's end actually purchase 9% more. If inflation has reduced the value of the dollar by 10%, our 9% positive investment return in dollars is actually about a 1% loss in economic value or purchasing power. Inflation is thus a measure of the decline in the purchasing power of the dollar.

Measure. The decline in purchasing power can be measured in many ways. Consumers may judge inflation in terms of the prices they pay for food and other goods; economists record this measure in the form of the consumer price index (CPI), which is based on sample prices in a "market basket" of purchases. We should note that consumer prices do not always behave like wholesale prices or commodity prices, and as a result, a dollar's worth varies depending on what is bought.

There is another measure of the dollar's value that reflects the average purchasing power of the dollar as it applies to all goods and services in the economy—the gross national product implicit price deflator (GNPIPD). The GNPIPD is computed and published quarterly by the U.S. Department of Commerce, Bureau of Economic Analysis.

Various cost indices are also available to the estimator. A government index listing is given by the *Statistical Abstract of the United States,* a yearly publication that includes material, labor, and construction costs. The Bureau of Labor Statistics publishes the monthly *Producer Price Index* and covers some 3,000 product groupings.

Average Inflation Rate. To account for the effect of inflation, we utilize an annual percentage rate that represents the annual increase in prices over a one-year period. Because the rate each year is based on the previous year's price, this inflation rate has a compounding effect. For example, prices that increase at the rate of 5% per year in the first year and 8% per year in the second year, with a starting base price of $100, will increase at an average inflation rate of 6.49%.

$$100(1 + 0.05)(1 + 0.08) = 113.40$$

first year

second year

Let f be the average annual inflation rate. Then we equate

$$100(1 + f)^2 = 113.40$$

$$f = 6.49\%$$

The inflation rate itself may be computed from any of the several available indices. With the CPI value, the annual inflation rate may be calculated from the expression

$$\text{Annual inflation rate for year } n = \frac{\text{CPI}_n - \text{CPI}_{n-1}}{\text{CPI}_{n-1}} \qquad (2.36)$$

For example, with $\text{CPI}_{1990} = 270$ and $\text{CPI}_{1989} = 260$, the annual inflation rate for year 1990 is

$$\frac{270 - 260}{260} = 0.0385 \text{ or } 3.85\%$$

As just indicated, we can easily compute the inflation rates for the years with known CPI values. However, most equivalence calculations for projects require the use of cash flow estimates that depend on expectations of *future* inflation rates. The methods used by economists to estimate future inflation rates are many and varied. Important factors to consider may include historical trends in rates, predicted economic conditions, professional judgment, and other elements of economic forecasting. The estimation of future inflation rates is certainly a difficult task; a complete discussion of this subject is beyond the scope of this text but can be found elsewhere [1]. Our interest here is in how we use these rates in equivalence calculations, when they are provided.

2.7.2 Explicit and Implicit Treatments of Inflation in Discounting

We will present three basic approaches for calculating equivalence values in an inflationary environment that allow for the simultaneous consideration of changes in earning power and changes in purchasing power. The three approaches are consistent and, if applied properly, should result in identical solutions. The first approach assumes that cash flow is estimated in terms of *actual dollars,* and the second uses the concept of *constant dollars.* The third approach uses a combination of actual and constant dollars and is discussed in Section 2.7.3.

Definition of Inflation Terminology. To develop the relationship between actual-dollar analysis and constant-dollar analysis, we will give precise definitions of several inflation-related terms, borrowed from Thuesen and Fabrycky [4].

Actual dollars represent the out-of-pocket dollars received or expended at any point in time. Other names for them are then-current dollars, current dollars, future dollars, inflated dollars, and nominal dollars.

Constant dollars represent the hypothetical purchasing power of future receipts and disbursements in terms of the purchasing dollars in some base year. (The base year is normally time zero, the beginning of the investment.) We will assume that the base year is always time zero unless specified otherwise. Other names are real dollars, deflated dollars, and today's dollars.

Market interest rate (i) represents the opportunity to earn as reflected by the actual rates of interest available in the financial market. The interest rates used in previous sections are actually market interest rates. (The designation i is used consistently throughout this book to represent interest rates available in the marketplace.) When the rate of inflation increases, there is a corresponding upward movement in market interest rates. Thus, the market interest rates include the effects of both the earning power and the purchasing power of money. Other names are combined interest rate, nominal interest rate, minimum attractive rate of return, and inflation-adjusted discount rate.

Inflation-free interest rate (i') represents the earning power of money isolated from the effects of inflation. This interest rate is not quoted by financial institutions and other investors and is therefore not generally known to the public. This rate can be computed, however, if the market interest rate and inflation rate are known. Naturally, if there is no inflation in an economy, i and i' should be identical. Other names are real interest rate, true interest rate, and constant-dollar interest rate.

General inflation rate (f) represents the average annual percentage of increase in prices of goods and services. The market inflation rate is expected to respond to this general inflation rate. *Escalation rate* (e) represents a specific inflation rate applicable to a specific segment of the economy. It is sometimes used in contracts.

It is important to recognize that there is a relationship between inflation and interest rate. For example, the historical rate on AAA bonds is about 2.5% to 3% above the general inflation rate as measured by the CPI [1]. In addition, the rate of return (ROR) required by well-managed companies on their investments must be at some level above the inflation rate. In the next section we will derive the mathematical relationships of i, i', and f.

Relationships of i, i', and f. We must first establish the relationship between actual dollars and constant dollars. Suppose we estimate a future single payment F' that occurs at the end of the nth period in terms of constant dollars (primes indicate constant dollars). To translate this constant-dollar amount into the actual dollars at the end of the nth period, we use

$$F = F'(1 + f)^n$$

Solving for F' yields

$$F' = F(1 + f)^{-n} \tag{2.37}$$

where F' = constant-dollar expression for the cash flow at the end of the nth period,

F = actual-dollar expression for the cash flow at the end of the nth period.

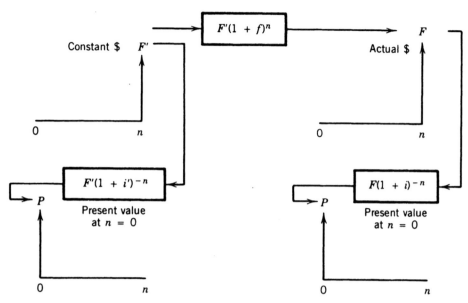

FIGURE 2.11 Relationships of i, i^1 and f.

As shown in Figure 2.11, to find the present value equivalent of this actual dollar, we should use the market interest rate i in

$$P = F(1 + i)^{-n} \qquad (2.38)$$

If the cash flow is already given in constant dollars with the inflation effect removed, we should use i' to account for only the earning power of the money. To find the present value equivalent of this constant dollar at i', we use

$$P = F'(1 + i')^{-n} \qquad (2.39)$$

The P values must be equal at time zero, and equating the results of Eqs. 2.38 and 2.39 yields

$$F(1 + i)^{-n} = F'(1 + i')^{-n}$$
$$= F(1 + f)^{-n}(1 + i')^{-n}$$
$$(1 + i)^{-n} = (1 + f)^{-n}(1 + i')^{-n}$$
$$(1 + i) = (1 + f)(1 + i')$$
$$= 1 + f + i' + i'f$$

or

$$i = i' + f + i'f \qquad (2.40)$$

Solving for i' yields

$$i' = \frac{i - f}{1 + f} \qquad (2.41)$$

As an example, say that the inflation rate is 6% per year and the market interest rate is known to be 15% per year. Calculating i' gives us

$$i' = \frac{0.15 - 0.06}{1 + 0.06} = 8.49\%$$

To summarize, the interest rate that is applicable in equivalence calculations depends on the assumptions used in estimating the cash flow. If the cash flow is estimated in terms of actual dollars, the market interest rate (i) should be used. If the cash flow is estimated in terms of constant dollars, the inflation-free interest rate (i) should be used. In subsequent sections we will give more detailed examples of how the two interest rates are used in equivalence calculations.

Actual-Dollar versus Constant-Dollar Analysis. If cash flow is represented in constant dollars (such as 1990 dollars), an inflation-free discount rate i (say 5% to 15%) may be appropriate for a profitable business. If cash flow is represented in inflated dollars, a market interest rate (say 15% to 25%) may be appropriate. Often, the difficulty lies in determining the nature of the cash flow. In this section, we will consider two cases and explain how the analyses in terms of actual and constant dollars can be used.

Case 1: Projections in physical units can often be translated into constant-dollar projections by using a constant-dollar price per unit and then converted to present value by using an inflation-free discount rate.

Example 2.12

SM Manufacturing Company makes electric meters of the type with which utility companies measure electricity consumption by users. SM has projected the sale of its meters by using data on new housing starts and deterioration and replacement of existing units. The price per unit should keep up with the wholesale price index (WPI). In 1990 the price per unit is $25. To achieve the production and sales projected in the following, SM needs to invest $75,000 now (in 1990). Other costs remain unchanged.

n	0	1	2	3	4	5	6	7
Unit Sales	—	1,000	1,100	1,200	1,200	1,300	1,300	1,200
$ Inflow	—	25,000	27,500	30,000	30,000	32,500	32,500	30,000

SM thinks it should earn a 5% inflation-free rate of return (ROR) on any investment.

This is an easy problem because all figures are in constant (1990) dollars. Just discount the dollar inflows at 5%. For example, present value would be

$$P = -75,000 + 25,000(1/1.05) + 27,500(1/1.05)^2$$
$$+ 30,000(1/1.05)^3 + 30,000(1/1.05)^4 + 32,500(1/1.05)^5$$
$$+ 32,500(1/1.05)^6 + 30,000(1/1.05)^7$$
$$= 95,386 \text{ in 1990 dollars} \quad \square$$

Case 2: If projections in dollars are made with numerical and statistical techniques, they will very likely reflect some inflationary trend. If they do, we should use a market interest rate or a two-step approach in which we first convert to constant dollars and then compute present value by using an inflation-free discount rate.

Example 2.13

U.S. Cola Company (USCC) is studying a new marketing scheme in southeast Georgia. By examining a similar project conducted from 1977 to 1989 and using nonlinear statistical regression, the analysts have projected additional dollar profits from this new marketing practice as follows.

Year	1 (1991)	2	3	4	5	6
Additonal Profit	100,000	120,000	150,000	200,000	150,000	100,000

An investment of $500,000 is required now (1990) to fund the project. USCC is accustomed to obtaining a 20% ROR on its projects during these inflation-ridden times.

Statistical regression on dollar sales inevitably reflects any inflationary trends during the study period (1977 to 1989 in this example), so we may conclude that the dollar profits are represented in inflated, actual dollars. The 20% discount rate was developed for today's inflationary economy, so it can be used to compute a present value:

$$P = -500,000 + 100,000(1/1.2) + 120,000(1/1.2)^2$$
$$+ 150,000(1/1.2)^3 + 200,000(1/1.2)^4$$
$$+ 150,000(1/1.2)^5 + 100,000(1/1.2)^6$$
$$= -56,306 \text{ in 1990 dollars}$$

(Note that in the sign convention used a minus sign means cash outflow.) $\quad \square$

Example 2.14

The scenario is the same as in example 2.13, but we assume that inflation is projected to be 9% per year, and we do the analysis by first converting to constant dollars. USCC expects at least a 10% inflation-free return on its investments. Noting that

$$(1 + 0.1)(1 + 0.09) = 1.990 \cong (1 + 0.2)$$

we judge this to be a reasonable translation. We first deflate the cash flow at 9%.

n	1	2	3	4	5	6
F'_n	91,743	101,002	115,828	141,685	97,490	59,627

Now we compute a present value using the constant-dollar cash flow with appropriate interest rate of 10%:

$$P = -500,000 + 91,743(1/1.1) + 101,002(1/1.1)^2$$
$$+ 115,828(1/1.1)^3 + 141,685(1/1.1)^4$$
$$+ 97,490(1/1.1)^5 + 59,627(1/1.1)^6$$
$$= -55,137 \text{ in 1990 dollars}$$

This value agrees closely with that obtained by using actual dollars and the market interest rate of 20%; the discrepancy comes from the fact that $1.199 \neq 1.200$. □

Composite Cash Flow Elements with Different Escalation Rates. The equivalence calculation examples in the previous sections were all based on the assumption that all cash flows respond to the inflationary trend in a uniform manner. Many project cash flows, however, are composed of several cash flow elements with different degrees of responsiveness to the inflationary trend. For example, the net cash flow elements for a certain project may comprise sales revenue, operating and maintenance costs, and taxes. Each element may respond to the inflationary environment to a varying degree. In computing the tax element alone, we need to isolate the depreciation element. With inflation, sales and operating costs are assumed to increase accordingly. Depreciation would be unchanged, but taxes, profits, and thus the net cash flow usually would be higher. (A complete discussion of the effect of inflation on the after-tax cash flow will be given in Chapter 4.) Now we will discuss briefly how we compute the equivalence value with such cash flows.

In complex situations there may be several inflation rates. For example, an apartment developer might project physical unit sales, building costs in actual dollars using a building cost index, and sales revenue in actual dollars using a real estate price index, and then find the equivalent present value using an interest rate that reflects the consumer price index.

Example 2.15

This more complex example illustrates the apartment building project. Base year cost per unit is $15,000 and selling price per unit is $20,000. The building cost index is projected to increase 11% next year and 10% more the following year. The real estate price index is expected to jump 15% next year and then level off at a 13% increase per year. We will use a market interest rate of 15%, hoping that it will yield an inflation-free return of 5% when the general inflation rate is 9% to 10% (to be precise, $f = 9.52\%$).

Item	n: 0	1	2	3
Units built	200	250	200	—
Units sold	—	200	250	200
Costs (thousands)	3,000	3,750(1.11)	3,000(1.11)(1.1)	—
Revenues (thousands)	—	4,000(1.15)	5,000(1.15)(1.13)	4,000(1.15)(1.13)^2
Net flow (thousands) (actual $)	−3,000	+438	+2,835	+5,874
(P/F, 15%, n)	1	0.8696	0.7561	0.6575

$$P = -3,000 + 438(0.8696) + 2,835(0.7561) + 5,874(0.6575)$$

$$P = \$3,387,000 \text{ in base year (time 0) dollars} \quad \square$$

2.7.3 Home Ownership Analysis during Inflation

A personal decision of wide and continuing interest is whether it is more economical to buy a home or to rent during an inflationary environment. In this section we will illustrate how this decision can be made on a rational basis by applying the concepts of actual and constant dollars.

Renting a House. To make a meaningful comparison, let's estimate the current rent of a two-bedroom apartment as $400 per month plus $60 per month for basic utilities (heating and cooling but not telephone, water, and sewer). Both costs have a tendency to increase with inflation, so let's project a 10% inflation rate, which gives us the following monthly costs per year.

n	1	2	3		10
Rent	400	440	484	$\cdots$	943
Utilities	60	66	73	$\cdots$	141

We selected a planning period of 10 years because realtors tell us that very few people live in the same house for the period of a home mortgage (typically 25 to 30 years). Of course, when you rent an apartment you are free to switch every year, and we'll assume a fairly uniform market of rents with no rent control (this situation occurs when the vacancy rate is 5% to 10%). Let's use a market interest rate of 15% (annual compounding) to compute the present value of apartment living costs (approximate, since we collapse all monthly flows to the year's end).

$$P = (-460)(12)/1.15 + (-506)(12)/(1.15)^2 + \cdots + (-1,084)(12)/(1.15)^{10}$$

$$= -39,610 \text{ in time 0 dollars}$$

Alternatively, we can compute an inflation-free discount rate i' to be used with constant dollars by applying Eq. 2.40.

$$0.15 = i' + 0.1 + 0.1i'$$

$$i' = 0.0455$$

We must also convert 460 to $460/1.1 = 418.18$. Thus, a present value using the constant-dollar cash flow is

$$P = (-418.18)(12)(P/A, \ 4.55\%, 10)$$

and

$$(P/A, \ 4.55\%, \ 10) = \left[\frac{(1.0455)^{10} - 1}{0.0455(1.0455)^{10}} \right] = 7.8933$$

so

$$P = (-418.18)(12)(7.8933)$$

$$= -39,610 \text{ in time 0 dollars}$$

Buying a House.   Now we must estimate the cash flow for a house or condominium. The purchase cost will be $60,000. "Wait a minute!" you say. "I've seen those $60,000 units and they're too old, too small, or too far away, or built like apartments." Right. It's difficult to compare the space and quality of an apartment with those of a house, but it is not fair to compare a two-bedroom apartment with a new, close-in home or condominium containing 1,500 or more square feet. Therefore, the $60,000 home is a more appropriate comparison. If you finally decide to spend $80,000, you're allocating more money to your residence than when you lived in apartments, but you'll get more space, privacy, convenience, return, and so forth.

We will try for 95% financing, which means that we need a $3,000 down payment plus about another $3,000 for closing costs, for a cash requirement of about $6,000.

The mortgage interest rate might be 14.5% (total $14.5/12 = 1.208\%$ per month) on a fixed-rate 30-year mortgage. So the monthly payment is

$$57{,}000 \, (A/P, \, 1.208\%, \, 360) = (57{,}000)\left[\frac{0.01208(1.01208)^{360}}{(1.01208)^{360} - 1}\right]$$

$$= (57{,}000)(0.012242)$$

$$= \$697.815 = \$698/\text{month}$$

The mortgage balance remaining after our 10-year comparison period is

$$697.815(P/A, \, 1.208\%, \, 240) = 697.815\left[\frac{(1.01208)^{240} - 1}{0.01208(1.1208)^{240}}\right]$$

$$= (697.815)(78.143) = \$54{,}529$$

We will have paid off less than 5% of the loan in 10 years, which is not unusual for these mortgages. Approximately 97% of our monthly payments will be interest, which is tax deductible:

$$(698)(12)(10) \ = \ \$83{,}760 \quad \text{total payments}$$

$$57{,}000 - 54{,}529 = \underline{\$ \ 2{,}471} \quad \text{principal repayments}$$

$$\$81{,}289 \quad \text{interest payments}$$

We will assume a 40%[1] marginal income tax rate (federal plus state) and sufficient other deductions to make the interest reduce our tax by

$$(698)(0.97)(0.40) = \$271/\text{month}$$

So the after-tax cost of the mortgage is only $698 − $271 = $427.

Real estate taxes are estimated to be $600 per year, or $50/month, and these are also tax deductible, which saves us $20/month for an after-tax cost of $30/month. These taxes will increase at about 10% per year.

Basic taxes and utilities will be about $60/month for a condominium and $100/month for a house, so let's use $80/month, with 10% inflation. Homeowner's insurance is slightly higher than renter's insurance, so we allow $100 per year. Maintenance can be another $300 per year. The monthly total of these items is $33/month, inflating at 10%. Our home will appreciate in value at about 7% per year and sell at

$$60{,}000(1.07)^{10} = \$118{,}029$$

After paying a 6% realtor's commission and the mortgage balance, we keep

$$(118{,}029)(0.94) - 54{,}529 = \$56{,}418$$

---

[1]A 30% tax rate may be more reasonable for many homeowners. We will leave this for the reader to do as an exercise (see Problem 2.23).

(We assume no capital gain tax on this amount.) Now we're ready to compute P.

$$P = -6,000 \qquad\qquad\qquad\qquad\qquad \text{constant dollars}$$

$$- (427)(12)(P/A,\ 15\%,\ 10) \qquad\qquad \text{actual dollars}$$

$$\left.\begin{aligned}
&- (30/1.1)(12)(P/A,\ 4.55\%,\ 10) \\
&- (80/1.1)(12)(P/A,\ 4.55\%,\ 10) \\
&- (33/1.1)(12)(P/A,\ 4.55\%,\ 10)
\end{aligned}\right\} \text{constant dollars}$$

$$+ 56,418(P/F,\ 15\%,\ 10) \qquad\qquad \text{actual dollars}$$

Note carefully that we use 15% for actual-dollars expenses and 4.55% for constant-dollars expenses. We could convert the real estate taxes, utilities, incremental insurance, and maintenance to actual dollars by using 10% and then using 15% for discounting, but that is too much work. Our method produces the same numerical results.

$$P = -6,000$$

$$- (427)(12)(5.0188)$$

$$- (130)(12)(7.8933)$$

$$+ (56,418)(0.2472)$$

$$= -30,080 \text{ in constant dollars}$$

This cost is $9,530 *less* than renting. In this example the present value costs in constant dollars for home ownership are about 76% of the present value costs for renting. The big difference comes from the fact that you are using $57,000 of someone else's money to buy an asset that resells at two times its purchase price. You pay interest on the loan, but this is partly offset by the rent you would pay in an apartment.

Notice that the house was assumed to appreciate at 7%, compared with a mortgage interest rate of 14.5% nominal (15.5% effective per year). Many people think home ownership makes sense only if the mortgage interest rate is below the real estate appreciation rate. This is not true, as the example demonstrates.

We also used a 15% market interest rate, versus 10% general inflation and 7% real estate inflation. We might question the sensitivity of the results to these factors. In Table 2.7 we show some results of a sensitivity analysis in which we vary the inflation rate, the real estate appreciation rate, and the rent. We can see that there is a wide range of parameter values where buying is better. In fact, many people have benefited financially from home ownership during inflation. The home ownership analysis could be based on the principle of monthly payment and monthly compounding without collapsing all monthly flows to year end. We will leave this for the reader to do as an exercise (see Problem 2.22).

Table 2.7 Sensitivity Analysis: Buy versus Rent Decision

Inflation f:	5%			10%			15%		
Market Interest i:	10%			15%			20%		
Real Estate Appreciation Rate: Rent	0%	2.5%	5%	5%	7.5%	10%	5%	10%	15%
350	−36.6	−36.6	−36.6	−35.3	−35.3	−35.3	−34.1	−34.1	−34.1
	−49.6	−43.5	−35.9	−34.8	−28.8	−21.4	−33.4	−24.6	−11.4
	136	119	98	99	82	61	98	72	33
400	−41.1	−41.1	−41.1	−39.6	−39.6	−39.6	−38.3	−38.3	−38.3
	−49.6	−43.5	−35.9	−34.8	−28.8	−21.4	−33.4	−24.6	−11.4
	121	106	87	88	73	54	87	64	30
450	−45.5	−45.5	−45.5	−43.9	−43.9	−43.9	−42.4	−42.4	−42.4
	−49.6	−43.5	−35.9	−34.8	−28.8	−21.4	−33.4	−24.6	−11.4
	109	96	79	79	66	49	79	58	27

NOTES: Each triplet of entries consists of present value of rental cash flow in thousands, present value of ownership cash flow in thousands, and percentage ratio of ownership flow to rental flow.

Other parameters:

5% down	$60,000 home cost	$80/month utilities (home)	$300/year maintenance (home)
5% closing costs	14.5% mortgage rate	$600/year real estate taxes	6% realtor's commission
30-year mortgage	40% marginal tax rate	$100/year incremental insurance	10-year planning period

2.8 SUMMARY

In this chapter we have examined the concept of the time value of money and the equivalence of cash flows. Discrete compound interest formulas have been derived for converting present sums, future sums, uniform series, gradient series, and geometric series to specified points in time. We also discussed the concepts of nominal interest rate and effective interest rate, which led to the idea of continuous compounding. Continuous-compounding formulas were then derived for both discrete and continuous cash flows.

We discussed the measures of inflation and the effects of inflation on equivalence calculations. We presented two basic approaches that may be used in equivalence calculations to offset the effects of changes in purchasing power. In the actual-dollar analysis, we include an inflation component in estimating cash flows so that a market interest rate is used to find the equivalence value. In the constant-dollar approach we express the cash flows in terms of base-year dollars and use an inflation-free interest rate to compute the equivalent value at the specified points in time. We also showed that if these approaches are applied correctly, they should lead to identical results.

REFERENCES

1. BUCK, J. R., and C. S. PARK, *Inflation and Its Impact on Investment Decisions,* Industrial Engineering and Management Press, Institute of Industrial Engineers, Norcross, Ga., 1984.
2. FLEISCHER, G. A., and T. L. WARD, "Classification of Compound Interest Models in Economic Analysis," *The Engineering Economist,* Vol. 23, No. 1, pp. 13–29, Fall 1977.
3. PARK, C. S., *Modern Engineering Economic Analysis,* Addison–Wesley, Reading, Mass., 1990.
4. THUESEN, G. J., and W. J. FABRYCKY, *Engineering Economy,* 7th edition, Prentice–Hall, Englewood Cliffs, N.J., 1989.
5. WHITE, J. A., M. H. AGEE, and K. E. CASE, *Principles of Engineering Economic Analysis,* 3rd edition, Wiley, New York, 1989.

PROBLEMS

2.1. A typical bank offers you a Visa credit card that charges interest on unpaid balance at a 1.5% per month compounded monthly. This means that the nominal interest (annual percentage) rate for this account is *A* and the effective annual interest rate is *B.* Suppose your beginning balance was $500 and you make only the required minimum *monthly* payment (payable at the end of each month) of $20 for next 3 months. If you made no new purchases with this card during this period, your unpaid balance will be *C* at the end of 3 months. What are the values of *A, B,* and *C?*

2.2. In January 1989, C&S, the largest mutual savings bank in Georgia, published the following information: interest, 7.55%; effective annual yield, 7.842%. The bank did not explain how the 7.55% is connected to the 7.842%, but you can figure out that the compounding scheme used by the bank should be _____.

2.3. How many years will it take an investment to double if the interest rate is 12% compounded (a) annually, (b) semiannually, (c) quarterly, (d) monthly, (e) weekly, (f) daily, and (g) continuously?

2.4. Suppose that $1,000 is placed in a bank account at the end of each *quarter* over the next 10 years. Determine the total accumulated value (future worth) at the end of 10 years where the interest rate is 8% compounded *quarterly*.

2.5. What equal-payment series is required to repay the following present amounts?
   a. $10,000 in 4 years at 10% interest compounded annually with 4 annual payments.
   b. $5,000 in 3 years at 12% interest compounded semiannually with 6 semiannual payments.
   c. $6,000 in 5 years at 8% interest compounded quarterly with 20 quarterly payments.
   d. $80,000 in 30 years at 9% interest compounded monthly with 360 monthly payments.

2.6. Suppose that $5,000 is placed in a bank account at the end of each quarter over the next 10 years. Determine the total accumulated value (future worth) at the end of 10 years when the interest rate is
   a. 12% compounded annually.   c. 12% compounded monthly.
   b. 12% compounded quarterly.   d. 12% compounded continuously.

2.7. What equal *quarterly* payments will be required to repay a loan of $10,000 over 3 years if the rate of interest is 8% compounded *continuously*?

2.8. Compute the present worth of cash flow that has a triangular pattern with 12% interest compounded continuously.

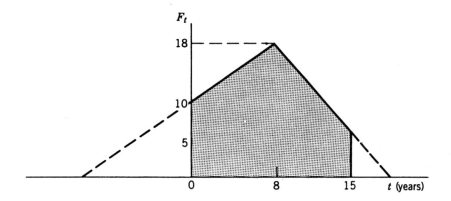

2.9. Suppose a uniformly increasing continuous cash flow (a ramp) accumulates $600 over 3 years. Find the present worth of this cash flow under continuous compounding at $r = 12\%$.

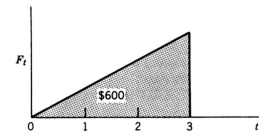

311

2.10. For computing the equivalent equal-payment series (A) of the following cash flow with $i = 10\%$, which of the following statements is (are) correct?

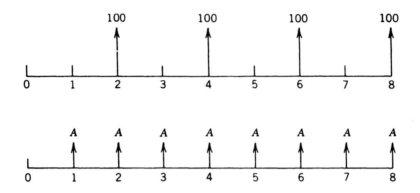

a. $A = 100(P/A, 10\%, 4)(A/P, 10\%, 8)$
b. $A = [100(P/F, 10\%, 2) + 100(P/F, 10\%, 4) + 100(P/F, 10\%, 6)$
      $+ 100(P/F, 10\%, 8)](A/P, 10\%, 8)$
c. $A = 100(A/F, 10\%, 2)$
d. $A = 100(P/A, 21\%, 4)(A/P, 10\%, 8)$
e. $A = 100(F/A, 10\%, 4)(A/F, 10\%, 8)$
f. $A = 100(F/A, 21\%, 4)(A/F, 10\%, 8)$

2.11. The following equation describes the conversion of a cash flow into an equivalent equal-payment series with $n = 8$. Draw the original cash flow diagram. Assume an interest rate of 10% compounded annually.

$A = [-1,000 - 1,000(P/F, 10\%, 1)](A/P, 10\%, 8)$

$\quad + [3,000 + 500(A/G, 10\%, 4)](P/A, 10\%, 4)(P/F, 10\%, 1)(A/P, 10\%, 8)$

$\quad + 750(F/A, 10\%, 2)(A/F, 10\%, 8)$

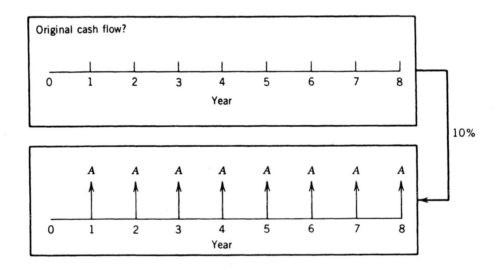

2.12. The following two cash flow transactions are said to be equivalent at 10% interest compounded annually. Find the unknown value X that satisfies the equivalence.

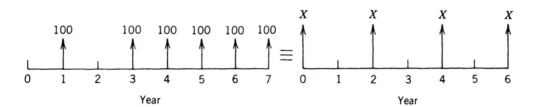

2.13. Suppose you have the choice of investing in (1) a zero-coupon bond that costs $513.60 today, pays nothing during its life, and then pays $1,000 after 5 years or (2) a municipal bond that costs $1,000 today, pays $67 in interest *semiannually*, and matures at the end of 5 years. Which bond would provide the higher *yield to maturity* (or return on your investment)?

2.14. You borrow B dollars from your bank, which adds on the total interest before computing the monthly payment (add-on interest). Thus, if the quoted nominal interest rate (annual percentage rate) is r% and the loan is for N months, the total amount that you agree to repay is

$$B + B(N/12)(r/100)$$

This is divided by N to give the amount of each payment, A.

$$A = B(1/N + r/1200)$$

This is called an add-on loan. But the true rate of interest that you are paying is somewhat more than r%, because you do not hold the amount of the loan for the full N months.

a. Find the equation to determine the true rate of interest i per month.

b. Plot the relationship between r and i as a function of N.

c. For $B = $10,000$, $N = 36$ months, and $r = 8$%, find the effective annual borrowing rate per year.

d. Identify the lending situation in which the true interest rate i per month approaches to $r/12$.

2.15. John Hamilton is going to buy a car worth $10,000 from a local dealer. He is told that the add-on interest rate is only 1.25% per month, and his monthly payment is computed as follows:

Installment period = 30 months

Interest = 30(0.0125)($10,000) = $3,750

Credit check, life insurance, and processing fee = $50

Total amount owed = $10,000 + $3,750 + $50 = $13,800

Monthly payment size = $13,800/30 = $460 per month

What is the effective rate that John is paying for his auto financing?

a. Effective interest rate per month?

b. Effective annual interest rate?

c. Suppose that John bought the car and made 15 such monthly payments ($460). Now he decides to pay off the remaining debt with one lump sum payment at the time of the sixteenth payment. What should the size of this payment be?

313

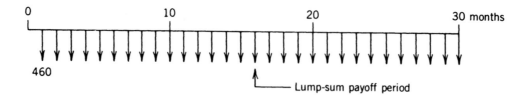

2.16. A pipeline was built 3 years ago to last 6 years. It develops leaks according to the relation

$$\log N = 0.07T - 2.42, \qquad T > 30$$

where N is the total number of leaks from installation and T is the time in months from installation. It costs $500 to repair a leak. If money is worth 8% per year, and without considering any tax effect, how much can be spent now for a cathodic system that will reduce leaks by 75%? (Adapted from F. C. Jelen and J. H. Black, *Cost and Optimization*, McGraw–Hill, New York, 1983.)

2.17. A market survey indicates that the price of a 10-oz jar of instant coffee has fluctuated over the last few years as follows:

Period	−4	−3	−2	−1	0	1
Price ($)	2.83	3.13	3.47	4.67	5.83	?

a. Assuming that the base period (price index = 100) is period −4 (four periods ago), compute the average price index for this instant coffee.
b. Estimate the price at time period 1, if the current price trend is expected to continue.

2.18. The annual operating costs of a small electrical generating unit are expected to remain the same ($200,000) if the effects of inflation are not considered. The best estimates indicate that the annual inflation-free rate of interest (i') will be 5% and the annual inflation rate (f) 6%. If the generator is to be used 3 more years, what is the present equivalent of its operating costs using *actual-dollar analysis?*

2.19. You want to know how much money to set aside now to pay for 1,000 gallons of home heating oil each year for 10 years. The current price of heating oil is $1.00 per gallon, and the price is expected to increase at a 10% compound price change each year for the next 10 years. The money to pay for the fuel oil will be set aside now in a bank savings account that pays 6% annual interest. How much money do you have to place in the savings account now, if payment for the fuel is made by end-of-year withdrawals?

2.20. An investment of $100,000 is required to expand a certain production facility in a manufacturing company. The firm estimates that labor costs will be $150,000 for the first year but will increase at the rate of 8% over the previous year's expenditure. Material costs, on the other hand, will be $400,000 for the first year but will increase at the rate of 10% per year due to inflation. If the firm's inflation-free interest rate (i') is 10% and the average general inflation rate (f) is expected to be 5% over the next 5 years, determine the total present equivalent operating expenses (with no tax consideration) for the project.

2.21. A couple with a 7-year-old daughter want to save for their child's college expenses in advance. Assuming that the child enters college at age 18, they estimate that an amount of $20,000 per year in terms of today's dollars will be required to support the child's college expenses for 4 years. The future inflation rate is estimated to be

6% per year and they can invest their savings at 8% compounded quarterly.

a. Determine the equal quarterly amounts the couple must save until they send their child to college.

b. If the couple has decided to save only $500 each quarter, how much will the child have to borrow each year to support her college education?

2.22. Consider the problem of renting versus buying a home given in Section 2.7.3. Recall that the analysis was performed on the basis of annual payments with annual compounding. Repeat the analysis using monthly payments and monthly compounding.

2.23. Consider again the problem of renting versus buying a home given in Section 2.7.3. Recall that the tax rate used in the analysis was 40%, which seems too high. Repeat the analysis using a tax rate of 30%. Does a lower tax rate make the buying option more attractive?

3
Transform Techniques in Cash Flow Modeling

3.1 INTRODUCTION

In Chapter 2 equivalence calculations were made by the proper use of the various interest formulas. In particular, with the interest rate and the compounding schemes specified, we showed how to convert various cash flow profiles into equivalent present values. In many situations, however, the cash flow patterns may take more complex forms than those discussed in Chapter 2. If they do, transform methods are often used to accomplish the same equivalence calculations with less computational effort and in a more routine manner. These methods are the Z-transform and Laplace transform methods. We will show in this chapter how they may be used in the modeling and analysis of economic situations involving either a discrete or a continuous time series of cash flow.

We will first discuss the concept of present value and its relationship to transform theory. Some useful properties of transforms will be presented, and their applications to economic model building will be discussed. Many examples are offered to aid the reader in understanding these powerful techniques. The reader will see that application of these transform formulas eliminates many of the calculations that are required when conventional interest formulas are used in complicated equivalence calculations.

3.2 Z-TRANSFORMS AND DISCRETE CASH FLOWS

3.2.1 The Z-Transform and Present Value

Consider that the function $f(n)$ describes the cash flow magnitude at the discrete point in time n. Then the equivalent present value of this cash flow series over an infinite time horizon at an interest rate i, assuming a discrete compounding principle, is

$$PV(i) = \sum_{n=0}^{\infty} f(n)(1 + i)^{-n} \tag{3.1}$$

Hill and Buck [6] recognized that the general form of the summation in (3.1) bears a striking resemblance to the definition of Z-transforms, the only difference being a definition of variables. That is, when a general discrete time series is described by a function $f(nT)$, where T is an equidistant time interval and n is an integer, the Z-transform of the time series $f(nT)$ is defined as

$$F(z) = \sum_{n=0}^{\infty} f(nT)z^{-n} \tag{3.2a}$$

With $T = 1$,

$$F(z) = \sum_{n=0}^{\infty} f(n)z^{-n} = Z\{f(n)\} \tag{3.2b}$$

where z is a complex variable. If we replace z with the interest rate $1 + i$ and set the constant-length time interval T to unity (that is, the compounding period is the unit of time, monthly or yearly), Eq. 3.2 becomes

$$F(z) = \sum_{n=0}^{\infty} f(n)(1 + i)^{-n} \tag{3.3}$$

where i is the interest rate for a compounding period. Throughout this chapter the value of T will be set to unity so that the compounding period can be assumed to be the unit of time. In the literature of mathematics, we find a transformation essentially the same as our Z-transform but expressed in positive powers of z:

$$F'(z) = \sum_{n=0}^{\infty} f(n)z^{n} \tag{3.4}$$

In this book we use the definition in (3.2) because the expressions for the corresponding Z-transform are analogous to those for present values. It should be obvious, however, that both transformations have the same purpose and application, and that one transform is converted to the other by the relations

$$F'(z) = F\left(\frac{1}{z}\right), \qquad F(z) = F'\left(\frac{1}{z}\right) \tag{3.5}$$

In the construction of Z-transforms, the following notation will be used. If $f(n)$ represents the discrete f function, $F(z)$ will represent the transform. In addition, as a shorthand notation, the transform pair will be denoted by $f(n) \leftrightarrow F(z)$. This double arrow is symbolic of the uniqueness of the one-to-one correspondence between $f(n)$ and $F(z)$. Thus, if $Z\{g(n)\} = G(z)$, we write $g(n) \leftrightarrow G(z)$. This lowercase–uppercase correspondence will be adhered to throughout this chapter.

For a cash flow sequence of infinite duration, the resulting Z-transform will be an infinite series involving inverse powers of z. This series can be expressed as a rational fraction in z, provided that the series converges. These so-called closed-form expressions will be especially convenient for our computations. For expressing a Z-transform as a ratio of polynomials in z, two important identities of infinite series will be needed:

$$\sum_{n=0}^{\infty} a^n = \frac{1}{1-a} \quad \text{provided } |a| < 1 \tag{3.6}$$

and

$$\sum_{n=0}^{\infty} (1+n)a^n = \frac{1}{(1-a)^2} \quad \text{provided } |a| < 1 \tag{3.7}$$

Now consider the sequence of function $f(n) = a^n$. The Z-transform is

$$F(z) = \sum_{n=0}^{\infty} f(n)z^{-n} = \sum_{n=0}^{\infty} a^n z^{-n} = \sum_{n=0}^{\infty} \left(\frac{a}{z}\right)^n$$

Using Eq. 3.6, we obtain

$$F(z) = \frac{1}{1 - a/z} = \frac{z}{z - a} \quad \text{if } \left|\frac{a}{z}\right| < 1 \tag{3.8}$$

In other words, the infinite geometric series a^n converges to $z/(z-a)$ if $|z| > |a|$. For ease of conversion, the table of transform pairs of $f(n)$ and $F(z)$ is provided (see Table 3.1).

Many cash flow transactions have a finite time duration. Because transforms are defined for series with infinite time horizons, it is necessary to introduce additional techniques to provide a methodology that is applicable to finite time horizons. We will examine some properties of the Z-transform in the following section.

3.2.2 Properties of the Z-Transform

Many useful properties of the Z-transform are discussed in the literature of mathematics, probability theory, and operations research [4,5,7]. We will focus on two important properties that are most relevant in equivalence calculations: linearity and translation.

Table 3.1 *A Short Table of Z-Transform Pairs*

Standard Pattern	Original Function, $f(n)$	Z-Transform, $F(z)$	Present Value of $f(n)$ Starting at $n=0$ and Continuous over the Infinite Time Horizon
Step (uniform series)	C	$C\left(\dfrac{z}{z-1}\right)$	$C\left(\dfrac{1+i}{i}\right)$
Ramp (gradient series)	Cn	$C\left[\dfrac{z}{(z-1)^2}\right]$	$C\left(\dfrac{1+i}{i^2}\right)$
Geometric	Ca^n	$C\left(\dfrac{z}{z-a}\right)$	$C\left(\dfrac{1+i}{1+i-a}\right)$
Decay	Ce^{-jn}	$C\left(\dfrac{z}{z-e^{-j}}\right)$	$C\left(\dfrac{1+i}{1+i-e^{-j}}\right)$
Growth	$C(1-e^{-jn})$	$C\left(\dfrac{z}{z-1}-\dfrac{z}{z-e^{-j}}\right)$	$C\left(\dfrac{1+i}{i}-\dfrac{1+i}{1+i-e^{-j}}\right)$
Impulse (single payment)	$C\delta(n-k)$	$C\left(z^{-k}\right)$	$C(1+i)^{-k}$

NOTE: C = pattern scale factor
    n = time index for compounding periods
    i = effective interest rate for a compounding period.
    a = pattern base factor
    j = pattern rate factor
    δ = impulse function
    k = number of time periods before the impulse occurs

Linearity. The Z-transform is a linear operation. Thus, when a sequence can be expressed as a sum of other sequences, the following result will be useful.

$$f(n) = C_1 f_1(n) + C_2 f_2(n) \leftrightarrow F(z)$$
$$f_1(n) \leftrightarrow F_1(z)$$
$$f_2(n) \leftrightarrow F_2(z)$$

then

$$F(z) = C_1 F_1(z) + C_2 F_2(z) \tag{3.9}$$

This linearity property makes it possible to combine component time forms and to amplify general time patterns by the scale factor C to represent the

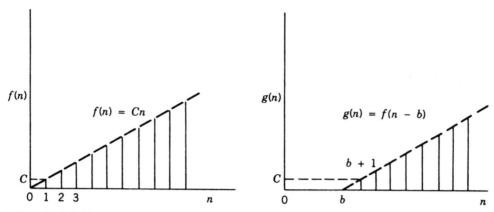

FIGURE 3.1 Ramp pattern transaction (gradient series).

proportion of the component. By adding it to or subtracting it from the scaled transforms of other components, we are able to describe the composite Z-transform of the entire stream of components.

Translation with Time Advance. To consider a composite of cash flows that start at various points in time, we seek the relation between the Z-transform of sequences and their shifted version. Consider the sequence $g(n)$ obtained from $f(n)$ by shifting $f(n)$ to the right by b units of time. This situation is illustrated in Figure 3.1, in which the function $f(n)$ takes a ramp pattern. Since the sequence $g(n)$ is 0 for $n < b$, we can define the sequence $g(n)$ in terms of $f(n)$ as

$$g(n) = \begin{cases} f(n-b) & \text{for } n \geq b \\ 0 & \text{for } n < b \end{cases} \tag{3.10}$$

To find the transform of this time-shifted function, we use the property of the unit step function. If we take the unit step function and translate it b units to the right to get $u(n - b)$, we obtain the function shown in Figure 3.2a. Mathematically, we denote this by

$$u(n-b) = \begin{cases} 1 & \text{for } n \geq b \\ 0 & \text{for } n < b \end{cases} \tag{3.11}$$

Notice that the shifted unit step function in Figure 3.2a has no values for $n < b$ but is equal to 1 for $n \geq b$. The product $f(n - b)u(n - b)$ will be zero for $n < b$ and will equal $f(n - b)$ for $n \geq b$. This product form shown in Figure 3.2c defines precisely the shifted ramp function we defined in Figure 3.1b. More generally, we define such a function as

$$g(n) = f(n-b)u(n-b) = \begin{cases} f(n-b) & \text{for } n \geq b \\ 0 & \text{for } n < b \end{cases} \tag{3.12}$$

321

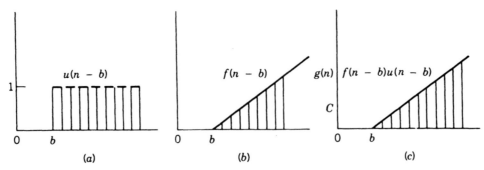

FIGURE 3.2 Graph of the ramp function with translation and cutoff.

Then the Z-transform of the above expression is defined as

$$G(z) = z^{-b} F(z) = (1 + i)^{-b} F(z) \tag{3.13}$$

The quantity z^{-b} in the Z-transform simply reflects the fact that the start of the function $f(n)$ has been shifted forward in time by b units. Thus, if $f(n) = Cn$, shifting $f(n)$ to the right by b units and taking its Z-transform generates $z^{-b}[Cz/(z - 1)^2]$. Expressing this in terms of the present value and replacing z with $(1 + i)$, we obtain $PV(i) = [C(1 + i)^{1 - b}]/i^2$.

Translation with Cutoff. Many realistic cash flow functions extend over finite time horizons. Another scheme of translation property is useful in finding the Z-transforms for these translated cash flow functions. Consider the function $g(n)$ shown in Figure 3.3c. This function is basically the truncated ramp function $f(n)$ in Figure 3.3b with the added feature of a delayed turn-on at time b, where b is an integer. By using the translation property discussed in the last section and multiplying the ramp function $f(n)$ by a unit step, we can express the desired truncated function $g(n)$ as

$$g(n) = f(n)u(n - b) = \begin{cases} f(n) & \text{for } b \leqslant n \\ 0 & \text{otherwise} \end{cases} \tag{3.14}$$

and the Z-transform of this product expression is

$$G(z) = z^{-b} Z\{f(n + b)\} \tag{3.15}$$

Unlike the situation in Figure 3.2c, the origin of the function $f(n)$ remains unchanged, but the first transaction begins at time b. Thus, it is important to recognize the functional distinction between $f(n)u(n - b)$ and $f(n - b)u(n - b)$. That is, an expression $f(n - b)u(n - b)$ similar to the one illustrated by Figure 3.2c will appear in shifting the sequence $f(n)$ to the right by b units in time; and its first transaction also starts at time b.

Now the Z-transform and present value expression for the ramp function

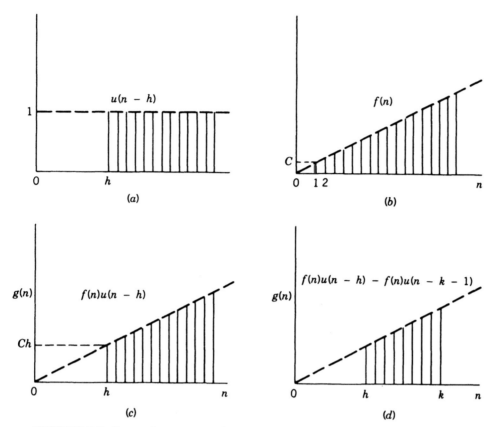

FIGURE 3.3 Ramp function with translation and cutoff.

with a delayed turn-on at time h shown in Figure 3.3c can easily be found. Since $f(n) = Cn$, the transform of $g(n)$ is

$$G(z) = z^{-h}Z\{f(n + h)\}$$

$$= z^{-h}Z\{Cn + Ch\}$$

$$= Cz^{-h}\left[\frac{z}{(z - 1)^2} + \frac{hz}{z - 1}\right]$$

$$= \frac{Cz^{1-h}}{(z - 1)^2}[1 + h(z - 1)] \tag{3.16}$$

By replacing z with $(1 + i)$, we obtain the present value expression

$$PV(i) = \frac{C(1 + i)^{1-h}}{i^2}(1 + hi) \tag{3.17}$$

Suppose we want to find the present value of the series shown in Figure 3.3d. This function is the same ramp function with the delayed turn-on at time h but also with a turn-off at time k, where h and k are integers. By using the property of the unit step function, we can express the desired ramp translation with turn-on and turn-off as follows.

$$g(n) = f(n)u(n - b) - f(n)u(n - k - 1) \qquad (3.18)$$

The transform of this function will be

$$
\begin{aligned}
G(z) &= z^{-b}Z\{f(n + b)\} - z^{-(k+1)}Z\{f(n + k + 1)\} \\
&= z^{-b}Z\{Cn + Cb\} - z^{-(k+1)}Z\{Cn + C(k + 1)\} \\
&= Cz^{-b}\left[\frac{z}{(z - 1)^2} + \frac{bz}{z - 1}\right] - Cz^{-(k+1)}\left[\frac{z}{(z - 1)^2} + \frac{(k + 1)z}{z - 1}\right] \\
&= \frac{C}{(z - 1)^2}(z^{1-b} - z^{-k}) + \frac{C}{z - 1}[bz^{1-b} - (k + 1)z^{-k}] \qquad (3.19)
\end{aligned}
$$

In terms of the present value expression, we have

$$PV(i) = \frac{C}{i^2}[(1 + i)^{1-b} - (1 + i)^{-k}] + \frac{C}{i}[b(1 + i)^{1-b} - (k + 1)(1 + i)^{-k}]$$

$$(3.20)$$

Example 3.1

As an example of the use of Eq. 3.20, suppose that estimates of certain end-of-year expenses are $300 for the third year, $400 for the fourth year, and $500 for the fifth year. If the effective interest rate is 15%, what is the equivalent present value?

The gradient series can be expressed as

$$f(n) = 100n \quad \text{where } 3 \le n \le 5$$

With $C = 100$, $b = 3$, $k = 5$, and $i = 0.15$, we obtain

$$PV(15\%) = \frac{100}{(0.15)^2}[(1.15)^{-2} - (1.15)^{-5}] + \frac{100}{0.15}[3(1.15)^{-2} - 6(1.15)^{-5}]$$

$$= \$674.54 \quad \square$$

Translation with Impulses. Suppose we want to find the transform of an impulse function $g(n)$ as given in Figure 3.4c. This type of impulse function may represent the salvage value of an item at time b, when the salvage value $f(n)$ decreases exponentially over time. To obtain the transforms of such impulse functions, we need to define a Kronecker delta function that corresponds to a unit impulse function as shown in Figure 3.4c. That is,

$$\delta(n - b) = \begin{cases} 1 & \text{for } n = b \\ 0 & \text{otherwise} \end{cases} \qquad (3.21)$$

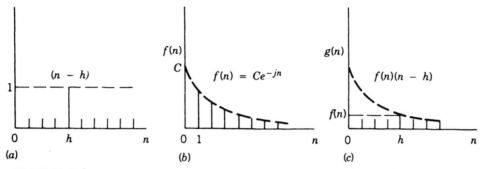

FIGURE 3.4 Kronecker delta function and translation with impulse.

By multiplying the salvage value function $f(n)$ by the unit impulse function, we obtain an expression in which the salvage value occurs only at time h, as desired. Formally, we may write this product expression as

$$g(n) = f(n)\delta(n - h) = \begin{cases} f(h) & \text{for } n = h \\ 0 & \text{otherwise} \end{cases} \qquad (3.22)$$

Since $f(h)$ is a constant and the transform of the shifted unit impulse function $\delta(n - h)$ is z^{-h}, the transform of the product form yields

$$G(z) = z^{-h}f(h) = f(h)(1 + i)^{-h} \qquad (3.23)$$

and this is exactly the present value expression for a single payment. If we define $f(h) = Ce^{-jh}$, we can find the present value expression

$$PV(i) = Ce^{-jh}(1 + i)^{-h} \qquad (3.24)$$

where j is the pattern rate factor for a decay function.

The linearity and translation properties just discussed provide many of the necessary analytical tools for finding the Z-transforms of realistic discrete time series encountered in economic analysis. Table 3.2 summarizes some other useful operational rules for the Z-transform. (See [7].)

3.2.3 Development of Present Value Models

We develop two types of present value models that correspond to the timing of the start of the original cash flow function. They are the extensive models and the simplified models.

Extensive Present Value Models. The extensive models represent cash flow functions that are shifted forward in time but switched on only at time h ($h \geq b$) and then terminated at time k ($k > h$) (see Figure 3.5). This function is basically the shifted ramp (gradient series) in Figure 3.1b with a delayed turn-on at time h and a turn-off at time k, where h and k are integers.

Table 3.2 *Some Properties of the Z-Transform*

Operational Rule	Original Function, $f(n)$	Z-Transform, $F(z)$
Linearity	$C_1 f_1(n) + C_2 f_2(n)$	$C_1 F_1(z) + C_2 F_2(z)$
Damping	$a^{-n} f(n)$	$F(az)$
Shifting to the right	$f(n - k)u(n - k), k \geq 0$	$z^{-k}F(z)$
Shifting to the left	$f(n+k), k \geq 0$	$z^k\left[F(z) - \sum_{n=0}^{k-1} f(n)z^{-n} \right]$
Differencing of $f(n)$	$\Delta f(n) = f(n + 1) - f(n)$	$(z - 1)F(z) - zf(0)$
	$\nabla f(n) = f(n) - f(n - 1)u(n - 1)$	$\dfrac{z - 1}{z}F(z)$
Summation of $f(n)$	$\displaystyle\sum_{j=0}^{n} f(j)$	$\dfrac{z}{z - 1}F(z)$
Periodic sequences	$f(n + k) = f(n)$, period k	$\dfrac{z^k}{z^k - 1}\displaystyle\sum_{n=0}^{k-1} f(n)z^{-n}$
Convolution	$f(n) * g(n)$	$F(z) * G(z)$

To find the correct transform, we use the translation properties of Eqs. 3.12 and 3.14. The function $g(n)$ can then be expressed by multiplying the shifted gradient series by a unit step function. The resulting functional expression is

$$g(n) = [u(n - b) - u(n - k - 1)]f(n - b) \qquad (3.25)$$

Since $f(n) = Cn$ (gradient series), we may rewrite $f(n - b)$ as

$$f(n - b) = C(n - b) = Cn - Cb = f(n) - f(b)$$

Thus, we may also rewrite $g(n)$ as

$$g(n) = f(n)[u(n - b) - u(n - k - 1)]$$
$$+ f(b)[u(n - k - 1) - u(n - b)] \qquad (3.26)$$

Note that $f(b)$ is a constant Cb. Using the transform results of Eq. 3.18, we obtain

$$G(z) = \frac{C}{(z - 1)^2}(z^{1-b} - z^{-k}) + \frac{C}{z - 1}[(b - b)z^{1-b}$$
$$- (k + 1 - b)z^{-k}] \qquad (3.27)$$

By replacing z with $1 + i$, we obtain the present value expression of this extensive model.

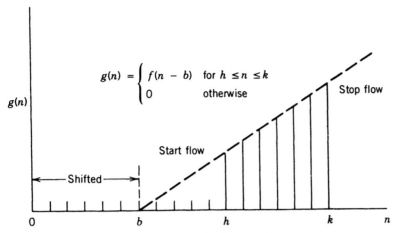

FIGURE 3.5 Extensive model of ramp time pattern.

$$PV(i) = \frac{C}{i^2}[(1 + i)^{1-b} - (1 + i)^{-k}] + \frac{C}{i}[(b - b)(1 + i)^{1-b}]$$
$$- (k + 1 - b)(1 + i)^{-k}] \tag{3.28}$$

If we use the conventional engineering economy notation, the present value of this shifted-gradient series is

$$PV(i) = [Cb(P/A, i, k - b + i) + C(P/G, i, k - b + 1)](P/F, i, b - 1) \tag{3.29}$$

If we converted these factor notations to algebraic form, the final form would be as long an expression as Eq. 3.28. Table 3.3 provides the extensive models of other discrete cash flow patterns.

Example 3.2

A 20-MW oil-burning power plant now under construction is expected to be in full commercial operation in 4 years from now. The fuel cost for this new plant is a function of plant size, thermal conversion efficiency (heat rate), and plant utilization factor. Because of inflation, the future price of oil will increase. The annual fuel cost is then represented by the following expression,

$$f(n) = (S)(H)(U)\left(\frac{8{,}760 \text{ hr/year}}{10^6}\right)P_0\,(1 + f)^{n-1}$$

where $f(n)$ = annual fuel cost at the end of the nth operating year,
  S = plant size in kW (1 MW = 1,000 kW),
  H = heat rate (Btu/kW·hr),
  U = plant utilization factor,
  f = average annual fuel inflation rate,
  P_0 = starting price of fuel per million Btu during the first year of operation.

Table 3.3 Extensive Discrete Present Value Models

Cash Flow Pattern	Function	Typical Cost Example	Present Value, $PV(i)$
(step cash flow diagram; C, b, h, k)	Step $g(n) = f(n - b)$ $= C$	Operating costs	$\dfrac{C}{i}[(1+i)^{1-b} - (1+i)^{-k}]$
(ramp cash flow diagram; slope $= C$, b, h, k)	Ramp $g(n) = f(n - b)$ $= C(n-b)$	Maintenance and deterioration	$\dfrac{C}{i^2}[(1+i)^{1-b} - (1+i)^{-k}]$ $+ \dfrac{C}{i}[(b-b)(1+i)^{1-b} - (k+1-b)(1+i)^{-k}]$
(decreasing ramp cash flow diagram; A, Slope $= -C$, b, h, k)	Decreasing Ramp $g(n) = f(n - b)$ $= A - C(n - b)$	Value depreciation costs	$\dfrac{(1+i)^{1-b}}{i}\left[A - \dfrac{C}{i} - C(b - b)\right]$ $- \dfrac{(1+i)^{-k}}{i}\left[A - \dfrac{C}{i} - C(k + 1 - b)\right]$
(geometric series cash flow diagram; b, h, k)	Geometric series $g(n) = f(n - b)$ $= Ca^{(n-b)}$	Inflationary costs	$\dfrac{Ca^{b-b}}{1+i-a}[(1+i)^{1-b} - a^{k+1-b}(1+i)^{-k}]$
(decay cash flow diagram; C, b, h, k)	Decay $g(n) = f(n - b)$ $= Ce^{-f(n-b)}$	Start-up and learning costs	$\dfrac{C(1+i)}{1+i-e^{-f}}\left[\dfrac{e^{-f(b-b)}}{(1+i)^b} - \dfrac{e^{-f(k+1-b)}}{(1+i)^{k+1}}\right]$
(growth cash flow diagram; C, b, h, k)	Growth $g(n) = f(n - b)$ $= C(1 - e^{-f(n-b)})$	Wear-in maintenance costs	$\dfrac{C(1+i)}{i(1+i-e^{-f})}\left[\dfrac{(1+i-e^{-f})-ie^{-f(b-b)}}{(1+i)^b}\right.$ $\left. - \dfrac{(1+i-e^{-f})-ie^{-f(k+1-b)}}{(1+i)^{k+1}}\right]$

Assume that $S = 20{,}000$ kW, $H = 10{,}000$ Btu/kW·hr, $U = 0.20$, $f = 0.07$, and $P_0 = \$4.5$ per million Btu during year 4. The expected life of the plant is 15 years. What is the present value of the total fuel cost at the beginning of construction (now) if the annual market rate of interest is 18%?

With the parameters as specified, the annual fuel cost function is

$$f(n) = 1{,}576{,}800 \, (1 + 0.07)^{n-1}, \quad 1 \le n \le 15$$

To find the present value of the total fuel cost at the beginning of construction, we rewrite $f(n)$ to obtain $g(n)$.

$$g(n) = f(n - 4)$$
$$= 1{,}576{,}800 \, (1 + 0.07)^{n-5}, \quad 5 \le n \le 19$$
$$= 1{,}473{,}645(1.07)^{n-4}$$

Now we can use the geometric series formula given in Table 3.3. We identify $C = 1{,}473{,}645$, $a = 1.07$, $b = 4$, $h = 5$, $k = 19$, and $i = 0.18$, which yield

$$PV(18\%) = \frac{1{,}473{,}645(1.07)}{0.11}[(1.18)^{-4} - (1.07)^{15} \, (1.18)^{-19}]$$
$$= \$5{,}689{,}941 \quad \square$$

Simplified Present Value Models. The simplified models are defined as those with cash flows that have no delayed turn-on ($b = 0$) and that terminate after k time units. The procedure for finding the Z-transform for this type of simplified form was illustrated in the previous section (see Figure 3.3d). Table 3.4 summarizes the present value models for some other common cash flow patterns. These simplified present value models correspond, in fact, to the traditional tabulated interest factors found in engineering economy textbooks. They simplify the use of this transform methodology when the modified features of cash flow patterns are not required.

3.2.4 Extension to Future and Annual Equivalent Models

The future equivalent values at the end of period N can easily be obtained from the present values shown in Tables 3.3 and 3.4 by multiplying through by $(1 + i)^N$. Similarly, annual equivalent values over period N are determined by multiplying the present values by the factor $i/[1 - (1 + i)^{-N}]$.

$$FV(i) = PV(i)[(1 + i)^N]$$
$$AE(i) = PV(i) \left[\frac{i}{1 - (1 + i)^{-N}} \right]$$

Consequently, all the Z-transforms in Tables 3.3 and 3.4 may be directly converted to a future or annual equivalent value by applying these elementary algebraic

Table 3.4 Simplified Discrete Present Value Models

Cash Flow Pattern	Function	Typical Cost Example	Present Value, $PV(i)$
	$f(n) = C$	Operating costs	$\dfrac{C}{i}[1 - (1 + i)^{-k}]$
	$f(n) = Cn$	Maintenance and deterioration	$\dfrac{C}{i^2}[1 - (1 + i)^{-k}]$ $+ \dfrac{C}{i}[1 - (k + 1)(1 + i)^{-k}]$
	$f(n) = A - Cn$	Value depreciation costs	$\dfrac{1}{i}\left(A - \dfrac{C}{i} - C\right)$ $- \dfrac{(1 + i)^{-k}}{i}\left[A - \dfrac{C}{i} - C(k + 1)\right]$
	$f(n) = Ca^n$	Inflationary costs	$\dfrac{Ca}{1 + i - a}[1 - a^k(1 + i)^{-k}]$
	$f(n) = Ce^{-jn}$	Start-up and learning costs	$\dfrac{C(1 + i)}{1 + i - e^{-j}}\left[\dfrac{e^{-j}}{1 + i} - \dfrac{e^{-j(k+1)}}{(1 + i)^{k+1}}\right]$
	$f(n) = C(1 - e^{-jn})$	Wear-in maintenance costs	$\dfrac{C(1 + i)}{1 + i - e^{-j}}\left[\dfrac{1 - e^{-j}}{i} - \dfrac{1 + i - e^{-j} - ie^{-j(k+1)}}{i(1 + i)^{k+1}}\right]$

manipulations as needed. All the Z-transforms derived in the previous sections are based on the assumption that the compounding periods and the payment occurrences coincide. In situations in which the compounding periods occur more frequently than the receipt of payments, one can find the effective interest rate for the payment period and use it in the Z-transforms developed in Tables 3.3 and 3.4 (see Section 2.4.2).

3.2.5 Applications of Z-Transforms

In this section we will demonstrate the application of the Z-transform to the solution of equivalence problems. Two uses will be illustrated: profit margin analysis and calculation of the present value of interest payments.

Profit Margin Analysis. Consider that a new production facility under construction is expected to be in full commercial operation 2 years from now. The plant is expected to have an initial profit margin of \$5 million per year. Find the present value of the total profit margin at 10% interest compounded annually for 20 years of operation if

i. Profit margin and plant performance stay level.

$$g(n) = 5, \quad 3 \le n \le 22$$

ii. Performance traces a learning curve whereby the profit margin grows in each year.

$$g(n) = 5(2 - e^{-0.10(n-3)}), \quad 3 \le n \le 22$$

iii. Performance traces the same growth curve, but the profit margin shrinks at a rate of $e^{-0.03(n-3)}$ so that

$$g(n) = 5e^{-0.03(n-3)}(2 - e^{-0.10(n-3)}), \quad 3 \le n \le 22$$

These three cases are illustrated in Figure 3.6.

For case i, the cash flow diagram is a shifted step function with $C = 5, b = 3, b = 3$, and $k = 22$. From Table 3.3 the equivalent present value for this shifted step function is

$$PV(i) = \frac{5}{0.1}[(1.1)^{-2} - (1.1)^{-22}] = 50(0.7036) = \underline{\$35.18}$$

For case ii, the growth cash flow function may be regarded as a linear combination of a shifted step function and a shifted decay function. That is,

$$\begin{aligned} \text{Growth function} &= \text{Step function} - \text{Decay function} \\ g(n) &= 5(2) - 5e^{-0.10(n-3)} \end{aligned}$$

Thus, for the step function, the corresponding parameters would be $C = 10, b = 3, b = 3$, and $k = 22$, and for the decay function they would be $C = 5, j = 0.10$,

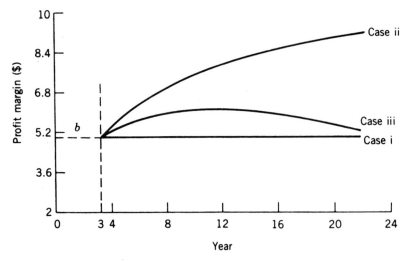

n	Case i	Case ii	Case iii
3	5	5	5
4	5	5.475813	5.313978
5	5	5.906346	5.562387
6	5	6.295909	5.754028
7	5	6.6484	5.896602
8	5	6.967347	5.996851
9	5	7.255942	6.060672
10	5	7.517073	6.093221
11	5	7.753355	6.099005
12	5	7.967152	6.08196
13	5	8.160603	6.045523
14	5	8.335645	5.992693
15	5	8.494029	5.926083
16	5	8.637341	5.847972
17	5	8.767016	5.76034
18	5	8.884349	5.664912
19	5	8.990518	5.563184
20	5	9.086582	5.456453
21	5	9.173506	5.345845
22	5	9.252158	5.232331

FIGURE 3.6 Profit margin analysis.

$b = 3$, $b = 3$, and $k = 22$. From Table 3.3 we obtain the Z-transform of this composite function as follows.

$$PV(i) = \frac{10}{0.1}\left[(1.1)^{-2} - (1.1)^{-22}\right] - \frac{5(1.1)}{1.1 - e^{-0.1}}\left[\frac{1}{(1.1)^3} - \frac{e^{-2.0}}{(1.1)^{23}}\right]$$

$$= 70.36 - 20.74 = \underline{\$49.61}$$

As expected, the total profit margin has increased significantly compared with case i, where no learning effect is appreciable.

For case iii, $g(n)$ is also a linear combination of two similar types of decay function. That is,

$$g(n) = 10e^{-0.03(n-3)} - 5e^{-0.13(n-3)}$$

The first decay function has parameter values of $C = 10, b = 3, b = 3, j = 0.03$, and $k = 22$. The second decay function has $C = 5, b = 3, b = 3, j = 0.13$, and $k = 22$. Thus, from Table 3.3 the Z-transform of this combination yields

$$PV(i) = \frac{10(1.1)}{1.1 - e^{-0.03}} \left[\frac{1}{(1.1)^3} - \frac{e^{-0.60}}{(1.1)^{23}} \right]$$

$$- \frac{5(1.1)}{1.1 - e^{-0.13}} \left[\frac{1}{(1.1)^3} - \frac{e^{-2.60}}{(1.1)^{23}} \right]$$

$$= 58.58 - 18.41 = \underline{\$40.17}$$

Analysis of Loan Transactions. The repayment schedule for most loans is made up of a portion for the payment of principal and a portion for the payment of interest on the unpaid balance. In economic analysis the interest paid on borrowed capital is considered as a deductible expense for income tax computation. Therefore, it is quite important to know how much of each payment is interest and how much is used to reduce the principal amount borrowed initially. To illustrate this situation, suppose that we want to develop an expression for the present value of the interest components of a uniform repayment plan. Let

A = the equal annual repayment amount,

B = the amount borrowed,

i_b = the borrowing interest rate per period,

N = the maturity of the loan (period).

Then the annual payments will be

$$A = B(A/P, i_b, N) = B \frac{i_b(1 + i_b)^N}{(1 + i_b)^N - 1} \tag{3.30}$$

Each payment is divided into an amount that is interest and a remaining amount for reduction of the principal. Let

I_n = portion of payment A at time n that is interest,

B_n = portion of payment A at time n that is used to reduce the remaining balance,

$A = I_n + B_n$, where $n = 1, 2, \ldots, N$,
U_n = unpaid balance at the end of period n, with $U_0 = B$.

The relation of these parameters is illustrated in Figure 3.7. Since the interest payment is based on the unpaid principal that remains at the end of each period, the interest accumulation in the first year is simply $i_b B$. Thus, the first payment A consists of an interest payment $i_b B$ and a principal payment of $A - i_b B$. The unpaid balance remaining after the first payment would be $U_1 = B - (A - i_b B) = B(1 + i_b) - A$. Consequently, the interest charge for the second year would be $i_b U_1$, and the size of the net principal reduction associated with the second payment would be $A - i_b U_1$. In other words, the unpaid balance remaining after the second payment would be

$$U_2 = U_1 - (A - i_b U_1)$$
$$= U_1(1 + i_b) - A \qquad (3.31)$$

The amount of principal remaining to be repaid right after making the nth payment can be found with the recursive relationship

$$U_n = U_{n-1}(1 + i_b) - A$$

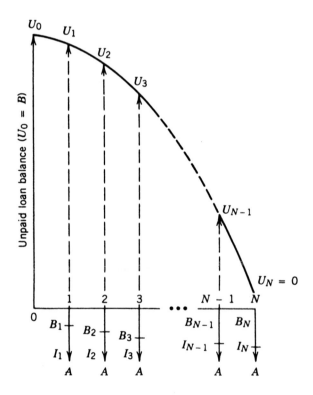

FIGURE 3.7 Loan transactions—unpaid balance as functions of B_n and I_n.

It follows immediately that

$$U_n = B(1 + i_b)^n - A[(1 + i_b)^{n-1} + (1 + i_b)^{n-2} + \cdots + 1]$$

$$= B(1 + i_b)^n - \frac{A}{i_b}[(1 + i_b)^n - 1]$$

$$= \left(B - \frac{A}{i_b}\right)(1 + i_b)^n + \frac{A}{i_b}, \qquad n = 0, 1, \ldots, N - 1 \qquad (3.32)$$

Now we can express the amount of interest payment required at the end of period $n + 1$.

$$I_{n+1} = i_b U_n$$

$$= \underbrace{(Bi_b - A)(1 + i_b)^n}_{\text{geometric series}} + \underbrace{A,}_{\substack{\text{step} \\ \text{function}}} \qquad n, = 0,1,\ldots, N - 1 \qquad (3.33)$$

Finally, the total present value of these interest payments at an interest rate of i over the loan life of N periods is defined as

$$PV(i) = \sum_{n=0}^{N-1} I_{n+1}(1 + i)^{-(n+1)} \qquad (3.34)$$

Let $g(n) = I_{n+1}$, where $g(n)$ is the sum of a geometric and a uniform series. From Table 3.4, the Z-transform of the geometric series portion is obtained by letting $a = (1 + i_b)$, $C = Bi_b - A$, $b = h = 1$, and $k = N$.

$$PV_1(i) = \frac{Bi_b - A}{i - i_b}[1 - (1 + i_b)^N(1 + i)^{-N}], \quad \text{where } i \neq i_b \qquad (3.35)$$

The transform of the step function portion is found by substituting $C = A$, $b = h = 1$, and $k = N$.

$$PV_2(i) = \frac{A}{i}[(1 - (1 + i)^{-N}] \qquad (3.36)$$

Finally, the transform of $g(n)$ *is found to be*

$$PV(i) = PV_1(i) + PV_2(i) \qquad .$$

$$= \frac{Bi_b - A}{i - i_b}\left[1 - \left(\frac{1 + i_b}{1 + i}\right)^N\right] + \frac{A}{i}[1 - (1 + i)^{-N}] \qquad (3.37)$$

To illustrate the use of this formula, suppose that $50,000 is borrowed at 8% annual interest and is to be repaid in ten equal annual payments. Determine the total present value of these interest payments associated with the loan transaction at a discount rate of 15%. Since we have $B = \$50,000$, $i_b = 8\%$, $N = 10$ years, and $i = 15\%$, the payment size A is

$$A = \$50,000(A/P, \ 8\%, \ 10) = \$7,451.47$$

Then the total present value is

$$PV(15\%) = \frac{\$50,000(0.08) - \$7,451.57}{0.15 - 0.08}\left[1 - \left(\frac{1.08}{1.15}\right)^{10}\right]$$

$$+ \frac{\$7,451.47}{0.15}\left[1 - \frac{1}{(1.15)^{10}}\right]$$

$$= -\$49,306.70(1 - 0.53365) + \$49,676.47(1 - 0.24718)$$

$$= \quad \$14,403.26$$

It may be of interest to compare the use of Eq. 3.37 with that of the conventional discounting formula developed by Brooking and Burgess [1]. They use the expression

$$PV(i) = B\left\{(A/P, \ i_b, \ N)\left[[(P/A, \ i, \ N) - \frac{(P/F, \ i_b, \ N) - (P/F, \ i, \ N)}{i - i_b}]\right]\right\}$$

$$= A\left[\frac{1 - (1 + i)^{-N}}{i} - \frac{(1 + i_b)^{-N} - (1 + i)^{-N}}{i - i_b}\right] \qquad (3.38)$$

Our method may be numerically verified with the traditional method as follows.

$$PV(15\%) = \$7,451.47(5.0188 - \frac{0.4632 - 0.2472}{0.07})$$

$$= \$7,451.47(5.0188 - 3.0857)$$

$$= \$14,404.47$$

The slight difference is due to rounding errors.

3.3 LAPLACE TRANSFORMS AND CONTINUOUS CASH FLOWS

Up to this point we have discussed only discrete cash flow functions. In this section we will extend the modeling philosophy to continuous cash flow functions. The Laplace transform method offers a modeling flexibility similar to that of the Z-transform for computing present values for many forms of continuous cash flow functions.

3.3.1 *Laplace Transform and Present Value*

As shown in Section 2.5.2, the present value of the infinite continuous cash flow streams, assuming continuous compounding, is given by the expression

$$PV(r) = \int_0^\infty f(t)e^{-rt}\, dt \tag{3.39}$$

where $f(t)$ = continuous cash flow function of the project,

r = nominal interest rate $[r = \ln(1 + i)]$,

t = time expressed in years,

e^{-rt} = discount function.

As Buck and Hill [2] recognized, the general form of this integral bears a close resemblance to the definition of the Laplace transforms. That is, if the function $f(t)$ is considered to be piecewise continuous, then the Laplace transform of $f(t)$, written $L\{f(t)\}$, is defined as a function $F(s)$ of the variable s by the integral

$$L\{f(t)\} = F(s) = \int_0^\infty f(t)e^{-st}\, dt \tag{3.40}$$

over the range of values of s for which the integral exists. Replacing s in Eq. 3.40 with the continuous compound interest rate r simply generates Eq. 3.39; thus, taking a Laplace transform on the cash flow function $f(t)$ is equivalent to computing the present value of the cash flow streams over an infinite horizon time.

In the construction of Laplace transforms, we will use the following notation. If $f(t)$ represents the time domain continuous function, then $F(s)$ will represent its transform. As for the Z-transform, this lowercase–uppercase correspondence will be used throughout the text. As a shorthand notation, the transform pair will be denoted by

$$f(t) \leftrightarrow F(s)$$

For example, to find the transform of a linear function $f(t) = t, t > 0$, we directly evaluate Eq. 3.40.

$$F(s) = \int_0^\infty te^{-st}\, dt = \frac{1}{s^2} \tag{3.41}$$

and find that the transform pair is

$$t \leftrightarrow \frac{1}{s^2}$$

The transforms of some causal time functions that are typically encountered are shown in Table 3.5. The function $u(t)$ in this table represents the unit

Table 3.5 *A Short Table of Laplace Transform Pairs** *

Standard Cash Flow Pattern	Cash Flow Function, $f(t)$	Laplace Transform, $F(s)$	Present Value, (Infinite), $PV(r)$
Unit step	$f(t) = u(t) = \begin{cases} 1 & t > 0 \\ 0 & \text{otherwise} \end{cases}$	$1/s$	$1/r$
Delayed unit step	$f(t) = u(t - b) \quad b > 0$	e^{-bs}/s	e^{-br}/r
Ramp	$f(t) = t$	$1/s^2$	$1/r^2$

Table 3.5 (Continued)

Standard Cash Flow Pattern	Cash Flow Function, $f(t)$	Laplace Transform, $F(s)$	Present Value, (Infinite), $PV(r)$
Decay	$f(t) = e^{-jt}$	$1/(s+j)$	$1/(r+j)$
Exponential	$f(t) = e^{jt}$	$1/(s-j)$	$1/(r-j)$
Growth	$f(t) = 1 - e^{-jt}$	$\dfrac{1}{s} - \dfrac{1}{s+j}$	$j/r(r+j)$

*See [7] for a complete Laplace function table.

step function with jump at $t = 0$, and $u(t - a)$ denotes the unit step function with jump at $t = a$. The special property of this function is discussed in the next section.

3.3.2 Properties of Laplace Transforms

In this section we will examine some useful operational properties of the Laplace transform. As in the Z-transform analysis, the properties most relevant to modeling cash flows are linearity and translation.

Linearity. If we define

$$f_1(t) \leftrightarrow F_1(s) \quad \text{and} \quad f_2(t) \leftrightarrow F_2(s)$$

then

$$c_1 f_1(t) + c_2 f_2(t) \leftrightarrow c_1 F_1(s) + c_2 F_2(s) \tag{3.42}$$

This follows from the linearity property of integrals of Eq. 3.40. Suppose we define $f(t)$ as

$$f(t) = 1 + t + \tfrac{1}{2} t^2$$

The transform is

$$L\{f(t)\} = L\{1\} + L\{t\} + L\{\tfrac{1}{2} t^2\}$$

Using Eqs. 3.42 and 3.40 along with the transform results in Table 3.5, we obtain

$$F(s) = \frac{1}{s} + \frac{1}{s^2} + \frac{1}{s^3}$$

Translation with Time Delay. Consider Figure 3.8, in which the function $g(t)$ is obtained from $f(t)$ by shifting the graph of $f(t)$ b units on the time scale to the right. Mathematically, we define such a function as

$$g(t) = \begin{cases} f(t - b) & \text{for } t \geq b \\ 0 & \text{for } t < b \end{cases} \tag{3.43}$$

To find the transform of this type of cash flow function that starts after a delay of b time units, we utilize the property of the unit step function $u(t)$. If we take the unit step function and translate it b units to the right to get $u(t - b)$, we obtain the function shown in Table 3.5. Mathematically, we denote this by

$$u(t - b) = \begin{cases} 1 & \text{for } t \geq b \\ 0 & \text{for } t < b \end{cases} \tag{3.44}$$

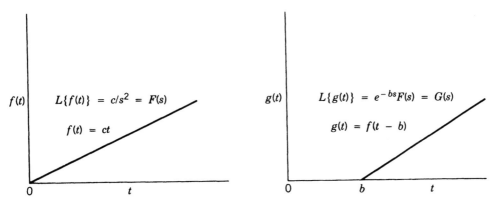

FIGURE 3.8 Translation of continuous ramp pattern.

Then the product $g(t)u(t - b)$ or $f(t - b)u(t - b)$ will be defined as

$$g(t) = f(t - b)u(t - b) = \begin{cases} f(t - b) & \text{for } t \geq b \\ 0 & \text{for } t < b \end{cases} \tag{3.45}$$

The Laplace transform of $g(t)$ given by Eq. 3.45 is

$$L\{g(t)\} = e^{-bs}F(s) \tag{3.46}$$

Accordingly, a cash flow that starts later than $t = 0$ can be treated as if it started immediately and then a correction for the delayed start can be made with the discount factor e^{-sb} ($= e^{-rb}$). This feature proves to be very useful when developing present value models with a composite of delayed turn-on cash flows.

Translation with Cutoff. Another translation property of interest is turning cash flow streams on and off as desired. To illustrate the concept, suppose we wish to find the Laplace transform of a ramp function with features of a delayed turn-on at time b and a turn-off at time k. This function is illustrated in Figure 3.9. Mathematically, we denote such a function by

$$g(t) = f(t)[u(t - b) - u(t - k)] \tag{3.47}$$

The first unit step begins the transactions at $t = b$ and the second stops the transactions at $t = k$. The Laplace transform of this $g(t)$ is defined by

$$G(s) = (e^{-bs} - e^{-ks})\left[F(s) + \frac{f(b)}{s}\right] \tag{3.48}$$

Some care must be exercised in using the time delay theorem. The reader should note the subtle functional difference that $f(t)u(t - b)$ is not a simple time-shifted function $[f(t - b)u(t - b)]$.

341

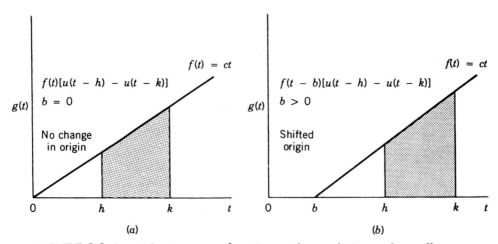

FIGURE 3.9 A continuous ramp function with translation and cutoff.

$$f(t)u(t - h) \neq f(t - h)u(t - h)$$

This difference is illustrated in Fig. 3.10. We can rewrite the function as

$$f(t)u(t - h) = f(t - h)u(t - h) + f(h)u(t - h) \qquad (3.49)$$

Since $f(h)$ is a constant, the Laplace transform of Eq. 3.49 is found by using Eq. 3.46:

$$L\{f(t)u(t - h)\} = e^{-hs}F(s) + \frac{f(h)e^{-hs}}{s}$$

$$= e^{-hs}L\{f(t + h)\} \qquad (3.50)$$

Therefore, the transform of Eq. 3.47 can be expressed as

$$L\{g(t)\} = G(s) = e^{-hs}L\{f(t + h\} - e^{-ks}L\{f(t + k)\} \qquad (3.51)$$

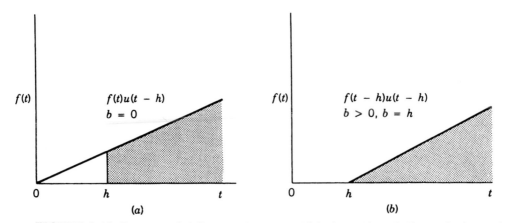

FIGURE 3.10 Functional difference between $f(t)u(t - h)$ and $f(t - h)u(t - h)$.

Example 3.3

Suppose a cash flow function is given by

$$f(t) = 5t, \qquad 10 \le t \le 20$$

Using Eq. 3.48 and Table 3.5, we obtain

$$G(s) = e^{-10s} L\{5(t + 10)\} - e^{-20s} L\{5(t + 20)\}$$

$$= e^{-10s}\left(\frac{5}{s^2} + \frac{50}{s}\right) - e^{-20s}\left(\frac{5}{s^2} + \frac{100}{s}\right)$$

$$= \frac{5}{s^2}\left(e^{-10s} - e^{-20s}\right) + \frac{50}{s}\left(e^{-10s} - 2e^{-20s}\right)$$

With a nominal interest rate of 10% ($r = s = 0.1$), the total present value is

$$PV(10\%) = \frac{5}{(0.1)^2}(e^{-1} - e^{-2}) + \frac{50}{0.1}(e^{-1} - 2e^{-2})$$

$$= 116.27 + 48.60 = \$164.87$$

Our method may be numerically verified by direct integration of the cash flow function.

$$PV(10\%) = \int_{10}^{20} 5te^{-0.1t}\, dt = \$165$$

Once again, the slight difference is due to rounding errors. □

Translations with Impulses.   Suppose we want to find the transform of an impulse function $f(t)$ shown in Figure 3.11. This type of impulse function may represent the salvage value of an asset at $t = b$ when the salvage value $f(t)$ decreases exponentially over time. To obtain the transform of such an impulse function, we need to define a Kronecker delta function that corresponds to a unit impulse at $t = b$. That is,

$$\delta(t - b) = \begin{cases} 1 & \text{for } t = b \\ 0 & \text{otherwise} \end{cases} \tag{3.52}$$

By multiplying the salvage value function $f(t)$ by the unit impulse function, we obtain

$$g(t) = f(t)\delta(t - b) = \begin{cases} f(b) & \text{for } t = b \\ 0 & \text{otherwise} \end{cases} \tag{3.53}$$

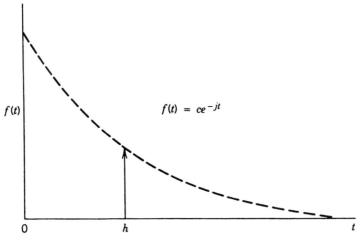

FIGURE 3.11 Example of an impulse cash flow function—decay.

Since $f(b)$ is a constant, the transform of the product form yields

$$g(s) = e^{-bs}f(b) \qquad (3.54)$$

which is the present value expression for a single payment.

Many other useful operational rules can be used in modeling continuous cash flow functions, such as scaling, periodic functions, and convolutions. These are summarized in Table 3.6. (See also Muth [7].)

3.3.3 Development of Continuous Present Value Models

Two types of present value models are needed, corresponding to the start of the original cash flow function. These are the extensive models and the simplified models. Figure 3.12 illustrates the modeling concept of both the extensive and the simplified forms of the ramp time form.

Extensive Present Value Models. The computational procedure for finding the correct extensive present value model was discussed in the previous section. Formulas for directly computing the present values of these extensive models of five common cash flow time forms are presented in Table 3.7. To examine the modeling concept again, consider the exponential time forms of cash flow given in Table 3.7.

Let $f(t) = ce^{jt}$, where c is the scale factor and j is the growth rate with time. To obtain a geometric time form shifted to the right by b time units, we define $g(t) = f(t - b)$. To denote the added feature of a delayed turn-on at $t = b$ and a turn-off at $t = k$, we write

$$g(t) = f(t - b)[u(t - b) - u(t - k)]$$

344

Table 3.6 *Summary of Operational Rules of the Laplace Transform*

Operational Rule	Original Function	Laplace Transform
Linearity	$C_1 f_1(t) + C_2 f_2(t)$	$c_1 F_1(s) + c_2 F_2(s)$
Change of scale	$f(at),\quad a > 0$	$\dfrac{1}{a} F(s)$
Shifting to the right	$f(t - a)u(t - a),\quad a > 0$	$e^{-as} F(s)$
Shifting to the left	$f(t + a),\quad a < 0$	$e^{as}\left[F(s) - \displaystyle\int_0^a e^{-st} f(t)\, dt\right]$
Damping	$e^{-at} f(t)$	$F(s + a)$
Differentiation of $F(s)$ function	$tf(t)$	$-\dfrac{d}{ds} F(s)$
Integration of $F(s)$ function	$\dfrac{f(t)}{t}$	$\displaystyle\int_s^\infty F(u)\, du$
Differentiation of $f(t)$	$\dfrac{d}{dt} f(t)$	$sF(s) - f(0^+)$
	$\dfrac{d^n}{dt^n} f(t)$	$s^n F(s) - s^{n-1} f(0^+)$ $- s^{n-2} fE(0^+) - \cdots$ $- f^{(n-1)}(0^+)$
Integration of $f(t)$	$\displaystyle\int_0^t f(u)\, du$	$\dfrac{1}{s} F(s)$
Periodic function	$f(t) = f(t + T),\quad T = \text{period}$	$F(s) = \dfrac{1}{1 - e^{-sT}}\displaystyle\int_0^T e^{-st} f(t)\, dt$
Convolution	$f_1(t) * f_2(t)$	$F_1(s) F_2(s)$

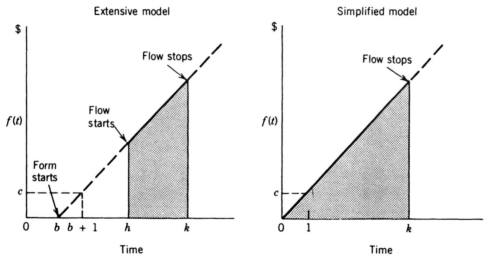

FIGURE 3.12 Features of extensive and simplified continuous models.

Table 3.7 Extensive Continuous Present Value Models

Time Form	$f(t)$	$PV(r)$	
Step	c	$\dfrac{c}{r}(e^{-br} - e^{-kr})$	
Ramp	ct	$\dfrac{c}{r^2}(e^{-br} - e^{-kr}) + \dfrac{c}{r}\left[(b - b)e^{-br} - (k - b)e^{-kr}\right]$	
Decay	ce^{-jt}	$\dfrac{ce^{+bj}}{r + j}(e^{-b(j+r)} - e^{-k(j+r)})$	
Growth	$c(1 - e^{-jt})$	$\dfrac{c}{r}(e^{-br} - e^{-kr}) - \dfrac{ce^{bj}}{r + j}(e^{-b(j+r)} - e^{-k(j+r)})$	
Exponential	ce^{jt}	$\dfrac{ce^{-bj}}{r - j}(e^{b(j-r)} - e^{k(j-r)}),\quad j \neq r$	

346

Since $f(t) = ce^{jt}$, $f(t - b) = ce^{j(t-b)}$. Therefore, we may rewrite $g(t)$ as

$$g(t) = ce^{j(t-b)}[u(t - b) - u(t - k)]$$
$$= (e^{-bj})(ce^{jt})[u(t - b) - u(t - k)]$$
$$= (e^{-bj})f(t)[u(t - b) - u(t - k)] \qquad (3.55)$$

From Eq. 3.47, the transform of $g(t)$ yields

$$L\{g(t)\} = e^{-bj}[e^{-bs}L\{f(t + b)\} - e^{-ks}L\{f(t + k)\}]$$

To evaluate $L\{f(t + b)\}$ and $L\{f(t + k)\}$, we simply expand the original function $f(t) = ce^{jt}$

$$L\{f(t + b)\} = \{ce^{j(t+b)}\} = ce^{jb}L\{f(t)\} = ce^{jb}F(s)$$
$$L\{f(t + k)\} = \{ce^{j(t+k)}\} = ce^{jk}L\{f(t)\} = ce^{jk}F(s)$$

Since $F(s) = 1/(s - j)$ for $f(t) = e^{jt}$, but with $s = r$, we have

$$L\{g(t)\} = \frac{ce^{-bj}}{r - j}\left(e^{b(j-r)} - e^{k(j-r)}\right) \qquad (3.56)$$

Example 3.4

Consider a cash inflow stream that starts at $t = 2$ (years) and increases $1,000 per year uniformly until $t = 10$. Table 3.7 reveals that the ramp is the proper time form for the cash flow. This time form has the scale parameter of $c = $1,000. Assume that the pattern starts at $b = 2$, the cash flow begins immediately after that at $b = 2$, and the flow stops at $k = 10$. The present value at the nominal rate of interest 10% is

$$PV(10\%) = \frac{\$1,000}{(0.1)^2} (e^{-0.2} - e^{-1}) + \frac{\$1,000}{0.1} (0 - 8e^{-1})$$

$$= \$45,085.13 - \$29,430.35 = \$15,654.78 \qquad \square$$

Simplified Present Value Models. When there is no shift in time form and no delayed turn-on, the extra factors in the extensive model become cumbersome. In other words, if $b = b = 0$, we can further simplify the formulas in Table 3.7. The reader may notice that the simplified models correspond to the traditional tabulated interest factors (funds flow factors) used in most engineering economy textbooks. These are summarized in Table 3.8.

Present Values of Impulse Cash Flows. Single instantaneous cash flows are referred to as "impulses" to distinguish them from the continuous flow streams examined in the previous sections. Frequently, it is necessary to describe a cash

Table 3.8 Simplified Continuous Present Value Models

Time Form	f(t)	PV(r)
Step	c	$\dfrac{c}{r}(1 - e^{-kr})$
Ramp	ct	$\dfrac{c}{r^2}(1 - e^{-kr} - rke^{-kr})$
Decay	ce^{-jt}	$\dfrac{c}{r+j}(1 - e^{-k(j+r)})$
Growth	$c(1 - e^{-jt})$	$\dfrac{c}{r}(1 - e^{-kr}) - \dfrac{c}{r+j}(1 - e^{-k(j+r)})$
Exponential	ce^{jt}	$\dfrac{c}{r-j}(1 - e^{k(j-r)})$

impulse that changes in magnitude over time according to some time form. As an example, a salvage value from the sale of a machine decreases gradually with the age of the machine, but the actual value received is a single flow at the time of disposal. Present value formulas corresponding to such a cash impulse, following the four time forms but occurring only at time T, are summarized in Table 3.9. These present value formulas are derived from Eq. 3.54.

Example 3.5

Suppose that the salvage value of an automobile can be described by a decay time form with an initial value of $6,000. The decay rate with time is given as 0.3. Find the present value of the salvage value that occurs at the end of 5 years at a nominal interest rate of 10% compounded continuously. Let $c = 6,000$, $r = 0.3$, $j = 0.1$, and $T = 5$. Then

$$PV(10\%) = ce^{-(j + r)T} = \$6,000e^{-2.0} = \$812.01 \quad \square$$

Table 3.9 *Present Values of Impulse Cash Flows*

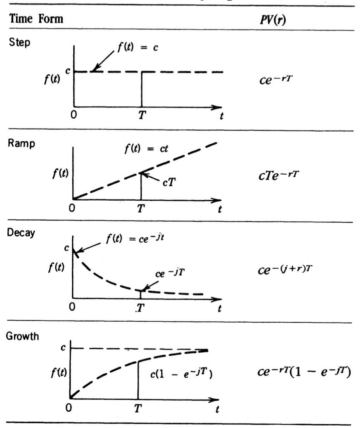

Time Form		PV(r)
Step	$f(t) = c$	ce^{-rT}
Ramp	$f(t) = ct$, cT	cTe^{-rT}
Decay	$f(t) = ce^{-jt}$, ce^{-jT}	$ce^{-(j+r)T}$
Growth	$c(1 - e^{-jT})$	$ce^{-rT}(1 - e^{-jT})$

3.3.4 Extension to Future and Annual Equivalent Models

The future equivalent values at the end of period T can easily be obtained from the present value formulas shown in Tables 3.7, 3.8, and 3.9 simply by multiplying through by e^{rT}. Similarly, annual values of equivalent cash flow streams are defined here as the annual cash flow of a step time form starting immediately, terminating at the same time as the equivalent stream, and possessing equal present value. Accordingly, the present value of a step (uniform) time form with the annual cash flow of $\bar{A}$ dollars may be equated to the present value formulas of the other time forms. Solving for $\bar{A}$ gives us the equivalent annual value.

Example 3.6

Consider Example 3.5 and find the equivalent annual value at a nominal interest rate of 10% compounded continuously. Since the present value of the ramp time form that extends over a 10-year period is $15,654.78, the annual equivalent cash flow stream of $\bar{A}$ dollars per year is determined as follows. From Table 3.8, the present value of the step time form with $b = h = 0$, $c = \bar{A}$, $k = 10$, and $r = 0.1$ yields

$$\frac{\bar{A}}{0.1}(1 - e^{-1}) = \$15,654.78$$

The satisfying value of $\bar{A}$ is the equivalent annual value, which is $\bar{A} = \$2,476.55$. □

3.3.5 Application of the Laplace Transform

Description of the Basic Inventory System. Consider the simplest imaginable type of inventory system in which there is only a single item. The demand rate for this item is assumed to be deterministic and a constant λ units per year. The fixed cost of placing an order in dollars is A. The unit cost of the item in dollars is C. Let I_0 be the inventory carrying charge (measured in the units of dollars per year per dollar of investment in inventory) exclusive of the rate of return (i.e., of the opportunity cost). We will further assume that the procurement lead time is a constant and that the system is not allowed to be out of stock at any point in time. Orders for the item are received in lots of Q units. The problem is to determine the optimal value of Q.

Figure 3.13 depicts the inventory behavior of this model with respect to time. Since the order quantity Q and the demand rate λ are constant, the inventory level of the first cycle T is

$$I(t) = Q - \lambda t, \qquad 0 \leq t \leq T \tag{3.57}$$

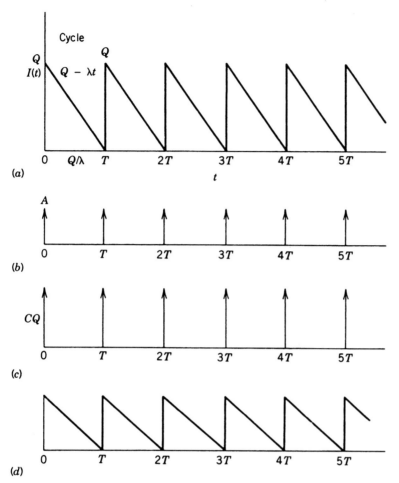

FIGURE 3.13 Inventory behavior: quantity and const as functions of time. (*a*) Inventory positions. (*b*) Ordering costs. (*c*) Purchase costs. (*d*) Inventory costs.

Note that $I(t) = 0$ at $t = T$ and $T = Q/\lambda$. Let

$r = $ the nominal interest rate,

$f(t)_1 = $ the ordering cost per cycle,

$f(t)_2 = $ the purchase cost per cycle,

$f(t)_3 = $ the inventory carrying cost per cycle.

Then the inventory cost for the first cycle is given by

$$f(t) = f(t)_1 + f(t)_2 + f(t)_3 \qquad (3.58)$$

where
$$f(t)_1 = A,$$
$$f(t)_2 = CQ,$$

$$f(t)_3 = I_0 C \int_0^T (Q - \lambda t)\, dt.$$

Equation 3.58 represents the inventory cost per cycle *without* considering the effect of the time value of money.

To find the present value of the inventory cost for the first cycle, we assume that the ordering and purchase costs will occur only at the beginning of the cycle, but that the inventory carrying cost will occur continuously over the cycle. With these assumptions, the Laplace transform of the inventory cost function is

$$F(s) = A + CQ + L\{I_0C(Q - \lambda t)\}$$
$$= A + CQ + I_0C\left[\frac{Q}{s} - \frac{\lambda}{s^2}(1 - e^{-sT})\right] \tag{3.59}$$

After substituting $s = r$ and $T = Q/\lambda$ back into Eq. 3.59, we find that the present value expression is

$$PV(r)_{cycle} = A + CQ + I_0C\left[\frac{Q}{r} - \frac{\lambda}{r^2}(1 - e^{-rQ/\lambda})\right] \tag{3.60}$$

Since the cycle repeats itself forever, we can use the Laplace transform property of periodic functions. If we denote the total inventory cost over infinite cycles as $g(t)$, $G(s)$ can be expressed in terms of the transform of the first cycle $F(s)$.

$$G(s) = F(s)\frac{1}{1 - e^{-sT}} \tag{3.61}$$

$$PV(r)_{total} = PV(r)_{cycle}\left(\frac{1}{1 - e^{-rQ/\lambda}}\right)$$
$$= \frac{1}{1 - e^{-rQ/\lambda}}\left(A + CQ + \frac{I_0CQ}{r}\right) - \frac{I_0C\lambda}{r^2} \tag{3.62}$$

Differentiating $PV(r)_{total}$ with respect to Q and equating the result to zero gives us

$$(1 - e^{-rQ/\lambda})\left(C + \frac{I_0C}{r}\right) - \left(A + CQ + \frac{I_0CQ}{r}\right)\left(\frac{r}{\lambda}e^{-rQ/\lambda}\right) = 0 \tag{3.63}$$

An exact analytical solution of (3.63) for Q is not normally possible, but a numerical solution may be obtained by using the Newton–Raphson method [8]. An approximate solution (within about 2%) can be obtained more easily, however, by using a second-order approximation for the exponential term.

$$e^{-rQ/\lambda} = 1 - \left(\frac{r}{\lambda}\right)Q + \left(\frac{r}{\lambda}\right)^2 Q^2\frac{1}{2!}$$
$$- \left(\frac{r}{\lambda}\right)^3 Q^3\frac{1}{3!} + \cdots \tag{3.64}$$

Since $0<r<1$ (in general), we can ignore the terms $(r/\lambda)^3$ and higher. Then, substituting the first three terms into Eq. 3.63 and solving for Q, we obtain

$$Q^* \triangleq \left[\frac{2A}{(I_0 + r)C}\right]^{1/2} \tag{3.65}$$

With $A = \$10$, $C = \$5/\text{unit}$, $I_0 = 0.1$, $r = 0.1$, and $\lambda = 100$ units per year, the optimal order quantity is about

$$Q^* \triangleq \left[\frac{2(15)(100)}{(0.1 + 0.2)5}\right]^{1/2} = 36.51$$

The numerical solution obtained by the Newton–Raphson method would be $Q^* = 36.23$.

3.4 SUMMARY

The Z-transform and the Laplace transform can be used in a wide variety of cash flow models, and in many situations these methodologies are more efficient than the traditional approach. This chapter was intended to (1) introduce the transform methodologies, (2) provide alternative techniques for modeling cash flows that are interrupted or impulses that follow a particular time form, and (3) demonstrate the use of this methodology in equivalence calculations. We do not recommend the transform analysis for modeling simple cash flow transactions because there is not much savings in computation. The transform analysis will provide definite computational advantages, however, for complex cash flow functions.

REFERENCES

1. BROOKING, S. A., and A. R. BURGESS, "Present Worth of Interest Tax Credit," *The Engineering Economist,* Vol. 21, No. 2, Winter 1976, pp. 111–117.
2. BUCK, J. R., and T. W. HILL, "Laplace Transforms for the Economic Analysis of Deterministic Problems in Engineering," *The Engineering Economist,* Vol. 16, No. 4, 1971, pp. 247–263.
3. BUCK, J. R., and T. W. HILL, "Additions to the Laplace Transform Methodology for Economic Analysis," *The Engineering Economist,* Vol. 20, No. 3, 1975, pp. 197–208.
4. GIFFIN, W. C., *Transform Techniques for Probability Modeling,* Academic Press, New York, 1975.
5. GRUBBSTROM, R. W., "On the Application of the Laplace Transform to Certain Economic Problems," *Management Science,* Vol. 13, No. 7, 1967, pp. 558–567.
6. HILL, T. W., and J. R. BUCK, "Zeta Transforms, Present Value, and Economic Analysis," *AIIE Transactions,* Vol. 6, No. 2, 1974, pp. 120–125.
7. MUTH, E. J., *Transform Methods with Applications to Engineering and Operations Research,* Prentice–Hall, Englewood Cliffs, N.J., 1977.

8. PARK, C. S., and Y. K. SON, "The Effect of Discounting on Inventory Lot Sizing Models," *Engineering Costs and Production Economics,* Vol. 16, No. 1, 1989, pp. 35–48.
9. REMER, D. S., J. C. TU, D. E. CARSON, and S. A. GANTY, "The State of the Art of Present Worth Analysis of Cash Flow Distributions," *Engineering Costs and Production Economics,* Vol. 7, No. 4, 1984, pp. 257–278.

PROBLEMS

3.1. Consider a cash flow stream for which the monthly profits are $1,000e^{-0.1n}$ for $n = 1, 2, 3, \ldots, 12$ months and the nominal interest rate is 12%. Find the present value under

    a. 12% compounded annually.   c. 12% compounded monthly.

    b. 12% compounded quarterly.   d. 12% compounded continuously.

3.2. Consider the discrete cash flow patterns shown in the accompanying illustration.

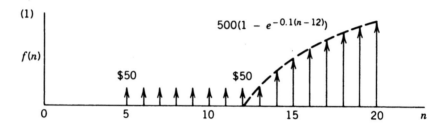

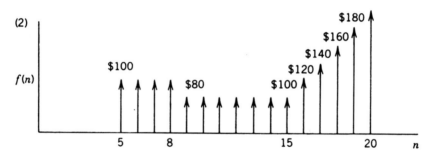

    a. Compute the present value of each cash flow series using the conventional interest formulas at $i = 10\%$.

    b. Compute the present value of each cash flow series using the discrete transform results at $i = 10\%$.

    c. Compute the annual equivalent value of each cash flow series over 20 years.

3.3. Consider the retirement schedule for a $100,000 bond issue by a city, which is to be proportional to the city's anticipated growth. If this anticipated growth tends to follow the general growth pattern of

$$f(n) = C(1 - e^{-0.087n})$$

and the bond interest rate is 5%, find an increasing repayment over 20 years.

3.4. Suppose you borrow $100,000 at an interest rate of 9% compounded monthly over 30 years to finance a home. If your interest rate is 1% per month, compute the present value of the total interest payment of the loan.

3.5. Consider the following cost and return components of a machine tool.
   a. The initial cost of $8,000.
   b. A uniform operating cost of $800 each year.
   c. Maintenance costs, which increase at a rate of $400 each year.
   d. Annual start-up costs, which decay at the rate of 1.0 from an upper limit of $1,000 initially.
   e. A single salvage value return, which decays at the rate of 0.5 with age from the initial cost of $8,000. Assume $i = 8\%$.
   Compute the present value of these five cash flow components over 10 years.

3.6. Consider a machine that now exists in condition j and generates earnings at the uniform continuous rate of A_j dollars per year. If at some time T the machine's condition changes from j to k, its earning rate will instantaneously change from A_j to A_k. We will inspect the machine exactly one year from now. You may treat the time value of money in terms of a nominal interest rate of r compounded continuously.
   a. If the machine's condition changes to k at time T, where T is in time interval between 0 and 1, what is the present value of its earnings for the year?
   b. If the machine remains in condition j for the entire year, what is the present value of its earnings for the year?

3.7. Suppose a uniformly increasing continuous cash flow (a ramp) accumulates $1,000 over 4 years. The continuous cash flow function is expressed as

$$f(t) = ct, \qquad 0 \le t \le 4$$

Assume that $r = 12\%$ compounded continuously.
   a. Find the slope c.
   b. Compute the present equivalent of this continuous series.
   c. Compute the future value of this continuous series.

3.8. Find the present value of the following quadratic cash flow at 10% interest compounded continuously,

$$f(t) = \$200 + 45t - 3t^2$$

   a. if $0 \le t \le 10$.
   b. if $0 \le t \le \infty$.

3.9. A chemical process for an industrial solvent generates a continuous after-tax cash flow $f(t)$ of $250,000 per year for a 10-year planning horizon.
   a. Find the present value of this cash flow stream over 10 years if money is worth 12% compounded continuously.
   b. The profit per year is expected to increase continuously because of increased productivity and can be expressed as

$$f(t) = 250,000(2.0 - e^{-0.2t})$$

   where t is time in years. Find the present value of this cash flow stream.
   c. Productivity increases as in part b, but competition reduces the profit continuously by 8% per year. Find the present value of the cash flow.

3.10. Consider the following simple inventory system. A stock of Q units is produced at a rate of a_p units per day for a period T_p. It is then necessary to leave the batch in stock for a period of T_d, during which sorting, inspection, and painting are carried out. A quantity Q_1 is then supplied to the assembly line at the rate of a units per day for a period T_c. The supply to the assembly is intermittent, so that after a supply period T_c there is an interval T_0 before supply is resumed for another period T_c, and so on. Assuming that the relationship between Q and a is defined as $Q = ka$, k is an integer, and b stands for a holding cost of one unit per unit time, answer the following questions.

   a. Draw the level of inventory position as a function of time t.

   b. Assuming continuous compounding at a nominal rate of r, find the expression of present value of the total inventory cost over one complete cycle. (One cycle is defined as a time interval in which the entire stock Q is depleted.)

   c. With $Q = 1,000$ units, $a_p = 10$ units/day, $T_p = 100$ days, $T_d = 50$ days, $a = 5$ units/day, $T_c = 80$ days, $T_0 = 55$ days, $b = \$5$ per unit per year, and $r = 12\%$ compounded continuously, find the total present value using the formula developed in part b.

3.11. Consider an inventory system in which an order is placed every T units of time. It is desired to determine the optimal value of Q by maximizing the average annual profit. This profit is the revenue less the sum of the ordering, purchasing, and inventory carrying costs. All demands will be met from inventory so that there are never any back orders or lost sales. We assume that the demand rate λ is known with certainty and does not change with time. If the on-hand inventory does not continually increase or decrease with each period, the quantity ordered each time will be $Q = \lambda T$. To minimize carrying charges, the on-hand inventory when a procurement arrives should be zero. Suppose that A is the fixed cost of placing an order, C is the cost of one unit, I is the inventory carrying charge, and R is the unit sales price. For simplicity, we select the time origin as a point just prior to the arrival of an order so that nothing is on hand at the time origin.

   a. If r is the nominal interest compounded continuously, find the optimal Q that maximizes the present value of all future profits.

   b. As a specific example, consider a situation in which $A = \$15$, $C = \$35$, $I = 0.10$, $r = 10\%$, $\lambda = 1,500$ units per year, and $R = \$60$ per unit.

3.12. Develop the Z-transform result for the decay function, $g(n) = Ce^{-j(n-b)}$, shown in Table 3.3.

3.13. Develop the Z-transform result for the growth function, $g(n) = C(1 - e^{-j(n-b)})$, shown in Table 3.3. Knowing that this growth function is the sum of C and $-Ce^{-j(n-b)}$, use the linearlity property.

3.14. Develop the Laplace transform result for the growth function shown in Table 3.7.

Outline

Part II: Evaluating Economic Performance of Companies and Projects

- Lecture slides on ratio analysis, discounted cash flows and transform techniques

- Chapters 2 and 3 of "Advanced Engineering Economics" by Park and Sharp-Bette

- Lecture slides on figures of merit

- Chapters 6 and 7 of "Advanced Engineering Economics" by Park and Sharp-Bette

Figures of Merit

> The Net Present Value Criterion

> The Future Value Criterion

> The Annual Equivalence Criterion

> The Internal Rate of Return Criterion

> Solomon's Average Rate of Return Criterion

> The Modified Internal Rate of Return Criterion

> The Benefit-Cost Ratios Criteria

> The Discounted Payback Period

> The Project Balance Concept

> Conventional, Potentially Profitable, Pure and Mixed Investments

Figures of Merit

➢A project net present value (NPV) is:

$$NPV\ (i) = \sum_{n=0}^{N} \frac{F_n}{(1+i)^n}$$

▪ **NPV Criterion:**

> ➢ Accept the project if $NPV\ (i) > 0$

> ➢ Remain indifferent if $NPV\ (i) = 0$

> ➢ Reject the project if $NPV\ (i) < 0$

Figures of Merit

➢ **"The" internal rate of return (IRR) of a project is "the" rate $i*$ for which:**

$$NPV(i^*) = 0$$

- **IRR Criterion:**
  - ➢ Accept the project if $i* > MARR$
  - ➢ Remain indifferent if $i* = MARR$
  - ➢ Reject the project if $i* < MARR$

Figures of Merit

➤ **A project NPV is:**

$$NPV(i) = \sum_{n=0}^{N} \frac{F_n}{(1+i)^n} = \sum_{n=0}^{N} \frac{b_n}{(1+i)^n} - \sum_{n=0}^{N} \frac{c_n}{(1+i)^n} = B - C$$

- **Aggregate B/C Ratio:**

$$R_A = \frac{B}{C}$$

- **Aggregate B/C Ratio Criterion:**

  ➤ Accept the project if $R_A > 1$

  ➤ Remain indifferent if $R_A = 1$

  ➤ Reject the project if $R_A < 1$

Figures of Merit

➢ **A project's outflows can be decomposed into two parts:**

- **I : the initial investment**

- **O = C − I : consists of annual operating and maintenance costs**

- **Netted B/C Ratio:**

$$R_N = \frac{B - O}{I}$$

- **Netted B/C Ratio Criterion:**

  ➢ Accept the project if $R_N > 1$

  ➢ Remain indifferent if $R_N = 1$

  ➢ Reject the project if $R_N < 1$

Figures of Merit

- **Lorie-Savage Ratio:**

$$L - S = \frac{B - C}{I}$$

- **Lorie-Savage Ratio Criterion:**

  ➢ Accept the project if $L\text{-}S > 0$

  ➢ Remain indifferent if $L\text{-}S = 0$

  ➢ Reject the project if $L\text{-}S < 0$

Figures of Merit

- **Generalized Project balance (PB):**

$$PB(i, j)_0 = F_0$$

$$PB(i, j)_n = \begin{cases} PB(i, j)_{n-1}(1+i) + F_n, \text{if } PB(i, j)_{n-1} \leq 0 \\ PB(i, j)_{n-1}(1+j) + F_n, \text{if } PB(i, j)_{n-1} > 0 \end{cases}$$

Where **j** is a conservative rate at which a company can invest recovered balances

- **GPB Criterion:**

  ➢ Accept the project if $PB(i,j)_N > 0$

  ➢ Remain indifferent if $PB(i,j)_N = 0$

  ➢ Reject the project if $PB(i,j)_N < 0$

Potentially Profitable
Conventional Investments

- **Investment:** $F_0 < 0$

- **Conventional (or simple) Investment:**
investment with only one change in the sign of
the cash flows

- **Potentially Profitable Investment:**
investment with a positive sum of net cash flows

- **Proposition:** a **potentially profitable
conventional investment has a unique
positive root**

- **Pure Investment:** no over-recovered balances at its largest root

  ➢ NPV (i^*) = 0 , NPV (i) <> 0 for $i > i^*$ and PB (i^*)$_n$ ≤ 0 for n=0,1,...,N-1

  $\Rightarrow$ All conventional investments are pure

- **Mixed Investment:** investment that is not pure

  ➢ Let j be the investment rate for over-recovered balances

  ➢ Let $i(j)$) be the interest rate at which the ending balance is zero: PB ($i(j),j$)$_N$ = 0

- **Generalized IRR criterion:**

  ➢Accept the project if $i(j) > \mathbf{MARR}$

  ➢Remain indifferent if $i(j) = \mathbf{MARR}$

  ➢Reject the project if $i(j) < \mathbf{MARR}$

Decision Rules for Selecting Among Multiple Alternatives

Incremental Approach

- **Rule:**

    ➢ Sort potentially profitable conventional investments by increasing order of the sum of their cash flows

    ➢ Compute incremental IRR and use IRR criterion to switch projects

Outline

Part II: Evaluating Economic Performance of Companies and Projects

- Lecture slides on ratio analysis, discounted cash flows and transform techniques

- Chapters 2 and 3 of "Advanced Engineering Economics" by Park and Sharp-Bette

- Lecture slides on figures of merit

- Chapters 6 and 7 of "Advanced Engineering Economics" by Park and Sharp-Bette

Measures
of Investment Worth
—Single Project

6.1 INTRODUCTION

In this chapter we focus primarily on evaluating individual projects by the application of various numerical criteria. In our analysis we treat investment projects as almost the same as securities (stocks, bonds, and so on). Both investment projects and securities normally require initial outlays in orger to provide a later sequence of cash receipts. The major difference is that investment projects are not marketable and securities are. When it is necessary to distinguish between projects and securities in our discussion, it will be done. Otherwise, the assumption can be made that the analyses are identical.

Ten different criteria are discussed in this chapter. The net present value (*PV*) criterion is considered the standard measure of investment, and the other measures are discussed and compared with it. The *PV* criterion and its economic interpretation by means of the project balance concept are discussed in Section 6.2. The internal rate of return (*IRR*) criterion, Solomon's average rate of return (*ARR*) criterion, and modified internal rate of return (*MIRR*) criterion are defined in Section 6.3 and are compared with the *PV* criterion. In Section 6.4 alternative measures, benefit–cost ratios, are presented, and again they are compared with the *PV* criterion. The payback period of an investment is discussed in Section 6.5. Finally, the time-dependent measure of investment worth is developed in Section 6.6. In discussing the various measures, we need to make certain assumptions about the investment settings.

6.1.1 Initial Assumptions

In the following investment worth analysis, we assume that the *MARR* (or cost of capital) is known to the decision maker. We also assume a stable, perfect capital market and complete certainty about investment outcomes. In a perfect capital market a firm can raise as much cash as it wants at the going rate of interest, or the firm has sufficient funds to accept all profitable investments. A perfect capital market makes it possible for a firm to invest as much cash as it wants at the market rate of interest. Since the firm may already have undertaken all profitable investments, the market rate of interest is assumed to measure the return on the firm's marginal investment opportunities. Having complete certainty about an investment means that the firm has perfect knowledge of the present and future cash flows associated with the project. Because of this knowledge, the firm finds it unnecessary to make any allowance for uncertainty in project evaluation.

These assumptions describe what might be called the ideal investment situation, quite different from the real-world situation. By setting aside certain complications, however, these assumptions will allow us to introduce the topic of investment analysis at a much simpler level than we otherwise could. In later chapters these assumptions will be removed and the analysis extended to more realistic situations, in which none of these assumptions is fully satisfied.

6.1.2 Notation

To discuss the various evaluation criteria, we will use the following common notation for cash flow representation.

n time, measured in discrete compounding periods

i opportunity interest rate (*MARR*), or market interest rate

C_0 initial investment at time 0, a positive amount

b_n revenue at end of period n, $b_n \geq 0$

c_n expense at the end of period n, $c_n \geq 0$

N project life

F_n net cash flow at the end of period n ($F_n = b_n - c_n$; if $b_n \geq c_n$, then $F_n \geq 0$; if $b_n < c_n$, then $F_n < 0$)

Figure 6.1 illustrates this notation with a cash flow diagram. Additional notation pertaining to a specific criterion will be defined later as necessary. It must be emphasized that all cash flows represent the *cash flows after taxes*.

6.2 THE NET PRESENT VALUE CRITERION

We will use the concept of equivalence to develop the net present value (*PV*) criterion for evaluating investment worth. The future value and annual equivalent criteria are variations of the *PV* criterion found by converting the *PV* into either the future value or the annual equivalent by using the same interest rate. In this section we define and discuss the interpretation of these three criteria.

6.2.1 Mathematical Definition

The PV Criterion.   Consider a project that will generate cash receipts of b_n at the end of each period n. The present value of cash receipts over the project life, B, is expressed by

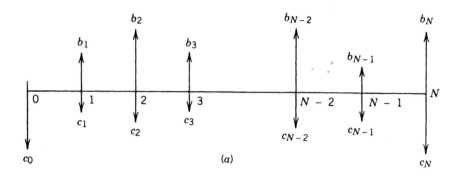

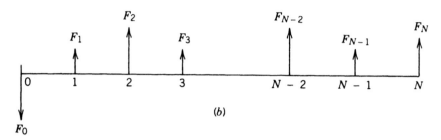

FIGURE 6.1. Notation conventions. (a) Gross cash flow. (b) Net cash flow.

$$B = \sum_{n=0}^{N} \frac{b_n}{(1 + i)^n} \qquad (6.1)$$

Assume that the cash expenses (including the initial outlay associated with the project) at the end of each period are c_n. The present value expression of cash expenses, C, is

$$C = \sum_{n=0}^{N} \frac{c_n}{(1 + i)^n} \qquad (6.2)$$

Then the PV of the project [denoted by $PV(i)$] is defined by the difference between B and C; that is,

$$PV(i) = \sum_{n=0}^{N} \frac{b_n - c_n}{(1 + i)^n} = \sum_{n=0}^{N} \frac{F_n}{(1 + i)^n} \qquad (6.3a)$$

The F_n will be positive if the corresponding period has a net cash inflow and negative if there is a net cash outflow. The foregoing computation of the PV is based on a rate of interest that remains constant over time. The PV could be computed with different rates of interest over time, in which case we would label the nth period's rate of interest as i_n. The PV expression is then

$$PV(i_n, n) = F_0 + \frac{F_1}{1 + i_1} + \frac{F_2}{(1 + i_1)(1 + i_2)} + \cdots \qquad (6.3b)$$

For simplicity, we assume here a single rate of interest in computing the *PV*. We further assume compounding at discrete points in time. A continuous compounding process or continuous cash flows can be handled according to the procedures outlined in Chapter 2.

A positive *PV* for a project represents a positive surplus, and we should accept the project if sufficient funds are available for it. A project with a negative *PV* should be rejected, because we could do better by investing in other projects at the opportunity rate or outside the market. The decision rule expressed simply is

> If $PV(i) > 0$, accept.
>
> If $PV(i) = 0$, remain indifferent.
>
> If $PV(i) < 0$, reject.

Future Value Criterion. As a variation of the *PV* criterion, the future value (*FV*) criterion measures the economic value of a project at the end of the project's life, *N*. Converting the project cash flows into a single payment concentrated at period *N* produces a cash flow equal to *FV*.

$$FV(i) = \sum_{n=0}^{N} F_n (1 + i)^{N-n}$$

$$= PV(i) (1 + i)^N \tag{6.4}$$

From another view, if we borrowed and lent at *i*, operated the project, and left all extra funds to accumulate at *i*, we would have a value equal to *FV(i)* at the end of period *N*. If this value is positive, the project is acceptable. If it is negative, the project should be rejected. As expected, the decision rule for the *FV* criterion is the same as that for the *PV* criterion.

> If $FV(i) > 0$, accept.
>
> If $FV(i) = 0$, remain indifferent.
>
> If $FV(i) < 0$, reject.

Annual Equivalent Criterion. The annual equivalent (*AE*) criterion is another basis for measuring investment worth that has characteristics similar to those of the *PV* criterion. This similarity is evident when we consider that any cash flow can be converted into a series of equal annual payments by first finding the *PV* for the original series and then multiplying the *PV* by the capital recovery factor.

$$AE(i) = PV(i) \left[\frac{i(1 + i)^N}{(1 + i)^N - 1} \right] = PV(i) (A/P, i, N) \tag{6.5}$$

Because the factor $(A/P, i, N)$ is positive for $-1 < i < \infty$, the *AE* criterion should provide a consistent basis for evaluating an investment project as the previous criteria have done.

> If $AE(i) > 0$, accept.
>
> If $AE(i) = 0$, remain indifferent.
>
> If $AE(i) < 0$, reject.

Example 6.1

This example will serve to illustrate the use of the *PV* criterion. Consider a project that requires a $1,000 initial investment with the following patterns of cash flow.

Cash Flow	0	1	2	3	4	5
			End of Period n			
Receipt (b_n)	$0	500	500	500	500	500
Expense (c_n)	$1,000	100	140	180	220	260
Net Flow (F_n)	$-$1,000	400	360	320	280	240

The cash flow diagram is shown in Figure 6.2. Assume the firm's *MARR* is 10%. Substituting F_n values into Eq. 6.3 and varying i values ($0 \le i \le 40\%$), we obtain Table 6.1 and Figure 6.3. We then find that the project's *PV* decreases monoto-

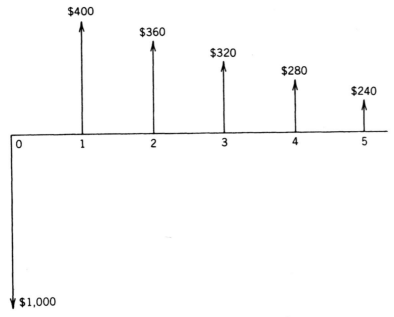

FIGURE 6.2. Cash flow diagram for Example 6.1.

Table 6.1 *Net Present Values PV(i)*
at Varying Interest Rate i, Example 6.1

i (%)	PV(i)	i (%)	PV(i)
0	$600.00	21%	−$19.5
1	556.96	22	−38.84
2	515.77	23	−57.30
3	476.33	24	−75.15
4	438.54	25	−92.43
5	402.31	26	−109.15
6	367.56	27	−125.34
7	334.21	28	−141.03
8	302.19	29	−156.23
9	271.42	30	−170.96
10	241.84	31	−185.25
11	213.40	32	−199.11
12	186.03	33	−212.56
13	159.68	34	−225.61
14	134.31	35	−238.29
15	109.86	36	−250.60
16	86.29	37	−262.56
17	63.55	38	−274.19
18	41.62	39	−285.49
19	20.45	40	−296.48
20	0		

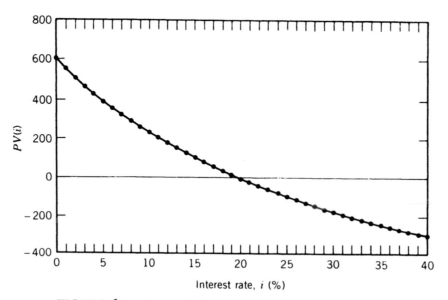

FIGURE 6.3. Plot of *PV(i)* as a function of *i*, Example 6.1.

nically with the firm's i. The project has a positive PV if the firm's interest rate ($MARR$) is below 20% and a negative PV if the $MARR$ is above 20%. At $i = 10\%$, the PV (the equivalent present value to the firm of the total surplus) is $241.84.`

Using Eqs. 6.4 and 6.5, we find

$$FV(10\%) = \$241.84(F/P, 10\%, 5) = \$389.49$$
$$AE(10\%) = \$241.84(A/P, 10\%, 5) = \$58.0$$

Since both $FV(10\%)$ and $AE(10\%)$ are positive, the project is considered viable under these criteria. □

6.2.2 Economic Interpretation Through Project Balance

An alternative way to interpret the economic significance of these criteria is through the project balance concept. In this section we define the project balance concept and then explain how these criteria are related to the terminal project balance.

Project Balance Concept. The *project balance* describes the net equivalent amount of dollars tied up in or committed to the project at each point in time over the life of the project. We will use $PB(i)_n$ to denote the project balance at the end of period n computed at the opportunity cost rate ($MARR$) of i. We will assume that the cost of having money tied up in the project is not incurred unless it is committed for the entire period. To show how the $PB(i)_n$ are computed, we consider the project described in Example 6.1. (See Figure 6.2.)

The project balance at the present time ($n = 0$) is just the investment itself.

$$PB(10\%)_0 = -\$1,000$$

At $n = 1$, the firm has an accumulated commitment of $1,100, which consists of the initial investment and the associated cost of having the initial investment tied up in the project for one period. However, the project returns $400 at $n = 1$. This reduces the firm's investment commitment to $700, so the project balance at $n = 1$ is

$$PB(10\%)_1 = -\$1,000(1 + 0.1) + \$400 = -\$700$$

This amount becomes the net amount committed to that project at the beginning of period 2. The project balance at the end of period 2 is

$$PB(10\%)_2 = -\$700(1 + 0.1) + \$360 = -\$410$$

This represents the cost of having $700 committed at the beginning of the second year along with the receipt of $360 at the end of that year.

We compute the remaining project balances similarly.

$PB(10\%)_3 = -\$410(1.1) + \$320 = -\$131.00$

$PB(10\%)_4 = -\$131(1.1) + \$280 = \$135.90$

$PB(10\%)_5 = \$135.90(1.1) + \$240 = \$389.49$

Notice that the firm fully recovers its initial investment and opportunity cost at the end of period 4 and has a profit of \$135.90. Assuming that the firm can reinvest this amount at the same interest rate ($i = 10\%$) in other projects or outside the market, the project balance grows to \$389.49 with the receipt of \$240 at the end of period 5. The project is then terminated with a net profit of \$389.49.

If we compute the present value equivalent of this net profit at time 0, we obtain

$$PV(10\%) = \$389.49(P/F, 10\%, 5) = \$241.84$$

The result is the same as that obtained when we directly compute the present value of the project at $i = 10\%$. Table 6.2 summarizes these computational results.

Mathematical Derivation. Defining the project balance mathematically based on the previous example yields the recursive relationship

$$PB(i)_n = (1 + i)PB(i)_{n-1} + F_n \qquad (6.6)$$

where $PB(i)_0 = F_0$ and $n = 0, 1, 2, \ldots, N$.

We can develop an alternative expression for the project balance from Eq. 6.6 by making substitutions as follows.

$$PB(i)_0 = F_0$$

$$PB(i)_1 = (1 + i)F_0 + F_1$$

$$PB(i)_2 = (1 + i)[(1 + i)F_0 + F_1] + F_2$$

$$= F_0(1 + i)^2 + F_1(1 + i) + F_2$$

so that at any period n

$$PB(i)_n = F_0(1 + i)^n + F_1(1 + i)^{n-1} + \cdots + F_n \qquad (6.7)$$

The terminal project balance is then expressed by

$$PB(i)_N = F_0(1 + i)^N + F_1(1 + i)^{N-1} + \cdots + F_N$$

$$= \sum_{n=0}^{N} F_n(1 + i)^{N-n}$$

$$= FV(i) \qquad (6.8)$$

Note that $PB(i)_N$ is the future value of the project.

Table 6.2 *Project Balance Computations for the Project in Example 6.1*

Item	n: 0	1	2	3	4	5
Beginning project balance, $PB(i)_{n-1}$	$0	−1,000	−700	−410	−131	+135.90
Interest owed, $i[PB(i)_{n-1}]$	$0	−100	−70	−41	−13.10	13.59
Cash receipt, F_n	−1,000	400	360	320	280	240
Ending project balance, $PB(i)_n$	−$1,000	−$700	−$410	−$131	$135.90	$389.49 $PB(i)_N$

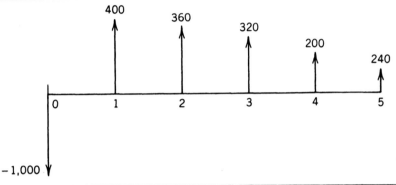

$$PV(10\%) = PB(10\%)_5(1 + 0.1)^{-5} = \$389.49(P/F, 10\%, 5) = \$241.84$$

$$PV(10\%) = -\$1,000 + 400(1.1)^{-1} + 360(1.1)^{-2} + 320(1.1)^{-3}$$
$$+ 280(1.1)^{-4} + 240(1.1)^{-5} = \$241.84$$

Economic Interpretation. If $PB(i)_N > 0$, we can say that the firm recovers the initial investment plus any interest owed, with a profit at the end of the project. If $PB(i)_N = 0$, the firm recovers only the initial investment plus interest owed and breaks even. If $PB(i)_N < 0$, the firm ends up with a loss by not being able to recover even the initial investment and interest owed. Naturally, the firm should accept a project only if $PB(i)_N > 0$. The present equivalent amount of this terminal profit is

$$PV(i) = \frac{PB(i)_N}{(1 + i)^N}$$

$$= \frac{FV(i)_N}{(1 + i)^N} \tag{6.9}$$

The factor $1/(1 + i)^N$ is always positive for $-1 < i < \infty$. This implies that the $PV(i)$ will be positive if and only if $PB(i)_N > 0$ [14].

Now the meaning of the PV criterion should be clear; accepting a project with $PV(i) > 0$ is equivalent to accepting a project with $PB(i)_N > 0$. Because the PV and the future value are measures of equivalence that differ only in the times at which they are stated, they should provide identical results. The analysis and discussion should also make clear why we consider PV as the baseline, or correct, criterion to use in a stable, perfect capital market with complete certainty.

6.3 INTERNAL RATE-OF-RETURN CRITERION

6.3.1 Definition of IRR

Mathematical Definition. The internal rate of return (*IRR*) is another time-discounted measure of investment worth similar to the *PV* criterion. The *IRR* of a project is defined as the rate of interest that equates the *PV* of the entire series of cash flows to zero. The project's *IRR, i^**, is defined mathematically by

$$PV(i^*) = \sum_{n=0}^{N} \frac{F_n}{(1 + i^*)^n} = 0 \qquad (6.10)$$

Multiplying both sides of Eq. 6.10 by $(1 + i^*)^N$, we obtain

$$PV(i^*)(1 + i^*)^N = \sum_{n=0}^{N} F_n(1 + i^*)^{N-n}$$

$$= FV(i^*) = 0 \qquad (6.11)$$

The left-hand side of Eq. 6.11 is, by definition, the future value (terminal project balance) of the project.

If we multiply both sides of Eq. 6.10 by the capital recovery factor, we obtain the relationship $AE(i^*) = 0$ (see Eq. 6.9). Alternatively, the *IRR* of a project may be defined as the rate of interest that equates the future value, terminal project balance, and annual equivalent value of the entire series of cash flows to zero.

$$PV(i^*) = FV(i^*) = PB(i^*)_N = AE(i^*) = 0 \qquad (6.12)$$

Computational Methods. Note that Eq. 6.11 is a polynomial function of i^*. A direct solution for such a function is not generally possible except for projects with a life of four periods or fewer. Instead, two approximation techniques are in general use, one using iterative procedures (a trial-and-error approach) and the other using Newton's approximation to the solution of a polynomial.

An iterative procedure requires an initial guess. To approximate the *IRR*, we calculate the *PV* for a certain interest rate (initial guess). If this *PV* is not zero, another interest rate is tried. A negative *PV* usually indicates that the choice is too high. We continue approximating until we reach the two bounds that contain the answer. We then interpolate to find the closest approximation to the *IRR*(s).

The Newton approximation to a polynomial $f(X) = 0$ is made by starting with an arbitrary approximation of X and forming successive approximations by the formula

$$X_{j+1} = X_j - \frac{f(X_j)}{f'(X_j)} \tag{6.13}$$

where $f'(X_j)$ is the first derivative of the polynomial evaluated at X_j. *The process is continued until we observe* $X_j \cong X_{j-1}$.

Example 6.2

Consider a project with cash flows $-\$100$, 50, and 84 at the end of periods 0, 1, and 2, respectively. The present value expression for this project is

$$PV(i) = -\$100 + \frac{50}{1+i} + \frac{84}{(1+i)^2}$$

Let $X = 1/(1 + i)$. Our polynomial, the present value function, is then

$$f(X) = -100 + 50X + 84X^2$$

The derivative of this polynomial is

$$f'(X) = 50 + 168X$$

Suppose the first approximation we make is

$$X_1 = 0.8696 \qquad (i = 0.15)$$

The second approximation is

$$X_2 = 0.8696 - \frac{-100 + 50(0.8696) + 84(0.8696)^2}{50 + 168(0.8696)}$$

$$= 0.8339$$

The third approximation is

$$X_3 = 0.8339 - \frac{-100 + 50(0.8339) + 84(0.8339)^2}{50 + 168(0.8339)}$$

$$= 0.8333$$

Further iterations indicate that $X = 0.8333$ or $i^* = 20\%$. (With any approximation we are limited by rounding, so when we get the same answer twice in the sequence of approximations, we stop.) □

Although the calculations in Newton's method are relatively simple, they are time-consuming if many iterations are required. The use of a computer is eventually necessary. (When we program the computer, it is wise to set tolerance limits on the degree of accuracy required to avoid unnecessary iterations.)

Uniqueness of i*.   The existence of a unique *IRR* is of special interest in applying the *IRR* investment worth criterion. Consider a project with cash flows of −$10, $47, −$72, and $36 at the end of periods 0, 1, 2, and 3, respectively. Applying Eq. 6.10 and solving for *i* gives us three roots: 20%, 50%, and 100%. This really should not surprise us, since Eq. 6.10 is a third-degree polynomial for the project. Here the plot of *PV* as a function of interest rate crosses the *i* axis several times, as illustrated in Figure 6.4. As we will see in later sections, multiple *IRRs* hinder the application of the *IRR* criterion, and we do not recommend the *IRR* criterion in such cases. In this section we will focus on the problem of whether a unique *IRR* for a project can be predicted by the cash flow stream.

One way to predict an upper limit on the number of positive roots of a polynomial is to apply Descartes' rule of signs.

> **Descartes' Rule.** The number of real positive roots of an *n*th-degree polynominal with real coefficients is never greater than the number of sign changes in the sequence of the coefficients.

Letting $X = 1/(1 + i)$, we can write Eq. 6.10 as

$$F_0 + F_1 X + F_2 X^2 + \cdots + F_N X^N = 0 \tag{6.14}$$

Thus, we need examine only the sign changes in F_n to apply the rule. For example, if the project has outflows followed by inflows, there is only one sign change and hence at most one real positive root.

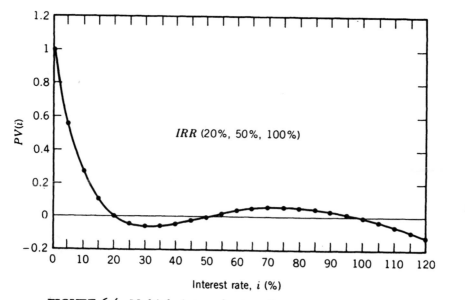

FIGURE 6.4. Multiple internal rates of return.

The Norstrom criterion [5] provides a more discriminating condition for the uniqueness of the root in the interval $(0 < i^* < \infty)$.

Norstrom Criterion. Consider a cash flow series $F_0, F_1, F_2, ..., F_N$. Form the auxiliary series $S_n = \sum_{j=0}^{n} F_j$, $n = 0, 1, ..., N$. If the series S_n starts negative and changes sign only once, there exists a unique positive real root.   (6.15)

Additional criteria for the uniqueness of roots do exist, but they are rather tedious to apply and will not be discussed here. Bernhard [5] discusses these additional criteria and provides another general method for detecting the uniqueness of *IRR*.

Example 6.3

To illustrate the use of both Descartes' rule and the Norstrom criterion, consider the following pattern of cash flows.

n	0	1	2
F_n	$-\$100$	$\$140$	$-\$10$

Descartes' rule implies that the maximum number of positive real roots is less than or equal to two, which indicates that there may be multiple roots. There are two sign changes in $F_n(-, +, -)$.

To apply the Norstrom criterion, we first compute the cumulative cash flow stream, S_n.

$$S_0 = F_0 = -\$100$$

$$S_1 = F_0 + F_1 = -\$100 + \$140 = \$40$$

$$S_2 = F_0 + F_1 + F_2 = \$40 - \$10 = \$30$$

The criterion indicates a unique positive, real root for the problem because there is only one sign change in the S_n series $(-, +, +)$. In fact, the project has a unique *IRR* at $i^* = 32.45\%$. □

6.3.2 Classification of Investment Projects

In discussing the *IRR* criterion, we need to distinguish between simple and nonsimple investments. Investment projects are further classified as pure or mixed investments.

Simple versus Nonsimple. A *simple* investment is defined as one in which there is only one sign change in the net cash flow (F_n). A *nonsimple* investment is one whose net cash outflows are not restricted to the initial period but are interspersed with net cash inflows throughout the life of the project. In other

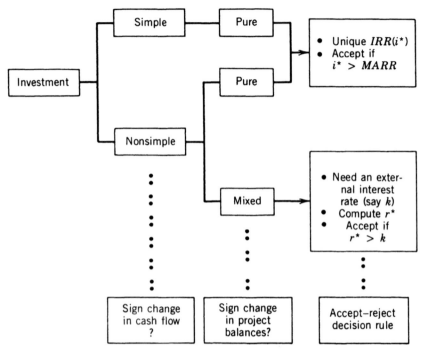

FIGURE 6.5. Classification of investment projects.

words, when there is more than one sign change in the net cash flow, the project is called a nonsimple project.

Pure versus Mixed. A *pure* investment is defined as an investment whose project balances computed at the project's *IRR*, $PB(i^*)_n$, are either zero or negative throughout the life of the project (with $F_0 < 0$). The implication of nonpositivity of $PB(i^*)_n$ for all values of n is that the firm has committed (or "lent") funds in the amount of $PB(i^*)_n$ dollars to the project for time n to time $n + 1$. In other words, the firm does not "borrow" from the project at any time during the life of the project.

A *mixed* investment, in contrast, is defined as any investment for which $PB(i^*)_n > 0$ for some values of n and $PB(i^*)_n \leq 0$ for the remaining values of n. These sign changes in $PB(i^*)_n$ indicate that at some times during the project's life $[PB(i^*)_n < 0]$ the firm acts as an "investor" in the project and at other times $[PB(i^*)_n > 0]$ the firm acts as a "borrower" from the project.

Classification by i_{min}. An alternative way of distinguishing between pure and mixed investments is to compute the value of i_{min}, the smallest interest rate that makes $PB(i)_n \leq 0$ for $n = 0, 1, 2, \ldots, N - 1$. Then we evaluate the sign of $PB(i_{min})_N$, the terminal project balance. If $PB(i_{min})_N \geq 0$, the project is a pure investment. If $PB(i_{min})_N < 0$, the project is a mixed investment.

If $PB(i_{min})_N > 0$, we can find some *IRR*, $i^* > i_{min}$, that will set $PB(i^*)_N$ to zero. Then use of a higher interest rate will simply magnify the negativity of $PB(i)_n$. Thus, the condition of $i^* \geq i_{min}$ will ensure the nonpositivity of $PB(i^*)_n$ for $0 \leq n \leq N - 1$. This is the definition of a pure investment.

If $PB(i_{min})_N < 0$, we can expect that $i^* < i_{min}$, which will set $PB(i^*)_N$ to zero. Because i_{min} is the minimum rate at which the nonpositivity condition $[PB(i_{min}) \leq 0]$ satisfies $0 \leq n \leq N - 1$, we know that $PB(i^*)_n$ is not always zero or negative for $0 \leq n \leq N - 1$. This implies that the project is a mixed investment.

Figure 6.5 illustrates the final classification scheme that provides the basis for the analysis of investments under the *IRR* criterion. Note that simple investments are always classified as pure investments. (See the proof in Bussey [6].) As we will see, the phenomenon of multiple *IRR*s occurs only in the situation of a mixed investment. Although a simple investment is always a pure investment, a pure investment is not necessarily a simple investment, as we will see in Example 6.4.

Example 6.4

We will illustrate the distinction between pure and mixed investments with numerical examples. Consider the following four projects with known i^* values.

End of Period	Project			
n	A	B	C	D
0	$-\$100$	$-\$100$	$-\$100$	$-\$100$
1	-100	140	50	470
2	200	-10	-50	-720
3	200		200	360
IRR	$i^* = 41.42\%$	$i^* = 32.45\%$	$i^* = 29.95\%$	$i^* = 20\%, 50\%, 100\%$

Table 6.3 summarizes the project balances from these projects at their respective *IRR*s. Project A is the only simple project; the rest are nonsimple. Projects A and C are pure investments, whereas projects B and D are mixed investments. As seen in project B, the existence of a unique *IRR* is a necessary but not a sufficient condition for a pure investment.

Table 6.3 *Project Balances, Example 6.4*

Project	IRR		End of Period n			
			0	1	2	3
A	41.42%	F_n	$-\$100$	-100	200	200
		$PB(i^*)_n$	$-\$100$	-241.42	-141.42	0
B	32.45%	F_n	$-\$100$	140	-10	
		$PB(i^*)_n$	$-\$100$	7.55	0	
C	29.95%	F_n	$-\$100$	50	-50	200
		$PB(i^*)_n$	$-\$100$	-79.95	-153.90	0
		F_n	$-\$100$	470	-720	360
	20%	$PB(20\%)$	$-\$100$	350	-300	0
	50%	$PB(50\%)$	$-\$100$	320	-240	0
D	100%	$PB(100\%)$	$-\$100$	270	-180	0

In distinguishing pure and mixed investments, we could use the i_{min} test. We will show how this is done for project D. Since $N = 3$, we need to consider $PB(i)_0$, $PB(i)_1$, and $PB(i)_2$.

$$PB(i)_0 = -100$$
$$PB(i)_1 = PB(i)_0(1 + i) + 470 = -100i + 370$$
$$PB(i)_2 = PB(i)_1(1 + i) - 720 = -100i^2 + 270i - 350$$

Since $PB(i)_0 < 0$, we find the smallest value of i that makes both $PB(i)_1$ and $PB(i)_2$ nonpositive. The minimum value is 370%. Now we evaluate $PB(i_{min})_3$ to find

$$PB(370\%)_3 = -720(4.70) + 360 = -\$3024 < 0$$

Since $PB(i_{min})_3 < 0$, project D is a mixed investment. □

6.3.3 IRR and Pure Investments

According to the *IRR* criterion, a pure investment should be accepted if its *IRR* is above the *MARR* (or cost of capital) to the firm. We will show why this decision rule can produce an accept–reject decision consistent with the *PV* criterion.

Recall that pure investments have the following characteristics.

1. Net investment throughout the life of the project.
2. Existence of unique i^*.
3. $PB(i^*)_n \leq 0$ for $0 \leq n \leq N - 1$, and $PB(i^*)_N = 0$.
4. $PB(i)_N \left[\dfrac{1}{(1 + i)^N} \right] = PV(i)$

and if $i = i^*$,

$$PB(i)_N = 0 \rightarrow PV(i) = 0$$

We will first consider computing $PB(i)_N$ with $i > i^*$. Here i is the *MARR* (or cost of capital) to the firm. Since $PB(i^*)_n \leq 0$ for $0 \leq n \leq N - 1$ and $PB(i^*)_N = 0$, the effect of a higher compounding rate is to magnify the negativity of these project balances. This implies that $PB(i)_N < PB(i^*)_N = 0$. From Eq. 6.9, this also implies that $PV(i) < 0$. If $i = i^*$, then $PB(i)_N = PB(i^*)_N = 0$ so that $PV(i) = 0$. If $i < i^*$, then $PB(i)_N > 0$, indicating that $PV(i) > 0$. Hence we accept the investment. This proves the equivalence of the *PV* and *IRR* criteria for accept–reject decisions concerning simple investments. These relationships are illustrated in Figure 6.6.

If $i < i^*$, accept.
If $i = i^*$, remain indifferent.
If $i > i^*$, reject.

When a firm makes a pure investment, it has funds committed to the project over the life of the project and at no time takes a loan from the project. Only in such a

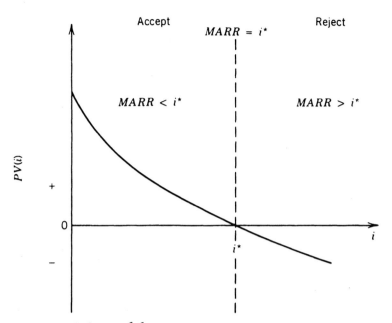

FIGURE 6.6. *PV(i)* of simple investment as a function of *i*.

situation is a rate of return concept *internal* to the project. Then the *IRR* can be viewed as the interest rate *earned* on the committed project balance (unrecovered balance, or negative project balance) of an investment, *not* the interest earned on the initial investment. The reader should keep this in mind, since it is a point not generally understood by many practitioners.

Example 6.5

Consider the project described in Example 6.1. (Note that the project is a simple and pure investment.) The project was acceptable at $i = 10\%$ by the *PV* criterion. We find that the *IRR* of this project is 20% by solving for i^* in Eq. 6.10.

$$PV(i^*) = -\$1,000 + \frac{\$400}{1 + i^*} + \frac{\$360}{(1 + i^*)^2} + \frac{\$320}{(1 + i^*)^3}$$

$$+ \frac{\$280}{(1 + i^*)^4} + \frac{\$240}{(1 + i^*)^5} = 0$$

Since $i^* > 10\%$, the project should be acceptable. The economic interpretation of the 20% is that the investment under consideration brings in enough cash to pay for itself in 5 years and also to provide the firm with a return of 20% on its invested capital over the project life.

Expressed another way, suppose that a firm obtains all its capital by borrowing from a bank at the interest rate of exactly 20%. If the firm invests in the project and uses the cash flow generated by the investment to pay off the principal and interest on the bank loan, the firm should come out exactly even on the transaction. If the firm can borrow the funds at a rate lower than 20%, the project should be profitable. If the borrowing interest rate is greater than 20%, acceptance of the project would result in losses. This break-even characteristic makes the *IRR* a popular criterion among many practitioners. ☐

6.3.4 IRR and Mixed Investments

Recall that the mixed investments have the following characteristics.

1. More than one sign change in cash flow.
2. Possibility of multiple rates of return.
3. Mixed signs in $PB(i^*)_n$.

The difficulty in mixed investments is determining which rate to use for the acceptance test, if any. The mixed signs in $PB(i^*)_n$ indicate that the firm has funds committed to the project part of the time [$PB(i^*)_n < 0$ for some values of n] and takes a "loan" from the project the rest of the time [$PB(i^*)_n > 0$ for some value of n]. Because of this lending and borrowing activity, there is no rate of return concept internal to the project. The return on such mixed investments tends to vary with the external interest rate (i.e., cost of capital) to the firm.

To circumvent this conceptual difficulty, we may modify the procedure for computation by compounding positive project balances at the cost of borrowing capital, k, and negative project balances at the return on invested capital (RIC), r. (We use the symbol r because the return on invested capital of a mixed project is generally not equal to the *IRR*, i^*, of the project.) Since the firm is never indebted to the project for pure investment, it is clear that k does not enter into the compounding process; hence this RIC is independent of k, the cost of capital to the firm. Two approaches may be used in computing r: the trial-and-error approach and the analytical approach.

Trial-and-Error Approach.   The trial-and-error approach is similar to finding a project's internal rate of return. For a given cost of capital, k, we first compute the project balances from an investment with a somewhat arbitrarily selected r value. Since it is hoped that projects will promise a return of at least the cost of capital, a value of r close to k is a good starting point for most problems. For a given pair of (k, r), we calculate the last project balance and see whether it is positive, negative, or zero. Suppose the last project balance $PB(r, k)_N$ is negative—what do we do then? A nonzero terminal project balance indicates that the guessed r value is not the true r value. We must lower the r value and go through the process again. Conversely, if the $PB(r, k)_N > 0$, we raise the r value and repeat the process.

Example 6.6

To illustrate the method described, consider the following cash flow of a project.

n	0	1	2
F_n	−$1,000	2,900	−2,080

Suppose that the cost of capital, k, is known to be 15%. For $k = 15\%$, we must compute r^* by trial and error.

For $k = 15\%$ and trial $r = 16\%$,

$$PB(16, 15)_0 = -1,000 \qquad\qquad\qquad = -\$1,000$$

$$PB(16, 15)_1 = -1,000(1 + 0.16) + 2,900 = \quad \$1,300 \quad [\text{use } r, \text{ since } PB(16, 15)_0 < 0]$$

$$PB(16, 15)_2 = \quad 1,300(1 + 0.15) - 2,080 = \quad -\$585 \quad [\text{use } k, \text{ since } PB(16, 15)_1 > 0]$$

The terminal project balance is not zero, indicating that r^* is not equal to our 16% trial r. The next trial value should be smaller than 16% because the terminal balance is negative (-585). After several trials, we conclude that for $k = 15\%$, r^* is approximately at 9.13%. To verify the results,

$$PB(9.13, 15)_0 = -1,000 \qquad\qquad\qquad = -\$1,000$$

$$PB(9.13, 15)_1 = -1,000(1 + 0.0913) + 2,900 = \quad \$1,808.70$$

$$PB(9.13, 15)_2 = \quad 1,808.70(1 + 0.15) - 2,080 = \quad 0$$

Since $r^* < k$, the investment is not profitable. Note that the project would also be rejected under the PV analysis at $MARR = i = k = 15\%$.

$$PV(15\%) = -1,000 + 2,900(P/F, 15\%, 1) - 2,080(P/F, 15\%, 2)$$
$$= -\$51.04 < 0 \quad \square$$

Analytical Approach. The most direct procedure for determining the functional relationship between r and k of a mixed investment is to write out the expression for the future value of the project. Since the project balance of a mixed investment is compounded at either r or k, depending on the sign of the project balance, the terminal (future) balance of the project, denoted by $PB(r, k)_N$, is a function of two variables. The following steps can be used to determine the *RIC*, r.

Step 1: Find $i_{\min}$ by solving for the smallest real rate for which all $PB(i_{\min})_n \le 0$, for $n = 1, \ldots, N - 1$. This is usually done by a trial-and-error method.

Step 2: Find $PB(i_{\min})_N$.
a. If $PB(i_{\min})_N \ge 0$, the project is a pure investment.
   (1) Find the *IRR*, i^*, for which $PB(i^*)_N = 0$; $i^* = r^*$ for a pure investment.
   (2) Apply the decision rules given in step 5.
b. If $PB(i_{\min})_N < 0$, the project is a mixed investment and it is necessary to proceed with step 3.

Step 3: Calculate $PB(r, k)_n$ according to the following.

$$PB(r, k)_0 = F_0$$

$$PB(r, k)_1 = PB(r, k)_0(1 + r) + F_1 \qquad \text{if } PB(r, k)_0 \le 0$$

$$ PB(r, k)_0(1 + k) + F_1 \qquad \text{if } PB(r, k)_0 > 0$$

$$\vdots$$

$$PB(r, k)_n = PB(r, k)_{n-1}(1 + r) + F_n \quad \text{if } PB(r, k)_{n-1} \le 0$$

$$ PB(r, k)_{n-1}(1 + k) + F_n \quad \text{if } PB(r, k)_{n-1} > 0$$

389

To determine the positivity or negativity of $PB(r, k)_n$ at each period, set $r = i_{min}$, knowing that $r \leq i_{min}$. (See Problem 6.10.)

Step 4: Determine the value of r^* by solving the equation $PB(r, k)_N = 0$.

Step 5: Apply the following set of decision rules to accept or reject the project.

> If $r^* > k$, accept.
>
> If $r^* = k$, remain indifferent.
>
> If $r^* < k$, reject.

Example 6.7

Consider the project cash flows given in Example 6.6.

End of Period n	0	1	2
Cash Flow F_n	$-\$1,000$	2,900	$-2,080$

There are two sign changes in the ordered sequence of cash flows $(-, +, -)$. The project has two *IRRs*, corresponding to $i^*_1 = 30\%$ and $i^*_2 = 60\%$. To derive the functional relationship between the return on invested capital, r, and the cost of capital, k, we apply the algorithm described in the preceding section.

Step 1: Find the i_{min} that satisfies the following two equations ($N = 2, N - 1 = 1$).

$$PB(i)_0 = -1,000 < 0$$

$$PB(i)_1 = -1,000(1 + i) + 2,900$$

$$= -1,000i + 1,900 \leq 0$$

Since $PB(i)_0 < 0$, we need only find the smallest i that satisfies $PB(i)_1 \leq 0$. The value of i_{min} is 190%.

Step 2: Calculate $PB(i_{min})_N$.

$$PB(i_{min})_2 = (-1,000i_{min} + 1900)(1 + i_{min}) - 2,080$$

$$= -2,080$$

Since $PB(i_{min})_2 < 0$, the project is a mixed investment.

Step 3: Calculate $PB(r, k)_n$.

$$PB(r, k)_0 = -1,000$$

Since $PB(r, k)_0 < 0$, we use r.

$$PB(r, k)_1 = -1,000(1 + r) + 2,900$$

$$= -1,000r + 1,900$$

Since r cannot exceed i_{min}, $PB(r, k)_1 \geq 0$. Then we use k.

$$PB(r, k)_2 = (-1,000r + 1,900)(1 + k) - 2,080$$

Step 4: Find the solution of $PB(r, k)_2 = 0$.

$$r = 1.9 - \frac{2.08}{1 + k} \tag{6.16}$$

The graph of Eq. 6.16 is shown in Figure 6.7. We observe the following characteristics.

1. First, since $\dfrac{dr}{dk} = \dfrac{2.08}{(1 + k)^2} > 0$, r is a monotonically increasing function of k. This means that the higher the cost that the firm places on borrowing funds from the project, the higher the return it will require on the invested capital.

2. Second, if we set $r = k$ in Eq. 6.16, we have $r = k = i^*$. Equation 6.16 intersects the 45° line $r = k$ twice, once at $k = 30\%$ and again at $k = 60\%$. With $r = k = i^*$, the terminal project balance $PB(r, k)_2$ decreases to $PB(i^*)_2 = 0$. Solving $PB(i^*)_2 = 0$ for i^* yields the *IRR* of the project. In other words, this mixed investment has multiple rates of return ($i_1^* = 30\%$, $i_2^* = 60\%$). Therefore, the roots i^* for mixed investment are the values of the return on invested capital, r, when the cost of borrowed money, k, is assumed to be equal to r.

3. Third, applying the decision rule, we have

If $30\% < k < 60\% \rightarrow r^* > k$,	accept the project.
If $k = 30\%$ or $k = 60\% \rightarrow r^* = k$,	remain indifferent.
If $k < 30\%$ or $k > 60\% \rightarrow r^* < k$,	reject the project.

4. Fourth, the decision we make will be consistent with the decision derived from applying the *PV* criterion when $i = MARR = k$. The *PV* of the project at an interest rate of k can be expressed as

$$PV(k) = -\$1,000 + \frac{\$2,900}{1 + k} - \frac{\$2,080}{(1 + k)^2} \tag{6.17}$$

which is also depicted in Figure 6.7.

The following comments about the *PV* function are in order. First, the *IRR* is by definition the solution to the equation $PV(k) = 0$. Therefore, we observe that $PV(k)$ intersects the horizontal axis at $k = 30\%$ and at $k = 60\%$. Second, since $PV(k)$ is positive only in the range $30\% < k < 60\%$, the *PV* criterion gives the same accept–reject signal as the *IRR* criterion. □

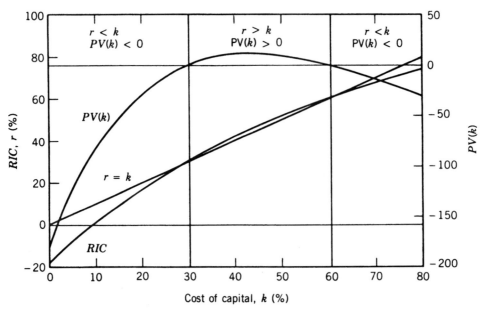

FIGURE 6.7. *RIC* and *PV* as functions of *k*, Example 6.7.

6.3.5 Modified Rate of Return

An alternative way of approaching mixed investments is to modify the procedure for computing the rate of return by making explicit and consistent assumptions about the interest rate at which intermediate receipts from projects may be reinvested. This reinvestment could be either in other projects or in the outside market. This procedure is similar to the previous use of two different rates (*r*, *k*) in the computation of the *project balance*. This section reviews some of the methods for applying the procedure.

Solomon's Average Rate of Return (ARR).   A different way of looking at a project is to ask the following question. Suppose we take the net revenues $F_n (F_n > 0)$ and reinvest them each year at *i*, letting them accumulate until time *N*. What rate of interest does investment C_0 have to earn to reach the same accumulated value in *N* periods [15]?

Mathematically, we wish to find *s* to solve the equation

$$\underbrace{C_0(1 + s)^N}_{\substack{\text{alternative} \\ \text{investment}}} = \underbrace{\sum_{n=1}^{N} F_n(1 + i)^{N-n}}_{\text{current investment}} \qquad (6.18)$$

With known *s*, the acceptance rule is

> If $s > i = MARR$, accept.
>
> If $s = i$, remain indifferent.
>
> If $s < i$, reject.

We can easily show that the *ARR* criterion is completely consistent with the *PV* criterion [2]. Recall that for a given project with $F_0 < 0$ but $F_n > 0$ for $1 \leq n \leq N$, the *PV* acceptance rule is

$$\sum_{n=0}^{N} F_n(1 + i)^{-n} > 0 \qquad (6.19)$$

Substituting C_0 for F_0 (note that $F_0 = -C_0$) gives us

$$C_0 < \sum_{n=1}^{N} F_n(1 + i)^{-n} \qquad (6.20)$$

Multiplying both sides of Eq. 6.18 by $(1 + i)^{-N}$ yields

$$C_0(1 + s)^N(1 + i)^{-N} = \sum_{n=1}^{N} F_n(1 + i)^{-n} \qquad (6.21)$$

By comparing Eqs. 6.20 and 6.21, we can deduce that

$$C_0(1 + s)^N(1 + i)^{-N} > C_0$$

or

$$(1 + s)^N > (1 + i)^N \qquad (6.22)$$

This implies that $s > i$, which is the *ARR* acceptance condition.

Example 6.8

Consider the cash flows shown in Figure 6.2, where $C_0 = \$1,000$, $F_1 = \$400$, $F_2 = \$360$, $F_3 = \$320$, $F_4 = \$280$, and $F_5 = \$240$. Substituting these values into Eq. 6.18, we obtain

$$1,000(1 + s)^5 = 400(1.1)^4 + 360(1.1)^3 + 320(1.1)^2 + 280(1.1) + 240$$

$$= \$2,000$$

Solving for s yields 15%. This tells us that we can invest $1,000 in the project, reinvest the proceeds at our opportunity rate (*MARR*) of 10%, and have $2,000 at time 5. If we do not wish to invest in the project but still wish to earn $2,000, the original $1,000 would have to earn 15% per period. Since the *MARR* is 10%, we are clearly better off accepting the project. If s had been less than $i = 10\%$, we would have rejected the project. □

Modified Internal Rate of Return (MIRR).   As a variation of the *ARR* procedure, we may make explicit the expected reinvestment rate of intermediate incomes

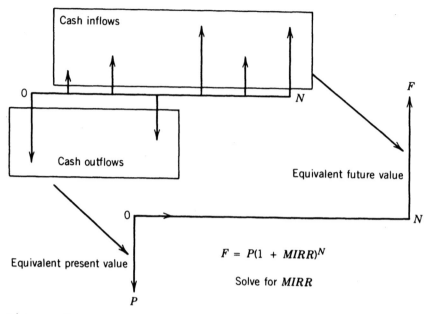

FIGURE 6.8. Illustration of the *MIRR* concept.

and costs and reduce them to an equivalent initial cost and a terminal project balance, a procedure known as the modified internal rate of return (*MIRR*) [12] or the external rate of return. In this way a unique *IRR* can be computed. This *MIRR* is defined by

$$\frac{\text{Future value of net cash inflow}}{\text{Present value of net cash outflow}}$$

$$= \frac{\displaystyle\sum_{n=0}^{N} \max(F_n, 0)(1 + i)^{N-n}}{-\displaystyle\sum_{n=0}^{N} \min(F_n, 0)(1 + i)^{-n}} = (1 + MIRR)^N \qquad (6.23)$$

where $\max(F_n, 0) = F_n$ if $F_n > 0$, otherwise $F_n = 0$; $\min(F_n, 0) = F_n$ if $F_n < 0$, otherwise $F_n = 0$; and i is the *MARR* to the firm. The meaning of the *MIRR* is illustrated in Figure 6.8.

By rearranging terms in Eq. 6.23, we can rewrite it as

$$\sum_{n=0}^{N} \max(F_n, 0)(1 + i)^{N-n} = \left[-\sum_{n=0}^{N} \min(F_n, 0)(1 + i)^{-n} \right](1 + MIRR)^N$$

$$(6.24)$$

If the cash outflow is restricted to the first period, $n = 0$, the *MIRR* is exactly the same as the *ARR*, s. The acceptance rule is then

> If *MIRR* > i, accept.
> If *MIRR* = i, remain indifferent.
> If *MIRR* < i, reject.

The *MIRR* will always give a unique solution and is also consistent with the *PV* criterion. The *MIRR* will always exceed the alternative rate whenever the investment sequence has a positive *PV* at i. This can be visualized from the following equations.

The project acceptance condition by the *PV* criterion is

$$\sum_{n=0}^{N} \max(F_n, 0)(1 + i)^{-n} \quad > \quad - \sum_{n=0}^{N} \min(F_n, 0)(1 + i)^{-n} \qquad (6.25)$$

$$\begin{array}{ccc} \text{Present value of} & > & \text{Present value of} \\ \text{net cash inflow} & & \text{net cash outflow} \end{array}$$

Multiplying both sides of Eq. 6.24 by $(1 + i)^{-N}$ yields

$$\sum_{n=0}^{N} \max(F_n, 0)(1 + i)^{-n}$$

$$= \left[- \sum_{n=0}^{N} \min(F_n, 0)(1 + i)^{-n} \right](1 + MIRR)^N (1 + i)^{-N} \qquad (6.26)$$

From the relation given in Eq. 6.25, we can say

$$\left[- \sum_{n=0}^{N} \min(F_n, 0)(1 + i)^{-n} \right](1 + MIRR)^N (1 + i)^{-N}$$

$$> - \sum_{n=0}^{N} \min(F_n, 0)(1 + i)^{-n} \qquad (6.27)$$

Simplifying the terms above gives

$$(1 + MIRR)^N > (1 + i)^N \qquad (6.28)$$

which indicates that *MIRR* > i.

There are three other variations of the *MIRR* [4], but these indices (including *ARR* and *MIRR*) have numerical values distinctly different from one another, and without additional information provided, these rates are considerably more complex to use than the simple *PV* criterion.

Example 6.9

Using an example from [4], we will illustrate the method of computing the *MIRR*. Assume that $i = 6\%$, and the cash flow components are

Cash Flow	n: 0	1	2	3
b_n	$0	3	2	25
c_n	$10	1	5	2
F_n	−$10	2	−3	23

Present value of net cash outflow $= +10 + 3(1 + 0.06)^{-2} = \$12.67$

Future value of net cash inflow $= 2(1 + 0.06)^2 + 23 = \$25.25$

Using Eq. 6.24, we find

$$25.25 = 12.67(1 + MIRR)^3$$

$$MIRR = 25.84\%$$

Since $MIRR > 6\%$, the project should be acceptable. Note that $PV(6\%) = \$8.53 > 0$, so the *MIRR* result is consistent with the *PV* criterion. □

6.4 BENEFIT–COST RATIOS

Another way to express the worthiness of a project is to compare the inflows with the investment. This leads to three types of benefit–cost ratios: the aggregate benefit–cost ratio (Eckstein *B/C*), the netted benefit–cost ratio (simple *B/C*), and the Lorie–Savage ratio.

Let B and C be the present values of cash inflows and outflows defined by Eqs. 6.1 and 6.2. We will split the equivalent cost C into two components, the initial capital expenditure and the annual costs accrued in each successive period. Assuming that an initial investment is required during the first m periods, while annual costs accrue in each period following, the components are defined as

$$I = \sum_{n=0}^{m} c_n(1 + i)^{-n} \tag{6.29}$$

$$C' = \sum_{n=m+1}^{N} c_n(1 + i)^{-n} \tag{6.30}$$

and $C = I + C'$.

The following example will be used to demonstrate the application of different B/C ratio criteria.

Cash Flow	n: 0	1	2	3	4	5
b_n	$0	0	10	10	20	20
c_n	$10	5	5	5	5	10
F_n	$-$10	-5	5	5	15	10

With $i = 10\%$, we define

$$N = 5$$

$$m = 1$$

$$B = 10(1.1)^{-2} + 10(1.1)^{-3} + 20(1.1)^{-4} + 20(1.1)^{-5} = \$41.86$$

$$C = 10 + 5(1.1)^{-1} + 5(1.1)^{-2} + 5(1.1)^{-3} + 5(1.1)^{-4}$$
$$+ 10(1.1)^{-5} = \$32.06$$

$$I = 10 + 5(1.1)^{-1} = \$14.55$$

$$C' = 5(1.1)^{-2} + 5(1.1)^{-3} + 5(1.1)^{-4} + 10(1.1)^{-5} = \$17.51$$

$$PV(10\%) = B - C = \$9.80$$

6.4.1 Benefit–Cost Ratios Defined

Aggregate B/C Ratio. The aggregate B/C ratio introduced by Eckstein [7] is defined as

$$R_A = \frac{B}{C} = \frac{B}{I + C'}, \qquad I + C' > 0 \tag{6.31}$$

To accept a project, the R_A must be greater than 1. Historically, this ratio was developed in the 1930s in response to the fact that in public projects the user is generally not the same as the sponsor. To have a better perspective on the user's benefits, we need to separate them from the sponsor's costs. If we assume that for a project b_n represents the user's benefits and c_n the sponsor's costs, the ratio is

$$R_A = \frac{41.86}{14.55 + 17.51} = 1.306$$

The ratio exceeds 1, which implies that the user's benefits exceed the sponsor's costs. Public projects usually also have benefits that are difficult to measure, whereas costs are more easily quantified. In this respect, the Eckstein B/C ratio lends itself readily to sensitivity analysis with respect to the value of benefits. We will discuss this measure in greater detail in Chapter 14.

Netted B/C Ratio. As an alternative expression in defining their terms, some analysts consider only the initial capital expenditure as a cash outlay, and equivalent benefits become net benefits (i.e., revenues minus annual outlays). This alternative measure is referred to as the *netted benefit–cost ratio, R_N*, and is expressed by

$$R_N = \frac{B - C'}{I}, \qquad I > 0 \tag{6.32}$$

The advantage of having the benefit–cost ratio defined in this manner is that it provides an index indicating the net benefit expected per dollar invested, sometimes called a *profitability index*. Again, for a project to remain under consideration, the ratio must be greater than 1. For our example, the R_N is

$$R_N = \frac{41.86 - 17.51}{14.55} = 1.674$$

Note that this is just a comparison of the present value of net revenues (F_n) with the present value of investment. Since $R_N > 1$, there is a surplus at time 0 and the project is favorable. The use of this criterion also had its origin in the evaluation of public projects in the 1930s.

Lorie–Savage Ratio. As a variation on R_N, the Lorie–Savage (*L–S*) ratio is defined as

$$L\text{-}S = \frac{B - C}{I} = \frac{B - C'}{I} - 1 = R_N - 1 > 0 \tag{6.33}$$

Here the comparison is between the surplus at time 0 and the investment itself. If the ratio is greater than 0, the project is favorable. Clearly, the R_N *B/C* and the *L–S B/C* ratios will always yield the same decision for a project, since both the ratios and their respective cutoff points differ by 1.0. For our example, *L–S* = 1.674 − 1 = 0.674 > 0. Thus the *L–S* ratio also indicates acceptance of the project.

6.4.2 Equivalence of B/C Ratios and PV

Using the notation in Section 6.4.1, we can state the *PV* criterion for project acceptance as

$$PV(i) = B - C$$
$$= B - (I + C') > 0. \tag{6.34}$$

By transposing the term ($I + C'$) to the right-hand side and dividing both sides by ($I + C'$), we have

$$\frac{B}{I + C'} > 1 \qquad (I + C' > 0)$$

which is exactly the decision rule for accepting a project with the R_A criterion. On the other hand, by transposing the term I to the right-hand side and dividing both sides of the equation by I, we obtain

$$\frac{B - C'}{I} > 1 \qquad (I > 0)$$

which is exactly the decision rule for accepting a project with the R_N criterion. In other words, use of R_A or use of R_N will lead to the same conclusion about the initial acceptability of a single project, as long as $I > 0$ and $I + C' > 0$. Notice that these B/C ratios will always agree with each other for an individual project, since I and C' are nonnegative.

$$\frac{B}{I + C'} > 1 \longleftrightarrow B > I + C' \longleftrightarrow B - C' > I$$

$$PV(i) = B - (I + C') > 0 \qquad\qquad \frac{B - C'}{I} > 1$$

$$\frac{B - C'}{I} - 1 > 0$$

Although *ARR* does not appear to be related to the benefit–cost ratios, it does, in fact, yield the same decisions for a project. From Eq. 6.18 we have

$$C_0(1 + s)^N = \sum_{n=1}^{N} F_n(1 + i)^{N-n}$$

Expressed differently,

$$I(1 + s)^N(1 + i)^{-N} = \sum_{n=1}^{N} F_n(1 + i)^{-n}$$

$$= B - C'$$

$$\frac{B - C'}{I} = \left(\frac{1 + s}{1 + i}\right)^N \qquad\qquad (6.35)$$

We require $s > i$ for project acceptance, so we must have

$$\frac{B - C'}{I} > 1$$

6.5 PAYBACK PERIOD

A popular rule-of-thumb method for evaluating projects is to determine the number of periods needed to recover the original investment. In this section we present two procedures for assessing the payback period of an investment.

6.5.1 Payback Period Defined

Conventional Payback Period. The payback period (*PP*) is defined as the number of periods it will take to recover the initial investment outlay. Mathematically, the payback period is computed as the smallest value of n that satisfies the equation

$$\sum_{n=0}^{n_p} F_n \geq 0 \tag{6.36}$$

This payback period (n_p) is then compared with the maximum acceptable payback period (n_{max}) to determine whether the project should be accepted. If $n_{max} > n_p$, the proposed project will be accepted. Otherwise, the project will be rejected.

   Obviously the most serious deficiencies of the payback period are that it fails to consider the time value of money and that it fails to consider the consequences of the investment after the payback period.

Discounted Payback Period. As a modification of the conventional payback period, one may incorporate the time value of money. The method is to determine the length of time required for the project's equivalent receipts to exceed the equivalent capital outlays.

   Mathematically, the discounted payback period Q is the smallest n that satisfies the expression

$$\sum_{n=0}^{Q} F_n(1 + i)^{-n} \geq 0 \tag{6.37}$$

where i is the *MARR*.

   If we multiply both sides of Eq. 6.37 by $(1 + i)^Q$, we should obtain

$$\sum_{n=0}^{Q} F_n(1 + i)^{Q-n} \geq 0 \tag{6.38}$$

Notice that Eq. 6.38 is the definition of project balance $PB(i)_n$. Thus, the discounted payback period is alternatively defined as the smallest n that makes $PB(i)_n \geq 0$.

6.5.2 Popularity of the Payback Period

Clearly, the payback period analysis is simple to apply and, in some cases, may give answers approximately equivalent to those provided by more sophisticated methods. A number of authors have tried to show an equivalence between the payback period and other criteria, such as *IRR*, under special circumstances [11]. For example, Gordon [8] interpreted the payback period as an indirect, though quick, measure of return. With a uniform stream of receipts, the reciprocal of the payback period is the *IRR* for a project of infinite life and is a good approximation to this rate for a long-lived project.

Weingartner [19] analyzed the basic reasons why the payback period measure is so popular in business. One reason is that the payback period can function like many other rules of thumb to shortcut the process of generating information and then evaluating it. Payback reduces the information search by focusing on the time when the firm expects to "be made whole again." Hence, it allows the decision maker to judge whether the life of the project past the break-even (bench mark) point is sufficient to make the undertaking worthwhile.

In summary, the payback period gives some measure of the rate at which a project will recover its initial outlay. This piece of information is not available from either the *PV* or the *IRR*. The payback period may not be used as a direct figure of merit, but it may be used as a constraint: no project may be accepted unless its payback period is shorter than some specified period of time.

Example 6.10

Suppose that a firm is considering a project costing \$10,000, the life of the project is 5 years, and the expected net annual cash flows at the end of the year are as follows (assume *MARR* = 10%).

Cash Flow	n: 0	1	2	3	4	5
F_n	−\$10,000	\$3,000	\$3,000	\$4,000	\$3,000	\$3,000
Cumulative F_n	−\$10,000	−7,000	−4,000	0	3,000	6,000
PV(10%)	−\$10,000	2,727	2,479	3,005	2,049	1,862
Cumulative present value	−\$10,000	−7,273	−4,794	−1,789	260	2,122

The conventional payback period is 3 years, whereas the discounted payback period is 3.87 years. This example demonstrates how consideration of the time value of money in payback analysis can produce different results. Clearly, this discounted measure is conceptually better than the conventional one, but both measures fail to indicate the overall profitability of the project. □

6.6 TIME-DEPENDENT MEASURE OF INVESTMENT WORTH

The project balance, which measures the equivalent loss or profit of an investment project as a function of time, is a recent development that provides additional insight into investment decisions. In Section 6.2.2 we defined the project balance and demonstrated its calculation both mathematically and through examples. This section presents particular characteristics of project balance profiles and their economic interpretation. We also discuss some possible measures of investment desirability based on these profiles. (The material presented in this section is based on the analysis given by Park and Thuesen [14].)

6.6.1 Areas of Negative and Positive Balances

Recall that the project balance is defined by

$$PB(i)_n = \sum_{j=0}^{n} F_j(1 + i)^{n-j}, \qquad n = 0, 1, 2, \ldots, N$$

By plotting $PB(i)_n$ as a function of time n, we can trace the time path of project balance as shown in Figure 6.9. This time path is referred to as the *project balance pattern*, and it provides the basic information about the attractiveness of a particular investment proposal as a function of its life. The shaded area represents the period of time during which the project balance has negative values, that is, the time during which the initial investment plus interest is not fully recovered. This area is referred to as the *area of negative balance (ANB)*. Mathematically, the area is represented by

$$ANB = \sum_{n=0}^{Q-1} PB(i)_n \tag{6.39}$$

where Q is the discounted payback period [the first period in which $PB(i)_n \geq 0$]. Since the value $PB(i)_n$ for $n < Q$ represents the magnitude of negative balance

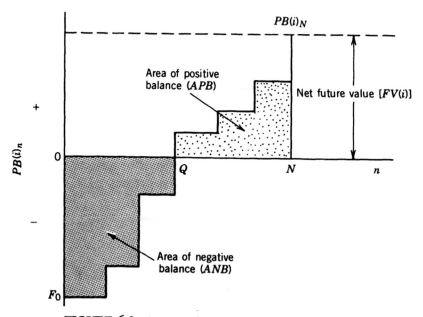

FIGURE 6.9. A general project balance diagram.

of the project at the end of period n, it is equivalent to the amount of possible loss if the project is terminated at this time. With certainty, the *ANB* can be interpreted as the total amount of dollars to be tied up for the particular investment option. The smaller the *ANB*, the more flexible the firm's future investment options. Therefore, the smaller the *ANB* for a project, the more attractive the project is considered, assuming that the expected terminal profits for other projects are the same.

Point Q on the horizontal axis in Figure 6.9 represents the discounted payback period, which indicates how long it will be before the project breaks even. Therefore, the smaller the Q for a project, the more desirable the project is considered, if other things are equal. (See the mathematical definition in Eq. 6.38.)

The stippled area in Figure 6.9 represents the period of time during which the $PB(i)_n$ maintains a positive project balance. This area is referred to as the *area of positive balance* (*APB*). The initial investment of the project has been fully recovered, so receipts during this time period contribute directly to the final profitability of the project. Symbolically, the area is represented by

$$APB = \sum_{n=Q}^{N-1} PB(i)_n \qquad (6.40)$$

The project balance diagram during these periods can be interpreted as the rate at which the project is expected to accumulate profits. This is certainly an important parameter which affects project desirability when decisions are made about the retirement of projects. Since the values $PB(i)_n$ for $n > Q$ represent the magnitude of positive project balance, there is no possible loss even though the project is terminated in a period before the end of its life or no additional receipts are received. Thus, $PB(i)_n$ becomes the net equivalent dollars earned.

Finally, the last project balance $PB(i)_N$ represents the net future value of the project (or terminal profit) at the end of its life. The *PV* of the project can be found easily by a simple transformation, shown in Eq. 6.9.

6.6.2. Investment Flexibility

To illustrate the basic concept of investment flexibility and its discriminating ability compared with the traditional measures of investment worth (e.g., *PV*), we consider the hypothetical investment situation shown in Figure 6.10a. Projects 1 and 2 have single-payment and uniform-series cash flows, respectively. Projects 3 and 4 are gradient series, one being an increasing gradient series and the other a decreasing gradient series. All the projects require the same initial investment and have a service life of 3 years. All the projects would have an equivalent future value of $63.40 at a *MARR* of 10% [or *PV*(10%) = $47.63]. This implies that no project is preferable to the others when they are compared on the basis of present value.

Plotting the project balance pattern for each project provides additional information that is not revealed by computing only present value equivalents

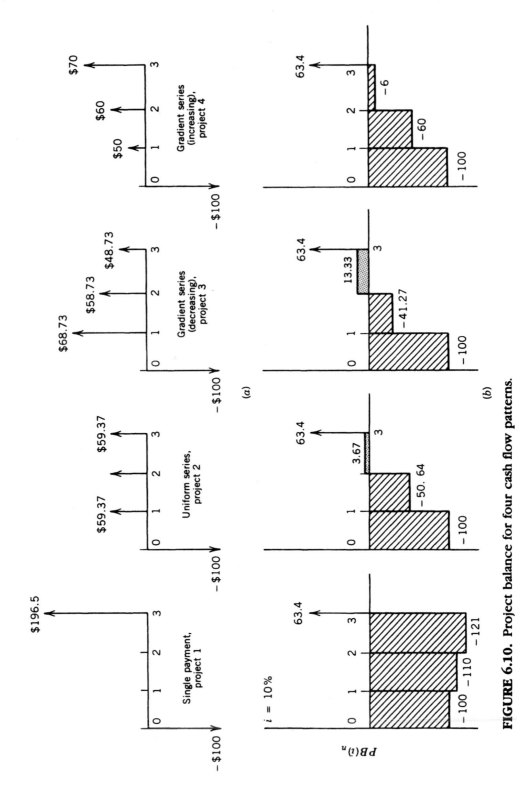

FIGURE 6.10. Project balance for four cash flow patterns.

Table 6.4 *Statistics of Project Balance Patterns for Projects 1, 2, 3, and 4*

Project Number	Cash Flow Pattern	Future Value FV(10%)	ANB	APB	Q
1	Single payment	$63.4	331.00	0	3
2	Uniform series	$63.4	150.63	3.67	2
3	Gradient series (decreasing)	$63.4	141.27	13.33	2
4	Gradient series (increasing)	$63.4	166.00	0	3

(see Figure 6.10*b*). For example, a comparison of project 1 with project 3 in terms of the shape of the project balance pattern shows that project 3 recovers its initial investment within 2 years, whereas project 1 takes 3 years to recover the same initial investment. This, in turn, indicates that project 3 would provide more flexibility in future investment activity to the firm than project 1. By selecting project 3, the investor can be sure of being restored to his or her initial position within a short span of time. Similar one-to-one comparisons can be made among all four projects. Table 6.4 summarizes the statistics obtained from the balance patterns for each project shown in Figure 6.10*b*.

Table 6.4 shows that project 3 appears to be most desirable, even though its terminal profitability is equal to those of the other projects, because its *ANB* is the smallest and its *APB* is the largest among the projects. As discussed in Section 6.6.1, the small value of *ANB* implies more flexibility in the firm's future investment activity. In other words, an early resolution of the negative project balance would make funds available for attractive investment opportunities that become

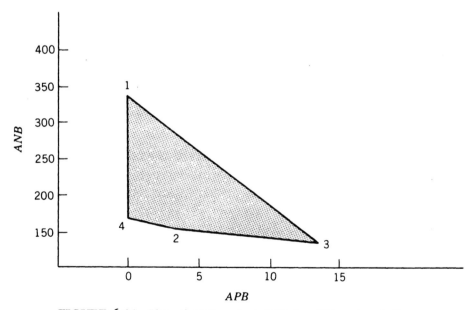

FIGURE 6.11. Plot of *APB* against *ANB* for different cash flow patterns.

available in the subsequent decision periods. One-to-one comparisons of the projects in terms of *ANB* and *APB* can be depicted graphically (see Figure 6.11). From Figure 6.9, it becomes evident that the project balance parameters such as *ANB* and *APB* reflect the changes in the cash flow patterns over time. Since project 3 represents the highest *APB* with the smallest *ANB*, project 3 appears to be the most desirable. Of course, the environment in which the decision is made and individual preferences will dictate which of these parameters should be used so that the economic implications of an investment project are fully understood.

6.7 SUMMARY

In this chapter we showed the following.

1. The *PV, FV,* and *AE* will always yield the same decision for a project. We consider *PV* as the baseline, or "correct," criterion to use in a stable, perfect capital market with complete certainty about investment outcomes.

2. The distinction between pure and mixed investments is needed to determine whether the return on invested capital is independent of the cost of capital.

3. Only for a pure investment is there a rate of return concept internal to the project. For pure investments, the *IRR* and *PV* criteria result in identical acceptance and rejection decisions.

4. The return on invested capital for a mixed project varies directly with the cost of capital. The phenomenon of multiple *IRR*s, which occurs only in the situation of a mixed investment, is actually a manifestation of the existence of this basic functional relationship. The *RIC* is consistent with the *PV* criterion.

5. *ARR* and *MIRR* will also always yield the same decision for a project, consistent with the *PV* criterion.

6. R_A, R_N, and *L–S* ratios will give the same accept–reject decisions for an individual project. The *PV* and these *B/C* ratios will always agree.

7. Neither the payback period nor the discounted payback period should be considered as a criterion, since they may not agree with *PV.* They may be used as additional constraints in the decision-making process, but they should be used with caution.

8. The project balance diagram provides quantitative information about four important characteristics associated with the economic desirability of an investment project. Two of these characteristics, net future value (terminal project balance) and discounted payback period, have generally been a part of conventional economic analyses. However, the other two characteristics, *ANB* and *APB*, have not been considered. Possible applications of the project balance indicate that a variety of measurements can be devised that reflect particular characteristics of the investment project under consideration. The project balance at the end of a project, $PB(i)_N$, is identical to the *FV* criterion.

In conclusion, we can say that the *PV* criterion is superior among the traditional measures of investment worth because of its ease of use, robustness, and consistency.

REFERENCES

1. BALDWIN, R. H., "How to Assess Investment Proposals," *Harvard Business Review*, Vol. 27, No. 3, pp. 98–104, May–June 1959.

2. BERNHARD, R. H., "Discount Methods for Expenditure Evaluation—A Clarification of Their Assumptions," *Journal of Industrial Engineering*, Vol. 18, No. 1, pp. 19–27, January–February 1962.

3. BERNHARD, R. H., "A Comprehensive Comparison and Critique of Discounting Indices Proposed for Capital Investment Evaluation," *The Engineering Economist*, Vol. 16, No. 3, pp. 157–186, Spring 1971.

4. BERNHARD, R. H., "Modified Rates of Return for Investment Project Evaluation—A Comparison and Critique," *The Engineering Economist*, Vol. 24, No. 3, pp. 161–167, Spring 1979.

5. BERNHARD, R. H., "Unrecovered Investment, Uniqueness of the Internal Rate and the Question of Project Acceptability," *Journal of Financial and Quantitative Analysis*, Vol. 12, No. 1, pp. 33–38, March 1977.

6. BUSSEY, L. E., *The Economic Analysis of Industrial Projects*, Prentice–Hall, Englewood Cliffs, N.J., 1978.

7. ECKSTEIN, O., *Water Resource Development: The Economics of Project Evaluation*, Harvard University Press, Cambridge, Mass., 1958.

8. GORDON, M., "The Payoff Period and the Rate of Profit," *Journal of Business*, Vol. 28, No. 4, pp. 253–260, October 1955.

9. KAPLAN, S., "A Note on a Method for Precisely Determining the Uniqueness or Nonuniqueness of the Internal Rate of Return for a Proposed Investment," *Journal of Industrial Engineering*, Vol. 26, No. 1, pp. 70–71, January–February 1965.

10. KAPLAN, S., "Computer Algorithms for Finding Exact Rates of Return," *Journal of Business*, Vol. 40, No. 4, pp. 389–392, October 1967.

11. LEVY, H., and M. SARNAT, *Capital Investment and Financial Decisions*, 2nd edition, Prentice–Hall, Englewood Cliffs, N.J., 1983.

12. LIN, S., "The Modified Internal Rate of Return and Investment Criterion," *The Engineering Economist*, Vol. 21, No. 4, pp. 237–248, Summer 1976.

13. MAO, J. C. T., *Quantitative Analysis of Financial Decisions*, Macmillan, Toronto, 1969.

14. PARK, C. S., and G. J. THUESEN, "Combining Concepts of Uncertainty Resolution and Project Balance for Capital Allocation Decisions," *The Engineering Economist*, Vol. 24, No. 2, pp. 109–127, Winter 1979.

15. SOLOMON, E., "The Arithmetic of Capital-Budgeting Decision," *Journal of Business*, Vol. 29, No. 2, pp. 124–129, April 1956.

16. TEICHROEW, D., A. A. ROBICHEK, and M. MONTALBANO, "Mathematical Analysis of Rates of Return under Certainty," *Management Science*, Vol. 11, No. 3, pp. 395–403, January 1965.

17. TEICHROEW, D., A. A. ROBICHEK, and M. MONTALBANO, "An Analysis of Criteria for Investment and Financing Decisions under Certainty," *Management Science*, Vol. 12, No. 3, pp. 151–179, November 1965.

18. WEINGARTNER, H. M., "The Excess Present Value Index: A Theoretical Basis and Critique," *Journal of Accounting Research*, Vol. 1, No. 2, pp. 213–224, Autumn 1963.
19. WEINGARTNER, H. M., "Some New Views on the Payback Period and Capital Budgeting Decision," *Management Science*, Vol. 15, No. 12, pp. B594–B607, August 1969.

PROBLEMS

All cash flows given in this problem set represent the cash flows after taxes, unless otherwise mentioned.

6.1. Consider the following sets of investment projects.

Project	After-Tax Cash Flows			
	$n: 0$	1	2	3
A	−$10,000	0	0	19,650
B	−$10,000	5,937	5,937	5,937
C	−$10,000	6,873	5,873	4,873
D	−$10,000	5,000	6,000	7,000

a. Compute the net present value of each project at $i = 10\%$.
b. Compute the project balance of each project as a function of the project year.
c. Compute the future value of each project at $i = 10\%$.
d. Compute the annual equivalent of each project at $i = 10\%$.

6.2. In Problem 6.1
a. Graph the net present value of each project as a function of i.
b. Graph the project balances (at $i = 10\%$) of each project as a function of n.
c. From the graphical results in part b of Problem 6.1, which project appears to be the safest to undertake if there is some possibility of premature termination of the projects at the end of year 2?

6.3. Consider the following set of independent investment projects.

Project	F_n						
	$n: 0$	1	2	3	4	5	6–20
1	−100	50	50	50	50	−750	100
2	−100	30	30	30	10	10	
3	−16	92	−170	100			

Assume $MARR(i) = 10\%$ for the following questions.
a. Compute the present value for each project and determine the acceptability of each project.
b. Compute the future value of each project at the end of each project period and determine its acceptability.
c. Compute the annual equivalent of each project and determine the acceptability of each project.
d. Compute the project value of each project at the end of 20 years with variable MARRs: 10% for $n = 0$ to $n = 10$ and 15% for $n = 11$ to $n = 20$.
e. Compute the project balance as a function of n for project 2.
f. Compute Solomon's average rate of return (*ARR*) for project 2, and determine the acceptability of the project.

g. Compute the modified internal rate of return (*MIRR*) for project 3 and determine the project's acceptability.

6.4. Consider the following project balance profiles for proposed investment projects.

Project	i	$PB(i)_0$	$PB(i)_1$	$PB(i)_2$	$PB(i)_3$	$PB(i)_4$	$PB(i)_5$
A	10%	−$1,000	−1,000	−900	−690	−359	105
B	0	−$1,000	−800	−600	−400	−200	0
C	15	−$1,000	−650	−348	−100	85	198
D	18	−$1,000	−680	−302	−57	233	575
E	20	−$1,000	−1,200	−1,440	−1,328	−1,194	−1,000
F	12.9	−$1,000	−530	−99	−211	−89	0

Project balance figures are rounded to dollars.

a. Compute the present value of each investment.
b. Determine the cash flows for each project.
c. Identify the future value of each project.
d. What would the internal rates of return be for projects B and F?

6.5. Consider the following sequence of cash flows.

Project	n: 0	1	2	3
A	−10	5	−5	20
B	100	−216	116	

a. Descartes' rule of sign indicates _____ possible rates of return for project A, but the Norstrom rule indicates _____ real root(s) because there are _____ sign change(s) in the S_n series. The rates of return is are _____.
b. For project B, determine the range of *MARR* for which the project would be acceptable.
c. Compute the *MIRR* for both projects. ($i = 6\%$)
d. Compute i_{min} for both projects and compute the return on invested capital at $k = 6\%$.

6.6. Consider the following set of investment projects.

Project	n: 0	1	2	3	4	5
1	−$10	60	−120	80		
2	−$225	100	100	100	100	
3		100	50	0	−230	
4	−$100	50	50	50	−100	600
5	−$100	300	−100	500		

a. Classify each project as either simple or nonsimple.
b. Compute the internal rate(s) of return for each project.
c. Classify each project as either a pure or a mixed investment.
d. Assuming that *MARR* = i = k = 10%, determine the acceptability of each project based on the rate-of-return principle.
e. For all mixed projects, compute the *MIRR*s.

6.7. Consider the following set of investment projects.

	After-Tax Cash Flow					
Project	n: 0	1	2	3	4	5
1	−60	70	−20	240		
2	−100	50	100			
3	−800	400	−100	400	400	−100
4	−160	920	−1,700	1,000		
5	−450	−200	700	−60	2,000	−500

  a. Compute the *PV* for each project. (i = 12%).
  b. Classify each project as either simple or nonsimple.
  c. Compute the internal rate(s) of return for each project.
  d. Classify each project as either a pure or a mixed investment.
  e. Assuming that *MARR* = i = k = 12%, determine the acceptability of each project based on the rate-of-return principle.

6.8. Consider the following set of investment projects.

	After-Tax Cash Flow				
Project	n: 0	1	2	3	4
1	−$10	−30	80	−30	
2	−$70	50	23	11	
3	−$50	25	102	−100	392
4	−$100	500	−600		
5	−$110	10	100	50	
6	−$10	60	−110	60	

  a. Classify each project as either simple or nonsimple.
  b. Compute the internal rate(s) of return for each project.
  c. Classify each project as either a pure or a mixed investment.
  d. Assuming that *MARR* = i = k = 10%, determine the acceptability of each project based on the rate-of-return principle.

6.9. Consider the following series of cash flows for an investment project.

n	0	1	2	3
F_n	−$500	1,000	3,000	−4,000

  a. Find i_{min} for this investment.
  b. Determine whether this is a mixed investment.
  c. If this is a mixed investment, derive the functional relationship between the *RIC*, r^*, and the cost of capital, k.
  d. Assume k = 10%. Determine the value of r^* and the acceptability of this investment.

6.10. Prove that $r \leq i_{min}$, in relation to the project balance.

6.11. Consider the following set of investment projects.

	After-Tax Cash Flow		
Project	n: 0	1	2
1	−$1,000	500	840
2	−$2,000	1,560	944
3	−$1,000	1,400	−100

Assume $MARR = i = 12\%$ in the following questions.
  a. Compute the internal rate of return for each project. If there is more than one rate of return, identify all the rates.
  b. Determine the acceptability of each project based on the rate-of-return principle.
6.12. Consider the projects described in Problem 6.3.
  a. Compute the rate of return (internal rate of return) for each project.
  b. Plot the present value as a function of interest rate (i) for each project.
  c. Classify each project as either simple or nonsimple. Then reclassify each project as either a pure or a mixed investment.
  d. Now determine the acceptability of each project by using the rate-of-return principle. Use $MARR(i) = 10\%$.
6.13. Consider the following investment project at $MARR = 10\%$.

Cash Flow	n: 0	1	2	3	4	5	6	7	8	9	10
b_n				100	100	200	300	300	200	100	50
c_n	$200	100	50	20	20	100	100	100	50	50	30
F_n	$-$$200	$-$100	$-$50	80	80	100	200	200	150	50	20

  a. Identify the values of N, m, B, C, I, and C'.
  b. Compute R_A, R_N, and the L–S ratio.
  c. Compute the $PV(10\%)$.
6.14. Consider the investment situation in which an investment of P dollars at $n = 0$ is followed by a series of equal annual positive payments A over N periods. If it is assumed that A dollars are recovered each year, with A being a percentage of P, the number of years required for payback can be found as a function of the rate of return of the investment. That is, knowing the relationship $A = P(A/P, i^*, N)$, or

$$A = P\left[\frac{i^*(1 + i^*)^N}{(1 + i^*)^N - 1}\right]$$

we can rewrite the relationship as

$$i^* = \frac{A}{P} - \frac{A}{P}\left(\frac{1}{1 + i^*}\right)^N$$

Note that A/P is the payback reciprocal, $R_p = 1/n_p$. Rearranging terms yields

$$R_p = \frac{i^*}{1 - (1 + i^*)^{-N}}$$

This relationship provides a convenient equation for carrying out a numerical analysis of the general relation between the payback reciprocal and the internal rate of return.
  a. Develop a chart that estimates the internal rate of return of a project as a function of payback reciprocal.
  b. Consider a project that requires an initial investment of $1,000 and has annual receipts of $500 for 5 years. This project has a payback period of 2 years, giving $R_p = 0.5$. Verify that the project has the internal rate of return of 41.04% from the chart developed in part a.
6.15. Johnson Chemical Company is considering investing in a new composite material processing project after a 3-year period of research and process development.

R&D cost: $3 million over a 3-year period, with an annual R&D growth rate of 50%/year ($0.63 million at the beginning of year 1, $0.95 million at the beginning of year 2, and $1.42 million at the beginning of year 3). These R&D expenditures will be expensed rather than amortized for tax purposes.

Capital investment: $5 million at the beginning of year 4, depreciated over a 7-year period using MACRS percentages.

Process life: 10 years.

Salvage value: 10% of initial capital investment at the end of year 10.

Total sales: $100 million (at the end of year 4) with a sales growth rate of 10%/year (compound growth) during the first 6 years and −10% (negative compound growth)/year for the remaining process life.

Out-of-pocket expenditures: 80% of annual sales.

Working capital: 10% of annual sales (considered as an investment at the beginning of each year and recovered fully at the end of year 10)

Marginal tax rate: 40%.

Minimum attractive rate of return (MARR): 18%.

a. Compute the net present value of this investment and determine whether the project should be pursued.
b. Compute the rate of return on this investment.
c. Compute the benefit–cost ratio for this investment.
d. Compute the annual equivalent for this project.

7

Decision Rules for Selecting among Multiple Alternatives

7.1. INTRODUCTION

In the previous chapter we presented ten different criteria for measuring the investment worth of an individual project. For an individual project all ten criteria yield consistent answers for the accept–reject decision. Which one to use is therefore a question of convenience and habit. When we *compare* projects, however, the situation is quite different. Naive or improper application of various criteria can lead to conflicting results. Fortunately, the *proper use of any of the ten criteria will always result in decisions consistent with PV analysis, which we consider the baseline, or "correct," criterion.*

In Section 7.2 we present some preliminary steps that must be taken before analysis can begin: formulating mutually exclusive alternatives and ordering them. Section 7.3 is the main part of the chapter, and here we present the criteria and decision rules for comparing alternatives. In Section 7.4 we examine some of the more detailed aspects of the "assumptions" behind the decision criteria and consider other writings on the subject. Section 7.5 treats the subject of unequal lives, which becomes important in service projects; benefits of service projects are unknown or not measured. Finally, there is a brief discussion of investment timing in Section 7.6.

As in Chapter 6, we assume that the *MARR* is known and that we operate in a stable, perfect capital market with complete certainty about the outcome of investments. The firm can therefore borrow funds at the *MARR* and invest any excess funds at the same rate. The firm's ability to borrow may be *limited,* however, which differs from the situation assumed in Chapter 6.

7.2. FORMULATING MUTUALLY EXCLUSIVE ALTERNATIVES

We need to distinguish between projects that are independent of one another and those that are dependent. We say that two or more projects are *independent* if the accept–reject decision of one has no influence, except for a possible budgetary reason, on the accept–reject decision of any of the others. We call this a *set of independent projects*. Typical examples are projects that derive revenues from different markets and require different technical resources.

Two or more projects are *mutually exclusive* if the acceptance of any one precludes the acceptance of any of the others. We call this a *set of mutually exclusive projects*. An example is a set of projects, each of which requires full-time use of a single, special-purpose machine. If we select a particular project, the machine becomes unavailable for any other use.

Two projects are *dependent* if the acceptance of one requires the acceptance of another. For example, the decision to add container ship dock facilities in an existing harbor may require a decision to increase the depth of the harbor channel. The container ship dock project is dependent on the channel project. Notice that the channel project does *not* depend on the dock project, however, since an increase in channel depth can benefit the conventional docks. If the channel project also depended on the container dock project, we would combine the two into one project.

Before applying any investment criterion to selecting among projects, we follow this procedure.

1. Reject any individual project that fails to meet the criterion acceptance test, *unless* some other project that passes the test depends on it. This step is not absolutely necessary, but it speeds later computations.
2. Form all possible, feasible *combinations* with the remaining projects. We call this step formulating mutually exclusive alternatives.
3. *Order* the alternatives formed in step 2, usually, but not always, by the investment required at time 0, c_0. If there is an overall budget limit, we may at this step eliminate any alternatives that exceed the limit.

Example 7.1

A chemical company is considering the manufacture of two products, A and B. The market demand for each of these products is independent of the demand for the other. Product A may be produced by either process x or process y, and product B by either process y or process z. It is inefficient to use more than one process to manufacture a particular product, and no process may be used to manufacture more than one product. *Formulate* all mutually exclusive investment alternatives. Table 7.1 presents the eight alternatives. The first one is the *do-nothing* alternative, which should always be included. We then list all alternatives that consist of a single product for manufacture, followed by all feasible combinations of two products. Since Ay and By are inherently mutually exclusive, we do not consider the combination. Nor do we consider combinations such as Ax, Ay, since they are mutually exclusive according to the problem statement. □

Table 7.1 *Mutually Exclusive Investment Alternatives, Example 7.1*

Alternative	Product–Process Combinations Included
1	None
2	Ax
3	Ay
4	By
5	Bz
6	Ax, By
7	Ax, Bz
8	Ay, Bz

Example 7.2

A marketing manager is evaluating strategies for three market areas, A, B, and C. The strategy selected in any one area is independent of that in any other area. Only one strategy is to be selected for each area. There are two strategies for A, 1 and 2; three for B, 1, 2, and 3; and three for C, 1, 2, and 3. Strategy 1 for any area is a do-nothing strategy. *Formulate* all mutually exclusive investment alternatives. Table 7.2 presents the $(2)(3)(3) = 18$ alternatives.   □

After formulating all possible, feasible combinations, we *treat* them as a set of mutually exclusive alternatives. The cash flow for any alternative is simply the sum of the cash flows of the included projects. Since we consider all possible, feasible combinations, we must obtain the optimal combination. The reason for defining mutually exclusive alternatives is related to the properties of an invest-

Table 7.2 *Mutually Exclusive Investment Alternatives, Example 7.2*

Alternative	Strategy Selected for Each Market Area			Alternative	Strategy Selected for Each Market Area		
	A	B	C		A	B	C
1	1	1	1	10	2	1	1
2	1	1	2	11	2	1	2
3	1	1	3	12	2	1	3
4	1	2	1	13	2	2	1
5	1	2	2	14	2	2	2
6	1	2	3	15	2	2	3
7	1	3	1	16	2	3	1
8	1	3	2	17	2	3	2
9	1	3	3	18	2	3	3

ment worth criterion. If we are considering the projects as wholly or partially independent, can we be sure our criterion will always lead to the best combination, no matter which project we examine first? With mutually exclusive alternatives we avoid this type of problem, because we have specific rules for ordering the alternatives before applying the investment worth criterion.

The *ordering* of the alternatives depends on which criterion is to be applied. There are four classifications.

1. Time 0 investment, c_0: order the alternatives by increasing c_0. Applies to PV, FV, AE, PB, and ARR.

2. I, the $PV(i)$ of initial investments $c_0, c_1, ..., c_m$: order by increasing I. Here i is the MARR. Applies to R_N and L–S.

3. C, the $PV(i)$ of all expenditures, consisting of initial investment plus annual expenses: order by increasing C. Again, i is the MARR. Applies to R_A and MIRR.

4. $PV(0\%)$ of all cash flows: order by increasing $PV(0\%)$. When there are ties, order by increasing first derivative of $PV(0\%)$. Applies to IRR and RIC.

These ordering rules are designed to facilitate the application of the criteria, as shown in the next section. They are not the only rules. For example, *any* ordering rule will work with PV, FV, AE, and PB. In addition, we can sometimes use ordering rule 1, based on c_0, with the other criteria, provided we modify the decision rules. These modifications often result in cumbersome variations and thus are usually avoided.

7.3 APPLICATION OF INVESTMENT WORTH CRITERIA

7.3.1 Total Investment Approach

This approach applies the investment criterion separately to each mutually exclusive alternative. Example 7.3 illustrates the approach.

Example 7.3

Two mutually exclusive alternatives, j and k, are being considered as shown in Table 7.3. Apply the various criteria to each alternative, using MARR = 10%. The results are shown in the lower part of Table 7.3. (The derivation of the results in the table is left as an exercise; see Problem 7.3.) □

Opposite Ranking Phenomenon.   Four of the criteria seem to indicate that alternative k is the better choice, whereas the other six give numerically higher ratings for j. We have here an example of the *opposite ranking phenomenon*. The cause of the discrepancy is that some of the criteria are *relative* measures of investment worth and others are *absolute* measures. The resolution of this conflict, for the situation of perfect capital markets and complete certainty, is given by the *incremental approach* in Section 7.3.2.

416

Table 7.3 *Total Investment Approach, Example 7.3*

Time	Alternative j			Alternative k		
	Outflow	Inflow	Net Flow	Outflow	Inflow	Net Flow
0	$1,000	0	−$1,000	$2,000	0	−$2,000
1	2,000	2,475	475	5,000	5,915	915
2	1,000	1,475	475	6,000	6,915	915
3	500	975	475	7,000	7,915	915

Criterion*	Value for j	Value for k	Alternative with Larger Value
PV	$181	$275	k
FV	$241	$367	k
AE	$ 73	$111	k
PB_N	$242	$367	k
IRR	20%	18%	j
ARR	16%	15%	j
MIRR	12%	11%	j
R_A	1.045	1.016	j
R_N	1.182	1.138	j
L–S	0.182	0.138	j

*i = 10% for all criteria.

At this point, we argue that *when we apply the total investment approach,* the *PV, FV, AE,* and *PB_N* give the *correct answer.* This is so because maximizing these criteria maximizes the future wealth of the firm. This point is proved in detail in Section 7.4.1. Before we resolve the discrepancies between *PV* and the other criteria, some special cases are considered.

Consistency Within Groups. The consistency within groups of the criteria is not coincidence but rather a fundamental characteristic. If the lifetimes of all alternatives are the same and −100% < *i*, it is easy to show that the following groups will always show internal consistency in ranking mutually exclusive alternatives.

PV, FV, AE and PB_N. The four criteria, *PV, FV, AE,* and *PB,* will always agree among themselves.
If

$$PV(i)_j < PV(i)_k$$

then

$$(F/P, i, N)PV(i)_j < (F/P, i, N)PV(i)_k$$

and

$$FV(i)_j < FV(i)_k$$

In addition,

$$(A/P, i, N)PV(i)_j < (A/P, i, N)PV(i)_k$$

and

$$AE(i)_j < AE(i)_k \qquad (7.1)$$

The $PB_N(i)$ is the same as $FV(i)$, so we complete the proof.

These criteria measure the surplus in an investment alternative over and above investment of $i = MARR$. It does not matter when we measure the surplus in comparing alternatives—at time 0, at time N, or spread equally over the life of the alternative. If one alternative has a greater time 0 surplus than another, its time N surplus will also be greater, and so forth. The surplus is measured in dollars (or other currency unit), and hence these criteria are *absolute* measures of investment worth. This argument again reinforces the *correctness of using PV, FV, AE, and PB_N with the total investment approach*.

For example, the addition of alternative m to j, where $PV(10\%)_m$ equals 0, does not change the PV measure of j:

Net Cash Flow	n: 0	1	2	3	PV(10%)
Alternative m	$-\$5,000$	0	0	6,655	0
Alternative j	$-\$1,000$	475	475	475	181
Alternative $j + m$	$-\$6,000$	475	475	7,130	181

R_N, L–S, and ARR. The Lorrie–Savage ratio L–S is simply the netted benefit–cost ratio minus one, or L–$S = R_N - 1$, so we need only compare Solomon's average rate of return, ARR, with R_N. In addition to equal lifetimes and $-100\% < i$, we assume the initial investment occurs only at time 0 (other outlays are annual operating expenses). Then $I = c_0$, and $R_N = (B - C')/c_0$. Assume

$$R_{Nj} > R_{Nk}$$

Then

$$\frac{B_j - C'_j}{c_{0j}} > \frac{B_k - C'_k}{c_{0k}}$$

or

$$\sum_{n=1}^{N} \frac{F_{nj}(1 + i)^{-n}}{c_{0j}} > \sum_{n=1}^{N} \frac{F_{nj}(1 + i)^{-n}}{c_{0k}}$$

where F_{nj} is the net cash flow for alternative j at the end of period n. In addition,

$$\sum_{n=1}^{N} \frac{F_{nj}(1 + i)^{N-n}}{c_{0j}} > \sum_{n=1}^{N} \frac{F_{nk}(1 + i)^{N-n}}{c_{0k}}$$

418

Substituting from Eq. 6.18, we have

$$(1 + s_j)^N > (1 + s_k)^N$$

and

$$s_j > s_k \qquad (7.2)$$

If the initial investment extends beyond time 0, the result need not hold (see Problem 7.16 at the end of the chapter).

R_A, MIRR. The aggregate benefit–cost ratio, R_A, and the modified internal rate of return as defined by Eq. 6.23, MIRR, will always agree. Assume

$$R_{Aj} > R_{Ak}$$

or

$$\frac{B_j}{I_j + C_j'} > \frac{B_k}{I_k + C_k'}$$

From the definitions of B, I, and C', Eqs. 6.1, 6.29, and 6.30, we substitute and obtain

$$\frac{\sum_{n=0}^{N} b_{nj}(1 + i)^{-n}}{\sum_{n=0}^{N} c_{nj}(1 + i)^{-n}} > \frac{\sum_{n=0}^{N} b_{nk}(1 + i)^{-n}}{\sum_{n=0}^{N} c_{nk}(1 + i)^{-n}}$$

Then

$$\frac{\sum_{n=0}^{N} b_{nj}(1 + i)^{N-n}}{\sum_{n=0}^{N} c_{nj}(1 + i)^{N-n}} > \frac{\sum_{n=0}^{N} b_{nk}(1 + i)^{N-n}}{\sum_{n=0}^{N} c_{nk}(1 + i)^{N-n}}$$

Using Eq. 6.23, we obtain

$$(1 + MIRR_j)^N > (1 + MIRR_k)^N$$

$$MIRR_j > MIRR_k \qquad (7.3)$$

IRR. The internal rate of return, IRR, or return on invested capital, RIC, for mixed investments does not necessarily agree with any of the other criteria.

Special Cases. In some special cases there will be agreement across some of the groups [2]. If each alternative has the same initial investment, the PV and R_N groups will give consistent rankings. If each alternative has a constant net cash flow during its lifetime, IRR (or RIC) will agree with the R_N group.

Modification of Criteria To Include Unspent Budget Amounts. Some authors advocate a modification of the investment criteria to include the effects of left-over funds [8,12]. Applying this concept to alternatives j and k with IRR, we would add to alternative j an additional investment of $1,000 earning interest at MARR = 10% and returning $1,000(A/P, 10\%, 3) = \$402$ each year. The argument is that we have $2,000 to invest at time 0; otherwise we would not consider alternative k. The augmented cash flow, designated by some as a *total cash flow*, becomes for alternative j

Time	Original Net Flow, Alternative j	Unspent 1,000 Earning 10%	Total Flow
0	−$1,000	−$1,000	−$2,000
1	475	402	877
2	475	402	877
3	475	402	877

The IRR for the total flow is 15%, which is less than the 18% for k. Thus, IRR, applied to the total cash flow, agrees with PV. Notice that this agreement between the criteria can be derived from the special cases just mentioned.

A similar approach has been proposed for benefit–cost ratios [8]. The extent to which the total cash flow approach ensures consistent ranking by the various criteria does not appear to have been fully examined. (See Problem 7.20 at the end of the chapter.) The following example illustrates opposite ranking with the same initial investment.

Example 7.4

Relevant summary data for alternatives p and q are given below. Evaluate the alternatives by using R_A and R_N. Here I is assumed to be c_0.

Item	Alternative p	Alternative q
Time 0 investment, c_0	$100	$100
PV of annual expenses, C'	10	0
PV of annual receipts, B	220	205

Computing R_A and R_N, we have

Ratio	Alternative p	Alternative q
R_A	2.00	2.05
R_N	2.10	2.05 □

420

In Example 7.4 alternative p has a smaller R_A value but a larger R_N value. Since the classification of a cash flow element as a user benefit or a sponsor cost is often arbitrary, the use of a total cash flow approach is questionable.

7.3.2 Incremental Analysis

Investment alternatives can have opposite ranking because some criteria are *relative* measures of investment worth. The resolution of the discrepancy requires incremental analysis. The general approach is as follows.

1. *Order* the investment alternatives by the ordering rule specified for the criterion in Section 7.2.
2. Apply the criterion to the cash flow of the first alternative.
3. a. If the criterion value is favorable, go to step 4.
   b. If the criterion value is unfavorable, select the next alternative in order. Continue until an alternative with a favorable criterion value is obtained. (If none is obtained, reject all alternatives.) Go to step 4.
4. Apply the criterion to the cash flow *difference* between the next alternative in order and the one most recently evaluated favorably.
5. Repeat step 4 until no more alternatives exist. Accept the last alternative for which the cash flow difference was evaluated favorably.

See Example 7.6 at the end of Section 7.3 for a comprehensive application of these rules.

Irrelevance of Ordering for PV, FV, AE, and PB_N. The ordering rule for criteria PV, FV, AE, and PB_N is by increasing time 0 investment, c_0. This rule is based on convention but is not required. For these four *absolute* measures of investment worth, the *ordering is irrelevant; furthermore, the incremental analysis always agrees with the total investment approach, which is optimal for perfect capital markets and complete certainty.*
If

$$PV(i)_j < PV(i)_k$$

then

$$PV(i)_{k-j} > 0 \tag{7.4}$$

by the definition of *PV* and the distributive rule of multiplication. In addition,

$$PV(i)_{k-j} = -PV(i)_{j-k} \tag{7.5}$$

and since the other three criteria always agree with *PV*, the ordering of alternatives is irrelevant for this group.

Applying these rules to Example 7.3, we obtain the ordering based on c_0: j, k. We have $PV(10\%)_j = \$181$, which is favorable.

We than examine the cash flow difference between k and j.

| n | Net Flow | | |
	Alt. j	Alt. k	$k - j$
0	$-\$1,000$	$-\$2,000$	$-\$1,000$
1	475	915	440
2	475	915	440
3	475	915	440

We have

$$PV(10\%)_{k-j} = -1,000 + 440 \overset{P/A,\ 10\%,\ 3}{(2.4869)} = \$94$$

There are no more alternatives, and we accept k, the last one for which the cash flow difference was evaluated favorably.

If we had started with the larger time 0 investment, we would have evaluated k and found it favorable with a PV of $275. The cash flow difference between j and k is

n	0	1	2	3
$j - k$, Cash Flow	$1,000	-440	-440	-440

The $PV(10\%)_{j-k} = -\$94$, and we again accept k.

Agreement on Increments Between PV and Other Criteria. Let us compare with PV any *one* of the other criteria, from the set IRR (or RIC), ARR, $MIRR$, R_A, R_N, L–S. We will use the ordering rule for the other criterion, since we just showed that for PV the ordering is irrelevant. The ordering rules are designed so that each increment appears to be an investment when evaluated by the criterion, as

Table 7.4 *Incremental Analysis, Example 7.3*

Criterion	Value for j	Favorable?	Next Increment	Value for Increment	Favorable?	Final Choice
PV	$181	Yes	$k-j$	$94	Yes	k
FV	$241	Yes	$k-j$	$125*	Yes	k
AE	$73	Yes	$k-j$	$38	Yes	k
PB_N	$242	Yes	$k-j$	$125	Yes	k
IRR	20%	Yes	$k-j$	15%	Yes	k
ARR	16%	Yes	$k-j$	14%	Yes	k
$MIRR$	12%	Yes	$k-j$	10.3%	Yes	k
R_A	1.045	Yes	$k-j$	1.007	Yes	k
R_N	1.182	Yes	$k-j$	1.093	Yes	k
L–S	0.182	Yes	$k-j$	0.093	Yes	k

*Values do not add to 367 because of rounding.

opposed to a loan, for example. Examining each increment by both criteria will yield the *identical sequence of accept–reject decisions,* because the other criterion *always agrees with PV for an individual project, or cash flow,* as shown in Chapter 6. Therefore, using *incremental analysis with any of the ten criteria will result in optimal decisions.* Some of the ordering rules may give different *sequences* of increments, but since each criterion agrees step by step with *PV,* and since *PV* is indifferent to ordering, the *final decisions will be the same.*

Table 7.4 contains the relevant data for all ten criteria as applied to Example 7.3. For each the ordering is *j, k.* Again, the derivation of table entries is left as an exercise; see Problem 7.4.

Alternative Derivations. In this section we provide some alternative algebraic derivations to show the correctness of incremental analysis. Space limits prevent us from presenting all of them, and some are left as chapter problems. These proofs also illustrate the logic behind the ordering rules.

R_N. If

$$R_{N,k-j} > 1$$

then

$$(B_{k-j} - C'_{k-j})/I_{k-j} > 1$$

and

$$B_{k-j} - C'_{k-j} > I_{k-j}$$

Since

$$I_{k-j} > 0 \quad \text{by the ordering rule,}$$
$$B_k - C'_k - I_k > B_j - C'_j - I_j$$

or

$$PV_k > PV_j \tag{7.6}$$

We can also reverse the step sequence. Thus, the netted benefit–cost ratio, when used with incremental analysis, always agrees with *PV.*

R_A. If

$$R_{A,k-j} > 1$$

then

$$B_{k-j}/C_{k-j} > 1$$

and

$$B_{k-j} > C_{k-j}$$

Since

$$C_{k-j} > 0 \quad \text{by the ordering rule}$$

$$B_k - C_k > B_j - C_j$$

or

$$PV_k > PV_j \tag{7.7}$$

Detailed Rules for IRR. Many practitioners apply *IRR* by using incremental analysis and ordering based on time 0 investment, c_0. Most of the time this presents no difficulties. Figure 7.1 shows the *PV* functions of the two alternatives j and k in Example 7.3. The ordering of alternatives by c_0 is first j, then k. If *MARR* $= i_1$, then $i_j^* > MARR$, so alternative j is favorable. The difference cash flow ($k - j$) has an *IRR* of $i_F > MARR$, so we accept k. (We call the *IRR* i_F for Fisher's intersection, described in Section 7.4.) From the graph in Figure 7.1, it is clear that $PV(i_1)_k > PV(i_1)_j$, so we are consistent with *PV*. If *MARR* $= i_2$, then again $i_j^* > MARR$. But the *IRR* for ($k - j$) is less than *MARR*, so our final choice is alternative j. Again, we have consistency with *PV*, since $PV(i_2)_k < PV(i_2)_j$.

But what if the ordering is first k, then j, and the *PV* functions are similar to those in Figure 7.1? The next example illustrates this situation.

Example 7.5

Compare the following two alternatives by using *IRR* with incremental analysis based on ordering by c_0, with *MARR* $= 10\%$.

n	Net Flow		
	Alt. w	Alt. j	$j - w$
0	$-\$900$	$-\$1,000$	$-\$100$
1	-350	475	825
2	915	475	-440
3	915	475	-440

The ordering by c_0 is first w, then j.

Examining w, we have $i_w^* = 19\% > 10\%$, so it is favorable. The difference cash flow has multiple sign changes, so multiple roots are possible. However, in the range 0 to 100% there is only one *IRR*: 16%. This value exceeds *MARR*, so we would accept j. However, $PV(10\%)_j = 181$, which is *less* than $PV(10\%)_w = 225$!

The explanation is that the cash flow difference ($j - w$) represents a borrowing activity, despite the negative time 0 flow. The *PV* function for ($j - w$) begins negative (which is characteristic of borrowing activities), crosses the horizontal axis near 16%, and then continues upward. The other root is at $i = 660\%$. (Applying *RIC*, we obtain $r_{j-w}^* = -38.64\%$ at $k = i = 10\%$, so we accept w.)

i	0	10	16	20	50	100	200	500	660	700
$PV(i)_{j-w}$	-155	-44	2	27	124	148	110	23	0	-5

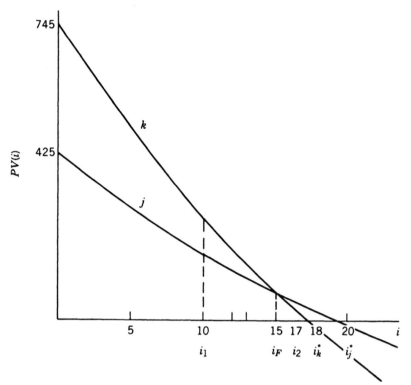

FIGURE 7.1. *IRR* for cash flow difference ($k - j$), Example 7.3.

From this example, it is clear that *ordering by c_0 for IRR* can lead to *incorrect results*.

Various other circumstances can cause problems for the practitioner accustomed to ordering by c_0. These include the situations in which the time 0 investment is the same for two alternatives. To remedy these difficulties, Wohl has recently developed a set of strict rules for applying *IRR* with incremental analysis [1, 13]. These rules result in complete consistency with *PV*.

For many applications the ordering rule based on *PV*(0%) clears up any inconsistencies between *IRR* and *PV*. When there are multiple roots, the *IRR* criterion can be replaced by return on invested capital, *RIC*. Multiple roots inevitably cause more computational work, whether we use *RIC*, the strict rules for *IRR* that require obtaining all roots, or plotting of the *PV* function. Plotting the *PV* function need be neither difficult nor time-consuming, and the plot contains at least as much information as is obtained by the other methods. In essence, we have argued for use of the *PV* criterion.

Example 7.6

We end this section with a comprehensive example that demonstrates the incremental analysis technique for several of the criteria. Three independent projects, A, B, and C, are to be evaluated by using *PV*, R_N, R_A, and *IRR*, with *MARR* = 10%. (Note that each of the four groups is represented.) There is a time 0 expenditure budget of $4,000. The cash flows for the three projects are given in the upper left portion of Table 7.5. Select the best project or projects.

Table 7.5 *Preliminary Data for Example 7.6*

Alternative: Project:	1 A	2 B	3 C	4 A + B	5 A + C	6 B + C
Outflows, $n = 0$	$1,000	900	3,000	1,900	4,000	3,900
1	$2,000	1,265	5,000	3,265	7,000	6,265
2	$1,000	6,000	5,000	7,000	6,000	11,000
3	$500	7,000	5,000	7,500	5,500	12,000
Inflows, $n = 0$	$0	0	0	0	0	0
1	$2,475	915	6,336	3,390	8,811	7,251
2	$1,475	6,915	6,336	8,390	7,811	13,251
3	$975	7,915	6,336	8,890	7,311	14,251
Net flows, $n = 0$	$-$1,000	$-900	$-3,000	$-1,900	$-4,000	$-3,900
1	$475	$-350	1,336	125	1,811	986
2	$475	915	1,336	1,390	1,811	2,251
3	$475	915	1,336	1,390	1,811	2,251
c_0	$1,000	900	3,000	1,900	4,000	3,900
m	0	2	0	0,2	0	2,0
$I(10\%)$	$1,000	7,009	3,000	8,009	4,000	10,009
$C'(10\%)$	$3,020	5,259	12,434	8,279	15,455	17,693
$C(10\%)$	$4,020	12,268	15,434	16,288	19,455	27,702
$PV(0\%)$	$425	580	1,008	1,005	1,433	1,588
$B(10\%)$	$4,202	12,493	15,757	16,695	19,958	28,250
$PV(10\%)$	$181	225	322	407	504	548
R_N	1.182	1.032	1.108	NA	NA	NA
R_A	1.045	1.018	1.021	NA	NA	NA
IRR, %	20.0	18.8	16.0	NA	NA	NA

NOTE: m is the period of the initial investments $c_0, c_1, ..., c_m$.

Preliminary screening. The lower left portion of Table 7.5 shows the relevant data for screening the projects individually. Each of the three projects, A, B, and C, is acceptable by each of the four criteria, PV, R_N, R_A, and IRR, using $MARR = 10\%$. (We expected the agreement on the individual projects by the criteria.)

Form investment alternatives. Since we know that the budget is $4,000 and that A, B, and C are independent, we can form three combinations: (A + B), (A + C), and (B + C). We thus have six investment alternatives (in addition to the do-nothing alternative). For the three alternatives composed of combinations of projects, the cash flows are shown in the upper right portion of Table 7.5, and the data needed for applying the criteria are shown in the lower right.

Order the alternatives. Here we apply the ordering rules specified in Section 7.2.

For PV, order by c_0:   alternatives 2, 1, 4, 3, 6, 5.
For R_N, order by I: alternatives 1, 3, 5, 2, 4, 6.

For R_A, order by C: alternatives 1, 2, 3, 4, 5, 6.

For *IRR*, order by *PV*(0%): alternatives 1, 2, 4, 3, 5, 6.

We are now ready to apply the incremental method with the four criteria.

PV(10%)

Alt. 2 vs. do nothing, or B vs. do nothing: $PV(10\%)_{2-0} = \$225 > 0$, so alt. 2 is *favorable*.

Alt. 1 vs. alt. 2, or A vs. B: $PV(10\%)_{1-2} = -\$44 < 0$, so alt. 1 is *not* favored over alt. 2. Note that we are using the relation $PV(i)_{x-y} = PV(i)_x - PV(i)_y$ to save ourselves some work. The cash flow difference $(1 - 2)$ is the same as $(A - B)$.

Alt. 4 vs. alt. 2, or $(A + B)$ vs. A: $PV(10\%)_{4-2} = \$182 > 0$, so alt. 4 is *favored* over alt. 2. Note that the difference $(4 - 2)$ is just the cash flow for A.

Alt. 3 vs. alt. 4, or C vs. $(A + B)$: $PV(10\%)_{3-4} = -\$85 < 0$, so alt. 3 is *not* favored over 4.

Alt. 6 vs. alt. 4, or $(B + C)$ vs. $(A + B)$: $PV(10\%)_{6-4} = \$141 > 0$, so alt. 6 is *favored* over alt. 4. The difference $(6 - 4)$ is the same as $(C - B)$.

Alt. 5 vs. alt. 6, or $(A + C)$ vs. $(B + C)$: $PV(10\%)_{5-6} = -\$44 < 0$, so alt. 5 is *not* favored over alt. 6. The difference $(5 - 6)$ is the same as $(A - B)$, which was evaluated earlier.

The last alternative favorably evaluated is 6, so we accept projects B and C with a total *PV* of *\$548*.

R_N, the netted benefit–cost ratio

Alt. 1 vs. do nothing, or A vs. do nothing: $R_{N,1-0} = 1.182 > 1$, so alt. 1 is *favorable*.

Alt. 3 vs. alt. 1, or C vs. A:

$$R_{N,3-1} = \frac{(\$15,757 - 4,202) - (\$12,434 - 3,020)}{\$3,000 - 1,000} = 1.071 > 1$$

so alt. 3 is *favored* over alt. 1.

Alt. 5 vs. alt. 3, or $(A + C)$ vs. C: The difference $(5 - 3)$ is the same as the cash flow for A. So $R_{N,5-3} = 1.182 > 1$, and alt. 5 is *favored* over alt. 3.

Alt. 2 vs. alt. 5, or B vs. $(A + C)$:

$$R_{N,2-5} = \frac{(\$12,493 - 19,958) - (\$5,259 - 15,455)}{\$7,009 - 4,000} = 0.908 < 1$$

so alt. 2 is *not* favored over alt. 5.

Alt. 4 vs. alt. 5, or $(A + B)$ vs. $(A + C)$:

$$R_{N,4-5} = \frac{(\$16,695 - 19,958) - (\$8,279 - 15,455)}{\$8,009 - 4,000} = 0.976 < 1$$

so alt. 4 is *not* favored over 5. The difference $(4 - 5)$ is the same as $(B - C)$.

Alt. 6 vs. alt. 5, or $(B + C)$ vs. $(A + C)$:

$$R_{N, 6-5} = \frac{(\$28,250 - 19,958) - (\$17,693 - 15,455)}{\$10,009 - 4,000} = 1.007 > 1$$

so alt. 6 is *favored* over alt. 5. The difference $(6 - 5)$ is the same as $(B - A)$.

We accept projects B and C, which constitute alternative 6, the last one favorably accepted. This decision agrees with *PV* analysis, as expected.

R_A, The aggregate benefit–cost ratio

Alt. 1 vs. do nothing, or A vs. do nothing: $R_{A, 1-0} = 1.045 > 1$, so alt. 1 is *favorable*.

Alt. 2 vs. alt. 1, or B vs. A:

$$R_{A, 2-1} = \frac{\$12,493 - 4,202}{\$12,268 - 4,020} = 1.005 > 1$$

so alt. 2 is *favored* over alt. 1.

Alt. 3 vs. alt. 2, or C vs. B:

$$R_{A, 3-2} = \frac{\$15,757 - 12,493}{\$15,434 - 12,268} = 1.031 > 1$$

so alt. 3 is *favored* over alt. 2.

Alt. 4 vs. alt. 3, or $(A + B)$ vs. C:

$$R_{A, 4-3} = \frac{\$16,695 - 15,757}{\$16,288 - 15,434} = 1.098 > 1$$

so alt. 4 is *favored* over alt. 3.

Alt. 5 vs. alt. 4, or $(A + C)$ vs. $(A + B)$: The difference $(5 - 4)$ is the same as $(C - B)$, which was evaluated in the comparison of alt. 3 vs. alt. 2. So $R_{A, 5-4} = 1.031 > 1$, and alt. 5 is *favored* over alt. 4.

Alt. 6 vs. alt. 5, or $(B + C)$ vs. $(A + C)$: The difference $(6 - 5)$ is the same as $(B - A)$, which was evaluated in the comparison of alt. 2 vs. alt. 1. So $R_{A, 6-5} = 1.005 > 1$, and alt. 6 is *favored* over alt. 5.

Again, our final selection is alternative 6, or projects B and C.

IRR, internal rate of return, and *RIC*, return on invested capital

Alt. 1 vs. do nothing, or A vs. do nothing: $i^*_{1-0} = 20.0\% > 10\%$, so alt. 1 is *favorable*.

Alt. 2 vs. alt. 1, or B vs. A: The difference cash flow is $+\$100, -825, +440, +440$. The multiple sign changes suggest two roots, and if we refer to

Example 7.5, we see that the roots are 16% and 660%. Applying *RIC*, we obtain $r^* = 15.03\%$, so alt. 2 is *favored* over alt. 1.

As an alternative, consider a more fundamental approach to the analysis of the cash flow for alt. 2 vs. alt. 1. In Example 7.5 the opposite cash flow, that is, $-\$100, +825, -440, -440$, was determined to be a borrowing activity. The cash flow $+100, -825, +440, +440$ is an investment activity, despite the initial inflow.

i	0	10	16	20	50	100
$PV(i)_{2-1}$	$\$155$	44	-2	-27	-124	-148

Notice that our decision here to accept the cash flow $+\$100, -825, +440, +440$ using $i = 10\%$ is consistent with the decision in Example 7.5 to reject the opposite cash flow using $i = 10\%$. With i^*_{2-1} near 16% > 10%, alt. 2 is *favored* over alt. 1.

Alt. 4 vs. alt. 2, or (A + B) vs. B: The difference cash flow is just that for A. So $i^*_{2-1} = 20.0\% > 10\%$, and alt. 4 is *favored* over alt. 2.

Alt. 3 vs. alt. 4, or C vs. (A + B): The difference cash flow is $-\$1,100, +1,211, -54, -54$. Again, we have multiple sign changes, but Norstrom's auxiliary series S_n is $-\$1,100, +111, +57, +3$. This guarantees a unique, positive, real root (see Section 6.3.1). With $i^*_{3-4} = 0.3\% < 10\%$, alt. 3 is *not* favored over alt. 4.

Alt. 5 vs. alt. 4, or (A + C) vs. (A + B): The difference cash flow is the same as (C − B), or $-\$2,100, +1,686, +421, +421$. This is a pure investment with a unique root of $i^*_{5-4} = 13.5\% > 10\%$, so alt. 5 is *favored* over alt. 4.

Alt. 6 vs. alt. 5, or (B + C) vs. (A + C): We have a repeat of the cash flow for alt. 2 vs. alt. 1, and $i^*_{6-5} = 16\% > 10\%$, so alt. 6 is *favored over alt. 5*.

Again, but after considerable work, our final selection is alternative 6, or projects B and C.

We thus arrive at the same final selection by using incremental analysis with each of the four criteria. □

Several conclusions are drawn from Example 7.6.

1. Correct ordering for evaluation is essential for all criteria except *PV* and the related *FV, AE,* and PB_N.

2. Although the ordering is different for each of the criteria used here, the final results are consistent with the fundamental criterion of *PV*.

3. The *IRR* criterion is particularly troublesome to apply, especially when we take differences between combination alternatives. The *RIC* concept is difficult to apply, and sometimes it is easier to obtain the *PV(i)* function.

4. *PV* with the *total investment approach* is by far the *easiest method* to apply. In this example we need to compute the *PV* of each of the three projects, add the appropriate *PVs* to obtain the *PV* of each combination alternative, and simply select the alternative with the largest *PV*.

7.4 REINVESTMENT ISSUES

We will begin this section with a simple example that puzzles most students when they encounter it for the first time.

Example 7.7.

Given projects A and B, which is preferred, project A with $MARR = 5\%$ or project B with $MARR = 10\%$?

	Cash Flows			
Project	n: 0	1	2	3
A	−$1,000	600	500	300
B	−$1,000	300	200	1,000

If we compute PVs, we obtain $PV(5\%)_A = \$284$, $PV(10\%)_B = \$189$. Most students (and practitioners, too) select project A because of its higher PV.

But how can we compare a PV computed at 5% with one computed at 10%? The interest rate used for discounting certainly implies something about reinvestment opportunities, as discussed in Chapter 5. Trying to compare the two projects as stated in the example is tantamount to trying to compare projects in different economic environments. Projects A and B might represent investment opportunities in two different countries, with different reinvestment rates and restrictions on repatriating cash flows. Or perhaps projects A and B occur in different regulatory environments, and the decision maker assumes that after project selection the firm will reinvest its cash flows in the chosen environment.

If we are eventually to recover the reinvested cash, by repatriating it in the one situation or by returning it to the firm's treasury in the second, it does not make sense to compare A and B by using PV. PV measures the surplus of funds a project generates over and above a minimum rate, and in this example the minimum rates differ. Instead, let's compute the total cash available at time 3 for each option.

Direct computation

Project A: $600(1.05)^2 + 500(1.05)^1 + 300 = \$1,487$

Project B: $300(1.1)^2 + 200(1.1)^1 + 1,000 = \$1,583$

Computation from PV

Project A: $(284 + 1,000)(1.05)^3 = \$1,486 \approx \$1,487$

Project B: $(189 + 1,000)(1.1)^3 = \$1,583$

We see that project B produces more cash at time 3, which is a direct result of the higher reinvestment rate, 10% for project B versus 5% for project A. It is clear that the reinvestment rate plays a crucial role in the analysis.   □

7.4.1 Net Present Value

Virtually all writers on engineering economics agree that the PV criterion is based on the assumption of reinvestment at the interest rate used for calculating *PV*. In Section 6.2 we assumed that positive cash flows would be reinvested at the outside, or market, interest rate, the same rate used for obtaining *PV*. In Chapter 5 we explained that the equity interest rate is the outside rate from the view of the equity holder. Whichever assumptions we make, we represent the rate by i.

In a perfect capital market we can borrow and lend unlimited amounts at the market interest rate. In this chapter we have modified that assumption to reflect a limited borrowing ability. But we still assume that we can *lend unlimited amounts* by investing at a market interest rate. This is the same as assuming reinvestment at the market interest rate. In this situation, maximizing *PV* is the same as maximizing the future cash of the firm.

Assume that we have two mutually exclusive alternatives, j and k, with cash flows F_{nj}, $n = 0, ..., N_j$, and F_{nk}, $n = 0, ..., N_k$. Further, assume that outlays occur only at time 0 and that we have a budget of M, which is greater than either time 0 outlay. The $MARR = i$. Select a horizon time N as the greater of N_j and N_k.

We have by definition

$$PV(i)_j = \sum_{n=0}^{N_j} F_{nj}(1 + i)^{-n}, \qquad PV(i)_k = \sum_{n=0}^{N_k} F_{nk}(1 + i)^{-n} \qquad (7.8)$$

Now let's obtain the future cash at time N for the three possible decisions. Say $N = N_j$, for example.

Decision 1, do nothing

$$\text{Future cash at time } N = M(1 + i)^N \qquad (7.9)$$

Unspent amounts are invested at i, which is consistent with the reinvestment assumption.

Decision 2, select j

Future cash at time N

$$= (M + F_{0j})(1 + i)^N + \sum_{n=1}^{N} F_{nj}(1 + i)^{N-n}$$

$$= M(1 + i)^N + \sum_{n=0}^{N} F_{nj}(1 + i)^{N-n}$$

$$= M(1 + i)^N + (1 + i)^N \sum_{n=0}^{N} F_{nj}(1 + i)^{-n}$$

$$= M(1 + i)^N + PV(i)_j(1 + i)^N \qquad (7.10)$$

The future cash is the same as for do nothing plus the $PV(i)_j$ shifted to time N. For j the $N_j = N$, so the shifted *PV* is the *FV*.

Decision 3, select k

Future cash at time N

$$= (M + F_{0k})(1 + i)^N + \sum_{n=1}^{N_k} F_{nk}(1 + i)^{N_k - n}(1 + i)^{N - N_k}$$

$$= M(1 + i)^N + \sum_{n=0}^{N} F_{nk}(1 + i)^{N - n}$$

$$= M(1 + i)^N + PV(i)_k(1 + i)^N \tag{7.11}$$

At the end of the project life the accumulated cash from reinvesting project inflows is left to earn interest until time N.

The *PV* of the do-nothing alternative is zero. In each case the future cash at time N is equal to the initial amount M times $(F/P, i, N)$ plus $PV(i)(F/P, i, N)$. Thus, by selecting the alternative with maximum $PV(i)$, we maximize future cash, assuming reinvestment at i.

Let us return to Example 7.7 and evaluate A and B with $i = 5\%$.

$$PV(5\%)_A = \$284, \qquad PV(5\%)_B = \$331$$

Here project B is preferred. Computing future cash amounts, we have

Project A: $(1,000 + 284)(1.05)^3 = \$1,486$

Project B: $(1,000 + 331)(1.05)^3 = \$1,541$

Again, project B is preferred, in agreement with our theoretical analysis.

7.4.2 Internal Rate of Return

Some authors have argued that implicit in the use of the *IRR* is an assumption of reinvestment at the project *IRR* [1, 3, 4]. It is difficult to prove or disprove what someone had in mind in stating the *IRR* criterion or using it. Instead, we show in this section the results of selecting alternatives with *IRR* under some special circumstances.

Let us first compute *IRR* for the projects in Example 7.7.

$$\text{Project A: } -\$1,000 + \frac{600}{1 + i} + \frac{500}{(1 + i)^2} + \frac{300}{(1 + i)^3} = 0$$

$$i_A^* = 21.48\%$$

$$\text{Project B: } -\$1,000 + \frac{300}{1 + i} + \frac{200}{(1 + i)^2} + \frac{1,000}{(1 + i)^3} = 0$$

$$i_B^* = 18.33\%$$

If we simply select A over B on the basis of its higher *IRR*, we would be in conflict with the *PV*s calculated at 5%: $1,486 for A and $1,541 for B.

We might ask whether there is a value i for which *PV* favors project A. The

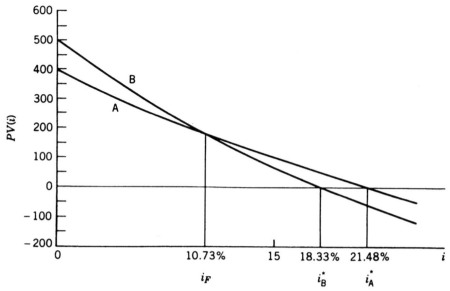

FIGURE 7.2. Fisher's intersection, Example 7.7.

PV curves for A and B are similar to those in Figure 7.1, with B starting higher than A but crossing the horizontal axis sooner. Figure 7.2 shows the curves for A and B. Clearly, *PV*(21.48%) is greater for A than for B. The point of intersection is at 10.73%. This point is also called *Fisher's intersection* or the *rate of return over cost* [5]. For any value of *i* equal to or greater than 10.73%, the *PV* criterion prefers project A. Fisher's intersection is also the *IRR* of the difference cash flow between A and B: $0, 300, 300, −700.

If we are uncertain about the reinvestment rate in selecting one of two alternatives, calculating Fisher's intersection can be useful. In our example any reinvestment rate greater than 10.73% would lead us to prefer A over B, and B would be favored at rates lower than 10.73%. This approach becomes cumbersome when more than two alternatives are compared.

Let us now examine the consequences of *assuming reinvestment at IRR*. If each investment alternative has its excess cash reinvested at its *IRR*, we could select among alternatives by choosing the one with the highest *IRR*. Say that alternative *j* has the highest *IRR*, i_j^*. Then for all others $PV(i_j^*)$ must be less than zero. (If we also have borrowing alternatives with upward-sloping *PV* curves, we must modify the acceptance rules.)

But how sensible is the assumption of reinvestment at *IRR*? Not very sensible at all. Do different *IRR*s imply different reinvestment rates? We don't think so. And with what should we compare the *IRR* if reinvestment is at that rate? The entire discussion is rather fruitless and provides little help for decision making.

The *IRR*, along with *RIC*, is a useful criterion when it is used with correct ordering and the incremental method. Capital that remains invested in a project grows at the *IRR* of the project, and cash released would be invested to grow at the *MARR* (or the cost of capital when this rate is used in *PV* calculation) [9]. When two alternatives are compared, Fisher's intersection is useful if the reinvestment rate is not known with certainty.

7.4.3 Benefit–Cost Ratio

A similar argument can be presented for the aggregate B/C ratio in relation to Fisher's intersection when we are comparing two alternatives [3]. We can demonstrate the logic by applying it to Example 7.7. We assume for simplicity that all investment and operating expenditures occur at time 0 and that the flows from time 1 to time 3 are benefits. Thus, we have

$$B_A = \frac{\$600}{1 + i} + \frac{500}{(1 + i)^2} + \frac{300}{(1 + i)^3}$$

$$I_A + C'_A = 1,000$$

$$B_B = \frac{\$300}{1 + i} + \frac{200}{(1 + i)^2} + \frac{1,000}{(1 + i)^3}$$

$$I_B + C'_B = 1,000$$

The i value for which the $B/(I + C')$ ratios are equal must satisfy the following expression.

$$\frac{\dfrac{\$600}{1 + i} + \dfrac{500}{(1 + i)^2} + \dfrac{300}{(1 + i)^3}}{1,000} = \frac{\dfrac{\$300}{1 + i} + \dfrac{200}{(1 + i)^2} + \dfrac{1,000}{(1 + i)^3}}{1,000}$$

or

$$\frac{\$300}{1 + i} + \frac{300}{(1 + i)^2} - \frac{700}{(1 + i)^3} = 0$$

But this last expression simply yields the *IRR* of the difference cash flow between A and B.

We conclude this section on reinvestment issues by observing that much has been written on the subject, but not all is of use in decision making. The reinvestment rate assumed is critical for alternative selection, and the assumed value should be based on the concepts in Chapter 5. Use of the *PV* criterion implies reinvestment at the rate used for *PV* calculations. Fisher's intersection is useful when comparing two alternatives, but it becomes cumbersome with more than two.

In the real world the reinvestment rates may depend on the time period and on which investments have been accepted. In Chapter 8 we present some mathematical programming approaches that can be used to model such problems.

7.5 COMPARISON OF PROJECTS WITH UNEQUAL LIVES

Comparing projects with unequal lives can be particularly troublesome, for a number of different situations must be considered. Furthermore, many of the methods presented in textbooks have underlying assumptions that are not always clearly stated. Unfortunately, competing projects often have unequal lives, especially in engineering studies for which only costs (not benefits) are known. Problems in this class are more difficult than those for which all benefits are known, and they require more assumptions to be made. Another aspect of the unequal-lives situation is that of repeatability. Decisions involving projects that are likely to be repeated can often be made conveniently by easier methods.

We thus have the following classifications of cases:

1. *Service projects,* for which no revenues or benefits are estimated, or the revenues or benefits do not depend on the project. Here we must select a *study period* common to all alternatives. There are two general cases.
    a. Repeatability is likely.
    b. Repeatability is unlikely.
2. *Revenue projects,* for which all benefits and costs are known. Here the *study period* may be different for each alternative, provided we have a well-specified reinvestment rate.
    a. Repeatability is likely.
    b. Repeatability is unlikely.

These four cases will lead to (and in some instances force us into making) various assumptions concerning reinvestment, salvage values, and characteristics of the repeated projects.

Notice that in this section we are not trying to determine the best life of any individual project that is likely to be repeated. This type of decision is covered in detail in Chapter 16. We now present some of the more common ways of treating unequal lives.

7.5.1 Common Service Period Approach

If the benefit from a project is needed for a much longer period than the individual life of the project, it may be convenient to assume repeatability of identical projects.

Example 7.8.

The Historical Society of New England must repaint its showcase headquarters building. The choice is between a latex paint that costs $12.00/gallon and an oil paint that costs $26.00/gallon. Each gallon would cover 500 square feet; labor is the same for both, 1 hour per 100 square feet at $18.00/hour. The latex paint has an estimated life of 5 years, compared with 8 years for the oil paint. With $i = 8\%$, which paint should be selected?

Let us assume that after either the 5- or the 8-year period the building would be repainted repeatedly with the same paint and that the same costs would apply, as shown in Figure 7.3. The lowest common multiple of 5 and 8 is 40, so we will use 40 as the *common service period.* This becomes the *study period.*

For latex paint, we have the initial painting and seven repaintings.

$$PV(8\%) = \left(\frac{\$12.00}{500} + \frac{\$18.00}{100}\right)[1 + (P/F, 8\%, 5) + (P/F, 8\%, 10)$$

$$+ \cdots + (P/F, 8\%, 35)]$$

$$= (\$0.204)[1 + \overset{P/A, \ 46.9\%, \ 7}{(1.9866)}] = \$0.609 \text{ per square foot}$$

Note: $1.469 = (1.08)^5$.

For oil paint, there are four repaintings plus the initial painting.

$$PV(8\%) = \left(\frac{\$26.00}{500} + \frac{\$18.00}{100}\right)[1 + (P/F, 8\%, 8) + (P/F, 8\%, 16)$$

$$+ \cdots + (P/F, 8\%, 32)]$$

$$= (\$0.232)[1 + \overset{P/A, \ 85.1\%, \ 4}{(1.0751)}] = \$0.481 \text{ per square foot}$$

Note: $1.851 = (1.08)^8$.

The *PV* of the oil paint per square foot is considerably less, so the oil paint should be the choice. □

In Example 7.8 a service period of 40 years seem reasonable. The number of repaintings needed with each type of paint will depend on the technology of paint, so we may or may not need exactly seven (latex) or four (oil) repaintings. The validity of the analysis also depends on the costs of paint and labor remaining constant. If we assume constant-dollar prices, this may be a reasonable assumption. But then our interest rate of 8% must represent an inflation-free rate i'. Thus, many assumptions are necessary to make the approach valid.

An easier way to solve Example 7.8 is to use annual equivalents. The *AE* of each 40-year cash flow is the same as that of the corresponding 5- or 8-year cash flow.

For latex paint, computing from a 5-year life, we have

$$AE(8\%) = \left(\frac{\$12.00}{500} + \frac{\$18.00}{100}\right)\overset{A/P, \ 8\%, \ 5}{(0.2505)} = \$0.0511 \text{ per square foot}$$

Computing from a 40-year period, we have

$$AE(8\%) = \$0.609 \overset{A/P, \ 8\%, \ 40}{(0.0839)} = \$0.0511 \text{ per square foot}$$

For oil paint, computing from an 8-year life, we have

$$AE(8\%) = \left(\frac{\$26.00}{500} + \frac{\$18.00}{100}\right)\overset{A/P, \ 8\%, \ 8}{(0.1740)} = \$0.0403 \text{ per square foot}$$

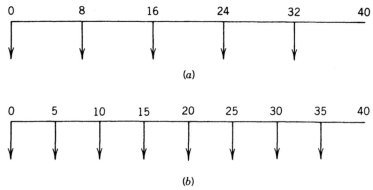

FIGURE 7.3. Common service period approach, Example 7.8: (*a*) oil, five paintings, (*b*) latex, eight paintings.

Computing from a 40-year period, we have

$$AE(8\%) = \$0.481\overset{A/P,\ 8\%,\ 40}{(0.0839)} = \$0.0403 \text{ per square foot}$$

With annual equivalents there is another possible interpretation regarding a common service period. We could assume that after the initial period, either 5 or 8 years, the building would be repainted with the type of paint that has the lower *AE* cost. Thus, if oil paint had the lower *AE* cost, the sequences would be

Latex paint (0 → 5), oil paint (5 →)

Oil paint (0 → 8), oil paint (8 →)

After time 5 the *AE* costs are the same. If latex paint had the lower *AE* cost, the sequences would be

Latex paint (0 → 5), latex paint (5 →)

Oil paint (0 → 8), latex paint (8 →)

After time 8 the *AE* costs are the same.

What circumstances would allow us to ignore the costs beyond time 5 when oil paint has the lower *AE* cost or time 8 when latex had the lower *AE* cost? An infinite service period with unchanging costs! Then we could simply look at the first 8 years; thereafter, costs would be identical. Actually, we do not need all these assumptions for reasonable accuracy in decision making. A long service period, say 30 years, and gradual changes in costs and technology will usually lead to the same decision about the initial choice of paint. Thus, we can minimize the *PV* of a long service period by selecting the alternative with the lower *AE* cost for an initial life.

The common service period approach is often used for analyzing *service projects,* for which no revenues or benefits are estimated or whose revenues or benefits are independent. The approach also can be applied to *revenue projects,* whose costs *and* benefits are known. In this situation we must be even more careful about our assumptions, especially regarding benefits.

7.5.2 Estimating Salvage Value of Longer-Lived Projects

If repeatability of projects is not likely for service projects, we must assume something about the salvage value of the longer-lived project. The next example shows how we can *explicitly* incorporate salvage values for assets with value remaining beyond the *required service period.*

Example 7.9

A highway contractor requires a ripper–bulldozer for breaking loose rock without the use of explosives, for a period of 3 years at about 2,000 hours/year. The smaller model, A, costs $300,000, has a life of 8,000 hours, and costs $40,000/year to operate. The larger model, B, costs $450,000, has a life of 12,000 hours, and costs $50,000/year to operate. Model B will perform adequately under all circumstances, whereas for model A some extra drilling is expected at an annual cost of $35,000. With a marginal tax rate of 40%, units of production depreciation, and $i = 15\%$, which model should be purchased?

Since either model's lifetime exceeds the required service period (also the *study period*) of 3 years, we must assume something about the used equipment at that time. Let us assume that after 3 years model A would be sold for $60,000 and model B for $190,000. The after-tax cash flows for each alternative are given in Table 7.6 and shown in Figure 7.4. Model A has the lower *PV* of costs and would be preferred. □

Table 7.6 *Explicit Salvage Values, Example 7.9*

Model	After-Tax Cash Flows (thousands)			
	n: 0	1	2	3
Model A				
Investment	−$300			
Depreciation, (300/8,000) (2,000) (0.4)		+$30	+30	+30
Operating costs, (40) (0.6)		−$24	−24	−24
Drilling costs, (35) (0.6)		−$21	−21	−21
Salvage value				+60
Tax credit on salvage, (75 − 60) (0.4)				+6
Totals	−$300	−15	−15	+51
Model B				
Investment	−$450			
Depreciation, (450/12,000) (2,000) (0.4)		+30	+30	+30
Operating costs, (50) (0.6)		−30	−30	−30
Salvage value				+190
Tax credit on salvage, (225 − 190) (0.4)				+14
Totals	−$450	0	0	+$204

$PV(15\%)_A = -\$291,$ $PV(15)_B = -\$316$

The outcome of Example 7.9 depends very much on the salvage values received for the used equipment. We estimated these values by using $1 - $ (hours used/lifetime in hours)$^{0.8}$. What effect would higher salvage values have, say with an exponent of 1.5 instead of 0.8?

Model A:

$$[1 - (0.75)^{1.5}](300,000) = \$105,000 \text{ salvage value}$$
$$\text{Change in cash flow} = (105,000 - 60,000)(0.6) = +\$27,000$$
$$\text{New } PV = -291,000 + 27,000/(1.15)^3 = -\$273,000$$

Model B:

$$[1 - (0.5)^{1.5}](450,000) = \$291,000 \text{ salvage value}$$
$$\text{Change in cash flow} = (291,000 - 190,000)(0.6) = +\$61,000$$
$$\text{New } PV = -316,000 + 61,000/(1.15)^3 = -\$276,000$$

The numbers have changed to the point that intangible factors are likely to determine the selection.

What would happen if we evaluate models A and B by using *AE*s for their respective lives? First, we need some terminal salvage values; assume 10%, which gives $30,000 and $45,000, respectively. Second, we need to make some assumption about the extra drilling costs for model A; assume they would continue during the fourth year. The annual cash flows would be, as in Table 7.6, $-\$15,000$ for model A and and $0 for model B. The positive salvage values

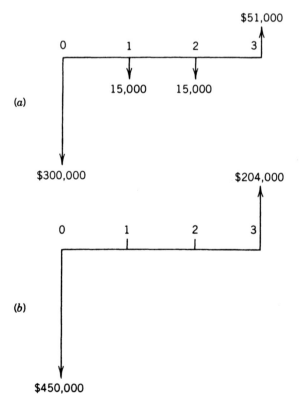

(a)

(b)

FIGURE 7.4. After-tax cash flows using explicit salvage value estimates, Example 7.9: (*a*) model A, (*b*) model B.

would result in depreciation recapture, so the net salvage proceeds would be $(30,000)(0.6) = \$18,000$ for model A and $(45,000)(0.6) = \$27,000$ for model B. Thus

$$AE(15\%)_A = -300,000\overset{A/P,\ 15\%,\ 4}{(0.3503)} - 15,000 + 18,000\overset{A/F,\ 15\%,\ 4}{(0.2003)}$$

$$= -\$116,485$$

$$AE(15\%)_B = -450,000\overset{A/P,\ 15\%,\ 6}{(0.2642)} + 0 + 27,000\overset{A/F,\ 15\%,\ 6}{(0.1142)}$$

$$= -\$115,807$$

The question at this point is not whether the foregoing analysis is valid, for the problem statement in Example 7.9 implies that it is not. (Many analysts use this method, nevertheless). Rather, we pose this question: Are there 3-year salvage values for models A and B that, when used in a 3-year analysis, yield these AE costs?

The answer is yes, and we can calculate the values as follows [7].

$$AE(15\%)_A = -300,000(A/P,\ 15\%,\ 3) - 15,000 + F_A(A/F,\ 15\%,\ 3)$$
$$= -116,485$$

or

$$AE(15\%)_A = -(300,000 - F_A)(0.4380) - 15,000 - F_A(0.15)$$
$$= -116,485$$

This gives $F_A = \$103,872$, net proceeds after taxes, which implies a selling price of $[103,872 - (0.4)(75,000)]/(0.6) = \underline{\$123,120}$. Similarly,

$$AE(15\%)_B = -(450,000 - F_B)\overset{A/P,\ 15\%,\ 3}{(0.4380)} - F_B(0.15) = -\$115,807$$

and $F_B = \$282,267$, net proceeds after taxes, giving a selling price of $[282,267 - (0.4)(225,000)]/(0.6) = \underline{\$320,445}$. (The derivation of the expression for selling price before depreciation recapture is left as an exercise; see Problem 7.24.)

These 3-year salvage values of $123,120 and $320,445 for models A and B, respectively, will result in AE costs of $-\$116,485$ and $-\$115,807$. From another point of view, if we make the selection decision between A and B by using AEs over 4 and 6 years, respectively, we are *implicitly* assuming these 3-year salvage values. Figure 7.5 shows these conversions. In Example 7.9 the contractor needs the equipment for only 3 years and will either sell the selected equipment after the 3-year period or use it elsewhere. If the equipment is sold, the contractor will receive a salvage value. If it is used elsewhere, the contractor considers the *unused value* to be equivalent to the implied salvage value [7, 10]. In this example we might be skeptical of 3-year salvage value ratios of 41% and 71% for bulldozer models A and B, respectively.

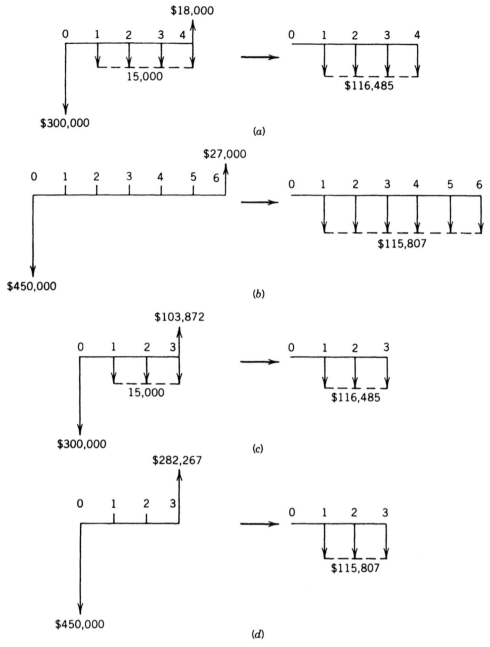

FIGURE 7.5. Conversions to annual equivalents, Example 7.9: (*a*) model A, original life; (*b*) model B, original life; (*c*) model A, 3-year life with implied salvage value; (*d*) model B, 3-year life with implied salvage value.

Sometimes one or more of the projects will have a life shorter than the required service period. One way to analyze such a situation is to *assume explicitly* how the requirement would be satisfied, for instance, by leasing an asset or by subcontracting. The *study period* then coincides with the *required service period,* which is desirable. If we use *AE* over the short life, we are *assuming explicitly* that we can lease an asset or subcontract for the remainder of the required service period at an annual cost equal to the *AE.*

441

In summary, when using *AEs* over the original, unequal lifetimes of projects, we are making *implicit* assumptions about salvage values or leasing costs at the end of the study period. Because most analysts do not understand these assumptions clearly and calculation of the implied values is not straightforward (especially for an after-tax analysis), we recommend that any salvage values and leasing costs used be *estimated explicitly*. The study period should equal the required service period. We do not recommend using *AEs* over unequal lifetimes for comparing service projects or using a study period different from the required service period.

7.5.3 Reinvestment Issues
When Revenues Are Known

The presentation in Section 7.4.1 proved that, when cash inflows are reinvested at *i*, we will maximize future cash by using *PV(i)* as a selection criterion. That proof applies for comparing projects with unequal lives as well as of those with equal lives. We thus have a way to compare revenue projects with unequal lives: use *PV(i)*. (If the reinvestment rate is not known, we must use the techniques presented in later chapters.)

7.5.4 Summary, Treatment of Unequal Lives

We summarize this section in terms of the classification given at the beginning.

1. Service projects
   a. Repeatability is likely.
      i. Use *AE* for each project's life. This is the easy method and is applicable in a greater variety of circumstances than the following method.
      ii. Use *PV* with a common service period. This is a tedious method and it requires or implies stricter assumptions than those in part i.
   b. Repeatability is not likely.
      i. *Explicitly* estimate salvage values for any assets with a remaining value at the end of the required service period. If an asset life falls short of the required service period, explicitly estimate the cost of leasing an asset or subcontracting.
      ii. Using *AE* for each project's life involves *implicit* estimates of salvage value or of the value of productive use after the required service period or both. This method should be used *only* if these implicit values are calculated and judged realistic.
2. Revenue projects
   a. Repeatability is likely.
      i. Use *AE* for each project's life.
      ii. Alternatively, use *PV* with a common service period.
   b. Repeatability is not likely. Use *PV* for each project's life.

It is particularly important to understand the assumptions underlying each of these methods.

7.6 DECISIONS ON THE TIMING OF INVESTMENTS

Sometimes it is possible to change the implementation timing of an investment. There are various reasons why this could occur, related to technology, marketing, production costs, financing costs, and so forth. We discuss briefly some of these situations and indicate how they can be treated analytically. For each situation it is understood that the same investment project with different implementation times should be treated as a set of mutually exclusive projects (a project would be implemented only once, if at all).

A rapidly *changing technology* may be a good reason to consider a timing change. Computer equipment, electronic instrumentation, aircraft, and the like change fast enough that a delay of one or two years in acquiring assets may result in significant differences in operating costs and performance capabilities. Such situations must be evaluated individually.

When the investment involves producing and marketing a product, the *product life cycle* should be considered [6].

PERIOD	CHARACTERISTICS
Early years	Product still being developed.
	High unit costs.
	Relatively small market.
Middle years	Product design is stable.
	Production economies have been achieved.
	Peak annual sales for product.
Late years	Product is being replaced by new ones.
	Annual sales are declining.

Companies with technological strengths try to be leaders and hope to get a marketing advantage by producing an item during its early years. Companies with production and marketing strengths avoid the high development costs and wait until the product design is stable; they will then attempt to produce and market the product at a lower price. During the late years of the product life cycle, the advantage rests with low-cost producers who have widespread marketing organizations. By evaluating its own capabilities, a company can decide how best to utilize its strengths.

Differential inflation rates for first cost have been used to argue for earlier construction of civil works and power plants. For methods for dealing with inflation, see Chapter 2. In the case of nuclear power plants, a positive differential inflation rate combined with more complex technology (related to safety measures) has brought about the cancellation of many planned facilities. Had they been constructed five or ten years earlier, they might have been successful investments.

Changing financing costs are often cited for delaying planned investments. Here we must be careful to separate the effects of raising more capital, perhaps by borrowing, from those of investment in a project. If the financing is not tied directly to the proposed project, a high borrowing cost should be viewed in the context of the company's overall cost of capital and capital structure; see Chapter 5. Viewed in this way, a high current borrowing cost may or may not raise the weighted-average cost of capital sufficiently to make a project undesirable. When borrowing costs are high, a company with financial strength may gain a significant market advantage by investing in new products and services. Delaying investments because of high rates may be shortsighted. Again, each situation must be evaluated by itself.

When we compare different timing decisions for the same project, a common point in time should be selected for the comparison. For example, *PV* at time 0 (a specific date) can be used. Here it is particularly important to have a good estimate of *MARR*, because different lateral time shifts of cash flows for two or more projects may distort the comparison if the *MARR* does not accurately reflect reinvestment opportunities.

7.7 SUMMARY

In this chapter we have shown how the proper use of any of the ten decision criteria presented in Chapter 6 will lead to correct decisions when we select among competing projects. The final selection will be consistent with *PV*, which is the correct, or baseline, criterion to use in a stable, perfect capital market with complete certainty. The necessary steps for proper use of a criterion are

1. Preliminary screening to eliminate unfavorable projects.
2. Forming mutually exclusive alternatives.
3. Ordering the alternatives (not always by the time 0 investment).
4. Applying the incremental procedure.

The total investment approach is guaranteed to work only with *PV*, *FV*, *AE*, and *PB*. Moreover, for these four criteria one can use arbitrary ordering with the incremental procedure. Detailed rules apply to *IRR* and make it particularly difficult to use properly.

Use of *PV* implies reinvestment at the rate used for computing *PV*. Since the other criteria, when used properly, give the same project selection, it can be argued that their use also implies reinvestment at the same rate. It is clear that the discount rate, designated *MARR*, must be selected carefully; see Chapter 5. Much has been written about the reinvestment rate implied by use of other criteria, especially *IRR*, but this criterion is of relatively little use for decision making, with the exception of Fisher's intersection.

When comparing projects with unequal lives, one must distinguish between service projects and revenue projects. The likelihood of repeatability affects the analysis techniques to be used. Finally, any salvage value assumptions should be stated clearly and treated explicitly.

This chapter is the last one dealing with "traditional" engineering economic analysis techniques. The next chapter considers more complex decision environments, still assuming certainty. Later chapters deal with variable cash flows and other uncertainties.

REFERENCES

1. Au, T., and T. P. Au, *Engineering Economics for Capital Investment Analysis,* Allyn and Bacon, Boston, 1983.

2. Bernhard, R. H., "A Comprehensive Comparison and Critique of Discounting Indices Proposed for Capital Investment Evaluation," *The Engineering Economist,* Vol. 16, No. 3, pp. 157–186, Spring 1971.

3. Bussey, L. E., *The Economic Analysis of Industrial Projects,* Prentice–Hall, Englewood Cliffs, N.J., 1978 (see Ch. 8).

4. DeGarmo, E. P., W. G. Sullivan, and J. R. Canada, *Engineering Economy,* 7th edition, Macmillan, New York, 1984 (see Chs. 5 and 6).

5. Fisher, I., *The Theory of Interest,* Macmillan, New York, 1930.

6. Kamien, M. I., and N. L. Schwartz, "Timing of Innovations under Rivalry," *Econometrica,* Vol. 40, No. 1, pp. 43–59, 1972.

7. Kulonda, D. J., "Replacement Analysis with Unequal Lives," *The Engineering Economist,* Vol. 23, No. 3, pp. 171–179, Spring 1978.

8. Levy, N. S., "On the Ranking of Economic Alternatives by the Total Opportunity ROR and B/C Ratios—A Note," *The Engineering Economist,* Vol. 26, No. 2, pp. 166–171, Winter 1981.

9. Lohmann, J. R., "The IRR, NPV and the Fallacy of the Reinvestment Rate Assumptions," *The Engineering Economist,* Vol. 33, No. 4, pp. 303–330, Summer 1988.

10. Saxena, U., and A. Garg, "On Comparing Alternatives with Different Lives," *The Engineering Economist,* Vol. 29, No. 1, pp. 59–70, Fall 1983.

11. Theusen, G. J., and W. J. Fabrycky, *Engineering Economy,* 7th edition, Prentice–Hall, Englewood Cliffs, N.J., 1989 (see Ch. 7, Sec. 8.3).

12. White, J. A., M. H. Agee, and K. E. Case, *Principles of Engineering Economic Analysis,* 3rd edition, Wiley, New York, 1989 (see Ch. 5).

13. Wohl, M., "A New Ordering Procedure and Set of Decision Rules for the Internal Rate of Return Method," *The Engineering Economist,* Vol. 30, No. 4, pp. 363–386, Summer 1985.

PROBLEMS

7.1. A company has the capability of manufacturing four products. There are three plants, with product capabilities as follows.

Plant A   Products 1, 2, 4
Plant B   Products 2, 3
Plant C   Products 1, 3, 4

For various reasons, the company does not produce the *same* product in more than *two* plants. In addition, any particular plant is used to produce only *one* product. Form all possible combinations of plants and products that the company should consider.

7.2. If there are four independent investment proposals A, B, C, and D, form all possible investment alternatives with them.

7.3. Apply the ten investment criteria to projects *j* and *k* in Example 7.3 to derive the results in Table 7.3.

7.4. Apply the incremental procedure to projects j and k in Example 7.3 to derive the results in Table 7.4.

7.5. Consider the four projects with cash flows as shown.

Project	n: 0	1	2	3
A	−1,000	900	500	100
B	−1,000	600	500	500
C	−2,000	900	900	800
D	+1,000	−402	−402	−402

Before proceeding to the questions, we will need to obtain FV for each project by using $MARR = 10\%$, 20%.

a. Explain why the FV criterion prefers A over B at 20% when it prefers B over A at 10%.

b. With $MARR = 10\%$, how much money would you have at time 3 if you invested $1,000 of your own money in A? In B?

c. Which of the following situations would you prefer?
   i. $MARR = 10\%$; you invest $1000 in B.
   ii. $MARR = 20\%$; you invest $1000 in A.
   Explain your answer.

d. With $MARR = 10\%$, how much money would you have at time 3 if you invested $2,000 of your own money in C?

e. Explain why the FV criterion prefers A over C at 10%, even though in situation d the cash at time 3 is greater than that in situation b (for project A).

f. What is the IRR for D? Would you accept D with $MARR = 20\%$? How would you modify the IRR acceptance rule when examining project D?

g. Suppose A and B are mutually exclusive projects. Which project would you select using $MARR$ of 10% and the IRR criterion?

7.6. Your company is faced with three independent proposals:

Project	n: 0	1	2	3
A	−1,000	500	500	500
B	−1,500	1,000	200	1,000
C	−3,000	1,300	1,300	1,300

a. With a budget of $3,000 at time 0 and $MARR = 8\%$, which project or projects should you choose? Use FV.

b. How much cash would you have at time 3? Answer this part by performing a minimum of computations.

c. Could you use IRR to obtain the answer to part a? Do you foresee any potential difficulties?

7.7. Consider the following three mutually exclusive projects. Each has a lifetime of 20 years and $MARR = 15\%$.

Project	Investment	Annual User Benefits	Annual Sponsor Costs
A	1,000	400	160
B	800	300	110
C	1,500	360	50

a. Select the best project, using the *PV* criterion.

b. Select the best project, using the aggregate benefit–cost ratio.

7.8. Consider the following four mutually exclusive projects. Use the incremental method with *PV* and the aggregate cost–benefit ratio to select the best project. Each has a lifetime of 20 years, and *MARR* = 8%.

Project	Investment	Annual User Benefits	Annual Sponsor Costs
A	978	500	100
B	1,180	492	60
C	1,390	550	120
D	1,600	630	140

7.9. Use *IRR* to select the best of the following three mutually exclusive projects. Each has a lifetime of 10 years, and *MARR* = 15%.

Project	Investment	Annual Net Cash Flow
A	5,000	1,400
B	10,000	2,500
C	8,000	1,900

7.10. Use *IRR* to select the best of the following three independent projects. Each has a lifetime of 5 years, and *MARR* = 8%. The investment budget is $13,000.

Project	Investment	Annual Net Cash Flow
A	5,000	1,319
B	7,000	1,942
C	8,500	2,300

7.11. Use the netted benefit–cost ratio to select the best of the following four mutually exclusive projects. Each has a lifetime of 5 years, and *MARR* = 12%.

Project	Investment	Annual Net Cash Flow
A	10,000	4,438
B	14,000	5,548
C	12,000	5,048
D	5,000	2,774

7.12. Rework Problem 7.11 with the assumption that the projects are independent and the investment budget is $16,000.

7.13. Listed are cash flows for three independent proposals. Use the netted benefit–cost ratio to select the best proposal or proposals with *MARR* = 12% and an investment budget of $34,000.

Project	n: 0	1	2	3	4
A	−10,000	4,175	4,175	4,175	4,175
B	−17,500	10,025	3,025	7,025	7,025
C	−15,000	6,025	6,025	6,025	6,025

7.14. Listed are data for three mutually exclusive proposals. Use the aggregate benefit–cost ratio to select the best proposal with $MARR = 10\%$.

	Proposal A		Proposal B		Proposal C	
n	Costs	Benefits	Costs	Benefits	Costs	Benefits
0	10,000	—	14,000	—	17,000	—
1	1,000	5,500	4,000	10,000	1,000	10,000
2	1,000	5,500	4,000	10,000	1,000	3,000
3	1,000	5,500	4,000	10,000	1,000	10,000
4	1,000	5,500	4,000	10,000	1,000	10,000

7.15. Apply *IRR* to the selection in problem 7.14.

7.16. Construct an example in which Solomon's average rate of return yields an answer inconsistent with the netted benefit–cost ratio. Use the total investment approach.

7.17. Prove that if each investment alternative has the same initial investment, then *PV* agrees with the netted benefit–cost ratio. Use the total investment approach.

7.18. Prove that if each investment alternative has a constant net cash flow during its lifetime, then *IRR* agrees with the netted benefit–cost ratio. Use the total investment approach. (Assume a common life).

7.19. What modifications are needed in the accept–reject rules for the aggregate benefit–cost ratio if the ordering for the incremental procedure is by the time 0 investment?

7.20. Prove, or disprove by counterexample, that consistency is obtained across all four groups of investment criteria. Use the total investment approach:
   a. When the total invested in each alternative is the same.
   b. When the total invested in each alternative is the same, and the lifetimes of all alternatives are the same.

7.21. Prove that incremental analysis with Solomon's average rate of return yields the same answer as *PV* analysis.

7.22. Use the *common service period* approach to compare the following two options. $MARR = 12\%$; ignore taxes.
   i. Initial cost of $1,000, annual costs of $300, salvage value of $100, 10-year lifetime.
   ii. Initial cost of $1,300, annual costs of $270, salvage value of $200, 12-year lifetime.
   Is the length of the common service period plausible?

7.23. A manufacturer requires a chemical finishing process for a product produced under contract for a period of 4 years. Three options are available.
   i. Process device A, which costs $100,000, has annual operating and labor costs of $60,000 and an estimated salvage value of $10,000 after 4 years.
   ii. Process device B, which costs $150,000, has annual operating and labor costs of $50,000 and an estimated salvage value of $30,000 after 6 years.
   iii. Subcontracting at $100,000 per year.
   a. Which option would you recommend? $MARR = 10\%$.
   b. What is the salvage value of process device B after 4 years that would cause the manufacturer to be indifferent in choosing between it and process device A?
   c. What options should the manufacturer consider if the required service period is 5 years? 7 years?

7.24. Derive the selling price before depreciation recapture for the assets in Example 7.9.

Outline

Part III: Corporate Finance

- Lecture slides on dividend policy, debt policy, WACC and optimal capital structure

- Chapters 5, 6, 7, 10, 11 and 12 of "Valuation: Measuring and Managing the Value of Companies" by McKinsey & Company, Koller, Goedhart and Wessels

Dividend Policy

- ➢ **The Dividend Controversy**

- ➢ **The Rightists**

- ➢ **Taxes and the Radical Left**

- ➢ **The Middle of the Roaders**

The Dividend Decision

Lintner's "stylized facts" on how dividends are determined)

1. Companies have long term target dividend payout ratios

2. Managers focus more on dividend changes than on absolute dividend levels

3. Dividend changes follow shifts in long-run sustainable levels of earnings

4. Managers are reluctant to make dividend changes that could be reversed

Dividend Policy is Irrelevant

Modigliani & Miller

Since investors do not need dividends to convert shares to cash, they will not pay a premium for firms with higher dividend payouts. In other words, dividend policy has no impact on firms' value

Dividends Increase Value

Dividends as Signals

Dividend increases send good news about earnings and cash flows. On the other hand, dividend cuts send bad news

Dividends Decrease Value

Tax Issues

Companies can convert dividends into capital gains by shifting their dividend policies. If dividends are taxed more heavily than capital gains, investors should favor capital gains

Debt Policy

➢ **Leverage in a Tax Free Environment**

➢ **How Leverage Affects Returns**

➢ **The Traditional Position**

Modigliani - Miller

Modigliani & Miller

When there are no taxes and capital markets function well, it makes no difference whether the firm borrows or individual shareholders borrow. Therefore, the market value of a company does not depend on its capital structure

Weighted Average Cost of Capital

Why Do We Use WACC

- **WACC of an asset is the weighed opportunity cost of all investors for putting their money into the asset given the risk of the asset. It therefore reflects:**

  - ➢ **The riskiness of the asset, and**

  - ➢ **The way the asset is financed**

Weighted Average Cost of Capital

WACC Tree

$$WACC = k_d (1-t)\frac{B}{V} + k_e \frac{S}{V} + k_p \frac{P}{V} + k_l (1-t)\frac{L}{V}$$

> k_d: cost of debt

> t: tax rate

> B: market value of debt

> V: market value of assets of company

> k_e: cost of equity

> S: market value of stocks

> k_p: cost of preferred stock

> P: market value of preferred stock

> k_l: cost of leases

> L: market value of leases

Weighted Average Cost of Capital

WACC Tree

$$WACC = k_d (1-t) \frac{B}{B+S} + k_e \frac{S}{B+S}$$

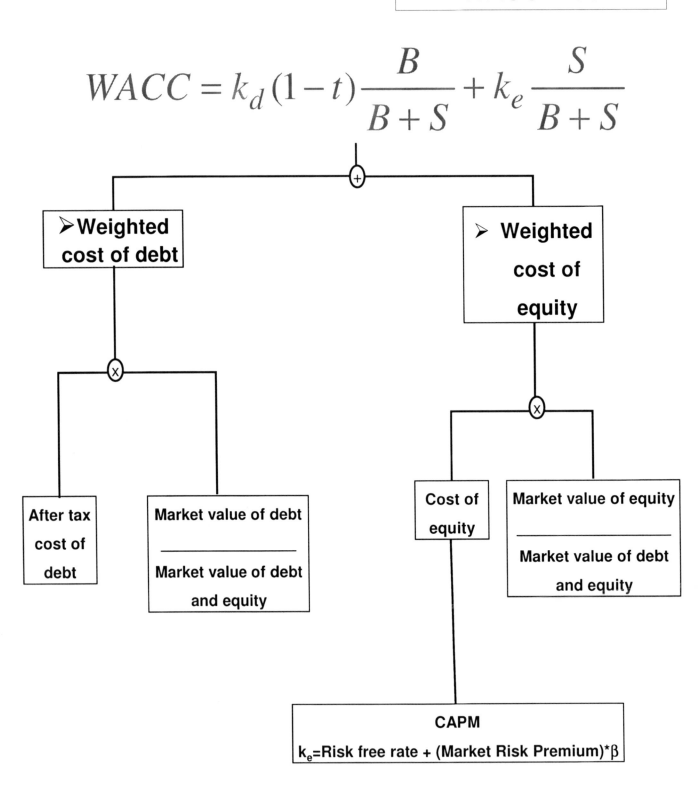

> Weighted cost of debt

> Weighted cost of equity

After tax cost of debt

$$\frac{\text{Market value of debt}}{\text{Market value of debt and equity}}$$

Cost of equity

$$\frac{\text{Market value of equity}}{\text{Market value of debt and equity}}$$

CAPM

k_e=Risk free rate + (Market Risk Premium)*β

Weighted Average Cost of Capital

Guidelines for
Estimating WACC
Parameters

➢ **For any security (including corporate debt and equity), the nominal rate required by the investors is a function of:**

- **The expected inflation over the life of the security**

- **The expected real rate over the life of the security**

- **The expected interest rate risk premium (if any)**

- **The expected risk premiums**

- **The expected illiquidity premium**

Weighted Average Cost of Capital

➤ **Average rates of return of various securities, 1926-1997**

(%/year)

Inflation	**3.2%**
Treasury Bills (3-month bills)	**3.8%**
Government Bonds	**5.3%**
Corporate Bonds	**5.8%**
Common Stocks (S&P 500)	**11.2%**
Small-firm Common Stocks	**12.9%**

Weighted Average Cost of Capital

Cost of Equity and CAPM

➤ **Cost of equity:**

$$k_e = E[r_e] = r_f + \beta_e.(E[r_m] - r_f)$$

$$\text{where } \beta_e = \frac{Cov(R_e, R_m)}{Var(R_m)}$$

- It takes into account the first four components in our security return decomposition (riskless rate takes into account the first three)

- For the riskless rate, use a long-term government bond rate and for the market risk premium, use the long-term realized risk premium of 3.5-4% (McK)

Weighted Average Cost of Capital (Finer Points)

- **Levering-Unlevering relationship:**

$$\beta_e = \beta_a + [\beta_a - \beta_d](1 - t_c) . \frac{B}{S}$$

This is the crucial formula as now, we can
compute a new β_e(and k_e) if we want to use a new
capital structure (**B/S**). This is true because:

- ✓ β_{assets} stays the same even if the capital
  structure changes as long as the projects
  (=assets) of the company do not change
- ✓ However, we should realize that in
  dramatic capital structure changes, β_{assets}
  changes

Cost of Financial Distress

Costs of Financial Distress: Costs arising from bankruptcy or distorted business decisions when close to bankruptcy

Market Value =   *Value if firm is all equity financed*

+ PV tax shield

- PV costs of financial distress

Cost of Financial Distress

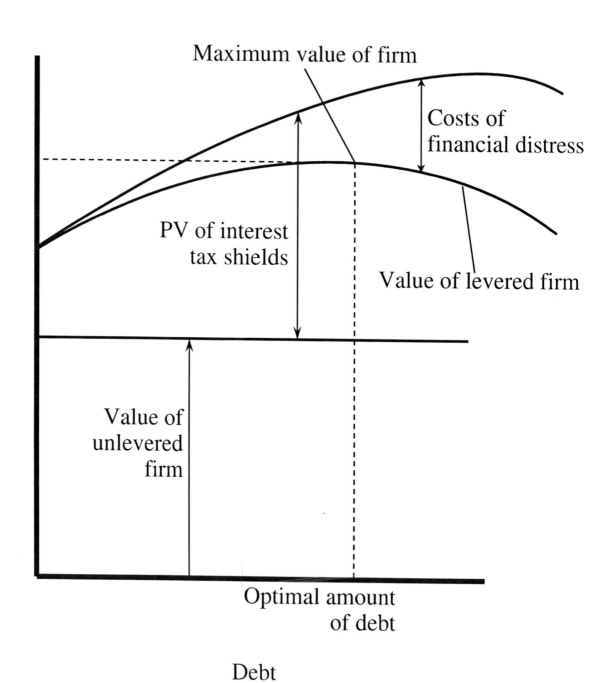

Outline

Part III: Corporate Finance

▪Lecture slides on dividend policy, debt policy, WACC and optimal capital structure

▪Chapters 5, 6, 7, 10, 11 and 12 of "Valuation: Measuring and Managing the Value of Companies" by McKinsey & Company, Koller, Goedhart and Wessels

Part Two

Core Valuation Techniques

5

Frameworks for Valuation

In Part One, we built a conceptual framework to show what drives value. In particular, a company's value is driven, first, by its ability to earn a return on invested capital (ROIC) greater than its weighted average cost of capital (WACC), and second, by its ability to grow. High returns and growth result in high cash flows, which in turn drives value.

Part Two offers a step-by-step guide for analyzing and valuing a company in practice, including technical details for properly measuring and interpreting the drivers of value. This chapter provides a high-level summary of valuation models based on discounted cash flow (DCF). We show how these models lead to *identical* results when applied correctly, and we illustrate how they differ in their ease of implementation.

Among the many ways to value a company (see Exhibit 5.1 on page 104 for an overview), we focus on two: enterprise DCF and discounted economic profit. When applied correctly, both valuation methods yield the same results; however, each model has certain benefits in practice. Enterprise DCF remains the favorite of many practitioners and academics because it relies solely on the flow of cash in and out of the company, rather than on accounting-based earnings (which can be misleading). Discounted economic profit is gaining in popularity because of its close link to economic theory and competitive strategy. Economic profit highlights whether a company is earning its cost of capital in a given year. Given the methods' identical results and complementary benefits of interpretation, we use both enterprise DCF and economic profit when valuing a company.

Both the enterprise DCF and economic profit models discount future streams at the weighted average cost of capital. WACC-based models work best when a company maintains a relatively stable debt-to-value ratio. If a company's debt-to-value mix is expected to change, WACC-based models can

471

Exhibit 5.1 Frameworks for DCF-Based Valuation

Model	Measure	Discount factor	Assessment
Enterprise discounted cash flow	Free cash flow	Weighted average cost of capital	Works best for projects, business units, and companies that manage their capital structure to a target level.
Economic profit	Economic profit	Weighted average cost of capital	Explicitly highlights when a company creates value.
Adjusted present value	Free cash flow	Unlevered cost of equity	Highlights changing capital structure more easily than WACC-based models.
Capital cash flow	Capital cash flow	Unlevered cost of equity	Compresses free cash flow and the interest tax shield in one number, making it difficult to compare performance among companies and over time.
Equity cash flow	Cash flow to equity	Levered cost of equity	Difficult to implement correctly because capital structure is embedded within cash flow. Best used when valuing financial institutions.

still yield accurate results but are more difficult to apply. When the company's capital structure is expected to change significantly, we recommend an alternative: adjusted present value (APV). Unlike WACC-based models, APV values the cash flow associated with capital structure (e.g., tax shields) separately from the cost of capital.

We conclude the chapter with a discussion of capital cash flow and equity cash flow valuation models. Because these two valuation models commingle operating performance and capital structure in cash flow, they lead more easily to mistakes in implementation. For this reason, we avoid capital cash flow and equity cash flow valuation models, except when valuing financial institutions, where capital structure is considered part of operations (for how to value financial institutions, see Chapter 25).

ENTERPRISE DISCOUNTED CASH FLOW MODEL

Enterprise valuation models value the company's operating cash flows. Equity valuation models, in contrast, value only the equity holder's claim against operating cash flows. In the 1950s, two Nobel laureates, Franco Modigliani and Merton Miller, postulated that the value of a company's economic assets must equal the value of the claims against those assets.

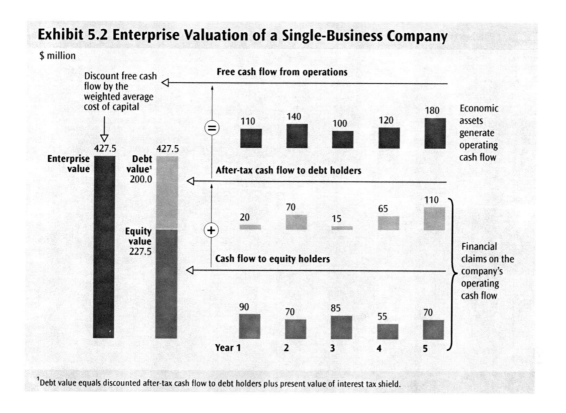

Exhibit 5.2 Enterprise Valuation of a Single-Business Company

$ million

¹Debt value equals discounted after-tax cash flow to debt holders plus present value of interest tax shield.

Thus, if we want to value the equity (and shares) of a company, we have two choices. We can value the company's operations and subtract the value of all nonequity financial claims (e.g., debt), or we can value the equity cash flows directly. In Exhibit 5.2, we demonstrate the relation between enterprise value and equity value. For this single-business company, equity can be calculated either directly at $227.5 million or by estimating enterprise value ($427.5 million) and subtracting debt ($200.0 million).

Although both methods lead to identical results when applied correctly, the equity method is difficult to implement in practice; matching equity cash flows with the correct cost of equity is challenging (for more on this, see the section on equity valuation later in this chapter). Consequently, to value a company's equity, we recommend valuing the enterprise first and then subtracting the value of any nonequity financial claims.[1]

In addition, the enterprise method is especially valuable when extended to a multibusiness company. As shown in Exhibit 5.3 on page 106, the enterprise value equals the summed value of the individual operating

[1] For financial institutions, such as banks and insurance companies, the choice, size, and structure of financial claims are directly linked to the company's operations (and thus are difficult to separate). In these situations, we prefer the equity cash-flow method. The valuation of financial institutions is addressed in Chapter 25.

Exhibit 5.3 Enterprise Valuation of a Multibusiness Company

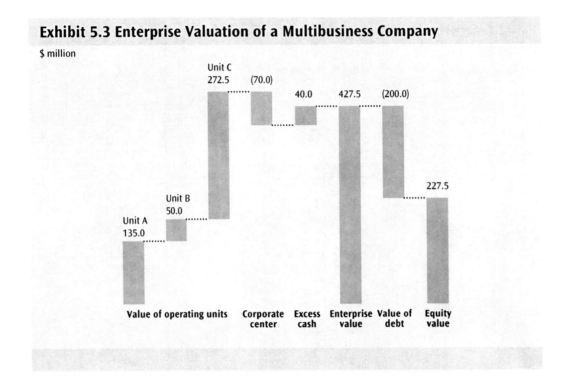

$ million

units less the present value of the corporate center costs, plus the value of nonoperating assets. Using enterprise discounted cash flow, instead of the equity cash flow model, enables you to value individual projects, business units, and even the entire company with a consistent methodology.

To value a company's common stock using enterprise DCF:

1. Value the company's operations by discounting free cash flow from operations at the weighted average cost of capital.

2. Value nonoperating assets, such as excess marketable securities, non-consolidated subsidiaries, and other equity investments. Combining the value of operating assets and nonoperating assets leads to enterprise value.

3. Identify and value all nonequity financial claims against the company's assets. Nonequity financial claims include (among others) fixed- and floating-rate debt, pension shortfalls, employee options, and preferred stock.

4. Subtract the value of nonequity financial claims from enterprise value to determine the value of common stock. To determine share price, divide equity value by the number of shares outstanding.

Exhibit 5.4 presents the results of an enterprise DCF valuation for Home Depot, the world's largest retailer of home improvement products.

Exhibit 5.4 Home Depot: Enterprise DCF Valuation

Year	Free cash flow (FCF) ($ million)	Discount factor (@ 9.3%)	Present value of FCF ($ million)
2004	1,930	0.915	1,766
2005	2,219	0.837	1,857
2006	2,539	0.766	1,944
2007	2,893	0.700	2,026
2008	3,283	0.641	2,104
2009	3,711	0.586	2,175
2010	4,180	0.536	2,241
2011	4,691	0.491	2,301
2012	5,246	0.449	2,355
2013	5,849	0.411	2,402
Continuing value	133,360	0.411	54,757
Present value of cash flow			75,928
Mid-year adjustment factor			1.046
Value of operations			**79,384**
Value of excess cash			1,609
Value of other nonoperating assets			84
Enterprise value			**81,077**
Value of debt			(1,365)
Value of capitalized operating leases			(6,554)
Equity value			**73,158**
Number of shares (at fiscal year-end 2003, million)			2,257
Estimated share value (in dollars)			**32.41**

To value Home Depot, future free cash flow is discounted to today's value and then summed across years. For simplicity, the first year's cash flow is discounted by one full year, the second by two full years, and so on. Since cash flows are generated throughout the year, and not as a lump sum, discounting in full-year increments understates the appropriate discount factor. Therefore, we adjust the present value by half a year,[2] leading to the value of operations of $79.4 billion.

To this value, add nonoperating assets (e.g., excess cash and other long-term nonoperating assets) to estimate Home Depot's enterprise value ($81.1 billion). From enterprise value, subtract the present value of nonequity

---

[2] A half-year adjustment is made to the present value for Home Depot because we assume cash flow is generated symmetrically around the midyear point. For companies dependent on year-end holidays, cash flows will be more heavily weighted toward the latter half of the year. In this case the adjustment should be smaller.

claims (traditional debt and capitalized operating leases) to arrive at Home Depot's estimated equity value ($73.2 billion). Dividing the equity value by the number of shares outstanding (2.3 billion) leads to an estimate of share value of $32.41. During the first half of 2004, Home Depot's stock price traded in the mid 30s.

Valuing Operations

The value of operations equals the discounted value of future free cash flow. Free cash flow equals the cash flow generated by the company's operations, less any reinvestment back into the business. Free cash flow is the cash flow available to *all* investors, and is *independent* of leverage. Consistent with this definition, free cash flow must be discounted using the weighted average cost of capital. The WACC is the company's opportunity cost of funds and represents a blended required return by the company's debt and equity holders.

Over the next few pages, we outline the enterprise DCF valuation process. Although we present it sequentially, valuation is an iterative process. To value operations, we analyze the company's historical performance; define and project free cash flow over the short, medium, and long run; and discount the projected free cash flows at the weighted average cost of capital.

Analyzing historical performance   Before projecting future cash flow, examine the company's historical financial performance. A good analysis will focus on the key drivers of value: return on invested capital, growth, and free cash flow. By thoroughly analyzing the past, we can document whether the company has created value, whether it has grown, and how it compares with its competitors.

Although ROIC and FCF are critical to the valuation process, they cannot be computed directly from a company's reported financial statements. Whereas ROIC and FCF are intended to measure the company's operating performance, financial statements mix operating performance, nonoperating performance, and capital structure. Therefore, to calculate ROIC and FCF, first reorganize the accountant's financial statements into new statements that separate operating items, nonoperating items, and financial structure.

This reorganization leads to two new terms: invested capital and net operating profits less adjusted taxes (NOPLAT). Invested capital represents the investor capital required to fund operations, without distinguishing how the capital is financed. NOPLAT represents the total after-tax operating income generated by the company's invested capital, available to *all* financial investors.

476

Exhibit 5.5 presents the historical NOPLAT and invested capital for Home Depot and one of its direct competitors, Lowe's. To calculate ROIC, divide NOPLAT by average invested capital. In 2003, Home Depot's return on invested capital equaled 18.2 percent (based on a two-year average of invested capital), which exceeds its weighted average cost of capital of 9.3 percent. A detailed discussion of invested capital and NOPLAT, as well as an in-depth historical examination of Home Depot and Lowe's, is presented in Chapter 7.

Next, use the reorganized financial statements to calculate free cash flow, which will be the basis for our valuation. Defined in a manner consistent with ROIC, free cash flow relies on NOPLAT and the change in invested capital. Unlike the accountant's cash flow statement (provided in the company's annual report), free cash flow is independent of nonoperating items and capital structure.

Exhibit 5.6 on page 110 presents historical free cash flow for both Home Depot and Lowe's. As seen in the exhibit, Home Depot is generating nearly

Exhibit 5.5 Home Depot & Lowe's: Historical ROIC Analysis

$ million

	Home Depot			Lowe's		
	2001	2002	2003	2001	2002	2003
Net sales	53,553	58,247	64,816	22,111	26,491	30,838
Cost of merchandise sold	(37,406)	(40,139)	(44,236)	(15,743)	(18,465)	(21,231)
Selling, general and administrative	(10,451)	(11,375)	(12,658)	(4,053)	(4,859)	(5,671)
Depreciation	(756)	(895)	(1,075)	(517)	(626)	(758)
Operating lease interest	288	260	276	106	106	114
Adjusted EBITA	5,228	6,098	7,123	1,904	2,647	3,292
Adjusted taxes	(2,020)	(2,117)	(2,040)	(654)	(825)	(1,069)
NOPLAT	**3,208**	**3,981**	**5,083**	**1,250**	**1,822**	**2,223**
Invested capital						
Operating working capital	2,552	2,746	2,674	1,634	1,451	1,363
Net property and equipment	15,375	17,168	20,063	8,653	10,352	11,945
Capitalized operating leases	5,459	5,890	6,554	2,189	2,373	2,762
Net other assets	(216)	(247)	(524)	134	145	211
Invested capital (excluding goodwill)	23,170	25,557	28,767	12,611	14,321	16,281
Acquired intangibles and goodwill	419	575	833	0	0	0
Cumulative amortization and unreported goodwill	46	54	55	730	730	730
Invested capital (including goodwill)	**23,635**	**26,185**	**29,655**	**13,341**	**15,051**	**17,012**
ROIC excluding goodwill (average)	14.5%	16.3%	18.7%	10.9%	13.5%	14.5%
ROIC including goodwill (average)	14.3%	16.0%	18.2%	10.3%	12.8%	13.9%

Exhibit 5.6 Home Depot and Lowe's: Historical Free Cash Flow

$ million

	Home Depot			Lowe's		
	2001	2002	2003	2001	2002	2003
NOPLAT	3,208	3,981	5,083	1,250	1,822	2,223
Depreciation	756	895	1,075	517	626	758
Gross cash flow	3,964	4,876	6,157	1,767	2,448	2,981
Investment in operating working capital	834	(194)	72	(203)	183	88
Net capital expenditures	(3,063)	(2,688)	(3,970)	(2,135)	(2,325)	(2,351)
Investment in capitalized operating leases	(775)	(430)	(664)	(547)	(184)	(389)
Investments in intangibles and goodwill	(113)	(164)	(259)	0	0	0
Decrease (increase) in other operating assets	105	31	277	(7)	(11)	(66)
Increase (decrease) in accumulated other comprehensive income	(153)	138	172	3	0	0
Gross investment	(3,165)	(3,307)	(4,372)	(2,889)	(2,336)	(2,719)
Free cash flow	**799**	**1,569**	**1,785**	**1,122**	**112**	**262**
After-tax interest income	33	49	36	15	13	9
Decrease (increase) in excess cash	(1,509)	383	(473)	(321)	(189)	(415)
Decrease (increase) in nonoperating assets	9	(24)	23	13	(7)	(140)
Discontinued operations	0	0	0	0	0	15
Cash flow available to investors	**(668)**	**1,977**	**1,371**	**(1,415)**	**(71)**	**(268)**
	2001	2002	2003	2001	2002	2003
After-tax interest expense	17	23	38	123	125	121
After-tax lease interest expense	177	162	170	66	65	71
Decrease (increase) in debt	88	140	(44)	(903)	78	60
Decrease (increase) in capitalized operating leases	(775)	(430)	(664)	(547)	(184)	(389)
Flows to debt holders	(492)	(105)	(500)	(1,261)	85	(138)
Dividends	396	492	595	60	66	87
Net shares repurchased (issued)	(572)	1,590	1,276	(213)	(222)	(217)
Flows to equity holders	(176)	2,082	1,871	(154)	(156)	(130)
Cash flow available to investors	**(668)**	**1,977**	**1,371**	**(1,415)**	**(71)**	**(268)**

$2 billion in free cash flow, whereas Lowe's free cash flow is barely positive. This isn't necessarily a problem for Lowe's. The company's free cash flow is small because it is reinvesting most of its gross cash flow to grow its business.

Projecting revenue growth, ROIC, and free cash flow To build an enterprise DCF valuation, we project revenue growth, return on invested capital, and free cash flow. Exhibit 5.7 graphs historical and projected ROIC and

Exhibit 5.7 ROIC and Revenue Growth Projections

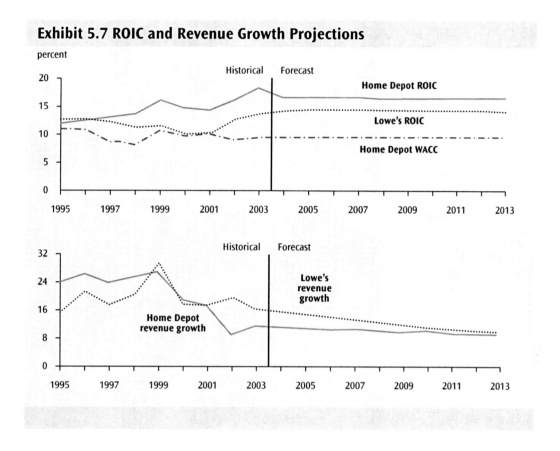

revenue growth for Home Depot and Lowe's. As the graphs demonstrate, the two companies are transitioning from a period of high growth (25 percent annually) into mature businesses with strong ROICs (well above Home Depot's 9.3 percent cost of capital) and lower growth rates (currently 10 to 15 percent but falling to 5 percent over the next 10 years).

Free cash flow, which is driven by revenue growth and ROIC, provides the basis for enterprise DCF valuation. Exhibit 5.8 on page 112 shows a summarized free cash flow calculation for Home Depot.[3] To forecast Home Depot's free cash flow, start with forecasts of NOPLAT and invested capital. Over the short run (the first few years), forecast all financial statement line items, such as gross margin, selling expenses, accounts receivable, and inventory. Moving farther out, individual line items become difficult to project. Therefore, over the medium horizon (5 to 10 years), focus on the company's key value drivers, such as operating margin, adjusted tax rate, and capital efficiency. At some point, even projecting key drivers on a

---

[3] Free cash flow does not incorporate any financing-related cash flows such as interest expense or dividends. A good stress test for an enterprise valuation model is to change future interest rates or dividend payout ratios and observe free cash flow. Free cash flow forecasts should *not* change when you adjust the cost of debt or dividend policy.

479

Exhibit 5.8 Home Depot: Free Cash Flow Summary

$ million

	Historical			Forecast		
	2001	2002	2003	2004	2005	2006
NOPLAT	3,208	3,981	5,083	5,185	5,741	6,342
Depreciation	756	895	1,075	1,193	1,321	1,459
Gross cash flow	3,964	4,876	6,157	6,378	7,062	7,801
Investment in operating working capital	834	(194)	72	(294)	(318)	(344)
Net capital expenditures	(3,063)	(2,688)	(3,970)	(3,399)	(3,708)	(4,036)
Investment in capitalized operating leases	(775)	(430)	(664)	(721)	(780)	(842)
Investments in intangibles and goodwill	(113)	(164)	(259)	(92)	(99)	(107)
Decrease (increase) in other operating assets	105	31	277	58	62	67
Increase (decrease) in accumulated other comprehensive income	(153)	138	172	0	0	0
Gross investment	(3,165)	(3,307)	(4,372)	(4,448)	(4,843)	(5,261)
Free cash flow	799	1,569	1,785	1,930	2,219	2,539

year-by-year basis becomes meaningless. To value cash flows beyond this point, use a continuing-value formula, described next.

Estimating continuing value At the point where predicting the individual key value drivers on a year-by-year basis becomes impractical, do not vary the individual drivers over time. Instead, use a perpetuity-based continuing value, such that:

$$\text{Value of Operations} = \frac{\text{Present Value of Free Cash Flow}}{during \text{ Explicit Forecast Period}} + \frac{\text{Present Value of Free Cash Flow}}{after \text{ Explicit Forecast Period}}$$

Although many continuing-value models exist, we prefer the key value driver model presented in Chapter 3. The key value driver formula is superior to alternative methodologies because it is based on cash flow and links cash flow to growth and ROIC. The key value driver formula is:

$$\text{Continuing Value}_t = \frac{\text{NOPLAT}_{t+1}\left(1 - \dfrac{g}{\text{RONIC}}\right)}{\text{WACC} - g}$$

The formula requires a forecast of net operating profits less adjusted taxes (NOPLAT) in the year following the explicit forecast period, the long-run

Exhibit 5.9 Home Depot: Continuing Value

$ million

NOPLAT $_{2014}$	12,415	
Return on incremental invested capital (RONIC)	9.3%	
NOPLAT growth rate in perpetuity (g)	4.0%	
Weighted average cost of capital (WACC)	9.3%	

$$\text{Continuing Value}_t = \frac{\text{NOPLAT}_{t+1}\left(1 - \frac{g}{\text{RONIC}}\right)}{\text{WACC} - g}$$

$$= 133,360$$

forecast for return on new capital (RONIC), the weighted average cost of capital (WACC), and long-run growth in NOPLAT (g).

Exhibit 5.9 presents an estimate for Home Depot's continuing value. Based on a final-year estimate of NOPLAT ($12.4 billion), return on new investment equal to the cost of capital (9.3 percent), and a long-term growth rate of 4 percent, the continuing value is estimated at $133.4 billion. This value is then discounted into today's dollars and added to the value from the explicit forecast period to determine Home Depot's operating value (see Exhibit 5.4).

Alternative methods and additional details for estimating continuing value are provided in Chapter 9.

Discounting free cash flow at the weighted average cost of capital   To determine the value of operations, discount each year's forecast of free cash flow for time and risk. When you discount any set of cash flows, make sure to define the cash flows and discount factor consistently. Since free cash flows are available to *all* investors, the discount factor for free cash flow must represent the risk faced by all investors. The weighted average cost of capital (WACC) blends the required rates of return for debt (k_d) and equity (k_e) based on their market-based target values. For a company financed solely with debt and equity, the WACC is defined as follows:

$$\text{WACC} = \frac{D}{D+E}k_d(1 - T_m) + \frac{E}{D+E}k_e$$

Note how the cost of debt has been reduced by the marginal tax rate (T_m). We do this because the interest tax shield has been *excluded* from free cash flow (remember, interest is tax deductible). Since the interest tax shield has value, it must be incorporated in the valuation. Enterprise DCF values the tax shield by reducing the weighted average cost of capital.

Why move the interest tax shields from free cash flow to the cost of capital? By calculating free cash flow as if the company were financed entirely

Exhibit 5.10 Home Depot: Weighted Average Cost of Capital

percent

Source of capital	Proportion of total capital	Cost of capital	Marginal tax rate	After-tax opportunity cost	Contribution to weighted average
Debt	8.3	4.7	38.2	2.9	0.2
Equity	91.7	9.9		9.9	9.1
WACC	**100.0**				**9.3**

with equity, we can compare operating performance across companies and over time without regard to capital structure. By focusing solely on operations, we can develop a cleaner picture of historical performance, and this leads to better forecasting.

Although applying the weighted average cost of capital is intuitive and relatively straightforward, it comes with some drawbacks. If you discount all future cash flows with a constant cost of capital, as most analysts do, you are implicitly assuming the company manages its capital structure to a target rate. For example, if a company plans to increase its debt-to-value ratio, the current cost of capital will understate the expected tax shields. Although the WACC can be adjusted for a changing capital structure, the process is complicated. In these situations, we recommend an alternative method such as adjusted present value.

The weighted average cost of capital for Home Depot is presented in Exhibit 5.10. For simplicity, the cost of capital in this valuation is based on the company's current capital structure. Since Home Depot has very little debt, the weighted average cost of capital (9.3 percent) is very close to Home Depot's cost of equity (9.9 percent). Chapter 10 provides a more formal discussion of WACC and its components.

This cost of capital is used to discount each year's forecasted cash flow, as well as the continuing value. The result is the value of operations.

Identifying and Valuing Nonoperating Assets

When measured properly, free cash flow from operations should not include any cash flows from nonoperating assets. Instead, nonoperating assets should be valued separately. Nonoperating assets can be segmented into two groups, marketable securities and illiquid investments.

Excess cash and marketable securities Statement of Financial Accounting Standards (SFAS) No. 115 (1993) and International Accounting Standards

(IAS) No. 39 (1998) require companies to report liquid debt and equity investments (e.g., excess cash and marketable securities) at a fair market value on the company's balance sheet.[4] Therefore, when valuing *liquid* nonoperating assets, use their most recent reported balance sheet value, rather than discount future nonoperating flows.

Illiquid investments, such as nonconsolidated subsidiaries When valuing a company from the inside, you should value illiquid investments by using enterprise DCF (i.e., project cash flow and discount at the appropriate cost of capital). If you are valuing the company from the outside, valuation of these assets is rough at best. Companies disclose very little information about illiquid investments, such as discontinued operations, excess real estate, nonconsolidated subsidiaries, and other equity investments.

For nonconsolidated subsidiaries, information disclosure depends on the level of ownership. When a company has some influence but not a controlling interest[5] in another company, it records its portion of the subsidiary's profits on its own income statement and the original investment plus its portion of reinvested profits on its own balance sheet. Use this information to create a simple cash flow statement. To discount the cash flow, use a cost of capital commensurate with the risk of the investment, not the parent company's cost of capital (this is why we recommend separation of operating and nonoperating assets).

When ownership is less than 20 percent, investments are reported at historical cost, and the company's portion of profits is recorded *only* when paid out to the parent. In most situations, you will see nothing more than the investment's original cost. In this case, use a multiple of the book value or a tracking portfolio to value the investment. Further details for valuing nonoperating assets are covered in Chapter 11.

Identifying and Valuing Nonequity Claims

Add the value of nonoperating assets to the value of operations to determine enterprise value. To estimate equity value, subtract any nonequity claims, such as debt, unfunded retirement liabilities, capitalized operating leases, and outstanding employee options. Common equity is a residual claimant, receiving cash flows only after the company has fulfilled its other contractual claims. In today's increasingly complex financial markets, *many* claimants have rights to a company's cash flow before equity

---

[4] Liquid investments can appear as either current or long-term assets. Their placement depends on when management intends to sell the assets.
[5] In the United States and Europe, this is generally accepted as between 20 percent and 50 percent ownership.

holders—and they are not always easy to spot. Enron collapsed in 2001 under the weight of hidden debt. The company signed agreements with the creditors of its nonconsolidated subsidiaries, promising to cover loan payments if the subsidiaries could not.[6] Since the subsidiaries were not consolidated, the debt never appeared on Enron's balance sheet, and investors dramatically overestimated the equity's value. When the loans were disclosed in November 2001, the company's stock price fell by more than 50 percent in a single week.

Here are the most common nonequity claims:

- *Debt:* If available, use the market value of all outstanding debt, including fixed and floating rate debt. If that information is unavailable, the book value of debt is a reasonable proxy, unless the probability of default is high or interest rates have changed dramatically since the debt was originally issued. Any valuation of debt, however, should be consistent with your estimates of enterprise value. (See Chapter 11 for more details.)

- *Unfunded retirement liabilities:* The recent weak performance of global stock markets and the rising cost of health care have left many companies with retirement liabilities that are partially unfunded. Although the actual shortfall is not reported on the balance sheet (only a smoothed amount is transferred to the balance sheet), the stock market clearly values unfunded retirement liabilities as an offset against enterprise value. Consider General Motors, which raised nearly $20 billion in debt to fund its pension deficit. The company's stock price actually rose during the month when the new debt was announced and issued. Investors knew a liability existed, even though it wasn't on the balance sheet.

- *Operating leases:* These represent the most common form of off-balance-sheet debt. Under certain conditions, companies can avoid capitalizing leases as debt on their balance sheet, although required payments must be disclosed in the footnotes.

- *Contingent liabilities:* Any other material off-balance-sheet contingencies, such as lawsuits and loan guarantees, will be reported in the footnotes.

- *Preferred stock:* Although the name denotes equity, preferred stock in well-established companies more closely resembles unsecured debt. Therefore, preferred-stock dividends (which are often predetermined and required) should be valued separately, using an appropriate risk-adjusted discount rate.

[6] D. Henry, "Who Else Is Hiding Debt: Moving Financial Obligations into Off-Book Vehicles Is Now a Common Ploy," *BusinessWeek* (January 2002), p. 36.

- *Employee options:* Each year, many companies offer their employees compensation in the form of options. Since options give the employee the right to buy company stock at a potentially discounted price, they can have great value. Employee options can be valued using traditional models, such as Black-Scholes, or advanced techniques such as lattice models.

- *Minority interest:* When a company controls a subsidiary but does not own 100 percent, the investment must be consolidated on the parent company's balance sheet, and the funding other investors provide is recognized on the parent company's balance sheet as minority interest. When valuing minority interest, it is important to realize the minority interest holder does not have a claim on the company's assets, but rather a claim on the subsidiary's assets. Thus, minority interest must be valued separately and not as a percentage of company value.

The identification and valuation of nonequity financial claims are covered in detail in Chapter 11.

A common mistake made when valuing companies is to double-count claims already deducted from cash flow. Consider a company with a pension shortfall. You have been told the company will make extra payments to eliminate the liability. If you deduct the present value of the liability from enterprise value, you should not model the extra payments within free cash flow; that would mean double-counting the shortfall (once in cash flow and once as a claim), leading to an underestimate of equity value.

Valuing Equity

Once you have identified and valued all nonequity claims, we can subtract the claims from enterprise value to determine equity value. Home Depot has traditional debt ($1.4 billion) and capitalized operating leases ($6.6 billion). To value Home Depot's common stock, we subtract each of these claims from Home Depot's enterprise value (see Exhibit 5.4).

To determine Home Depot's share price, divide the estimated common-stock value by the number of undiluted shares outstanding. Do not use diluted shares. We have already valued convertible debt and employee stock options separately. If we were to use diluted shares, we would be double-counting the options' value.

At the end of fiscal year 2003, Home Depot had 2.3 billion shares outstanding. Dividing the equity estimate of $73.2 billion by 2.3 billion shares generates an estimated value of $32 per share. The estimated share value assumes Home Depot can maintain its current ROIC over the forecast period and the growth rate will remain strong, decaying gradually over the next 10 years from its current level of 11 percent to 4 percent in the continuing value. During the first half of 2004, the Home Depot's actual stock price traded between $32 and $38 per share.

ECONOMIC-PROFIT-BASED VALUATION MODELS

The enterprise DCF model is a favorite of academics and practitioners alike because it relies solely on how cash flows in and out of the company. Complex accounting can be replaced with a simple question: Does cash change hands? One shortfall of enterprise DCF, however, is that each year's cash flow provides little insight into the company's performance. Declining free cash flow can signal either poor performance or investment for the future. The economic profit model highlights how and when the company creates value yet leads to a valuation that is identical to that of enterprise DCF.

As stated in Chapter 3, economic profit measures the value created by the company in a single period and is defined as follows:

$$\text{Economic Profit} = \text{Invested Capital} \times (\text{ROIC} - \text{WACC})$$

Since ROIC equals NOPLAT divided by invested capital, we can rewrite the equation as follows:

$$\text{Economic Profit} = \text{NOPLAT} - (\text{Invested Capital} \times \text{WACC})$$

In Exhibit 5.11, we present economic profit calculations for Home Depot using both methods. Since Home Depot has been earning returns greater than its cost of capital, its historical economic profit is positive. Given the company's strong competitive position, we also project positive economic profits going forward. Not every company has positive economic profit. In fact, many companies earn an accounting profit (net income greater than zero) but do not earn their cost of capital.

To demonstrate how economic profit can be used to value a company—and to demonstrate its equivalence to enterprise DCF, consider a stream of growing cash flows valued using the growing-perpetuity formula:

$$\text{Value}_0 = \frac{\text{FCF}_1}{\text{WACC} - g}$$

In Chapter 3, we transformed this cash flow perpetuity into the key value driver model. The key value driver model is superior to the simple cash flow perpetuity model, because it explicitly models the relation between growth and required investment. Using a few additional algebraic

Exhibit 5.11 Home Depot: Economic Profit Summary

$ million

	Historical 2001	2002	2003	Forecast 2004	2005	2006
Method 1						
Return on invested capital	15.0%	16.8%	19.4%	17.5%	17.4%	17.4%
Weighted average cost of capital	10.1%	9.0%	9.3%	9.3%	9.3%	9.3%
Economic spread	4.9%	7.9%	10.1%	8.2%	8.1%	8.1%
Invested capital	21,379	23,635	26,185	29,655	32,910	36,432
Economic profit	1,048	1,857	2,645	2,424	2,677	2,950
Method 2						
Invested capital	21,379	23,635	26,185	29,655	32,910	36,432
Weighted average cost of capital	10.1%	9.0%	9.3%	9.3%	9.3%	9.3%
Capital charge	2,159	2,124	2,438	2,761	3,064	3,392
NOPLAT	3,208	3,981	5,083	5,185	5,741	6,342
Capital charge	2,159	2,124	2,438	2,761	3,064	3,392
Economic profit	1,048	1,857	2,645	2,424	2,677	2,950

steps (see Appendix A) and the assumption that the company's ROIC on new projects equals historical ROIC, we can transform the cash flow perpetuity into a key value driver model based on economic profits:

$$\text{Value}_0 = \text{Invested Capital}_0 + \frac{\text{Invested Capital}_0 \times (\text{ROIC} - \text{WACC})}{\text{WACC} - g}$$

Finally, we substitute the definition of economic profit:

$$\text{Value}_0 = \text{Invested Capital}_0 + \frac{\text{Economic Profit}_1}{\text{WACC} - g}$$

As can be seen in the economic-profit-based key value driver model, the operating value of a company equals its book value of invested capital plus the present value of all future value created. In this case, the future economic profits are valued using a growing perpetuity, because the company's economic profits are increasing at a constant rate over time. More generally, economic profit can be valued as follows:

$$\text{Value}_0 = \text{Invested Capital}_0 + \sum_{t=1}^{\infty} \frac{\text{Invested Capital}_{t-1} \times (\text{ROIC}_t - \text{WACC})}{(1 + \text{WACC})^t}$$

Since the economic profit valuation was derived directly from the free cash flow model (see Appendix B for a proof of equivalence), any valuation based on discounted economic profits will be identical to enterprise DCF. To assure equivalence, however, you must:

- Use beginning-of-year invested capital (i.e., last year's value).
- Use the same invested-capital number for both economic profit and ROIC. For example, ROIC can be measured either with or without goodwill. If you measure ROIC without goodwill, invested capital must also be measured without goodwill. All told, it doesn't matter how you define invested capital, as long as you are consistent.

Exhibit 5.12 presents the valuation results for Home Depot using economic profit. Economic profits are explicitly forecasted for 10 years; the

Exhibit 5.12 Home Depot: Economic Profit Valuation

Year	Invested capital[1] ($ million)	ROIC (percent)	WACC (percent)	Economic profit ($ million)	Discount factor (@ 9.3%)	Present value of economic profit ($ million)
2004	29,655	17.5	9.3	2,424	0.915	2,217
2005	32,910	17.4	9.3	2,677	0.837	2,241
2006	36,432	17.4	9.3	2,950	0.766	2,259
2007	40,235	17.4	9.3	3,242	0.700	2,271
2008	44,329	17.3	9.3	3,556	0.641	2,278
2009	48,729	17.3	9.3	3,890	0.586	2,281
2010	53,445	17.3	9.3	4,247	0.536	2,278
2011	58,488	17.2	9.3	4,627	0.491	2,270
2012	63,870	17.2	9.3	5,031	0.449	2,258
2013	69,600	17.2	9.3	5,458	0.411	2,241
Continuing value				57,671	0.411	23,679
Present value of economic profit						46,273
Invested capital[1] $_{2004}$						29,655
Invested capital plus present value of economic profit						75,928
Mid-year adjustment factor						1.046
Value of operations						**79,384**
Value of excess cash						1,609
Value of other nonoperating assets						84
Enterprise value						**81,077**
Value of debt						(1,365)
Value of capitalized operating leases						(6,554)
Equity value						**73,158**

[1]Invested capital is measured at the beginning of the year.

remaining years are valued using an economic profit continuing-value formula.[7] Comparing the equity value from Exhibit 5.4 with that of Exhibit 5.12, we see that the value of Home Depot's stock is the same, regardless of the method.

The benefit of economic profit becomes apparent when we examine the drivers of economic profit, ROIC and WACC, on a year-by-year basis in Exhibit 5.12. Notice how the valuation depends heavily on Home Depot's ability to maintain current levels of ROIC (17.5 percent) well above the WACC (9.3 percent). If the company's markets become saturated, growth could become elusive, and some companies might compete on price to steal market share. If this occurs, ROICs will drop, and economic profits will revert to zero. Explicitly modeling ROIC as a primary driver of economic profit will prominently display this analysis. Conversely, the free cash flow model fails to show this dynamic. Free cash flow could continue to grow, even as ROIC falls.

Another insight generated by the economic profit model occurs when comparing a company's value of operations with its invested capital. For Home Depot, the estimated operating value ($79.4 billion) exceeds the company's invested capital ($29.7 billion) by more than $49.7 billion.

ADJUSTED PRESENT VALUE MODEL

When building an enterprise DCF or economic profit valuation, most financial analysts discount all future flows at a *constant* weighted average cost of capital. Using a constant WACC, however, assumes the company manages its capital structure to a target debt-to-value ratio.

In most situations, debt grows in line with company value. But suppose the company planned to significantly change its capital structure. Indeed, companies with significant debt often pay it down as cash flow improves, thus lowering their future debt-to-value ratios. In these cases, a valuation

---

[7] To calculate continuing value, you can use the economic-profit-based key value driver formula, but only if RONIC equals historical ROIC in the continuing-value year. If RONIC going forward differs from the final year's ROIC, then the equation must be separated into current and future economic profits:

$$\text{Continuing Value}_t = \underbrace{\frac{IC_t(ROIC_{t+1} - WACC)}{WACC}}_{\text{Current Economic Profits}} + \underbrace{\frac{PV(\text{Economic Profit}_{t+2})}{WACC - g}}_{\text{Future Economic Profits}}$$

such that

$$PV(\text{Economic Profit}_{t+2}) = \frac{NOPLAT_{t+1}\left(\dfrac{g}{RONIC}\right)(RONIC - WACC)}{WACC}$$

based on a constant WACC would overstate the value of the tax shields. Although the WACC can be adjusted yearly to handle a changing capital structure, the process is complex. Therefore, we turn to an alternative model: adjusted present value.

The adjusted present value (APV) model separates the value of operations into two components: the value of operations as if the company were all-equity financed and the value of tax shields that arise from debt financing:[8]

$$\begin{matrix} \text{Adjusted} \\ \text{Present Value} \end{matrix} = \begin{matrix} \text{Enterprise Value as if the} \\ \text{Company Was All-Equity Financed} \end{matrix} + \begin{matrix} \text{Present Value of} \\ \text{Tax Shields} \end{matrix}$$

The APV valuation model follows directly from the teachings of Modigliani and Miller, who proposed that in a market with no taxes (among other things), a company's choice of financial structure will not affect the value of its economic assets. Only market imperfections, such as taxes and distress costs, affect enterprise value.

When building a valuation model, it is easy to forget these teachings. To see this, imagine a company (in a world with no taxes) that has a 50-50 mix of debt and equity. If the company's debt has an expected return of 5 percent and the company's equity has an expected return of 15 percent, its weighted average cost of capital would be 10 percent. Suppose the company decides to issue more debt, using the proceeds to repurchase shares. Since the cost of debt is lower than the cost of equity, it would appear that issuing debt to retire equity should lower the WACC, raising the company's value.

This line of thinking is flawed, however. In a world without taxes, a change in capital structure would *not* change the cash flow generated by operations, nor the risk of those cash flows. Therefore, neither the company's enterprise value nor its cost of capital would change. So why did we think it would? When adding debt, we adjusted the weights, but we failed to properly increase the cost of equity. Since debt payments have priority over cash flows to equity, adding leverage increases the risk to equity holders. When leverage rises, they demand a higher return. Modigliani and Miller postulated this increase would perfectly offset the change in weights.

In reality, taxes play a part in decision making, and capital structure choice therefore *can* affect cash flows. Since interest is tax deductible, profitable companies can lower taxes by raising debt. But, if the company relies

---

[8] In this book, we focus on the tax shields generated by interest. On a more general basis, the APV values *any* incremental cash flows associated with capital structure, such as tax shields, issue costs, and distress costs. Distress costs include direct costs, such as court-related fees, and indirect costs, such as the loss of customers and suppliers.

too heavily on debt, the company's customers and suppliers may fear bankruptcy and walk away, restricting future cash flow (academics call this distress costs or deadweight costs). Rather than model the effect of capital structure changes in the weighted average cost of capital, APV explicitly measures and values the cash flow effects of financing separately.

To build an APV-based valuation, value the company as if it were all-equity financed. Do this by discounting free cash flow by the unlevered cost of equity (what the cost of equity would be if the company had no debt). To this value, add any value created by the company's use of debt. Exhibit 5.13 values Home Depot using adjusted present value. Since we assume that Home Depot will manage its capital structure to a target debt-to-value level of 9.3 percent, the APV-based valuation leads to the same value for equity as

Exhibit 5.13 Home Depot: Valuation Using Adjusted Present Value

Year	Free cash flow ($ million)	Interest tax shield (ITS)	Discount factor (@ 9.5%)	Present value of FCF ($ million)	Present value of ITS ($ million)
2004	1,930	113	0.914	1,763	103
2005	2,219	120	0.835	1,852	100
2006	2,539	128	0.763	1,936	98
2007	2,893	136	0.697	2,016	95
2008	3,283	145	0.636	2,090	92
2009	3,711	153	0.581	2,158	89
2010	4,180	162	0.531	2,220	86
2011	4,691	171	0.485	2,276	83
2012	5,246	180	0.443	2,326	80
2013	5,849	189	0.405	2,369	77
Continuing value	129,734	3,626	0.405	52,550	1,469
Present value				73,557	2,372

Present value of FCF using unlevered cost of equity	73,557
Present value of interest tax shields (ITS)	2,372
Present value of FCF and ITS	75,928
Mid-year adjustment factor	1.046
Value of operations	**79,384**
Value of excess cash	1,609
Value of other nonoperating assets	84
Enterprise value	**81,077**
Value of debt	(1,365)
Value of capitalized operating leases	(6,554)
Equity value	**73,158**

491

did enterprise DCF (see Exhibit 5.4) and economic profit (see Exhibit 5.12). A simplified proof of equivalence between enterprise DCF and adjusted present value can be found in Appendix C. The following subsections explain APV in detail.

Value Free Cash Flow at Unlevered Cost of Equity

When valuing a company using the APV, we explicitly separate the unlevered value of operations (V_u) from any value created by financing, such as tax shields (V_{txa}). For a company with debt (D) and equity (E), this relation is as follows:

$$V_u + V_{txa} = D + E \tag{1}$$

A second result of Modigliani and Miller's work is that the total risk of the company's assets, real and financial, must equal the total risk of the financial claims against those assets. Thus, in equilibrium, the blended cost of capital for operating assets (k_u, which we call the unlevered cost of equity) and financial assets (k_{txa}) must equal the blended cost of capital for debt (k_d) and equity (k_e):

$$\underbrace{\frac{V_u}{V_u + V_{txa}} k_u}_{\text{Operating Assets}} + \underbrace{\frac{V_{txa}}{V_u + V_{txa}} k_{txa}}_{\text{Tax Assets}} = \underbrace{\frac{D}{D+E} k_d}_{\text{Debt}} + \underbrace{\frac{E}{D+E} k_e}_{\text{Equity}} \tag{2}$$

In the corporate finance literature, academics combine Modigliani and Miller's two equations to solve for the cost of equity—to demonstrate the relation between leverage and the cost of equity. In Appendix D, we algebraically rearrange equation 2 to solve for the levered cost of equity:

$$k_e = k_u + \frac{D}{E}\left(k_u - k_d\right) - \frac{V_{txa}}{E}\left(k_u - k_{txa}\right)$$

As this equation indicates, the cost of equity depends on the unlevered cost of equity plus a premium for leverage, less a reduction for the tax deductibility of debt.

Determining the unlevered cost of equity with market data To use the APV, we need to discount projected free cash flow at the unlevered cost of equity, k_u. However, none of the variables (including k_u) on the left side of equation 2 can be observed. Only the values on the right—that is, those related to debt and equity—can be estimated directly. Because there are so many unknowns and only one equation, we must impose additional restrictions to solve for k_u.

Method 1: Assume k_{txa} equals k_u   If you believe the risk associated with tax shields (k_{txa}) equals the risk associated with operating assets (k_u), equation 2 can be simplified dramatically (see Appendix D):

$$k_u = \frac{E}{D+E}k_d + \frac{D}{D+E}k_e \tag{3}$$

We can now determine the unlevered cost of equity because it now relies solely on observable variables, that is, those related to debt and equity. In fact, k_u looks very similar to the weighted average cost of capital, without the interest tax shield.

Equation 3 can be rearranged to solve for the levered cost of equity:

$$k_e = k_u + \frac{D}{E}(k_u - k_d) \tag{4}$$

Note that when the company has no debt ($D = 0$), k_e equals k_u. This is why k_u is referred to as the unlevered cost of equity.

Method 2: Assume k_{txa} equals k_d   If you believe the risk associated with tax shields (k_{txa}) is comparable to the risk of debt (k_d), equation 2 can be rearranged to solve for the unlevered cost of equity:

$$k_u = \frac{D - V_{txa}}{D - V_{txa} + E}k_d + \frac{E}{D - V_{txa} + E}k_e \tag{5}$$

In this equation, k_u relies on observable variables, such as the market value of debt, market value of equity, cost of debt, and cost of equity, as well as one unobservable variable: the present value of tax shields (V_{txa}). To use equation 4, discount expected future tax shields at the cost of debt (to remain consistent) and *then* solve for the unlevered cost of equity.

Many practitioners further refine the last equation by imposing an additional restriction: that the absolute dollar level of debt is constant. If the dollar level of debt is constant, the annual expected tax shield equals $(D \times k_d) \times$

T_m, where T_m equals the marginal tax rate. Applying a no-growth perpetuity formula allows us to value the tax shield:

$$V_{txa} = \frac{(D \times k_d) \times T_m}{k_d} = D \times T_m$$

Substituting $D \times T_m$ for the value of the tax shield in the last equation leads to:

$$k_u = \frac{(1-T_m)D}{(1-T_m)D+E} k_d + \frac{E}{(1-T_m)D+E} k_e \tag{6}$$

Although equation 6 is quite common in practice, its use is limited because the assumptions are extremely restrictive.

Choosing the appropriate formula Which formula should you use to back-solve for the unlevered cost of equity, k_u? It depends on how you see the company managing its capital structure going forward and whether the debt is risk free. If you believe the company will manage its debt-to-value to a target level (the company's debt will grow with the business), then the value of the tax shields will track the value of the operating assets. Thus, the risk of tax shields will equal the risk of operating assets (k_{txa} equals k_u). The majority of companies have relatively stable capital structures (as a percentage of expected value), so we favor the first method.

If you believe the debt to equity ratio will not remain constant, then the value of interest tax shields will be more closely tied to the value of forecasted debt, rather than operating assets. In this case, the risk of tax shields is equivalent to the risk of debt (when a company is unprofitable, it cannot use interest tax shields, the risk of default rises, and the value of debt drops). In this case, equation 5 better approximates the unlevered cost of equity.[9] This situation occurs frequently in periods of high debt such as financial distress and leveraged buyouts.

Value Tax Shields and Other Capital Structure Effects

To complete an APV-based valuation, forecast and discount capital structure side effects such as tax shields, security issue costs, and distress costs. Since Home Depot has little chance of default, we estimated the company's future interest tax shields using the company's promised yield to maturity and marginal tax rate (see Exhibit 5.14). To calculate the expected interest

[9] Even if a company's tax shields are predetermined for a given period, eventually they will track value. For instance, successful leveraged buyouts pay down debt for a period of time, but once the debt level becomes reasonable, debt will more likely track value than remain constant.

Exhibit 5.14 Home Depot: Forecast of Interest Tax Shields

Year	Prior year net debt ($ million)	Expected interest rate (percent)	Interest payment ($ million)	Marginal tax rate (percent)	Interest tax shield ($ million)
2004	6,310	4.7	295	38.2	113
2005	6,737	4.7	315	38.2	120
2006	7,179	4.7	336	38.2	128
2007	7,637	4.7	357	38.2	136
2008	8,107	4.7	379	38.2	145
2009	8,589	4.7	402	38.2	153
2010	9,081	4.7	425	38.2	162
2011	9,579	4.7	448	38.2	171
2012	10,081	4.7	472	38.2	180
2013	10,583	4.7	495	38.2	189
Continuing value	11,082	4.7	518	38.2	198

payment in 2004, multiply the prior year's net debt of $6.3 billion by the expected yield of 4.7 percent (net debt equals reported debt plus capitalized operating leases minus excess cash). This led to an expected interest payment of $295 million. Next multiply the expected interest payment by the marginal tax rate of 38.2 percent, for an expected interest tax shield of $113 million in 2004.

Home Depot's conservative use of debt makes tax shield valuation straightforward. For companies with significant leverage, the company may not be able to fully use the tax shields (it may not have enough profits to shield). If there is a significant probability of default, you must model *expected* tax shields, rather than the tax shields based on promised interest payments. To do this, reduce each promised tax shield by the cumulative probability of default.

CAPITAL CASH FLOW MODEL

When a company actively manages its capital structure to a target debt-to-value level, both free cash flow (FCF) and the interest tax shield (ITS) are discounted at the unlevered cost of equity, k_u:

$$V = \sum_{t=1}^{\infty} \frac{FCF_t}{(1+k_u)^t} + \sum_{t=1}^{\infty} \frac{ITS_t}{(1+k_u)^t}$$

In 2000, Richard Ruback of the Harvard Business School argued there is no need to separate free cash flow from tax shields when both flows are discounted by the same cost of capital.[10] He combined the two flows and named the resulting cash flow (FCF plus interest tax shields) capital cash flow (CCF):

$$V = \text{PV(Capital Cash Flows)} = \sum_{t=1}^{\infty} \frac{\text{FCF}_t + \text{ITS}_t}{(1 + k_u)^t}$$

Given that Ruback's assumptions match those of the weighted average cost of capital, the capital cash flow and WACC-based valuations will lead to identical results. In fact, we now have detailed three distinct but identical valuation methods created solely around how they treat tax shields: WACC (tax shield valued in the cost of capital), APV (tax shield valued separately), and CCF (tax shield valued in the cash flow).

Although FCF and CCF lead to the same result when debt is proportional to value, we believe free cash flow models are superior to capital cash flow models. Why? By keeping NOPLAT and FCF independent of leverage, we can cleanly evaluate the company's operating performance over time and across competitors. A clean measure of historical operating performance leads to better forecasts.

CASH-FLOW-TO-EQUITY VALUATION MODEL

In each of the preceding valuation models, we determined the value of equity indirectly by subtracting nonequity claims from enterprise value. The equity cash flow model values equity directly by discounting cash flows to equity at the cost of equity, rather than at the weighted average cost of capital.[11]

Exhibit 5.15 details the cash flows to equity for Home Depot. Cash flow to equity can be computed by reorganizing free cash flow found in Exhibit 5.6 or using the traditional method in Exhibit 5.15. In the traditional method, cash flow to equity starts with net income. Next, noncash expenses are added back, and investments in working capital, fixed assets, and nonoperating assets are subtracted. Finally, any increases in nonequity financing such as debt are added, and decreases in nonequity financing are subtracted. Alternatively, we can compute cash flow to equity as dividends

---

[10] Richard S. Ruback, "Capital Cash Flows: A Simple Approach to Valuing Risky Cash Flows," Social Science Research Network (March 2000).

[11] The equity method can be difficult to implement correctly because capital structure is embedded in the cash flow. This makes forecasting difficult. For companies whose operations are related to financing, such as financial institutions, the equity method is appropriate. We discuss valuing financial institutions in Chapter 25.

Exhibit 5.15 Home Depot: Equity Cash Flow Summary

$ million

	Historical 2001	2002	2003	Forecast 2004	2005	2006
Net income	3,044	3,664	4,304	4,796	5,318	5,882
Depreciation	756	895	1,075	1,193	1,321	1,459
Amortization	8	8	1	0	0	0
Increase (decrease) in deferred taxes	(6)	173	605	214	237	262
Gross cash flow	3,802	4,740	5,985	6,203	6,876	7,603
Investment in operating working capital	834	(194)	72	(294)	(318)	(344)
Investment in net long-term assets	(3,224)	(2,683)	(3,780)	(3,433)	(3,745)	(4,076)
Decrease (increase) in excess cash	(1,509)	383	(473)	(177)	(191)	(207)
Investment in other nonoperating assets	9	(24)	23	(9)	(10)	(11)
Increase (decrease) in short-term debt	207	(211)	509	(44)	(54)	(66)
Increase (decrease) in long-term debt	(295)	71	(465)	(73)	(91)	(112)
Cash flow to equity	**(176)**	**2,082**	**1,871**	**2,173**	**2,466**	**2,788**
	2001	2002	2003	2004	2005	2006
Dividends	396	492	595	663	735	813
Share repurchases (issued)	(572)	1,590	1,276	1,510	1,731	1,975
Cash flow to equity	**(176)**	**2,082**	**1,871**	**2,173**	**2,466**	**2,788**

plus share repurchases minus new equity issues. Both methods generate identical results.

To value Home Depot, we discount projected equity cash flows at the cost of equity (see Exhibit 5.16 on p. 130). Unlike enterprise-based models, no adjustments are made for nonoperating assets, debt, or capitalized operating leases. Rather, they are included as part of the equity cash flow.

Once again, note how the valuation, derived using equity cash flows, matches each of the prior valuations.[12] This occurs because we have modeled

---

[12] When performing a stand-alone equity cash flow valuation, you can calculate the continuing value by using a simple growing perpetuity:

$$V_e = \frac{\text{Net Income}\left(1 - \dfrac{g}{\text{ROE}}\right)}{k_e - g}$$

To tie the free cash flow and equity cash flow models, you must convert free cash flow continuing-value inputs into equity cash flow inputs. We did this using:

$$\text{Net Income}\left(1 - \frac{g}{\text{ROE}}\right) = \frac{\text{NOPLAT}\left(1 - \dfrac{g}{\text{ROIC}}\right)}{1 + \dfrac{D}{E}\left(1 - \dfrac{k_e - (1-T)k_d}{k_e - g}\right)}$$

497

Exhibit 5.16 Home Depot: Cash-Flow-to-Equity Valuation

Year	Cash flow to equity ($ million)	Discount factor (@ 9.9%)	Present value of CFE ($ million)
2004	2,173	0.910	1,978
2005	2,466	0.828	2,042
2006	2,788	0.754	2,101
2007	3,143	0.686	2,155
2008	3,530	0.624	2,203
2009	3,954	0.568	2,245
2010	4,416	0.517	2,282
2011	4,917	0.470	2,312
2012	5,459	0.428	2,336
2013	6,044	0.389	2,353
Continuing value	122,492	0.389	47,695
Present value of cash flow to equity			69,702
Midyear adjustment amount			3,456
Equity value			**73,158**

Home Depot's debt-to-value ratio at a constant level. If debt-to-value instead changes over time, the equity model becomes difficult to implement and can lead to conceptual errors. For example, if leverage is expected to rise, the cost of equity must be adjusted to reflect the additional risk imposed on equity holders. Although formulas exist to adjust the cost of equity, many of the best-known formulas are built under restrictions that may be inconsistent with the way you are implicitly forecasting the company's capital structure via the cash flows. This will cause a mismatch between cash flows and the cost of equity, resulting in an incorrect valuation.

Unwittingly changing the company's capital structure when using the cash-flow-to-equity model occurs too easily—and that is what makes the model so risky. Suppose you plan to value a company whose debt-to-value ratio is 15 percent. You believe the company will pay extra dividends, so you increase debt to raise the dividend payout ratio. Presto! Increased dividends lead to higher equity cash flows and a higher valuation. Even though operating performance has not changed, the equity value has mistakenly increased. What happened? Using new debt to pay dividends causes a rise in net debt to value. Unless you adjust the cost of equity, the valuation will rise incorrectly.

Another shortcoming of the direct equity approach occurs when valuing a company by business unit. The direct equity approach requires allocating debt and interest expense to each unit. This creates extra work yet provides few additional insights.

OTHER APPROACHES TO DISCOUNTED CASH FLOW

You may also come across two variants of enterprise DCF:

1. Using real instead of nominal cash flows and discount rates
2. Discounting pretax cash flows instead of after-tax cash flows

These approaches are well suited only to limited circumstances.

Using Real Cash Flows and Discount Rates

Companies can be valued by projecting cash flow in real terms (e.g., in constant 2004 dollars) and discounting this cash flow at a real discount rate (e.g., the nominal rate less expected inflation). But most managers think in terms of nominal rather than real measures, so nominal measures are often easier to communicate. In addition, interest rates are generally quoted nominally rather than in real terms (excluding expected inflation). Also, since historical financial statements are stated in nominal terms, projecting future statements in real terms is difficult and confusing.

A second difficulty occurs when calculating and interpreting ROIC. The historical statements are nominal, so historical returns on invested capital are nominal. But if the projections for the company use real rather than nominal forecasts, returns on new capital are also real. Projected returns on total capital (new and old) are a combination of nominal and real, so they are impossible to interpret. The only way around this is to restate historical performance on a real basis. This is a complex and time-consuming task. The extra insights gained rarely equal the effort (except in extremely high-inflation environments described in Chapter 22).

Discounting Pretax Cash Flow

For purposes of valuing internal investment opportunities, individual project cash flows are sometimes calculated without taxes. The pretax cash flow is then discounted by a pretax "hurdle rate" (the market-based cost of capital multiplied by 1 plus the marginal tax rate) to determine a pretax value.

This method, however, leads to three fundamental inconsistencies. First, the government calculates taxes on profits after depreciation, not on cash flow after capital expenditures. By discounting pretax cash flow at the pretax cost of capital, you implicitly assume capital investments are tax deductible when made, not as they are depreciated. Furthermore, short-term investments, such as accounts receivable and inventory, are never tax deductible. Selling a product at a profit is what leads to incremental taxes, not holding inventory. By discounting pretax cash flow at the pretax cost of capital, you incorrectly assume investments in operating working capital are tax deductible. Finally, it can be shown that even when net investment equals depreciation, the final result will be downward biased—and the larger the cost of capital, the larger the bias. This bias occurs because the method is only an approximation, not a formal mathematical relation. Because of these inconsistencies, we recommend against discounting pretax cash flows at a pretax hurdle rate.

ALTERNATIVES TO DISCOUNTED CASH FLOW

To this point, we have focused solely on discounted cash flow models. Two additional valuation techniques exist: multiples (comparables) and real options.

Multiples

Assume that you have been asked to value a company that is about to go public. Although you project and discount free cash flow to derive an enterprise value, you worry that your forecasts lack precision. One way to place your DCF model in the proper context is to create a set of comparables. One of the most commonly used comparables is the enterprise-value-to-earnings before interest, taxes, and amortization (EV/EBITA) multiple. To apply the EV/EBITA multiple, look for a set of comparable companies, and multiply a representative EV/EBITA multiple by the company's EBITA. For example, assume the company's EBITA equals $100 million and the typical EV/EBITA multiple in the industry is 15×. Multiplying 15 by $100 million leads to an estimated value of $1.5 billion. Is the enterprise DCF valuation near $1.5 billion? If not, what enables the company to earn better (or worse) returns or grow faster (or slower) than other companies in the industry?

Although the concept of multiples is simple, the methodology is misunderstood and often misapplied. Companies within an industry will have different multiples for valid economic reasons. Computing a representative multiple ignores this fact. In addition, common multiples, such as the price-to-earnings ratio, suffer from the same capital structure problems as equity cash flows. In Chapter 12, we demonstrate how to build and interpret forward-looking comparables, independent of capital structure and other nonoperating items.

Real Options

In 1997 Robert Merton and Myron Scholes won the Nobel Prize in Economics for developing an ingenious method to value derivatives that avoids the need to estimate either cash flows or the cost of capital. (Fischer Black would have been named as a third recipient, but the Nobel Prize is not awarded posthumously.) Their model relies on what today's economists call a "replicating portfolio." They argued that if there exists a portfolio of traded securities whose future cash flows perfectly mimic the security you are attempting to value, the portfolio and security must have the same price. As long as we can find a suitable replicating portfolio, we need not discount future cash flows.

Given the model's power, there have been many recent attempts to translate the concepts of replicating portfolios to corporate valuation. This valuation technique is commonly known as real options. Unlike those for financial options, however, replicating portfolios for companies and their projects may be difficult to create. Therefore, although options-pricing models may teach powerful lessons, today's applications are limited. We cover valuation using options-based models in Chapter 20.

SUMMARY

This chapter described the most common DCF valuation models, with particular focus on the enterprise DCF model and the economic profit model. We explained the rationale for each model and reasons why each model has an important place in corporate valuation. The remaining chapters in Part Two describe a step-by-step approach to valuing a company:

- Chapter 6: Thinking about Return on Invested Capital and Growth
- Chapter 7: Analyzing Historical Performance
- Chapter 8: Forecasting Performance
- Chapter 9: Estimating Continuing Value
- Chapter 10: Estimating the Cost of Capital
- Chapter 11: Calculating and Interpreting Results
- Chapter 12: Using Multiples for Valuation

These chapters explain the technical details of valuation, including how to calculate free cash flow from the accounting statements and how to create and interpret the valuation through careful financial analysis.

REVIEW QUESTIONS

1. What process should a manager employ to compute corporate valuation? In your answer, differentiate between the choice of a process to be followed and the choice of valuation model.

2. Describe the enterprise DCF valuation model.

3. How does growth and return on invested capital drive free cash flow? Illustrate with an example employing constant and nonconstant growth rates.

4. In terms of the enterprise DCF model, how would a manager increase corporate value?

5. Describe the economic profit model. Identify the differences between the economic profit model's value drivers compared to the enterprise DCF model value drivers.

6. Under what conditions would the discounted dividend model of equity value incorrectly define corporate value?

7. Under what circumstances would an executive select the adjusted present value (APV) model of corporate valuation over either the enterprise DCF model or the economic profit model?

8. Why is it important to compute the company's unlevered cost of equity when the APV model is used to determine corporate value?

9. When would a manager use real versus nominal cash flows and rates to value entities?

10. You have been asked to value a stable company (i.e., no growth) whose revenues are $100 million and operating margins are 10 percent. Since the company is not growing, working capital is constant and capital expenditures are spent only to replace depreciation. The company has $50 million in debt outstanding and has a cost of debt equal to 5 percent (the company's bonds trade at par, so interest payments can be computed using the cost of debt). The company has 10 million shares outstanding and its stock is trading at $10.50. The company has a cost of equity equal to 10 percent. The company faces a tax rate of 40 percent.

   a. Compute free cash flow.

   b. Assuming the current capital structure proxies the target capital structure, estimate the weighted average cost of capital.

   c. Using a no-growth perpetuity (FCF divided by WACC), estimate the company's enterprise value, the company's equity value, and its stock price. Is the company undervalued?

   d. If interest taxes shields are discounted at the unlevered cost of equity, what is the unlevered cost of equity?

   e. Compute enterprise value using adjusted present value. How does your result differ from part c?

6

Thinking about Return on Invested Capital and Growth

A fully developed discounted cash flow model can be complex. Models that forecast each line item on the income statement and balance sheet can include hundreds of numbers, if not thousands. But in the forest of numbers, it is all too easy to forget the fundamentals: A company's value depends on its return on invested capital (ROIC) and its ability to grow. All other considerations—gross margins, cash tax rates, collection periods, and inventory turns—are, well, just details.

By focusing on ROIC and growth, you can place your forecasts in the proper context. You can measure how well the model's projections fit with the capabilities of the company and the competitive dynamics of the industry. Consider the following example. You are valuing a company in the commodity chemicals business. The company projects operating costs to drop by 3 percent per year over the next 10 years, but because the industry is highly competitive, cost reductions are usually passed on to the consumer. Therefore, you project that the price will fall 2 percent annually. Combined with expected growth in volume, your forecasts lead to a healthy growth in cash flow and a high valuation. After further analysis, however, you realize that because costs are dropping faster than price, ROIC grows from 8 percent to 20 percent over the forecast period. What initially appears to be a reasonable forecast translates to returns on capital not likely to be seen in a commodity business.

Now consider a second model, one that focuses on the economics of the business and not the details. To demonstrate the power of a simple yet insightful model, we present Exhibit 6.1 on page 136, which shows a set of realistic projections for a hypothetical company. We forecast only three line

Exhibit 6.1 The Fundamental Drivers of Value

Forecast	Year 1	2	3	4	5	6	7
Revenue growth (percent)	15.0	14.0	13.0	12.0	11.0	10.0	9.0
After-tax operating margin (percent)	3.0	6.0	8.2	20.0	16.4	11.7	8.3
Capital turns	1.0	1.0	1.1	1.1	1.1	1.2	1.2
ROIC (percent)	3.0	6.0	9.0	22.0	18.0	14.0	10.0

items: revenue growth, after-tax operating margins, and capital turns (the ratio of sales to invested capital). We assume the company's cost of capital equals 10 percent and current revenues equal $1 billion. No other projections are made.

Using the enterprise DCF method outlined in Chapter 5, we value the hypothetical company based solely on the forecasts presented in Exhibit 6.1. The results are presented in Exhibit 6.2. To determine future revenues, we grow current revenues by the forecasted growth rates. After-tax operating profit equals revenue multiplied by after-tax operating margin. To calculate invested capital, we divide each year's revenue by projected capital turnover. Free cash flow equals after-tax operating profit less the increase in invested capital. Adding forecasted discounted free cash flow to continuing value leads to enterprise value.[1] We have been able to build a relatively sophisticated free cash flow model based on only *three* projections.

If simple models provide the necessary flexibility to value a company, why do so many complicated models exist? In some cases, the details *are* unnecessary. In fact, extraneous details can cloud the drivers that really matter. You should make detailed line item forecasts only when they increase the accuracy of key value driver forecasts. For example, perhaps the ROIC you forecast requires dropping the inventory holding period from 50 days to 35 days, an operational improvement beyond the capabilities of the company.

We start the chapter by examining economic theory and how competitive dynamics should affect long-term corporate performance. In the second part of the chapter, we analyze ROIC and growth from an empirical perspective, presenting 40 years of data on the size, timing, and sustainability of ROIC and growth. We find that the typical company's returns on capital gradually regress toward a median ROIC of 9 percent, but many companies show persistence even over 15-year periods. Fast revenue growth,

---

[1] We assume economic profits are zero (i.e., ROIC equals the cost of capital) beyond year 7. When economic profits equal zero, the enterprise value of a company equals its book value. Therefore, the continuing value in year 7 equals the book value of invested capital. To determine today's value, invested capital in year 7 is discounted by seven years.

Exhibit 6.2 A Valuation Based on Fundamentals

$ million

	Year 0	1	2	3	4	5	6	7
Revenues	1,000.0	1,150.0	1,311.0	1,481.4	1,659.2	1,841.7	2,025.9	2,208.2
Operating profits[1]	25.0	34.5	78.7	121.2	331.8	301.4	236.4	184.0
Invested capital	950.0	1,150.0	1,311.0	1,346.8	1,508.4	1,674.3	1,688.2	1,840.2
Free cash flow								
Operating profits[1]		34.5	78.7	121.2	331.8	301.4	236.4	184.0
Net investment		(200.0)	(161.0)	(35.8)	(161.6)	(165.9)	(14.0)	(151.9)
Free cash flow		(165.5)	(82.3)	85.5	170.2	135.5	222.4	32.1
Discount factor		0.91	0.83	0.75	0.68	0.62	0.56	0.51
Discounted cash flow		(150.5)	(68.0)	64.2	116.3	84.1	125.5	16.5
Valuation								
PV(explicit forecasts)	188.1							
Continuing value	944.3							
Enterprise value	1,132.4							

[1]After-tax.

on the other hand, is fleeting. Even the fastest growers struggle to maintain high growth rates, regressing to the long-run median of 6 percent real growth within five years.

A FRAMEWORK FOR VALUE CREATION

In Chapter 3, we introduced a simple, yet powerful, valuation formula that we call the key value driver formula. Derived directly from the growing cash flow perpetuity, the key value driver formula formalized the direct relation between ROIC, growth, and a company's valuation. For some companies, especially companies in mature industries, the key value driver formula works quite well.

For companies growing quickly, however, the key value driver formula is overly restrictive in its assumptions. In many cases, ROIC will change over time as companies and their product markets evolve. Exhibit 6.3 on page 138 presents a *general* pattern for ROIC over time for a single-product company (later in this chapter, we demonstrate how this pattern can take different shapes). The ability to create value for this hypothetical company can be measured in two dimensions: the level of peak ROIC and the sustainability of returns in excess of the cost of capital. In this example, the peak ROIC occurs where the vertical arrow marks the spread between ROIC and cost of capital. The horizontal arrow represents sustainability; the longer a company creates value (ROIC greater than WACC), the greater

Exhibit 6.3 A General Model of Value Creation

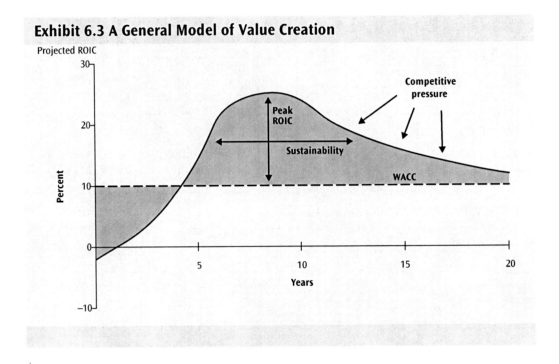

its enterprise value. When it can no longer protect its competitive position, as marked by the downward arrows of competitive pressure, economic theory predicts its ROIC will regress to WACC such that enterprise value equals the book value of invested capital. (Empirical evidence, however, demonstrates this may not be the case; more on this later.)

To better understand the components of value creation, we first examine peak ROIC. Consider the following representation of return on invested capital:

$$\text{ROIC} = (1-T)\frac{(\text{Unit Price} - \text{Unit Cost}) \times \text{Quantity}}{\text{Invested Capital}}$$

This version of ROIC is identical to the traditional definition of ROIC: NOPLAT divided by invested capital. We segment the ratio, however, into taxes (T), revenue and cost per unit, as well as quantity, to highlight the potential sources of value creation that you should consider when valuing a company.[2] The formula generates a series of questions. Can the company charge a price premium for its products or services? Does the company have lower unit costs than its competition? Can the company sell more products per dollar of invested capital? To justify high future ROICs, you *must* identify at least one source of competitive advantage.

[2] We introduce *units* to motivate a discussion surrounding price, cost, and volume. The formula, however, is not specific to manufacturing. Units can represent the number of hours billed, patients seen, transactions processed, and so on.

Price premium   In commodity markets, companies are price takers. Price takers must sell at the market price to generate business. Alternatively, a price setter has control over the price it charges. To enable price setting, a company cannot sell a commoditized product. It must find a way to differentiate its product so that its competition, if any, is limited.

The beverage company Coca-Cola is a price setter. For the company's primary products, Coke and Diet Coke, Coca-Cola can charge a price well in excess of its marginal costs because most consumers choose soft drinks based on taste, preference, and brand image, not on price. Coca-Cola customers are extremely loyal and rarely switch brands, even when faced with a generic, low-priced alternative. Coke's power to charge a price premium can be seen in the company's ROIC and valuation. At year-end 2003, Coke's ROIC was 48 percent, excluding goodwill, and its enterprise value equaled $125 billion, more than 11 times its book value of invested capital.

Be careful, however. Consumer brand loyalty does not guarantee immunity to competition. Consumer preferences change over time (consider the recent low-carb diet craze in the United States), and as products change, customers may migrate to competing offerings.

Cost competitiveness   A second driver of high ROIC is a company's ability to sell products and services at a lower cost than the competition. The discount retailer Wal-Mart is a low-cost operator. Wal-Mart is well known for using its substantial purchasing volume to lower its costs and force better terms from its suppliers. The company also invests heavily in computing power and other technologies to continually improve its cost position. It stands at the forefront of RFID, a new technology that electronically identifies when inventory enters a stockroom, reaches the main floor, and leaves the store.[3] Data collected is sent to Wal-Mart's Internet-based software, Retail Link, which allows the retailer's 30,000 suppliers to check inventory and sales in near real time. To lower costs further, the company is developing software that will trigger a business process, such as automated restocking or purchasing.

Capital efficiency   Even if profits per unit (or transaction) are small, a company can generate significant value by selling more products per dollar of invested capital than its competition. In the airline industry, an aircraft generates revenue when it is transporting passengers, not when it sits on the ground empty. Thus, the more an airline flies each aircraft in a given day, the more value it can create.

Southwest Airlines is an example of a company with superb capital efficiency. The typical Southwest aircraft can land, deplane, board, and take off

---

[3] L. Sullivan, "Wal-Mart's Way: Heavyweight Retailer Looks Inward to Stay Innovative in Business Technology," *Information Week* (September 27, 2004): 36.

in well under an hour. Conversely, this turnaround process at network carriers, such as American and United, averages over two hours per flight. This difference enables Southwest to spend more time in the air and less time on the ground.

The differences in ground time can be traced directly to differences in corporate strategy. First, Southwest flies point-to-point and does not rely on a hub; network carriers use hubs. A network carrier lands every flight at the same time, transfers passengers, and takes off at the same time. Not only does the congestion cause delays, but any late arrivals cause further delays throughout the system. A point-to-point airline does not face these constraints. Second, Southwest uses a single plane type, whereas network carriers use many. If a pilot calls in sick, an airline that has only one plane type can use any available pilot in the system. A network carrier might have an available pilot, but unless the pilot is certified to fly the given aircraft, the aircraft will sit empty until a qualified pilot becomes available.

Sustainability

To generate a high value, a company must not only excel at pricing power, cost competitiveness, or capital efficiency, but also must be able to sustain this competitive advantage over long periods. If the company cannot prevent competition from duplicating its efforts, high ROIC will be short-lived, and the company's value will be low. Consider a major cost improvement recently implemented by the airlines. The self-service kiosk allows passengers to purchase a ticket or print a boarding pass without waiting in line. From the airlines' perspective, fewer ground personnel can handle more people. So why has this cost improvement not translated into high ROICs for the airlines? Since every company has access to the technology, any cost improvements are passed directly to the consumer in the form of lower prices.

A company can maintain pricing power or a cost advantage only if the company maintains a barrier to imitation (from existing competition) or a barrier to entry (from new competition). The complexity of Microsoft's primary product, Windows, makes switching to an alternative unattractive for individuals and companies. Once users have become well versed in the platform, they are unlikely to switch to a new competitor. Even Linux, a low-cost alternative to Windows, has struggled to gain market share as system administrators and end users remain wary of learning a new way of computing. Or consider Wal-Mart, which located its first stores in rural communities. Rather than build a small store on the town's main street, as did Woolworth, Wal-Mart builds large-scale stores on the outskirts of town. Wal-Mart uses its size to dictate low prices and good terms from its suppliers; but more importantly, by building such a large store in an isolated community, it prevents other large, low-cost competitors from entering the market. A competitor such as Target or Costco could enter the community but, given the scale required to match Wal-Mart's prices, would generate instant overcapacity in the region.

Examples of Peak ROIC and Sustainability

The general pattern of ROIC and sustainability provided in Exhibit 6.3 is flexible and can describe different companies. Some companies have peak ROICs that are very high but offer little sustainability. Other companies have peak ROICs near the cost of capital but can generate excess returns over an extremely long period. Two examples with varying levels of peak ROIC and sustainability are Intel and Johnson & Johnson.

Intel has twice sustained high ROICs over the last 30 years. Exhibit 6.4 plots ROIC for Intel between 1973 and 2003. During that time, Intel has had two distinct periods of significant value creation. In its early life, the company was a pioneer in the computer chips that store data, commonly known as random access memory (RAM) chips. Intel created value for nearly 10 years, but the Japanese government made RAM a high priority, and companies such as NEC and Fujitsu began to flood the market with similar chips at lower prices. The price competition was so intense that it nearly drove Intel out of business. With a financial infusion from IBM, the company reinvented itself, creating the new "brains" of the personal computer. Through

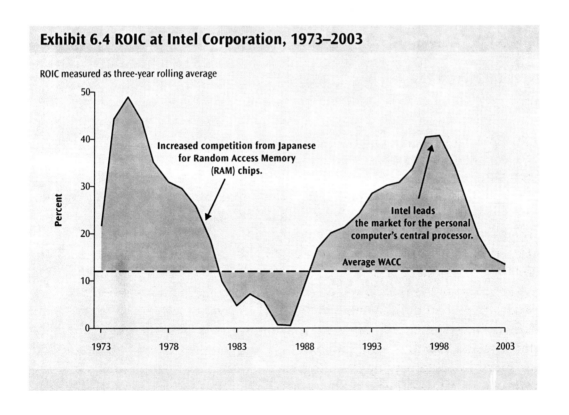

Exhibit 6.4 ROIC at Intel Corporation, 1973–2003

ROIC measured as three-year rolling average

an informal partnership with Microsoft, Intel led the personal-computer microprocessor market. By the late 1990s, however, competitors such as Advanced Micro Devices (AMD) began making inroads, forcing Intel to broaden its product line to include lower-priced chips. Facing increased competition and a general downturn in technology, Intel could no longer post the enormous ROICs of the mid-1990s. Today, Intel is still profitable and remains a strong player in microprocessors for personal computers, but the challenge for Intel is to capture the next major technology shift.

Economic theory dictates that companies earning returns in excess of their cost of capital will invite competition. Yet some companies are able to protect their primary product lines while concurrently expanding into new markets. One such example is Johnson & Johnson. Historically, Johnson & Johnson has earned strong returns on capital through its patented pharmaceuticals and branded consumer products lines, such as Tylenol and Johnson's Baby Shampoo. Through strong brands and capable distribution, the company has been able to maintain a price premium, even in the face of new entrants and alternative products. More recently, the company broadened its product portfolio to health care include medical devices and diagnostics, given the strength of the healthcare industry and expected growth as the baby boomers age.

As shown in Exhibit 6.5, which plots Johnson & Johnson's ROIC over the past 30 years, the company has maintained an ROIC greater than the

Exhibit 6.5 ROIC at Johnson & Johnson, 1973–2003

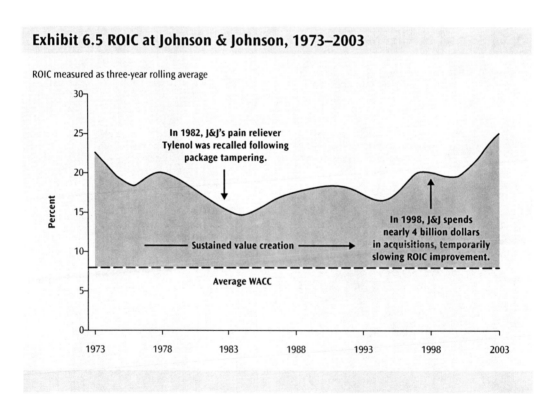

ROIC measured as three-year rolling average

In 1982, J&J's pain reliever Tylenol was recalled following package tampering.

Sustained value creation

In 1998, J&J spends nearly 4 billion dollars in acquisitions, temporarily slowing ROIC improvement.

Average WACC

cost of capital during the entire period. In fact, given the strength of health care in the 1990s, returns have actually risen from the 1980s. Only the Tylenol tampering scare of the 1980s and the high cost of acquisitions in the late 1990s have dampened the company's continually strong performance.

Recouping Initial Investments or Early Losses

Not every company generates positive spreads. When companies are not earning returns in excess of their cost of capital (or are even losing money), you must assess two questions: (1) How long will it take before the company starts creating value? and (2) How large will the initial investments (or losses) be? We represent these two dimensions as arrows in Exhibit 6.6. The horizontal arrow represents the time to break-even (from a value creation perspective), and the vertical arrow represents the depth of value destruction.

One company that invested for years before creating value (or even earning a profit) is Amgen. Today, Amgen is a global biotechnology company that develops, manufactures, and markets therapeutics based on cellular biology and medicinal chemistry. Founded in 1980 with approximately $20 million in venture capital, the company burned through cash for nearly 10 years. In 1983, company scientists cloned the human protein erythropoietin (EPO), which eventually led to the drug Epogen, a treatment for anemia. Immediately following the drug's FDA approval in 1989, the company's ROIC skyrocketed to nearly 60 percent (see Exhibit 6.7 on p. 144).

Exhibit 6.6 ROIC Projections: Value Destruction at Young Companies

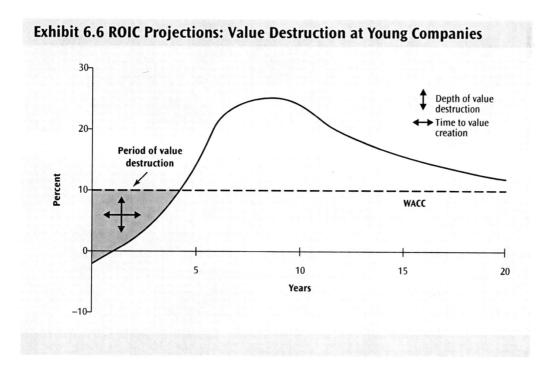

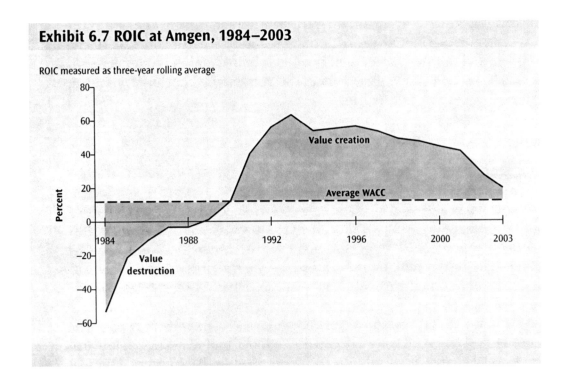

Exhibit 6.7 ROIC at Amgen, 1984–2003

But standing in 1984, how could you predict the depth and length of value destruction? Once EPO was cloned in 1983, it became crucial to thoroughly analyze how much additional research (in dollar terms) would be needed to bring the product to market. In addition, how much would have to be spent for marketing and distribution? Since the drug would not generate cash until it gained FDA approval, it is also necessary to estimate expected time until approval. When considering approval, the FDA will ask: Is the drug truly revolutionary, or just incremental? How would the drug be administered? What are the side effects? The answer to each of these questions has a direct impact on approval time.

AN EMPIRICAL ANALYSIS OF RETURN ON INVESTED CAPITAL

In the previous section, we outlined the economic factors to consider when valuing a company. Any forecasts you develop for ROIC should be consistent with the company's core competencies, its competitive advantage, and industry economics. As a second step, benchmark your forecasts against the *actual* long-run historical performance of other companies. By comparing forecasts with historical industry benchmarks, you can assess whether your forecasts of future performance are reasonable in the context of other companies.

To help place forecasts of ROIC and growth in the proper context, we present the historical financial performance (using ROIC and revenue growth) for more than 5,000 U.S.-based nonfinancial companies over the past 40 years. Our results are generated from McKinsey & Company's corporate performance database, which relies on financial data provided by Standard & Poor's Compustat. Our key findings are as follows:

- The median ROIC between 1963 and 2003 was 9.0 percent and remained relatively constant throughout the period.[4] ROIC does, however, vary dramatically across companies, with only half of observed ROICs between 5 percent and 15 percent.

- Median ROIC differs by industry and growth, but not by company size. Industries that rely on sustainable advantages, such as patents and brands, tend to have high median ROICs (11 percent to 18 percent), whereas companies in basic industries, such as transportation and utilities, tend to earn low ROICs (6 percent to 8 percent).

- Individual-company ROICs gradually regress toward medians over time but are somewhat persistent. Fifty percent of companies that earned ROICs greater than 20 percent in 1994 were still earning at least 20 percent 10 years later.

To analyze historical corporate performance, we first measured median ROIC for each of the past 40 years. In Exhibit 6.8 on page 146, median ROIC is plotted between 1963 and 2003 for U.S.-based nonfinancial companies. ROIC is presented with and without goodwill. The aggregate median ROIC without goodwill equals 9.0 percent, and annual medians oscillate in a relatively tight range between 6.9 percent and 10.6 percent. This oscillation is not random, but instead is tied directly to the overall growth of the economy. When regressing median ROIC versus gross domestic product (GDP), we found that a 100-basis-point increase in GDP growth translates to a 20-basis-point increase in median ROIC.

Although a given year's median ROIC depends on the level of economic growth, it demonstrates no long-term trend. At first, the lack of an upward trend in ROIC may appear counterintuitive; especially given productivity increases over the past 40 years. The U.S. Department of Labor reports manufacturing workers were approximately 3.5 times more productive in 2003 than they were in 1963. So why have productivity increases not translated into improved financial performance? In most industries, healthy competition has transferred the benefits from internal improvements to customers and employees in the form of lower prices and higher salaries, instead of adding to corporate profits.

---

[4] Throughout this section, we report aggregate median ROICs over the entire sample period. To determine an aggregate median ROIC, we average each year's median.

Exhibit 6.8 ROIC for Nonfinancial Companies

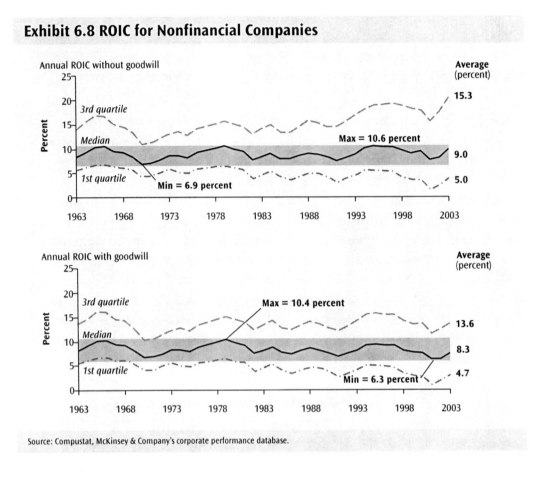

Source: Compustat, McKinsey & Company's corporate performance database.

Although median ROICs show little change over the past 40 years, the cross-sectional spread of company ROICs has increased. Over the entire period, half the companies typically had ROICs between 5.0 percent and 15.3 percent. Yet, since 1986, this spread has gradually widened, driven primarily by companies on the top end. In many cases, this improvement has occurred in industries with strong barriers to entry, such as patents or brands, where the drops in raw-material prices and increased productivity have not been transferred to other stakeholders.

The ROIC spreads across companies do not widen, however, when ROIC is measured with goodwill. This implies that top companies are acquiring other top performers yet paying full price for the acquired performance.

To further analyze the spread of ROIC across companies, we present a histogram in Exhibit 6.9. Each bar measures the percentage of observations within a certain range. For instance, approximately 17 percent of the sample has an ROIC between 5.0 percent and 7.5 percent. The aggregate distribution is quite wide, with only half the sample between 5 percent and 15 percent. In fact, in any given year, a particular company can have ROICs well below 0 or above 40 percent. However, 84 percent of the sample had ROIC *below* 20 per-

Exhibit 6.9 ROIC Distribution for Nonfinancial Companies

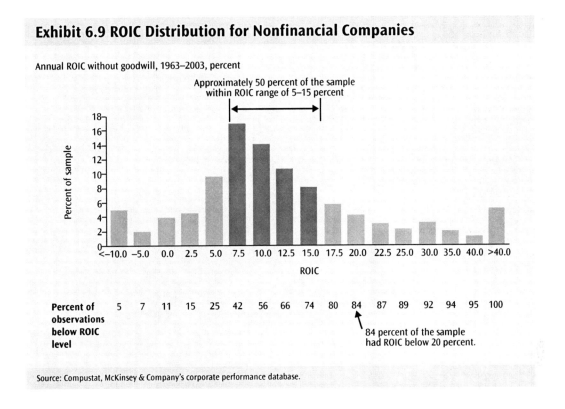

Annual ROIC without goodwill, 1963–2003, percent

Source: Compustat, McKinsey & Company's corporate performance database.

cent. Thus, if you project sustained ROICs above 20 percent, you must believe the company is truly exceptional, as only one in six companies achieved this level of performance in a typical year.

Return on Invested Capital by Industry, Size, and Growth

Using aggregate data overlooks the fact that companies with certain characteristics are likely to have different levels of performance. Ideally, we would provide a comprehensive list of segmentation, tying median ROICs directly to the economic principles of pricing power, financial discipline, and competitive barriers to entry. This way, a valuation forecast could be benchmarked against true comparables, rather than overall aggregates. These characteristics, however, are mostly unobservable and difficult to measure quantitatively. Therefore, we instead segmented our sample using proxies, such as industry (different industries have varying competitive barriers to entry), size (for economies of scale), and growth (for the intensity of competition).

In our first segmentation, we examined median ROIC by industry. In Exhibit 6.10 on page 148, we rank 20 nonfinancial industries by median ROIC (based on performance over the past 40 years). To construct an industry, we used S&P's Global Industry Classifications Standard. Each industry classification is broad and encompasses many companies. As the

Exhibit 6.10 ROIC by Industry Group[1]

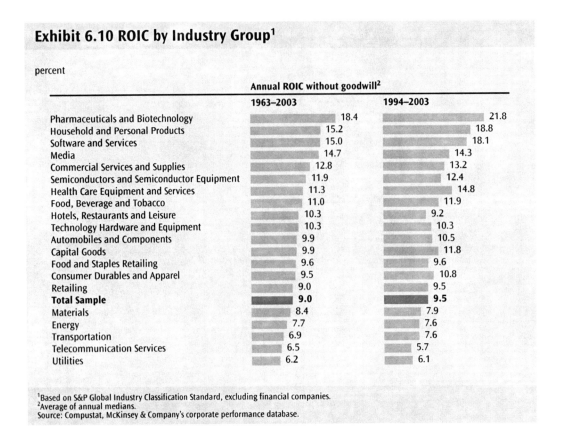

percent

	Annual ROIC without goodwill[2]	
	1963–2003	1994–2003
Pharmaceuticals and Biotechnology	18.4	21.8
Household and Personal Products	15.2	18.8
Software and Services	15.0	18.1
Media	14.7	14.3
Commercial Services and Supplies	12.8	13.2
Semiconductors and Semiconductor Equipment	11.9	12.4
Health Care Equipment and Services	11.3	14.8
Food, Beverage and Tobacco	11.0	11.9
Hotels, Restaurants and Leisure	10.3	9.2
Technology Hardware and Equipment	10.3	10.3
Automobiles and Components	9.9	10.5
Capital Goods	9.9	11.8
Food and Staples Retailing	9.6	9.6
Consumer Durables and Apparel	9.5	10.8
Retailing	9.0	9.5
Total Sample	**9.0**	**9.5**
Materials	8.4	7.9
Energy	7.7	7.6
Transportation	6.9	7.6
Telecommunication Services	6.5	5.7
Utilities	6.2	6.1

[1]Based on S&P Global Industry Classification Standard, excluding financial companies.
[2]Average of annual medians.
Source: Compustat, McKinsey & Company's corporate performance database.

exhibit demonstrates, financial performance varies significantly across industries. Industries that have identifiable sustainable advantages, such as patents and brands, tend to generate higher returns.[5] Pharmaceutical and biotechnology companies had a median ROIC of 18.4 percent; whereas companies in commodity (and often regulated) industries, such as transportation and utilities, had much lower ROICs—6.9 percent and 6.2 percent, respectively. Although performance differs at the extremes, the center is concentrated. Half the industries had median ROICs between 9 percent and 12 percent.

Although not reported, the industry ranking does not vary materially over time. Comparing median ROICs for the 10-year period ending in 2003 versus the entire sample leads to few changes in order (only ROICs of health care equipment companies are noticeably higher). Thus, industry membership can be an important predictor of performance.

We next segment the sample by size and growth. In Exhibit 6.11, we present the median ROICs for 30 separate subgroupings (five categories by

[5]Since R&D and advertising are not capitalized, ROIC will be upward-biased for industries with significant intangible assets. Capitalizing intangible assets, however, requires subjective assessments on amortization periods. Therefore, we present raw results without capitalizing R&D and advertising.

Exhibit 6.11 ROIC Segmented by Size and Growth

Annual ROIC without goodwill, 1963 to 2003

Three-year real growth rate (percent)	Revenues				
	<$200M	$200M–$500M	$500M–$1B	$1B–$2.5B	>$2.5B
<0	3.3%	5.2%	6.0%	6.5%	7.0%
0–5	8.0%	7.7%	8.0%	8.1%	9.1%
5–10	8.9%	9.3%	9.6%	9.5%	10.3%
10–15	10.8%	10.9%	11.2%	10.9%	11.8%
15–20	11.9%	11.1%	11.7%	11.5%	11.9%
>20	12.4%	11.9%	11.8%	11.8%	11.6%

ROIC increases with higher growth rate

No clear relation between size and performance

Source: Compustat, McKinsey & Company's corporate performance database.

total revenue and six categories by revenue growth), each of which has roughly the same number of companies. Moving from the top of this chart to the bottom, we find that median ROICs consistently increase as revenue growth increases, regardless of company size. Do not, however, misinterpret these results. We do *not* believe growth causes strong performance. A company that grows by stealing market share through price reductions is unlikely to maintain high margins—and lower margins often lead to lower ROICs. So why the positive correlation?

First, certain underlying factors enable *both* growth and ROIC. In rapidly expanding sectors with barriers to entry (e.g., high fixed costs), current capacity cannot fulfill continually increasing market demand. Since buyers exceed suppliers, prices and margins remain strong. If growth unexpectedly slows, however, so that industry capacity cannot be filled, companies often lower prices to generate the volume required to cover fixed costs. In this case, as growth drops, so does ROIC.

Second, companies with high ROICs have more incentives and greater opportunities to grow. A company earning a strong ROIC in its core business can create significant value by increasing growth (as demonstrated in

Chapter 3). Conversely, a company with returns at or below the cost of capital is unlikely to create value by accepting new projects (unless economies of scale lower unit costs). In addition, a company with a poor track record for earning high returns on capital in its core business is unlikely to attract funding for new opportunities.

Unlike growth, a company's size (as measured by revenues) shows no clear relation with ROIC. Despite the common perception that economies of should continually lower unit costs, many companies often reach minimum efficient scale at relatively small sizes. At this point, any incremental growth comes at the same unit cost, or even slightly higher costs, as bureaucratic inefficiency and other inflexibilities begin to dominate. To see this, one merely needs to examine Southwest Airlines, a company with only 35 percent of the revenues of American Airlines yet eight times the equity valuation (as of year-end 2004). Or consider Nucor Steel, a company with only 80 percent of the revenues of United States Steel yet 1.5 times the valuation.

Return on Invested Capital Decay Rates

When a company generates ROICs greater than its cost of capital, it invites competition. But how fast does the competition typically replicate a business, steal share, and force lower prices? In Exhibit 6.12, we address this question by forming portfolios based on ROIC. For instance, in each year,

Exhibit 6.12 ROIC Decay Analysis: Nonfinancial Companies

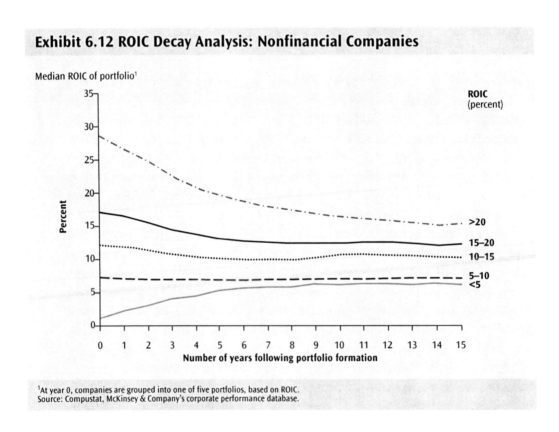

[1] At year 0, companies are grouped into one of five portfolios, based on ROIC.
Source: Compustat, McKinsey & Company's corporate performance database.

we aggregated all companies earning an ROIC greater than 20 percent into a single portfolio. We then tracked the median ROIC for each portfolio over the next 15 years.

Exhibit 6.12 demonstrates a pattern of mean reversion. Companies earning high returns tend to fall gradually over the next 15 years, and companies earning low returns tend to rise over time. Only the portfolio containing companies generating returns between 5 percent and 10 percent (mostly regulated companies) remains constant.

An important result of Exhibit 6.12 is the continued persistence of superior performance beyond 10 years. Although the best companies cannot maintain their current performance, their ROIC does *not* fully regress to the aggregate median of 9 percent. Instead, the top portfolio's median ROIC drops from 29 percent to 15 percent. Since a company's continuing value is highly dependent on long-run forecasts of ROIC and growth, this result has important implications for corporate valuation. Basing a continuing value on the economic concept that ROIC will approach WACC is overly conservative for the *typical* company generating high ROICs (continuing value is the focus of Chapter 9).

When benchmarking historical decay, it is important to segment results by industry (especially if industry is a proxy for competitive barriers to entry). In Exhibit 6.13, we plot the ROIC decay rates for the Consumer Staples

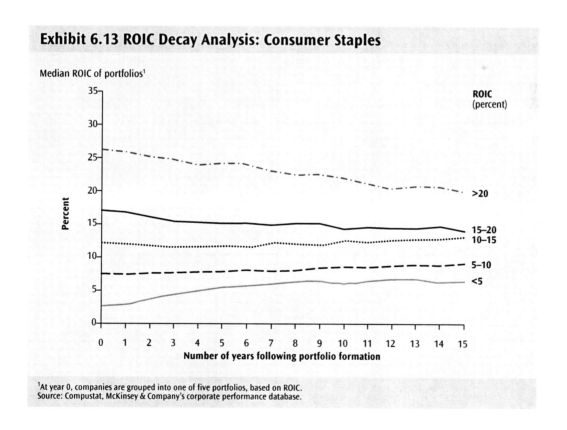

Exhibit 6.13 ROIC Decay Analysis: Consumer Staples

Median ROIC of portfolios[1]

[1]At year 0, companies are grouped into one of five portfolios, based on ROIC.
Source: Compustat, McKinsey & Company's corporate performance database.

segment of the Food and Staples industry. As the exhibit demonstrates, ROICs once again regress to the mean but at a much slower rate than seen in the full sample. Top performers in Consumer Staples have a median ROIC of 26 percent, which drops to 20 percent after 15 years. (Top performers in the entire sample dropped to 15 percent.) Even after 15 years, the *original* class of best performers still outperforms the worst performers by more than 13 percent.

Although decay rates examine the *rate* of regression toward the mean, decay rates present only aggregate results, not the spread of potential future performance. Does every company generating returns greater than 20 percent eventually migrate to 15 percent, or do some companies actually generate higher returns? Conversely, do some top performers become poor performers? To address this question, we present ROIC transition probabilities in Exhibit 6.14. An ROIC transition probability measures the probability that a company will migrate from one ROIC grouping to another in 10 years. For instance, a company generating an ROIC less than 5 percent in 1994 had a 43 percent chance of earning less than 5 percent in 2003. Transition probabilities read from left to right, and the rows must sum to 100 percent.

As seen in Exhibit 6.14, both high and low performers demonstrate significant persistence in performance. This pattern was consistent throughout the 40-year period. Companies with an ROIC below 5 percent, companies between 5 and 10 percent, and companies greater than 20 percent have a 43 percent, 40 percent, and 50 percent probability, respectively, of remaining in the same grouping 10 years later. Only companies with ROICs between 10 and 20 percent show little persistence. Companies that earn between 10 and 15 percent can land in any grouping 10 years later with roughly equal probability.

The results are clear: ROIC varies across companies and industries in a systematic fashion. And for many companies, these differences are persistent—even in the face of ever more competitive markets.

Exhibit 6.14 ROIC Transition Probability, 1994–2003

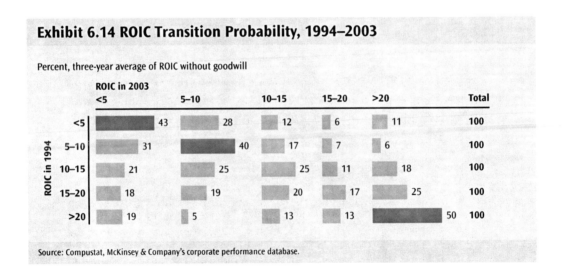

Percent, three-year average of ROIC without goodwill

| ROIC in 1994 | ROIC in 2003 | | | | | Total |
	<5	5–10	10–15	15–20	>20	
<5	43	28	12	6	11	100
5–10	31	40	17	7	6	100
10–15	21	25	25	11	18	100
15–20	18	19	20	17	25	100
>20	19	5	13	13	50	100

Source: Compustat, McKinsey & Company's corporate performance database.

AN EMPIRICAL ANALYSIS OF CORPORATE GROWTH

Today's public companies are under tremendous pressure to grow. Sell-side analysts set aggressive growth targets for revenues, earnings per share, and cash flow. Yet growth creates value only when a company's new customers, projects, or acquisitions generate returns greater than the risk-adjusted cost of capital. Finding good projects becomes increasingly difficult as industries become ever more competitive and companies grow ever larger. To generate revenue growth of 26.3 percent in 1990, Wal-Mart added 57,000 new employees. By 2003, the company was so large that it added approximately 100,000 employees, yet grew revenue by only 4.8 percent. To replicate 1990's revenue growth at 2003 productivity levels, Wal-Mart would have needed to add nearly half a million people in a single year—aggressive by any standards.

To help place expectations of long-term growth in a realistic context, we present data on the level and persistence of corporate growth over the past 40 years. Our analysis of revenue growth mirrors that of ROIC, except we now use three-year rolling averages to moderate distortions caused by currency fluctuations and merger and acquisition (M&A) activity.[6] Ideally, we would report statistics on *organic* revenue growth, but current reporting standards do not require companies to disclose the effects of currencies and M&A on revenue growth. Algorithms can be applied to dampen distortions but require overly stringent assumptions.[7] We therefore report raw results.

In addition, all corporate growth results are analyzed using real, rather than nominal, data. We do this because even mature companies saw a dramatic increase in revenue during the 1970s as inflation increased prices. Therefore, to compare growth rates over different time periods, we strip out the effect of inflation by using annual changes in the consumer price index. If you plan to use these data to drive growth forecasts in a valuation model, you *must* add expected inflation to the real results we present. (For more on modeling inflation consistently, see Chapter 22.)

Our general results concerning revenue growth (measured in real terms, except where noted) are as follows:

- The median revenue growth rate between 1963 and 2003 equals 6.3 percent in real terms and 10.2 percent in nominal terms. Real revenue growth fluctuates more than ROIC, ranging from 1.8 percent in 1975 to 10.8 percent in 1998.

---

[6] For more detail on how to define and separate organic, M&A, and currency-driven revenue growth, see Chapter 7.

[7] Acquired growth can be estimated by analyzing the increase in goodwill plus impairments, but doing this has two drawbacks. First, acquired revenue must be estimated using a goodwill-to-revenue ratio. However, profitable companies will have higher ratios, so applying an industry average ratio can cause systematic distortions. Second, goodwill exists only when companies use purchase accounting. Companies that used pooling for M&A would still be incorrectly estimated.

- High growth rates decay very quickly. Companies growing faster than 20 percent (in real terms) typically grow at only 8 percent within 5 years and 5 percent within 10 years.

- Extremely large companies struggle to grow. Excluding the first year, companies entering the *Fortune* 50 grow at an average of only 1 percent (above inflation) over the following 15 years.

We start by examining aggregate levels and trends of corporate growth. Exhibit 6.15 presents median (real) revenue growth rates between 1963 and 2003. The annualized median revenue growth rate between 1963 and 2003 equals 6.3 percent and oscillates between 1.8 percent and 10.8 percent. Median revenue growth demonstrates no trend over time. Even so, real revenue growth of 6.3 percent is quite high, especially when compared with real GDP growth in the United States at 3.3 percent. Why the difference?

Possible explanations abound. They include self-selection, specialization and outsourcing, global expansion, the use of medians, and nonorganic growth. First, companies with good growth opportunities need capital to grow. Since public markets are large and liquid, high-growth companies are more likely to be publicly traded than privately held. We measure only publicly traded companies, so our growth results are likely to be higher. Second, as companies become increasingly specialized and outsource more services, new companies, not picked up by GDP, will grow and develop quickly. Consider Electronic Data Systems (EDS), a company that provides information technology (IT) and data services. As companies move IT from

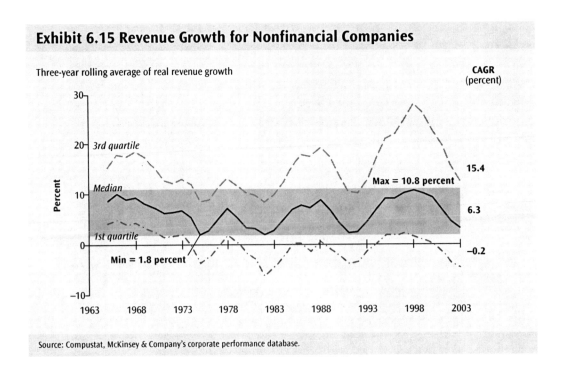

Exhibit 6.15 Revenue Growth for Nonfinancial Companies

Source: Compustat, McKinsey & Company's corporate performance database.

internal management to EDS, GDP will not change, since it measures aggregate output. Yet EDS's high growth will be part of our sample. A third explanation is that many of the companies in our sample create products and generate revenue outside the United States. This revenue will not be picked up by GDP. Fourth, a significant portion of U.S. GDP is driven by large companies, which tend to grow more slowly. Since we measure the median corporate growth rates, the median company is typically small, and small public companies grow faster. Finally, although we use rolling averages and medians, we can only dampen the effects of M&A and currency fluctuations, not eliminate them entirely.

In addition to mapping median growth, Exhibit 6.15 reveals a second point: beginning in 1973, one-quarter of all companies actually shrank in real terms in a given year. Thus, although most companies publicly project healthy growth over the next five years, reality dictates that many mature firms will shrink in real terms. When you perform a valuation of a mature business, treat projections of strong growth skeptically.

Like the results concerning ROIC, the spread of growth rates across industries varies dramatically. In Exhibit 6.16, we present median revenue growth rates for 20 industries. The median Software and Services company has grown by 20 percent between 1963 and 2003, Semiconductors

Exhibit 6.16 Revenue Growth by Industry Group[1]

percent

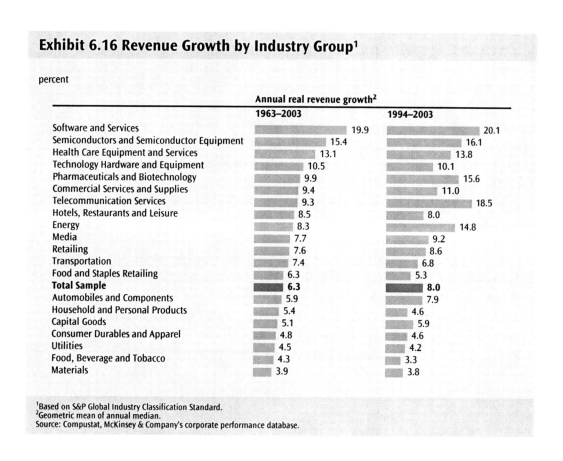

	Annual real revenue growth[2]	
	1963–2003	1994–2003
Software and Services	19.9	20.1
Semiconductors and Semiconductor Equipment	15.4	16.1
Health Care Equipment and Services	13.1	13.8
Technology Hardware and Equipment	10.5	10.1
Pharmaceuticals and Biotechnology	9.9	15.6
Commercial Services and Supplies	9.4	11.0
Telecommunication Services	9.3	18.5
Hotels, Restaurants and Leisure	8.5	8.0
Energy	8.3	14.8
Media	7.7	9.2
Retailing	7.6	8.6
Transportation	7.4	6.8
Food and Staples Retailing	6.3	5.3
Total Sample	**6.3**	**8.0**
Automobiles and Components	5.9	7.9
Household and Personal Products	5.4	4.6
Capital Goods	5.1	5.9
Consumer Durables and Apparel	4.8	4.6
Utilities	4.5	4.2
Food, Beverage and Tobacco	4.3	3.3
Materials	3.9	3.8

[1]Based on S&P Global Industry Classification Standard.
[2]Geometric mean of annual median.
Source: Compustat, McKinsey & Company's corporate performance database.

and Semiconductor Equipment has grown at 15 percent, and Health Care Equipment and Services has grown by 13 percent. Basic staples—such as Consumer Durables and Apparel; Utilities; Food, Beverage, and Tobacco; and Materials—all have grown less than 5 percent in real terms, only slightly higher than real GDP growth.

Yet, unlike the ROIC ranking, the ranking of industries based on growth varies over time. Between 1994 and 2003, Pharmaceuticals and Biotechnology, Telecommunication Services, and Energy each grew at rates well above long-term averages. For Energy, the recent level of higher growth is primarily driven by M&A, as energy companies consolidated during the 1990s (U.S. energy consumption rose by only 1 percent from 1994 to 2003). For Pharmaceuticals and Biotechnology and for Telecommunication Services, the results are a mixture of organic growth and M&A. Although significant consolidation took place during the 1990s, organic pharmaceutical revenues rose substantially with the development of many blockbuster drugs.

Decay Rates for Corporate Growth

Developing an accurate revenue growth forecast is critical to valuation. Yet building tempered projections is challenging, especially given the upward bias shown by research analysts and the media. For instance, empirical research has found that analysts are overly optimistic in their earnings forecasts following initial public offerings (IPOs) relative to a control sample.[8] This upward forecast bias also holds on a broader scale. In Exhibit 6.17, we plot analyst forecasts of aggregate earnings for the S&P 500 versus actual results from 1985 through 2000. Each line plots median earnings forecasts for a particular year and shows how they changed as actual results came closer. In nearly every year, the actual results are lower than forecast. In addition, the longer the forecast (measured up to four years), the more overly optimistic the forecast typically is.

To keep long-term corporate growth rates in their proper perspective, we present historical growth decay rates over the past 40 years. Companies were segmented into five portfolios, depending on their growth rate at portfolio formation. In Exhibit 6.18 on page 158, we plot how each portfolio's median company grows over time. As the exhibit shows, growth decays very quickly; for the typical company, high growth is not sustainable. Within three years, the difference across portfolios dampens considerably, and by year 5, the highest-growth portfolio outperforms the lowest-growth portfolio by less than 5 percentage points. Within 10 years, this difference

[8] R. Rajan and H. Servaes, "Analyst Following of Initial Public Offerings," *Journal of Finance*, 52(3) (1997): 507–529.

Exhibit 6.17 Aggregate EPS Forecasts for S&P 500 Constituents

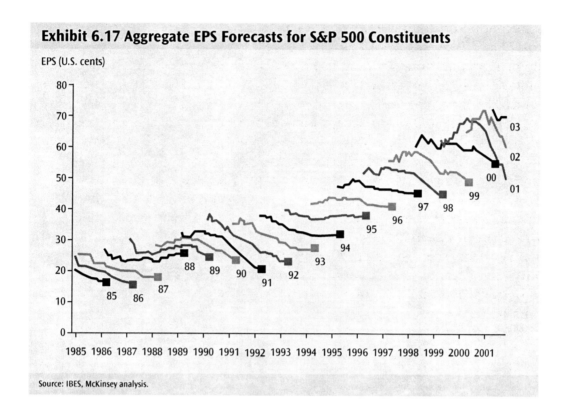

Source: IBES, McKinsey analysis.

drops to less than 2 percentage points. Comparing the decay of growth with that of ROIC, we see that although ROIC is persistent (top companies outperform bottom companies by more than 10 percentage points after 15 years), growth is not.

So why do companies struggle to maintain growth? As with ROIC, strong growth at high returns on capital attracts competition. More importantly, size, saturation, and growth itself are to blame. As the company grows, its revenue base increases, and growing at 20 percent on $200 billion of revenue is much harder than growing at 20 percent on $200 million. Remember, a company that grows at 20 percent will double in size in less than four years. Growth at this rate places many demands on the company and its management, making future growth ever more difficult.

Moreover, since every product market has a limited size, even the best performers must eventually track market growth. Most large companies struggle to grow once they reach a certain size. Exhibit 6.19 on page 159 reports results compiled by the Corporate Executive Board concerning the real revenue growth rate surrounding entrance into the *Fortune* 50.[9] Although

---

[9] Corporate Executive Board, "Stall Points: Barriers to Growth for the Large Corporate Enterprise" (1998).

Exhibit 6.18 Revenue Growth Decay Analysis

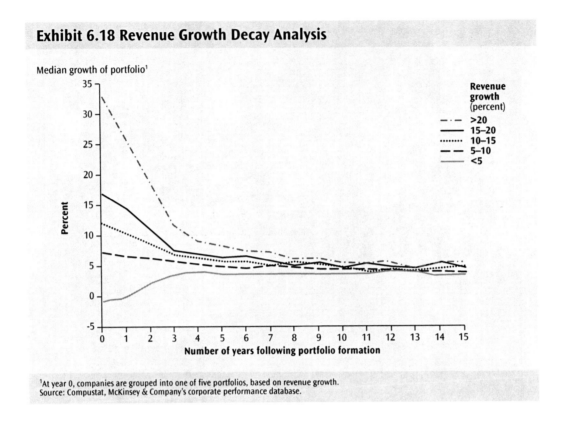

Median growth of portfolio[1]

Revenue growth (percent)
- –·– >20
- —— 15–20
- ········ 10–15
- – – 5–10
- —— <5

Number of years following portfolio formation

[1]At year 0, companies are grouped into one of five portfolios, based on revenue growth.
Source: Compustat, McKinsey & Company's corporate performance database.

growth is strong before companies enter the *Fortune* 50 (often because of acquisitions), growth drops dramatically after inclusion. In the five years before entrance, real revenue growth varies between 9 percent and 20 percent. And although the year immediately following entrance is high (28.6 percent), in every subsequent year, growth is quite low. In fact, during 5 of the 15 years after inclusion, companies actually shrink (in real terms).

In analyzing Exhibits 6.18 and 6.19 it becomes evident that the *typical* firm cannot maintain supernormal revenue growth. But are there companies that can beat the norm? In short, the answer is no. Exhibit 6.20, which reports the transition probabilities from one grouping to another, shows that maintaining high growth is uncommon. For example, 67 percent of the companies reporting less than 5 percent revenue growth in 1994 continued to report growth below 5 percent 10 years later. The same is also true for high-growth companies: 56 percent of companies growing faster than 20 percent in 1994 grew at real rates below 5 percent 10 years later. Only 13 percent of high-growth companies maintained 20 percent real growth 10 years later, most of which was probably driven by acquisitions.

Exhibit 6.19 Revenue Growth Rate Falls Dramatically for Companies Reaching Fortune 50

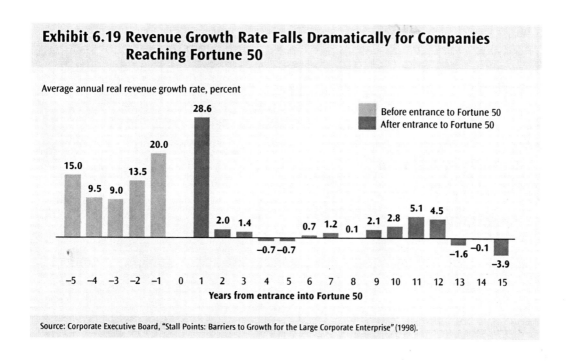

Source: Corporate Executive Board, "Stall Points: Barriers to Growth for the Large Corporate Enterprise" (1998).

SUMMARY

A valuation based on discounted cash flow is only as good as the model's forecasts. Yet, all too often, we get caught up in the details of a company's financial statements and forget the economic fundamentals: A company's valuation is driven by ROIC and growth. Thus, when you perform a valuation, it is critical to evaluate how your forecasts of ROIC and growth relate to the economics of the industry and how your results compare with the historical performance of companies that came before.

Exhibit 6.20 Revenue Growth Transition Probability, 1994–2003

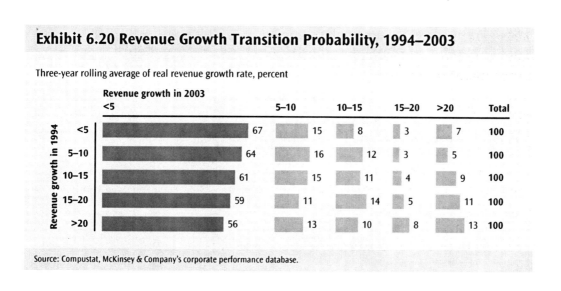

Source: Compustat, McKinsey & Company's corporate performance database.

527

In this chapter, we have explored elements of value creation: price premium, cost competitiveness, capital efficiency, and sustainability. If you plan to forecast large returns on capital and high levels of growth, make sure you can explicitly point to the company's source of competitive advantage. In addition, make sure any forecasts—even those for which the company's advantages are clear—are within reasonable historical bounds. Otherwise, you may generate an unrealistic valuation and find yourself caught in yet another speculative bubble.

REVIEW QUESTIONS

1. Identify and discuss three sources of competitive advantage that could lead to increases in ROIC.

2. Referring to the key value driver formula, explain why this formula might work well for an established company, whereas for either a startup or rapidly growing company, the key value driver formula is inappropriate.

3. Explain how proper "branding" of corporate products could lead to sustained periods of high ROIC.

4. What factors would lead ROIC to be significantly different across industrial lines? Why might companies operating within the pharmaceutical and biotechnology industries be able to sustain higher ROICs than firms in the technology hardware and equipment and the retailing industries?

5. What does economic theory predict about long-run ROIC? Is historical evidence consistent with these predictions?

6. How might the key value driver approach to corporate valuation be adjusted to incorporate the unique growth characteristics of a non-constant growth firm?

7. Why might large firms experience lower rates of growth than smaller firms? What is the danger of having a large company attempt to match the growth of a small company?

7

Analyzing Historical Performance

Understanding a company's past is essential for forecasting its future. For that reason, we begin the valuation process by analyzing historical performance. Since the financial statements are not designed for valuation, historical analysis can be challenging. To properly evaluate a company's performance, it is therefore necessary to rearrange the accounting statements, dig for new information in the footnotes, and, where information is missing, make informed assumptions. Only then will the company's previous performance, competitive position, and ability to generate cash in the future come into focus. To analyze a company's historical performance:

- Reorganize the financial statements to reflect economic, instead of accounting, performance, creating such new terms as net operating profit less adjusted taxes (NOPLAT), invested capital, and free cash flow (FCF).

- Measure and analyze the company's return on invested capital (ROIC) and economic profit to evaluate the company's ability to create value.

- Break down revenue growth into its four components: organic revenue growth, currency effects, acquisitions, and accounting changes.

- Assess the company's financial health and capital structure to determine whether it has the financial resources to conduct business and make short- and long-term investments.

The final section of this chapter covers advanced issues in financial analysis, such as capitalizing expenses (e.g., operating leases and R&D), stock-based compensation, retirement plans, provisions and loss reserves, and inflation. Immediately following this chapter, we apply the principles to Heineken, the Dutch brewer. The Heineken case continues through Part Two of the book.

REORGANIZING THE ACCOUNTING STATEMENTS: KEY CONCEPTS

Most companies report in their financial statements return on assets (ROA), return on equity (ROE), and cash flow from operations (CFO). Nonoperating items such as nonoperating assets and capital structure, however, bias these measures.[1] To properly ground our historical analysis, we need to separate operating performance from nonoperating items and the financing obtained to support the business. The resulting measures, ROIC and FCF, are independent of leverage and focus solely on the operating performance of a business.

To build ROIC and FCF, we need to reorganize the balance sheet to create invested capital and likewise reorganize the income statement to create net operating profit less adjusted taxes (NOPLAT). Invested capital represents the total investor capital required to fund operations, without distinction to how the capital is financed. NOPLAT represents the total after-tax operating income (generated by the company's invested capital) that is available to *all* financial investors. (Although choice of capital structure will affect valuation, this will be handled through the cost of capital, *not* through ROIC or FCF.) Return on invested capital and free cash flow both rely on NOPLAT and invested capital. ROIC is defined as

$$\text{ROIC} = \frac{\text{NOPLAT}}{\text{Invested Capital}}$$

and free cash flow is defined as

FCF = NOPLAT + Noncash Operating Expenses − Investment in Invested Capital

By combining noncash operating expenses, such as depreciation with investment in invested capital, we can also express FCF as[2]

FCF = NOPLAT − Net Increase in Invested Capital

---

[1] As financial leverage rises, net income will fall due to increased interest expenses. This will cause return on assets to fall, even if the operating performance remains unchanged. Return on equity also commingles operating performance with financial leverage. Specifically, ROE rises with leverage when ROIC is greater than the company's after-tax interest rate on debt, and it falls with leverage when ROIC is less than the company's after-tax interest rate.

[2] This follows directly from the relation that invested capital$_{t+1}$ equals invested capital$_t$ plus investment in invested capital minus any noncash charges that reduce invested capital.

Invested Capital: Key Concepts

To build an economic balance sheet that separates a company's operating assets from its nonoperating assets and financial structure, we start with the traditional balance sheet. The accountant's balance sheet is bound by the most fundamental rule of accounting,

$$\text{Assets} = \text{Liabilities} + \text{Equity}$$

For single-product companies, assets consist primarily of operating assets (OA), such as receivables, inventory, and property, plant, and equipment (PP&E). Liabilities consist of operating liabilities (OL), such as accounts payable and accrued salaries, and interest-bearing debt (D), such as notes payable and long-term debt. Equity (E) will consist of common stock, possibly preferred stock, and retained earnings. Using this more explicit breakdown of assets, liabilities, and equity leads to an expanded version of the balance sheet relation:

$$\text{Operating Assets} = \text{Operating Liabilities} + \text{Debt} + \text{Equity}$$

The traditional balance sheet equation, however, mixes operating liabilities and investor capital on the right side of the equation. Moving operating liabilities to the left side of the equation leads to "invested capital":

$$\text{Operating Assets} - \text{Operating Liabilities} = \textbf{Invested Capital} = \text{Debt} + \text{Equity}$$

With this new equation, we have rearranged the balance sheet to better reflect invested capital used for operations, and net financing provided by investors to fund operations. Note how invested capital can be calculated using the *operating* method, that is, operating assets minus operating liabilities, or the *financing* method, which equals debt plus equity.

For most companies, our last equation is overly simplistic. Assets consist not only of core operating assets, but also of nonoperating assets, such as marketable securities, prepaid pension assets, nonconsolidated subsidiaries, and other equity investments. Liabilities consist not only of operating liabilities and interest-bearing debt, but also of debt equivalents (DE), such as unfunded retirement liabilities and restructuring reserves, and equity equivalents (EE), such as deferred taxes and income-smoothing provisions (we explain equivalents in detail later in the chapter). Expanding our original balance sheet equation:

OA		NOA		OL		D + DE		E + EE
Operating	+	Nonoperating	=	Operating	+	Debt and	+	Equity and
Assets		Assets		Liabilities		Its Equivalents		Its Equivalents

Exhibit 7.1 An Example of Invested Capital

$ million

Accountant's Balance Sheet				Invested Capital				
Assets	Prior year	Current year			Prior year	Current year		
Inventory	200	225		Inventory	200	225	Operating liabilities
Net PP&E	300	350		Accounts payable	(125)	(150)	are netted against
Equity investments	15	25		Operating working capital	75	75	operating assets.
Total assets	515	600					
				Net PP&E	300	350	
Liabilities and equity				Invested capital	375	425	
Accounts payable	125	150					Nonoperating assets
Interest-bearing debt	225	200		Equity investments	15	25	are not included in
Common stock	50	50		Total funds invested	390	450	invested capital.
Retained earnings	115	200		**Total funds invested**			
Total liabilities and equity	515	600		Interest-bearing debt	225	200	
				Common stock	50	50	
				Retained earnings	115	200	
				Total funds invested	390	450	

Rearranging leads to the derivation of "total funds invested":

$$
\underset{\substack{\text{Invested} \\ \text{Capital}}}{\text{OA} - \text{OL}} + \underset{\substack{\text{Nonoperating} \\ \text{Assets}}}{\text{NOA}} = \underset{\substack{\text{Funds} \\ \text{Invested}}}{\text{Total}} = \underset{\substack{\text{Debt and} \\ \text{Its Equivalents}}}{\text{D} + \text{DE}} + \underset{\substack{\text{Equity and} \\ \text{Its Equivalents}}}{\text{E} + \text{EE}}
$$

From an investing perspective, total funds invested equals invested capital plus nonoperating assets. From the financing perspective, total funds invested equals debt and its equivalents, plus equity and its equivalents. Exhibit 7.1 rearranges the balance sheet into invested capital for a simple hypothetical company with only a few line items. A more sophisticated example, using real companies, is developed in the next section.

Net Operating Profit Less Adjusted Taxes: Key Concepts

Invested capital makes no distinction between debt and equity. Rather, invested capital combines the two sources of investor funds and treats them equally. In a similar fashion, net operating profit less adjusted taxes (NOPLAT) aggregates the operating income generated by invested capital. Unlike net income, NOPLAT includes profits available to both debt holders and equity holders.

To calculate NOPLAT, we reorganize the accountant's income statement (see Exhibit 7.2) in three fundamental ways. First, interest is not sub-

Exhibit 7.2 An Example of NOPLAT

$ million

Accountant's income statement	Current year
Revenues	1,000
Operating costs	(700)
Depreciation	(20)
Operating profit	280
Interest	(20)
Nonoperating income	4
Earnings before taxes (EBT)	264
Taxes	(66)
Net income	198

NOPLAT	Current year
Revenues	1,000
Operating costs	(700)
Depreciation	(20)
Operating profit	280
Operating taxes[1]	(70)
NOPLAT	210
After-tax nonoperating income[1]	3
Total income to all investors	213
Reconciliation with net income	
Net income	198
After-tax interest[1]	15
Total income to all investors	213

Taxes are calculated on operating profits.

Do not include income from any asset excluded from invested capital as part of NOPLAT.

Treat interest as a financial payout to investors, not an expense.

[1]Assumes a flat tax of 25% on all income.

tracted from operating profit. Interest is considered a payment to the company's financial investors, not an operating expense. By reclassifying interest as a financing item, we make NOPLAT independent of the company's capital structure.

Second, when calculating after-tax operating profit, exclude any nonoperating income, gains, or losses generated from assets that were excluded from invested capital. Mistakenly including nonoperating income in NOPLAT, without including the assets in invested capital, will lead to an inconsistent definition of ROIC (the numerator and denominator will consist of different elements).

Finally, since reported taxes are calculated after interest and nonoperating income, they are a function of nonoperating items and capital structure. Keeping NOPLAT focused solely on operations requires that the effects of interest expense and nonoperating income also be removed from taxes. To calculate operating taxes, start with reported taxes, add back the tax shield caused by interest expense, and remove the taxes paid for nonoperating income. The resulting operating taxes should equal the hypothetical taxes that would be reported by an all-equity, pure operating company.

You may wonder how we will take into account the value of the tax shield. Given that interest is tax deductible, the deduction provides an important source of value to the company. But rather than model tax shields in NOPLAT, we will model all financing costs (including interest and its tax shield) in the cost of capital. Similarly, taxes for nonoperating income must be accounted for, and should be netted directly against the nonoperating income, *not* as part of NOPLAT.

Return on Invested Capital: Key Concepts

With our newly reorganized financial statements, we can now measure total investor capital and the after-tax operating income generated from those investments. ROIC measures the ratio of NOPLAT to invested capital:

$$ROIC = \frac{NOPLAT}{Invested\ Capital}$$

Since NOPLAT and invested capital are independent of financial structure and nonoperating assets, so is ROIC. And by using ROIC, we can now measure how the company's *core* operating performance has changed and how the company compares with its competitors, without the effects of financial structure and other nonoperating items distorting the analysis.

Free Cash Flow: Key Concepts

To value a company's core operations, we discount projected free cash flow at an appropriate risk-adjusted cost of capital. Free cash flow is the after-tax cash flow available to *all* investors: debt holders and equity holders. Unlike "cash flow from operations" reported in a company's financial statement, free cash flow is independent of financing and nonoperating items. It can be thought of as the after-tax cash flow—as if the company held only core operating assets and financed the business entirely with equity. Free cash flow is defined as:

FCF = NOPLAT + Noncash Operating Expenses − Investments in Invested Capital

As shown in Exhibit 7.3, free cash flow excludes nonoperating flows and items related to capital structure. Unlike the accountant's cash flow statement, the free cash flow statement starts with NOPLAT (versus net income). As discussed earlier, NOPLAT excludes nonoperating income and interest expense. Instead, interest (and its tax shield) is treated as a financing cash flow.

Net investments in nonoperating assets and the gains, losses, and income associated with these nonoperating assets are *not* included in free cash flow. Instead, nonoperating cash flows should be valued separately. Combining free cash flow and nonoperating cash flow leads to cash flow available to investors. As is true with total funds invested and profit available to all investors, cash flow available to investors can be calculated using two methodologies: "origin of cash flow" and "to whom the cash flow belongs." Although the two seem redundant, using both methods can help you avoid line item omissions and classification pitfalls.

534

Exhibit 7.3 An Example of Free Cash Flow

$ million

Accountant's cash flow statement	Current year		Free cash flow	Current year
Net income	198		NOPLAT	210
Depreciation	20		Depreciation	20
Decrease (increase) in inventory	(25)		Gross cash flow	230
Increase (decrease) in accounts payable	25			
Cash flow from operations	218		Decrease (increase) in inventory	(25)
			Increase (decrease) in accounts payable	25
Capital expenditures	(70)		Capital expenditures	(70)
Decrease (increase) in equity investments	(10)		Gross investment	(70)
Cash flow from investing	(80)			
			Free cash flow	160
Increase (decrease) in interest-bearing debt	(25)			
Increase (decrease) in common stock	0		After-tax nonoperating income	3
Dividends	(113)		Decrease (increase) in equity investments	(10)
Cash flow from financing	(138)		Cash flow available to investors	153
			After-tax interest expense	15
			Increase (decrease) in interest-bearing debt	25
			Increase (decrease) in common stock	0
			Dividends	113
			Cash flow available to investors	153

- Treat interest as a financial payout to investors, not as an expense.
- Investments in operating items are subtracted from gross cash flow.
- Cash flow from nonoperating assets should be evaluated separately from core operations.

REORGANIZING THE ACCOUNTING STATEMENTS: IN PRACTICE

Reorganizing the statements can be difficult, even for the savviest analyst. Which items are operating assets? Which are nonoperating? Which items should be treated as debt? As equity? In the following pages, we address these questions through an examination of Home Depot, the world's largest home improvement retailer, with stores located throughout North America. The company has grown rapidly over the past 10 years, generating strong returns and cash flow. But its core markets have become increasingly saturated, and the company now faces new challenges.

Invested Capital: In Practice

Invested capital equals operating assets minus operating liabilities. Total funds invested equals invested capital plus nonoperating assets. Alternatively,

Exhibit 7.4 Home Depot and Lowe's: Historical Balance Sheet

$ million

	Home Depot			Lowe's		
Assets	2001	2002	2003	2001	2002	2003
Cash and cash equivalents	2,477	2,188	2,826	799	853	1,446
Short-term investments	69	65	26	54	273	178
Receivables, net	920	1,072	1,097	166	172	131
Merchandise inventories	6,725	8,338	9,076	3,611	3,068	4,584
Other current assets	170	254	303	291	302	348
Total current assets	10,361	11,917	13,328	4,920	5,568	6,687
Net property and equipment	15,375	17,168	20,063	8,653	10,352	11,945
Long-term investments	83	107	84	22	29	169
Acquired intangibles and goodwill	419	575	833	0	0	0
Other assets	156	244	129	141	160	241
Total assets	26,394	30,011	34,437	13,736	16,109	19,042
Liabilities and equity	**2001**	**2002**	**2003**	**2001**	**2002**	**2003**
Short-term debt	211	0	509	159	79	77
Accounts payable	3,436	4,560	5,159	1,715	1,943	2,366
Accrued salaries	717	809	801	347	394	409
Deferred revenue	933	998	1,281	0	0	0
Other accrued expenses	1,204	1,668	1,804	796	1,162	1,516
Total current liabilities	6,501	8,035	9,554	3,017	3,578	4,368
Long-term debt	1,250	1,321	856	3,734	3,736	3,678
Deferred income taxes	189	362	967	305	478	657
Other long-term liabilities	372	491	653	6	15	30
Net common stock and paid-in capital	5,503	3,913	2,637	2,192	2,414	2,631
Retained earnings	12,799	15,971	19,680	4,482	5,887	7,677
Accumulated other comp income	(220)	(82)	90	1	1	1
Total liabilities and equity	26,394	30,011	34,437	13,736	16,109	19,042

total funds invested equals debt and its equivalents plus equity and its equivalents:

$$\underset{\substack{\text{Invested} \\ \text{Capital}}}{\text{OA} - \text{OL}} + \underset{\substack{\text{Nonoperating} \\ \text{Assets}}}{\text{NOA}} = \underset{\substack{\text{Total} \\ \text{Funds} \\ \text{Invested}}}{\text{Total}} = \underset{\substack{\text{Debt and} \\ \text{Its Equivalents}}}{\text{D} + \text{DE}} + \underset{\substack{\text{Equity and} \\ \text{Its Equivalents}}}{\text{E} + \text{EE}}$$

In Exhibit 7.4, we present balance sheets for Home Depot and Lowe's (a direct competitor of Home Depot). We next set each element of the preceding equation against those figures.

For simplicity, we previously defined invested capital as operating assets minus operating liabilities (OA – OL). Most financial analysts, however, separate invested capital into operating working capital (current operating assets less current operating liabilities), fixed assets (e.g., net property, plant,

536

Exhibit 7.5 Home Depot and Lowe's: Invested Capital Calculation

$ million

	Home Depot			Lowe's		
	2001	2002	2003	2001	2002	2003
Working cash	1,027	1,117	1,243	424	508	591
Receivables, net	920	1,072	1,097	166	172	131
Merchandise inventories	6,725	8,338	9,076	3,611	3,968	4,584
Other current assets	170	254	303	291	302	348
Operating current assets	8,842	10,781	11,719	4,491	4,950	5,654
Accounts payable	3,436	4,560	5,159	1,715	1,943	2,366
Accrued salaries	717	809	801	347	394	409
Deferred revenue	933	998	1,281	0	0	0
Other accrued expenses	1,204	1,668	1,804	796	1,162	1,516
Operating current liabilities	6,290	8,035	9,045	2,858	3,499	4,291
Operating working capital	2,552	2,746	2,674	1,634	1,451	1,363
Net property and equipment	15,375	17,168	20,063	8,653	10,352	11,945
Capitalized operating leases[1]	5,459	5,890	6,554	2,189	2,373	2,762
Net other assets	(216)	(247)	(524)	134	145	211
Invested capital (excluding goodwill)	23,170	25,557	28,767	12,611	14,321	16,281
Acquired intangibles and goodwill	419	575	833	0	0	0
Cumulative amortization and pooled goodwill[2]	46	54	55	730	730	730
Invested capital (including goodwill)	23,635	26,185	29,655	13,341	15,051	17,012
Excess cash	1,519	1,136	1,609	429	618	1,033
Long-term investments	83	107	84	22	29	169
Total funds invested	25,237	27,428	31,348	13,792	15,698	18,213

	2001	2002	2003	2001	2002	2003
Short-term debt	211	0	509	159	79	77
Long-term debt	1,250	1,321	856	3,734	3,736	3,678
Capitalized operating leases[1]	5,459	5,890	6,554	2,189	2,373	2,762
Debt and debt equivalents	6,920	7,211	7,919	6,082	6,188	6,517
Deferred income taxes	189	362	967	305	478	657
Cumulative amortization and pooled goodwill[2]	46	54	55	730	730	730
Net common stock and paid-in-capital	5,503	3,913	2,637	2,192	2,414	2,631
Retained earnings	12,799	15,971	19,680	4,482	5,887	7,677
Accumulated other comp income	(220)	(82)	90	1	1	1
Equity and equity equivalents	18,317	20,218	23,429	7,709	9,510	11,696
Total funds invested	25,237	27,428	31,348	13,792	15,698	18,213

[1]Capitalized operating lease adjustments are detailed in Exhibit 7.21.
[2]Goodwill and cumulative amortization adjustments are detailed in Exhibit 7.6.

and equipment), intangible assets (e.g., goodwill), and net other long-term operating assets (net of long-term operating liabilities). Exhibit 7.5 demonstrates this line-by-line aggregation for Home Depot and Lowe's. In the following subsections, we examine each element in detail.

Operating working capital Operating working capital equals operating current assets, net of operating current liabilities. Operating current assets comprise all current assets necessary for the operation of the business, including working cash balances, trade accounts receivable, inventory, and prepaid expenses. Specifically *excluded* are excess cash and marketable securities, that is, cash greater than the operating needs of the business.[3] Excess cash generally represents temporary imbalances in the company's cash position and is discussed later in this section.

Non-interest-bearing operating current liabilities include those liabilities that are related to the ongoing operations of the firm. The most common operating liabilities are those related to suppliers (accounts payable), employees (accrued salaries), customers (deferred revenue),[4] and the government (income taxes payable). If a liability is deemed operating versus financial, it should be netted from operating assets to determine invested capital.

Some argue that operating liabilities, such as accounts payable, are a form of financing and should be treated no differently than debt. This would lead to an *inconsistent* definition of NOPLAT and invested capital. NOPLAT is the income available to both debt and equity holders and therefore, when determining ROIC, should be divided by debt plus equity. Although a supplier may charge customers implicit interest for the right to pay in 30 days, the charge is an indistinguishable part of the price, and hence an indistinguishable part of the cost of goods sold. Since cost of goods sold is subtracted from revenue to determine NOPLAT, operating liabilities must be subtracted from operating assets to determine invested capital.[5]

Net property, plant, and equipment   The book value of net property, plant, and equipment (e.g., production equipment and facilities) is always included in operating assets. Situations that require using the market value or replacement cost are discussed in the section on advanced issues.

Acquired intangibles and goodwill   Whether to include acquired intangibles and goodwill as part of invested capital depends on the type of analysis being performed. To prepare for these later analyses, measure invested capital with and without goodwill. Then, to properly evaluate goodwill, make two adjustments. First, unlike other fixed assets, goodwill does not wear out, nor is it replaceable. Therefore, adjust reported goodwill upward

---

[3] In the company's financial statements, accountants often distinguish between cash and marketable securities, but not between working cash and excess cash. We provide guidance on distinguishing working from excess cash later in the chapter.

[4] Retailers, such as Home Depot and Lowe's, receive customer prepayments from gift cards, prepaid product installations, and anticipated customer returns (for which funds are received but revenue is not recognized).

[5] Alternatively, we could add back the estimated financing cost associated with any operating liabilities to NOPLAT and not subtract the operating liabilities from operating assets. This approach, however, requires information not readily available.

Exhibit 7.6 Home Depot and Lowe's: Adjustments to Goodwill

$ million

Home Depot	1999	2000	2001	2002	2003
Reported goodwill	311	314	419	575	833
Adjustments for merger accounting	0	0	0	0	0
Cumulative amortization and impairments	30	38	46	54	55
Adjusted goodwill	341	352	465	629	888

Lowe's	1999	2000	2001	2002	2003
Reported goodwill	0	0	0	0	0
Adjustments for merger accounting	730	730	730	730	730
Cumulative amortization and impairments	0	0	0	0	0
Adjusted goodwill	730	730	730	730	730

to recapture historical amortization and impairments.[6] (To maintain consistency, amortization and impairments will not be deducted from revenues to determine NOPLAT).

Second, any unrecorded goodwill (due to the old pooling of interest/merger accounting) must be added to recorded goodwill. Consider Lowe's acquisition of Eagle Garden & Hardware. Since the acquisition was recorded using pooling, no goodwill was recognized. Had Lowe's used purchase accounting, the company would have recorded $730 million in goodwill.[7] To include pooling transactions, estimate and record the incremental goodwill while simultaneously adjusting equity to represent the value of shares given away.

In Exhibit 7.6, cumulative amortization and impairments are added back to Home Depot's recorded goodwill. The exhibit also shows Lowe's recapitalized goodwill from the Eagle Garden & Hardware acquisition.

Net other long-term operating assets   If other long-term assets and liabilities are small—and not detailed by the company—we can assume that they are operating. To determine net other long-term operating assets, subtract other long-term liabilities from other long-term assets. This figure should be included as part of invested capital.

[6] The recent implementation of new accounting standards (in 2001 for the United States and 2005 for Europe) radically changed the way that companies account for acquisitions. Today, whether paid in cash or stock, acquisitions must be recorded on the balance sheet using the purchase methodology. Second, goodwill is no longer amortized. Instead, the company periodically tests the level of goodwill to determine whether the acquired business has lost value. If it has, goodwill is impaired (written down).

[7] On the final day of trading, Eagle had 29.1 million shares outstanding at a price of $37.75. Thus, Lowe's paid approximately $1.1 billion. According to its last 10-Q, Eagle had only $370 million in total equity. Goodwill equals $1.1 billion less $370 million, or $730 million.

If, however, the other long-term assets account is relatively large, it might include nonoperating items such as deferred tax assets, prepaid pension assets, intangible assets related to pensions, nonconsolidated subsidiaries, and other equity investments. Nonoperating items should not be included in invested capital.

Long-term liabilities can also include operating and nonoperating items. Long-term *operating* liabilities are liabilities that result directly from an ongoing operating activity. For instance, Home Depot warranties some products beyond one year, collecting customer funds today but recognizing the revenue only as the warranty expires. Most long-term liabilities are not operating liabilities, but rather what we deem debt and equity equivalents. These include unfunded pension liabilities, unfunded postretirement medical costs, restructuring reserves, and deferred taxes.

Where can you find the breakdown of other assets and other liabilities? In some cases, companies provide a table in the footnotes. Most of the time, however, you must work through the footnotes, note by note, searching for items aggregated within other assets and liabilities. For instance, in 2003, Lockheed Martin detailed an intangible asset related to pensions in the pension footnote but nowhere else in its annual report.

Hidden assets and their respective financing   Up to now, we have focused on reorganizing items that appear on the balance sheet. But there are two other items that accountants fail to capitalize: operating leases and investments masquerading as expenses (e.g., research and development). If these hidden assets are significant, we recommend the following adjustments:

- When a company leases an asset under certain conditions, it need not record either an asset or a liability. To properly compare across companies with different leasing policies, you should include the value of the lease as an operating asset, with a corresponding debt recorded as a financing item. Otherwise, companies that lease assets will appear "capital light" relative to identical companies that purchase the assets.

- Given the conservative principles of accounting, accountants expense research and development (R&D), advertising, and certain other expenses in their entirety, even when the economic benefits of the expense continue beyond the current reporting period. If possible, R&D and other quasi investments should be capitalized *and* amortized in a manner similar to capital expenditures. Equity should be adjusted correspondingly to balance the invested capital equation.

The specific treatment of operating leases and R&D expenses is detailed later in this chapter.

Nonoperating assets   Invested capital represents the capital necessary to operate a company's core business. In addition to invested capital, companies can also own nonoperating assets, both liquid and illiquid. Liquid assets include excess cash, marketable securities, and certain financing receivables (e.g., credit card receivables). Illiquid assets include equity investments and excess pension assets. We address excess cash, illiquid investments, and other nonoperating assets like excess pension assets next.

Excess cash and marketable securities   Do not include excess cash in invested capital. By its definition, excess cash is unnecessary for core operations. Rather than mix excess cash with core operations, therefore, you should analyze and value excess cash separately.

Given its liquidity and low risk, excess cash will earn very small returns. Therefore, failing to separate excess cash from core operations will incorrectly depress the company's apparent ROIC. Home Depot's ROIC in 2003 was 18.2 percent. Had excess cash been included as part of invested capital, Home Depot's ROIC would have been incorrectly measured as 17.4 percent.

Companies do not disclose how much cash they deem necessary for operations. Nor does the accountant's definition of cash versus marketable securities distinguish working cash from excess cash. To estimate the size of working cash, we examined the cash holdings of the S&P 500 nonfinancial companies. Between 1993 and 2000, the companies with the smallest cash balances held cash just below 2 percent of sales. If this is a good proxy for working cash, any cash above 2 percent should be considered excess.[8]

This aggregate figure, however, is not a rule. Required cash holdings vary by industry. For instance, one study found that companies in industries with higher cash flow volatility hold higher cash balances.[9] To assess the *minimum* cash needed to support operations, look for a minimum clustering of cash to revenue across the industry.

Illiquid investments, nonconsolidated subsidiaries, and other equity investments   If possible, interest-generating customer loans (e.g., credit card receivables and other long-term customer financing), nonconsolidated subsidiaries, and other equity investments should be measured and valued separately from invested capital. Evaluating customer financing and equity investments

---

[8] Companies in economies with poor shareholder protections tend to hold more cash. Therefore, in economies with poor shareholder protections, median (or bottom quartile) cash holdings might overestimate the amount of working cash truly needed. A. Dittmar, J. Mahrt-Smith, and H. Servaes "International Corporate Governance and Corporate Cash Holdings," *Journal of Financial and Quantitative Analysis* (forthcoming).

[9] T. Opler, L. Pinkowitz, R. Stulz, and R. Williamson, "The Determinants and Implications of Corporate Cash Holdings," *Journal of Financial Economics*, 52(1) (1999): 3–46.

separately requires excluding these accounts from invested capital *and* excluding their respective income from NOPLAT. Companies do not always clearly separate sources of income, so we are sometimes forced to aggregate certain nonoperating assets within invested capital.

Prepaid and intangible pension assets If a company runs a defined-benefit plan for its employees, it must fund the plan each year. And if a company funds its plan faster than its pension expenses dictate, under U.S. Generally Accepted Accounting Principles (GAAP), the company can recognize a portion of the excess assets on the balance sheet. Pension assets are considered a nonoperating asset and not part of invested capital. Their value is important to the equity holder, so they will be valued later, but separately from core operations. We examine pension assets in detail in the section on advanced issues.

Total funds invested can be calculated as invested capital plus nonoperating assets, or as the sum of net debt, equity, and equity equivalents. We next examine the right-hand side of the "total funds invested" equation.

Other nonoperating assets Other nonoperating assets, such as excess real estate and discontinued operations, should also be excluded from invested capital.

Debt Debt includes any short-term or long-term interest-bearing liability. Short-term debt includes commercial paper, notes payable, and the current portion of long-term debt. Long-term debt includes fixed debt, floating debt, and convertible debt with maturities of more than a year.

Debt equivalents such as retirement liabilities and operating leases If a company's defined-benefit plan is underfunded, it must recognize a portion of the underfunding as a liability. The amount of underfunding is not an operating liability. Rather, we treat unfunded pension expenses and unfunded postretirement medical expenses as a debt equivalent (and treat the net interest expense associated with these liabilities as nonoperating). It is as if the company must borrow money to fund the plan.

Treating unfunded retirement expenses as debt might seem hypothetical, but for some companies the issue has become real. In June 2003, General Motors issued $17 billion in debt, using the proceeds to reduce its pension shortfall, not to fund operations.[10]

---

[10] R. Barley and C. Evans, "GM Plans Record Bond Sale Thursday to Plug Pension Gap," Reuters News (June 26, 2003).

As discussed in the section on hidden assets, a company with substantial operating leases should capitalize those leases, recognizing them both as an asset and as a debt. The resulting liability from capitalizing operating leases should be treated as a debt equivalent. For some companies, such as retailers, operating leases can increase debt dramatically. This helps explain why some retailers, such as the Gap, have sub-A credit ratings even with minimal formal debt.

Other debt equivalents, such as reserves for plant decommissioning and restructuring, are discussed in the section on advanced issues.

Equity (E)   Equity includes original investor funds, such as common stock and additional paid-in capital, as well as investor funds reinvested into the company such as retained earnings and accumulated other comprehensive income (AOCI). In the United States, AOCI consists primarily of currency adjustments and aggregate unrealized gains and losses from liquid assets whose value has changed but have not yet been sold. Any stock repurchased and held in the treasury should be deducted from total equity.

Equity equivalents such as deferred taxes   In certain situations, companies will expense a future cost that has no corresponding cash outlay. Since the expense is noncash, both an expense and an offsetting liability are recognized. The most common noncash expenses are deferred taxes and reserves created for the purpose of income smoothing. Each of these liabilities is an equity equivalent, not an operating liability, so it should *not* be subtracted from operating assets. These liabilities should remain on the right side of the invested-capital equation.

The most common equity equivalent, deferred taxes, arises primarily from tax incentives that governments provide to encourage investment.[11] In many countries, companies use straight-line depreciation to determine taxes reported in their financial statements but can use accelerated depreciation to compute actual taxes owed.[12] Since the delay in taxes is temporary, a liability is recognized. For growing companies, the financial statements will overstate the company's actual tax burden. Thus, rather than using the taxes reported on the income statement to compute NOPLAT, we recommend using taxes actually paid. Using cash taxes, however, means no deferred tax account needs to be recognized. Instead, adjust retained earnings to balance the financial statements. This is why deferred taxes are considered an equity equivalent.

---

[11] In addition to deferred taxes arising from investment, deferred taxes also arise from nonoperating items, such as pensions. When this is the case, deferred taxes should be aggregated with (or netted against) their corresponding nonoperating item. See the company's footnotes for a full breakdown of deferred taxes.

[12] Although not every country allows reported taxes to differ from actual taxes, the practice is becoming more prevalent.

NOPLAT: In Practice

To determine the after-tax income generated by invested capital, we calculate net operating profits less adjusted taxes (NOPLAT). NOPLAT represents total income generated from operations available to all investors. To determine NOPLAT for Home Depot and Lowe's, we turn to their respective income statements (see Exhibit 7.7) and convert the income statement into NOPLAT (see Exhibit 7.8).

Net operating profit (NOP or EBITA) NOPLAT starts with earnings before interest, taxes, and amortization of goodwill (EBITA), which equals revenue less operating expenses (e.g., cost of goods sold, selling costs, general and administrative costs, depreciation).

Nonoperating income, gains, and losses To remain consistent with the calculation of invested capital, calculate NOPLAT without interest income, gains, and losses from the corresponding assets that have been excluded. Historical returns on excess cash and other nonoperating assets should be calculated and evaluated separately.

Income adjustments for hidden assets In the section on invested capital, we outlined certain assets not on the balance sheet: operating leases and capitalized R&D. Corresponding adjustments must also be made to the income statement:

Exhibit 7.7 Home Depot and Lowe's: Historical Income Statement

$ million	Home Depot			Lowe's		
	2001	2002	2003	2001	2002	2003
Net sales	53,553	58,247	64,816	22,111	26,491	30,838
Cost of merchandise sold	(37,406)	(40,139)	(44,236)	(15,743)	(18,465)	(21,231)
Selling, general and administrative	(10,451)	(11,375)	(12,658)	(4,053)	(4,859)	(5,671)
Depreciation	(756)	(895)	(1,075)	(517)	(626)	(758)
Amortization	(8)	(8)	(1)	0	0	0
EBIT	4,932	5,830	6,846	1,798	2,541	3,178
Interest and investment income	53	79	59	25	21	15
Interest expense	(28)	(37)	(62)	(199)	(203)	(195)
Discontinued operations	0	0	0	0	0	15
Earnings before taxes	4,957	5,872	6,843	1,624	2,359	3,013
Income taxes	(1,913)	(2,208)	(2,539)	(601)	(888)	(1,136)
Net earnings	3,044	3,664	4,304	1,023	1,471	1,877

Exhibit 7.8 Home Depot and Lowe's: NOPLAT Calculation

$ million

	Home Depot			Lowe's		
	2001	2002	2003	2001	2002	2003
Net sales	53,553	58,247	64,816	22,111	26,491	30,838
Cost of merchandise sold	(37,406)	(40,139)	(44,236)	(15,743)	(18,465)	(21,231)
Selling, general and administrative	(10,451)	(11,375)	(12,658)	(4,053)	(4,859)	(5,671)
Depreciation	(756)	(895)	(1,075)	(517)	(626)	(758)
Operating lease interest	288	260	276	106	106	114
Adjusted EBITA	5,228	6,098	7,123	1,904	2,647	3,292
Operating cash taxes	(2,020)	(2,117)	(2,040)	(654)	(825)	(1,069)
NOPLAT	3,208	3,981	5,083	1,250	1,822	2,223
Operating taxes						
Reported taxes	1,913	2,208	2,539	601	888	1,136
Taxes on interest income	(20)	(30)	(23)	(9)	(8)	(6)
Tax shield on interest expense	11	14	24	75	78	74
Tax shield on lease interest expense	111	98	105	40	41	44
Operating taxes on EBITA	2,014	2,290	2,645	707	998	1,248
Decrease (increase) in deferred taxes	6	(173)	(605)	(53)	(173)	(179)
Operating cash taxes on EBITA	2,020	2,117	2,040	654	825	1,069
Reconciliation with net income	**2001**	**2002**	**2003**	**2001**	**2002**	**2003**
Net earnings	3,044	3,664	4,304	1,023	1,471	1,877
Increase in deferred taxes	(6)	173	605	53	173	179
Goodwill amortization	8	8	1	0	0	0
Adjusted net income	3,046	3,845	4,910	1,076	1,644	2,056
After-tax interest expense	17	23	38	123	125	121
After-tax lease interest expense	177	162	170	66	65	71
Loss (gain) from discontinued operations	0	0	0	0	0	(15)
Total income available to investors	3,240	4,030	5,119	1,265	1,835	2,232
After-tax interest income	(33)	(49)	(36)	(15)	(13)	(9)
NOPLAT	3,208	3,981	5,083	1,250	1,822	2,223

- Operating lease payments, which consist of interest and depreciation, are expensed within EBITA. Since interest is a financing flow, add back the implied interest expense to determine EBITA and NOPLAT.
- If you decide to capitalize R&D, the R&D expense must not be deducted from revenue to calculate operating profit. Instead, deduct amortization of past R&D, using a reasonable amortization schedule.

Operating leases and capitalized R&D are detailed in the section on advanced issues later in this chapter. Pension expenses and loss provisions may require further adjustments to income. The section on advanced issues also discusses these topics.

Operating cash taxes on EBITA Since nonoperating items also affect reported taxes, they must be adjusted to an all-equity, operating level. Since interest expense is deductible before taxes, highly leveraged companies will have smaller tax burdens. Although a smaller tax burden can lead to a higher valuation, we recommend valuing all financing effects in the weighted average cost of capital (WACC) or valuing them separately using adjusted present value (APV)—but *not* as part of after-tax operating income.

For Home Depot, compute operating taxes for core operations by starting with reported taxes ($2,539). Next, eliminate the taxes paid on the nonoperating income generated by the company's nonoperating assets ($23). Finally, eliminate the interest expense tax shield (from both traditional debt and capitalized operating leases) by adding the incremental taxes the companies would have paid had Home Depot been entirely financed with equity ($24 and $105 respectively). Home Depot's calculation is as follows:

$ Millions	2001	2002	2003
Reported taxes	1,913	2,208	2,539
Subtract: Taxes on interest income	(20)	(30)	(23)
Add: Tax shield on interest expense	11	14	24
Add: Tax shield on operating lease interest expense	111	98	105
Operating taxes	2,014	2,290	2,645

To eliminate the tax effects of each nonoperating item, multiply each line item's dollar amount by the company's *marginal* tax rate. The marginal tax rate is defined as the tax rate on an extra dollar of income.[13] To calculate marginal taxes, it is necessary to examine the company's financial footnotes. Home Depot reports the following tax schedule in footnote 3 of its annual report:

Tax Rate	2001	2002	2003
Income taxes at federal statutory rate (1)	35.0%	35.0%	35.0%
State income taxes, net of federal (2)	3.5	2.7	3.2
Foreign rate differences	0.1	0.0	−0.4
Other, net	0.0	0.0	−0.6
Accountant's effective (average) tax rate	38.6%	37.6%	37.1%
Marginal tax rate (1 + 2)	38.5%	37.7%	38.2%

[13] Marginal taxes do not equal average taxes, which are computed by dividing reported taxes by earnings before taxes. In fact, whereas marginal taxes are relatively constant, average taxes can vary dramatically. Walt Disney's average tax rate varied between 35 percent and 82 percent from 2001 to 2003, whereas its marginal tax rate varied between 37 percent and 42 percent.

For adjusting reported taxes, marginal taxes are those taxes the company would pay if the financing or nonoperating item were eliminated. If the company eliminated leverage, it would be required to pay additional federal income taxes (line item 1) and state taxes (2). If foreign taxes (3) are based on income and debt is raised abroad, they are marginal. If, however, foreign taxes are based on revenues or debt is raised solely at home, they are not marginal; taxes would not increase as leverage decreased. Whether other taxes (4) are marginal requires further investigation. In this case, we assume they are not. For Home Depot, the marginal tax rate is merely the sum of the federal and state income taxes (1 + 2).

Finally, we recommend using the cash taxes actually paid, versus the taxes reported.[14] The simplest way to calculate cash taxes is to subtract the increase in deferred tax liabilities from operating taxes on EBITA. As shown in Exhibit 7.1, Home Depot's deferred tax liabilities have been growing over time, so reported taxes overstate actual cash taxes. Subtracting the increase in deferred taxes leads to cash taxes:

$ Millions	2001	2002	2003
EBITA	5,228	6,098	7,123
(All-equity) operating taxes on EBITA	2,014	2,290	2,645
Decrease (increase) in deferred taxes	6	(173)	(605)
Operating cash taxes on EBITA	2,020	2,117	2,040
Operating tax rate	38.5%	37.6%	37.1%
× (1 − percent deferred)	−0.3%	7.6%	22.9%
Operating cash tax rate	38.6%	34.7%	28.6%

The cash tax rate at Home Depot has been falling because a greater percentage of operating taxes have been deferred. In 2003, Home Depot was able to defer 22.9 percent of its operating taxes on EBITA.

Reconciliation to net income   To ensure that the reorganization is complete, we recommend reconciling net income to NOPLAT (see the bottom of Exhibit 7.8). To reconcile NOPLAT, start with net income and add back the increase in deferred tax liabilities and goodwill amortization. Next, add back *after-tax* interest expense from both debt and capitalized operating leases. This determines the profits available to all investors. To calculate NOPLAT, subtract after-tax gains and income from nonoperating assets, and you are done. We do this for Home Depot in Exhibit 7.8.

---

[14] If a company reported cash taxes on the income statement, the deferred tax liability would no longer exist, and an offsetting adjustment to retained earnings would be made. Thus, when using cash taxes, you should treat the deferred tax liability as an equity equivalent.

Free Cash Flow: In Practice

Free cash flow is defined as:

$$FCF = NOPLAT + Noncash\ Operating\ Expenses - Investments\ in\ Invested\ Capital$$

Exhibit 7.9 builds the free cash flow calculation and reconciles free cash flow to cash flow available to investors for both Home Depot and Lowe's. The components of free cash flow are as follows:

Gross cash flow   Gross cash flow represents the cash flow generated by the company's operations. It represents the cash available for investment and investor payout, without having to sell nonoperating assets (e.g., excess cash) or raise additional capital. Gross cash flow has two components:

1. *NOPLAT:* As previously defined, net operating profits after taxes are the operating profits available to all investors.
2. *Noncash operating expenses:* Some expenses deducted from revenue to generate NOPLAT are noncash expenses. To convert NOPLAT into cash flow, add back noncash expenses. The two most common noncash expenses are depreciation and employee stock options.[15] Do not add back goodwill amortization and impairments to NOPLAT; they were not subtracted in calculating NOPLAT.

Gross investment   To grow, companies must reinvest a portion of their gross cash flow back into the business. To determine free cash flow, subtract gross investment from gross cash flow. We segment gross investment into four primary areas:

1. *Change in operating working capital:* Growing a business requires investment in operating cash, inventory, and other components of working capital. Operating working capital excludes nonoperating assets, such as excess cash, and financing items, such as short-term debt and dividends payable.
2. *Net capital expenditures:* Net capital expenditures equals investments in property, plant, and equipment, less the book value of any PPE

---

[15] Even though stock options are a noncash expense, they represent value being transferred from shareholders to company employees. Therefore, if you choose to add back noncash compensation to NOPLAT, you must value noncash compensation separately. If you choose not to add back noncash compensation to NOPLAT, there is no need to value them separately. They will be part of enterprise value.

Exhibit 7.9 Home Depot and Lowe's: Historical Free Cash Flow

$ million

	Home Depot			Lowe's		
	2001	2002	2003	2001	2002	2003
NOPLAT	3,208	3,981	5,083	1,250	1,822	2,223
Depreciation	756	895	1,075	517	626	758
Gross cash flow	3,964	4,876	6,157	1,767	2,448	2,981
Investment in operating working capital	834	(194)	72	(203)	183	88
Net capital expenditures	(3,063)	(2,688)	(3,970)	(2,135)	(2,325)	(2,351)
Investment in capitalized operating leases	(775)	(430)	(664)	(547)	(184)	(389)
Investments in intangibles and goodwill	(113)	(164)	(259)	0	0	0
Increase (decrease) in other operating assets	105	31	277	(7)	(11)	(66)
Increase (decrease) in accumulated other comprehensive income	(153)	138	172	3	0	0
Gross investment	(3,165)	(3,307)	(4,372)	(2,889)	(2,336)	(2,719)
Free cash flow	**799**	**1,569**	**1,785**	**1,122**	**112**	**262**
After-tax interest income	33	49	36	15	13	9
Decrease (increase) in excess cash	(1,509)	383	(473)	(321)	(189)	(415)
Decrease (increase) in nonoperating assets	9	(24)	23	13	(7)	(140)
Discontinued operations	0	0	0	0	0	15
Cash flow available to investors	**(668)**	**1,977**	**1,371**	**(1,415)**	**(71)**	**(268)**
	2001	2002	2003	2001	2002	2003
After-tax interest expense	17	23	38	123	125	121
After-tax lease interest expense	177	162	170	66	65	71
Decrease (increase) in debt	88	140	(44)	(903)	78	60
Decrease (increase) in capitalized operating leases	(775)	(430)	(664)	(547)	(184)	(389)
Flows to debt holders	(492)	(105)	(500)	(1,261)	85	(138)
Dividends	396	492	595	60	66	87
Net shares repurchased (issued)	(572)	1,590	1,276	(213)	(222)	(217)
Flows to equity holders	(176)	2,082	1,871	(154)	(156)	(130)
Cash flow available to investors	**(668)**	**1,977**	**1,371**	**(1,415)**	**(71)**	**(268)**

sold. Net capital expenditures are estimated by taking the change in *net* property, plant, and equipment plus depreciation. Do not estimate capital expenditures by taking the change in gross PP&E. Since gross PP&E drops when companies retire assets (which has no cash implications), the change in gross PP&E will often understate the actual amount of capital expenditures.

3. *Change in capitalized operating leases:* To keep the definitions of NOPLAT, invested capital, and free cash flow consistent, include investments in capitalized operating leases in gross investment.[16]

4. *Investment in acquired intangibles and goodwill:* For acquired intangible assets, where cumulative amortization has been added back, we can estimate investment by computing the change in net acquired intangibles. For intangible assets that are being amortized, use the same method as determining net capital expenditures (by taking the change in *net* intangibles plus amortization).

5. *Change in other long-term operating assets, net of long-term liabilities:* Subtract investments in other net *operating* assets. As with invested capital, do not confuse other long-term *operating* assets with other long-term nonoperating assets, such as equity investments and excess pension assets. Changes in equity investments need to be evaluated—but should be measured separately.

Since companies translate foreign balance sheets into their home currency, changes in accounts will capture both true investments (which involve cash) and currency-based restatements (which are merely accounting adjustments). Removing the currency effects line item by line item is impossible. But we can partially undo their effect by subtracting the increase in the equity item titled "foreign currency translation effect," which in the United States is found within the accumulated other comprehensive income account (AOCI).[17] By subtracting the increase, we undo the effect of changing exchange rates.[18]

Reinvestment ratio Once gross cash flow and gross investment are calculated, we can compare them by dividing gross investment by gross cash flow. The faster the company is growing, the higher the ratio will be. If the ratio is rising without a corresponding increase in growth, examine

---

[16] Since capitalized operating leases are an artificial computation to allow for comparison across companies, we are modeling cash flows that do not really occur. Therefore, some analysts model capitalized operating leases only for ROIC and not for free cash flow. To calculate FCF independent of capitalized operating leases, do not add back after-tax interest when calculating NOPLAT, do not take the change in capitalized operating leases when calculating gross investment, and do not subtract their present value when valuing the company.

[17] Another source of AOCI equals unrealized gains and losses from marketable securities. Each period, marketable securities are *marked to market,* even if the gains and losses are unrealized. Thus, a change in marketable securities might not represent a nonoperating cash flow, but rather an adjustment to their market value. Combining unrealized gains and losses in AOCI with changes in marketable securities will give a more accurate picture of marketable security purchases and sales (which are located in the nonoperating section of cash flow to investors).

[18] For more information on currency adjustments, see FASB Statement 52.

whether the company's investments are taking longer to blossom than expected, or whether the company is adding capital inefficiently.

Cash flow available to investors Although not included in free cash flow, cash flows related to nonoperating assets are valuable in their own right and must be evaluated separately:

$$\begin{array}{c} \text{Present Value} \\ \text{of Company's} \\ \text{Free Cash Flow} \end{array} + \begin{array}{c} \text{Present Value of After-Tax} \\ \text{Nonoperating Cash Flow} \\ \text{and Marketable Securities} \end{array} = \begin{array}{c} \text{Total Value} \\ \text{of} \\ \text{Enterprise} \end{array}$$

To reconcile free cash flow with total cash flow available to investors, include the following nonoperating cash flows:

- *Cash flow related to excess cash and marketable securities:* Excess cash and marketable securities generate cash flow through interest income and asset sales. When you add investment income to cash flow, it must be added-back on an after-tax basis, using the marginal tax rate. This is necessary because NOPLAT includes taxes only on operating profit, not total earnings.

- *Cash flow from other nonoperating assets:* Similar to the treatment of excess cash, add other nonoperating income and gains (or subtract losses) less increases in other nonoperating assets (or add decreases). It is best to combine nonoperating income and changes in nonoperating assets; otherwise a distorted picture could emerge. Consider a company that impaired a $100 million equity investment. If we examine the change in equity investments alone, it appears that the company sold $100 million in nonoperating assets. But this assessment is misleading because no cash actually changed hands; the asset was merely marked down. If we combine the $100 million change (positive cash flow) with the $100 million reported loss (negative cash flow) from the income statement, we see the true impact is zero.

Total financing flow Cash flow available to investors should be identical to total financing flow. That is, it flows to or from all investors. By modeling cash flow to *and* from investors, you will catch mistakes otherwise missed. Financial flows include flows related to debt, debt equivalents, and equity:

- *After-tax interest expenses:* After-tax interest should be treated as a financing flow. When computing after-tax interest, use the same marginal tax rate used for NOPLAT.

- *Debt issues and repurchases:* The change in debt represents the net borrowing or repayment on *all* the company's interest-bearing debt, including short-term debt, long-term debt, and capitalized operating leases.

- *Dividends:* Dividends include all cash dividends on common and preferred shares. Dividends paid in stock have no cash effects and should be ignored.

- *Share issues and repurchases:* When new equity is issued or shares are repurchased, three accounts will be affected: common stock, additional paid-in capital, and treasury shares. Although different transactions will have varying affects on the individual accounts, we focus on the aggregate change of the three accounts combined. In Exhibit 7.9, we refer to the aggregate change as "Net Shares Repurchased."

- *Change in debt and equity equivalents:* Since accrued pension liabilities and accrued postretirement medical benefits are considered debt equivalents (see advanced topics for more on issues related to retirement benefits), their changes should be treated as a financing flow. Although deferred taxes are treated as an equity equivalent, they should not be included in the financing flow because they are already included as part of NOPLAT.

With our financial statements now reorganized to reflect economic performance versus accounting performance, we are ready to analyze a company's return on invested capital, operating margins, and capital efficiency.

ANALYZING RETURNS ON INVESTED CAPITAL

Having reorganized the financial statements, we have a clean measure of total invested capital and its related after-tax operating income. Return on invested capital (ROIC) measures the ratio of NOPLAT to invested capital:

$$\text{ROIC} = \frac{\text{NOPLAT}}{\text{Invested Capital}}$$

If an asset is included in invested capital, the income related to that asset should be in NOPLAT. Similarly, if a liability is netted against operating assets to determine invested capital, its related expense should be deducted from revenue to determine NOPLAT. Defining the numerator and denominator consistently in this manner is the most important part of correctly calculating the ROIC.

Since profit is measured over an entire year (whereas capital is measured only at a point in time), we also recommend that you average starting

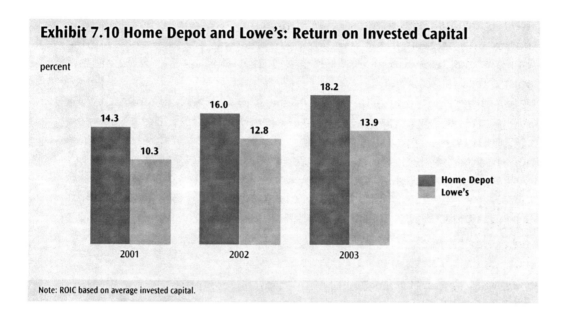

Exhibit 7.10 Home Depot and Lowe's: Return on Invested Capital

percent

18.2
16.0
14.3
13.9
12.8
10.3

Home Depot
Lowe's

2001   2002   2003

Note: ROIC based on average invested capital.

and ending invested capital. Companies that report ROIC in their annual reports often use starting capital. If new assets acquired during the year generate additional income, using only starting capital will overestimate the true ROIC.

Using the NOPLAT and invested capital figures calculated for Home Depot and Lowe's in Exhibits 7.5 and 7.8, we measure the return on invested capital for each company. As can be seen in Exhibit 7.10, Home Depot's ROIC in 2003 exceeds Lowe's ROIC by about 4 percentage points. Both companies have improved their respective ROIC from 2001 to 2003.

Since it focuses solely on a company's operations, ROIC is a better analytical tool for understanding the company's performance than return on equity (ROE) and return on assets (ROA). Return on equity mixes operating performance with capital structure, making peer group analysis and trend analysis less meaningful. Return on assets (even when calculated on a preinterest basis) is inadequate because the ratio double counts any implicit financing charged by suppliers—in the numerator as part of cost of goods sold (COGS) and in the denominator as part of total assets.

Analyzing Return on Invested Capital with and without Goodwill

ROIC should be computed both with and without goodwill because each ratio analyzes different things. For instance, a company that purchases another at a premium to book must spend real resources to acquire valuable economic assets. If the company does not properly compensate investors for the funds spent (or shares given away), it will destroy value. Thus, when you measure historical performance for the company's shareholders, ROIC should be measured with goodwill.

Conversely, ROIC excluding goodwill measures the company's internal performance and is useful for comparing operating performance across companies and for analyzing trends. It is not distorted by the price premiums paid for acquisitions made to build the company.

For both Home Depot and Lowe's, goodwill is a relatively small part of invested capital, but for companies that rely on acquisitions, the choice can make a big difference. In 2003, Procter & Gamble continued its string of acquisitions by purchasing Wella, the German hair-care products company. As a result of this and other acquisitions, P&G had $13.5 billion in cumulative goodwill and $13.8 billion of organic invested capital. As can be seen in the following table, the inclusion of goodwill reduces Procter & Gamble's ROIC by nearly half:

	2000	2001	2002	2003
ROIC excluding goodwill (%)	26.3	24.8	33.2	41.2
ROIC including goodwill (%)	17.8	16.5	19.6	21.3

Economic Profit

In Chapter 5, we demonstrated that the value of a company's operations equals the book value of its invested capital plus the discounted present value of economic profits. Economic profits are calculated as follows:

$$\text{Economic Profit} = \text{Invested Capital} \times (\text{ROIC} - \text{WACC})$$

For an alternative definition of economic profit, substitute NOPLAT/Invested capital for ROIC, and cancel terms:

$$\text{Economic Profit} = \text{NOPLAT} - (\text{Invested Capital} \times \text{WACC})$$

Because it measures whether a company is using its capital more effectively than could be done in the capital markets, economic profit is a powerful tool. In 2003, Home Depot generated $5.1 billion in NOPLAT, yet its capital charge was only $2.4 billion. As can be seen in Exhibit 7.11, both Home Depot and Lowe's were creating value.

Profitable companies do not always create value. In fact, if the capital charge (defined as WACC times invested capital) exceeds NOPLAT, then the company is actually destroying value.

Do not confuse economic profit, which measures how profitably the company used its capital versus the capital markets, with a company's change in market value. In fiscal year 2003, Home Depot generated $2.6 billion in economic profit. During the same year, the company paid $595 mil-

Exhibit 7.11 Home Depot and Lowe's: Economic Profit Calculation

$ million

	Home Depot			Lowe's		
	2001	2002	2003	2001	2002	2003
Invested capital[1]	21,379	23,635	26,185	10,965	13,341	15,051
Weighted average cost of capital	10.1%	9.0%	9.3%	9.8%	8.8%	9.1%
Capital charge	2,159	2,124	2,438	1,071	1,175	1,373
NOPLAT	3,208	3,981	5,083	1,250	1,822	2,223
Capital charge	(2,159)	(2,124)	(2,438)	(1,071)	(1,175)	(1,373)
Economic profit	1,048	1,857	2,645	179	647	850

[1]Invested capital is measured at the beginning of the year.

lion in dividends, and its stock appreciated by $26.4 billion. This generated a total return to shareholders (TRS) of $27.0 billion, substantially more than the economic profit. Economic profit and total returns to shareholders measure different aspects of value: Economic profit measures the one-year performance on *historical book capital*. The change in market value measures changing expectations about *future* economic profits. In Home Depot's case, the market raised its expectations of the company's future performance, based on recent improvements in profitability.

Decomposing Return on Invested Capital to Build an Integrated Perspective

Compared with both its weighted average cost of capital and that of its archrival Lowe's, Home Depot has been earning a superior return on invested capital. But what is driving this performance? Can it be sustained? To better understand ROIC, split apart the ratio as follows:

$$\text{ROIC} = (1 - \text{Cash Tax Rate}) \times \frac{\text{EBITA}}{\text{Revenues}} \times \frac{\text{Revenues}}{\text{Invested Capital}}$$

The preceding equation is one of the most powerful equations in financial analysis. It demonstrates that a company's ROIC is driven by its ability to maximize profitability (operating margin), optimize capital efficiency (turns), or minimize taxes.

Each of these components can be further disaggregated into their respective components, so that each expense and capital item can be compared with revenues. Exhibit 7.12 on page 188 shows how the components can be organized into a tree. On the right side of the tree are operational

Exhibit 7.12 Home Depot and Lowe's: Return on Invested Capital, 2003

percent

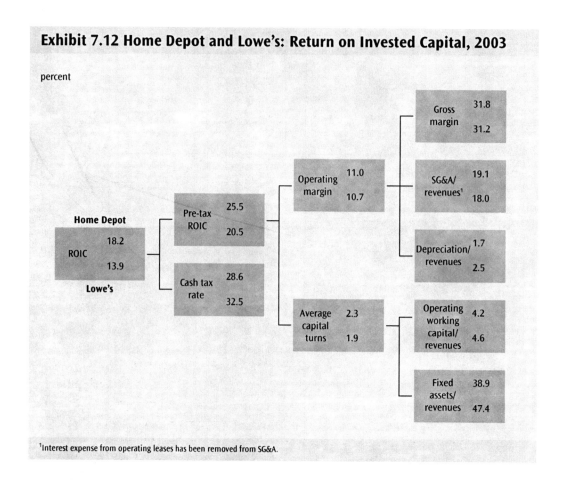

¹Interest expense from operating leases has been removed from SG&A.

drivers, over which the manager has control. As we read from right to left, each subsequent box is a function of the boxes to its right. For example, pretax ROIC equals operating margin times capital turnover, and operating margin equals gross margin less SG&A/revenues less depreciation/revenues.

Once you have calculated the historical value drivers, compare them with the drivers of other companies in the same industry. Integrate this perspective with an analysis of the industry structure (opportunities for differentiation, entry/exit barriers, etc.) and a qualitative assessment of the company's strengths and weaknesses.

What is the source of Home Depot's ROIC advantage over Lowe's? Is the advantage sustainable? By examining the ROIC tree in Exhibit 7.12, we can see that Home Depot benefits from a more efficient use of capital and a better cash tax rate. Moving to the right, we see that this capital efficiency comes primarily from fixed assets, which in turn come from more revenues per dollar of store investment. Is this because Home Depot's stores are more efficient or operating at higher-traffic locations? Perhaps, but after further investigation, it appears that a typical Lowe's store is newer and

Exhibit 7.13 Home Depot and Lowe's: Operating Current Assets in Days

Number of days

	Home Depot			Lowe's		
	2001	2002	2003	2001	2002	2003
Operating cash	7.0	7.0	7.0	7.0	7.0	7.0
Receivables, net	6.3	6.7	6.2	2.7	2.4	1.6
Merchandise inventories	45.8	52.2	51.1	59.6	54.7	54.3
Other current assets	1.2	1.6	1.7	4.8	4.2	4.1
Operating current assets	60.3	67.6	66.0	74.1	68.2	66.9

thus more expensive than Home Depot's average store.[19] Newer stores may be a burden today (from a turns perspective) but could be an advantage going forward.

Line item analysis A comprehensive valuation model will convert every line item in the company's financial statements into some type of ratio. For the income statement, most items are taken as a percentage of sales. (Exceptions exist, however: Taxes should be calculated as a percentage of pretax profits, to determine an average tax rate, not as a percentage of sales.)

For the balance sheet, each line item can also be taken as a percentage of revenues (or for inventories and payables, to avoid the bias caused by changing prices, as a percentage of cost of goods sold). For operating current assets and liabilities, you can also convert each line item into "days," using the following formula:

$$\text{Days} = 365 \times \frac{\text{Balance Sheet Item}}{\text{Revenues}}$$

Although days and a percentage of sales perform a similar cross-company and trend analysis, the use of days lends itself to a more operational interpretation.[20] As can be seen in Exhibit 7.13, the average inventory holding time (using revenue as a base) for Home Depot has risen from 46 to 51 days, whereas the inventory holding time for Lowe's has dropped from 60 to 54. The use of days shows us that what used to be a sizable advantage for Home Depot has turned into a virtual dead heat.

---

[19] M. E. Lloyd, "Lowe's Execs: Younger Stores, New Programs Distinguish Company," Dow Jones Newswires (May 28, 2004).

[20] If the business is seasonal, operating ratios such as inventories should be calculated using quarterly data.

Exhibit 7.14 Discount Carrier and Network Carrier: Operating Statistics

Operating statistic	Discount carrier 2003	Network carrier 2003
Total revenues ($ millions)	1,000.0	10,000.0
Labor expenses ($ millions)	252.4	4,767.3
Number of employees	5,773.2	53,070.7
Available seat miles (millions)	10,942.9	101,017.1

Source: Company 10-Ks.

Nonfinancial analysis   In an external analysis, ratios are often confined to financial performance. If you are working from inside a company, however, or if the company releases operating data, link operating drivers directly to return on invested capital. By evaluating the operating drivers, you can better assess the sustainability of financial spreads among competitors.

Consider airlines, which are required to release a tremendous amount of operating data. Exhibit 7.14 details operating data from two airlines, a point-to-point discount carrier and a full-service network carrier. The exhibit includes the first two line items from each airline's income statement, total revenue and labor expenses, as well as two operating statistics, total employees and available seat miles (ASMs).[21]

Dividing labor expenses by total revenue (as part of ROIC) shows that the network carrier's labor costs (47.7 percent of revenues) are nearly twice as high as the discount carrier's labor costs (25.2 percent of revenues). But what is driving this differential? Are the discounter's employees more productive? Or are they paid less? Is it that the discount carrier can charge a price premium for its product? To answer these questions, we disaggregated labor expenses to revenue, using the following equation:

$$\frac{\text{Labor Expenses}}{\text{Revenues}} = \frac{\text{Labor Expenses}}{\text{Total Employees}} \times \frac{\text{Total Employees}}{\text{ASMs Flown}} \times \frac{\text{ASMs Flown}}{\text{Revenues}}$$

Note how each term's denominator cancels the next term's numerator, leaving us with the original ratio. Each term has a specific operating interpretation. The first term represents the average salary per full-time employee; the second measures the productivity of each full-time employee (number of employees required to fly one billion ASMs); and the third measures the number of miles flown to generate one dollar of revenue. Companies that can charge a price premium (for such services as frequent-flier miles) need to fly fewer miles per dollar of revenue.

---

[21] Airlines use available seat miles as a proxy for unit capacity. Available seat miles equal the total number of seats available for passengers times the number of miles the airline flies.

Exhibit 7.15 Operational Drivers of Labor Expenses to Revenues

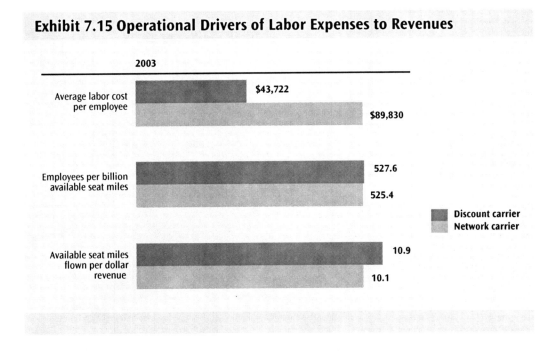

Exhibit 7.15 illustrates the comparative drivers of total labor expenses for both airlines. Note that the numbers of employees required to fly one billion ASMs are nearly identical (528 employees for the discount carrier versus 525 for the network carrier). The numbers of miles flown to generate one dollar of revenue are also comparable (10.9 miles for the discount carrier and 10.1 for the network carrier). What really drives the difference is average salaries.[22] Based on the calculation, the discounter's employees earn half the salary ($43,722) of their counterparts at the network carrier ($89,830). To assess the network carrier's ability to survive and prosper, we must ask whether the company can close this gap. If it cannot, financial performance will remain poor, and its outlook remains bleak.

ANALYZING REVENUE GROWTH

In Chapter 3 we determined that the value of a company is driven by ROIC, WACC, and growth. Until now, growth has been defined solely as the growth in cash flows. But what drives the long-term growth in cash flows? Assuming profit margins and reinvestment rates stabilize to a long-term level, long-term growth in cash flows will be directly tied to long-term growth in revenues. And by analyzing historical revenue growth, we can assess the potential for growth going forward.

[22] Since the number of employees is reported only once a year, labor costs per employee are only a proxy for average salary. Also, labor costs per employee might differ across airlines because of differences in mix. Both airlines might pay identical salaries for the same position, but the network carrier might employ more higher-paid positions.

Exhibit 7.16 IBM: Revenue Growth Analysis

percent

	2001	2002	2003
Organic revenue growth	0.5	(1.8)	(2.6)
Acquisitions	0.5	2.1	5.4
Divestitures	0.0	(3.3)	0.0
Currency effects	(3.9)	(2.5)	7.0
Reported revenue growth	(2.9)	(5.5)	9.8

Calculating revenue growth directly from the income statement will suffice for most companies. The year-to-year revenue growth results sometimes can be misleading, however. The three prime culprits affecting revenue growth are the effects of changes in currency values for multinational companies, mergers and acquisitions, and changes in accounting policies.

Exhibit 7.16 demonstrates how misleading raw year-to-year revenue growth figures can be. In 2003, when IBM announced its first rise in reported revenues in three years, it became the subject of a *Fortune* magazine cover story.[23] "Things appear to be straightening out dramatically," reported *Fortune*. "Last year Palmisano's company grew for the first time since 2000, posting a 10 percent revenue jump." Although IBM's revenues had technically risen 9.8 percent, *organic revenues* (those attributable to the company's core business, independent of currency fluctuations, acquisitions and divestitures, and accounting changes) actually fell 2.6 percent. Indeed, the rise in IBM's revenue was directly attributable to the general weakening of the U.S. dollar and its acquisitions of Rational Software and of PricewaterhouseCooper's (PwCC) consulting business.

Currency Effects

Multinational companies conduct business in many currencies. At the end of each reporting period, these revenues are converted to the currency of the reporting company. If foreign currencies are rising in value relative to the company's home currency, this translation, at better rates, will lead to higher revenue numbers. Thus, a rise in revenue may not reflect increased pricing power or greater quantities sold, but just a depreciation of the company's home currency.

---

[23] D. Kirkpatrick and C. Tkaczyk, "Inside Sam's $100 Billion Growth Machine," *Fortune* (June 14, 2004), p. 80.

Companies with extensive foreign business will often comment about revenue growth, using current as well as constant exchange rates. IBM discloses a "year-to-year revenue change" of 9.8 percent but a "year-to-year constant currency" revenue change of only 2.8 percent. Thus, had currencies remained at their prior-year levels, IBM revenue would have been $83.5 billion, rather than the $89.1 billion reported.

Mergers and Acquisitions

Growth through acquisition may have very different ROIC characteristics from internal growth because of the sizable premiums a company must pay to acquire another company. Therefore, it is important to understand how companies have been generating historical revenue growth—through acquisition or internally.

Stripping the effect of acquisitions from reported revenues is difficult. Unless an acquisition is material, company filings do not need to detail or even report an acquisition. For larger acquisitions, a company will sometimes report pro forma statements that recast historical financials as though the acquisition was completed at the beginning of the fiscal year. Revenue growth, then, should be calculated using the pro forma revenue numbers. If the target company publicly reports its own financial data, pro forma statements can be constructed manually by combining revenue of the acquirer and target for the prior year. But beware: The bidder will often include only partial-year revenues from the target for the period *after* the acquisition is completed. To remain consistent, reconstructed prior years also must include only partial-year revenue.

In its 2003 annual report, IBM did not create historical pro forma revenues to account for its February 2003 acquisition of Rational Software. To properly analyze IBM's 2003 organic growth rate, therefore, we create our own estimated historical pro formas (see Exhibit 7.17, p. 194). Since the acquisition closed at the end of February, IBM's 2003 revenue included 10 months of Rational Software's revenues, whereas IBM's 2002 revenues did not. To make the two years comparable, add 10 months of Rational Software's historical revenues to IBM's.

In October 2002, IBM acquired PwCC. IBM's 2003 revenue included an entire year of PwCC revenue, whereas 2002 included only three months of PwCC. To make the two years comparable, add nine months of PwCC's 2002 revenues to IBM's 2002 revenues.[24] Combining IBM's reported revenue with its partial-year revenue from the two acquisitions results in a 2002 pro forma revenue of $85.7 billion. Comparing 2003's constant-currency revenue

---

[24] We assume PwCC was purchased in its entirety by IBM (since PwCC was a private company, a full analysis is difficult). If only a portion of the business were purchased, our estimate of acquired growth would shrink.

Exhibit 7.17 IBM: Calculating Organic Revenue Growth

$ million	Transaction date	Estimated 2002 revenue	Partial year adjustment	Revenue adjustments
IBM reported 2002 revenue				81,186.0
Ten months of Rational Software revenue	2/21/2003	689.8	10/12	574.8
Nine months of PwCC revenue	10/1/2002	5,200.0	9/12	3,900.0
IBM adjusted 2002 revenue				85,660.8
IBM 2003 "constant currency" revenue				83,459.2
IBM adjusted growth rate				(2.6%)

Source: Hoovers On-Line (for Rational Software) and Gartner Group (for PwCC).

of $83.5 billion with the pro forma prior-year revenues of $85.7 billion shows a *decline* in organic revenues of 2.6 percent.

Accounting Changes and Irregularities

Each year, the Financial Accounting Standards Board in the United States and the International Accounting Standards Board make recommendations concerning the financial treatment of certain business transactions. Most changes in revenue recognition policies do not come as formal pronouncements from the boards themselves, but from task forces that issue topic notes. Companies then have a set amount of time to implement the required changes. Changes in a company's revenue recognition policy can significantly affect revenues from year to year.

Consider Emerging Issues Task Force (EITF) 01-14 from the Financial Accounting Standards Board, which concerns reimbursable expenses. Before 2002, U.S. companies accounted for reimbursable expenses by ignoring the pass-through. Today, U.S. companies can recognize the reimbursement as revenue and the outlay as an expense. Although operating profits were unaffected, this dramatically increased year-by-year revenue comparisons for some companies from 2001 to 2002.[25]

If an accounting change is material, a company will document the change in its section on management discussion and analysis (MD&A) and will also recast its historical financial statements. Some companies do not fully document changes in accounting policy, and this can lead to distorted views of performance. For example, a change in consolidation policy can in-

---

[25] One such company, Total System Services (TSYS), a credit-card-processing company, changed its recognition of reimbursable expenses in 2002. From 2001 to 2002, the company increased revenues from $650 million to $955 million, but $250 million of the $305 million in new revenues was attributable solely to the accounting change. Since the change was material, TSYS recast its previous year's financial statements and discussed the change in its management discussion and analysis.

flate revenue growth artificially. In the extreme case, a company that consolidates equity investments one by one can generate artificial revenue growth for years.

Decomposing Revenue Growth to Build an Integrated Perspective

Once the effects of mergers and acquisitions, currency translations, and accounting changes have been removed from the year-to-year revenue growth numbers, analyze revenue growth from an operational perspective. The most standard breakdown is:

$$\text{Revenues} = \frac{\text{Revenue}}{\text{Unit}} \times \text{Units}$$

Using this formula, determine whether prices or quantities are driving growth. Do not, however, confuse revenue per unit with price—they can be different. If revenue per unit is rising, the change could be due to rising prices. Or the company could be shifting its product mix from low-priced to high-priced items.

The operating statistics that companies choose to report (if any) depend on the norms of the industry and the practices of competitors. For instance, most retailers provide information on the number of stores they operate, the number of square feet in those stores, and the number of transactions they conduct annually. By relating different operating statistics to total revenues, we can build a deeper understanding of the business. Consider this retailing standard:

$$\text{Revenues} = \frac{\text{Revenue}}{\text{Stores}} \times \text{Stores}$$

Using the operating statistics reported in Exhibit 7.18, we discover Home Depot not only has more stores than Lowe's, but also generates more revenue

Exhibit 7.18 Home Depot and Lowe's: Operating Data

Operating data	Home Depot			Lowe's		
	2001	2002	2003	2001	2002	2003
Revenue ($ millions)	53,553	58,247	64,816	22,111	26,491	30,838
Number of stores	1,333	1,532	1,707	744	854	952
Number of transactions (millions)	1,091	1,161	1,246	402	466	521
Square feet (thousands)	116,901	157,335	182,649	80,700	94,794	108,528

Source: Company 10-Ks; missing figures estimated using alternative 10-K data.

Exhibit 7.19 Home Depot and Lowe's: Revenue Growth Analysis, 2003

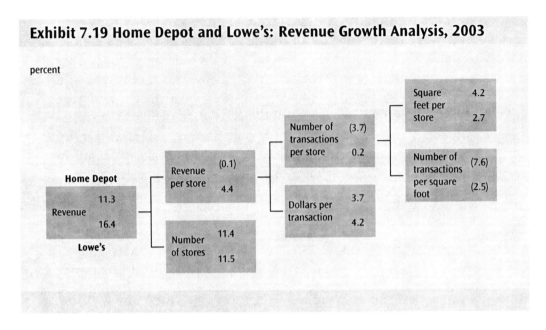

per store ($38 million per store for Home Depot versus $32.4 million for Lowe's). Using the three operating statistics, we can build ratios on revenues per store, transactions per store, square feet per store, dollars per transaction, and number of transactions per square foot.

Although operating ratios are powerful in their own right, what can really change one's thinking about performance is how the ratios are changing over time. Exhibit 7.19 organizes each ratio into a tree similar to the ROIC tree built earlier. Rather than report a calculated ratio, such as revenues per store, however, we report the *change* in the ratio and relate this back to the growth in revenue. At Home Depot and Lowe's, revenues are growing at rates above 10 percent. That growth is respectable by any standard. For Home Depot, however, new store openings, rather than an increase in revenues per store, have been driving growth.

The implications of this analysis are extremely important, to the point that financial analysts have a special name for growth in revenue per store: *comps,* shorthand for "comparables," or year-to-year same-store sales.[26] Why is this revenue growth important? First, new store development is an investment choice, whereas same-store sales growth reflects store-by-store operating performance. Second, new stores require large capital investments, whereas comps growth requires little incremental capital. Higher revenues and less capital lead to higher capital turns, which lead to higher ROIC.

[26] Exhibit 7.19 reports only a proxy for comps, as it calculates revenue per store growth directly from each company's reported operating statistics. Given the statistic's importance, both Home Depot and Lowe's report their own calculation of comps growth, defining it as same-store sales for stores open at least one year. How the companies treat closed stores in calculating comps growth is unclear. According to their annual reports, comps growth for Home Depot in 2003 was 3.8 percent, while comps growth for Lowe's was 6.7 percent.

CREDIT HEALTH AND CAPITAL STRUCTURE

To this point, we have focused on the operations of the company and its ability to create value. We have examined the primary drivers of value: a company's return on invested capital, organic revenue growth, and free cash flow. In the final step of historical analysis, we focus on how the company has financed its operations. What proportion of invested capital comes from creditors instead of from equity investors? Is this capital structure sustainable? Can the company survive an industry downturn?

To determine how aggressive a company's capital structure is, we examine two related but distinct concepts, liquidity (via coverage) and leverage. Liquidity measures the company's ability to meet short-term obligations, such as interest expenses, rental payments, and required principal payments. Leverage measures the company's ability to meet obligations over the long term. Since this book's focus is not credit analysis, we detail only a few ratios that credit analysts use to evaluate a company's credit health.

Coverage

To measure the company's ability to meet short-term obligations, compute two ratios: the traditional interest coverage ratio and a more advanced measure, EBITDAR to interest expense plus rental expense.[27] Interest coverage is calculated by dividing either EBITA or EBITDA by interest. The first ratio, EBITA to interest, measures the company's ability to repay interest using profits without having to cut expenditures intended to replace depreciating equipment. The second coverage ratio, EBITDA to interest, measures the company's ability to meet short-term financial commitments, using both current profits and the depreciation dollars earmarked for replacement capital. Although EBITDA provides a good measure of extremely short-term ability to meet interest payments, most companies cannot survive very long without replacing worn assets.

Like the interest coverage ratio, the ratio of EBITDAR to interest expense plus rental expense measures the company's ability to meet its known future obligations, including the effect of operating leases. For many companies, especially retailers, including rental expenses is a critical part of understanding the financial health of the business. Assuming Home Depot can maintain its current level of EBITDAR, it should have no problems meeting either its interest or rental expense commitments (see Exhibit 7.20 on p. 198).[28]

---

[27] EBITDAR is a common acronym for earnings before interest, taxes, depreciation, amortization, and rental expenses.

[28] Profitable, stable companies with small amounts of debt have little bankruptcy risk but forgo the tax benefits of debt. We discuss optimal capital structure in Chapter 17.

Exhibit 7.20 Home Depot: Measuring Coverage

$ million

	1999	2000	2001	2002	2003
EBITA	3,803	4,199	4,940	5,838	6,847
EBITDA	4,258	4,792	5,696	6,733	7,922
EBITDAR	4,647	5,271	6,218	7,266	8,492
Interest	28	21	28	37	62
Rental expense	389	479	522	533	570
Interest plus rental expense	417	500	550	570	632
EBITA / Interest	135.8	199.9	176.4	157.8	110.4
EBITDA / Interest	152.1	228.2	203.4	182.0	127.8
EBITDAR / Interest plus rental	11.1	10.5	11.3	12.7	13.4

Source: Home Depot 10-Ks.

Leverage

To better understand the power (and danger) of leverage, consider the relationship between return on equity (ROE) and return on invested capital (ROIC):

$$ROE = ROIC + \left[ROIC - (1-T)k_d\right]\frac{D}{E}$$

As the formula demonstrates, a company's ROE is a direct function of its ROIC, its spread of ROIC over its after-tax cost of debt, and its book-based debt-to-equity ratio. Consider a company earning an ROIC of 10 percent, whose after-tax cost of debt is 5 percent. To raise its ROE, the company can either increase its ROIC (through operating improvements) or increase its debt-to-equity ratio (by swapping debt for equity). Although each strategy can lead to an identical change in ROE, increasing the debt-to-equity ratio makes the company's ROE more sensitive to changes in operating performance (ROIC). Thus, while increasing the debt-to-equity ratio can increase ROE, it does so by increasing the risks faced by shareholders.

To assess leverage, measure the company's (market) debt-to-equity ratio over time and against peers. Does the leverage ratio compare favorably with the industry? How much risk is the company taking? We answer these and other questions related to leverage in depth in Chapter 17.

Payout Ratio

The dividend payout ratio equals total common dividends divided by net income available to common shareholders. We can better understand the company's financial situation by analyzing the payout ratio in relation to its cash flow reinvestment ratio (examined earlier). On one hand, if the company has a high dividend payout ratio and a reinvestment ratio greater than 1, then it must be borrowing money to fund negative free cash flow, to pay interest, or to pay dividends. But is this sustainable? On the other hand, a company with positive free cash flow and low dividend payout is probably paying down debt (or aggregating excess cash). In this situation, is the company passing up the valuable tax benefits of debt or hoarding cash unnecessarily?

General Consideration for Historical Analysis

Although it is impossible to provide a comprehensive checklist for analyzing a company's historical financial performance, here are some things to keep in mind:

- Look back as far as possible (at least 10 years). Long-time horizons will allow you to determine whether the company and industry tend to revert to some normal level of performance, and whether short-term trends are likely to be permanent.
- Disaggregate value drivers, both ROIC and revenue growth, as far as possible. If possible, link operational performance measures with each key value driver.
- If there are any radical changes in performance, identify the source. Determine whether the change is temporary or permanent, or merely an accounting effect.

ADVANCED ISSUES

Until now, we have focused on the issues you will typically encounter when analyzing a company. Depending on the company, you may come across difficult (and technical) accounting issues that can affect the estimation of NOPLAT, invested capital, economic profit, and free cash flow. Note, however, that not every issue will lead to material differences in ROIC and growth. Before collecting extra data and estimating required unknowns, decide whether the adjustment will further your understanding of a company and its industry. This section discusses the adjustments most likely to affect results.

Operating Leases

When a company borrows money to purchase an asset, the asset and debt are recorded on the company's balance sheet, and interest is deducted from operating profit. If instead, the company leases that same asset from another company (the *lessor*), it records only the periodic rental expense associated with the lease.[29] Therefore, a company that chooses to lease its assets will have artificially low operating profits (because rental expenses include the implicit interest expense) and artificially high capital productivity (because the assets do not appear on the lessee's balance sheet).

To properly compare operating margins and capital productivity across companies and over time, convert the operating leases into purchased assets and corresponding debt. This is done in two steps. First, value the operating leases. Capitalize the asset value on the balance sheet, and add the implied debt as a liability. (If you do this, remember to increase the company's debt-to-value level in the cost of capital to reflect the higher debt.) Second, break down the rental expense into two components—interest expense and depreciation. Since interest expense is a financing item, the implied interest payment should be added back to EBITA, and taxes should be adjusted to remove the interest tax shield.

To derive the value of operating leases, we examine the determinants of rental expense.[30] To properly compensate the lessor, the rental expense includes compensation for the cost of financing the asset (at the cost of debt, k_d) and the periodic depreciation of the asset (for which we assume straight-line depreciation). Thus, the periodic rental expense equals:

$$\text{Rental Expense}_t = \text{Asset Value}_{t-1} \left(k_d + \frac{1}{\text{Asset Life}} \right)$$

To estimate the asset's value, we rearrange the equation:

$$\text{Asset Value}_{t-1} = \frac{\text{Rental Expense}_t}{k_d + \dfrac{1}{\text{Asset Life}}}$$

In 2003, Home Depot had $570 million in rental expenses. Assuming an average asset life of 20 years and using Home Depot's cost of debt of 4.7 percent, 2002's operating leases are valued at $5.89 billion. Next, we make adjustments to EBITA, operating taxes, and invested capital (see Exhibit 7.21). To determine adjusted EBITA in 2003, we add back the implied interest of operating leases ($276 million) by multiplying the operating lease value

---

[29] SFAS 13 details certain situations when leases must be capitalized (the asset and associated debt must be recorded on the balance sheet). For example, if the asset is transferred to the lessee at the end of the lease, the lease must be capitalized.

[30] We would like to thank McKinsey colleagues Steven Bond, S. R. Rajan, and Werner Rehm for deriving this method of valuing capitalized operating leases.

Exhibit 7.21 Home Depot and Lowe's: Capitalizing Operating Leases

$ million

	Home Depot			Lowe's		
	2001	2002	2003	2001	2002	2003
Reported EBITA	4,940	5,838	6,847	1,798	2,541	3,178
Implied interest	288	260	276	106	106	114
Adjusted EBITA	5,228	6,098	7,123	1,904	2,647	3,292
Operating taxes						
Cash taxes	1,909	2,019	1,935	614	784	1,026
Tax shield on lease interest expense	111	98	105	40	41	44
Adjusted cash taxes	2,020	2,117	2,040	654	825	1,069
NOPLAT (using rental expense)	3,031	3,819	4,912	1,184	1,757	2,152
NOPLAT (capitalizing operating leases)	3,208	3,981	5,083	1,250	1,822	2,223

	Home Depot			Lowe's		
	2001	2002	2003	2001	2002	2003
Invested capital	18,176	20,296	23,101	11,152	12,678	14,250
Capitalized operating leases	5,459	5,890	6,554	2,189	2,373	2,762
Invested capital (with operating leases)	23,635	26,185	29,655	13,341	15,051	17,012
ROIC (using rental expense)	17.4%	19.9%	22.6%	11.6%	14.7%	16.0%
ROIC (capitalizing operating leases)	14.3%	16.0%	18.2%	10.3%	12.8%	13.9%

($5,890 million) times the cost of debt (4.7 percent). The tax shield associated with operating lease interest equals the marginal tax rate (38.2 percent) times the implied interest expense ($276 million). In addition, we increase invested capital by the value of the operating leases.

When we convert from rental expense to capitalized operating leases, Home Depot's ROIC (based on average capital) drops from 22.6 percent to 18.2 percent in 2003. The drop for Lowe's is smaller, but significant nonetheless. However, the smaller percentage does not necessarily imply less value creation. Why? Because the cost of capital will also be lower after adjusting downward for operating leases (we discuss the cost of capital in Chapter 10).

Expensed Investment: Advertising and Research and Development

When a company builds a plant or purchases equipment, the asset is capitalized on the balance sheet and depreciated over time. Conversely, when a company creates an intangible asset, such as a brand name or patent, the entire outlay must be expensed immediately.[31] For firms with significant intangible assets, such as technology companies and pharmaceuticals, failure to recognize intangible assets can lead to a significant underestimation of a company's invested capital and, thus, overstate ROIC.

When you evaluate performance internally, many expenses, such as brand building, customer development, research and development, and training, should be capitalized and amortized (for purposes of internal economic evaluation, not external reporting). But when you examine a company from the outside, you can only evaluate two expensed investments: advertising and research and development (R&D).

The first step in capitalizing an expense like R&D is to choose an amortization period, for example 10 years. Use product and industry characteristics to guide your choice. Next, using the financial statements from 10 years prior (or whatever the amortization period is), treat the year's R&D no differently than you would capital expenditures. This means eliminating the R&D expenditure from the income statement and placing the amount on the balance sheet. Repeat the process for the next year, except that you also deduct R&D amortization from both the income statement (as an expense) and the balance sheet (as a deduction to accumulated R&D).

In Exhibit 7.22, we demonstrate the process by capitalizing R&D expenses for Merck. To adjust 2003 EBITA, start with the original EBITA ($8,651 million), add back the current year's R&D ($3,280 million), and subtract the current amortization ($1,936 million) of the accumulated R&D asset. This leads to an adjusted EBITA of $9,995 million. Although EBITA will change, taxes should *not* be adjusted when capitalizing R&D. The R&D tax shield is real and is related to operations (unlike the interest tax shield). Therefore, the tax shield should remain as part of operations.

To adjust Merck's invested capital, start with 2002's accumulated R&D ($12,163 million), add 2003's R&D ($3,280 million), and subtract 2003's amortization ($1,936 million). Thus, by the end of 2003, Merck's accumulated R&D (based on a 10-year asset life) was $13,506 million. As the exhibit shows, by 2003 nearly one-third of Merck's adjusted invested capital consisted of capitalized R&D. When R&D is expensed, Merck's return on average invested capital is estimated at 21.5 percent. When R&D is capitalized, ROIC drops to 15.2 percent.

Unlike ROIC, free cash flow will not change when expenses are capitalized. When an expense is capitalized, the expense is moved from gross cash flow to gross investment. But since both are components of free cash flow, it remains unaffected. Since amortization is noncash, it also has no

---

[31] Although most development must be expensed, companies can capitalize software development after the product becomes technologically feasible. According FASB's Statement of Position 86, development costs can be capitalized and straight-line amortized over the estimated economic life of the product.

Exhibit 7.22 Merck: Capitalizing R&D

$ million

	1999	2000	2001	2002	2003
EBITA	7,594	9,089	9,728	9,668	8,651
Annual R&D expenditure	2,119	2,344	2,456	2,677	3,280
Annual amortization	(1,347)	(1,484)	(1,633)	(1,780)	(1,936)
Adjusted EBITA	8,367	9,949	10,552	10,565	9,995
Operating taxes (at 38% of EBITA)	(2,886)	(3,454)	(3,697)	(3,674)	(3,288)
NOPLAT	5,481	6,495	6,855	6,891	6,707

	1999	2000	2001	2002	2003
Beginning balance	8,809	9,582	10,442	11,265	12,163
Annual R&D expenditure	2,119	2,344	2,456	2,677	3,280
Annual amortization (10 year life)	(1,347)	(1,484)	(1,633)	(1,780)	(1,936)
Ending accumulated R&D	9,582	10,442	11,265	12,163	13,506
Invested capital	26,533	29,266	33,243	33,885	28,545
Accumulated R&D	9,582	10,442	11,265	12,163	13,506
Adjusted invested capital	36,114	39,707	44,508	46,047	42,051
ROIC (R&D expensed)	22.1%	23.3%	21.9%	20.5%	21.5%
ROIC (R&D capitalized)	16.1%	17.1%	16.3%	15.2%	15.2%

effect (it is deducted to compute NOPLAT but added back to calculate gross cash flow). Thus, capitalizing R&D should have no effect on valuation (beyond how it changes your perceptions of the company's future ability to create value).

Employee Stock Options

By the end of 2003, Home Depot employees held options to buy 2.5 million shares of the company's stock. An alternative to cash compensation, options give the right, but not the obligation, to buy company stock at a specified price. Given the unlimited upside (and limited downside), options can be extremely valuable to the employee. Yet before 2005, companies in the United States and Europe were not required to report the value of options granted as a compensation expense.[32] In fact, before the rule changes requiring expensing, only 117 of the companies in the S&P 500 voluntarily expensed employee stock options. Therefore, to assure

[32] Since January 1, 2005, European listed companies are required under IFRS to reflect the cost of all share-based payments, including employee stock options, as an expense. In 2004, the Financial Accounting Standards Board announcedits intention to require U.S. listed companies to expense stock-based compensation starting June 15, 2005.

Exhibit 7.23 Home Depot: 10-K Note on Stock-Based Compensation

$ million

	2001	2002	2003
Net earnings, as reported	3,044	3,664	4,304
Stock-based compensation expense included in reported net earnings, net of related tax effects	13	10	42
Total stock-based compensation expense determined under fair value based method for all awards, net of related tax effects	(257)	(260)	(279)
Pro forma net earnings	2,800	3,414	4,067

Source: Home Depot 10-K, 2003.

consistency across years, it is important to analyze and expense historical stock-based compensation.

If the company did not expense options historically, we recommend estimating the impact on ROIC. To determine the value of options not included in Home Depot's income statement, we take the difference between net earnings ($4,304 million) and pro forma net earnings ($4,067 million) found in the company's footnotes (see Exhibit 7.23). For Home Depot, this difference equals $237 million. Since this is an after-tax number, it must be converted to a pretax value, using the company's marginal tax rate (38.2 percent). The pretax compensation expense, estimated at $383 million,[33] is then deducted from EBITA.

Since ROIC is based on cash taxes, and since option expenses are not tax deductible at the time of grant, no adjustment should be made to taxes. For companies that expense options, reported taxes are based on income after option expenses, even though the options are not deductible until exercise. Therefore, accountants create a deferred tax account (since cash taxes are higher than reported taxes). Convert reported taxes to cash taxes (for companies that expense options) by subtracting the increase in deferred tax assets from reported taxes. NOPLAT equals adjusted EBITA less cash taxes.

No adjustment should be made to invested capital. When a company issues options, it is essentially transferring a portion of ownership from one group (current shareholders) to another (employees).

To value a company with significant employee options, you have two choices for treating future stock options compensation: include the future options granted as part of operations (and hence part of free cash flow) or value them separately. Subsequently, the process for adjusting free cash

---

[33] Home Depot's estimated options expense is less than 5 percent of EBIT. For some companies, especially technology companies, the options expense can be quite large. In 2003, Yahoo reported $238 million in net income. Had the company expensed employee stock option grants, net income would have fallen 85 percent to $35 million.

Exhibit 7.24 Treatment of Provisions and Reserves

Classification	Examples	Treatment in NOPLAT	Treatment in invested capital	Treatment in valuation
Ongoing operating provisions	Product returns and warranties	Deduct provision from revenue to determine NOPLAT.	Deduct reserve from operating assets to determine invested capital.	Provision is already part of free cash flow.
Long-term operating provisions	Plant decommissioning costs and retirement plans	Deduct operating portion from revenue to determine NOPLAT and treat interest portion as nonoperating.	Treat reserve as a debt equivalent.	Deduct reserve's present value from the value of operations.
Nonoperating provisions	Restructuring charges, such as expected severance due to layoffs	Convert provision into cash provision and treat as nonoperating.	Treat reserve as a debt equivalent.	Deduct reserve's present value from the value of operations.
Income smoothing provision	Provisions for the sole purpose of income smoothing	Eliminate provision by converting accrual provision into cash provision.	Treat reserve as an equity equivalent.	Since income smoothing provisions are noncash, there is no effect.

flow depends on the choice of valuation method. We defer this discussion to Chapter 11.

Provisions and Reserves

Provisions are *noncash* expenses that reflect future costs or expected losses.[34] Companies take provisions by reducing current income and setting up a corresponding reserve as a liability (or deducting the amount from the relevant asset).

For the purpose of analyzing and valuing a company, we categorize provisions into one of four types: ongoing operating provisions, long-term operating provisions, nonoperating restructuring provisions, or provisions created for the purpose of smoothing income (transferring income from one period to another). Based on the characteristics of each provision, adjust the financial statements to better reflect the company's true operating performance. For example, ongoing operating provisions are treated like any other operating expense, whereas restructuring provisions are converted from an accrual to a cash basis and treated as nonoperating. Exhibit 7.24 summarizes the four provision types.

[34] A note on terminology: In the United States, the term *provision* refers to an income statement expense (a charge against income to reflect decline in the value of an asset or expected loss), and the term *reserve* refers to its corresponding liability. In continental Europe, the terms are used interchangeably.

Exhibit 7.25 Provisions and Reserves in the Financial Statements

$ million

Income statement	Year 1	Year 2	Year 3	Year 4
Revenue	1,000	1,200	1,400	1,600
Operating costs	(550)	(660)	(910)	(880)
Provision for product returns	(100)	(120)	(140)	(160)
Provision for plant decommissioning	(24)	(27)	(30)	0
Income smoothing provision	(40)	(40)	80	0
EBITA	286	353	400	560
Provision for restructuring	0	(30)	0	0
Net income	286	323	400	560

Balance sheet	Year 0	Year 1	Year 2	Year 3	Year 4
Operating assets	700	840	980	1,120	0
Reserve for product returns	150	180	210	240	0
Reserve for plant decommissioning	119	144	170	0	0
Reserve for restructuring	0	0	30	0	0
Reserve for income smoothing	0	40	80	0	0
Equity	431	476	490	880	0
Liabilities and shareholder equity	700	840	980	1,120	0

Although reclassification leads to better analysis, the way you adjust the financials for provisions should not affect the company's valuation (no matter how you classify a provision). The company's valuation depends on how and when cash flows through the business, not on accrual-based accounting.

In Exhibit 7.25, we present the financial statements for a hypothetical company that recognizes four types of provisions: a provision for future product returns, an environmental provision for decommissioning the company's plant in four years, an artificial provision for smoothing income, and a restructuring provision for future severance payments. In this example, we reorganized forecasted statements rather than historical statements (whose analysis would be the same) to also demonstrate how each would be treated from a valuation perspective. For simplicity, we assume the company pays no taxes and has no debt.

The process for adjusting the financial statements depends on the type of provision. We use Exhibit 7.26 to discuss each provision in turn. All numbers in parentheses refer to year 1 financials.

Provisions related to ongoing operations When a company expects that some of its products will be returned, warranties a product, or self-insures

Exhibit 7.26 ROIC with Provisions and Reserves

$ million

NOPLAT	Year 1	Year 2	Year 3	Year 4
Reported EBITA	286	353	400	560
Interest associated with plant decommissioning	12	14	17	0
Increase (decrease) in inc. smoothing reserve	40	40	(80)	0
NOPLAT	337	407	337	560
Reconciliation to net income				
Net income	286	323	400	560
Interest associated with plant decommissioning	12	14	17	0
Increase (decrease) in inc. smoothing reserve	40	40	(80)	0
Provision for restructuring	0	30	0	0
NOPLAT	337	407	337	560

Invested capital	Year 0	Year 1	Year 2	Year 3	Year 4
Operating assets	700	840	980	1,120	0
Reserve for product returns	(150)	(180)	(210)	(240)	0
Invested capital	550	660	770	880	0
Reserve for plant decommissioning	119	144	170	0	0
Reserve for restructuring	0	0	30	0	0
Reserve for income smoothing	0	40	80	0	0
Equity	431	476	490	880	0
Invested capital	550	660	770	880	0
ROIC (on beginning of year capital)		61.4%	61.7%	43.8%	63.6%

a service, it must create a liability when that product or service is sold. If the reserve is related to the ongoing operations and grows in step with sales, the reserve should be treated the same as other noninterest-bearing liabilities (e.g., accounts payable). Specifically, the provision should be deducted from revenues to determine EBITA, and the reserve ($180) should be netted against operating assets ($840). Since the provision and reserve are treated as operating items, they appear as part of free cash flow and should not be valued separately.

Long-term operating provisions Sometimes, when a company decommissions a plant, it must pay for cleanup and other costs. Assume our hypothetical company owns a plant that operates for 10 years and requires $200 million in decommissioning costs. Rather than expense the cash outflow in a lump sum at the time of decommissioning, the company builds a reserve as if the company borrowed the money gradually over time. Thus, if the company borrowed $12.5 million annually at 10 percent, the debt (recorded as a reserve) would grow to $200 million by the plant's final year of operation.[35] If the provision is material, it will be recorded in the company's footnotes as follows:

	Year			
	0	1	2	3
Balance Sheet				
Starting reserve	96.8	119.1	143.5	170.4
Plant decommissioning expense (1)	12.5	12.5	12.5	12.5
Interest cost (2)	9.7	11.9	14.4	17.0
Decommissioning payout	0.0	0.0	0.0	(200.0)
Ending reserve	119.1	143.5	170.4	0.0
Income Statement				
Reported provision (1 + 2)	22.2	24.5	26.9	29.6

In year 1, two years before decommissioning, the reported provision is $24.5 million. The provision consists of the $12.5 million annual decommissioning expense and $11.9 million in hypothetical interest expense (the interest that would have been paid if the company gradually borrowed the decommissioning expense). Therefore, when calculating adjusted EBITA, add back $11.9 million to reported EBITA to remove the interest charges.

To measure NOPLAT and invested capital consistently, treat the reserve ($144 million in year 1) as a source of debt-based capital (and not netted against operating assets to determine invested capital). When you treat the plant closure reserve as a debt equivalent, the final payment will not flow through free cash flow. Therefore, for companies that use the present value methodology with implied interest, the current reported reserve ($119.1 million in year 0) should be subtracted from the value of operations ($1,000.2 million) to determine equity value (see Exhibit 7.27).

One-time restructuring provisions   When management decides to restructure a company, it will often recognize certain future expenses (e.g., severance) immediately. We recommend treating one-time provisions as nonoperating and treating the corresponding reserve as a debt equivalent. In year 2, our hypothetical company declared a $30 million restructuring provision, which will be paid in year 3. Since the restructuring is nonoperating, it is not deducted from revenues to determine NOPLAT. Rather, it is included in the reconciliation to net income. Because we plan to value the provision on a cash basis, the noncash reserve is treated as a debt equivalent and is not netted against operating asset to determine invested capital.

---

[35] A company that borrows $CF annually at R percent will owe $FV at the end of N years:

$$CF = \frac{R \times FV}{(1+R)^N \left[1 - \frac{1}{(1+R)^N}\right]}$$

Exhibit 7.27 Enterprise DCF with Provisions and Reserves

$ million

	Year 1	Year 2	Year 3	Year 4	
NOPLAT	337	407	337	560	
Net investment in invested capital	(110)	(110)	(110)	880	
Free cash flow	227	297	227	1,440	
From the investor's perspective:					
Provision for restructuring	0	30	0	0	**Present**
(Increase) decrease in restructuring reserve	0	(30)	30	0	**value at 10%**
Cash-based restructuring provision	0	0	30	0	22.5
Interest associated with plant decommissioning	12	14	17	0	
(Increase) decrease in plant closure reserve	(24)	(27)	170	0	
Dividends	240	310	10	1,440	
Free cash flow	227	297	227	1,440	

Free cash flow valuation

	Year 1	Year 2	Year 3	Year 4
Free cash flow	227	297	227	1,440
Discount factor (at 10%)	0.91	0.83	0.75	0.68
Discounted cash flow	206.8	245.8	170.9	983.5

	Year 0	
Value of operations	1,607	
PV (restructuring provision)	(22.5)	Debt equivalent (present value)
Reserve for plant decommissioning	(119.1)	Debt equivalent (reported at time = 0)
Equity value	1,465.4	

Since nonoperating income (and expenses) does not flow through free cash flow, the restructuring expense must be valued separately on a cash basis. To convert accrual-based restructuring expenses to cash, start with the restructuring expense, and subtract the increase in the restructuring reserve. In year 2, this leads to a cash flow of $0 (see Exhibit 7.27). In year 3, this leads to a cash flow of –$30 million. The estimated present value of the nonoperating cash flow stream equals $22.5 million, which must be deducted from the value of operations to determine equity value.

Income-smoothing provisions In some countries, provisions can be manipulated to smooth earnings. In Exhibit 7.25, our hypothetical company was able to show a smooth growth in reported EBITA and net income by using a smoothing provision. Although we title the account "provision for income smoothing," actual companies use wording more subtle, such as "other provisions." For our hypothetical company, a provision was recorded

577

in years 1 and 2, and was reversed in year 3.[36] By using an income-smoothing provision, the company hid its year 3 decline in operating performance (operating costs rose from 70 percent to 80 percent of sales).

To properly evaluate the company's performance, eliminate any income-smoothing provisions. Do this by adding the income-smoothing provision back to reported EBITA (essentially undoing the income-smoothing provision). In this way, we are converting the provision to a cash (vs. accrual) basis and subsequently need to treat the reserve as an equity equivalent (the process is identical to deferred taxes). Since income-smoothing provisions are entirely noncash, no adjustment must be made to the company's valuation.

Provisions and taxes   In most situations, provisions are tax deductible only when cash is dispersed, not when the provision is reported. Thus, most provisions will give rise to deferred tax assets. We recommend using cash taxes when including provisions in the DCF valuation. This requires netting deferred tax assets against deferred tax liabilities (from depreciation) and subtracting the increase in net deferred tax liabilities from adjusted taxes.

Pensions and Postretirement Medical Benefits

Pension and postretirement medical benefits are a special case of long-term provisions described in the previous section. Retirement benefits differ from other long-term provisions primarily because they (although not always) are prefunded with cash. The cash is held in an off-balance-sheet account titled "plan assets." Since the expected (dollar) return on plan assets is included as part of reported EBITA, retirement provisions can lead to serious distortions in operating performance. Thus, we reorganize the financial statements by allocating pension expenses, prepaid pension assets, and unfunded pension liabilities into operating and nonoperating items.

Pension expenses are composed of four primary items: service cost, interest cost on plan liabilities, expected return on plan assets, and recognized gains and losses.[37] Exhibit 7.28 presents the 10-K pension note for Lockheed Martin. To determine the portion of pension expense that is compensation (and hence operating), we combine service cost and amortization of prior service cost, which represents today's value of promised retirement payments. In 2003, Lockheed Martin had $640 million in service cost and $79 million in prior service cost, for a total operating expense of $719 million.

---

[36] Provisions for income smoothing are often categorized as "general" or "other" provisions.

[37] For more on pension accounting, see D. Kieso, J. Weygandt, and T. Warfield, *Intermediate Accounting* (Hoboken, NJ: Wiley, 2004).

Exhibit 7.28 Lockheed Martin: 10-K Note on Retirement Plans

$ million

	2001	2002	2003	
Service cost	523	565	640	} Operating
Amortization of prior service cost	64	72	79	
Interest cost	1,357	1,401	1,453	} Nonoperating
Expected return on plan assets	(2,177)	(2,162)	(1,748)	
Recognized net actuarial losses (gains)	(117)	(33)	62	
Amortization of transition asset	(4)	(3)	(2)	
Total net pension expense (income)	(354)	(160)	484	

Source: Lockheed Martin 10-K, 2003.

The remaining items, interest cost and plan returns (both expected and the portion of unexpected returns being recognized), are related to the relative performance of the plan assets, not the operations of the business. If the return on plan assets happened to equal the interest cost on the pension liability, the two would cancel, and only the service cost would remain. Since plan assets fluctuate (with the performance of the market), these two items will not cancel. Consider the bull market of the late 1990s. Strong stock returns drove pension assets up; this raised the expected dollar return on plan assets, driving down reported pension expense. Lockheed Martin's 2001 expected dollar returns were so large, in fact, that the company reported a net pension gain as part of EBITA, rather than as a net expense. As the market fell over the next two years, asset values fell as well. Lockheed Martin wound up adding more than $460 million to its reported operating costs, none of which was actually related to operations.

To remove plan performance from operating expenses (see Exhibit 7.29), we increase reported EBITA ($1,976 million) by the interest cost

Exhibit 7.29 Lockheed Martin: EBITA Pension Adjustment

$ million

	2001	2002	2003
Revenue	23,990	26,578	31,824
EBITA	1,787	1,949	1,976
Add: interest cost[1]	1,357	1,401	1,453
Subtract: return on plan assets[2]	(2,298)	(2,198)	(1,688)
Adjusted EBITA	846	1,152	1,741
EBITA/Revenues (raw)	7.4%	7.3%	6.2%
EBITA/Revenues (adjusted for pension)	3.5%	4.3%	5.5%

[1]Interest cost disclosed in Lockheed Martin 10-K (see Exhibit 7.28).
[2]Return on plan assets equals expected returns plus recognized net actuarial losses plus amortization of transition asset disclosed in Lockheed Martin 10-K (see Exhibit 7.28).

($1,453 million) and decrease it by the combined return on plan assets ($1,688 million). This lowers EBITA in 2003 by more than $200 million. Consider the impact on Lockheed Martin's operating margin over the past three years. In actuality, Lockheed Martin's (adjusted) operating margins have been steadily improving, even though the income statement hides this fact.

Since pension expenses are tax deductible, remove nonoperating pension expenses from reported taxes. At Lockheed Martin's marginal tax rate of 33.1 percent, reported taxes would be increased by $481 million ($1,453 million × 33.1 percent), and decreased by $559 million ($1,688 million × 33.1 percent) to determine operating taxes.

Pension accounting will also affect invested capital. When the reported pension expenses differ from cash payments to the plan, the difference is recorded on the company's balance sheet. The recorded asset (when cash payments exceed expenses) or liability (when expenses exceed cash payments) either is unrelated to operations (e.g., when pension assets rise) or is a debt the company owes (when cash payments are smaller than the present value of the promised benefit). Therefore, any assets should be treated as nonoperating, and any liabilities should be treated as debt equivalents.

Since prepaid pension assets and unfunded liabilities are moved to the balance sheet over long periods of time (under U.S. GAAP and IFRS), they do not reflect current valuation of the plan assets and liabilities. To determine the actual present value of the funding shortfall, you must consult the company's footnotes. (For more on pension valuation, see Chapter 11.)

Minority Interest

A minority interest occurs when a third party owns some percentage of one the company's consolidated subsidiaries. If a minority interest exists, treat the balance sheet amount as an equity equivalent. Treat the earnings attributable to minority interest as a financing cost similar to interest, with an appropriate adjustment for income taxes. Thus, NOPLAT (for use with ROIC and FCF) will exclude the effects of minority interest. After-tax minority interest should be a financing flow.

Inflation

While ROIC provides the single best measure for evaluating the operational performance of a company, it can be distorted by inflation. Consider a company earning $10 in NOPLAT on $100 in invested capital. If inflation doubles both prices and costs, profits will also double. Yet since invested capital is measured at cost, it will remain constant. With profits doubling and capital remaining constant, ROIC will artificially double from 10 percent to 20 percent. If the company's cost of capital equals 10 percent, does this mean the company is now creating value? Probably not. An identical company started today with similar capacity and similar features would require $200 in investment (based on the inflated currency), earn $20, and have an ROIC of 10 percent. Since the two companies are identical from an operating perspective, the older company should not appear superior.[38]

If inflation is significant, such long-term assets as net PP&E should be adjusted upward for inflation. Working backward, you must decompose the fixed assets into layers based on when they were purchased. Each layer is then revalued using a price index. Since depreciation is also based on historical cost, it should be increased as well. Do not adjust taxes, however. Taxes are based on historical depreciation, and increasing depreciation would overestimate the tax shield. To calculate an inflation-adjusted ROIC, divide adjusted NOPLAT by the adjusted invested capital. Since ROIC is now in real terms (excluding inflation), it must be compared with the real cost of capital. (See Chapter 22 for an example of this approach.)

Market versus Book-Invested Capital

The traditional measure of ROIC divides NOPLAT by book-invested capital. Thus, ROIC represents the rate of return on original cost (less depreciation). Although this provides a good ex-post measure of performance, it should not be used to make entry and exit decisions. Consider a company that built a facility for $1 billion. The facility is currently generating $10 million in NOPLAT. Because the facility's 1 percent ROIC is well below its 10 percent cost of capital, the CEO recommends selling the facility. But what if the facility is worth only $50 million on the open market? In this case, the rate of return (based on market-based opportunity costs) is 20 percent. At this price, the CEO would be better off keeping the facility, assuming profits remain constant.

An Alternative Measure: Cash Flow Return on Investment

For companies with large, uneven capital expenditures, ROIC may vary systematically over the asset's life, and this can give a distorted picture about when value is created. In this case, it may be helpful to convert ROIC into a measure similar to internal rate of return (IRR). One common measure based on the principles of IRR is CFROI (cash flow return on investment).[39]

---

[38] In this example, we argue the two companies are comparable because only inflation causes differences in ROIC. If, however, the older company were able to purchase assets at a discount (for a reason other than inflation), it would have a true competitive advantage. Thus, using replacement cost to handle inflation can improperly mask superior performance.

[39] For more information, see B. Madden, *CFROI Valuation: A Total System Approach to Valuing the Firm* (Oxford: Butterworth-Heinemann, 1999).

Consider a livery company that plans to purchase a new taxi for $20,000. The vehicle will operate for four years. Since revenues are independent of the taxi's age, the taxi will earn relatively constant profits over the four years. Assume the company's NOPLAT, invested capital, and ROIC per taxi are as follows:

	Year ($ Thousands)				
	0	1	2	3	4
Revenues		100.0	100.0	100.0	100.0
Operating costs		(93.0)	(93.0)	(93.0)	(93.0)
Depreciation		(5.0)	(5.0)	(5.0)	(5.0)
NOPLAT		2.0	2.0	2.0	2.0
Invested capital	20.0	15.0	10.0	5.0	0.0
ROIC (on beginning of year capital)		10%	13%	20%	40%

Note how the investment's ROIC rises from 10 percent to 40 percent over its life. If the company's cost of capital is 15 percent, it appears that the investment destroys value during its first two years but creates value during the last two years.

Alternatively, you could calculate the internal rate of return for each taxi. Using the classic IRR formula, you would find the taxi earns an IRR of 15 percent over its life. Calculating IRR, however, requires making subjective forecasts, so it does not offer a consistent measure of historical performance.

CFROI removes the subjectivity of year-by-year forecasting yet provides a smoothed measure. To calculate CFROI in a given year, use the traditional IRR methodology of setting the net present value to 0 and then solving for the discount rate. To avoid the subjectivity of forecasting, CFROI assumes a fixed cash flow for a fixed number of periods (the company's estimated asset life). To calculate CFROI, we need three components: the initial investment, the annual cash flow, and residual value. The initial investment equals the gross invested capital measured in the prior period (gross invested capital equals invested capital plus accumulated deprecation). The annual cash flow equals NOPLAT plus depreciation. The residual value equals NOPLAT plus depreciation, plus the return of the original working capital.

Exhibit 7.30 calculates the CFROI in 2003 for Home Depot. To measure initial investment, we add 2002's invested capital ($25,557 million) to 2002's accumulated depreciation ($3,565 million). The annual gross cash flow over 20 years is $6,157 million (as measured by 2003 gross cash flow), and the final year's return of 2002 working capital equals $2,746 million. Using Excel's goal seek function, we arrive at an internal rate of return (CFROI) of 20.7 percent.

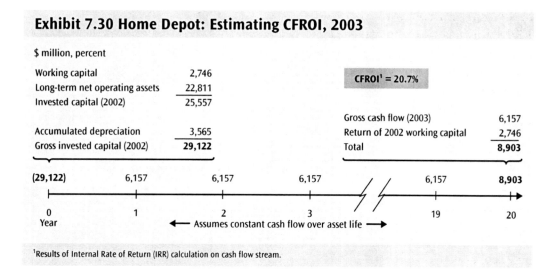

Exhibit 7.30 Home Depot: Estimating CFROI, 2003

$ million, percent

Working capital	2,746	**CFROI[1] = 20.7%**	
Long-term net operating assets	22,811		
Invested capital (2002)	25,557		
		Gross cash flow (2003)	6,157
Accumulated depreciation	3,565	Return of 2002 working capital	2,746
Gross invested capital (2002)	**29,122**	Total	**8,903**

(29,122)	6,157	6,157	6,157	6,157	8,903
0	1	2	3	19	20

Year

← Assumes constant cash flow over asset life →

[1] Results of Internal Rate of Return (IRR) calculation on cash flow stream.

CFROI captures the lumpiness of the investment better than ROIC. But it is complex to calculate and requires assumptions about the company's estimated asset life. Weighing the simplicity of ROIC versus the smoothness of CFROI, we suggest using CFROI only when companies have the following characteristics:

- Lumpy capital expenditure patterns
- Long-lived fixed assets (over 15 years)
- Large fixed assets to working capital

HEINEKEN CASE

To wrap up this chapter and each of the next four chapters, we present a case study, Heineken N.V.[40] This case will illustrate the concepts from each of the chapters and provide a comprehensive integration of the pieces of an enterprise DCF valuation and economic profit valuation.

Heineken, based in the Netherlands, is the world's third largest beer company, behind Anheuser-Busch and SABMiller. Its main brands are the popular Heineken and Amstel beers. In 2003, the last historical year prior to our valuation, Heineken had net turnover (revenues) of €9.3 billion and employed more than 61,000 people worldwide. The company is also the most international brewer: only 6 percent of its volume comes from the Netherlands. Heineken earns 57 percent of net turnover in Western Europe,

[40] The authors would like to thank Meg Smoot and Yasser Salem for their support of the analysis of Heineken. This case was prepared before the merger of Interbrew and AmBev. The combined company, InBev, is now the world's largest brewer.

Exhibit 7.31 Heineken: Historical Income Statements

€ million

	1998	1999	2000	2001	2002	2003
Net turnover	5,453	6,164	7,014	7,937	9,011	9,255
Raw materials and consumables	(2,593)	(2,890)	(3,246)	(3,645)	(4,011)	(4,461)
Marketing and selling expenses	(790)	(964)	(1,107)	(1,281)	(1,585)	(1,131)
Staff costs	(1,042)	(1,132)	(1,301)	(1,417)	(1,642)	(1,832)
EBITDA	1,028	1,178	1,360	1,594	1,773	1,831
Depreciation	(369)	(379)	(439)	(469)	(491)	(578)
EBITA	659	799	921	1,125	1,282	1,253
Amortization of goodwill	0	0	0	0	0	(31)
Operating profit	659	799	921	1,125	1,282	1,222
Interest paid	(53)	(80)	(109)	(118)	(146)	(180)
Interest received	42	39	43	47	37	40
Profit before tax	648	759	855	1,054	1,173	1,082
Taxation	(235)	(265)	(277)	(327)	(364)	(319)
Results of nonconsolidated participating interest (after tax)	44	51	59	45	48	101
Minority interest	(12)	(28)	(16)	(57)	(62)	(66)
Income before extraordinary items	445	516	621	715	795	798
Extraordinary items (after tax)	0	0	0	52	0	0
Net profit	**445**	**516**	**621**	**767**	**795**	**798**
Shareholders' equity						
Position as of 1 January	2,316	2,299	2,618	2,396	2,758	2,543
Exchange differences	0	0	0	0	(107)	(152)
Reclassification of dividend payable	0	0	0	0	0	94
Revaluations	(69)	35	60	72	32	41
Goodwill written off	(278)	(106)	(778)	(320)	(778)	0
Net profit for the year	445	516	621	767	795	798
Dividends	(115)	(125)	(125)	(157)	(157)	(157)
Position as of 31 December	**2,299**	**2,618**	**2,396**	**2,758**	**2,543**	**3,167**

12 percent in Central/Eastern Europe, 17 percent in North America, 9 percent in Africa and the Middle East, and the remaining 5 percent in the Asia/Pacific region. In addition, only 30 percent of its volume comes from its flagship brands; the rest is from Heineken-owned regional brands.

In this chapter of the case study, we analyze Heineken's historical performance, summarize the beer market, and compare Heineken's performance with the market.

REORGANIZATION OF THE FINANCIAL STATEMENTS

Exhibits 7.31 through 7.38 detail the historical financial analysis of Heineken. Exhibits 7.31 and 7.32 present Heineken's income statement and balance sheet for the years 1998 through 2003, using the British nomenclature that Heineken uses in its English annual report (for example, "turnover" refers to revenues). Exhibits 7.33 through 7.35 present the calculations of Heineken's NOPLAT, invested capital, and

Exhibit 7.32 Heineken: Historical Balance Sheets

€ million

	1998	1999	2000	2001	2002	2003
Operating cash	109	123	140	159	180	185
Excess cash and marketable securities	839	1,084	684	1,016	598	1,231
Accounts receivable	667	746	858	985	1,066	1,205
Stocks (inventory)	452	490	550	692	765	834
Other current assets	108	157	166	207	204	174
Total current assets	2,175	2,600	2,398	3,059	2,813	3,629
Tangible fixed assets	2,605	2,964	3,250	3,605	4,133	5,053
Goodwill	0	0	0	0	0	1,093
Nonconsolidated participating interests	256	189	279	183	412	433
Deferred tax assets	0	0	35	30	22	18
Other financial fixed assets	233	233	301	318	401	671
Total assets	5,270	5,986	6,263	7,195	7,781	10,897
Short-term debt	347	488	428	570	1,039	1,113
Accounts payable	412	457	529	620	629	745
Tax payable	221	289	288	335	322	392
Dividend payable	58	87	78	107	105	16
Other current liabilities	422	538	569	603	554	644
Total current liabilities	1,460	1,860	1,892	2,235	2,649	2,910
Long-term debt	522	490	875	797	1,215	2,721
Deferred tax liabilities	273	295	312	357	381	415
Retirement liabilities	47	48	100	112	352	526
Other provisions	125	158	158	133	133	133
Restructuring provision	289	269	406	422	115	293
Total long-term liabilities	1,255	1,260	1,851	1,821	2,196	4,088
Shareholders' equity	2,299	2,618	2,396	2,758	2,543	3,167
Minority interest	256	248	124	381	393	732
Total equity	2,555	2,866	2,520	3,139	2,936	3,899
Total liabilities and shareholders' equity	5,270	5,986	6,263	7,195	7,781	10,897

free cash flow for each year. Exhibit 7.36 shows the calculations of Heineken's economic profit. The remaining exhibits offer the backup calculations and ratios to be used for forecasting.

Heineken made a significant acquisition in 2003 and changed its accounting policy for discounts provided to distributors and retailers. Therefore, its 2003 results are not directly comparable with those of prior years. For 2003, we calculate ROIC using end-of-year capital rather than average or beginning capital (our standard practice) because Heineken's 2003 income statement contains most of a year's income from the acquired company but its beginning balance sheet contains none of the acquired company's capital.

In our analysis of Heineken's financial statements, several accounting issues merit special attention:

Exhibit 7.33 Heineken: Historical NOPLAT

€ million

	1999	2000	2001	2002	2003
EBITA	799	921	1,125	1,282	1,253
Adjustment for retirement related liability	2	4	4	14	21
Increase/(decrease) in other provisions	34	(0)	(25)	0	0
Adjusted EBITA	835	925	1,104	1,296	1,274
Taxes on EBITA	(280)	(302)	(353)	(406)	(375)
Increase/(decrease) in deferred tax liability	22	(18)	50	32	38
NOPLAT	**577**	**606**	**801**	**922**	**937**
Taxes on EBITA					
Reported taxes	(265)	(277)	(327)	(364)	(319)
Tax shield on interest paid	(28)	(38)	(41)	(50)	(62)
Taxes on interest received	14	15	16	13	14
Tax shield on retirement related liabilities	(1)	(1)	(2)	(5)	(7)
Taxes on EBITA	**(280)**	**(302)**	**(353)**	**(406)**	**(375)**
Reconciliation to net profit					
Net profit	516	621	767	795	798
Increase/(decrease) in other provisions	34	(0)	(25)	0	0
Increase/(decrease) in deferred tax liability	22	(18)	50	32	38
Extraordinary items	0	0	(52)	0	0
Minority interest	28	16	57	62	66
Results of nonconsolidated participating interests	(51)	(59)	(45)	(48)	(101)
Amortization of goodwill	0	0	0	0	31
Adjusted net profit	549	560	752	841	832
Interest paid after tax	52	71	77	96	118
Interest expense on retirement related liabilities	1	3	3	9	14
Total income available to investors	603	633	832	946	964
Interest received after tax	(26)	(28)	(31)	(24)	(26)
NOPLAT	**577**	**606**	**801**	**922**	**937**

- *Net turnover:* Beginning in 2003, Dutch reporting rules changed the method for determining net turnover. Now all discounts and excise duties directly attributable to the turnover must be deducted from gross turnover to determine net turnover. Before 2003, net turnover included excise duties collected from customers. Heineken then showed the transmittal of these duties to the government as an expense. To improve comparability, we have shown net turnover less excise duties for all years. Heineken does not disclose the necessary prior-year information to adjust for discounts.

Exhibit 7.34 Heineken: Historical Invested Capital

€ million

	1998	1999	2000	2001	2002	2003
Operating current assets	1,336	1,516	1,714	2,043	2,215	2,398
Operating current liabilities	(1,055)	(1,284)	(1,386)	(1,558)	(1,505)	(1,781)
Operating working capital	282	232	328	485	710	617
Tangible fixed assets	2,605	2,964	3,250	3,605	4,133	5,053
Operating invested capital (before goodwill)	2,887	3,196	3,578	4,090	4,843	5,670
Goodwill	0	0	0	0	0	1,093
Cumulative goodwill written off and amortized	1,046	1,152	1,930	2,250	3,028	3,059
Operating invested capital (after goodwill)	3,932	4,348	5,508	6,340	7,871	9,822
Excess cash and marketable securities	839	1,084	684	1,016	598	1,231
Nonconsolidated participating interests	256	189	279	183	412	433
Other financial fixed assets	233	233	301	318	401	671
Total investor funds	**5,261**	**5,853**	**6,772**	**7,857**	**9,282**	**12,157**
Shareholders' equity	2,299	2,618	2,396	2,758	2,543	3,167
Cumulative goodwill written off and amortized	1,046	1,152	1,930	2,250	3,028	3,059
Minority interest	256	248	124	381	393	732
Other provisions	125	158	158	133	133	133
Net deferred taxes	273	295	277	327	359	397
Dividend payable	58	87	78	107	105	16
Adjusted equity	4,056	4,558	4,963	5,956	6,561	7,504
Debt	869	978	1,303	1,367	2,254	3,834
Retirement liabilities	47	48	100	112	352	526
Restructuring provision	289	269	406	422	115	293
Total investor funds	**5,261**	**5,853**	**6,772**	**7,857**	**9,282**	**12,157**

- *Acquisitions and treatment of goodwill:* Heineken has consistently used acquisitions for growth, generating more than €3.1 billion in goodwill over the last five years. Before 2003, Heineken followed Dutch accounting policies that permitted the immediate write-off of goodwill. In 2003, these rules were changed, and Heineken began capitalizing and amortizing goodwill. To estimate invested capital with goodwill, we add back the cumulative goodwill written off.

- *Results from nonconsolidated participating interests:* Results from nonconsolidated participating interests represent Heineken's share of income from companies that are not consolidated in its financial statements. Heineken reports these on an after-tax basis. Therefore, when estimating NOPLAT, we do not adjust for taxes on this income.

- *Revaluation reserves:* Each year, Heineken makes an adjustment to its equity called a "revaluation reserve." Although the details of this adjustment are not disclosed, it is most likely due to foreign-currency translation adjustments and

Exhibit 7.35 Heineken: Historical Cash Flow

€ million

	1999	2000	2001	2002	2003
Operating cash flows					
NOPLAT	577	606	801	922	937
Depreciation	379	439	469	491	578
Gross cash flow	956	1,045	1,270	1,413	1,515
(Increase) decrease in working capital	50	(97)	(156)	(225)	93
Capital expenditures	(703)	(665)	(752)	(1,094)	(1,609)
Gross investment	(653)	(762)	(908)	(1,319)	(1,516)
Free cash flow before goodwill	303	283	362	93	0
Investment in goodwill	(106)	(778)	(320)	(778)	(1,124)
Free cash flow after goodwill	197	(495)	42	(685)	(1,124)
After tax interest received	26	28	31	24	26
(Increase) decrease in excess marketable securities	(245)	400	(333)	418	(633)
Results of nonconsolidated participating interests	51	59	45	48	101
(Increase) decrease in nonconsolidated participating interests	67	(90)	96	(229)	(21)
Other nonoperating cash flows	1	(68)	35	(83)	(270)
Cash flow to investors	96	(166)	(84)	(506)	(1,921)
Financing flows					
After tax interest paid	52	71	77	96	118
Interest on retirement liabilities	1	3	3	9	14
Minority interest (income statement)	28	16	57	62	66
(Increase) decrease in minority interest	8	124	(257)	(12)	(339)
(Increase) decrease in debt	(109)	(325)	(64)	(887)	(1,580)
(Increase) decrease in retirement liabilities	(1)	(52)	(12)	(240)	(174)
(Increase) decrease in restructuring provisions	20	(137)	(16)	307	(178)
(Increase) decrease in dividends payable	(28)	9	(29)	2	(5)
Dividends	125	125	157	157	157
Total financing flows	96	(166)	(84)	(506)	(1,921)

fixed-asset revaluations. We have treated changes in these reserves as nonoperating cash flows.

- *Dividends:* Following changes in Dutch reporting standards in 2003, the year-end equity is reported inclusive of dividends declared but not yet paid. Before 2003, dividends were deducted from equity when declared and shown as a liability until paid to shareholders.

Exhibit 7.36 Heineken: Historical Economic Profit

€ million, percent

Before goodwill	1999	2000	2001	2002	2003
After-tax ROIC (on beginning of year invested capital)	20.0%	18.9%	22.4%	22.5%	16.5%
WACC	8.7%	8.3%	8.4%	7.7%	7.7%
Spread	**11.3%**	**10.6%**	**14.0%**	**14.8%**	**8.8%**
Invested capital (beginning of year)	2,887	3,196	3,578	4,090	5,670
Economic profit	**326**	**340**	**500**	**607**	**501**
NOPLAT	577	606	801	922	937
Capital charge	(251)	(265)	(301)	(315)	(437)
Economic profit	**326**	**340**	**500**	**607**	**501**
After goodwill					
After-tax ROIC (on beginning of year invested capital)	14.7%	13.9%	14.5%	14.5%	9.5%
WACC	8.7%	8.3%	8.4%	7.7%	7.7%
Spread	**6.0%**	**5.6%**	**6.1%**	**6.8%**	**1.8%**
Invested capital (beginning of year)	3,932	4,348	5,508	6,340	9,822
Economic profit	**235**	**245**	**338**	**433**	**181**
NOPLAT	577	606	801	922	937
Capital charge	(342)	(361)	(463)	(488)	(756)
Economic profit	**235**	**245**	**338**	**433**	**181**

- *Taxes:* The statutory tax rate in the Netherlands has been 35 percent in recent years. That rate will be used to calculate the marginal taxes related to interest income and expense.

- *Excess cash:* We have assumed that any cash and marketable securities above 2 percent of turnover are excess to the needs of the business operations. This assumption is approximately the minimum cash level we have historically observed for similar companies. Excess cash is treated as a nonoperating asset, rather than as working capital.

- *Other financial fixed assets:* Other financial fixed assets are primarily loans to customers and related parties.

- *Pension plans:* At the end of 2003, Heineken had an unfunded pension liability of €526 million, primarily related to pensions and annuities that have not been insured with third parties. Unlike U.S. companies, Heineken's financial statements do not disclose the components of pension expense (the portion of expense that is related to interest expense or investment income), so we have assumed a net interest expense at 4 percent of the liability is included in pension expense in operating costs. In estimating NOPLAT, we have reclassified this amount from operating costs to interest expense. (We normally would not adjust for such a small amount, but we do so here to illustrate the technique.)

Exhibit 7.37 Heineken: Historical Operating Ratios

percent

Operating ratios	1999	2000	2001	2002	2003
Adjusted EBITA/net turnover	13.5	13.2	13.9	14.4	13.8
Raw materials, consumables and services/net turnover	46.9	46.3	45.9	44.5	48.2
Marketing and selling expenses/net turnover	15.6	15.8	16.1	17.6	12.2
Staff costs/net turnover	18.4	18.5	17.9	18.2	19.8
Depreciation[1]/net turnover	12.0	12.7	12.6	11.8	11.3
Return on invested capital (beginning)					
Tangible fixed assets/net turnover	48.1	46.3	45.4	45.9	54.6[2]
Working capital/net turnover	4.6	3.3	4.1	5.4	7.7
Net turnover/invested capital (times)	2.1	2.2	2.2	2.2	1.9
Pre-tax ROIC	28.9	28.9	30.9	31.7	26.3
Cash tax rate	30.9	34.5	27.5	28.9	26.4
After-tax ROIC	20.0	18.9	22.4	22.5	19.4[2]
After-tax ROIC (including goodwill)	14.7	13.9	14.5	14.5	11.9[2]
Return on invested capital (average)					
Average tangible fixed assets/net turnover	45.2	44.3	43.2	42.9	54.6[2]
Working capital/net turnover	4.2	4.0	5.1	6.6	7.2
Net turnover/invested capital	2.0	2.1	2.1	2.0	1.6
Pre-tax ROIC	27.5	27.3	28.8	29.0	22.5
After-tax ROIC	19.0	17.9	20.9	20.6	16.5[2]
After-tax ROIC (including goodwill)	13.9	12.3	13.5	13.0	9.5[2]
Growth rates					
Revenue growth rate	13.0	13.8	13.2	13.5	2.7
Adjusted EBITA growth rate	24.7	10.8	19.4	17.3	(1.7)
NOPLAT growth rate	38.6	4.9	32.3	15.0	1.7
Invested capital growth rate	10.7	12.0	14.3	18.4	17.1
Net Income growth rate	16.1	20.3	23.5	3.7	0.4
Investment rates					
Gross investment rate	68.3	72.9	71.5	93.4	100.0
Net investment rate	47.5	53.3	54.9	89.9	100.0
Financing					
Coverage (adjusted EBITA/interest)	10.0	8.4	9.5	8.8	7.0
Cash coverage (gross CF/interest)	11.9	9.6	10.8	9.7	8.4
Debt/total book capitalization	29.9	33.2	36.3	45.0	60.1
Debt/total market capitalization	6.1	6.1	7.6	17.2	24.5
Market value of operating invested capital/book value on invested capital	5.4	6.1	4.7	2.8	3.0
Market value of operating invested capital/adjusted EBITA	21.0	24.0	17.0	11.0	13.0

[1]Depreciation excluding value adjustments.
[2]Ending invested capital used for calculations of ROIC.

Exhibit 7.38 Heineken: Supporting Calculations

€ million

	1999	2000	2001	2002	2003
Change in working capital					
Increase (decrease) in operating cash	14	17	18	21	5
Increase (decrease) in accounts receivable	78	112	127	81	139
Increase (decrease) in stocks	38	60	142	73	69
Increase (decrease) in other current assets	49	9	41	(3)	(30)
(Increase) in accounts payable	(46)	(72)	(91)	(9)	(116)
(Increase) decrease in tax payable	(68)	1	(47)	13	(70)
(Increase) decrease in other current liabilities	(116)	(31)	(34)	49	(90)
Net change in working capital	**(50)**	**97**	**156**	**225**	**(93)**
Capital expenditures					
Increase (decrease) in tangible fixed assets	359	286	355	528	920
Depreciation	379	439	469	491	578
Exchange differences	0	0	0	107	152
Revaluation	(35)	(60)	(72)	(32)	(41)
Capital expenditures (net of disposals)	**703**	**665**	**752**	**1,094**	**1,609**
Investment in goodwill					
Increase (decrease) in goodwill	0	0	0	0	1,093
Increase (decrease) in cumulative goodwill written off and amortized	106	778	320	778	31
Investment in goodwill	**106**	**778**	**320**	**778**	**1,124**
Other nonoperating cash flows					
Extraordinary items	0	0	52	0	0
(Increase) decrease in other financial fixed assets	1	(68)	(17)	(83)	(270)
Nonoperating cash flows	**1**	**(68)**	**35**	**(83)**	**(270)**

- *Deferred taxes:* Heineken has €397 million in net deferred taxes, which we have treated as an equity equivalent, adjusting NOPLAT for the change each year and adding it to equity in the total investor funds reconciliation.

- *Provisions:* We have divided Heineken's provisions—other than pensions and deferred taxes—into restructuring provisions (related to specific plant closings and layoffs) and other provisions (the general income-smoothing provisions that European companies sometimes use), based on information from its footnotes. Similar to deferred taxes, income-smoothing provisions are treated as equity equivalents. Restructuring provisions are treated as a debt equivalent, meaning they are not considered part of NOPLAT, and the change in their value is treated like the change in debt in calculating investor funds and financing flows, as explained earlier in this chapter.

INDUSTRY BACKGROUND

To provide a context for analyzing Heineken's performance, we first outline the competitive landscape of the beer industry. The industry has long been fragmented, regional, and slow growing. Over the five years to 2003, worldwide beer consumption grew 2.0 percent annually in volume terms. Volume is expected to increase by another 2.1 percent per year from 2004 to 2008, primarily from growth in emerging markets (see Exhibit 7.39).

In the past few years, the beer industry has experienced a flurry of mergers and acquisitions, though it remains fragmented. The top 3 brewers have a combined market share of only 23 percent worldwide, and the top 20 brewers have a combined market share of only 61 percent. This fragmentation is due in large part to regional oligopolies. In the top 20 markets by size, the top two players have large market shares, with an average combined market share of 68 percent. However, the leading players vary from country to country (see Exhibit 7.40).

Even as the major brewers have expanded outside their home markets, competition has remained local. The main reasons include consumer preferences for local brands and tastes, high government tariffs, regulations, and limited opportunities for economies of scale or scope across national borders. As a result, when brewers have entered new markets, they typically have focused on transferring skills, such as marketing, rather than building globally integrated businesses. The strength of local com-

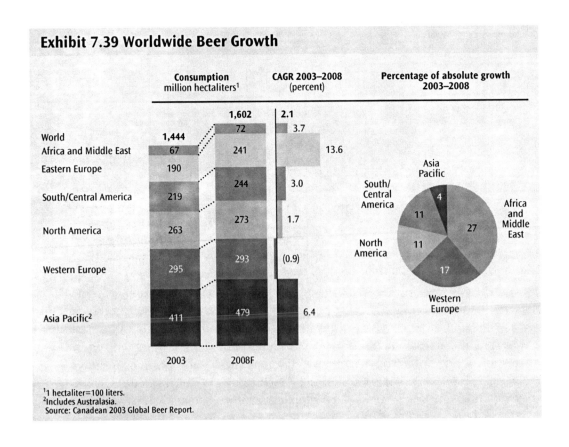

Exhibit 7.39 Worldwide Beer Growth

[1]1 hectaliter=100 liters.
[2]Includes Australasia.
Source: Canadean 2003 Global Beer Report.

Exhibit 7.40 Beer Industry: National Market Share

percent

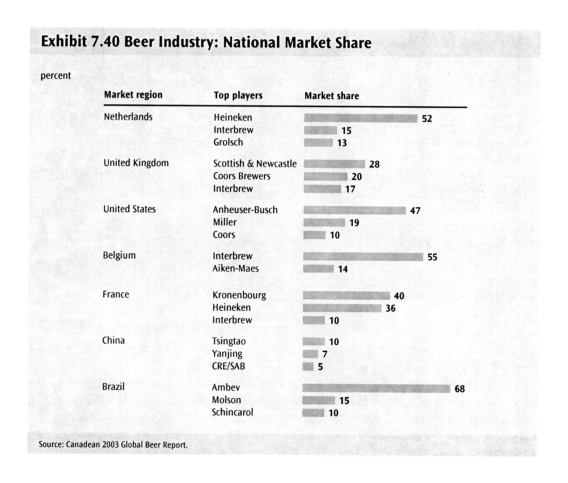

Market region	Top players	Market share
Netherlands	Heineken	52
	Interbrew	15
	Grolsch	13
United Kingdom	Scottish & Newcastle	28
	Coors Brewers	20
	Interbrew	17
United States	Anheuser-Busch	47
	Miller	19
	Coors	10
Belgium	Interbrew	55
	Aiken-Maes	14
France	Kronenbourg	40
	Heineken	36
	Interbrew	10
China	Tsingtao	10
	Yanjing	7
	CRE/SAB	5
Brazil	Ambev	68
	Molson	15
	Schincarol	10

Source: Canadean 2003 Global Beer Report.

petition has kept the pace of industry consolidation slow, as local brewers do not feel the need to sell their businesses to the majors to remain competitive.

As tastes converge, technology improves, transportation costs decline, and brewers learn how to better leverage their expertise and brand names, the industry will slowly begin to reach consumers on a global scale. For 6 of the top 10 breweries, at least 20 percent of the volume growth since 1990 has come through acquisitions.

Brewers adopt two distinct strategies: They either specialize by focusing on a specific link in the value chain or become a geographic integrator. The specialization strategy involves focusing on product development, brewing, packaging, distribution, or marketing, and then becoming the global leader in one or two of these tasks. Diageo's Guinness, for example, has focused on a product with a unique flavor supported by aggressive global marketing. Boston Beer Company runs a "virtual" beer company in which it controls product development and marketing but contracts out most production. Geographic integrators such as Heineken and Interbrew, in contrast, purchase underperforming breweries or breweries in developing countries and apply best practices in brewing, distribution, and marketing.

Exhibit 7.41 Heineken: Revenue Growth Analysis

percent

	2000	2001	2002	2003	CAGR 00–03
Organic volume growth	2.0	1.0	2.0	1.5	1.6
Price increase/mix change	3.0	4.0	4.0	3.5	3.6
Underlying organic growth	5.0	5.0	6.0	5.0	5.2
Acquisitions (first time consolidations)	7.0	6.0	7.0	8.0	7.0
Currency changes	1.0	2.0	(1.0)	(4.0)	(0.5)
Accounting change/other	0.8	0.2	1.5	(6.3)	(1.0)
Revenue growth	13.8	13.2	13.5	2.7	10.7

HEINEKEN'S GROWTH AND ROIC

To evaluate Heineken's financial performance, we compared it with other large, publicly traded beer companies: Anheuser-Busch, SABMiller, Coors, and Interbrew (now InBev after the merger with AmBev).

From 1999 through 2003, Heineken increased its revenues by 10.7 percent per year (see Exhibit 7.41). However, organic growth (volume, price increase, and mix) has driven only half of total revenue growth, about 5 percent per year. Acquisitions have added 7 percent per year. The remaining difference is due to currency effects and accounting changes. In 2003, currency changes, primarily the decline in the U.S. dollar, reduced Heineken's revenues by 4 percent. In addition, Heineken changed its method of ac-

Exhibit 7.42 Beer Industry: Revenue Growth Analysis, 1999–2003

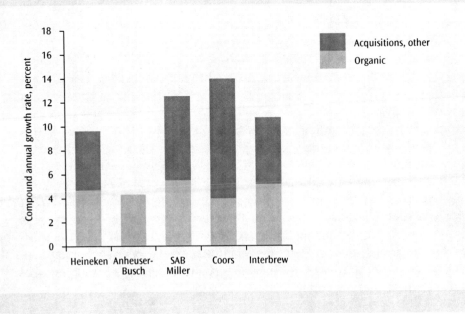

counting for discounts provided to retailers and distributors. Beginning in 2003, turnover (revenue) is shown net of discounts. This accounting change reduced turnover by 6.3 percent in 2003. Heineken does not disclose enough information to restate prior years. This accounting change had no impact on profits, but margins appear to be higher (the same profit divided by smaller turnover).

Exhibit 7.42 compares Heineken's revenue growth with that of its peers. Overall growth from 1999 to 2003 varies from 4.8 percent for Anheuser-Busch to 15.5 percent for Coors. However, these results are not comparable due to acquisitions, accounting changes, and currency effects. The distribution of organic growth was very narrow, ranging from 4.8 percent to 6.1 percent, with Heineken right in the middle.

As all of the companies have similar organic growth rates, the most important driver for explaining the differences in value across peers is ROIC. Heineken increased its ROIC excluding goodwill from 19.4 percent in 1999 to 21.1 percent in 2002 (see Exhibit 7.43). Then ROIC fell in 2003 to 16.5 percent. The decline was largely due to the weaker economics of the Austrian brewer BBAG, which Heineken acquired in 2003. In addition, Heineken's margins were hurt by competition in some markets and by lower margins on beer exported from Europe to the United States, due to the weakening of the

Exhibit 7.43 Beer Industry: Value Drivers

percent

ROIC (including goodwill)	1999	2000	2001	2002	2003
Heineken	13.9	12.3	13.5	13.0	9.5
Anheuser-Busch	16.1	17.2	18.7	21.1	23.8
SABMiller	21.0	27.5	23.6	18.1	12.5
Coors	11.2	12.0	12.2	12.5	6.9
Interbrew	8.2	8.7	10.8	9.7	10.5
ROIC (excluding goodwill)					
Heineken	19.0	17.9	20.9	20.6	16.5
Anheuser-Busch	16.9	18.0	19.6	22.1	24.9
SABMiller	24.7	35.6	36.0	34.3	36.6
Coors	11.6	12.5	13.0	21.3	13.9
Interbrew	13.3	14.6	19.0	18.8	22.1
Operating margin					
Heineken	13.5	13.2	13.9	14.4	13.8
Anheuser-Busch	25.9	26.5	27.1	28.2	29.1
SABMiller	13.8	16.4	19.1	20.3	14.4
Coors	6.3	6.7	7.2	8.3	6.8
Interbrew	10.1	10.4	13.5	13.5	14.1
Capital turnover					
Heineken	2.0	2.1	2.1	2.0	1.6
Anheuser-Busch	1.4	1.5	1.5	1.7	1.8
SABMiller	2.7	2.8	2.6	2.5	3.9
Coors	3.0	2.9	2.9	3.9	3.2
Interbrew	2.0	1.9	1.8	1.8	2.0

U.S. dollar. Heineken's EBITA margin declined from 14.4 percent in 2002 to 13.8 percent in 2003. In addition, BBAG is more capital intensive. Heineken's capital turnover, which had been constant from 1999 to 2002 at 2.1 times, declined to 1.6 times in 2003. (Remember that we used Heineken's ending invested capital to calculate ROIC in 2003.)

We also estimated Heineken's ROIC including goodwill to see the impact of acquisitions. Including goodwill reduces Heineken's ROIC about four to six percentage points in each of the last five years. In 2003, Heineken's ROIC including goodwill was 9.6 percent versus 16.5 percent without goodwill.

Anheuser-Busch and SABMiller had the best underlying performance, with 2003 ROICs before goodwill of 24.9 percent and 36.6 percent, respectively. While Busch's high ROIC comes from strong margins, increasing from 25.9 percent in 1999 to 29.1 percent in 2003, SABMiller was the leader in invested capital turnover, increasing from 2.7 in 1999 to 3.9 in 2003. Exhibit 7.44 shows the breakdown of the capital turnover for each company during 2003. Heineken's low capital turnover has primarily resulted from much higher working capital needs than those of its peers.

Although SABMiller has the highest ROIC excluding goodwill, the company is in line with its peers when taking into account the effects of acquisitions at 12.5 percent in 2003. Since Anheuser-Busch has primarily grown organically, its ROIC including goodwill is roughly the same excluding goodwill at 23.8 percent. Coors has had slight improvements in both margins and capital turnover over the last five years. Interbrew has had constant turnover but has increased margins from 10.1 percent in 1999 to 14.1 percent in 2003. However, ROIC including goodwill has deteriorated for Coors and has increased only slightly for Interbrew, going from 1999 levels of 11.2 percent and 8.2 percent, respectively, to 6.9 percent and 10.5 percent, respectively, in 2003.

PERFORMANCE IN THE STOCK MARKET

As a final assessment of historical performance, we compared the stock market performance of these companies, using two indicators: TRS and the ratio of market value to invested capital. In terms of TRS, Heineken has struggled during the last five years. It is the only company out of its peers to have negative TRS when measured over the one, three, and five years to 2003 (see Exhibit 7.45). Over that period, Heineken's

Exhibit 7.44 Beer Industry: Capital Turnover Analysis, 2003

percent

Company	Working capital/ revenue	Net PPE/ revenue	Other assets/ revenue	Goodwill/ revenue	Capital turnover excluding goodwill	Capital turnover including goodwill
Heineken	7.2	54.6	0.0	11.8	1.6	1.4
Anheuser-Busch	(2.0)	59.5	(1.7)	2.5	1.8	1.7
SABMiller	(2.4)	29.2	(1.0)	49.8	3.9	1.3
Coors	2.2	34.9	(5.7)	31.8	3.2	1.6
Interbrew	0.1	48.7	0.9	55.1	2.0	1.0

shareholder returns have averaged −5 percent per year, much lower than for Anheuser-Busch, at 12 percent, and SABMiller, at 11 percent. (These percentages are based on local currencies, not in a common currency. We tested total returns in U.S. dollars and found the relative performance to be the same.) The market set high standards for Heineken. Unfortunately, Heineken has been unable to keep pace with expectations.

We also compared Heineken's market-value-to-invested-capital ratio with that of its peers. Market-value-to-invested-capital compares the company's market value (both debt and equity) to the amount of capital that has been invested in the company (fixed assets, working capital, and investments in intangibles from acquisitions); it measures the market's perception of the company's ability to create wealth. Heineken's value places it in line with its peers at a market-value-to-invested-capital ratio of 1.6. This means that the market assigns a value of $1.60 for every dollar invested in the company. Anheuser-Busch was the only company that truly stood out from its peers, with a market-value-to-invested-capital ratio of 6.1. Busch's high value to invested capital including goodwill is primarily driven by a greater ROIC including goodwill: 23.8 percent in 2003 versus its peer average of 12.9 percent.

Exhibit 7.45 Beer Industry: Stock Market Performance

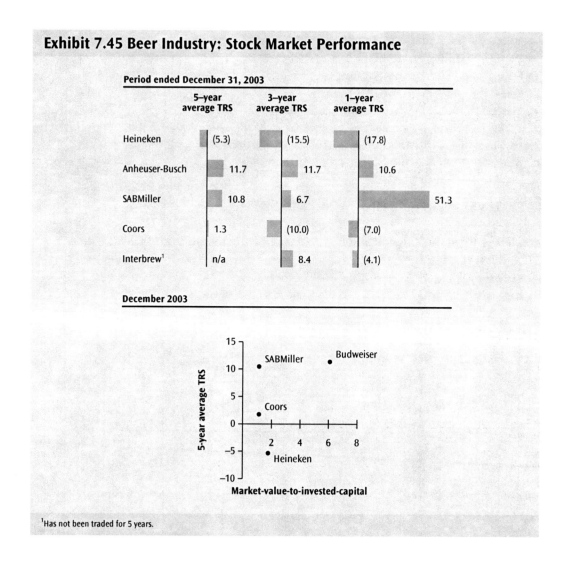

Period ended December 31, 2003

	5–year average TRS	3–year average TRS	1–year average TRS
Heineken	(5.3)	(15.5)	(17.8)
Anheuser-Busch	11.7	11.7	10.6
SABMiller	10.8	6.7	51.3
Coors	1.3	(10.0)	(7.0)
Interbrew[1]	n/a	8.4	(4.1)

December 2003

[1]Has not been traded for 5 years.

597

Exhibit 7.46 Beer Industry: Value Multiples

Excluding goodwill	Value/invested capital	Operating value/EBITA	2003 ROIC (percent)	1999–2003 ROIC (percent)
Heineken	2.8	12.1	16.5	19.0
Anheuser-Busch	6.4	15.7	24.8	20.3
SABMiller	4.5	11.0	36.6	33.5
Coors	2.8	12.3	13.9	14.5
Interbrew	4.0	13.7	22.1	17.6
Including goodwill				
Heineken	1.6	12.1	9.5	12.5
Anheuser-Busch	6.1	15.7	23.8	19.4
SABMiller	1.5	11.0	12.5	20.5
Coors	1.4	12.3	6.9	11.0
Interbrew	1.2	13.7	10.5	9.6

The matrix on the bottom of Exhibit 7.45 shows TRS and market-value-to-invested-capital simultaneously. Heineken is valued in line with Coors and SABMiller, but the market historically had high expectations for Heineken, so its TRS is lower. Anheuser-Busch had high value to invested capital as well as high TRS. Anheuser-Busch positively surprised the market during this period.

Heineken is valued at 12.1 times EBITA, in line with SABMiller, Coors, and Interbrew but below Anheuser-Busch at 15.7 times (see Exhibit 7.46). As the exhibit shows, all the peers have similar organic growth, so it is no surprise that differences in ROIC (without goodwill) drive the differences in earnings multiples.

LIQUIDITY, LEVERAGE, AND FINANCIAL HEALTH

Heineken's debt increased significantly in 2003, due to acquisitions. Despite the higher debt, interest coverage in 2003 was 7.2 times, a strong investment-grade level and also in line with peers (see Exhibit 7.47). Heineken retains significant financial flexibility for additional acquisitions or to weather difficult periods.

Exhibit 7.47 Beer Industry: Credit Ratios

Company	Adjusted EBITA $ million	Interest expense $ million	Adjusted EBITA/ interest expense	Gross cash flow/ interest expense	Debt to MV of investor funds (percent)
Heineken	1,605	227	7.1	8.4	24.5
Anheuser-Busch	3,201	376	8.5	2.8	14.5
SABMiller	1,198	163	7.3	6.9	33.8
Coors	272	70	4.0	6.0	33.9
Interbrew	996	131	8.0	10.0	21.2

REVIEW QUESTIONS

1. Why is it important to convert the balance sheet and income statement to reflect economic performance versus accounting performance?

2. Identify and explain the key steps to restate the company's balance sheet and income statement.

3. How do operating assets differ from nonoperating assets? How do operating assets differ from invested capital? Why is this differentiation important?

4. How does a manager adjust the income statement to compute NOPLAT? Why are the adjustments important?

5. Explain how net income differs from free cash flow. Why is the difference important when valuing a corporation?

6. Define ROIC. How does ROIC differ from ROA or ROI? Explain the process and importance of decomposing the ROIC ratio.

7. How does a corporation's choice of pension plan (defined contribution versus defined benefit) impact the computation of ROIC? What additional factors must be evaluated when computing invested capital, NOPLAT, and ROIC?

8. When should goodwill be included in the computation of ROIC?

Historical Balance Sheet for MKM, Inc.

$ millions	2003	2004
Cash	5	10
Marketable securities	155	107
Inventory	250	300
Current assets	410	417
Property, plant, and equipment	400	500
Equity investments at cost	100	75
Total assets	910	992
Accounts payable	200	210
Current portion of long-term debt	20	20
Current liabilities	220	230
Long-term debt	200	200
Equity	100	100
Retained earnings	390	462
Total liabilities and shareholder equity	910	992

Historical Income Statement for MKM, Inc.

$ millions	2003	2004
Revenue	810	880
Operating expenses	-600	-640
Depreciation	-80	-90
Operating profit	130	150
Interest income	5	5
Interest expense	-10	-10
Loss on equity investment	0	-25
Earnings before taxes	125	120
Taxes	-50	-48
Net income	75	72

9. Assuming the marginal tax rate equals 40 percent, compute MKM's EBITDA, NOPLAT, Invested Capital, and ROIC (for simplicity, use year-end invested capital). Is ROIC increasing or decreasing?

10. Decompose MKM's ROIC and explain how each component of the decomposition leads to an integrated perspective of performance. Address whether operating margins or capital turnover is driving the drop in ROIC.

11. Develop an economic profit statement for MKM. Assume an 11.1 percent weighted average cost of capital. Interpret the results from year to year.

12. Compute MKM's free cash flow in 2004. How can the company have negative free cash flow, even though it is creating value?

13. Compute MKM's interest coverage ratio. Is the interest coverage ratio improving?

10

Estimating the Cost of Capital

To value a company using enterprise DCF, we discount free cash flow by the weighted average cost of capital (WACC). The weighted average cost of capital represents the opportunity cost that investors face for investing their funds in one particular business instead of others with similar risk.

The most important principle underlying successful implementation of the cost of capital is consistency between the components of WACC and free cash flow. Since free cash flow is the cash flow available to all financial investors (debt, equity, and hybrid securities), the company's WACC must include the required return for each investor. In addition, the duration and risk of the financial securities used to estimate the WACC must match that of the free cash flow being discounted. To assure consistency, the cost of capital must meet several criteria:

- It must include the opportunity costs from *all* sources of capital—debt, equity, and so on—since free cash flow is available to all investors, who expect compensation for the risks they take.

- It must weight each security's required return by its target market-based weight, not by its historical book value.

- It must be computed after corporate taxes (since free cash flow is calculated in after-tax terms). Any financing-related tax shields not included in free cash flow must be incorporated into the cost of capital or valued separately (as done in the adjusted present value).

- It must be denominated in the same currency as free cash flow.

- It must be denominated in nominal terms when cash flows are stated in nominal terms.

For most companies, discounting free cash flow at the WACC is a simple, accurate, and robust method of corporate valuation. If, however, the company's target capital structure is expected to change significantly, for instance in a leveraged buyout (LBO), a constant WACC can overstate (or understate) the impact of interest tax shields. In this situation, discount free cash flow at the unlevered cost of equity, described later in this chapter, and value tax shields and other financing effects separately (as described in Chapter 5).

To determine the weighted average cost of capital, calculate its three components: the cost of equity, the after-tax cost of debt, and the company's target capital structure. Since *none* of the variables are directly observable, we employ various models, assumptions, and approximations to estimate each component.

In this chapter, we begin by defining the components of WACC and introducing the assumptions underlying these metrics. The next three sections detail how to estimate the cost of equity, cost of debt, and target capital structure, respectively. The chapter concludes with a discussion of WACC estimation when the company employs a complex capital structure, using hybrid securities such as convertible debt.

WEIGHTED AVERAGE COST OF CAPITAL

In its simplest form, the weighted average cost of capital is the market-based weighted average of the after-tax cost of debt and cost of equity:

$$\text{WACC} = \frac{D}{V}k_d(1-T_m) + \frac{E}{V}k_e$$

where D/V = Target level of debt to enterprise value using market-based (not book) values

E/V = Target level of equity to enterprise value using market-based values

k_d = Cost of debt

k_e = Cost of equity

T_m = Company's marginal income tax rate

For companies with other securities, such as preferred stock, additional terms must be added to the cost of capital, representing each security's expected rate of return and percentage of total enterprise value.

The cost of capital does not include expected returns of operating liabilities, such as accounts payable. Required compensation for funds from customers, suppliers, and employees is included in operating expenses, such as cost of goods sold, so it is already incorporated in free cash flow. Including operating liabilities in the WACC would incorrectly double-count their cost of financing.

Exhibit 10.1 Home Depot: Weighted Average Cost of Capital

percent

Source of capital	Proportion of total capital	Cost of capital	Marginal tax rate	After-tax opportunity cost	Contribution to weighted average
Debt	8.3	4.7	38.2	2.9	0.2
Equity	91.7	9.9		9.9	9.1
WACC	**100.0**				**9.3**

To determine the cost of equity, we rely on the capital asset pricing model (CAPM), one of many theoretical models that convert a stock's risk into expected return.[1] The CAPM uses three variables to determine a stock's expected return: the risk-free rate, the market risk premium (i.e., the expected return of the market over risk-free bonds), and the stock's beta. In the CAPM, beta measures a stock's co-movement with the market and represents the stock's ability to further diversity the market portfolio. Stocks with high betas must have excess returns that exceed the market risk premium; the converse is true for low-beta stocks.

To approximate the cost of debt for an investment-grade firm, use the company's yield to maturity on its long-term debt. For companies with publicly traded debt, calculate yield to maturity directly from the bond's price and promised cash flows. For companies with illiquid debt, use the company's debt rating to estimate the yield to maturity. Since free cash flow is measured without interest tax shields, measure the cost of debt on an after-tax basis.

Finally, the after-tax cost of debt and cost of equity should be weighted using target levels of debt to value and equity to value. For mature companies, the target capital structure is often approximated by the company's current debt-to-value ratio, using market values of debt and equity. As will be explained later, you should not use book values.

In Exhibit 10.1, we present the WACC calculation for Home Depot. The company's cost of equity was determined using the CAPM, which led to a required equity return of 9.9 percent. To apply the CAPM, we used the December 2003 10-year U.S. government bond rate of 4.3 percent, a market risk premium of 4.5 percent, and a relevered industry beta of 1.23. As a

---

[1] Depending on the context, we use the terms *expected return, required return,* and *opportunity cost* interchangeably. Expected return refers to an investor's expected return on a security, given its level of risk. Financial managers refer to a "required return" because the return on an internal project must exceed the expected return on comparable investments. Otherwise, the investor would generate better returns outside the company. This is why the term *opportunity cost* also is quite common.

proxy for Home Depot's pretax cost of debt, we used the yield to maturity on AA-rated debt (4.7 percent). In Chapter 7, we estimated Home Depot's marginal tax rate at 38.2 percent, so its after-tax cost of debt equals 2.9 percent. Finally, we assume Home Depot will maintain a current debt-to-value ratio of 8.3 percent going forward.[2] Adding the weighted contributions from debt and equity, we arrive at a WACC equal to 9.3 percent.

We discuss each component of the weighted average cost of capital next.

ESTIMATING THE COST OF EQUITY

To estimate the cost of equity, we must determine the expected rate of return of the company's stock. Since expected rates of return are unobservable, we rely on asset-pricing models that translate risk into expected return.

The most common asset-pricing model is the capital asset pricing model (CAPM). Other models include the Fama-French three-factor model and the arbitrage pricing theory (APT). The three models differ primarily in how they define risk. The CAPM defines a stock's risk as its sensitivity to the stock market,[3] whereas the Fama-French three-factor model defines risk as a stock's sensitivity to three portfolios: the stock market, a portfolio based on firm size, and a portfolio based on book-to-market ratios. The CAPM is the most common method for estimating expected returns, so we begin our analysis with that model.

Capital Asset Pricing Model

Because the CAPM is discussed at length in modern finance textbooks,[4] we will not delve into the theory here. Instead, we focus on best practices for implementation.

The CAPM postulates that the expected rate of return on any security equals the risk-free rate plus the security's beta times the market risk premium:

$$E(R_i) = r_f + \beta_i [E(R_m) - r_f]$$

---

[2] Net debt equals reported debt plus the present value of operating leases, less excess cash. Although net debt to value at 8.3 percent is probably overly conservative, there is no evidence that Home Depot plans to increase its debt-to-value ratio.

[3] In theory, the market portfolio represents the value-weighted portfolio of all assets, both traded (such as stocks) and untraded (such as a person's skill set). Throughout this chapter, we use a well-diversified stock portfolio, such as the S&P 500 or the Morgan Stanley Capital International World Index, as a proxy for the market portfolio.

[4] For example, Richard Brealey and Stewart Myers, *Principles of Corporate Finance* (New York: McGraw-Hill, 2002); and Thomas Copeland, Fred Weston, and Kuldeep Shastri, *Financial Theory and Corporate Policy* (Boston: Addison-Wesley, 2005).

where $E(R_i)$ = Security i's expected return

r_f = Risk-free rate

β_i = Stock's sensitivity to the market

$E(R_m)$ = Expected return of the market

In the CAPM, the risk-free rate and market risk premium (defined as the difference between $E(R_m)$ and r_f) are common to all companies; only beta varies across companies. Beta represents a stock's incremental risk to a diversified investor, where risk is defined by how much the stock covaries with the aggregate stock market. Consider General Mills, a cereal manufacturer, and Cisco, a maker of network routers. Consumer cereal purchases are relatively independent of the stock market's value, so the beta for General Mills is low; we estimated it at 0.4. Based on a risk-free rate of 4.3 percent and a market risk premium of 5 percent, the cost of equity for General Mills is estimated at 6.3 percent (see Exhibit 10.2). In contrast, technology companies tend to have high betas. When the economy struggles, the stock market drops, and companies stop purchasing new technology. Thus, Cisco's value is highly correlated with the market's value, and its beta is high. Based on a beta of 1.4, Cisco's expected rate of return is 11.3 percent. Since General Mills offers greater protection against market downturns than Cisco, investors are willing to pay a premium for the stock, driving down expected returns. Conversely, since Cisco offers little diversification to the market portfolio, the company must earn higher returns to entice investors.

Although the CAPM is based on solid theory (the 1990 Nobel Prize in Economics was awarded to the model's primary author, William Sharpe),

Exhibit 10.2 The Capital Assets Pricing Model (CAPM)

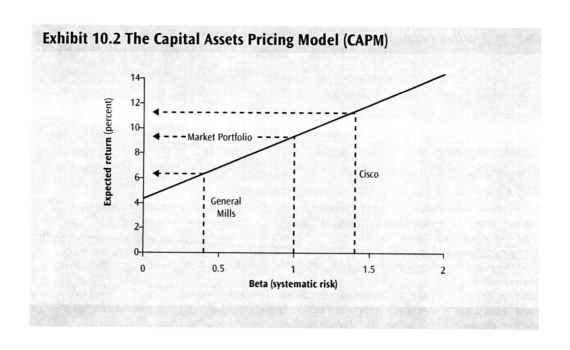

the model provides little guidance for implementation. For instance, when valuing a company, which risk-free rate should you use? How do you estimate the market risk premium and beta? In the following section, we address these issues. Our general conclusions are as follows:

- To estimate the risk-free rate in developed economies, use highly liquid, long-term government securities, such as the 10-year zero-coupon strip.
- Based on historical averages and forward-looking estimates, the appropriate market risk premium is currently between 4.5 and 5.5 percent.
- To estimate a company's beta, use an industry-derived unlevered beta levered to the company's target capital structure.

Estimating the risk-free rate   To estimate the risk-free rate, we look to government default-free bonds.[5] Government bonds come in many maturities. For instance, the U.S. Treasury issues bonds with maturities ranging from one month to 20 years. Since different maturities can generate different yields to maturity, which maturity should you use?

Ideally, each cash flow should be discounted using a government bond with a similar maturity. For instance, a cash flow generated 10 years from today should be discounted by a cost of capital derived from a 10-year zero-coupon government bond. We prefer zero-coupon government strips because long-term government bonds make interim interest payments,[6] causing their effective maturity to be shorter than their stated maturity.

In practice, few people discount each cash flow using a matched maturity. For simplicity, most choose a single yield to maturity from one government bond that best matches the entire cash flow stream being valued. For U.S.-based corporate valuation, the most common proxy is the 10-year government bond (longer-dated bonds such as the 30-year Treasury might match the cash flow stream better, but their illiquidity can cause stale prices and yield premiums). When valuing European companies, we prefer the 10-year German Eurobond. German bonds have higher liquidity and lower credit risk than bonds of other European countries. (In most cases, the differences across European bonds are insignificant.) Note that we use *local* government bond yields to estimate the risk-free rate. To handle issues

[5] In its most general form, the risk-free rate is defined as the return on a portfolio (or security) that has no covariance with the market (represented by a CAPM beta of 0). Hypothetically, one could construct a zero-beta portfolio, but given the cost and complexity of designing such a portfolio, we recommend focusing on long-term government *default-free* bonds. Although not necessarily *risk free*, long-term government bonds in the United States and Western Europe have extremely low betas.

[6] Introduced in 1985, Treasury STRIPS stands for "Separate Trading of Registered Interest and Principal of Securities." The STRIPS program enables investors to hold and trade the individual components of Treasury notes and bonds as separate securities.

Exhibit 10.3 Government Strip Yields, December 2003

percent

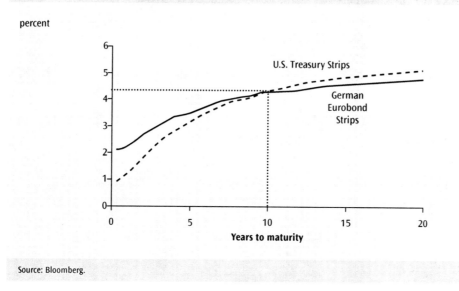

Source: Bloomberg.

like inflation consistently, we must ensure that cash flows and the cost of capital are denominated in the same currency.

In Exhibit 10.3, we plot the yield to maturity for various U.S. and German zero-coupon strips versus their years to maturity (a relation commonly known as the yield curve or term structure of interest rates). As of December 2003, the 10-year U.S. and German treasury strips were both trading at 4.3 percent.

If you are valuing a company or long-term project, do *not* use a short-term Treasury bill to determine the risk-free rate. When finance textbooks calculate the CAPM, they typically use a short-term Treasury rate because they are estimating expected returns for the next *month*. As can be seen in Exhibit 10.3, short-term Treasury bills (near the *y*-axis) traded well below 10-year bonds (0.9 percent versus 4.3 percent) in December 2003. Investors typically demand higher interest rates from long-term bonds when they believe short-term interest rates will rise over time. Using the yield from a short-term bond as the risk-free rate in a valuation fails to recognize that a bondholder must reinvest at higher rates when the short-term bond matures. Thus, the short-term bond rate misestimates the opportunity cost of investment for longer-term projects.

Estimating the market risk premium Sizing the market risk premium—the difference between the market's expected return and the risk-free rate—is arguably the most debated issue in finance. The ability of stocks to outperform bonds over the long run has implications for corporate valuation, portfolio composition, and retirement savings. But similar to a stock's expected return, the expected return on the market is unobservable. And since no single model for estimating the market risk premium has gained universal acceptance, we present the results of various models.

Methods to estimate the market risk premium fall in three general categories:

1. Estimating the future risk premium by measuring and extrapolating historical excess returns.

2. Using regression analysis to link current market variables, such as the aggregate dividend-to-price ratio, to project the expected market risk premium.

3. Using DCF valuation, along with estimates of return on investment and growth, to reverse engineer the market's cost of capital.

None of today's models precisely estimate the market risk premium. Still, based on evidence from each of these models, we believe the market risk premium as of year-end 2003 was just under 5 percent.

Historical market risk premium Investors, being risk-averse, demand a premium for holding stocks rather than bonds. If the level of risk aversion hasn't changed over the last 75 years, then historical excess returns are a reasonable proxy for future premiums (assuming measurement issues, such as survivorship bias, aren't overly problematic). To best measure the risk premium using historical data, follow these guidelines:

• Calculate the premium relative to long-term government bonds.
• Use the longest period possible.
• Use an arithmetic average of longer-dated intervals (such as five years).
• Adjust the result for econometric issues, such as survivorship bias.

Use long-term government bonds When calculating the market risk premium, compare historical market returns with the return on 10-year government bonds. As discussed in the previous section, long-term government bonds better match the duration of a company's cash flows than do short-term bonds.

Use the longest period possible When using historical observations to predict future results, the issue is what length of history to examine. If the market risk premium is stable, a longer history will reduce estimation error. Alternatively, if the premium changes and estimation error is small, a shorter period is better. To determine the appropriate historical period, we consider any trends in the market risk premium compared with the noise associated with short-term estimates.

To test for the presence of a long-term trend, we regress the U.S. market risk premium versus time. Over the last 100 years, no statistically significant trend is observable.[7] Based on regression results, the average excess return has fallen by 3.3 basis points a year, but this result is well below its standard error (leading to a low t-statistic). In addition, premiums calculated over sub-periods, even as long as 10 years, are extremely noisy. For instance, U.S. stocks outperformed bonds by 18 percent in the 1950s but offered no premium in the 1970s. Given the lack of any discernible trend and the significant volatility of shorter periods, you should use the longest time series possible.

Use arithmetic average of longer-dated intervals   When reporting market risk premiums, most data providers report an annual number, such as 6.2 percent per year. But how do they convert a century of data into an annual number? And is an annualized number even important?

Annual returns can be calculated using either an arithmetic average or a geometric average. An arithmetic (simple) average sums each year's observed premium and divides by the number of observations:

$$\text{Arithmetic Average} = \frac{1}{T}\sum_{t=1}^{T}\frac{1+R_m(t)}{1+r_f(t)} - 1$$

A geometric average compounds each year's excess return and takes the root of the resulting product:

$$\text{Geometric Average} = \left(\prod_{t=1}^{T}\frac{1+R_m(t)}{1+r_f(t)}\right)^{1/T} - 1$$

The choice of averaging methodology will affect the results. For instance, between 1903 and 2002, U.S. stocks outperformed long-term government bonds by 6.2 percent per year when averaged arithmetically. Using a geometric average, the number drops to 4.4 percent. This difference is not random; arithmetic averages always exceed geometric averages when returns are volatile.

So which averaging method on historical data best estimates the *expected* future rate of return? To estimate the mean (expectation) for any random variable, well-accepted statistical principles dictate that the arithmetic average is the best unbiased estimator. Therefore, to determine a security's

---

[7]Some authors, such as Lewellen, argue that the market risk premium does change over time—and can be measured using financial ratios, such as the dividend yield. We address these models separately. J. Lewellen, "Predicting Returns with Financial Ratios," *Journal of Financial Economics*, 74(2) (2004): 209–235.

expected return for one period, the best unbiased predictor is the arithmetic average of many one-period returns. A one-period risk premium, however, can't value a company with many years of cash flow. Instead, long-dated cash flows must be discounted using a compounded rate of return. But when compounded, the arithmetic average will be *biased* upward (too high).

This bias is caused by estimation error and autocorrelation in returns. Let's examine the effect of estimation error first. To estimate the mean of a distribution, statistical theory instructs you to average the observations. In a finite sample, the sample average (R_A) will equal the true mean (μ) plus an error term (ε):

$$R_A = \mu + \varepsilon$$

Sometimes the error term is positive, so the sample average overestimates the true mean, and at other times, the error term is negative. But the average error term equals 0, so the sample average is an unbiased estimator of the true mean.

To value a cash flow *beyond* one period, we must determine the discount factor by raising R_A to a given power. For instance, to estimate a two-period discount rate, we calculate R_A squared. Squaring R_A leads to the following equation:

$$R_A = (\mu + \varepsilon)^2 = \mu^2 + \varepsilon^2 + 2\mu\varepsilon$$

Since the true mean, μ, is a constant and the expectation of ε is 0, the expectation of $2\mu\varepsilon$ equals 0. The expectation of ε^2, however, is not 0, but a positive number (the square of any nonzero number is greater than zero). Therefore, R_A^2 will be greater than μ^2 (the true mean squared), and a compounded sample average will be too high.

The compounded arithmetic average will also be biased upward when returns are negatively autocorrelated (meaning low returns follow high returns and high returns follow low returns). Although there is disagreement in the academic community, the general consensus is that the aggregate stock market exhibits negative autocorrelation.[8] In this case, the arithmetic mean is biased upward.

---

[8] Empirical evidence presented by James Poterba, Lawrence Summers, and others indicates that a significant long-term negative autocorrelation exists in stock returns. See J. Poterba and L. Summers, "Mean Reversion in Stock Prices," *Journal of Financial Economics* (October 1988): 27–60. However, subsequent studies by Matthew Richardson and others challenge the statistical significance of earlier studies. See M. Richardson, "Temporary Components of Stock Prices: A Skeptic's View," *Journal of Business and Economic Statistics*, 11 (1993): 199–207.

Exhibit 10.4 Expected Value When Returns Exhibit Negative Autocorrelation

	Potential return	Unconditional probability					
	20%	50%					
	(10%)	50%					

Scenario	Current value	Return in period one	Return in period two	Future value	Expected value when returns are independent		Expected value when returns are negatively autocorrelated	
1	100	1.2	1.2	144	25%	36.0	15%	21.6
2	100	1.2	0.9	108	25%	27.0	35%	37.8
3	100	0.9	1.2	108	25%	27.0	35%	37.8
4	100	0.9	0.9	81	25%	20.3	15%	12.2
					100%	110.3	100%	109.4

To better understand the effect of negative autocorrelation, consider a portfolio that can either grow by 20 percent or fall by 10 percent in a given period (see Exhibit 10.4). Since both returns are equally likely, the one period average return equals 5 percent. In addition, if returns are independently and identically distributed, after two periods there is:

1. A 25 percent probability that an initial investment of $100 will grow to $144

2. A 50 percent probability (two equally probable scenarios) that $100 will grow to $108

3. A 25 percent probability that $100 will shrink to $81

The expected value in two periods equals $110.3, the same as if $100 had grown consistently at the *arithmetic* average of 5 percent for two periods. But if the four scenarios are not equally likely, the expected value in two periods will not equal $110.3. For instance, if there is a 70 percent probability that low returns will be followed by high returns (or vice versa), the expected value in two periods is only $109.4. In this case, compounding the arithmetic mean will lead to an upward bias in expected return.

To correct for the bias caused by estimation error and negative autocorrelation in returns, we have two choices. First, we can calculate multiperiod holding returns directly from the data, rather than compound single-period averages. Using this method, a cash flow received in five years will be discounted by the average five-year market risk premium, not by the annual

Exhibit 10.5 Cumulative Returns for Various Intervals, 1903–2002

percent

Arithmetic mean of	Number of observations	Cumulative returns			Annualized returns	
		U.S. stocks	U.S. government bonds	U.S. excess return	U.S. excess returns	Blume estimator
1-year holding periods	100	11.3	5.3	6.2	6.2	6.2
2-year holding periods	50	24.1	10.9	12.6	6.1	6.1
4-year holding periods	25	49.9	23.1	23.0	5.3	6.0
5-year holding periods	20	68.2	29.5	32.3	5.8	5.9
10-year holding periods	10	165.6	72.1	70.1	5.5	5.6

Source: Ibbotson Associates, McKinsey analysis.

market risk premium compounded five times.[9] In Exhibit 10.5, we present arithmetic averages for holding periods of 1, 2, 4, 5, and 10 years. To avoid placing too little weight on either early or recent observations, we use nonoverlapping returns. The downside of this method is that 5- and 10-year holding periods have very few observations. As shown in the exhibit, the annualized excess return trends downward from 6.2 percent to 5.5 percent as the length of the holding period increases.

Alternatively, researchers have used simulation to show that an estimator proposed by Marshall Blume best adjusts for problems caused by estimation error and autocorrelation of returns:[10]

$$R = \frac{T-N}{T-1}R_A + \frac{N-1}{T-1}R_G$$

where T = Number of historical observations
N = Forecast period
R_A = Arithmetic average
R_G = Geometric average

In the last column of Exhibit 10.5, we report Blume's estimate for the market risk premium. Blume's method generates the same downward-trending estimate of the market risk premium (albeit more smoothly than the raw holding period averages). Based on both estimation techniques, it appears 5.5 percent is a reasonable approximation for *historical* excess returns.

[9] Jay Ritter writes, "There is no theoretical reason why one year is the appropriate holding period. People are used to thinking of interest rates as a rate per year, so reporting annualized numbers makes it easy for people to focus on the numbers. But I can think of no reason other than convenience for the use of annual returns." J. Ritter, "The Biggest Mistakes We Teach," *Journal of Financial Research*, 25 (2002): 159–168.

[10] D. C. Indro and W. Y. Lee, "Biases in Arithmetic and Geometric Averages Premia," *Financial Management*, 26(4) (Winter 1997); M. E. Blume, "Unbiased Estimators of Long Run Expected Rates of Return," *Journal of the American Statistical Association*, 69(347) (September 1974).

Survivorship bias   Other statistical difficulties exist with historical risk premiums. According to one argument,[11] even properly measured historical premiums can't predict future returns, because the observable sample will include only countries with strong historical returns. Statisticians refer to this phenomenon as survivorship bias. The U.S. market outperformed all others during the twentieth century, averaging 4.3 percent in real terms (deflating by the wholesale price index) versus a median of 0.8 percent for other countries.[12] A concurring study[13] notes that the −100 percent returns from China, Russia, and Poland are too often ignored in discussions of stock market performance.

Since it is unlikely that the U.S. stock market will replicate its performance over the next century, we adjust downward the historical arithmetic average market risk premium. Using data from Philippe Jorion and William Goetzmann, we find that between 1926 and 1996, the U.S. arithmetic annual return exceeded the median return on a set of 11 countries with continuous histories dating to the 1920s by 1.9 percent in real terms, or 1.4 percent in nominal terms. If we subtract a 1 percent to 2 percent survivorship bias from the long-term arithmetic average of 5.5 percent, the difference implies the future range of the U.S. market risk premium should be 3.5 to 4.5 percent.

Market risk premium regressions   Although we find no long-term trend in the historical risk premium, many argue that the market risk premium is predictable using observable variables, such as the aggregate dividend-to-price ratio, the aggregate book-to-market ratio, or the aggregate ratio of earnings to price.

The use of current financial ratios to estimate the expected return on stocks is well documented and dates back to Charles Dow in the 1920s. The concept has been tested by many authors.[14] To predict the market risk premium using financial ratios, excess market returns are regressed against a financial ratio, such as the market's aggregate dividend-to-price ratio:

$$R_m - r_f = \alpha + \beta \ ln\left(\frac{\text{Dividend}}{\text{Price}}\right) + \varepsilon$$

[11] S. Brown, W. Goetzmann, and S. Ross, "Survivorship Bias," *Journal of Finance* (July 1995): 853–873.

[12] P. Jorion and W. Goetzmann, "Global Stock Markets in the Twentieth Century," *Journal of Finance,* 54(3) (June 1999): 953–974.

[13] Elroy Dimson, Paul Marsh, and Michael Staunton, *Triumph of the Optimists* (Princeton: Princeton University Press, 2002).

[14] E. Fama and K. French, "Dividend Yields and Expected Stock Returns," *Journal of Financial Economics,* 22(1) (1988): 3–25; R. F. Stambaugh, "Predictive Regressions," *Journal of Financial Economics,* 54(3) (1999): 375–421; and J. Lewellen, "Predicting Returns with Financial Ratios," *Journal of Financial Economics,* 74(2) (2004): 209–235.

Exhibit 10.6 Expected Market Risk Premium Based on Dividend Yield

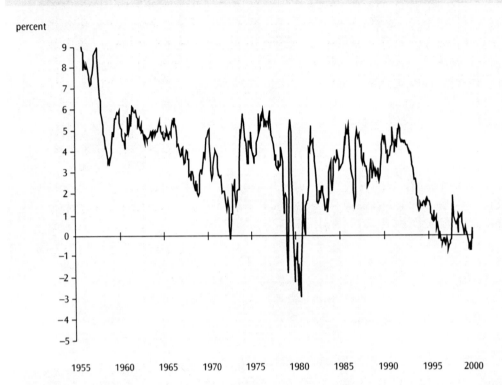

Source: Lewellen (2004), Goyal and Welch (2003), McKinsey analysis.

Using advanced regression techniques unavailable to earlier authors, Jonathan Lewellen found that dividend yields *do* predict future market returns. But as shown in Exhibit 10.6, the model has a major drawback: the risk premium prediction can be negative (as it was in the late 1990s). Other authors question the explanatory power of financial ratios, arguing that a financial analyst relying solely on data available at the time would have done better using unconditional historical averages (as we did in the last section) in place of more sophisticated regression techniques.[15]

Forward-looking models   A stock's price equals the present value of its dividends. Assuming dividends are expected to grow at a constant rate, we can rearrange the growing perpetuity to solve for the market's expected return:

$$P = \frac{DIV}{k_e - g} \quad \text{converts to} \quad k_e = \frac{DIV}{P} + g$$

In the previous section, we reviewed regression models that compare market returns (k_e) to the dividend-price ratio (DIV/P). Using a simple re-

---

[15] A. Goyal and I. Welch, "Predicting the Equity Premium with Dividend Ratios," *Management Science*, 4, 9(5) (2003): 639–654.

gression, however, ignores valuable information and oversimplifies a few market realities. First, the dividend-price yield itself depends on the expected growth in dividends (g), which simple regressions ignore (the regression's intercept is determined by the data). Second, dividends are only one form of corporate payout. Companies can use free cash flow to repurchase shares or hold excess cash for significant periods of time; consider Microsoft, which accumulated more than $50 billion in liquid securities before paying its first dividend.

Using the principles of discounted cash flow, along with estimates of growth, various authors have attempted to reverse engineer the market risk premium. Two studies used analyst forecasts to estimate growth,[16] but many argue that analyst forecasts focus on the short term and are severely upward biased. Fama and French use long-term dividend growth rates as a proxy for future growth, but they focus on dividend yields, not on available cash flow.[17] Alternatively, our own research has focused on *all* cash flow available to equity holders, as measured by a modified version of the key value driver formula (detailed in Chapter 3):[18]

$$k_e = \frac{\text{Earnings}\left(1 - \dfrac{g}{\text{ROE}}\right)}{P} + g \ \text{ such that } \ \text{CF}_e = \text{Earnings}\left(1 - \frac{g}{\text{ROE}}\right)$$

Based on this formula, we used the long-run return on equity (13 percent) and the long-run growth in real GDP (3.5 percent) to convert a given year's S&P 500 median earnings-to-price ratio into the cost of equity.[19]

Exhibit 10.7 on page 312 plots the nominal and real expected market returns between 1962 and 2002. The results are striking. After stripping out inflation, the expected market return (*not* excess return) is remarkably constant, averaging 7.0 percent. For the United Kingdom, the real market return is slightly more volatile, averaging 6.0 percent. Based on these results, we estimate the current market risk premium by subtracting the current real long-term risk-free rate from the real equity return of 7.0 percent (for U.S. markets). At year-end 2003, the yield on a U.S. Treasury inflation-protected security (TIPS) equaled 2.1 percent. Subtracting 2.1

---

[16] J. Claus and J. Thomas, "Equity Premia as Low as Three Percent? Evidence from Analysts' Earnings Forecasts for Domestic and International Stocks," *Journal of Finance*, 56(5) (October 2001): 1629–1666; and W. R. Gebhardt, C. M. C. Lee, and B. Swaminathan, "Toward an Implied Cost of Capital," *Journal of Accounting Research*, 39(1) (2001): 135–176.

[17] Eugene F. Fama and Kenneth R. French, "The Equity Premium," Center for Research in Security Prices Working Paper No. 522 (April 2001).

[18] Marc H. Goedhart, Timothy M. Koller, and Zane D. Williams, "The Real Cost of Equity," *McKinsey on Finance* (Autumn 2002): 11–15.

[19] Using a two-stage model (i.e., short-term ROE and growth rate projections, followed by long-term estimates) did not change the results in a meaningful way.

Exhibit 10.7 Real and Nominal Expected Market Returns

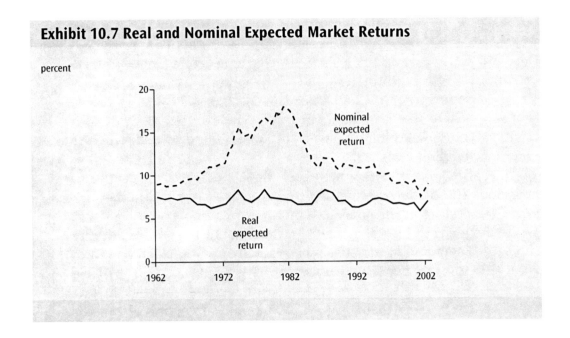

percent from 7.0 percent gives an estimate of the risk premium at just under 5 percent.

Although many in the finance profession disagree about how to measure the market risk premium, we believe 4.5 to 5.5 percent is an appropriate range. Historical estimates found in most textbooks (and locked in the mind of many), which often report numbers near 8 percent, are too high for valuation purposes because they compare the market risk premium versus short-term bonds, use only 75 years of data, and are biased by the historical strength of the U.S. market.

Estimating beta   According to the CAPM, a stock's expected return is driven by beta, which measures how much the stock and market move together. Since beta cannot be observed directly, we must *estimate* its value. To do this, we first measure a raw beta using regression and then improve the estimate by using industry comparables and smoothing techniques. The most common regression used to estimate a company's raw beta is the market model:

$$R_i = \alpha + \beta R_m + \varepsilon$$

In the market model, the stock's return (not price) is regressed against the market's return.

In Exhibit 10.8, we plot 60 months of Home Depot stock returns versus S&P 500 returns between 1999 and 2003. The solid line represents the "best

Exhibit 10.8 Home Depot: Stock Returns versus S&P 500 Returns, 1999–2003

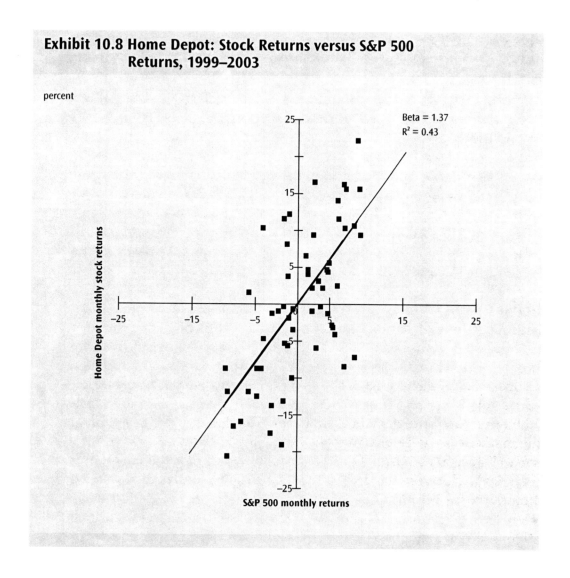

percent

Beta = 1.37
$R^2 = 0.43$

Home Depot monthly stock returns

S&P 500 monthly returns

fit" relation between Home Depot's stock returns and the stock market. The slope of this line is commonly denoted as beta. For Home Depot, the company's raw beta (slope) is 1.37. Since typical betas range between 0 and 2, with the value-weighted average beta equaling 1, this raw result implies Home Depot is riskier than the typical stock.

But why did we choose to measure Home Depot's returns in months? Why did we use five years of data? And how precise is this measurement? The CAPM is a one-period model and provides little guidance on implementation. Yet, based on certain market characteristics and a variety of empirical tests, we reach several conclusions:

- Raw regressions should use at least 60 data points (e.g., five years of monthly returns). Rolling betas should be graphed to examine any systematic changes in a stock's risk.

617

- Raw regressions should be based on monthly returns. Using shorter return periods, such as daily and weekly returns, leads to systematic biases.

- Company stock returns should be regressed against a value-weighted, well-diversified portfolio, such as the S&P 500 or MSCI World Index.

Next, recalling that raw regressions provide only estimates of a company's true beta, we improve estimates of a company's beta by deriving an unlevered industry beta and then relevering the industry beta to the company's target capital structure. If no direct competitors exist, you should adjust raw company betas by using a smoothing technique. We describe the basis for our conclusions next.

Measurement period   Although there is no common standard for the appropriate measurement period, we follow the practice of data providers such as Standard & Poor's and Value Line, which use five years of monthly data to determine beta. Using five years of monthly data originated as a rule of thumb during early tests of the CAPM.[20] In subsequent tests of optimal measurement periods, researchers confirmed five years as appropriate.[21] Not every data provider uses five years. The data service Bloomberg, for instance, creates raw betas using two years of weekly data.

Because estimates of beta are imprecise, however, plot the company's rolling 60-month beta to visually inspect for structural changes or short-term deviations. For instance, changes in corporate strategy or capital structure often lead to changes in risk for stockholders. In this case, a long estimation period would place too much weight on stale data.

In Exhibit 10.9, we graph IBM's raw beta between 1985 and 2004. As the exhibit shows, IBM's beta hovered near 0.7 in the 1980s but rose dramatically in the mid-1990s and now measures near 1.3. This rise in beta occurred during a period of great change for IBM, as the company moved from hardware (such as mainframes) to services (such as consulting). Subsequently, using a long estimation period (for instance, 10 years) would underestimate the risk of the company's new business model.

Frequency of measurement   In 1980, Nobel laureate Robert Merton argued that estimates of covariance, and subsequently beta, improve as returns are

---

[20] F. Black, M. Jensen, and M. Scholes, "The Capital Asset Pricing Model: Some Empirical Tests," in *Studies in Theory of Capital Markets*, ed. M. Jensen (New York: Praeger, 1972).

[21] Alexander and Chervany tested the accuracy of estimation periods from one to nine years. They found four-year and six-year estimation periods performed best but were statistically indistinguishable. G. Alexander and N. Chervany, "On the Estimation and Stability of Beta," *Journal of Financial and Quantitative Analysis*, 15 (1980): 123–137.

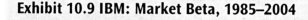

Exhibit 10.9 IBM: Market Beta, 1985–2004

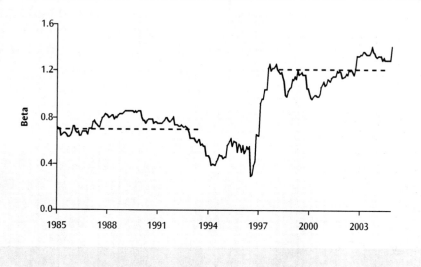

measured more frequently.[22] Implementing Merton's theory, however, has proven elusive. Empirical problems make high-frequency beta estimation unreliable. Therefore, we recommend using monthly data.

Using daily or even weekly returns is especially problematic when the stock is rarely traded. An illiquid stock will have many reported returns equal to zero, not because the stock's value is constant but because it hasn't traded (only the last trade is recorded). Consequently, estimates of beta on illiquid stocks are biased downward. Using longer-dated returns, such as monthly returns, lessens this effect. One proposal for stocks that trade infrequently even on a monthly basis is to sum lagged betas.[23] In lagged-beta models, a stock's return is simultaneously regressed on concurrent market returns and market returns from the prior period. The two betas from the regression are then summed.

A second problem with using high-frequency data is the bid/ask bounce. Periodic stock prices are recorded at the last trade, and the recorded price depends on whether the last trade was a purchase (using the ask price) or a sale (using the bid price). A stock whose intrinsic value remains unchanged will therefore "bounce" between the bid and ask price, causing distortions in beta estimation. Using longer-period returns dampens this distortion.

---

[22] R. Merton, "On Estimating the Expected Return on the Market," *Journal of Financial Economics,* 8 (1980): 323–361.

[23] M. Scholes and J. T. Williams, "Estimating Betas from Nonsynchronous Data," *Journal of Financial Economics,* 5 (1977): 309–327. See also E. Dimson, "Risk Measurement When Shares Are Subject to Infrequent Trading," *Journal of Financial Economics,* 7 (1979): 197–226.

Over the past few years, promising research on high-frequency beta estimation has emerged, spawned by improvements in computing power and data collection. One study used five-minute returns to measure beta, and the estimation method produced more accurate measurements than the standard 60-month rolling window.[24] Since that research was limited to highly liquid stocks, however, we continue to focus on longer-dated intervals in practice.

The market portfolio In the CAPM, the market portfolio equals the value-weighted portfolio of all assets, both traded (such as stocks and bonds) and untraded (such as private companies and human capital). Since the true market portfolio is unobservable, a proxy is necessary. For U.S. stocks, the most common proxy is the S&P 500, a value-weighted index of large U.S. companies. Outside the United States, financial analysts rely on either a regional index like the MSCI Europe Index or the MSCI World Index, a value-weighted index comprising large stocks from 23 developed countries (including the United States).

Most well-diversified indexes, such as the S&P 500 and MSCI World Index, are highly correlated (the two indexes had an 85.4 percent correlation between 1999 and 2003). Thus, the choice of index will have little effect on beta. For instance, Home Depot's beta with respect to the S&P 500 is 1.37, whereas the company's beta with respect to the MSCI World Index is nearly identical at 1.35. Do *not*, however, use a local market index. Most countries are heavily weighted in only a few industries and, in some cases, a few companies. Consequently, when measuring beta versus a local index, you are not measuring market-wide systematic risk, but rather a company's sensitivity to a particular industry.

The internet bubble distorted the market portfolio In the late 1990s, equity markets rose dramatically, but this increase was confined primarily to extremely large capitalization stocks and stocks in the telecommunications, media, and technology sectors (commonly known as TMT). Historically, TMT stocks contribute approximately 20 percent of the market value of the S&P 500. Between 1999 and 2001, this percentage rose to nearly 50 percent. And as the market portfolio changed, so too did industry betas. As shown by the historical betas for 10 industries in Exhibit 10.10, betas related to TMT rose dramatically during the tech boom, while betas outside the TMT sector fell. For instance, between 1990 and 1997, the food industry had an average beta of 0.85. Immediately following the tech boom, the food industry's beta dropped to zero.

---

[24] T. Bollerslev and B. Y. B. Zhang, "Measuring and Modeling Systematic Risk in Factor Pricing Models Using High-Frequency Data," *Journal of Empirical Finance*, 10 (2003): 533–558.

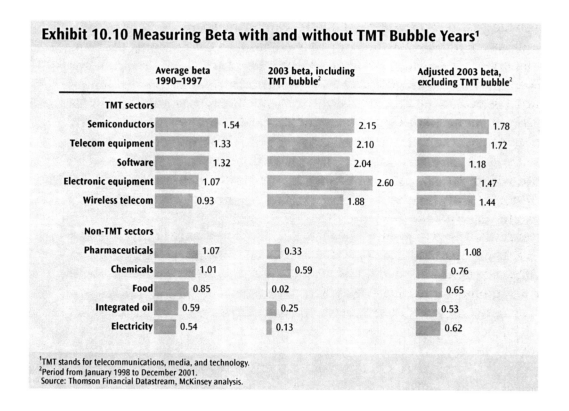

Exhibit 10.10 Measuring Beta with and without TMT Bubble Years[1]

	Average beta 1990–1997	2003 beta, including TMT bubble[2]	Adjusted 2003 beta, excluding TMT bubble[2]
TMT sectors			
Semiconductors	1.54	2.15	1.78
Telecom equipment	1.33	2.10	1.72
Software	1.32	2.04	1.18
Electronic equipment	1.07	2.60	1.47
Wireless telecom	0.93	1.88	1.44
Non-TMT sectors			
Pharmaceuticals	1.07	0.33	1.08
Chemicals	1.01	0.59	0.76
Food	0.85	0.02	0.65
Integrated oil	0.59	0.25	0.53
Electricity	0.54	0.13	0.62

[1] TMT stands for telecommunications, media, and technology.
[2] Period from January 1998 to December 2001.
Source: Thomson Financial Datastream, McKinsey analysis.

But will these new, widely dispersed, betas continue? Probably not. Since 2001, the market portfolio has returned to its traditional composition. Therefore, betas are likely to normalize as well. To this end, we argue that estimates of future beta should exclude observations from 1998 to 2001.[25] Remember, the end goal is not to measure beta historically, but rather to use the historical estimate as a predictor of future value. In this case, recent history isn't very useful and should not be overweighted.

Improving estimates of beta: Industry betas   Estimating beta is an imprecise process. Earlier, we used historical regression to estimate Home Depot's raw beta at 1.37. But the regression's R-squared was only 43 percent, and the standard error of the beta estimate was 0.20. Using two standard errors as a guide, we feel confident Home Depot's true beta lies between 0.97 and 1.77—hardly a tight range.

To improve the precision of beta estimation, use industry, rather than company-specific, betas.[26] Companies in the same industry face similar

---

[25] André Annema and Marc Goedhart, "Better Betas," *McKinsey on Finance* (Winter 2003): 10–13.
[26] If unlevered industry betas are drawn from the same distribution, the standard error of the industry average equals the volatility of the beta distribution divided by the square root of the number of observations. Thus, the standard error of an industry beta falls as the number of beta observations rises.

operating risks, so they should have similar operating betas. As long as estimation errors across companies are uncorrelated, overestimates and underestimates of individual betas will tend to cancel, and an industry median (or average) beta will produce a superior estimate.[27]

Simply using the median of an industry's raw betas, however, overlooks an important factor: leverage. A company's beta is a function of not only its operating risk, but also the financial risk it takes. Shareholders of a company with more debt face greater risks, and this increase is reflected in beta. Therefore, to compare companies with similar operating risks, we must first strip out the effect of leverage. Only then can we compare beta across an industry.

To undo the effect of leverage (and its tax shield), we rely on the theories of Franco Modigliani and Merton Miller (M&M), introduced in Chapter 5. According to M&M, the weighted average risk of a company's financial claims equals the weighted average risk of a company's economic assets. Using beta to represent risk, this relation is as follows:

$$\underbrace{\frac{V_u}{V_u + V_{txa}}\beta_u}_{\substack{\text{Operating} \\ \text{Assets}}} + \underbrace{\frac{V_{txa}}{V_u + V_{txa}}\beta_{txa}}_{\substack{\text{Tax} \\ \text{Asset}}} = \underbrace{\frac{D}{D+E}\beta_d}_{\text{Debt}} + \underbrace{\frac{E}{D+E}\beta_e}_{\text{Equity}}$$

where V_u = Value of the company's operating assets
V_{txa} = Value of the company's interest tax shields
D = Market value of the company's debt
E = Market value of the company's equity

In Appendix D, we rearrange the equation to solve for the beta of equity (β_e). This leads to:

$$\beta_e = \beta_u + \frac{D}{E}(\beta_u - \beta_d) - \frac{V_{txa}}{E}(\beta_u - \beta_{txa})$$

To simplify the formula further, most practitioners impose two additional restrictions.[28] First, because debt claims have first priority, the beta of

---

[27] Statistically speaking, the sample average will have the lowest mean squared error. However, because sample averages are heavily influenced by outliers, we recommend examining both the mean and median beta.

[28] In Chapter 5, we detailed alternative restrictions that can be imposed to simplify the general equation regarding risk. Rather than repeat the analysis, we focus on the least restrictive assumption for mature companies: that debt remains proportional to value. For a full discussion of which restrictions to impose and how they affect the cost of capital, please see the section on adjusted present value in Chapter 5.

debt tends to be low. Thus, many assume (for simplicity) the beta of debt is 0. Second, if the company maintains a constant capital structure, the value of tax shields will fluctuate with the value of operating assets and beta of the tax shields (β_{txa}) will equal the beta of the unlevered company (β_u). Setting β_{txa} equal to β_u eliminates the final term:

$$\beta_e = \beta_u \left(1 + \frac{D}{E} \right) \tag{1}$$

Thus, a company's equity beta equals the company's operating beta (commonly known as the unlevered beta) times a leverage factor. As leverage rises, so will the company's equity beta. Using this relation, we can convert equity betas into unlevered betas. Since unlevered betas focus solely on operating risk, they can be averaged across an industry (assuming industry competitors have similar operating characteristics).

To estimate an industry-adjusted company beta, use the following four-step process. First, regress each company's stock returns against the S&P 500 to determine raw beta. In Exhibit 10.11 on page 320, we report regression betas for Home Depot (1.37) and Lowe's (1.15). Next, to unlever each beta, calculate each company's market-debt-to-equity ratio. To calculate net debt ($6.310 billion for Home Depot), add the book value of reported debt ($1.365 billion) to the estimated value of operating leases ($6.554 billion) and then subtract excess cash ($1.609 billion).[29] To determine equity value ($80.101 billion), we multiply the company's stock price ($35.49) by the number of shares outstanding (2.257 billion). With debt and equity in hand, compute debt to equity (.079). Applying equation 1 leads to an unlevered beta of 1.27 for Home Depot and 1.02 for Lowe's. In step three, determine the industry unlevered beta by calculating the median (in this case, the median and average betas are the same).[30] In the final step, relever the industry unlevered beta is to each company's *target* debt-to-equity ratio (using current market values as proxies).

Unlevered cost of equity   As demonstrated, we can unlever an equity beta in order to improve beta estimation for use in the CAPM and WACC. We also can use unlevered industry betas to estimate a company's unlevered cost of equity. To estimate the unlevered cost of equity for use in an adjusted present value (APV) valuation, simply apply the CAPM to the industry unlevered beta.

---

[29] The process for valuing operating leases and excess cash is detailed in Chapter 7.
[30] In most valuations, more than two company betas are available. For Home Depot, Lowe's is the only publicly traded competitor. As a general rule, use as many direct comparables as possible.

Exhibit 10.11 Determining the Industry Beta

$ million

Capital structure	Home Depot	Lowe's
Debt	1,365	3,755
Operating leases	6,554	2,762
Excess cash	(1,609)	(948)
Total net debt	6,310	5,569
Shares outstanding (millions)	2,257	787
Share price ($)	35.49	55.39
Market value of equity	80,101	43,592
Debt/equity	0.079	0.128

Beta calculations	Home Depot	Lowe's
Raw beta (step 1)	1.37	1.15
Unlevered beta (step 2)	1.27	1.02
Industry average unlevered beta (step 3)	1.14	1.14
Relevered beta (step 4)	1.23	1.30

Improving estimates of beta: Smoothing   For well-defined industries, an industry beta will suffice. But if few direct comparables exist, an alternative is beta smoothing. Consider the simple smoothing process used by Bloomberg:

$$\text{Adjusted Beta} = (.33) + (.67) \text{ Raw Beta}$$

Using this formula "smooths" raw estimates toward 1. For instance, a raw beta of 0.5 leads to an adjusted beta of 0.67, while a raw beta of 1.5 leads to an adjusted beta of 1.34. Bloomberg's smoothing mechanism dates back to Blume's observation that betas revert to the mean.[31] Today, more advanced smoothing techniques exist.[32] Although the proof is beyond the scope of this book, the following adjustment will reduce beta estimation error:

$$\beta_{adj} = \frac{\sigma_\varepsilon^2}{\sigma_\varepsilon^2 + \sigma_b^2}(1) + \left(1 - \frac{\sigma_\varepsilon^2}{\sigma_\varepsilon^2 + \sigma_b^2}\right)\beta_{raw}$$

---

[31] M. Blume, "Betas and Their Regression Tendencies," *Journal of Finance,* 30 (1975): 1–10.
[32] For instance, see P. Jorion, "Bayes-Stein Estimation for Portfolio Analysis," *Journal of Financial and Quantitative Analysis,* 21 (1986): 279–292.

where σ_ε = The standard error of the regression beta

σ_b = The cross-sectional standard deviation of all betas

The raw regression beta receives the most weight when the standard error of beta from the regression (σ_ε) is smallest. In fact, when beta is measured perfectly ($\sigma_\varepsilon = 0$), the raw beta receives all the weight. Conversely, if the regression provides no meaningful results (σ_ε is very large), you should set beta equal to 1.

For Home Depot, the standard error of the beta estimate equals 0.20, and in 2004 the cross-sectional standard deviation of beta (across all S&P 500 stocks) equaled 0.590. Therefore, the adjusted beta equals 0.103 + $(1 - 0.103) \times 1.37$, or 1.33.

Alternatives to the CAPM: Fama-French Three-Factor Model

In 1992, Eugene Fama and Kenneth French published a paper in the *Journal of Finance* that received a great deal of attention because they concluded, "In short, our tests do not support the most basic prediction of the SLB [Sharpe-Lintner-Black] Capital Asset Pricing Model that average stock returns are positively related to market betas."[33] At the time, theirs was the most recent in a series of empirical studies that questioned the usefulness of estimated betas in explaining the risk premium on equities. Among the factors negatively or positively associated with equity returns were the size of the company, a seasonal (January) effect, the degree of financial leverage, and the firm's book-to-market ratio.[34] Based on prior research and their own comprehensive regressions, Fama and French concluded that equity returns are inversely related to the size of a company (as measured by market capitalization) and positively related to the ratio of a company's book value to its market value of equity.

Given the strength of Fama and French's empirical results, the academic community has begun measuring risk with a model commonly known as the Fama-French three-factor model. With this model, a stock's excess returns are regressed on excess market returns (similar to the CAPM), the excess

[33] E. Fama and K. French, "The Cross-Section of Expected Stock Returns," *Journal of Finance* (June 1992): 427–465.

[34] R. Blanz, "The Relationship between Return and the Market Value of Common Stocks," *Journal of Financial Economics* (March 1981): 3–18; M. Reinganum, "Misspecification of Capital Asset Pricing: Empirical Anomalies Based on Earnings Yields and Market Values," *Journal of Financial Economics* (March 1981): 19–46; S. Basu, "The Relationship between Earnings Yield, Market Value and Return for NYSE Common Stocks: Further Evidence," *Journal of Financial Economics* (June 1983): 129–156; L. Bhandari, "Debt/Equity Ratio and Expected Common Stock Returns: Empirical Evidence," *Journal of Finance* (April 1988): 507–528; D. Stattman, "Book Values and Stock Returns," *The Chicago MBA: A Journal of Selected Papers* (1980): 25–45; and B. Rosenberg, K. Reid, and R. Lanstein, "Persuasive Evidence of Market Inefficiency," *Journal of Portfolio Management* (1985): 9–17.

Exhibit 10.12 Home Depot's Fama-French Cost of Equity

Factor	Average monthly premium (percent)	Average annual premium (percent)	Regression beta	Contribution to expected return (percent)
Market risk premium		4.5	1.35	6.1
SMB premium	0.25	3.0	(0.04)	(0.1)
HML premium	0.36	4.4	(0.10)	(0.5)
Premium over risk free rate				5.5
			Risk free rate	4.3
			Cost of equity	9.8

returns of small stocks over big stocks (SMB), and the excess returns of high book-to-market stocks over low book-to-market stocks (HML).[35] Because the risk premium is determined by a regression on the SMB and HML stock portfolios, a company does not receive a premium for being small. Instead, the company receives a risk premium if its stock returns are correlated with those of small stocks or high book-to-market companies. The SMB and HML portfolios are meant to replicate unobservable risk factors, factors that caused small companies with high book-to-market values to outperform their CAPM expected returns.

To run a Fama-French regression, we need monthly returns for three portfolios: the market portfolio, the SMB portfolio, and the HML portfolio. Given the model's popularity, Fama-French portfolio returns are now available from professional data providers.

We use the Fama-French three-factor model to estimate Home Depot's cost of equity in Exhibit 10.12. To determine the company's three betas, regress Home Depot stock returns against the excess market portfolio, SMB, and HML. The regression in Exhibit 10.12 used monthly returns and was specified as follows:

$$R_i - r_f = \alpha + \beta_1 (R_m - r_f) + \beta_2 (R_S - R_B) + \beta_3 (R_H - R_L) + \varepsilon$$

As the exhibit indicates, Home Depot's traditional beta remains unchanged, but its cost of equity is lower in the Fama-French model because Home Depot is correlated with other large companies (small companies outperform large companies) and other companies with a low book-to-market ratio (high book-to-market companies outperform low book-to-

---

[35] For a complete description of the factor returns, see E. Fama and K. French, "Common Risk Factors in the Returns on Stocks and Bonds," *Journal of Financial Economics*, 33 (1993): 3–56.

market companies). Based on the historical annualized premiums for SMB (3.0 percent) and HML (4.4 percent), Home Depot's cost of capital equals 9.8 percent, versus 10.4 percent according to the standard CAPM. (These values are not comparable to the cost of equity presented in Exhibit 10.1, which used industry betas.)

The Fama-French model suffers from the same implementation issues as the CAPM. For instance, how much data should you use to determine the each factor's risk premium? Since 1926, small companies have outperformed large companies, but since 1982, they have not. Should returns be regressed using monthly data? Should regressions use five years of data? Given the model's recent development, many of these questions are still under investigation.

Alternatives to the CAPM: The Arbitrage Pricing Theory

Another alternative to the CAPM, the arbitrage pricing theory (APT), resembles a generalized version of the Fama-French three-factor model. In the APT, a security's actual returns are *fully* specified by k factors and random noise:

$$\tilde{R}_i = \alpha + \beta_1 \tilde{F}_1 + \beta_2 \tilde{F}_2 + \cdots + \beta_k \tilde{F}_k + \varepsilon$$

By creating well-diversified factor portfolios, it can be shown that a security's expected return must equal the risk-free rate plus the cumulative sum of its exposure to each factor times the factor's risk premium (λ):

$$E[R_i] = r_f + \beta_1 \lambda_1 + \beta_2 \lambda + \cdots + \beta_k \lambda_k$$

Otherwise, arbitrage is possible (positive return with zero risk).

On paper, the theory is extremely powerful. Any deviations from the model result in unlimited returns with no risk. In practice, implementation of the model has been elusive, as there is little agreement about how many factors there are, what the factors represent, or how to measure the factors. For this reason, use of the APT resides primarily in the classroom.

In Defense of Beta

Fama and French significantly damaged the credibility of the CAPM and beta. Today, most academics rely on three-factor models to measure historical risk and return. Even so, the three-factor model has its critics. To start, the CAPM is based on solid theory about risk and return (albeit with strong assumptions), whereas the Fama-French model is based purely on empirical evidence. Although the latter model has been loosely tied to risk factors such as illiquidity (size premium) and default risk (book-to-market premium), no theory has gained universal acceptance.

In addition, S. P. Kothari, Jay Shanken, and Richard Sloan argue that beta may work better than portrayed in Fama and French. They point out that Fama and French's statistical tests were of low enough power that the tests could not reject a nontrivial (beta-related) risk premium of 6 percent over the post-1940 period.[36] Second, when they used annual returns, rather than monthly returns, to estimate beta (to avoid seasonality in returns), they found a significant linear relationship between beta and returns. Finally, they argue that the economic magnitude of size is quite small, and book-to-market premiums could be a result of survivorship bias.

Other research argues that the Fama-French three-factor model historically outperforms the CAPM because either beta or the market portfolio has been improperly measured. In a recent study, a one-factor model based on time-varying conditional betas eliminated the book-to-market effect.[37] Another article argues that regressions based on equity-only portfolios, such as the S&P 500, leads to the incorrect measurement of beta.[38] This mismeasurement is correlated with leverage, which in turn is correlated with size and book-to-market. When the researchers controlled for leverage, excess returns associated with HMB and SML disappeared.

The bottom line? It takes a better theory to kill an existing theory, and we have yet to see the better theory. Therefore, we continue to use the CAPM while keeping a watchful eye on new research in the area.

ESTIMATING THE AFTER-TAX COST OF DEBT

To estimate the cost of debt, use the yield to maturity of the company's long-term, option-free bonds. Technically speaking, yield to maturity is only a proxy for expected return, because the yield is actually a *promised* rate of return on a company's debt (it assumes all coupon payments are made on time and the debt is paid in full). An enterprise valuation based indirectly on the yield to maturity is therefore theoretically inconsistent: expected free cash flows should not be discounted by a promised yield. For companies with highly rated debt, however, this inconsistency is

---

[36] S. Kothari, J. Shanken, and R. Sloan, "Another Look at the Cross-Section of Expected Returns," *Journal of Finance* (December 1995).

[37] A. Ang and J. Chen, "CAPM over the Long Run: 1926–2001," (working paper, Los Angeles: University of Southern California, 2004).

[38] M. Ferguson and R. Shockley, "Equilibrium 'Anomalies,'" *Journal of Finance*, 58(6) (2003): 2549–2580.

immaterial, especially when compared with the estimation error surrounding beta and the market risk premium. Thus, for estimating the cost of debt for a company with investment-grade debt (debt rated at BBB or better), yield to maturity is a suitable proxy.

When calculating yield to maturity, use *long-term* bonds. As discussed earlier, short-term bonds do not match the duration of the company's free cash flow. To solve for yield to maturity (ytm), reverse engineer the discount rate required to set the present value of the bond's promised cash flows equal to its price:

$$\text{Price} = \frac{\text{Coupon}}{(1 + \text{ytm})} + \frac{\text{Coupon}}{(1 + \text{ytm})^2} + \cdots + \frac{\text{Face} + \text{Coupon}}{(1 + \text{ytm})^N}$$

Ideally, yield to maturity should be calculated on liquid, option-free, long-term debt. If the bond is rarely traded, the bond price will be stale. Using stale prices will lead to an outdated yield to maturity. Yield to maturity will also be distorted when corporate bonds have attached options, such as callability or convertibility, as their value will affect the bond's price but not its promised cash flows.

Bond Ratings and Yield to Maturity

For companies with only short-term bonds or bonds that rarely trade, determine yield to maturity by using an indirect method. First, determine the company's credit rating on unsecured long-term debt. Next, examine the average yield to maturity on a portfolio of long-term bonds with the same credit rating. Use this yield as a proxy for the company's implied yield on long-term debt.

Investing in corporate debt is not risk free. Each year, a number of companies default on their obligations. In 2002, corporate bond defaults reached $163.6 billion worldwide. Since the probability of default is critical to bond pricing, professional rating agencies, such as Standard & Poor's (S&P) and Moody's, will rate a company's debt. To determine a company's bond rating, a ratings agency will examine the company's most recent financial ratios, analyze the company's competitive environment, and interview senior management. Corporate bond ratings are freely available to the public and can be downloaded from rating agency Web sites. For example, consider Home Depot. On June 10, 2004, Moody's reaffirmed its credit rating for Home Depot at Aa3 for its long-term debt. During that same time period, S&P rated Home Depot slightly higher at AA. In this case, the two agencies' ratings were different. Split ratings occur, but relatively infrequently.

Exhibit 10.13 Yield Spread over U.S. Treasuries by Bond Rating, December 2003

Basis points

				Maturity in Years			
Rating	1	2	3	5	7	10	30
Aaa/AAA	34	28	35	21	22	28	50
Aa1/AA+	37	31	33	34	40	29	62
Aa2/AA	39	33	34	35	42	34	64
Aa3/AA−	40	34	36	37	43	37	65
A2/A	57	49	49	57	65	48	82
Baa2/BBB	79	91	96	108	111	102	134
Ba2/BB	228	245	260	257	250	236	263
B2/B	387	384	384	349	332	303	319

Source: Bloomberg.

Once you have a rating, convert the rating into a yield to maturity. Exhibit 10.13 presents U.S. corporate yield spreads over U.S. government bonds. All quotes are presented in basis points, where 100 basis points equals 1 percent. Since Home Depot is rated AA by S&P and Aa3 by Moody's, we estimate that the 10-year yield to maturity is between 34 and 37 basis points over the 10-year Treasury. Adding 34 basis points to the risk-free rate of 4.34 percent equals 4.68 percent.

Using the company's bond ratings to determine the yield to maturity is a good alternative to calculating the yield to maturity directly. Never, however, approximate the yield to maturity using a bond's coupon rate. Coupon rates are set by the company at time of issuance and only approximate the yield if the bond trades near its par value. When valuing a company, you must estimate expected returns relative to *today's* alternative investments. Thus, when you measure the cost of debt, estimate what a comparable investment would earn if bought or sold today.

Below-Investment-Grade Debt

In practice, few financial analysts distinguish between expected and promised returns. But for debt below investment grade, using the yield to maturity as a proxy for the cost of debt can cause significant error.

To better understand the difference between expected returns and yield to maturity, consider the following example. You have been asked to value a one-year zero-coupon bond whose face value is $100. The bond is risky; there is a 25 percent chance the bond will default and you will recover only half the final payment. Finally, the cost of debt (not yield to maturity), estimated using the CAPM, equals 6 percent. Based on this information,

Exhibit 10.14 Beta by Bond Class, 1990–2000

Asset class	Beta
Treasury bonds	0.19
Investment-grade corporate debt	0.27
High-yield corporate debt	0.37

Source: Lehman Brothers, "Global Family of Indices, Fixed Income Research"; Morgan Stanley Capital International; U.S. Treasury, Paul Sweeting.

you estimate the bond's price by discounting expected cash flows by the cost of debt:

$$\text{Price} = \frac{E[CF]}{1+k_d} = \frac{(.75)(\$100)+(.25)(\$50)}{1.06} = \$82.55$$

Next, to determine the bond's yield to maturity, place promised cash flows, rather than expected cash flows, into the numerator. Then solve for the yield to maturity:

$$\text{Price} = \frac{\text{Promised}[CF]}{1+\text{ytm}} = \frac{\$100}{1+\text{ytm}} = \$82.55$$

The $82.55 price leads to a 21.1 percent yield to maturity, *much* higher than the cost of debt. So what drives the yield to maturity? Three factors: the cost of debt, the probability of default, and the recovery rate. When the probability of default is high and the recovery rate is low, the yield to maturity will deviate significantly from the cost of debt. Thus, for companies with high default risk and low ratings, the yield to maturity is a poor proxy for the cost of debt.

To estimate the cost of high-yield debt, we rely on the CAPM (a general pricing model, applicable to any security). Bond indexes are used to generate betas, since individual bonds rarely trade. Exhibit 10.14 presents the market beta for investment-grade and high-yield bonds. As reported in the exhibit, high-yield bonds have a beta 0.1 higher than investment-grade bonds. Assuming a 5 percent market risk premium, this translates to a premium of 0.5 percent over investment-grade bonds. Thus, to calculate the cost of debt for a company with debt rated BB or below, use the BBB yield to maturity and add 0.5 percent.

Incorporating the Interest Tax Shield

To calculate free cash flow (using techniques detailed in Chapter 7), we compute taxes as if the company were entirely financed by equity. By using all-equity taxes, we can make comparisons across companies and over time, without regard to capital structure. Yet, since the tax shield has value, it must be accounted for. In an enterprise DCF using the WACC, the tax shield is valued as part of the cost of capital. To value the tax shield, reduce the cost of debt by the marginal tax rate:

$$\text{After-Tax Cost of Debt} = \text{Cost of Debt} \times (1 - T_m)$$

Chapter 7 detailed how to calculate the marginal tax rate for historical analysis. For use in the cost of capital, you should calculate the marginal tax rate in a consistent manner, with one potential modification to account for the timing of future tax payments. According to research by John Graham, the statutory marginal tax rate overstates the *future* marginal tax rate because of rules related to tax-loss carryforwards, tax-loss carrybacks, investment tax credits, and alternative minimum taxes.[39] For instance, when a company loses money, it will receive a cash credit only if it has been profitable in the past three years; otherwise, it must carry the loss forward until it is once again profitable.

Graham uses simulation to estimate the realizable marginal tax rate on a company-by-company basis. For investment-grade companies, use the statutory rate. For instance, because Home Depot is highly profitable, Graham's model estimates the company's future marginal statutory tax rate at the full 35 percent. The typical company, however, does not always fully use its tax shields. Graham estimates the marginal tax rate is on average 5 percentage points below the statutory rate.

USE TARGET WEIGHTS TO DETERMINE COST OF CAPITAL

With our estimates of the cost of equity and cost of debt, we can now blend the two expected returns into a single number. To do this, we use the target weights of debt and equity to enterprise value, on a market (not book) basis:

$$\text{WACC} = \frac{D}{V} k_d (1 - T_m) + \frac{E}{V} k_e$$

Using market values to weight expected returns in the cost of capital follows directly from the formula's derivation (see Appendix C for a derivation of free cash flow and WACC). But consider a more intuitive explanation: the WACC represents the expected return on an *alternative* investment with identical risk. Rather than reinvest in the company, management could return capital to investors, who could reinvest elsewhere. To return capital without changing the capital structure, management can repay debt and re-

---

[39] J. Graham, "Debt and the Marginal Tax Rate," *Journal of Financial Economics*, 41 (1996): 41–73; and J. Graham, "Proxies for the Corporate Marginal Tax Rate," *Journal of Financial Economics*, 42 (1996): 187–221.

purchase shares, but must do so at their *market* value. Conversely, book value represents a sunk cost, so it is no longer relevant.

The cost of capital should rely on target weights, rather than current weights, because at any point, a company's current capital structure may not reflect the level expected to prevail over the life of the business. The current capital structure may merely reflect a short-term swing in the company's stock price, a swing that has yet to be rebalanced by management. Thus, using today's capital structure may cause you to overestimate (or underestimate) the value of tax shields for companies whose leverage is expected to drop (or rise).

Many companies are already near their target capital structure. If yours is not, decide how quickly the company will achieve the target. In the simplest scenario, the company will rebalance immediately and maintain the new capital structure. In this case, using the target weights and a constant WACC (for all future years) will lead to a reasonable valuation. If you expect the rebalancing to happen over a significant period of time, then use a different cost of capital each year, reflecting the capital structure at the time. In practice, this procedure is complex; you must correctly model not only the weights, but also the changes in the cost of debt and equity (because of increased default risk and higher betas). For extreme changes in capital structure, modeling enterprise DCF using a constant WACC can lead to significant error. In this case, value the company with adjusted present value (APV).

To develop a target capital structure for a company, use a combination of three approaches:

1. Estimate the company's current market-value-based capital structure.
2. Review the capital structure of comparable companies.
3. Review management's implicit or explicit approach to financing the business and its implications for the target capital structure.

Estimating Current Capital Structure

To determine the company's current capital structure, measure the market value of all claims against enterprise value. For most companies, the claims will consist primarily of debt and equity (we address more complex securities in the last section). If a company's debt and equity are publicly traded, simply multiply the quantity of each security by its most recent price. Most difficulties arise when securities are not traded such that prices can be readily observed.

Debt If an observable market value is not readily available, you can value debt securities at book or use discounted cash flow. In most cases, book value reasonably approximates the current market value. This will not be

ESTIMATING THE COST OF CAPITAL

the case, however, if interest rates have changed dramatically since the time of issuance or the company is in financial distress. In these two situations, the current price will differ from book value because either expected cash flows have changed (increased probability of default lowers expected cash flow) or the discount rate has changed (interest rates drive discount rates) from their original levels.[40]

In these situations, value each bond separately by discounting promised cash flows at the appropriate yield to maturity. Promised cash flows will be disclosed in the notes of a company's annual report. Determine the appropriate yield to maturity by examining the yields from comparably rated debt with similar maturities.

Debt equivalent claims   Next, value off-balance-sheet debt, such as operating leases and pension liabilities. As detailed in Chapter 7, operating leases can be valued using the following formula:

$$\text{Lease Value}_{t-1} = \frac{\text{Rental Expense}_t}{k_d + \dfrac{1}{\text{Asset Life}}}$$

Only include operating leases in debt if you plan to adjust free cash flow for operating leases as well. Consistency between free cash flow and the cost of capital is paramount. Any pension adjustments made to free cash flow must be properly represented in the debt portion of the cost of capital. Specifically, if you add back any tax shields during adjustments to NOPLAT, you must account for the tax shields in the present value of pension liabilities and the cost of debt.

Equity   If common stock is publicly traded, multiply the market price by the number of shares *outstanding*. The market value of equity should be based on shares outstanding in the capital market. Therefore, do not use shares issued, as they may include shares repurchased by the company.

At this point, you may be wondering why you are valuing the company if you are going to rely on the market's value of equity in the cost of capital. Shouldn't we be using the estimated equity value? The answer is no. Remember, we are only estimating today's market value to frame management's philosophy concerning capital structure. To value the company, use *target* weights.

For privately held companies, no market-based values are available. In this case, you must determine equity value (for the cost of capital) either using a

---

[40] For floating-rate bonds, changes in Treasury rates won't affect value, since coupons float with Treasury yields. Changes in market-based default premiums, however, will affect the market value of floating-rate bonds, since bonds are priced at a fixed spread above Treasury yields.

multiples approach or through DCF iteratively. To perform an iterative valuation, assume a reasonable capital structure, and value the enterprise using DCF. Using the estimate of debt to enterprise value, repeat the valuation. Continue this process until the valuation no longer materially changes.

Minority interest   If minority interest—claims by outside shareholders on a portion of a company's business (often a subsidiary acquired by the company)—is publicly traded, then you can determine their approximate value directly from the market price for the shares. When the minority interest is not publicly traded, you must estimate its current value. To do this, apply a company-specific or industry price-to-earnings ratio directly to the income generated for minority interest.

Review Capital Structure of Comparable Companies

To place the company's current capital structure in the proper context, compare its capital structure with those of similar companies. Exhibit 10.15 presents the median debt-to-value levels for 11 industries. As the exhibit shows, industries with heavy fixed investment in tangible assets tend to have higher debt levels. High-growth industries, especially those

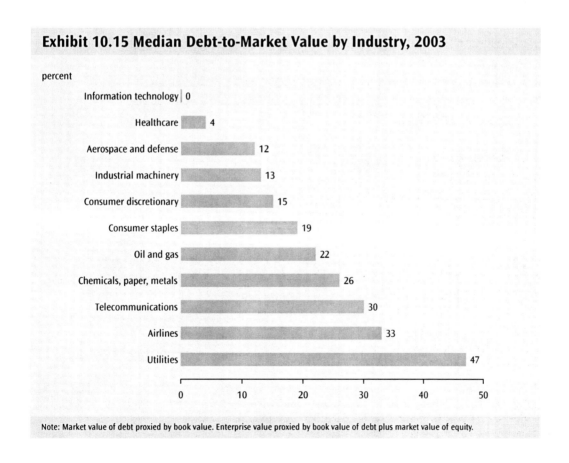

Exhibit 10.15 Median Debt-to-Market Value by Industry, 2003

percent

Industry	Percent
Information technology	0
Healthcare	4
Aerospace and defense	12
Industrial machinery	13
Consumer discretionary	15
Consumer staples	19
Oil and gas	22
Chemicals, paper, metals	26
Telecommunications	30
Airlines	33
Utilities	47

Note: Market value of debt proxied by book value. Enterprise value proxied by book value of debt plus market value of equity.

with intangible investments, tend to use very little debt. Economy-wide, the median debt-to-value ratio for the S&P 500 is 13.1 percent, and the median debt-to-equity ratio is 19.7 percent.

Having a company with a different capital structure is perfectly acceptable, but you should understand why. For instance, is the company by philosophy more aggressive or innovative in the use of debt financing, or is the capital structure only a temporary deviation from a more conservative target? Often, companies finance acquisitions with debt they plan to quickly retire or refinance with a stock offering. Alternatively, is there anything different about the company's cash flow or asset intensity that can explain the difference? Always use comparables to help you assess the reasonableness of estimated debt-to-equity levels.

Review Management's Philosophy

As a final step, review management's historical financing philosophy (or question management outright). Has the current team been actively managing the company's capital structure? Is the management team aggressive in its use of debt? Or is it overly conservative? Consider UPS, a company with a well-known conservative culture. Although cash flow is strong and stable, the company rarely issues debt. From a financing perspective, it doesn't need to issue additional securities; investments can be funded with current profits. Since the company is primarily employee owned, there is little threat of outside takeover. Therefore, UPS is unlikely to increase its target debt-to-value ratio anytime soon.

Over the long run, one would expect most companies to aim toward a target capital structure that minimizes cost of capital. We will address the choice of capital structure in Chapter 17.

COMPLEX CAPITAL STRUCTURES

The weighted average cost of capital is determined by weighting each security's expected return by its proportional contribution to total value. For a complex security, such as convertible debt, measuring expected return is challenging. Is a convertible bond like straight debt, enabling us to use the yield to maturity? Is it equity, enabling us to use the CAPM? In actuality, it is neither, so we recommend an alternative method.

If the treatment of hybrid securities will make a material difference in valuation results,[41] we recommend using adjusted present value (APV). In the APV, enterprise value is determined by discounting free cash flow at

---

[41] If the hybrid security is unlikely to be converted, it can be treated as traditional debt. Conversely, if the hybrid security is well "in the money," it should be treated as traditional equity. In these situations, errors are likely to be small, and a WACC-based valuation remains appropriate.

the unlevered cost of equity. The value of incremental cash flows related to financing, such as interest tax shields, is then computed separately. To determine the company's unlevered cost of equity, use the unlevered industry beta. This avoids the need to compute company specific components, such as the debt-to-equity ratio, a required input in the unlevering equation.

In some situations, you may still desire an accurate representation of the cost of capital. In these cases, split hybrid securities into their individual components. For instance, you can replicate a convertible bond by combining a traditional bond with a call option on the company's stock. You can further disaggregate a call option into a portfolio consisting of a risk-free bond and the company's stock. By converting a complex security into a portfolio of debt and equity, you once again have the components required for the traditional cost of capital. The process of creating replicating portfolios to value options is discussed in Chapter 20.

HEINEKEN CASE

In the case for this chapter, we explain how we estimated Heineken's WACC. Our estimate of Heineken's WACC is 7.5 percent as of the end of February 2004, as shown in Exhibit 10.16, based on a target market value capital structure of 10 percent debt to 90 percent equity, with the cost of equity at 8.0 percent and pretax cost of debt at 4.5 percent.

Our estimate of Heineken's target capital structure (10 percent debt to 90 percent equity) is based on historical analysis. Heineken's current capital structure using market values is 24 percent debt to 76 percent equity, as shown in Exhibit 10.17 on page 334, but the current capital structure is higher than Heineken's historical norm (see Exhibit 10.18 on p. 334). Heineken historically has had less than 10 percent debt. Its debt in 2002 and 2003 is higher because of recent acquisitions. In light of Heineken's excess cash balances, significant cash flow, and conservative dividend, we expect the company to reduce its debt levels significantly within a few years. So we selected a conservative long-term capital structure of 10 percent debt.

Exhibit 10.16 Heineken: Weighted Average Cost of Capital

percent

	Target capital structure	Cost	Tax benefit	Weighted cost
Debt	10.0	4.5	35	0.3
Common equity	90.0	8.0		7.2
Total	100.0			7.5

Exhibit 10.17 Heineken: Current Capital Structure

	Book value € million	Percent of total capitalization	Market value € million	Percent of total capitalization
Short term debt	1,113	14	1,113	6
Long term debt	2,721	33	2,809	15
Retirement related liabilities	526	6	526	3
Total debt	4,360	53	4,448	24
Common equity	3,167	38	13,171	71
Minority interest	732	9	1,030	5
Total equity	3,899	47	14,201	76
Total capitalization	8,259	100	18,649	100

Even though we did not use Heineken's year-end 2003 capital structure, we present its calculation in Exhibit 10.17, as follows:

- *Short-term debt:* Short-term debt matures within one year, so in most cases, book value approximates market value.

- *Long-term debt:* None of Heineken's debt is publicly traded, so market quotes were unavailable. Heineken supplied limited information on its long-term debt issues. For the debt instruments for which we had information, we used the current face value, years to maturity, coupon rate, and opportunity cost of debt to estimate the market value by discounting the expected cash flows to the present (see Exhibit 10.19). For long-term debt where no information was available, we assumed the current book value was a reasonable proxy for market value.

Exhibit 10.18 Heineken: Historical Capital Structure

Debt/(debt and equity) at market value

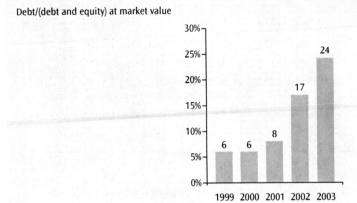

638

Exhibit 10.19 Heineken: Market Value of Long-Term Debt

Debt issue	Coupon rate percent	Book value € million	Year of maturity	Market value € million
Bond loan from credit institution	4.4	497	2010	496
Bond loan from credit institution	5.0	596	2013	624
Loan from credit institution	5.3	387	2008	414
Loan from credit institution	4.1	506	2008	540
Other issues		735		735
Total long-term debt		**2,721**		**2,809**

- *Retirement-related liabilities:* We estimated the market value of net retirement-related liabilities to be equal to the actuarial value in the footnotes, which for Heineken also equals its book value.

- *Common equity:* In late February 2004, the market value of Heineken's equity was €13.2 billion, based on a share price of €33.65 and a total of 392 million shares outstanding.

- *Minority interest:* To estimate a market value for minority interest, we applied a peer-average P/E multiple of 15.6 to Heineken's minority-interest income in 2003. Given minority-interest income in 2003 of 66 million, we estimated the market value of minority interest to be €1.0 billion.

We estimated the cost of Heineken's debt and equity as follows:

- *Cost of debt:* We assumed that Heineken's opportunity cost of debt equals that of the similarly rated companies (as expressed as a premium over the risk-free rate). Although Heineken has not been rated by S&P or Moody's, we have assumed that its rating would be similar to highly rated beer companies. In the Netherlands, the default premium for investment-grade companies comparable to Heineken was about 40 basis points in February 2004. Since the euro risk-free rate in February was 4.1 percent, the opportunity cost of debt is 4.5 percent before taxes, or 2.9 percent after taxes.

- *Cost of equity:* Using the capital asset pricing model, we estimated Heineken's cost of equity to be 8.0 percent based on a euro risk-free rate of 4.1 percent,[42] a market risk premium of 5.2 percent,[43] and a levered beta of approximately 0.75 rounded. The levered beta is based on the median of the unlevered betas for a sample of brewers (0.66), shown in Exhibit 10.20 on page 336, relevered to Heineken's target capital structure (debt-to-value ratio of 10 percent). To un-lever and relever the betas, we used the formula $\beta_l = \beta_u \times (1 + D/E)$, as explained

---

[42] We used the yield on German treasury bonds for the risk-free rate, as they are the most liquid and have the lowest yield to maturity.

[43] The market risk premium is based on a 7.0 percent real return on equities less the real return on the risk-free rate of 1.8 percent at the time of the Heineken valuation.

Exhibit 10.20 Beer Industry Unlevered Betas

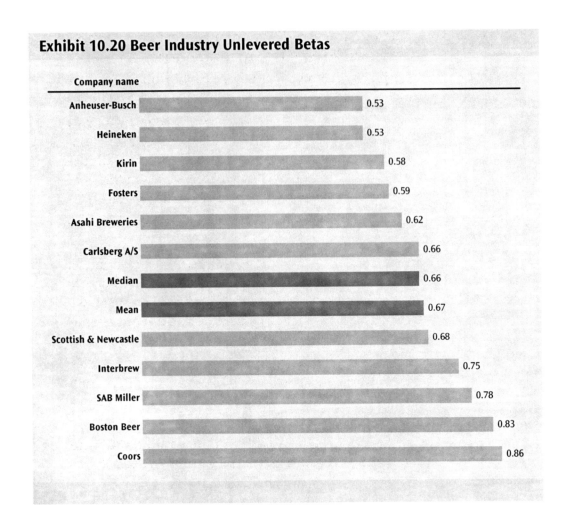

earlier in this chapter. In the brewing industry, the range of unlevered betas was 0.53 to 0.86, and the median and mean were almost identical (0.66 and 0.67, respectively). As we mentioned earlier, individual companies' betas are difficult to measure, so we typically use the industry median rather than a company's measured beta unless we have specific reasons to believe that the company's beta should differ from the industry.

REVIEW QUESTIONS

1. Identify and describe five key principles of computing WACC.
2. Present, in its simplest form, the WACC formula. Why should a manager compute an after-tax cost of debt and not an after-tax cost of equity when determining WACC?
3. Present, in its simplest form, the $E(R_i)$ formula, based upon the CAPM. What should a manager consider when selecting an appropriate risk free rate of return?

4. How does an arithmetic average differ from a geometric average? When might one approach be preferred over the other?

5. What is survivorship bias? How does survivorship bias impact a manager's computation and use of historical market returns?

6. Using an average of historical returns to determine the market risk premium is often described as backward looking while reverse engineering the key value driver formula is described as forward looking. Identify the differences between the two approaches in terms of the data used in the computation of $E[R_i]$ or k_e for each model.

7. Identify three key characteristics of the raw data needed for computing the CAPM.

8. What is the purpose of unlevering beta? What useful information can be gained from comparing the unlevered beta of a company compared to the unlevered beta of its industry? What is the purpose of relevering the industry's beta by the market value of your corporation's debt position?

9. Identify the strengths and weaknesses of the three $E[R_i]$ or k_e models presented in Chapter 10 (CAPM, APT, and Fama-French). Which model would you recommend a manager select to compute a company's estimate of $E[R_i]$ or k_e? Explain.

10. What is the basis for using the company's target capital structure versus the current capital structure when estimating WACC?

11

Calculating and Interpreting Results

After finishing your financial projections and continuing-value estimate, you are ready to conclude your valuation. In this chapter, we show how to take the final steps to create a complete valuation:

- Discount forecasted cash flows or economic profits and continuing value to determine the present value of operations.
- Calculate equity value from the present value of operations by adding the value of nonoperating assets and subtracting the value of nonequity claims.
- Use scenarios to deal better with the uncertainty underlying the final valuation.
- Examine valuation results to ensure that your findings are technically correct, your assumptions realistic, and your interpretations plausible.

This chapter focuses on calculating and interpreting results for the two most widely used approaches: enterprise DCF and discounted economic profit. In Chapter 5, we also discussed several valuation alternatives such as the APV, capital cash flow, and cash-flow-to-equity approach. To a large extent, the key messages about calculation and interpretation of results also apply to the alternative approaches. When they do not, we will state this explicitly.

CALCULATE VALUE OF OPERATIONS

From the free cash flow and economic profit projections, calculate the present value of operations in three steps: discount free cash flows, discount continuing value, and sum the resulting values to determine the value of operations.

Discount Free Cash Flows

The first step is to discount each year's free cash flow (or economic profit) to the present, using the WACC. For most valuations, future cash flow is discounted by a constant WACC. If you have chosen to vary the WACC over time, however, ensure that you are consistent in the way you discount future cash flows.[1] A time-varying WACC is appropriate if the yield curve is sharply increasing or decreasing or if significant changes are expected in, for example, the capital market weights for debt and equity, the cost of debt, or the tax rate. Such changes could occur for a company that is at a very low or high leverage and will converge to a sustainable, long-term capital structure. In that case, however, the APV approach is preferable, because it more easily allows for explicit modeling of the capital structure and debt-related tax shields over time.

Discount the Continuing Value

Next, discount the continuing value to the present. If you calculate continuing value using the perpetuity-based approach we presented in Chapter 9, bear in mind that the continuing value is already expressed as a value in the last year of the explicit forecast period. Therefore, you should discount it by the number of years in the explicit forecast. For example, if the forecast has 10 years, discount the continuing value by 10 years, not 11 years. In addition, if WACC varies over the explicit forecast period, remember to follow the approach described in the previous section when discounting continuing value.

Calculate the Value of Operations

The third and final step is to add the present value of free cash flow in the explicit period to the present value of the continuing value. The resulting value is called the value of operations. In the economic profit approach, invested capital at the beginning of the forecast period must be added to discounted economic profits and continuing value.[2]

---

[1] If the WACC varies over time, ensure that the discount factor DF_T for the free cash flow in year T is properly defined as:

$$DF_T = \prod_{t=1}^{T}(1 + WACC_t)$$

where $WACC_t$ = Cost of capital for year t

[2] This should be the invested capital at the end of the last historical year.

The value of operations should be adjusted for midyear discounting. We often assume that cash flows occur continuously throughout the year rather than in a lump sum at the end of the year. To adjust for this discrepancy, we grow the discounted value of operations at the WACC for six months.

CALCULATE EQUITY VALUE

Discounting cash flows or economic profits to obtain the value of operations was fairly straightforward. Calculating the equity value from the value of operations is a bit more complex. For all the valuation approaches discussed in Chapter 5, except the cash-flow-to-equity approach, there are two general rules:

1. All assets and liabilities whose cash flows are not included in the DCF value of operations must be separately valued and added to or subtracted from the DCF valuation. This holds for both on-balance-sheet and off-balance-sheet assets and liabilities (see Exhibit 11.1 on p. 342).

2. The best valuation approach for these assets and liabilities depends on the degree to which their value changes with the DCF value of operations. For example, the value of employee stock options and convertible bonds will increase as the value of operations increases, and your valuation approach should reflect this.

   - If there is a strong dependency between nonoperating assets and nonequity claims on one hand and the value of operations on the other, make sure the assumptions underlying your estimates are fully consistent with those underlying the DCF value of operations. This applies to employee stock options, convertible bonds, debt in distressed companies, and sometimes to nonconsolidated subsidiaries.[3]

   - If there is little or no dependency, as in the case of marketable securities, you can use the current market value when available or perform a DCF valuation if not. Use book values only when they are a good approximation of market value or as a method of last resort.

[3] Assume that your DCF valuation of operations implies a value per share significantly above the current market price per share. In this case, you should not deduct convertibles or options as nonequity claims at their current market value but at the higher value implied by your DCF results. Similarly, the current market value of nonconsolidated subsidiaries may need upward adjustment if their operations are closely related to those of the parent company. Finally, if the company is in financial distress with debt trading at a significant discount, deducting debt at the current market value will lead to an overestimation of equity value because the value of debt should increase with the value of operations.

Exhibit 11.1 Example Valuation Buildup

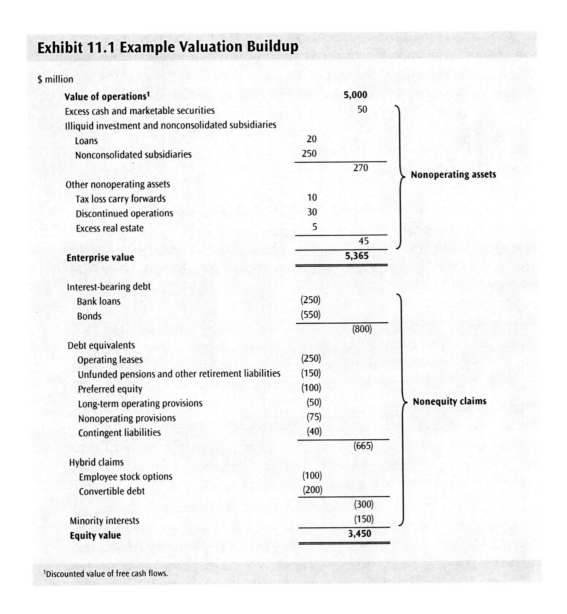

$ million

Value of operations[1]		**5,000**
Excess cash and marketable securities		50
Illiquid investment and nonconsolidated subsidiaries		
Loans	20	
Nonconsolidated subsidiaries	250	
		270
Other nonoperating assets		
Tax loss carry forwards	10	
Discontinued operations	30	
Excess real estate	5	
		45
Enterprise value		**5,365**
Interest-bearing debt		
Bank loans	(250)	
Bonds	(550)	
		(800)
Debt equivalents		
Operating leases	(250)	
Unfunded pensions and other retirement liabilities	(150)	
Preferred equity	(100)	
Long-term operating provisions	(50)	
Nonoperating provisions	(75)	
Contingent liabilities	(40)	
		(665)
Hybrid claims		
Employee stock options	(100)	
Convertible debt	(200)	
		(300)
Minority interests		(150)
Equity value		**3,450**

Nonoperating assets

Nonequity claims

[1]Discounted value of free cash flows.

If you have applied the cash-flow-to-equity approach, there are fewer adjustments to the DCF result because the valuation already represents an estimate of the (undiluted) equity value. However, in some cases, you must still adjust for outstanding stock options or other convertible securities.

Nonoperating Assets

When reorganizing the company's accounting statements in Chapter 7, we classified particular assets as nonoperating assets. Cash flows related to these assets are not included in the free cash flow (or economic profit), and therefore are not accounted for in the value of operations. Although not included in operations, they still represent value to the shareholder. Thus, you must assess the present value of each nonoperating asset separately and add the resulting value to the value of operations. In this section, we identify the most common nonoperating assets and describe how to handle these in the valuation.

If necessary, you should take into account any special circumstances that could affect shareholders' ability to capture the full market value of these assets. For example, if the company has announced it will sell off a nonoperating asset in the near term, you should deduct the estimated capital gains taxes (if any) on the asset from its market value.

Excess cash and marketable securities Nonoperating assets that can be converted into cash on short notice and at low cost are classified as excess cash and marketable securities. Under U.S. GAAP and IFRS, companies must report such assets at their fair market value on the balance sheet. Therefore, you can use the most recent book values as a proxy for the market value—unless you have reason to believe they have significantly changed in value since the reporting date (as in the case of high-risk equity holdings).

In general, we do not recommend valuing highly liquid nonoperating assets if the market values are available. If you decide to perform a DCF valuation of nonoperating securities, estimate meaningful cash flow projections, and discount these at the appropriate cost of capital, which in general is *not* equal to the company's WACC. For example, discounting future cash flows from government bonds and Treasury bills at the company's WACC will lead to an undervaluation because the appropriate cost of capital is the risk-free rate.

Illiquid investments and nonconsolidated subsidiaries This category of nonoperating assets typically includes loans and equity stakes in subsidiaries that are not consolidated in the company's financial statements. These assets are not easily converted into cash, so they are recorded on the balance sheet at historical cost, not at fair market value.

For *loans* to other companies, use the reported book value. This is a reasonable approximation of market value if the loans were given at fair market terms and if the borrower's credit risk and general interest rates have not changed significantly since issuance. If this is not the case, you should perform a separate DCF valuation of the promised interest and principal payments at the yield to maturity for corporate bonds with similar risk and maturity.

Nonconsolidated subsidiaries are companies in which the parent company holds a noncontrolling equity stake. Under U.S. GAAP and IFRS, this generally applies to equity stakes below 50 percent.[4] Because the parent company does not have formal control over these subsidiaries, their financials are not

---

[4] See Chapter 21 for more details on consolidation under U.S. GAAP and IFRS.

consolidated. Under U.S. GAAP and IFRS, there are two ways in which non-consolidated subsidiaries can appear in the parent company's accounts:

1. For equity stakes between 20 percent and 50 percent, the parent company is assumed to have *influence but not control* over the subsidiary. The equity holding in the subsidiary is reported in the parent balance sheet at the investment's historical cost plus profits and additional investment, less dividends received. The parent company's portion of the subsidiary's profits is shown below EBIT on the income statement.

2. For equity stakes below 20 percent, the parent company is assumed to have *no influence*. The equity holdings are shown at historical cost on the parent's balance sheet. The parent's portion of the subsidiary's dividends is included below EBIT on the income statement.

The best approach to handling these subsidiaries depends on the information available:

- If the subsidiary is publicly listed, use the market value for the company's equity stake. Verify that the market value is indeed a good indicator of intrinsic value. In some cases, these listed subsidiaries have very limited free float and/or very low liquidity, so the share price may not properly reflect current information.

- If the subsidiary is not listed but you have access to its financial statements, perform a separate DCF valuation of the equity stake. Discount the cash flows at the appropriate cost of capital, which is not necessarily the parent company's WACC. Also, when completing the parent valuation, include only the value of the parent's *equity stake* and not the subsidiary's entire enterprise value or equity value.

If the parent company's accounts are the only source of financial information for the subsidiary, we suggest the following alternatives:

- *Simplified cash-flow-to-equity valuation:* This is a feasible approach when the parent has a 20 to 50 percent equity stake, because the subsidiary's net income and approximate book equity[5] are disclosed in the parent's accounts. Build forecasts for how the key value drivers (net income growth and return on equity) will develop, so you can project future cash flows to equity. Discount these cash flows at the cost of equity for the subsidiary in question and not at the parent company's WACC.

- *Multiples valuation:* If the parent has a 20 to 50 percent equity stake, you can also build a valuation based on the price-to-earnings and/or

---

[5] The book value of the subsidiary equals the historical acquisition cost plus retained profits, which is a reasonable approximation of book equity. In case any goodwill is included in the book value of the subsidiary, this should be deducted.

market-to-book multiple. Net income and approximate book equity for the subsidiary are available, and you can estimate an appropriate multiple from a group of listed peers.

- *Tracking portfolio:* For parent equity stakes below 20 percent, you may have no information beyond the investment's original cost, that is, the book value shown in the parent's balance sheet. Even applying a multiple is difficult because neither net income nor the *current* book value of equity is reported. If you know when the stake was acquired, you can approximate its current market value by adding the relative price increase for a portfolio of comparable stocks over the same holding period.

You should triangulate your results as much as possible, given the lack of precision for these valuation approaches.

Other nonoperating assets The preceding categories are typically the most significant nonoperating assets from a valuation perspective. But companies can also have several other types of nonoperating assets such as tax loss carryforwards, excess real estate, and pension assets, to name a few. These assets are not necessarily reported separately on a company's balance sheet, so they can be hard to identify.

Tax loss carryforwards—or net operating losses (NOLs), as they are called in the United States—represent accumulated historical losses that a company can use to compensate future tax charges. Tax loss carryforwards are included in the tax assets on the balance sheet and discussed in the company's footnotes. From an outsider's perspective, it is difficult to accurately estimate the true value of tax loss carryforwards, because they do not necessarily offset the cash taxes as derived from the consolidated income statement. For example, for companies with foreign subsidiaries, you would need to know tax losses and future taxable profits on a country-by-country basis, because domestic tax losses cannot offset foreign taxable profits, and vice versa.

Do not confuse tax loss carryforwards with ongoing deferred tax assets as defined in Chapter 7. Ongoing deferred tax assets should not be included in nonoperating assets because they are already explicitly accounted for in the calculation of the cash tax rate.

Estimate the value of the tax loss carryforwards separately and not as part of free cash flow. Create a separate account for the accumulated tax loss carryforwards, and forecast the development of this account by adding any future losses and subtracting any future taxable profits on a year-by-year basis. For each year in which the account is used to offset taxable profits, discount the tax savings at the cost of debt.[6] Some practitioners

---

[6] If the tax loss carryforwards are relatively small compared with near-term taxable profits, the amount of future tax savings will not fluctuate much with the company's profitability, and the cost of debt is most appropriate. The higher the tax losses relative to near-term profits, the more

simply set the carryforward's value at the tax rate times the accumulated tax losses.

A second, more complex alternative, is to adjust both the tax rate used in the free cash flow projections and in the WACC during years for which the company can offset (part of) its tax charges. In this case, the value of tax loss carryforwards is included in the DCF value of operations and should not be double counted as a nonoperating asset.

Discontinued operations are businesses being sold or closed down. The earnings from discontinued operations are explicitly shown in the income statement, and the associated net asset position is disclosed on the balance sheet. Because discontinued operations are no longer part of a company's operations, their value should not be modeled as part of free cash flow or included in the DCF value of operations. Under U.S. GAAP and IFRS, the assets and liabilities associated with the discontinued operations are written down to their fair value and disclosed as a net asset on the balance sheet, so the most recent book value is usually a reasonable approximation.[7]

Excess real estate and other unutilized assets are assets no longer required for the company's operations. As a result, any cash flows that the assets could generate are excluded from the free cash flow projection, and the assets are not included in the DCF value of operations. Identifying these assets in an outside-in valuation is nearly impossible unless they are specifically disclosed in the company's footnotes. Therefore, including their value separately as a nonoperating asset is often limited to internal valuations. For excess real estate, use the most recent appraisal value when available. Alternatively, estimate the real estate value either by using an appraisal multiple such as value per square meter or by discounting expected future cash flows from rentals at the appropriate cost of capital. Of course, be careful to exclude any *operating* real estate from these figures, because that value is implicitly included in the free cash flow projections and value of operations.

We do not recommend a separate valuation for unutilized operating assets unless they are expected to be sold in the near-term. If the financial projections for the company reflect growth, the value of any underutilized assets should instead be captured in lower future capital expenditures.

Surpluses in a company's pension funds show up as net *pension assets* in the balance sheet. We will describe in detail how to value pension assets during our discussion of pension liabilities.

---

the value of tax savings will fluctuate with profits, and the more appropriate the unlevered cost of capital becomes. This is consistent with our recommendation in Chapter 5 to use the unlevered cost of capital to discount the expected future tax savings from the interest on debt.

[7] Any upward adjustment to the original book value of assets and liabilities is limited to the cumulative historical impairments on the assets. Thus, the fair market value of discontinued operations *could* be higher than the net asset value disclosed in the balance sheet.

Nonequity Claims

The value of operations plus nonoperating assets equals the enterprise value. To calculate the value of common equity, you need to deduct the value of all the nonequity claims from the enterprise value. Although nonequity claims include a long array of items, they can be grouped into four categories (shown in Exhibit 11.1):

1. Debt such as bonds, short-term and long-term bank loans
2. Debt equivalents such as operating leases, pensions, specific types of provisions, preferred stock, and contingent liabilities (e.g., outstanding claims from litigation)
3. Hybrid claims such as employee stock options and convertible bonds
4. Minority interests

For the purpose of exposition, we use the term *nonequity claims* to represent all financial claims other than those from current common stockholders. For example, even though convertible debt and employee options can be converted into common equity, we group them under nonequity claims. Note that even in a discounted-cash-flow-to-equity valuation, you must deduct the value of employee stock options and convertible debt or convertible preferred equity[8] to estimate the value of common equity.

In this section, we provide an overview of the most frequently encountered nonequity claims and recommend how to include them in a company valuation.

Debt Corporate debt comes in many forms: commercial paper, notes payable, fixed and floating bank loans, corporate bonds, and capitalized leases. If the debt is relatively secure and actively traded, use its market value. If the debt instrument is not traded, discount the promised interest payments and the principal repayment at the yield to maturity to estimate current value. The book value of debt is a reasonable approximation for fixed-rate debt if interest rates and default risk have not significantly changed since the debt issuance. For floating-rate debt, market value is not sensitive to interest rates, and book value is a reasonable approximation if the company's default risk has been fairly stable.

For companies in *financial distress*, you must be careful when valuing debt. For distressed companies, the value of the debt will be at a significant discount to its book value and will fluctuate with the value of the enterprise. Essentially, the debt has become similar to equity: its value will depend

---

[8] For convertible debt (preferred equity), only the interest (preferred dividend) payments are included in the equity cash flow projections. The value of the conversion option still needs to be deducted from the equity DCF result.

directly on your estimate for the enterprise value, and you should not simply deduct the current market value of debt. If sound economic forecasts put your DCF estimate of enterprise value significantly above its current market value and you deduct the current market value of debt to determine equity, you are underestimating the true value of debt and overestimating the equity value. The reason is that as the enterprise value increases, the value of debt increases as well.

For distressed companies, apply an integrated-scenario approach to value operations as well as equity. For each scenario, estimate the enterprise value conditional on your financial forecasts, deduct the full value[9] of the debt and other nonequity claims,[10] and calculate the equity value as the residual (which should be zero for any scenario where the conditional enterprise value is less than the value of debt plus other nonequity claims). Next, weight each scenario's conditional value of equity by its probability of occurrence to obtain an estimate for the value of equity. In the same way, you can calculate the point estimates for enterprise value and debt value (for an example, see the section on scenario valuation later in this chapter).

Operating leases   These are the most common form of off-balance-sheet debt. Under certain restrictions, companies can avoid capitalizing leases on their balance sheet. For these so-called operating leases, rental charges are included in operating costs, and required future payments are disclosed in the notes to the balance sheet.

Following the guidelines outlined in Chapter 7, capitalize the value of the operating leases as part of invested capital and as a debt-equivalent liability. Add the estimated after-tax interest component from the lease back to operating profit on the income statement. By doing this, you effectively treat the leased assets as if they were owned and financed with straight debt. Therefore, you need to deduct the capitalized value of operating leases as a nonequity claim. Estimate this value with the following formula:

$$\text{Capitalized Operating Leases} = \text{Asset Value} = \frac{\text{Rental Expense}}{\left(k_d + \dfrac{1}{\text{Asset Life}} \right)}$$

where k_d = Cost of debt

Unfunded pension and other postretirement liabilities   Unfunded retirement liabilities should be treated as debt-equivalents. They can make a signif-

[9] That is, the value of the debt for a nondistressed company—typically close to book value.
[10] All nonequity claims need to be included in the scenario approach for distressed companies. The order in which they are entitled to claim the enterprise value will make a difference for the value of debt and other claims, but not for the equity value.

Exhibit 11.2 Distribution of Unfunded US Pension Liability by Industry

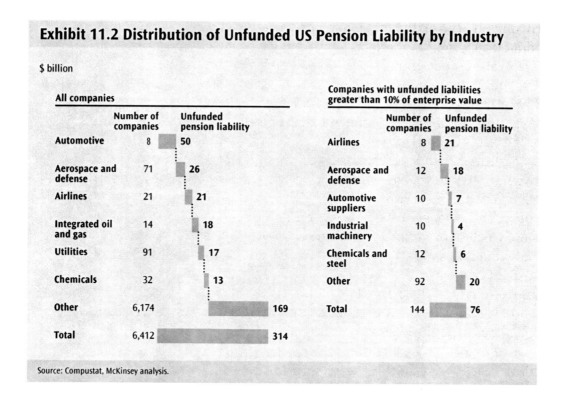

$ billion

Source: Compustat, McKinsey analysis.

icant difference when calculating equity value, especially for older companies. As Exhibit 11.2 shows, unfunded pension liabilities are significant, amounting to $314 billion for listed U.S. companies in 2002. These liabilities are concentrated in the automotive, aerospace, airline, oil and gas, and utility sectors.

Postretirement liabilities typically originate from pension plans and postretirement medical benefit plans. Plans are designated as either defined contribution or defined benefit. If a plan is structured on a *defined-contribution* basis, it is not relevant from a valuation perspective. In this case, the company makes fixed contributions into a fund, whose investment performance determines an employee's eventual benefits. The company is only liable to contribute a predetermined amount, and the employees bear the risk of inadequate performance of fund assets.

However, for *defined-benefit* plans, the company is obliged to provide specific retirement benefits to employees irrespective of the actual performance of the plan's funds. Under U.S. GAAP and IFRS, the fair market value of the plan's assets and liabilities are disclosed in the financial statements, but only in the footnotes. The resulting surplus (deficit) should be added to (subtracted from) enterprise value on an after-tax basis.

Do not use the book value of net retirement assets or liabilities as reported on the balance sheet. That amount does not include all of the capital gains and losses on the fund assets, nor recent changes to the fund's liabilities.

We illustrate our recommended approach through an analysis of the retirement liabilities for a large U.S. company. Exhibit 11.3 on page 350 shows a

653

Exhibit 11.3 Company Pension and Postretirement Liabilities, 2004

$ million

2004 Balance Sheet			2004 Notes to the balance sheet		
			Change in benefit obligation	Pension	Non-pension
Current assets			**Obligation at beginning of year**	**1,798**	**373**
Cash and cash equivalents	32		Acquisition adjustment	–	–
Accounts receivable	490		Service cost	50	4
Inventories	795		Interest cost	111	23
Other current assets	164		Plan amendments	(3)	(21)
Total current assets	**1,481**		Actuarial loss	23	(19)
			Participant contributions	3	–
Plant assets, net of depreciation	1,901		Curtailment/special termination benefits	3	–
Goodwill	1,900		Benefits paid	(119)	(27)
Other intangible assets	1,095		Foreign currency adjustment	27	–
Other assets	298		**Benefit obligation at end of year**	**1,893**	**333**
Total assets	**6,675**				
			Change in fair value of plan assets		
Current liabilities			Fair value at beginning of year	1,472	
Notes payable	810		Acquisition adjustment	–	
Payable to suppliers and others	607		Actual return on plan assets	184	
Accrued liabilities[1]	607		Employer contributions	65	
Dividend payable	65		Participants contributions	3	
Accrued income taxes	250		Benefits paid	(115)	
Total current liabilities	**2,339**		Foreign currency adjustment	18	
			Fair value at end of year	**1,627**	
Long-term debt	2,543				
Nonpension postretirement benefits	298		**Funded status recognized**		
Other liabilities	621		**Funded status at end of year**	**(266)**	**(333)**
Total liabilities	**5,801**		Unrecognized prior service cost	42	(33)
			Unrecognized loss	661	49
Shareowners' equity			**Net amount recognized**	**437**	**(317)**
Preferred stock	0				
Capital stock	20		**Amounts recognized**		
Additional paid-in capital	264		Prepaid benefit cost (included in Other Assets)	103	
Earnings retained in the business	5,642		Intangible asset (incl. in Other Intangible Assets)	27	
Capital stock in treasury	(4,848)		Accumulated other comprehensive loss	307	
Accum. other comprehensive loss	(204)		**Net amount recognized**	**437**	
Total shareowners' equity	**874**				
Total liabilities and equity	**6,675**				

[1]The current portion of nonpension postretirement liabilities included in accrued liabilities was $19 million at August 1, 2004 and August 3, 2003.

summary of the company's balance sheet and the overview of retirement liabilities in the footnotes. As of August 2004, the balance sheet has just one specific entry for retirement-related liabilities of $298 million. However, this is an incomplete picture. First, this liability represents only the nonpension postretirement benefits that the company provides. The assets and liabilities for pension benefits are hidden within other entries in the balance sheet.

Second, under U.S. GAAP, the amounts recognized in the balance sheet for pension and other retirement liabilities do not necessarily represent the fair value of the liabilities. In fact, for many companies, the book values in the balance sheet differ significantly from the fair value.

The notes to the balance sheet provide critical information for analyzing and valuing the company's retirement liabilities. Focus first on the pension benefits. The fair value of the total pension liabilities is $1,893 million, whereas the fair value of the fund assets is $1,627 million. Because of this underfunding, the pension plan represents a net liability to the company with a fair value of $266 million. However, since a portion of the losses and prior costs for the plan are classified as unrecognized losses and costs under U.S. GAAP, the book value in the balance sheet is higher. This occurs because annual gains and losses from plan assets are not charged to the income statement immediately, but only gradually over the course of several years. In our example, the company recognizes the pension plan as a net asset of $437 million (instead of a net liability of $266 million). The notes discuss how this net amount is spread out across multiple balance sheet categories: Other Assets, Other Intangible Assets, and Shareholders' Equity.

For the nonpension postretirement benefits, the fair value of the liability is $333 million, another net liability because there are no fund assets. Again, this value differs from the $317 million recognized as book value on the balance sheet—although not by a large amount. The book amount corresponds to the $298 million explicitly shown as a line item on the balance sheet plus an additional $19 million included in Accrued Liabilities.

In this case, the company's total net liability at fair value equals $599 million ($266 million for pension benefits plus $333 million for nonpension retirement benefits). On an after-tax basis, this converts to $389 million, which should be subtracted from enterprise value as a nonequity claim.[11]

To avoid double counting, make sure all other nonequity claims or nonoperating assets do not include retirement assets and liabilities. For example, in our case, $103 million of pension assets are included on the balance sheet under Other Assets. In the event you classify Other Assets as nonoperating assets, you should at least take out the $103 million before adding Other Assets to the equity value buildup.

Preferred equity The name *preferred equity* is somewhat misleading; preferred stock more closely resembles unsecured debt than equity and should be treated as a debt equivalent. Preferred stock dividends are similar to interest payments because they are often predetermined and can be withheld only under special conditions. If preferred equity is traded, use the market

---

[11] This example uses a nominal tax rate of 35 percent.

value to deduct from enterprise value. In other cases, make a separate DCF valuation, discounting the expected preferred dividends in perpetuity at the cost of unsecured debt.

Other debt equivalents This category includes all remaining liabilities for which no cash flows are included in the company's free cash flow projections. Here we discuss two examples: provisions and contingent liabilities.

Certain *provisions* other than retirement-related liabilities need to be deducted as nonequity financial claims. Following the guidelines in Chapter 7, we distinguish four types of provisions:

1. Ongoing operating provisions (e.g., for warranties and product returns) are already accounted for in the free cash flows and should therefore not be deducted from enterprise value.

2. Long-term operating provisions (e.g., for plant-decommissioning costs) should be deducted from enterprise value as debt equivalents. Because these provisions cover cash expenses that become payable in the long term, they are typically recorded at the discounted value in the balance sheet. In this case, there is no need to perform a separate DCF analysis, and you can use the book value of the liability in your valuation. Note that the book value does not equal the present value of all future expenses because the provision is gradually accumulated over the years until the expense becomes payable (see Chapter 7 for more details).

3. Nonoperating provisions (e.g., for restructuring charges resulting from layoffs) must be deducted from enterprise value as a debt equivalent. Although a discounted value would be ideal, the book value from the balance sheet is often a reasonable approximation. These provisions are recorded at a nondiscounted value because outlays are usually in the near term.

4. Income-smoothing provisions do not represent actual future cash outlays, so they should not be deducted from enterprise value. These provisions were common in several European countries but will disappear after 2005, when most European countries adopt IFRS.

Contingent liabilities are usually not disclosed in the balance sheet but are separately discussed in the notes to the balance sheet. Examples are possible liabilities from pending litigation and loan guarantees. When possible, estimate the associated expected after-tax cash flows (if the costs are tax deductible), and discount these at the cost of debt. Unfortunately, assessing the probability of such cash flows materializing is difficult, so the valuation should be interpreted with caution. Therefore, estimate the value of contingent liabilities for a range of probabilities to provide some boundaries on your final valuation.

Employee stock options   Many companies offer their employees stock options as part of their compensation. Options give the holder the right, but not the obligation, to buy company stock at a specified price, known as the exercise price. Since employee stock options have long maturities and the company's stock price could eventually rise above the exercise price, options can have great value.

Employee stock options affect a company valuation in two ways. First, the value of options that will be granted in the future needs to be captured in the free cash flow projections or in a separate DCF valuation, following the guidelines in Chapter 7. When captured in the free cash flow projections, the value of future options grants is included in the value of operations and should not be treated as a nonequity claim. Second, the value of options currently outstanding must be subtracted from enterprise value as a nonequity claim. Note, however, that the value of the options will depend on your estimate of enterprise value, and your option valuation should reflect this.

Under U.S. GAAP and IFRS, the notes disclose considerable information about employee options, including the number of options currently outstanding grouped by exercise prices and maturities, as well as the number of options that are vested. In general, employee options are unvested at the time of granting. Options can be exercised or sold only after they are vested, which usually happens over several years of continuous employment. For valuation purposes, deduct the value of all vested options. For unvested options, make an adjustment to account for the likelihood that some employees will leave the company and never exercise their options.

The following approaches can be used for valuing employee options:

- We recommend using the estimated market value from *option-valuation models,* such as Black-Scholes or more advanced binomial (lattice) models. Under U.S. GAAP and IFRS, the notes to the balance sheet report the total value of all employee stock options outstanding, as estimated by such option-pricing models. Note that this value is a good approximation only if your estimate of share price is close to the one underlying the option values in the annual report. Otherwise, you need to create a new valuation using an option-pricing model. The notes disclose the information required for valuation.[12]

- A second method, the *exercise value approach,* provides only a lower bound for the value of employee options. It assumes that all options are exercised immediately and thereby ignores the time value of the options. The resulting valuation error increases as options have longer time to maturity, the company's stock has higher volatility,

---

[12] For more on the valuation of employee stock options, see, for example, J. Hull and A. White, "How to Value Employee Stock Options," *Financial Analysts Journal,* 60(1) (January/February 2004): 114–119.

Exhibit 11.4 Employee Stock Options Example

Company data			Option value method	Exercise value method
Enterprise value ($ million)	11,000	Enterprise value ($ million)	11,000	11,000
Debt value ($ million)	(1,000)	Debt value ($ million)	(1,000)	(1,000)
Nondiluted equity value ($ million)	10,000	Option exercise proceeds ($ million)		900
Number of shares nondiluted	90.0	Option value ($ million)	(481)	
Value per share nondiluted	111.1	Equity value ($ million)	9,519	10,900
Stock options		Number of shares nondiluted	90.0	90.0
Number of options outstanding	10.0	Number of new shares	–	10.0
Option exercise price	90.0	Number of shares diluted	90.0	100.0
Option maturity (years)	5.0			
Stock volatility (annualized percent)	35.0	Value per share	105.8	109.0
Risk free rate (percent)	5.5			

and the company's share price is closer to the exercise price. Given that a more accurate valuation is already disclosed in the annual report, we do not recommend this method. However, it is still quite common among practitioners.

Exhibit 11.4 provides a brief example of these two methods. Assume that you have estimated the enterprise value of a company at $11 billion. The company has straight debt with a market value of $1 billion and 10 million unexercised, fully vested stock options. The number of common shares currently outstanding is 90 million. The exercise price for all options is $90, which will acquire one share of common stock. If you did not value the options separately but simply divided the nondiluted equity value by the number of undiluted shares, you would overestimate the value per share at $111.1 instead of the true value of $105.8, derived next.

The column titled "Option value method" in Exhibit 11.4 shows the equity value per share when employee options are incorporated using an option valuation model. We assume a remaining time to maturity of five years for the options, a risk-free rate of 5.5 percent, and a volatility of the company's stock of 35 percent. Applying a Black-Scholes option-pricing model adjusted for the dilution effect, the estimated market value of the options amounts to $481 million.[13] The value per share of common equity is then $105.8.

---

[13] For illustration purposes, we adjusted the Black-Scholes option price only for the dilution effect of new-share issuance by multiplying the option price by the following expression:

$$\frac{\text{Number of Existing Shares Outstanding}}{\left(\text{Number of Existing Shares Outstanding} + \text{Number of New Shares Issued}\right)}$$

The exercise value method overestimates the value per share of common equity because it assumes immediate conversion of all options. The only advantage of the method is that it is simple to apply. Assuming full conversion, the company in this example receives $900 million in exercise proceeds and would have to provide 10 million common shares to the option holders. In the exercise value method, the company either retains the exercise proceeds or uses these to repay debt so that the resulting equity value will amount to $10.9 billion. Taking into account the 10 million shares handed out to the options holders, the resulting value per share is $109.

In this simplified example, the valuation error from applying the exercise value method is only 3 percent. However, for companies with a relatively large number of options outstanding or exercise prices well above the current stock price, the difference can be quite significant.

Convertible debt   Convertible bonds are corporate bonds that can be exchanged for common equity at a predetermined conversion ratio. A convertible bond is essentially a package of a straight corporate bond plus a call option on equity (the conversion option).[14] Because the conversion option can have significant value, this form of debt requires treatment different from that of regular corporate debt.

The value of convertibles depends on the enterprise value. In contrast to straight debt, neither the book value nor the simple DCF value of bond cash flows is a good proxy for the value of convertibles. If the convertible bonds are actively traded, you could use their market values, but these are suitable only if your estimated stock price is near the traded stock price. If not, there are two alternatives:

1. We recommend using an *option-based valuation* for convertible debt. In contrast to the treatment of stock options, however, annual reports do not provide any information on the value of convertible debt. Accurate valuation of convertible bonds with option-based models is not straightforward, but following methods outlined by John Ingersoll,[15] you can apply an adjusted Black-Scholes option-pricing model for a reasonable approximation.

2. The *conversion value approach* assumes that all convertible bonds are immediately exchanged for equity and ignores the time value of the

[14] See R. Brealey and S. Myers, *Principles of Corporate Finance*, 7th ed. (New York: McGraw-Hill, 2002), ch. 23. If you are doing a discounted-cash-flow-to-equity valuation, you subtract only the value of the conversion option from your DCF valuation. The straight-debt component of the convertible debt has already been included in the equity cash flows.

[15] The convertible bond can be modeled as a call option on the fraction of equity that the bondholders receive after conversion, with the face value of the bond as exercise price. See J. Ingersoll, "A Contingent Claims Valuation of Convertible Securities," *Journal of Financial Economics*, 4 (1977): 289–322.

conversion option. It leads to reasonable results when the conversion option is deep in the money, meaning the bond is more valuable when converted into equity than held for future coupon and principal payments.

We illustrate both methods in Exhibit 11.5. This exhibit presents an example similar to the one used for the valuation of stock options. In this case, the company has no options outstanding but instead 10 million convertible bonds with a face value of $100. The coupon is 2 percent per year, and the bonds have five years to maturity. The cost of debt is 6.5 percent. The conversion ratio for the bonds is 0.8, meaning 10 bonds can be converted into 8 common shares of equity.

Using a simple convertible-bond valuation model, we estimate a value of $108.2 per bond. This value consists of the present value of coupons and principal repayment of $81.3 plus a conversion option value of $26.9. Deducting the value of all convertible bonds and straight debt from the enterprise value, we arrive at an equity value of $8,918 million and a value per share of $99.1.

Under the conversion value approach, we convert all bonds into equity and simply divide the undiluted equity value by a total of $90 + 0.8 \times 10 = 98$ shares. In contrast to the exercise of stock options, there is no cash inflow

Exhibit 11.5 Convertible Debt Example

Company data			Convertible valuation method	Conversion value method
Enterprise value ($ million)	11,000	Enterprise value ($ million)	11,000	11,000
Debt value ($ million)	(1,000)	Debt value ($ million)	(1,000)	(1,000)
Convertibles face value ($ million)	(1,000)	Convertibles value ($ million)	(1,082)	–
Nondiluted equity value ($ million)	9,000	**Equity value ($ million)**	**8,918**	**10,000**
Number of shares nondiluted	90.0			
Value per share nondiluted	100.0	Number of shares nondiluted	90.0	90.0
		Number of new shares	–	8.0
Convertible bond		**Number of shares diluted**	90.0	98.0
Number of bonds	10			
Face value	100.0	**Value per share**	**99.1**	**102.0**
Coupon rate (percent)	2.0			
Years to maturity	5			
Conversion ratio	0.8			
Value per bond				
Bond component	81.3			
Conversion option	26.9			
Total	108.2			
Stock volatility (annualized percent)	35.0			
Risk free rate (percent)	5.5			
Cost of debt (percent)	6.5			

for the company. Instead, we exclude the value of the convertible bonds from the nonequity claims. This leads to an estimated value per share of $102, which overestimates the true value.

Minority interests When a company controls a subsidiary without full ownership, the subsidiary's financial statements still must be fully consolidated in the group accounts. Without any further adjustment, the full value of the subsidiary would be improperly included in the parent company valuation. Therefore, you need to deduct the value of the third-party minority stake in the subsidiary as a nonequity financial claim.

Because minority stakes are to a certain extent the mirror image of nonconsolidated subsidiaries, the recommended valuation for minority interest is similar to that of nonconsolidated subsidiaries; see the corresponding section for more details. If the minority stake is publicly listed, as in the case of minority carve-outs (see Chapter 16), use the proportional market value owned by outsiders to deduct from enterprise value. Alternatively, you can perform a separate valuation using a DCF approach, multiples, or a tracking portfolio, depending on the amount of information available. Remember, however, that minority interest is a claim on a subsidiary, not the entire company. Thus, any valuation should be directly related to the subsidiary and not the company as a whole.

Calculating Value per Share

The final step in a valuation is to calculate the value per share. Assuming that you have used an option-based-valuation approach for all options and convertible securities, you should divide the total equity value by the number of *undiluted* shares outstanding. Use the undiluted number of shares because the values of convertible debt and stock options have already been deducted from the enterprise value as nonequity claims.

The number of shares outstanding is the gross number of shares issued, less the number of shares held in treasury. Most U.S. and European companies report the number of shares issued and those held in treasury under shareholders' equity. However, some companies show treasury shares as an investment asset, which they are not from an economic perspective. Treat them, instead, as a reduction in the number of shares outstanding.

If you use the conversion and exercise value method to account for convertible debt and stock options, you generate a different value for equity and should divide by the *diluted* number of shares.

VALUATION UNDER MULTIPLE SCENARIOS

The purpose of valuing a company is often to guide a management decision related to acquisition, divestiture, or adoption of internal strategic initiatives. Since most of these decisions involve uncertainty and risk, consider making financial projections under multiple scenarios. The scenarios should reflect different assumptions regarding future macroeconomic, industry, or business developments, as well as the corresponding strategic response by the company. Collectively, the scenarios should capture the future states of the world that would have the most impact on future value creation and a reasonable chance of occurrence.

Assess how likely it is that the key assumptions underlying each scenario will change, and assign each scenario a probability of occurrence. When analyzing the scenarios, critically review your assumptions on the following variables:

- *Broad economic conditions:* How critical are these forecasts to the results? Some industries are more dependent on basic economic conditions than others. Home building, for example, is highly correlated with the overall health of the economy. Branded food processing, in contrast, is less affected by broad economic trends.
- *Competitive structure of the industry:* A scenario that assumes substantial increases in market share is less likely in a highly competitive and concentrated market than in an industry with fragmented and inefficient competition.
- *Internal capabilities of the company* that are necessary to achieve the business results predicted in the scenario: Can the company develop its products on time and manufacture them within the expected range of costs?
- *Financing capabilities of the company* (which are often implicit in the valuation): If debt or excess marketable securities are excessive relative to the company's targets, how will the company resolve the imbalance? Should the company raise equity if too much debt is projected? Should the company be willing to raise equity at its current market price?

Complete the alternative scenarios suggested by the preceding analyses. The process of examining initial results may well uncover unanticipated questions that are best resolved by creating additional scenarios. In this way, the valuation process is inherently circular. Performing a valuation often provides insights that lead to additional scenarios and analyses. Scenarios not only help you deal with the uncertainty in your financial projections, they also enable you to value nonoperating assets and nonequity claims more consistently, as we discussed in the beginning of this chapter.

In Exhibit 11.6, we provide a simplified example of a scenario approach to DCF valuation. The company being valued faces great uncertainty because of a new product launch for which it has spent considerable R&D.

Exhibit 11.6 Example of a Scenario Approach to DCF Valuation

$, percent

Financial projections

Scenario #1

	2004	2005	2006	2007	2008	2009	2010	CV
Growth (percent)	5.0	6.0	8.0	9.0	6.0	5.0	3.5	3.5
Operating margin[1] (percent)	7.5	10.0	12.0	10.0	10.0	10.0	10.0	
Capital turns	1.00	1.00	1.05	1.10	1.05	1.00	1.00	
ROIC (percent)	7.5	10.0	12.6	11.0	10.5	10.0	10.0	10.0
Revenues	3,000	3,180	3,434	3,743	3,968	4,167	4,312	
NOPLAT	225	318	412	374	397	417	431	
Invested capital	3,000	3,180	3,271	3,403	3,779	4,167	4,312	
NOPLAT		318	412	374	397	417	431	431
Net investment		(180)	(91)	(132)	(376)	(387)	(146)	
Free cash flow (FCF)		138	321	242	21	29	285	7,253
Discount factor		0.93	0.87	0.80	0.75	0.70	0.65	0.65
PV(FCF)		128	278	195	16	20	185	4,700

Scenario #1

Value of operations	5,522
Nonoperating assets	614
Interest-bearing debt	(3,500)
Equity value	2,635

67% Probability

Scenario #2

	2004	2005	2006	2007	2008	2009	2010	CV
Growth (percent)	5.0	3.0	(1.0)	(1.0)	1.5	1.5	1.5	1.5
Operating margin[1] (percent)	7.5	5.0	3.0	2.0	3.0	4.0	6.5	
Capital turns	1.00	1.03	1.00	0.97	0.97	0.97	0.97	
ROIC (percent)	7.5	5.2	3.0	1.9	2.9	3.9	6.3	7.5
Revenues	3,000	3,090	3,059	3,029	3,074	3,120	3,167	
NOPLAT	225	155	92	61	92	125	206	
Invested capital	3,000	3,000	3,059	3,122	3,169	3,217	3,265	
NOPLAT		155	92	61	92	125	206	206
Net investment		–	(59)	(63)	(47)	(48)	(48)	
Free cash flow (FCF)		155	33	(3)	45	77	158	2,786
Discount factor		0.93	0.87	0.80	0.75	0.70	0.65	0.65
PV(FCF)		144	28	(2)	34	54	102	1,805

Scenario #2

Value of operations	2,165
Nonoperating assets	241
Interest-bearing debt	(2,406)
Equity value	–

33% Probability

Probability weighted equity value: 1,766

Note: WACC: 7.5%, Tax rate: 35%, Debt at face value: $3,500.
[1] After-tax operating margin.

If the product succeeds, revenue growth will nearly double over the next few years. Returns on capital will peak at above 12 percent and remain at 10 percent in perpetuity. If the product launch fails, however, growth will continue to erode as the company's current products become obsolete. Operating margins and returns on capital will decline to levels below the cost of capital. The company only earns its cost of capital in the long term beyond 2010.

The two scenarios in Exhibit 11.6 reflect this double-or-quit future. Under the favorable scenario, the DCF value of operations equals $5,522. The nonoperating assets consist primarily of nonconsolidated subsidiaries, and given their own reliance on the product launch, they are valued at the implied NOPLAT multiple for the parent company, $614. We next deduct the face value of the debt outstanding at $3,500, as the bond was issued at par and interest rates have not changed significantly since the debt was issued. The resulting equity value is $2,635 million.

Under the unfavorable scenario, the product launch fails and the DCF value of operations is only $2,165. In this scenario, the value of the subsidiaries is much lower ($241), as their business outlook has deteriorated due to the failure of the new product. The value of the debt is no longer $3,500 in this scenario. Instead, the debt holders would end up with $2,406 by seizing the enterprise. Obviously, the common equity would have no value.

Given the approximately two-thirds probability of success for the product, the probability-weighted equity value across both scenarios amounts to $1,766. Note that the probability-weighted value of the debt would be $3,139—below its face value.

When using the scenario approach, make sure to generate a complete valuation buildup from value of operations to equity value. For example, using a scenario approach solely for the value of operations and subsidiaries and then deducting debt at its face value would seriously underestimate the equity value. In this case, the equity value would be $361 too low ($3,500 face value minus $3,139 probability-weighted value of debt).[16] A similar argument holds for nonoperating assets.

By creating scenarios, you can also better understand the company's key priorities. In our example, it appears that searching for ways to improve the financial performance in the downside scenario by, for example, reducing costs or cutting capital expenditures is unlikely to affect shareholder value, unless the changes can generate at least $1,100 in present value. Given the current operating profit of $225, this seems unlikely. In contrast,

---

[16] This also explains why using the market price of bonds or debt in your valuation can lead to errors if the bonds trade at a significant discount to their face value due to default risk (see this chapter's discussion on the treatment of debt as a nonequity claim). Deducting the market price of such bonds from the probability-weighted value of operations would be correct only if your assumptions on default scenarios and probabilities precisely reflect those of bond investors in the capital market.

increasing the odds of a successful launch has a much greater impact on shareholder value. Increasing the success probability from two-thirds to three-fourths would boost shareholder value by 12 percent.

VERIFYING VALUATION RESULTS

After estimating the equity value, you should perform several checks to test the logic of your results, minimize the possibility of errors, and ensure that you have a good understanding of the forces driving the valuation.

Consistency Check

The first series of checks concerns the logic of your model and valuation: Are the outcomes consistent with your assumptions?

Ensure that all *checks and balances* in your model are in place. Your model should reflect the following fundamental equilibrium relations:

- For the unadjusted financial statements, does the balance sheet balance in every year? Does the net income flow correctly into dividends paid and retained earnings? Are the sources of cash equal to the uses of cash?

- For the rearranged financial statements, does the sum of invested capital plus nonoperating assets balance with the financing sources? Is NOPLAT identical when calculated top down from sales and bottom up from net income? Does net income correctly link to dividends and retained earnings in adjusted equity? Does the change in excess cash and debt line up with the cash flow statement?

If these relations do not hold, there is a logical error in the model.

The next step is to check that your valuation results correctly reflect *value driver economics.* If the projected returns on invested capital are above the WACC, the value of operations should be above the book value of invested capital. If, in addition, growth is high, value of operations should be considerably above book value. If not, a computational error has probably been made. Compare your valuation results with a back-of-the-envelope value estimate based on the key value driver formula, taking long-term average growth and return on capital as key inputs.

Finally, make sure that patterns of *key financial and operating ratios* are consistent with economic logic:

- Are the patterns intended? For example, does invested capital turnover increase over time for sound economic reasons or simply because you modeled future capital expenditures as a fixed percentage of revenues? Are future cash tax rates changing dramatically because you forecasted deferred tax assets as a percentage of revenues or operating profit?

- Are the patterns reasonable? Avoid large step-changes in key assumptions from one year to the next because these will distort key ratios and could lead to false interpretations. For example, a strong single-year improvement in capital efficiency could make capital expenditures in that year negative, leading to an unrealistically high cash flow.

- Is a steady state reached for the company's economics by the end of the explicit forecasting period, that is, when you apply a continuing-value formula? A company achieves a steady state only when its free cash flows are growing at a constant rate. If this is not the case, extend the explicit forecast period while keeping the key performance ratios constant.

Sensitivity Analysis

The second step is to check whether your model's results are robust under alternative assumptions. Start with the *key value drivers* such as growth and return on invested capital, which you can further break down into operating margins and capital turnover. If you change the projected growth and returns, does the valuation change in the way it should? For example, if the return on invested capital is near the WACC, is value fairly insensitive to changes in growth, as it should be? If you increase capital turnover assumptions, do ROIC and value rise?

Next, dive deeper into the model's logic and check how changes in sector-specific *operating value drivers* affect the final valuation. For example, if you increase customer churn rates for a telecommunications company, does company value decrease? Can you explain with back-of-the-envelope estimates why the change is so large (or so small)?

Plausibility Analysis

Once you believe the model's logic is correct, you should test whether the final results are plausible.

If the company is listed, compare your results with the *market value.* If your estimate is far from the market value, do not jump to the conclusion that the market is wrong. Your default assumption should be that the market is right, unless you have specific indications that not all relevant information has been incorporated in the share price, for example due to low free float or low liquidity of the stock.

Perform a sound *multiples analysis.* Calculate the implied forward-looking valuation multiples of the operating value over, for example, EBITA, and compare these with equivalently defined multiples of traded peer-group companies. We explain in Chapter 12 how to do a proper multiples analysis. Make sure you can explain any significant differences with peer-group companies in terms of the companies' value drivers and underlying business characteristics or strategy.

The Art of Valuation

Valuation can be highly sensitive to small changes in assumptions about the future. Take a look at the sensitivity of a typical company with a forward-looking P/E ratio of 15 to 16. Increasing the cost of capital for this company by 0.5 percentage points will decrease the value by approximately 10 percent. Changing the growth rate for the next 15 years by 1 percentage point annually will change the value by about 6 percent. For high-growth companies, the sensitivity is even greater. The sensitivity is highest when interest rates are low, as they have been since the late 1990s.

In light of this sensitivity, it should be no surprise that the market value of a company fluctuates over time. Historical volatilities for a typical stock over the past several years have been around 25 percent per annum. Taking this as an estimate for future volatility, the market value of a typical company could well fluctuate around its expected value by 15 percent over the next month.[17]

We typically aim for a valuation range of plus or minus 15 percent, which is similar to the range used by many investment bankers. Even valuation professionals cannot always generate exact estimates. In other words, keep your aspirations for precision in check.

HEINEKEN CASE

In this chapter's case, we complete and analyze the Heineken valuation. First, we calculate the equity value of Heineken for the business-as-usual scenario. We then value

---

[17] Based on a 95 percent confidence interval for the end-of-month price of a stock with an expected return of 9 percent per year.

the other two scenarios we developed for the case in Chapter 8. Finally, we estimate a probability-weighted value.

VALUE IN THE BUSINESS-AS-USUAL SCENARIO

Exhibits 11.7 and 11.8 show the calculation of the value of Heineken's operations, using the DCF and economic profit approaches, respectively. Under both methods, the value of Heineken's operations is €16.855 billion.

The value of operations includes a midyear adjustment equal to one-half of a year's value discounted at Heineken's WACC. This is to adjust for the fact that we conservatively discounted the free cash flows and economic profits as if they were entirely realized at the end of each year, when, in fact, cash flows occur (cycles notwithstanding) evenly throughout the year. The six-month factor assumes that cash flows will come in on average in the middle of the year.

Under the business-as-usual scenario, Heineken's equity value is €13.466 billion, or €34.35 per share, as shown in Exhibit 11.9 on page 366. To calculate the market equity value, we added the market value of nonoperating assets such as excess cash, financial fixed assets, and nonconsolidated participating interests to the value of operations; this sum is the enterprise value. We then subtract debt, retirement liabilities, minority interest, and the restructuring provision to obtain the equity value.

Exhibit 11.7 Heineken: DCF Valuation

€ million

	Free cash flow	Discount factor	Present value of FCF
2004	(107)	0.9302	(100)
2005	181	0.8653	156
2006	320	0.8050	258
2007	477	0.7488	357
2008	648	0.6966	452
2009	975	0.6480	632
2010	1,009	0.6028	608
2011	1,039	0.5607	583
2012	1,071	0.5216	558
2013	1,103	0.4852	535
2014	1,136	0.4513	513
2015	1,170	0.4199	491
2016	1,205	0.3906	471
2017	1,241	0.3633	451
2018	1,278	0.3380	432
Continuing value	29,173	0.3380	9,860
Operating value			16,257
Mid-year adjustment factor			1.04
Operating value (discounted to current month)			**16,855**

Exhibit 11.8 Heineken: Economic Profit Valuation

€ million

	Economic profit before goodwill	Discount factor	Present value of economic profit
2004	512	0.9302	476
2005	540	0.8653	467
2006	570	0.8050	459
2007	597	0.7488	447
2008	618	0.6966	431
2009	619	0.6480	401
2010	637	0.6028	384
2011	656	0.5607	368
2012	676	0.5216	353
2013	696	0.4852	338
2014	717	0.4513	324
2015	739	0.4199	310
2016	761	0.3906	297
2017	784	0.3633	285
2018	807	0.3380	273
Continuing value	18,387	0.3380	6,214
Present value of economic profit			11,826
Invested capital excluding goodwill (beginning of forecast)			5,670
Less: present value of investments in goodwill			(1,239)
Value of operations			16,257
Mid-year adjustment factor			1.04
Operating value (discounted to current month)			16,855

Heineken's enterprise value includes three nonoperating assets:

1. Financial fixed assets of €671 million are primarily receivables from customers. We valued these loans at book value.

2. Nonconsolidated participating interests are less than 50 percent investments in other companies. We valued these at a multiple of income from these investments, similar to the multiples for all brewers. Heineken's share of income from these companies was €30 million in 2003 (excluding a one-time gain from the sale of investments of €71 million), which we multiplied by a typical brewer's multiple of 16 to estimate the value of Heineken's interest at €480 million.

3. Heineken's excess cash of €1.231 billion is valued at book value.

By adding the nonoperating assets to the value of operations, we determine an enterprise value of €19.237 billion. The value of Heineken's debt, minority interest, and retirement liabilities were estimated in Chapter 10 when we estimated Heineken's

Exhibit 11.9 Heineken: Value of Equity

€ million

Value of operations	16,855
Value of financial fixed assets	671
Value of nonconsolidated participating interests	480
Excess cash	1,231
Enterprise value	**19,237**
Value of debt	(3,922)
Value of retirement liabilities	(526)
Minority interest	(1,030)
Restructuring provision	(293)
Equity value	**13,466**
Number of shares outstanding (million)	392
Value per share	**€34.35**

cost of capital. We also subtract the restructuring provision, which we expect to be paid out in the next year. (Since the payout of the restructuring provision will not flow through free cash flow, it must be subtracted here.) There is no adjustment for executive stock options because Heineken does not use options to compensate its managers.

The value of operations for the business-as-usual case is about three times the invested capital (excluding goodwill). This is consistent with Heineken's projected ROIC being about twice its cost of capital with modest growth. (With zero growth, the ratio of DCF value to invested capital will equal the ratio of ROIC to WACC.)

ADDITIONAL SCENARIOS AND PROBABILITY WEIGHTING

We also valued the other two scenarios for Heineken, the operating-improvement scenario and the aggressive-acquisitions scenario. The results are summarized in Exhibit 11.10.

In the operating-improvement scenario, we projected that Heineken could improve margins and capital turnover near to the peak levels it achieved over the last five years. This brings Heineken's ROIC up to 21 percent by the end of the forecast, versus 15 percent in the business-as-usual scenario. Under the operating-improvement scenario, Heineken's value is €47.00 per share, a 37 percent premium to the business-as-usual scenario.

For the aggressive-acquisitions scenario, we forecast growth from acquisitions at the five-year average historical level of 7.2 percent from 2005 to 2010, then slowing

Exhibit 11.10 Heineken: Summary of Scenario Values

	Scenario		
	Operating capital utilization improvements	Business as usual	High premium acquisitions
Average revenue growth, 2004–2008 (percent)	6.5	6.5	10.2
Average EBITA/turnover 2004–2008 (percent)	13.8	12.6	12.6
Average ROIC (excluding goodwill) 2004–2008 (percent)	20.0	16.0	16.0
Enterprise value (€ million)	23.9	19.2	15.1
Equity value (€ million)	18.4	13.5	9.6
Equity value per share (€ million)	46.97	34.35	24.55
Probability	25%	60%	15%
Expected value per share		€36.03	

by 1 percent per year. Under this scenario, competition for acquisitions heats up, and Heineken is forced to pay high premiums to continue its acquisition growth. We forecast goodwill to increase to 150 percent of revenues from acquisitions during the acquisition year. Operating performance remains constant. Under the aggressive-acquisitions scenario, Heineken's value is €24.55 per share, a 29 percent discount relative to the business-as-usual case.

Finally, we weighted the scenario values with probabilities and arrived at an estimated value of €36.03 per share, as shown in Exhibit 11.10. The estimated value is about 7 percent higher than Heineken's market value of €33.65 per share as of February 2004. We assigned a higher probability to the upside scenario because we believe that the recent pressures on margins will force Heineken management to focus on operating improvement rather than acquisition growth. That said, the temptation of growth through acquisitions is always lurking and may overcome the focus on operations.

While the scenario approach estimates a value close to the market value, the real insight from the scenario approach is the spread of values. Even in the case of a profitable but modestly growing company like Heineken, the spread of values across the scenarios is plus or minus 30 percent, a substantial opportunity (or risk) for both investors and managers.

Finally, we conducted a sensitivity analysis to complement the scenario analysis. Exhibit 11.11 on page 368 summarizes the impact on Heineken's value when we change the forecasts for revenue growth, margins, capital turnover, and cost of capital. It is impossible to compare the sensitivities directly, because we don't know whether the changes in variables are equally likely or difficult. For example, we don't know whether it is more or less difficult to increase capital turnover by 0.1 times or to increase margins by 1 percent.

671

Exhibit 11.11 Heineken: Sensitivity Analysis

	Base value 2004–2008 (percent)	Change	Change in equity value (€ billions)	(percent)
Organic revenue growth	3.0	1.0 %	1.6	11.5
Adjusted EBITA margin	12.7	1.0 %	1.8	13.0
Capital turnover	1.6	0.1 times	0.2	1.1
WACC	7.5	(0.5) %	2.4	17.5

In any case, it is evident that Heineken's value is highly sensitive to changes in its cost of capital (a 17 percent change in value for a 0.5 percentage point change in WACC). Given the uncertainty in estimating WACC, this suggests a range of accuracy for the valuation. On the operating front, the value is moderately sensitive to both revenue growth and margin, although we suspect that margin increases might be more achievable and sustainable than accelerating growth in a mature market like beer.

REVIEW QUESTIONS

1. From a manager's perspective, what is the purpose of computing the firm's enterprise value?

2. Once a manager computes enterprise value, what additional process steps need to be undertaken to determine the value of its equity position? Compare and contrast these additional steps to those of the cash-flow-to-equity model.

3. Identify the accounting standards specifying the manner and methods to be followed when consolidating a subsidiary's financial statements into those of the parent's financial statements.

4. If a parent company is not able to consolidate a subsidiary's financial position, explain how the degree of equity ownership impacts the parent company's cash flow position.

5. Discuss the relationship of the following nonoperating assets to the estimation of enterprise value: tax loss carry forwards, discontinued operations, investment in excess real estate, and investments in underutilized assets.

6. Identify and define the basic categories of nonequity claims. Discuss how each of the following nonequity claims could lead to significant adjustments to a corporate valuation model: preferred equity and convertible bonds, employee stock options, and unfunded pension liabilities.

7. What should a company consider when estimating the value of employee stock options? Identify the main factors that impact the value of employee stock options.

8. Define scenario analysis. What benefits are likely to accrue to a manager when scenario analysis is undertaken in conjunction with computing enterprise value?

9. Identify the steps that should be taken to verify the results obtained from estimating enterprise value.

10. How are convertible debt instruments defined in an annual report? Discuss the impact of the financial statement treatment of convertible debt to the estimation of equity value.

12

Using Multiples
for Valuation

Discounted cash flow analysis is the most accurate and flexible method for valuing projects, divisions, and companies. Any analysis, however, is only as accurate as the forecasts it relies on. Errors in estimating the key ingredients of corporate value—ingredients such as a company's ROIC, growth rate, and WACC—can lead to mistakes in valuation and, ultimately, to strategic errors.

A careful multiples analysis—comparing a company's multiples versus those of comparable companies—can be useful in making such forecasts and the DCF valuations they inform more accurate. Properly executed, such an analysis can help test the plausibility of cash flow forecasts, explain mismatches between a company's performance and that of its competitors, and support useful discussions about whether the company is strategically positioned to create more value than other industry players. As you seek to understand why a company's multiples are higher or lower than those of the competition, multiples analysis can also generate insights into the key factors creating value in an industry.

Yet multiples are frequently misunderstood and even more often misapplied. Many financial analysts, for example, calculate an industry-average price-to-earnings (P/E) ratio and multiply it by a company's earnings to establish a "fair" valuation. The use of the industry average, however, overlooks the fact that companies, even in the same industry, can have drastically different expected growth rates, returns on invested capital, and capital structures. The P/E ratio can exhibit flaws even when comparing companies with identical prospects, since it commingles operating and nonoperating items. By contrast, a carefully designed multiples analysis *can* provide valuable insights about a company and its competitors.

675

In this chapter, we step through the process of how to create, interpret, and apply multiples in a valuation setting. We examine how to choose which multiples are the most effective and how to create multiples that reflect a company's core operations. Although many claim multiples are an easy-to-apply valuation method, the converse is true. As you will see, a well-done multiples analysis requires many of the same adjustments (and effort) as traditional DCF.

COMPARABLES ANALYSIS: AN EXAMPLE

Each week, investment banking research analysts report the stock market performance of Home Depot and other American retailers by creating a valuation *comps* table (*comps* means "comparable companies"). Exhibit 12.1 is an abridged version of a typical valuation summary. We use the exhibit to demonstrate how multiples are created and reported.

Reported in the summary are each company's week-end closing price and market capitalization. The table also reports analyst projections for each company's earnings per share (EPS). To compare the valuations across companies, each company's share price is divided by the projected EPS to obtain a forward-looking P/E ratio. To derive Home Depot's forward-looking P/E ratio of 13.3, divide its week-end closing price of $33 by its projected 2005 EPS of $2.48. Although the calculation is not detailed in the summary tables, a forward-looking enterprise-value-to-EBITDA ratio is also reported.

A challenge of using these ratios involves selecting the appropriate companies for comparison. For the period covered in Exhibit 12.1, Home

Exhibit 12.1 Hardline Retailing Valuation Summary, July 2004

Hardline retailing	Ticker	Stock price ($) July 23, 2004	Market capitalization $ million	Earnings per share (EPS), ($)[1] 2004	2005	Foward-looking multiples, 2005 EBITDA[2]	P/E
Home improvement							
Home Depot	HD	33.00	74,250	2.18	2.48	7.1	13.3
Lowe's	LOW	48.39	39,075	2.86	3.36	7.3	14.4
Home furnishing							
Bed Bath & Beyond	BBBY	34.89	10,697	1.58	1.83	9.9	19.1
Linens 'n Things	LIN	25.86	1,152	1.86	2.13	5.1	12.1
Consumer electronics							
Best Buy	BBY	47.11	15,537	2.88	3.41	6.3	13.8
Circuit City	CC	13.58	2,708	0.55	0.61	4.4	22.3
Benchmark index							
S&P 500	SPX	1,086.20		64.74	69.76		15.6

[1] Credit Suisse First Boston (CSFB) analysts' projections for EPS by calendar year.
[2] EBITDA = earnings before interest, taxes, depreciation, and amortization; EBITDA and P/E are reported by calendar year.
Source: *Hardlines Retailing: Weekly Review*, CSFB, New York, July 26, 2004.

Depot and its primary competitor, Lowe's, traded at nearly identical multiples. The price-to-earnings ratios for the two companies differed by only 8 percent, and their enterprise-to-EBITDA ratios differed by only 3 percent. This similarity does not hold, however, when we expand the set of comparables. For the entire hardline retailing group, enterprise multiples vary from 4.4 to 9.9. Why such a large range? Investors have different expectations for each company's ability to create value going forward. Therefore, from a valuation perspective, not every company in the sample is truly comparable.

Understanding what drives these systematic differences in multiples is critical to using multiples appropriately. We discuss the drivers of multiples next.

WHAT BESIDES GROWTH DRIVES MULTIPLES?

Many investors and corporate managers swayed by the teachings of Wall Street pundits believe that multiples are driven by earnings growth. David and Tom Gardner of The Motley Fool investor web site write, "The P/E generally reflects the market's expectations for the growth of a given company."[1] Academics further this perception in their own writings. In their core finance text, Professors Richard Brealey and Stewart Myers write, "The high P/E shows that investors think that the firm has good growth opportunities, that its earnings are relatively safe and deserve a low [cost of capital], or both."[2]

Growth does indeed drive multiples, but *only* when combined with a healthy return on invested capital. To see how both ROIC and growth drive multiples, we reexamine the key value driver formula, introduced in Chapter 3:

$$V = \frac{\text{NOPLAT}\left(1 - \dfrac{g}{\text{ROIC}}\right)}{\text{WACC} - g}$$

The key value driver is a cash-flow-based formula that has been rearranged to focus on NOPLAT, ROIC, growth (g), and the WACC. To build a pretax enterprise-value multiple, disaggregate NOPLAT into EBITA and the company's cash tax rate (T):

---

[1] David Gardner and Tom Gardner, "The Fool Ratio: The Growth Rate Examined," www.fool.com/School/TheGrowthRate.htm.

[2] Many readers interpret "good growth opportunities" as implying "plentiful growth opportunities." This is incorrect. Instead, Brealey and Myers write "good growth opportunities" to imply "value-creating growth opportunities." This difference is critical. Richard Brealey and Stewart Myers, *Principles of Corporate Finance* (New York: McGraw-Hill, 2002).

$$V = \frac{\text{EBITA}(1-T)\left(1-\dfrac{g}{\text{ROIC}}\right)}{\text{WACC} - g}$$

and divide both sides by EBITA:

$$\frac{V}{\text{EBITA}} = \frac{(1-T)\left(1-\dfrac{g}{\text{ROIC}}\right)}{\text{WACC} - g}$$

The resulting equation is an algebraic representation of a commonly used multiple, enterprise value to EBITA. The multiple is similar to the P/E ratio but focuses on enterprise value, rather than equity. (We return to this fundamental difference in the next section.) From the equation, four factors drive the enterprise-value-to-EBITA multiple: the company's growth rate, return on invested capital, the cash tax rate, and the cost of capital. In most situations, the average cash tax rate and cost of capital will be similar across companies within the industry (because they face the same tax policies and have similar operating risks). This similarity does *not* hold for ROIC and growth, which can vary dramatically across companies, even within an industry. Thus, the same industry can include companies with drastically different multiples for perfectly valid reasons.

To demonstrate how different values of ROIC and growth will generate different multiples, Exhibit 12.2 uses the key value driver formula to create a set of hypothetical multiples for a company whose cash tax rate equals 30

Exhibit 12.2 How ROIC and Growth Drive Multiples

Enterprise value to EBITA[1]

Long-term growth rate (percent)	Return on invested capital (percent)				
	6	9	15	20	25
4.0	4.7	7.8	10.3	11.2	11.8
4.5	3.9	7.8	10.9	12.1	12.8
5.0	2.9	7.8	11.7	13.1	14.0
5.5	1.7	7.8	12.7	14.5	15.6
6.0	n/a	7.8	14.0	16.3	17.7

[1]Based on the key value driver formula, assuming a 30 percent cash tax rate and a 9 percent cost of capital.

percent and whose cost of capital equals 9 percent, rates similar to those for Home Depot.[3] In the exhibit, high multiples result from high returns on invested capital *and* from high growth rates.

As Exhibit 12.2 demonstrates, the enterprise-value-to-EBITA multiple increases with growth only if the company's ROIC is greater than the cost of capital. When ROIC equals the WACC, the enterprise-value-to-EBITA multiple is constant and equals $(1 - T)/WACC$. In this example, the WACC is 9 percent, and expected cash taxes are 30 percent, so the enterprise-value multiple is estimated at 7.8 times, regardless of expected growth. (Home Depot's actual enterprise value multiple of 2005 EBITA equals 8.7.) The exhibit also demonstrates that different combinations can lead to the same results. If the company grows at 6 percent and generates a 15 percent return on invested capital, it will have the same multiple (according to the formula) as if the company grew at only 5 percent but generated returns of 25 percent.

BEST PRACTICES FOR USING MULTIPLES

A thoughtful multiples analysis can provide valuable insights about a company and its competitors. Conversely, a poor analysis can result in confusion. In Exhibit 12.3 on page 376, we create a set of multiples analyses for Home Depot using various methodologies. For each comparison, we compute whether Home Depot is trading at a premium (i.e., has a higher multiple) to other companies or trading at a discount. In the first comparison, a trailing P/E ratio (based on earnings from the last fiscal year) is computed to benchmark Home Depot against all hardline retailers. Based on this comparison, the company trades at a 19 percent discount to its "peers." This discount is misleading, however, because the backward-looking price-to-earnings ratio measures past performance, not future performance, which is the basis for value. The ratio also commingles operating, nonoperating, and financial characteristics. Therefore, we make a series of adjustments to focus on future operating performance.

Because the listed retailers are extremely diverse, with varying prospects for ROIC and growth, we first reduce the peer group to Home Depot's closest competitor, Lowe's. (We would prefer to include other home improvement competitors, such as Menards, but it and other large-scale home improvement retailers are not publicly traded.) After this adjustment, the trailing P/E ratio discount drops to 17 percent. We next replace historical earnings with estimates for next year's earnings, which further lowers the discount to 8 percent.

---

[3] The key value driver formula is a perpetuity-based formula that assumes ROIC and growth never change. Since this assumption is overly restrictive for most companies, we use the formula to demonstrate levers, rather than predict accurate enterprise-value multiples.

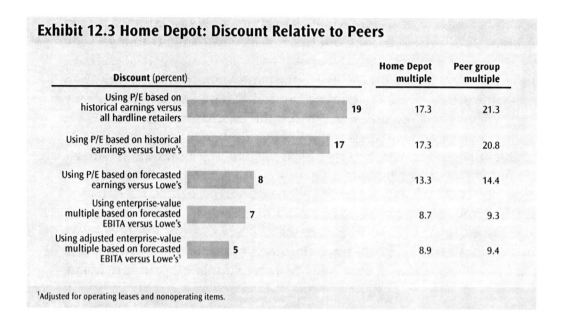

Exhibit 12.3 Home Depot: Discount Relative to Peers

Discount (percent)		Home Depot multiple	Peer group multiple
Using P/E based on historical earnings versus all hardline retailers	19	17.3	21.3
Using P/E based on historical earnings versus Lowe's	17	17.3	20.8
Using P/E based on forecasted earnings versus Lowe's	8	13.3	14.4
Using enterprise-value multiple based on forecasted EBITA versus Lowe's	7	8.7	9.3
Using adjusted enterprise-value multiple based on forecasted EBITA versus Lowe's[1]	5	8.9	9.4

[1] Adjusted for operating leases and nonoperating items.

To improve the comparison further, we switch to an enterprise-value multiple. This avoids any bias caused by capital structure and nonoperating gains and losses. Using an enterprise-value-to-EBITA multiple causes the difference to drop to 7 percent. Finally, we strip out excess cash and adjust for capitalized operating leases (the same two adjustments we made when calculating Home Depot's enterprise DCF value) from the enterprise-value multiple. Based on the adjusted enterprise-value multiple, Home Depot and Lowe's trade within 5 percent of one another.

As the Home Depot example demonstrates, using the wrong multiple can lead to errors in assessment and potentially valuation. When we used trailing P/E to compare Home Depot with the hardline retailers, the company seemed to be undervalued by 20 percent. But with an adjusted enterprise-value multiple, the valuation differences are small.

To apply multiples properly, use the following four best practices:

1. Choose comparables with similar prospects for ROIC and growth.

2. Use multiples based on forward-looking estimates.

3. Use enterprise-value multiples based on EBITA to mitigate problems with capital structure and one-time gains and losses.

4. Adjust the enterprise-value multiple for nonoperating items, such as excess cash, operating leases, employee stock options, and pension expenses (the same items for which we adjusted ROIC and free cash flow).

Choose Comparables with Similar Prospects

To analyze a company using comparables, you must first create a peer group. Most analysts start by examining the company's industry. But how do you define an industry? Sometimes, a company lists its competitors in its annual report. If the company doesn't disclose its competition, you can use an industry classification system such as Standard Industrial Classification (SIC) codes.[4] Home Depot's SIC code, however, contains more than 20 companies, many of which are not directly comparable because they sell very different products or rely on different business models. A slightly better but proprietary system is the Global Industry Classifications Standard (GICS) system, recently developed by Standard & Poor's and Morgan Stanley. A recent study found GICS classifications do a significantly better job of explaining cross-sectional variations in valuation multiples, forecasted and realized growth rates, R&D expenditures, and key financial ratios.[5]

Once you have collected a list and properly measured the multiples, the digging begins. You must answer a series of questions: Why are the multiples different across the peer group? Do certain companies in the group have superior products, better access to customers, recurring revenues, or economies of scale? If these strategic advantages translate to superior ROIC and growth rates, better-positioned companies should trade at higher multiples. You must understand what products they sell, how they generate revenue and profits, and how they grow. Only then will a company's multiple appear in the appropriate context with other companies.

In general, we recommend analyzing a set of multiples to better understand how a company is valued relative to its peers. In limited situations, you may need a representative multiple for use in valuation. For example, valuing minority interest from an outside perspective is difficult using traditional DCF because the required information to reconstruct cash flows is unavailable. (See Chapter 11 for more on minority interest.) Although missing information can be estimated, an alternative is to apply a representative earnings-based multiple to minority interest.

To develop a representative multiple, first limit the set to companies with similar characteristics, as we described above. Next, compute the median or harmonic mean of the sample.[6] To calculate the harmonic mean, compute the peer group's average EBITA-to-enterprise-value ratio (the reciprocal of the traditional ratio), and then take the reciprocal of the average. Do not use the average multiple outright, which can lead to major

---

[4] Beginning in 1997, SIC codes were replaced by a major revision called the North American Industry Classification System (NAICS). The NAICS six-digit code not only provides for newer industries, but also reorganizes the categories on a production/process-oriented basis. The Securities and Exchange Commission (SEC), however, still lists companies by SIC code.

[5] S. Bhojraj, C. M. C. Lee, and D. Oler, "What's My Line? A Comparison of Industry Classification Schemes for Capital Market Research" (working paper, Ithaca, NY: Cornell University, May 2003), http://ssrn.com/abstract=356840.

[6] Malcolm Baker and Richard Ruback use simulation to demonstrate that the harmonic mean leads to superior results. M. Baker and R. S. Ruback, "Estimating Industry Multiples" (working paper, Cambridge, MA: Harvard Business School, 1999).

distortions. Companies whose earnings are small on a temporary basis will have extremely large multiples that will inappropriately dominate the average. The sample median is less sensitive to outliers.

In some industries, the peer group will contain companies with negative earnings. For these companies, the multiples are not meaningful. In most situations, these companies can be excluded from the peer set because they are not comparable (a company with poor prospects should not be used to value a company with good prospects). If you are truly unclear about your company's future prospects, then including only companies with positive earnings will bias the industry multiple. In this case, switch to a multiple whose denominator is positive. Companies with negative earnings often have positive EBITDA and always have positive sales. Use this option sparingly, however. Moving up the income statement imposes further restrictions on the comparability of margins, returns on capital, and so on.

The retailers examined in Exhibit 12.1 are "pure play" businesses, meaning the vast majority of their revenues and profits come from one business type. When valuing or analyzing a company with multiple business units, each with different prospects for ROIC and growth, you should use a separate peer group for each business unit. (For more on valuing multibusiness companies, see Chapter 19.)

Use Forward-Looking Multiples

When building a multiple, the denominator should use a forecast of profits, rather than historical profits. Unlike backward-looking multiples, forward-looking multiples are consistent with the principles of valuation—in particular, that a company's value equals the present value of future cash flow, not sunk costs.

Empirical evidence shows that forward-looking multiples are indeed more accurate predictors of value. One empirical study examined the characteristics and performance of historical multiples versus forward industry multiples for a large sample of companies trading on the New York Stock Exchange (NYSE), the American Stock Exchange (AMEX), and NASDAQ.[7] When companies were measured versus their industry, their historical earnings-to-price (E/P) ratios had 1.6 times the standard deviation of one-year forward E/P ratios (6.0 percent versus 3.7 percent). In addition, the study found forward-looking multiples led to greater pricing accuracy.[8] The median pricing error equaled 23 percent for historical multiples and 18

---

[7] J. Liu, D. Nissim, and J. Thomas, "Equity Valuation Using Multiples," *Journal of Accounting Research*, 40 (2002): 135–172.

[8] To forecast a company's price, the authors multiplied the company's earnings by the industry median multiple. Pricing error equals the difference between forecasted price and actual price, divided by actual price.

percent for one-year forecasted earnings. Two-year forecasts worked even better, lowering the median pricing error to 16 percent.

Other research, which used multiples to predict the price of 142 initial public offerings, also found multiples based on forecasted earnings outperformed those based on historical earnings.[9] As the analysis moved from multiples based on historical earnings to multiples based on one- and two-year forecasts, the average pricing error fell from 55.0 percent to 43.7 percent to 28.5 percent, respectively, and the percentage of firms valued within 15 percent of their actual trading multiple increased from 15.4 percent to 18.9 percent to 36.4 percent.

Based on the principles of valuation and on empirical evidence, we recommend building multiples based on forecasted profits, not on historical profits.[10] If you must use historical data, make sure to use the most recent data possible and eliminate any one-time events.

Use Enterprise-Value Multiples

Although widely used, the price-earnings multiple has two major flaws. First, the price-earnings ratio is systematically affected by capital structure. Second, unlike EBITA, net income is calculated after nonoperating gains and losses. Thus, a nonoperating loss, such as a noncash write-off, can significantly lower earnings (without a comparable effect on value), causing the P/E ratio to be artificially high. Given the shortcomings of P/E ratios, we recommend using forward-looking enterprise-value multiples—debt plus equity to forecasted EBITA.[11] The following paragraphs examine the effects of capital structure and one-time items in detail.

Throughout this book, we have focused on the drivers of operating performance—ROIC, growth, and free cash flow—because the traditional ratios, such as return on assets and return on equity, commingle the effects of operations and capital structure. The same principles hold true with multiples. Price-earnings multiples commingle expectations about operating performance, capital structure, and nonoperating items.

To effectively analyze valuation multiples across an industry, we need a multiple that is independent of capital structure. The price-to-earnings ratio does not meet this criterion. In Appendix E, we derive the explicit

---

[9] M. Kim and J. R. Ritter, "Valuing IPOs," *Journal of Financial Economics,* 53(3) (1999): 409–437.

[10] A cautionary note about using forward multiples: Some analysts forecast future earnings by assuming an industry multiple and backing out the required earnings based on the current price. In this case, any multiples you calculate will merely reflect the analyst's assumptions about the appropriate forward multiple, and dispersion (even when warranted) will be nonexistent.

[11] If the company has nonoperating assets, such as excess cash or nonconsolidated subsidiaries, the enterprise-value ratio must be adjusted. Otherwise, the numerator (which includes the value from nonoperating assets) and the denominator (which excludes their income) will be inconsistent. We discuss adjustments in the next section.

Exhibit 12.4 The Relation between Leverage and P/E

Price to earnings multiple[1]

Debt to value	Price to earnings for an all-equity company				
	10	15	20	25	40
10%	9.5	14.6	20.0	25.7	45.0
20%	8.9	14.1	20.0	26.7	53.3
30%	8.2	13.5	20.0	28.0	70.0
40%	7.5	12.9	20.0	30.0	120.0
50%	6.7	12.0	20.0	33.3	n/m

[1]Assumes a cost of debt equal to 5% and no taxes.

relation between a company's actual P/E ratio and its unlevered P/E ratio (PE_u)—the P/E ratio as if the company were entirely financed with equity. Assuming no taxes, a company's P/E ratio can be expressed as follows:

$$\frac{P}{E} = \bar{K} + \frac{\bar{K} - PE_u}{\left(\frac{D}{V}\right)(k_d)(PE_u) - 1} \quad \text{such that } \bar{K} = \frac{1}{k_d}$$

where k_d = cost of debt
      D/V = the ratio of debt to value

As the formula demonstrates, when the unlevered P/E equals the reciprocal of the cost of debt, the numerator of the fraction equals zero, and leverage has no effect on the P/E ratio. For companies with large unlevered P/Es (i.e., companies with significant opportunities for future value creation), P/E systematically increases with leverage. Conversely, companies with small unlevered P/Es would exhibit a drop in P/E as leverage rises.

Based on this formula for the P/E ratio, Exhibit 12.4 compares the relation between leverage and P/E. To build the table, we assume a cost of debt equal to 5 percent and no taxes. For unlevered P/E ratios greater than 20, the P/E ratio increases with leverage. This occurs because, for high-P/E companies, the drop in equity (which occurs when debt is used to repurchase shares) is less than the drop in earnings (because of new interest). For companies with significantly high unlevered P/Es, such as 40, increased leverage will cause the levered P/E to explode. In this example, a company with an unlevered P/E of 40 and debt to value of 50 percent is not meaningful, because interest causes earnings to be negative.

An alternative to the P/E ratio is enterprise value to EBITA. In a world with no taxes and no distress costs, the enterprise-value-to-EBITA ratio is unaffected by leverage. In actuality, even the enterprise-value-to-EBITA ratio depends somewhat on a company's capital structure. The reason is that although EBITA is independent of capital structure, enterprise value is higher for companies with more efficient capital structures. Remember, enterprise value depends on ROIC, growth, *and* the weighted average cost of capital. Thus, improvements in WACC translate to increases in enterprise value.

In theory, we would like to remove the present value of tax shields and distress costs from enterprise value. This would allow us to create a purely operating multiple, completely independent of a company's capital structure. In practice, the complexity of removing these effects outweighs the potential errors they cause if left in place.

A second problem with the P/E ratio is that earnings include many nonoperating items, such as restructuring charges and write-offs. Since many nonoperating items are one-time events, multiples based on P/Es can be misleading. In 2002, AOL-Time Warner wrote off nearly $100 billion in goodwill and other intangibles. Even though EBITA equaled $6.4 billion, the company recorded a $98 billion loss. Since earnings were negative, the company's 2002 P/E ratio was meaningless.

Adjust Enterprise-Value Multiple for Nonoperating Items

Although EBITA is superior to earnings for calculating multiples, even enterprise-value multiples must be adjusted for nonoperating items included within enterprise value or reported EBITA. This is similar to the discussion in Chapter 7, where we demonstrated how financial statements based on today's accounting principles commingle operating and nonoperating items. This caused us to reorganize the company's financial statements, allowing us to compute ROIC and free cash flow, both of which are independent of capital structure and nonoperating items.

To build a clean set of multiples, we apply the same principles. The market-based enterprise value must be adjusted for nonoperating items, such as excess cash and operating leases. Although reported EBITA appears independent of nonoperating items, it *must* be adjusted as well. For instance, reported EBITA includes the implicit interest expense from operating leases. Failing to adjust EBITA can generate misleading results. See Chapter 7 for a detailed description of the reorganization process; here are the most common adjustments:

- *Excess cash and other nonoperating assets:* Since EBITA excludes interest income from excess cash, enterprise value should not include excess cash either. To calculate an enterprise-value multiple, sum the market values of debt and equity, subtract excess cash, and divide the remainder by EBITA. The same holds true for other nonoperating assets, whose income is not part of EBITA. Nonoperating assets must be evaluated separately.

- *Operating leases:* Companies with significant operating leases will have an artificially low enterprise value (because we are ignoring the value of lease-based debt) and an artificially low EBITA (because rental expense includes interest costs). To calculate an enterprise-value multiple, add the value of leased assets to the market value of debt and equity. Add back the implied interest expense to EBITA.

- *Employee stock options:* For companies that fail to expense stock options, EBITA will be artificially high. To properly calculate an enterprise-value multiple, subtract the after-tax value of *newly issued* employee option grants from EBITA (as reported in the footnotes). To adjust enterprise value, add the present value of employee grants *outstanding* to the sum of debt and equity. Enterprise value should be adjusted for any company with outstanding options, regardless of its expensing policy.

- *Pensions:* To adjust enterprise value, add the after-tax present value of pension liabilities to debt plus equity. To remove the nonoperating gains and losses related to plan assets, start with EBITA, add the pension interest expense, and deduct the recognized returns on plan assets (as reported in the footnotes).

To see the distortions caused by nonoperating assets, consider once again the multiples analysis presented in Exhibit 12.1. Best Buy trades at a premium to Circuit City Stores, according to their respective enterprise-value multiples (6.3 versus 4.4), but it trades at a discount based on P/E ratios (13.8 versus 22.3). So which is it, premium or discount? In reality, Circuit City's P/E multiple is meaningless. In July 2004, Circuit City's total equity value was approximately $2.7 billion, but the company held nearly $1 billion in cash. Since cash generates very little income, the P/E ratio of cash is very high (a 2 percent after-tax return on investment translates to a P/E of 50). Thus, the extremely high P/E of cash will artificially increase the P/E of Circuit City's operating business. When we remove cash from equity value ($2,708 million – $990 million) and divide by earnings less after-tax interest income ($122 million – $8 million), Circuit City's P/E drops from 22.3 to 15.1.

In Exhibit 12.5, we adjust the enterprise multiples of Home Depot and Lowe's for excess cash and operating leases. To adjust enterprise value, we start with Home Depot's market value of debt plus equity ($75.6 billion), add back the value of leased assets ($6.6 billion), and subtract excess cash ($1.6 billion). This leads to an adjusted enterprise value of $80.6 billion. Next, we adjust 2005 estimated EBITA ($8.7 billion) for implied interest on operating leases ($340 million). Before adjustments, Home Depot's enterprise-value multiple is within 6.6 percent of that for Lowe's. After adjustments, the difference drops to 5.1 percent.

Exhibit 12.5 Home Depot and Lowe's: Adjusted to Enterprise Value Multiples

$ million	Home Depot	Lowe's	
Outstanding debt	1,365	3,755	
Market value of equity	74,250	39,075	
Enterprise value	75,615	42,830	
Capitalized operating leases	6,554	2,762	
Excess cash	(1,609)	(1,033)	
Adjusted enterprise value	80,560	44,559	
2005 EBITA	8,691	4,589	
Implied interest from leases	340	154	
Adjusted 2005 EBITA	9,031	4,743	
	Home Depot	**Lowe's**	**Difference**
Raw enterprise value multiple	8.7	9.3	(6.6%)
Adjusted enterprise value multiple	8.9	9.4	(5.1%)

Throughout this chapter, we emphasize enterprise-value multiples based on EBITA. This approach enables us to tie the enterprise-value multiple directly to the key value driver formula. A common alternative to the EBITA multiple is the EBITDA multiple.[12] Many financial analysts use EBITDA multiples because depreciation is a noncash expense, reflecting sunk costs, not future investment.

To see this, consider two companies, each of which owns a machine that produces identical products. Both machines have the same cash-based operating costs, and each company's products sell for the same price. If one company paid more for its equipment (for whatever reason—perhaps poor negotiation), it will have higher depreciation going forward and, thus, lower EBITA. Valuation, however, is based on discounted cash flow, not discounted profits. And since both companies have identical cash flow, they should have identical values.[13] We would therefore expect the two companies to have identical multiples. Yet, because EBITA differs across the two companies, their multiples will differ as well.

Since valuation is based on future cash flows, EBITDA might seem superior to EBITA. But this is not always the case. Exhibit 12.6 on page 384 presents two companies that differ in only one aspect. Company A manufactures its

---

[12] EBITDA stands for earnings before interest, taxes, depreciation, and amortization.

[13] Since depreciation is tax deductible, a company with higher depreciation will have a smaller tax burden. Lower taxes lead to higher cash flows and a higher valuation. Therefore, even companies with identical EBITDAs will have different EBITDA multiples. The distortion, however, is less pronounced.

Exhibit 12.6 Comparing EBITA and EBITDA Multiples

$ million	Company A	Company B	
Revenues	100	100	
Raw materials	(10)	(35)	Company B outsources manufacturing to another company
Operating costs	(40)	(40)	
EBITDA	50	25	
Depreciation	(30)	(5)	
EBITA	20	20	

Multiples	Company A	Company B
Enterprise value ($ million)	150.0	150.0
Enterprise value / EBITDA	3.0	6.0
Enterprise value / EBITA	7.5	7.5

products using its own equipment, whereas Company B outsources manufacturing to a supplier. Since Company A owns its equipment, it recognizes significant depreciation—in this case, $30 million. Company B has less equipment, so its depreciation is only $5 million. However, Company B's supplier will include its own depreciation costs in its price, and Company B will subsequently pay more for its raw materials. Because of this difference, Company B generates EBITDA of only $25 million, versus $50 million for Company A. This difference in EBITDA will lead to differing multiples. Yet, when Company A's depreciation is accounted for, both companies trade at 7.5 times EBITA.

When computing the enterprise-value-to-EBITDA multiple in the previous example, we failed to recognize that Company A (the company that owns its equipment) will have to expend cash to replace aging equipment. Since capital expenditures are recorded as an investing cash flow they do not appear on the income statement, causing the discrepancy. Some analysts overcome this reinvestment problem by adjusting EBITDA for expected investments in working capital and property, plant, and equipment. This adjustment is highly subjective (capital expenditures are lumpy, so smoothing is required) and can result in a negative denominator, making the multiple meaningless.

ALTERNATIVE MULTIPLES

Although we have so far focused on enterprise-value multiples based on EBITA and EBITDA, other multiples can prove helpful in certain situations.

In the following subsections, we discuss three alternatives: the price-to-sales ratio, the price-to-earnings-growth ratio (known as the PEG ratio), and regression-based analysis using nonfinancial data.

Price-to-Sales Multiples

Generally speaking, price-to-sales multiples are not particularly useful for explaining company valuations. As shown earlier, an enterprise-value-to-EBITA multiple assumes similar growth rates and returns on incremental capital. An enterprise-value-to-sales multiple imposes an additional important restriction: similar operating margins on the company's existing business. For most industries, this restriction is overly burdensome.

The multiples chart in Exhibit 12.7 is often analyzed by investment bankers. In the chart, Home Depot's stock value is estimated using peer multiples. Each horizontal set of dots represents a different multiple. The top row estimates Home Depot's stock price based on each peer company's enterprise-value-to-sales ratio, the middle row uses an enterprise-value-to-EBITA ratio, and the bottom row shows a price-to-earnings ratio. The vertical line represents Home Depot's actual stock price at the time of the analysis and intersects Home Depot's actual multiples.

In this example, Circuit City trades at 0.1 times forecasted sales; applying that ratio to Home Depot's forecasted revenues would place Home Depot's stock price at $4 per share. At the other extreme, Bed, Bath, & Beyond trades at 1.7 times sales, generating an estimate of $60 for Home Depot's stock. Thus, we have narrowed the company's stock price to somewhere between $4 and $60 per share—a range too wide to provide any useful insight.

Given how imprecise price-to-sales ratios are, limit their use to situations where the company in question or its peers have extremely small or

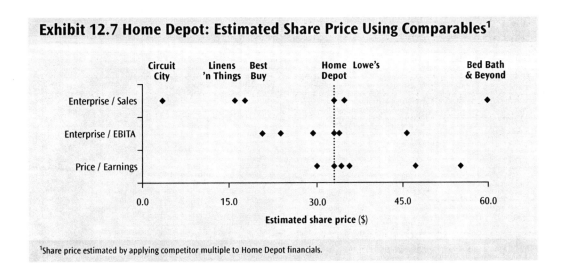

Exhibit 12.7 Home Depot: Estimated Share Price Using Comparables[1]

[1]Share price estimated by applying competitor multiple to Home Depot financials.

even negative operating profits. Revenue multiples are most common to venture capital because many start-ups will not turn a profit for years. If your situation demands a price-to-sales multiple, make sure to follow the fundamental principles presented in this chapter: Use enterprise value, not equity value; use forward-looking sales projections; and focus on companies with similar growth, ROICs, and expected operating margins.

PEG Ratios

Whereas a price-to-sales ratio further restricts the enterprise-value-to-EBITA multiple by assuming operating margins are common across companies, the price-earnings-growth (PEG) ratio is more flexible than the enterprise-value-to-EBITA ratio, because it allows expected growth to vary across companies. If you use a PEG ratio, you can expand a company's peer group to include competitors that are in different stages of their life cycle (from a growth perspective).

Traditionally, PEG ratios are calculated by dividing the P/E ratio by expected growth in earnings per share, but our modified version is based on the enterprise-value multiple:

$$\text{Adjusted PEG Ratio} = 100 \times \frac{\text{Enterprise-Value Multiple}}{\text{Expected EBITA Growth Rate}}$$

Exhibit 12.8 calculates the adjusted PEG ratios for our sample of retailers. To calculate Home Depot's adjusted PEG ratio (0.6 times), divide the company's forward-looking enterprise-value multiple (7.1 times) by its expected operating profit growth rate (11.8 percent). Based on the adjusted PEG ratio, Home Depot trades at a significant premium to Lowe's. Using the

Exhibit 12.8 Adjusted PEG Ratio

Hardline retailing	2005 enterprise multiple	Expected profit growth	Adjusted PEG ratio
Home improvement			
Home Depot	7.1	11.8	0.60
Lowe's	7.3	17.2	0.42
Home furnishing			
Bed Bath & Beyond	9.9	16.1	0.61
Linens 'n Things	5.1	15.4	0.33
Consumer electronics			
Best Buy	6.3	18.8	0.34
Circuit City	4.4	7.6	0.58

Source: CSFB estimates on hardline retailing, July 26, 2004.

key value driver formula as our guide, this is not surprising. Since the PEG ratio controls only for growth, companies with higher ROICs *should* trade at higher levels. According to analyst estimates, Home Depot's ROIC is expected to equal 17 percent, whereas the estimate of ROIC for Lowe's is only 14 percent.

The PEG ratio's ability to analyze companies with varying growth rates appears to give it a leg up on the standard enterprise-value multiple. Yet the PEG ratio has its own drawbacks that can lead to valuation errors. First, there is no standard time frame for measuring expected growth. You may find yourself wondering whether to use one-year, two-year, or long-term growth. Exhibit 12.8 used analyst projections for two-year expected EBITA growth.

Second, PEG ratios assume a linear relation between multiples and growth, such that no growth implies zero value. Exhibit 12.9 uses the average PEG ratio to value a hypothetical industry with five companies. Each company has a long-term expected ROIC of 15 percent, has a WACC equal to 9 percent, and pays cash taxes at 30 percent. The five hypothetical companies differ only in their growth rates (which vary from 2 percent to 6 percent). Using the key value driver formula, we estimate each company's enterprise-value multiple. Note how the dotted line, which plots enterprise value versus

Exhibit 12.9 PEG Ratio Estimation Error

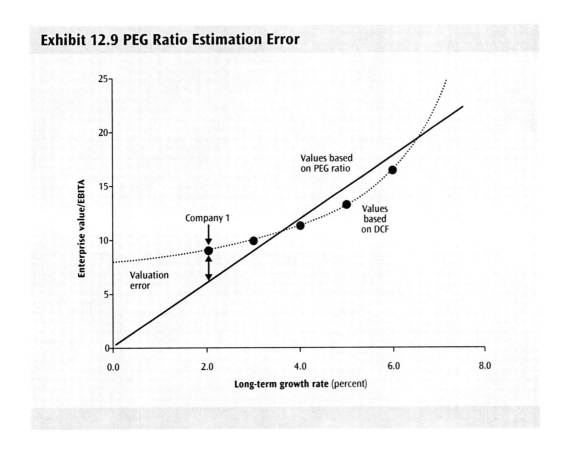

growth, is curved and has a positive intercept (even zero-growth firms have positive values). Conversely, the PEG ratio is linear and has a zero intercept. Since PEG is multiplied by growth to approximate firm value, a company with constant profits would have an implied value of zero. As a result, the typical application of industry PEG ratios will systematically undervalue companies with low growth rates.

To avoid undervaluing low-growth companies, some financial analysts (and most academics) use a regression analysis to determine a representative multiple. The regression is based on the following equation:

$$EV/EBITA_i = a + b \, (Expected \; Growth_i)$$

For the six hardline retailers presented in Exhibit 12.8, this regression leads to an intercept of 3.5 and a slope coefficient of 0.2. Thus, a zero-growth company should be valued at 3.5 times EBITA, not zero, and a company expected to grow at 5 percent would be valued at 4.5 times EBITA. This regression analysis, however, does not adjust for the nonlinear relation between growth and value. More advanced regression techniques can be employed, but unless the sample is large, the regression often fails to provide useful insight.

Multiples Based on Nonfinancial (Operational) Data

In the late 1990s, numerous companies went public with meager sales and negative profits. For many financial analysts, valuing the young companies was a struggle because of the great uncertainty surrounding potential market size, profitability, and required investments. Financial multiples that normally provide a benchmark for valuation were rendered useless because profitability (measured in any form) was often negative.

To overcome this shortcoming, academics and practitioners alike relied on nonfinancial multiples, which compare enterprise value to one or more nonoperating financial statistics, such as web site hits, unique visitors, or number of subscribers. In 2000, *Fortune* reported market-value-to-customer multiples for a series of Internet companies.[14] *Fortune* determined Yahoo was trading at $2,038 per customer, Amazon.com was trading at $1,400 per customer, and NetZero at $1,140 per customer. The article suggested that "Placing a value on a Website's customers may be the best way to judge an [Internet] stock."

[14] E. Schonfeld, "How Much Are Your Eyeballs Worth?" *Fortune* (February 21, 2000), pp. 197–200.

To use a nonfinancial multiple effectively, you must follow the same guidelines outlined earlier in this chapter. The nonfinancial metric must be a reasonable predictor of future value creation, and thus somehow tied to ROIC and growth. In the example cited previously, Yahoo trades at a higher multiple than Amazon.com because Yahoo's incremental costs per user are much smaller, an advantage that translates into higher profits.

Nonfinancial measures did play an important role in the early valuation of Internet stocks. The first academic study about Internet valuations examined a sample of 63 publicly traded Internet firms in the late 1990s.[15] The study found that the number of unique visitors to a web site or the number of pages on a site viewed per visit were directly correlated to a company's stock price even after controlling for the company's current financial performance. The power of a given nonfinancial metric, however, depended on the company. For portal and content companies such as Yahoo, page views and unique visitors were both correlated to a company's market value. For e-tailers such as Amazon.com, only the page views per visit were correlated with value. Evidently, the market believed "stopping by" would not translate to future value for e-tailers.

For Internet companies in the late 1990s, investors focused on nonfinancial metrics because early financial results were unrelated to long-term valuation creation. As the industry matured, however, financial metrics became increasingly important. Later research found gross profit and R&D spending became increasingly predictive, whereas nonfinancial data lost power.[16] This research indicates a return to traditional valuation metrics even for the "new economy" stocks, as the relevance of nonfinancial metrics diminished over the 24-month testing period.

Two cautionary notes about using nonfinancial multiples to analyze and value companies: First, nonfinancial multiples should be used only when they provide incremental explanatory power above financial multiples. If a company cannot translate visitors, page views, or subscribers into profits and cash flow, the nonfinancial metric is meaningless, and a multiple based on financial forecasts is better. Second, nonfinancial multiples, like all multiples, are *relative* valuation tools. They measure one company's valuation relative to another, normalized by some measure of size. They do not measure absolute valuation levels. To value a company correctly, one must always remember to ask: Is a value of $2,038 per customer too much?

---

[15] B. Trueman, M. H. F. Wong, and X. J. Zhang, "The Eyeballs Have It: Searching for the Value in Internet Stocks," *Journal of Accounting Research*, 38 (2000): 137–162.
[16] P. Jorion and E. Talmor, "Value Relevance of Financial and Non Financial Information in Emerging Industries: The Changing Role of Web Traffic Data" (working paper no. 021, London Business School Accounting Subject Area, 2001).

SUMMARY

Of the available valuation tools, discounted cash flow continues to deliver the best results. However, a thoughtful multiples analysis merits a place in your tool kit as well. When that analysis is careful and well reasoned, it not only provides a useful check of your DCF forecasts but also provides critical insights into what drives value in a given industry. Just be sure that you analyze the underlying reasons that multiples differ from company to company. When possible, base your analysis on forward-looking numbers. Focus on enterprise value and remove nonoperating items from your analysis. Never view multiples as a shortcut. Instead, approach your multiples analysis with as much care as you bring to DCF analysis.

REVIEW QUESTIONS

1. Compare and contrast the following relative valuation models: P/E Model, PEG Model, P/B Model, P/S Model.

2. Why is it important that management perform a supplemental valuation analysis employing a relative valuation model?

3. Discuss the importance of selecting comparable companies when estimating the appropriate relative valuation model.

4. Identify and discuss the four best practices applied to the construction of a relative valuation multiplier.

5. Compare and contrast the relative P/E valuation model to the DCF valuation model.

6. How does the relative valuation model differ from the enterprise valuation model?

Outline

Part IV: Additional Topics

- Lecture slides on deterministic capital budgeting

- Chapter 8 of "Advanced Engineering Economics" by Park and Sharp-Bette

- Lecture slides on utility theory

- Chapter 9 of "Advanced Engineering Economics" by Park and Sharp-Bette

Deterministic Capital Budgeting

> ### Pure Capital Rationing with no lending or borrowing allowed

- **Primal formulation**

$$\text{max} \qquad Z = \sum_{j=1}^{J} p_j . x_j$$

$$\text{subject to} \qquad -\sum_{j=1}^{J} a_{nj} . x_j \leq M_n \ , \quad n = 0,1,...,N$$

$$x_j \leq 1 \qquad , \quad j = 1,2,...,J$$

$$x_j \geq 0 \qquad , \quad j = 1,2,...,J$$

Where:

> p_j is the present value of project j

> x_j is the project selection variable

> M_n is the budget limit at time n

> N is the end of the planning period

Deterministic Capital Budgeting

> Pure Capital Rationing with no lending or borrowing allowed

- **Complementary slackness conditions**

$$\rho_n^*(M_n + \sum_{j=1}^{J} a_{nj} x_j^*) = 0 \qquad , \quad n = 0,1,...,N$$

$$x_j^*(\mu_j^* - p_j - \sum_{n=0}^{N} a_{nj} \rho_n^*) = 0 \quad , \quad j = 1,2,...,J$$

$$\mu_j^*(1 - x_j^*) = 0 \qquad\qquad , \quad j = 1,2,...,J$$

> ➤ The complementary slackness conditions hold at the optimal solution

Deterministic Capital Budgeting

Pure Capital Rationing with no lending or borrowing allowed

- **Economic interpretation: the present value of a project plus the sum of the cash flows over the horizon "discounted" by the dual variables is:**

  ➢ Non-positive for a rejected project

  ➢ Exactly zero for a partially funded project

  ➢ Non-negative for a fully funded project

- **Primal formulation with one lending, one borrowing rate, and unlimited borrowing capacity**

max
$$Z = \sum_{j=1}^{J} \hat{a}_j . x_j + v_N - w_N$$

subject to
$$-\sum_{j=1}^{J} a_{0j}.x_j + v_0 - w_0 \le M_0$$

$$-\sum_{j=1}^{J} a_{nj}.x_j - (1+r_l)v_{n-1} + v_n + (1+r_b)w_{n-1} - w_n \le M_n \ , \quad n = 1,...,N$$

$$v_n, w_n \ge 0 \quad , \quad n = 0,1,...,N$$
$$0 \le x_j \le 1 \quad , \quad j = 1,2,...,J$$

Where:
- ➤ r_l is the lending rate
- ➤ r_b is the borrowing rate

- **Let us distinguish three scenarios for a project j. Using the dual formulation and complementary slackness, we obtain:**

  - ➤ The project is rejected

  $$\hat{a}_j + \sum_{n=0}^{N} a_{nj} \rho_n^* \leq 0$$

  - ➤ The project is partially funded

  $$\hat{a}_j + \sum_{n=0}^{N} a_{nj} \rho_n^* = 0$$

  - ➤ The project is fully funded

  $$\hat{a}_j + \sum_{n=0}^{N} a_{nj} \rho_n^* \geq 0$$

- **Other insights from duality and complementary slackness**

  - ➤ Dual variables:

$$\rho_N^* = 1$$

$$(1 + r_l)\rho_{n+1}^* \le \rho_n^* \le (1 + r_b)\rho_{n+1}^* \;, \quad n = 0,1,....N-1$$

  - ➤ In period of borrowing

$$w_n > 0 \Rightarrow \quad \begin{aligned} v_n &= 0 \\ \rho_n^* &= (1 + r_b)\rho_{n+1}^* \end{aligned}$$

  - ➤ In period of lending

$$v_n > 0 \Rightarrow \quad \begin{aligned} w_n &= 0 \\ \rho_n^* &= (1 + r_l)\rho_{n+1}^* \end{aligned}$$

Outline

Part IV: Additional Topics

- Lecture slides on deterministic capital budgeting

- Chapter 8 of "Advanced Engineering Economics" by Park and Sharp-Bette

- Lecture slides on utility theory

- Chapter 9 of "Advanced Engineering Economics" by Park and Sharp-Bette

8

Deterministic Capital Budgeting Models

8.1 INTRODUCTION

In the previous chapter we determined that we should select from among multiple alternatives by choosing the one with the maximum net present value (*PV*) or by using the incremental approach with one of several criteria. There are two important characteristics of the problems solved in the previous chapter.

1. We could easily formulate and list all mutually exclusive alternatives of interest.
2. There is an underlying assumption of ability to borrow and lend unlimited amounts at a single, fixed interest rate. When budget limits are imposed, the borrowing ability at time 0 is restricted, and we are left with a single, fixed interest rate for future lending, or reinvestment.

In this chapter we relax these assumptions. We consider problems in which budget limits are imposed during several time periods, the projects have interdependencies, and there are different, but known, borrowing and lending opportunities. In short, we examine problems for which it would be exceedingly difficult to specify all mutually exclusive alternatives. This type of analysis is called capital budgeting. In keeping with the sense of Part Two of this book, we assume certainty with respect to all information. Linear programming (LP) is a convenient tool for analyzing such situations, and we give a brief introduction to its use in Section 8.2.

We will also see that *PV* maximization is not necessarily our best objective, for different reinvestment rates are possible. In the pure capital rationing model (Section 8.3), which allows no external borrowing and lending, this situation has been the focus of much academic controversy during the last twenty years. We include a brief review of the major arguments, not from the view of favoring any

705

one of them but rather to give the reader an important historical perspective on the subject.

The inclusion of borrowing and lending opportunities (Section 8.4) leads to more realistic operational models. In some situations the previously mentioned academic controversy disappears, and in others it reappears. Weingartner's horizon model (Section 8.5) provides the analyst with a convenient way of avoiding these issues, while yielding solutions consistent with *PV* analysis of situations allowing unlimited borrowing and lending. Bernhard's general model (Section 8.6) allows for the use of dividends and other terms in the objective function, and for a variety of linear and nonlinear constraints.

In Section 8.7 we finally consider the situation of integer restrictions, which we have avoided until now because it requires more difficult mathematical analysis. Multiple objectives are discussed in Section 8.8. Following the summary, the chapter ends with a case study illustrating the application of Bernhard's general model to a dividend-terminal-wealth problem.

8.2 THE USE OF LINEAR PROGRAMMING MODELS

Because linear programming models are so widely used in capital budgeting, we present a brief introduction here. In this section we illustrate the application of LP in a typical example. A word of caution is in order here: the example given is *not* intended to represent the best principles of capital budgeting but *rather to illustrate* the use of LP. The various methods of capital budgeting (for the deterministic case) are given in the following sections.

Example 8.1

Table 8.1 presents data for Example 8.1, which concerns five investment projects. There are budget limits of $4,400 and $4,000 at time 0 and time 1, respectively; these limits do not apply to any funds generated by the projects themselves. We note the sign convention that inflows are positive and outflows negative. Most of the projects require investment during the first two years before they return any funds. All the projects are simple investments with unique, positive, real *IRR*s, and for a sufficiently low *MARR*, say 20%, all have positive *PV*s. But from the budget limits it is clear that we cannot accept all of them; hence the capital rationing problem. Moreover, project 5 starts to provide cash inflow at time 1, when all the others require outflows, so we would like to consider this advantage of project 5. (The solution to Example 8.1 follows in the text). □

8.2.1 Criterion Function To Be Optimized
A variety of criterion functions could be optimized.

- Maximize the *PV* of the cash flows of the selected projects.
- Maximize the *IRR* of the total cash flow of the selected projects.

Table 8.1 *Data for Example 8.1*

Cash Flow at Time	Project				
	1	2	3	4	5
0	−$1,000	−$1,200	−$2,000	−$2,500	−$3,000
1	−2,000	−2,400	−2,100	−1,300	900
2	2,000	2,500	3,000	2,000	1,400
3	2,900	3,567	3,000	2,000	1,600
4	0	0	1,308	2,000	1,800
5	0	0	0	2,296	955
PV(20%)	$400	600	700	850	900
IRR, %	29.1	31.3	29.7	28.9	32.2

Budgets for external sources of funds: $n = 0$, $4,400; $n = 1$, $4,000

- Maximize the "utility" of the dividends that can be paid from the cash flows of the selected projects.
- Maximize the cash that can be accumulated at the end of the planning period.

Other functions could be used. The important thing is that the function is clearly expressed in terms of the decision variables for project acceptance or rejection and that it is (we hope) linear.

Let us see, for *illustration* purposes, the *PV* of the cash flows of the selected projects,

$$\text{Max} \sum_j p_j x_j \tag{8.1}$$

where p_j is the *PV* of project j, using $i = MARR$, and
x_j is a project selection variable, with $0 \le x_j \le 1$.

Using a *MARR* value of $i = 20\%$, we obtain

j	1	2	3	4	5
p_j	$400	600	700	850	900

Thus Eq. 8.1 becomes, for Example 8.1,

$$\max \$400x_1 + 600x_2 + 700x_3 + 850x_4 + 900x_5 \tag{8.2}$$

The project selection variables are continuous in this linear formulation. A value of $x_j = 0$ means that the project is not selected, a value of $x_j = 1$ implies complete acceptance, and a fractional values implies partial acceptance. We will leave aside the question of the practicality of fractional acceptance. In some industries, such as oil and gas exploration, fractional acceptance is common practice; generally, though, it is not possible to accept fractional projects without changing the nature of their cash flows. (We will consider integer restrictions in Section 8.7.)

8.2.2 Multiple Budget Periods

The budget limits for Example 8.1 can be expressed by linear constraints on the selection variables,

$$-\sum_j a_{nj} x_j \le M_n, \qquad n = 0, 1, ..., N \qquad (8.3)$$

where a_{nj} = cash flow for project j at time n, inflows having a plus sign, and outflows a minus sign,

M_n = budget limit on externally supplied funds at time n, and

N = end of the planning period.

Notice that M_n represents only the funds from sources other than the projects. The equation states that project outflows minus project inflows at time n must be less than the budget limit on funds from other sources at time n. A negative value for M_n implies that the set of selected projects must *generate* funds. (Equation 8.3 states that cash outflows $\le$ cash inflows + M_n). Note that the absence of a budget limit is not equivalent to M_n being zero; the former implies a positive, unbounded M_n value. Equations of the type (8.3) are usually called budget constraints or cash balance equations. Inflows and outflows for borrowing, lending, and dividend payments may also be included; these are discussed in later sections.

Applying the equation to Example 8.1, we obtain two constraints,

$n = 0$: $\quad \$1,000x_1 + 1,200x_2 + 2,000x_3 + 2,500x_4 + 3,000x_5 \le 4,400$

$n = 1$: $\quad \$2,000x_1 + 2,400x_2 + 2,100x_3 + 1,300x_4 - 900x_5 \le 4,000 \quad (8.4)$

The advantage of project 5 at time 1 is clearly apparent here; setting $x_5 = 1$ increases the amount available for other projects by $900. There are no stated limits for times 2, 3, 4, and 5, so we need not write constraints for these times.

8.2.3 Project Limits and Interdependencies

The limits on the selection variables given following Eq. 8.1 are presented here again.

$$x_j \le 1, \qquad j = 1, \ldots, J \qquad (8.5)$$

The nonnegativity constraints are expressed separately:

$$x_j \ge 0, \qquad j = 1, \ldots, J \qquad (8.6)$$

It is also possible to have interdependencies among project selection variables. Some common types are the following.

1. Mutual exclusivity—when a subset of projects form a mutually exclusive set.

$$x_j + x_k + x_m \leq 1 \qquad (8.7)$$

The selection of one project precludes the selection of either of the other two in Eq. 8.7. Note that a complete interpretation is possible only if the x_j are restricted to integers.

2. Contingency—when execution of one project depends on execution of another.

$$x_j - x_k \leq 0 \qquad (8.8)$$

Here x_j cannot be selected unless x_k is also selected.

3. Complementary and competitive projects—when the selection of two projects changes the cash flows involved. For complementary projects inflows are greater than the sum of the individual project inflows; the opposite is true for competitive projects. Such situations can be handled by defining a new project for the combination and then establishing mutual exclusivity,

$$x_j + x_k + x_m \leq 1$$

where x_m is a combination of j and k. (If there are many such situations, the method becomes cumbersome.)

We will not impose interdependencies in Example 8.1, in order to keep the duality analysis simple at this point. That type of treatment is given in Section 8.5.

8.2.4 LP Formulation of Lorie–Savage Problem

In LP terminology, the *primal problem* formulation of the capital budgeting problem is given symbolically and numerically by Table 8.2. This version summarizes the relationships that have been presented so far in this chapter. This version of the problem is also designated as the LP formulation of the Lorie–Savage problem [15], after the two economists who stated the original form of the project selection problem. Their concern with the problem came from the inadequacies of the *IRR* method to deal with budget limitations and project interdependencies. Our analysis in the next section follows closely the work of Weingartner [20], who applied LP to the Lorie–Savage problem.

8.2.5 Duality Analysis

For every *primal problem* in linear programming, there is a related *dual problem* formulation. Table 8.3 presents both the symbolic and numeric versions of the dual problem for Example 8.1. The dual formulation is a minimization problem stated in terms of the ρ_n and μ_n. By making appropriate conversions from minimization to maximization and from $\geq$ to $\leq$, we can easily show that the dual formulation of the problem in Table 8.3 is the same as the formulation given in Table 8.2. In other words, the dual of the dual is the primal, and our specific designations are based on habit and convenience.

709

Table 8.2 *Primal Problem Formulation for Maximizing PV for Example 8.1 (Lorie–Savage Formulation)*

Symbolic

$$\text{Max} \sum_j p_j x_j \tag{8.1}$$

s.t.*

$$[\rho_n] \qquad -\sum_j a_{nj} x_j \leq M_n, \qquad n = 0, 1, \ldots, N \tag{8.3}$$

$$[\mu_j] \qquad x_j \leq 1, \qquad j = 1, \ldots, J \tag{8.5}$$

$$x_j \geq 0, \qquad j = 1, \ldots, J \tag{8.6}$$

where p_j = PV of project j using $i = MARR$,
$\quad x_j$ = project selection variable,
$\quad a_{nj}$ = cash flow for project j at time n; inflows have a plus sign, outflows have a minus sign,
$\quad M_n$ = budget limit on externally supplied funds at time n,
$\quad N$ = end of the planning period,
$\quad \rho_n, \mu_j$ = dual variables for the primal constraints.

Numeric

$$\text{Max } \$400x_1 + 600x_2 + 700x_3 + 850x_4 + 900x_5 \tag{8.2}$$

s.t.

$$[\rho_0] \quad \$1,000x_1 + 1,200x_2 + 2,000x_3 + 2,500x_4 + 3,000x_5 \leq \$4,400$$

$$[\rho_1] \quad \$2,000x_1 + 2,400x_2 + 2,100x_3 + 1,300x_4 - 900x_5 \leq \$4,000 \tag{8.4}$$

$$
\begin{aligned}
[\mu_1] \quad & x_1 && \leq 1 \\
[\mu_2] \quad & \quad x_2 && \leq 1 \\
[\mu_3] \quad & \qquad x_3 && \leq 1 \qquad (8.5) \\
[\mu_4] \quad & \qquad\quad x_4 && \leq 1 \\
[\mu_5] \quad & \qquad\qquad x_5 && \leq 1
\end{aligned}
$$

$$\text{All } x_j \geq 0, j = 1, \ldots, 5 \tag{8.6}$$

*The abbreviation s.t. stands for subject to.

The economic interpretation of the dual problem is to establish prices for each of the scarce resources so that the minimum total possible would be paid for the consumption of the resources, while ensuring that the resources used for any project cost as much as or more than the value of the project, the project PV in this case [5]. We have two categories of resources here. The first category is cash, represented by cash at time 0 and by cash at time 1; the dual variables ρ_0 and ρ_1 represent the prices, respectively. The second category consists of the projects themselves: a project is considered a scarce resource in the sense that we have the opportunity to execute only one of each. The dual variables $\mu_1, \ldots, \mu_5$ correspond to the upper-bound constraints of the projects and represent the respective prices for the project opportunities.

Table 8.3 *Dual Problem Formulation for Example 8.1, Solution to Primal and Dual*

Symbolic

$$\text{Min} \sum_n \rho_n M_n + \sum_j \mu_j \tag{8.9}$$

s.t.
$[x_j]$
$$-\sum_n a_{nj}\rho_n + \mu_j \geq p_j, \quad j = 1, \ldots, J \tag{8.10}$$

$$\rho_n \geq 0, \quad n = 0, 1, \ldots, N \tag{8.11}$$

$$\mu_j \geq 0, \quad j = 1, \ldots, J \tag{8.12}$$

where ρ_n = dual variable for budget constraint,
μ_j = dual variable for project upper bound.

Numeric

Min $\quad 4{,}400\rho_0 + 4{,}000\rho_1 + \mu_1 + \mu_2 + \mu_3 + \mu_4 + \mu_5 \tag{8.13}$

s.t.

$[x_1]$	$+1{,}000\rho_0$	$+ 2{,}000\rho_1$	$+ \mu_1$				≥ 400
$[x_2]$	$+1{,}200\rho_0$	$+ 2{,}400\rho_1$		$+ \mu_2$			≥ 600
$[x_3]$	$+2{,}000\rho_0$	$+ 2{,}100\rho_1$			$+ \mu_3$		≥ 700
$[x_4]$	$+2{,}500\rho_0$	$+ 1{,}300\rho_1$				$+ \mu_4$	≥ 850
$[x_5]$	$+3{,}000\rho_0$	$- 900\rho_1$				$+ \mu_5$	≥ 900

$$(8.14)$$

$$\rho_n, \mu_j \geq 0$$

Solution

Primal variables: $x_1 = 0.22, x_2 = 1.00, x_3 = 0.0, x_4 = 1.0, x_5 = 0.16$

Dual variables: $\rho_0 = 0.3130, \rho_1 = 0.0435$
$\quad\quad\quad\quad\quad \mu_1 = 0.0, \mu_2 = 120.0, \mu_3 = 0.0, \mu_4 = 10.9, \mu_5 = 0.0$

Objective function value: **$1,682**

If the primal problem is feasible and bounded, there is an optimal solution to both problems. At such an optimum we have, from the dual constraint,

$$\mu_j^* \geq p_j + \sum_n a_{nj}\rho_n^* \tag{8.15}$$

where the asterisk refers to values of the primal and dual variables at the optimum. We know from complementary slackness [5] that if $x_j^* > 0$, the dual constraint is met exactly, and since all dual variables are nonnegative, we have

$$0 \leq \mu_j^* = p_j + \sum_n a_{nj}\rho_n^* \tag{8.16}$$

The μ_j^* represents the opportunity value of project j, and it is equal to the PV plus the cash inflows less any cash outflows evaluated by the ρ_n^*. Hence, for all projects that are accepted fractionally or completely,

$$-\sum_n a_{nj}\rho_n^* \leq p_j \tag{8.17}$$

Equation 8.17 states that in order for a project to be accepted, its PV must be equal to or greater than the cash outflows minus cash inflows evaluated by the ρ_n^*.

Again from complementary slackness, if $x_j^* < 1$, then $\mu_j^* = 0$. So for fractionally accepted projects (8.17) becomes

$$-\sum_n a_{nj}\rho_n^* = p_j \tag{8.18}$$

For rejected projects we also have $\mu_j^* = 0$ and, using Eq. 8.15,

$$-\sum_n a_{nj}\rho_n^* \geq p_j \tag{8.19}$$

In other words, the cash outflows minus cash inflows, evaluated by the ρ_n^*, exceed (or equal) the PV of the project.

We can demonstrate these conditions by using the optimal values of the LP problem given in Table 8.3. For project 1, fractionally accepted, applying (8.18) gives

$$(\$1,000)(0.313) + (2,000)(0.0435) = \$400 = PV$$

The value of cash inflows minus outflows equals the PV.

For project 2, completely accepted, applying (8.16) gives

$$\mu_2^* = \$600 - (1,200)(0.313) - (2,400)(0.0435) = \$120 > 0$$

The opportunity cost of the project is $120, the difference between the PV and the cash outflows minus the cash inflows.

For project 3, rejected, applying (8.19) gives

$$(\$2,000)(0.313) + (2,100)(0.0435) = \$717 \geq \$700$$

Here the cash outflows minus inflows are worth more than the PV, which explains the rejection.

.These types of project evaluation, or project pricing, with the dual variables, are fundamental to the LP modeling and analysis of capital budgeting problems. We will see more of this type of analysis in the following sections.

8.3 PURE CAPITAL RATIONING MODELS

The type of model given in Table 8.2 has been extensively analyzed, criticized, and modified during the last twenty years. In this section we attempt to summarize the major arguments so that the reader will obtain a historical perspective on the situation. We do not go into great detail, because the arguments are presented better elsewhere [21] and because the major conclusion to be drawn is that the pure capital rationing (PCR) model is of extremely limited applicability. This fact reinforces the fundamental notion that one must fully understand the assumptions embedded in any mathematical model before attempting to use it.

8.3.1 Criticisms of the PV Model

Among the first to criticize the PV model (as in Table 8.2) were Baumol and Quandt [3]. They identified three major flaws.

1. There is no provision in the model for investment outside the firm or for dividend payments.
2. The model does not provide for carryover of unused funds from one period to the next.
3. Assuming that we have an appropriate discount rate i for computing the PV of each project, this rate is valid in general only for the situation of unlimited borrowing and lending at that rate. Since we have borrowing limits implicitly stated in the budget constraints, an externally determined discount rate is inappropriate.

The first two objections can easily be overcome. For example, investment outside the firm, including lending activities, can easily be represented by new projects. Define project 6 to be lending from time 0 to time 1 at 15%. Then we set $a_{06} = -1$ and $a_{16} = 1.15$ and place no upper bound (or a very large bound) on x_6. Similarly, variables can be defined for divided payments and included in the budget constraints. We would also need to include dividends in the objective function, which implies knowledge of the discount rate appropriate for the owner(s) or shareholders of the firm in order to discount correctly the future dividends. Later, we will see some different methods for including dividends in the objective function.

The third objection is a serious one and requires more attention. To illustrate the difficulties arising from it, let us analyze Example 8.2.

Example 8.2

Table 8.4 presents the data for Example 8.2 along with the optimal LP solution. Example 8.2 is somewhat similar to Example 8.1: projects 1, 2, and 4 are the same; projects 3 and 5 are slightly changed so their PVs are negative; project 6 is added to the set; and the budget limits are changed.

Notice that projects 2 and 4 are completely accepted, as they were in

Table 8.4 *Data and Solution for Example 8.2*

Cash Flow at Time	Project					
	1	2	3	4	5	6
0	−$1,000	−$1,200	−$2,000	−2,500	−$3,000	$1,000
1	−2,000	−2,400	−2,100	−1,300	900	−700
2	2,000	2,500	3,000	2,000	1,400	−700
3	2,900	3,567	2,621	2,000	1,600	0
4	0	0	0	2,000	211	0
5	0	0	0	2,296	0	0
PV (20%)	$400	600	−150	850	−250	−70

Budgets for external sources of funds: $n = 0$, \$3,000; $n = 1$, \$5,000

Solution

Primal variables: $x_1 = 0.30$, $x_2 = 1.0$, $x_3 = 0.0$, $x_4 = 1.0$, $x_5 = 0.0$, $x_6 = 1.0$

Dual variables: $\rho_0 = 0.3189$, $\rho_1 = 0.0405$

$\mu_1 = 0.0$, $\mu_2 = 120.0$, $\mu_3 = 0.0$, $\mu_4 = 0.0$, $\mu_5 = 0.0$, $\mu_6 = 220.5$

Objective function value: \$1,500

Example 8.1. The dual variables for the budget constraints, ρ_0 and ρ_1, do not have their optimal values changed much, so the pricing of projects 2 and 4 is similar.

Project 2: $\mu_2 = \$120 = \$600 - (1,200)(0.3189) - (2,400)(0.0405)$

Project 4: $\mu_4 = 0 = \$850 - (2,500)(0.3189) - (1,300)(0.0405)$

Here we have an example of a completely accepted project with $\mu_j = 0$. Project 1 is again accepted fractionally, and it prices out at zero.

Project 1: $\mu_1 = 0 = \$400 - (1,000)(0.3189) - (2,000)(0.0405)$

We can demonstrate Eq. 8.19 for a rejected project with negative PV.

Project 3: $(\$2,000)(0.3189) + (2,100)(0.0405) = 723 > -150$

This result is hardly surprising since project 3 has only outflows during the critical times and has a negative PV.

The real surprise is that project 6, with a negative PV of −\$70, is accepted. Pricing out by using Eq. 8.16 yields

Project 6: $\mu_6 = \$221 = -70 + (1,000)(0.3189) - (700)(0.0405)$

The value of the \$1,000 inflow at time 0, less the value of the \$700 outflow at time 1, more than overcomes the negative PV and makes project 6 desirable. (The \$700 outflow at time 2 is worth zero since there is no constraint on money at this time.) The extra $1,000 when it is needed most enables us to select more of the other projects and thereby increase the overall *PV* of the projects selected. □

Project 6 in Example 8.2 has the cash flow pattern of a borrowing activity. Since its *IRR* = 26%, we are effectively borrowing at a periodic rate of 26% in order to maximize overall *PV* at 20%! This example clearly demonstrates the philosophical conflict in using an interest rate for *PV* maximization when we are faced with a budget limitation. If we have available a borrowing opportunity at a different, higher interest rate, we could be induced to borrow at a rate higher than that used for computing *PV*. The budget limits, in effect, invalidate the use of an externally determined discount rate. The inclusion of lending opportunities and dividend payments does not solve the difficulty, so various authors have attempted other approaches, some of which are discussed in the following.

8.3.2 Consistent Discount Factors

In reformulating the *PV* model to eliminate the incompatibility presented, Baumol and Quandt defined a model in which the discount rates between periods are determined by the model itself [3]. On the basis of our previous notation, their revised model is

$$\operatorname*{Max}_{x_j, \rho_n} \sum_n \sum_j a_{nj} \frac{\rho_n}{\rho_0} x_j \tag{8.20}$$

s.t.[1]
$[\rho_n]$

$$-\sum_j a_{nj} x_j \leq M_n, \qquad n = 0, 1, ..., N \tag{8.3}$$

$$x_j \geq 0, \qquad j = 1, ..., J \tag{8.6}$$

The terms ρ_n/ρ_0 represent the discount factors from time 0 to time n. Whenever the discount factors are so defined, we will designate them as *consistent discount factors*. Notice the absence of project upper-bound constraints (8.5).

A typical dual constraint has the form

$$-\sum_n a_{nj} \rho_n \geq \sum_n a_{nj} \frac{\rho_n}{\rho_0} \tag{8.21}$$

or

$$\left(-1 - \frac{1}{\rho_0}\right) \sum_n a_{nj} \rho_n \geq 0$$

But the dual variables are nonnegative, so

$$\sum_n a_{nj} \rho_n \leq 0$$

---

[1]The abbreviation s.t. stands for subject to.

In the primal objective function the term ρ_0 can be placed before the summation signs; thus each coefficient of x_j is nonpositive. The objective function must therefore have an optimal solution of zero with all $x_j = 0$. In addition, the solution to the dual objective function

$$\operatorname*{Min}_{\rho_n} \sum_n M_n \rho_n \qquad (8.22)$$

with $M_n > 0$ will be zero, with all $\rho_n = 0$. The zero value of ρ_0 in the denominator of the primal objective function (8.20) renders that function indeterminate.

With this line of reasoning, Baumol and Quandt rejected *PV* models. They then formulated a model with an objective function that is linear in dividend payments. We will not present this model here but instead examine the PCR line that was pursued by others.

Atkins and Ashton [1] criticized the approach of Baumol and Quandt because there were no upper-bound constraints on the projects and the consequent interpretation of dual variables was absent. The discount factors ρ_n/ρ_0 are determined by the marginal productivities of capital in the various time periods. In the absence of upper bounds on projects, any project that is accepted is also partially rejected. Hence, the discounted cash flow of that project *must* be zero.

The implication of this reasoning is that projects must have upper bounds placed on them to avoid the phenomenon of each accepted (and, at the same time, rejected) project having a *PV*, based on consistent discount factors $d_n = \rho_n/\rho_0$, equal to zero. In addition, the Atkins and Ashton model allows for funds to be carried forward at a lending rate of interest. The final modification is the interpretation of the discount factors when one of the ρ_n becomes zero: the equivalent form $\rho_n = d_n \rho_0$ avoids these difficulties.

The method for finding a *consistent optimal solution* (an optimal set of x_j and $d_n = \rho_n/\rho_0$) consists of identifying and evaluating the Kuhn–Tucker stationary points [17] of the problem. In the PCR model there are potentially many consistent solutions, whereas in the situation with lending there is only one solution. In general, this is a rather unsatisfactory procedure because of the large number of such points.

Freeland and Rosenblatt [8] pursued the PCR model (with project upper-bound constraints) further and obtained several interesting results.

- The value of the objective function at a consistent optimal solution equals

$$\frac{1}{2} \sum_j \mu_j^* \quad \text{(property 2)}.$$

- For the PCR case (no lending or borrowing allowed) an objective function value different from zero can be obtained only if some of the M_n values have opposite signs.
- If the objective function value for a consistent optimal solution is not zero, there are alternative optimal discount factors d_n.

716

A more recent article by Hayes [12] on the same topic has further clarified the issue for the situation in which *all budgets are fully expended.* Hayes's analysis assumes upper bounds on projects and lending from one period to the next, but his major result does not depend on the lending activities. If the budgets are fully utilized in all periods except the last (the horizon), the optimal set of projects is independent of discount factors and may be obtained by maximizing the cash at the end of the last period (at the horizon). To see why this result is true, let us reexamine the *PV* model.

$$\text{Max} \sum_{n} \sum_{j} a_{nj} d_n x_j \qquad (8.23)$$

s.t.

$$[\rho_n] \qquad -\sum_{j} a_{nj} x_j = M_n, \qquad n = 0, 1, ..., N - 1 \qquad (8.24)$$

$$[\rho_N] \qquad -\sum_{j} a_{Nj} x_j + l_N = M_N \qquad (8.25)$$

$$x_j \le 1, \qquad j = 1, ..., J \qquad (8.5)$$

$$x_j \ge 0, \qquad j = 1, ..., J \qquad (8.6)$$

where d_n = discount factor for time n,
  l_n = cash left over at time N, the horizon,

and the other terms are as defined previously. Note that the budget constraints 8.24 and 8.25 are equalities, reflecting the assumption about cash being used up each period. The l_N term measures any leftover cash at time N, the horizon, the only time we are allowed to have excess cash in this model.

To obtain the desired result, let us split the objective function.

$$\text{Max} \sum_{j} a_{Nj} d_N x_j + \sum_{n=0}^{N-1} \sum_{j} a_{nj} d_n x_j \qquad (8.26)$$

Now we can substitute the constraints into the objective function.

$$\text{Max}\; d_N (l_N - M_N) - \sum_{n=0}^{N-1} d_n M_n = \text{Max}\; d_N l_N - \sum_{n=0}^{N} d_n M_n \qquad (8.27)$$

Since the summation in Eq. 8.27 is a constant for fixed values of d_n, it may be dropped without affecting the solution, and by dividing out the constant d_N we are left with

$$\text{Max}\; l_N \qquad (8.28)$$

subject to constraints 8.24, 8.25, 8.5, and 8.6.

Appropriate discount factors may be obtained by the usual form $d_n = \rho_n/\rho_0$ with $\rho_0 = 1$ or any positive constant. With all budget constraints at equality, it is easy to show that $\rho_{n-1} \geq \rho_n$; therefore, no possibility exists of zero dual variables. In summary, the discount factors are irrelevant for project selection!

The foregoing result is important because it emphasizes the fact that the dual variables for the budget constraints reflect the marginal productivities of capital in the respective time periods. Since all cash flows are automatically reinvested in this closed system, any consumption choices by the owner or owners of the firm have been expressed by the values set for the M_n.

In this section we appear to have presented numerous models, summarized extensive analyses, and arrived at very little in terms of a useful *PV* model. That is precisely true. All the arguments and discussion repeatedly point to the following types of conclusions and statements.

- In any *PV* model the budget constraint dual variables must reflect the marginal productivities of capital.

- Project upper-bound constraints and lending activities must be included in order to have a meaningful formulation.

- For certain types of closed systems, in which all budgets are fully expended, the projects are selected by maximizing cash at the horizon.

We will return to this last point in Section 8.5. In the meantime, we will discuss in more detail the inclusion of lending and borrowing opportunities in the *PV* model.

8.4 NET PRESENT VALUE MAXIMIZATION WITH LENDING AND BORROWING

8.4.1 Inclusion of Lending Opportunities

We can define a lending project as an outflow of cash in one period followed by an inflow, with interest, at a later period. Define v_n to be the amount lent at time n, to be repaid at time $n + 1$ with interest r_n. We then have coefficients $a_{nj} = -1$ and $a_{n+1,j} = 1 + r_n$. We will define as many lending variables as there are time periods with budget constraints. There are no limits on lending.

Notice that we have defined only one-period loans, which is the common practice. Multiple-period lending could easily be included. The following are some typical examples, all with a constant lending rate.

	a_{nj}		
Period	Case 1: Lump Sum Payment	Case 2: Interest Only During Period, Principal at End of Last Period	Case 3: Equal Payments
n	-1	-1	-1
$n + 1$	0	r	$(A/P, r, 2)$
$n + 2$	$(1 + r)^2$	$1 + r$	$(A/P, r, 2)$

718

The number of variables tends to become somewhat unwieldy with this approach, however, compared with the benefits derived from distinguishing between short-term and long-term lending rates. If the projects consist mainly of financial instruments, it is important to work at this level of detail [11]. Otherwise, the approximation of multiple-period lending with successive one-period lending usually suffices.

The objective function coefficients for the lending activities can be obtained by straightforward discounting at $i = MARR$. Applying this concept to case 2, we have

$$PV = -1 + \frac{r}{1+i} + \frac{1+r}{(1+i)^2}$$

The resulting PV may be positive or negative, depending on whether r is greater than or smaller than i, respectively.

If one-period lending opportunities are included in the PV model, and lending is always preferred to doing nothing, we can solve an equivalent problem by simply maximizing the amount of cash at the horizon [1,8]. This result is similar to that obtained by Hayes, as described in Section 8.3.2. With attractive lending opportunities present, all budgets will be fully expended, and Hayes's result can be applied directly.

8.4.2 Inclusion of Borrowing Opportunities

We should note that the inclusion of unlimited lending opportunities still has not resolved the philosophical conflict between using an interest rate for PV maximization and having budget constraints. If borrowing opportunities are also unlimited, it appears that we have eliminated the conflict. But in that case we really do not need budget constraints and LP to solve our project selection problem. Investment projects with an IRR less than the lending rate would always be rejected, and those with an IRR greater than the borrowing rate would be accepted. The selection problem would concern only projects with an IRR between the lending and borrowing rates.

There remain two difficulties with such an approach. The first is that we rarely have unlimited borrowing opportunities at one interest rate. (In a practical sense, only an agency of the U.S. government can borrow unlimited amounts). Typically, we can borrow, but only up to a limit. Some of the models presented in the next section have this feature. The second difficulty is related to the interpretation of the interest rate used for PV calculations. If the (different) lending and borrowing rates are specified, any other discount rate must presumably reflect the time preferences of the owners of the firm. There is no philosophical conflict in having three distinct rates for lending by the firm, borrowing by the firm, and discounting to reflect the owners' time preferences. But in this case we need to include dividends in the objective function, as shown in Section 8.6 and Appendix 8.A.

We have again failed to develop a rational *PV* model. The reasons here are similar to those for the PCR case. In the face of limits on borrowing, the decisions about selecting projects must be related, through the interrelationships among project combinations and budget amounts, to the decisions for dividend payments [21]. The marginal productivities of capital from one period to the next determine the dual variables ρ_n. Any attempt to ignore these two realities in constructing a project selection model or procedure is bound to have major conceptual flaws.

8.5. WEINGARTNER'S HORIZON MODEL

Many of the conceptual issues discussed in the previous two sections can be avoided by ignoring *PV* and concentrating on accumulated cash as the objective. Such models are called horizon models. They typically include borrowing and lending activities and may have other constraints added. These models represent an empirical approach to capital budgeting and should therefore be judged mainly on this basis. The presentation in this section, which is based largely on Weingartner [20], presumes the use of LP and hence allows fractional projects.

8.5.1 Equal Lending and Borrowing Rates

The simplest type of horizon model contains budget constraints, project upper bounds, and lending and borrowing opportunities at a common, fixed rate.

Example 8.3

Table 8.5 presents the data for Example 8.3, and Table 8.6 presents both the symbolic and numeric primal formulations. The projects, 1 through 6, are the same as for Example 8.2. The budget amounts are slightly different from those in Example 8.2, being $3,000, $5,000, and $4,800 at times 0, 1, and 2, respectively. We are using 20% for both borrowing and lending, with no limits on either. The horizon is at time 2, so we are trying to maximize the accumulated cash at this time. Most of the projects, however, have cash flows after time 2, so we discount at 20% these flows back to time 2. For example, $\hat{a}_1$ represents the $2,900 inflow at time 3 for project 1, discounted at 20% for one period, or $2,900/1.2 = $2,417.

The objective function in this horizon model is $v_2 - w_2$, the accumulated cash available (for lending) at time 2, plus the value of posthorizon flows, represented by the $\hat{a}_j$. The cash balance equations 8.30 and 8.31 are similar to those for the *PV* model. A typical constraint says that cash outflows from projects, plus current lending, plus repayment with interest of previous-period borrowing, minus repayment with interest of previous-period lending, minus current borrowing must be less than or equal to the amount of externally supplied funds. The project upper bounds and nonnegativity restrictions complete the model. For simplicity, we have not included any project dependency or exclusivity constraints. (The solution to Example 8.3 follows in the text.) □

Table 8.5 *Data for Examples 8.3 and 8.5 (Horizon Is Time 2)*

Variable Type		Project 1	2	3	4	5	6
Cash Flow							
at Time	0	−$1,000	−$1,200	−$2,000	−$2,500	−$3,000	$1,000
Same for	1	−2,000	−2,400	−2,100	−1,300	900	−700
Examples 8.3	2	2,000	2,500	3,000	2,000	1,400	−700
and 8.5	3	2,900	3,567	2,621	2,000	1,600	0
	4	0	0	0	2,000	211	0
	5	0	0	0	2,296	0	0
Example 8.3 $\hat{a}_j$		$2,417	2,973	2,184	4,384	1,480	0
Example 8.5 $\hat{a}_j$		$2,230	2,744	2,016	3,767	1,356	0

Budgets (M_n)	$n = 0$	$n = 1$	$n = 2$
Example 8.3	$3,000	5,000	4,800
Example 8.5	$1,000	2,000	4,800
Lending rates	$n = 0 \rightarrow 1$	$n = 1 \rightarrow 2$	$n = 2 \rightarrow 3$
Example 8.3	20%	20%	20%
Example 8.5	15%	15%	15%
Borrowing rates	$n = 0 \rightarrow 1$	$n = 1 \rightarrow 2$	$n = 2 \rightarrow 3$
Example 8.3	20%	20%	20%
Example 8.5	30%	30%	30%
Borrowing limits	$n = 0 \rightarrow 1$	$n = 1 \rightarrow 2$	$n = 2 \rightarrow 3$
Example 8.5 only	None	1,000	None

The LP solution of the horizon model in Example 8.3 is straightforward and quick, requiring less than one second of time for both processing and input–output on a mainframe computer. Table 8.7 contains the solution for Example 8.3. Projects 1, 2, and 4 were accepted completely, and projects 3, 5, and 6 were rejected. In addition, there was borrowing of $1,700 at time 0 and $2,740 at time 1. At time 2 a total cash accumulation of $8,012 was available for lending.

There is more to the solution of this horizon problem than the numerical results, however. We note several features of the solution.

- The dual variables ρ_n are powers of 1.2.
- The dual variables μ_j for accepted projects are equal to the *FV*(20%) of these projects.
- Projects with positive *PV*(20%) were accepted and those with negative *PV* (20%) were rejected.

These features are not coincidental but rather are characteristic of the horizon model as presented in Table 8.6. We can verify this by examining the dual formulation, given in Table 8.8.

Table 8.6 *Primal Problem Formulation For Horizon Model for Example 8.3*

Symbolic

$$\text{Max}_{x_j,v_n,w_n} \sum_j \hat{a}_j x_j + v_N - w_N \tag{8.29}$$

s.t.

$$[\rho_0] \qquad -\sum_j a_{0j} x_j + v_0 - w_0 \le M_0 \tag{8.30}$$

$$[\rho_n] \qquad -\sum_j a_{nj} x_j - (1+r)v_{n-1} + v_n + (1+r)w_{n-1} - w_n \le M_n,$$

$$n = 1, 2, \ldots, N \tag{8.31}$$

$$[\mu_j] \qquad\qquad\qquad x_j \le 1, \qquad j = 1, \ldots, J \tag{8.5}$$

$$x_j \ge 0, \qquad j = 1, \ldots, J \tag{8.6}$$

$$v_n, w_n \ge 0, \qquad j = 0, \ldots, J \tag{8.32}$$

where $\hat{a}_j$ = horizon time value of cash flows beyond horizon
x_j = project selection variable
a_{nj} = cash flow for project j at time n; inflows have a plus sign, outflows have a minus sign
v_n = lending amount from time n to time $n + 1$
w_n = amount borrowed from time n to time $n + 1$
r = interest rate for borrowing and lending
M_n = budget limit on externally supplied funds at time n
N = horizon, end of the planning period
ρ_n, μ_j = dual variables

Numeric

$$\text{Max } \$2{,}417x_1 + 2{,}973x_2 + 2{,}184x_3 + 4{,}384x_4 + 1{,}480x_5 + v_2 - w_2$$

s.t.

$$[\rho_0] \quad \$1{,}000x_1 + 1{,}200x_2 + 2{,}000x_3 + 2{,}500x_4 + 3{,}000x_5 - 1{,}000x_6$$
$$+ v_0 - w_0 \le 3{,}000$$

$$[\rho_1] \quad \$2{,}000x_1 + 2{,}400x_2 + 2{,}100x_3 + 1{,}300x_4 - 900x_5 + 700x_6$$
$$- 1.2v_0 + v_1 + 1.2w_0 - w_1 \le 5{,}000$$

$$[\rho_2] \quad -\$2{,}000x_1 - 2{,}500x_2 - 3{,}000x_3 - 2{,}000x_4 - 1{,}400x_5 + 700x_6$$
$$- 1.2v_1 + v_2 + 1.2w_1 - w_2 \le 4{,}800$$

$$[\mu_1] \qquad x_1 \qquad\qquad\qquad\qquad\qquad \le 1$$

$$[\mu_2] \qquad\qquad x_2 \qquad\qquad\qquad\qquad \le 1$$

$$[\mu_3] \qquad\qquad\qquad x_3 \qquad\qquad\qquad \le 1$$

$$[\mu_4] \qquad\qquad\qquad\qquad x_4 \qquad\qquad \le 1$$

$$[\mu_5] \qquad\qquad\qquad\qquad\qquad x_5 \qquad \le 1$$

$$[\mu_6] \qquad\qquad\qquad\qquad\qquad\qquad x_6 \le 1$$

all $x_j \ge 0$, $j = 1, \ldots, 6$

all $v_n, w_n \ge 0$, $n = 0, 1, 2$

Table 8.7 *Solution to Examples 8.3 and 8.5*

Variable Type	Objective Function	Example 8.3, $17,786	Example 8.5, $9,210
Project selection	x_1	1.0	0
	x_2	1.0	1.0
	x_3	0	0
	x_4	1.0	0.151
	x_5	0	0
	x_6	0	0.577
Lending	v_0	0	0
	v_1	0	0
	v_2	$8,012	$5,898
Borrowing	w_0	$1,700	0
	w_1	2,740	$1,000
	w_2	0	0
Budget constraint dual variable	ρ_0	1.44	1.622
	ρ_1	1.20	1.317
	ρ_2	1.00	1.0
Project upper-bound dual variable	μ_1	577	0
	μ_2	865	137
	μ_3	0	0
	μ_4	1.224	0
	μ_5	0	0
	μ_6	0	0
Borrowing limit dual variable	β_1	—	0.017

From (8.36) and (8.37) we have $\rho_n^* = 1$. The value of $1 at time N is $1 in the optimal solution because we do not have time to do anything with it. Similarly, from (8.34) and (8.35) we obtain

$$1 + r \le \frac{\rho_n^*}{\rho_{n+1}^*} \le 1 + r, \qquad n = 0, ..., N - 1 \qquad (8.38)$$

or

$$\frac{\rho_n^*}{\rho_{n+1}^*} = 1 + r \qquad (8.39)$$

and

$$\rho_n^* = \rho_{n+1}^*(1 + r) = \rho_{n+2}^*(1 + r)^2 = \cdots = \rho_{n+N-n}^*(1 + r)^{N-n}$$
$$= \rho_N^*(1 + r)^{N-n} = (1 + r)^{N-n} \qquad (8.40)$$

The interpretation of the ρ_n^* now becomes clear: they are compound interest factors that reflect the value at the horizon, time N, of an additional dollar at time n.

723

Table 8.8 *Dual Problem Formulation for Horizon Model with Common, Fixed Rate for Borrowing and Lending*

$$\text{Min} \sum_n \rho_n M_n + \sum_j \mu_j \qquad (8.9)$$

s.t.

$[x_j]$	$-\sum_n a_{nj}\rho_n + \mu_j \geq \hat{a}_j,$ $\qquad j = 1, \ldots, J$	(8.33)
$[v_n]$	$\rho_n - (1 + r)\rho_{n+1} \geq 0,$ $\qquad n = 0, \ldots, N - 1$	(8.34)
$[w_n]$	$-\rho_n + (1 + r)\rho_{n+1} \geq 0,$ $\qquad n = 0, \ldots, N - 1$	(8.35)
$[v_N]$	$\rho_N \geq 1$	(8.36)
$[w_N]$	$-\rho_N \geq -1$	(8.37)
	$\rho_n \geq 0, \qquad n = 0, 1, \ldots, N - 1$	(8.11)
	$\mu_j \geq 0, \qquad j = 1, \ldots, J$	(8.12)

The analysis of (8.33) is similar to that of (8.10) in Section 8.2.5. If $x_j^* > 0$, the dual constraint is met exactly, and

$$0 \leq \mu_j^* = \hat{a}_j + \sum_n a_{nj}\rho_n^* \qquad (8.41)$$

Substituting for ρ_n^* from (8.40), we have

$$\mu_j^* = \hat{a}_j + \sum_n a_{nj}(1 + r)^{N-n} \qquad (8.42)$$

The right side of (8.42) is simply the net future value (*FV*) at time *N* of the cash flows for project *j*. The $\hat{a}_j$ term is the value of posthorizon flows discounted back to time *N*, and the summation is the forward compounding of the other cash flows. For fractionally accepted projects $\mu_j^* = 0$, and thus (8.42) equals zero. For rejected projects x_j^* and μ_j^* are both equal to zero, so

$$0 \geq \hat{a}_j + \sum_n a_{nj}(1 + r)^{N-n} \qquad (8.43)$$

The horizon model with a common, fixed rate for borrowing and lending thus will accept only projects with nonnegative *FV(r)*, or *PV(r)*, and the *FV(r)* of any rejected project is nonpositive. This agreement between the LP model and the *PV* criterion reassures us that the model performs as intended. Actually, we would expect the model to perform precisely in this manner, since the unlimited borrowing and lending opportunities at interest rate r are equivalent to the assumptions underlying the *PV* criterion.

8.5.2. Lending Rates Less Than Borrowing Rates

Clearly, an LP model that yields the same answers as *PV* analysis is of little use. The true power of the LP model is the ability to represent a great variety of investment opportunities and restrictions, lending and borrowing opportunities, scarce resource restrictions, and so forth. In this section we modify the horizon model of the previous section by having a borrowing rate higher than the lending rate. The only modification needed in the model is in the cash balance equation 8.31, which becomes

$$[\rho_n] \qquad -\sum_j a_{nj}x_j - (1 + r_l)v_{n-1} + v_n + (1 + r_b)w_{n-1}$$

$$- w_n \le M_n, \qquad n = 1, 2, ..., N \qquad (8.44)$$

where r_l = lending interest rate,
r_b = borrowing interest rate.

The corresponding changes in the dual problem affect constraints 8.34 and 8.35, which become, respectively,

$$[v_n] \qquad \rho_n - (1 + r_l)\rho_{n+1} \ge 0, \qquad n = 0, \ldots, N-1 \qquad (8.45)$$

$$[w_n] \qquad -\rho_n + (1 + r_b)\rho_{n+1} \ge 0, \qquad n = 0, \ldots, N-1 \qquad (8.46)$$

Instead of (8.38) and (8.39), we obtain

$$1 + r_l \le \frac{\rho_n^*}{\rho_{n+1}^*} \le 1 + r_b, \qquad n = 0, ..., N - 1 \qquad (8.47)$$

The ratio of the dual variables for the cash balance equations is now restricted to the range (including end points) between the lending and borrowing interest factors. From complementary slackness [5] we can deduce that if we are lending money at time n ($v_n > 0$), then (8.45) and the left part of (8.47) are satisfied as equality. If we are borrowing at time n ($w_n > 0$), then (8.46) and the right side of (8.47) are satisfied as equality. This makes sense, because the lending activity implies that extra dollars at time n would also be lent, leading to 1.2 times the extra dollars at the horizon as extra dollars at time $n + 1$, and so forth.

Example 8.4

We can demonstrate these results with Example 8.4, for which both data and solution are shown in Table 8.9. There are four projects, six budget limits, a

Table 8.9 *Data and Solution for Example 8.4 (Lending Rate Less Than Borrowing Rate)*

Cash Flow at Time	Project				
	1	2	3	4	Budget
0	−600	−$1,200	−$900	−$1,500	$270
1	360	480	360	420	150
2	330	360	330	480	30
3	60	0	300	510	0
4	−150	660	270	540	−60
5	330	510	240	540	0
$\hat{a}_j$	150	300	150	330	—

$r_l = 0.2, r_b = 0.3, N = 5$

Solution

$x_1 = 1.0$	$v_0 = 0$	$w_0 = 420$	$\rho_0 = 2.754$
$x_2 = 0$	$v_1 = 0$	$w_1 = 0$	$\rho_1 = 2.119$
$x_3 = 0.1$	$v_2 = 393$	$w_2 = 0$	$\rho_2 = 1.728$
$x_4 = 0$	$v_3 = 561$	$w_3 = 0$	$\rho_3 = 1.440$
$\mu_1 = 67$	$v_4 = 490$	$w_4 = 0$	$\rho_4 = 1.200$
$\mu_2 = 0$	$v_5 = 943$	$w_5 = 0$	$\rho_5 = 1.000$
$\mu_3 = 0$			
$\mu_4 = 0$			

lending rate of 20%, a borrowing rate of 30%, and a horizon at time 5. The negative budget at time 4 means we must generate $60 to be used elsewhere in the firm. Only project 1 is accepted completely; project 3 is accepted fractionally, and the other two are rejected. There are borrowing at time 0 and lending at times 2 through 5. We can demonstrate how Eq. 8.47 indicates borrowing or lending by taking the ratios of the dual variables.

$\rho_0^*/\rho_1^* = 1.3$ borrowing at time 0

$\rho_1^*/\rho_2^* = 1.23$ neither at time 1

$\rho_2^*/\rho_3^* = 1.2$ lending at time 2

$\rho_3^*/\rho_4^* = 1.2$ lending at time 3

$\rho_4^*/\rho_5^* = 1.2$ lending at time 4   □

Everything seems to work according to theory in Example 8.4, but how do we explain the ratio ρ_1^*/ρ_2^* of 1.23, which is strictly between the limits? And if there are no restrictions on borrowing, why is project 3 accepted only fractionally? To answer these questions, let us assume two hypothetical situations in Example 8.3. First, assume everything is as before except that we borrow at time

1, forcing the ratio to be 1.3. The new dual variables can then be obtained as follows.

$$\rho_5 = 1.0$$
$$\rho_4 = \rho_5(1.2) = 1.2$$
$$\rho_3 = \rho_4(1.2) = 1.44$$
$$\rho_2 = \rho_3(1.2) = 1.728$$
$$\rho_1 = \rho_2(1.3) = 2.246$$
$$\rho_0 = \rho_1(1.3) = 2.920$$

Now let us find the corresponding value of μ_3 from Eq. 8.41. In LP terminology, we are pricing out the activity vector for project 3.

$$\$150 + (-900)(2.920) + (360)(2.246) + (330)(1.728)$$
$$+ (300)(1.44) + (270)(1.2) + (240)(1.0) = -\$103$$

The negative value means that we would not introduce project 3 into the LP solution, given the values for the ρ_n. In other words, given the other borrowing and lending activities, we are not justified in borrowing at 30% at time 1 in order to accept more of project 3.

Now assume everything is as in the original solution in Table 8.9, except that we lend at time 1, forcing the ratio to be 1.2. The new dual variables are obtained as before, and the pricing of the activity vector yields

$$\rho_5 = 1.0$$
$$\rho_4 = \rho_5(1.2) = 1.2$$
$$\rho_3 = \rho_4(1.2) = 1.44$$
$$\rho_2 = \rho_3(1.2) = 1.728$$
$$\rho_1 = \rho_2(1.2) = 2.074$$
$$\rho_0 = \rho_1(1.3) = 2.696$$

$$\$150 + (-900)(2.696) + (360)(2.074) + (330)(1.728)$$
$$+ (300)(1.44) + (270)(1.2) + (240)(1.0) = \$37$$

The positive value means that if we were lending money at time 1, given the other borrowing and lending activities, we could improve our situation by accepting project 3. The best action is to accept as much as possible without borrowing at time 1. This turns out to be 10%. What has happened is that the marginal productivity of cash at time 1 is determined by project 3.

8.5.3 Inclusion of Borrowing Limits, Supply Schedule of Funds

Another typical restriction in the horizon model is a limit on the amount borrowed at a particular time. Example 8.5 is a slight variation on Example 8.3.

727

Example 8.5

Table 8.5 presents the relevant data. The project cash flows are the same, the budgets at times 0 and 1 are reduced, the lending rate is 15%, the borrowing rate is 30%, and a \$1,000 limit on borrowing is imposed at time 1. In anticipation of future borrowing at 30%, the $\hat{a}_j$ have been computed by using a discount rate of 30%. The solution for Example 8.5 is given in Table 8.7. Only one project, number 2, is accepted completely, and 4 and 6 are accepted fractionally. The only borrowing activity is at time 1, at the limit of \$1,000. □

To analyze the results of Example 8.5, we need to add one more constraint to the primal problem.

$$[\beta_1] \qquad\qquad w_1 \leq 1,000 \qquad\qquad (8.48)$$

The changes in the dual formulation are in the objective function and in Eq. 8.46.

$$\text{Min} \sum_n \rho_n M_n + \sum_j \mu_j + 1,000\beta_1 \qquad\qquad (8.49)$$

$$[w_1] \qquad\qquad -\rho_1 + (1 + r_b)\rho_2 + \beta_1 \geq 0 \qquad\qquad (8.50)$$

Instead of (8.47) we have

$$(1 + r_l)\rho_2^* \leq \rho_1^* \leq (1 + r_b)\rho_2^* + \beta_1^* \qquad\qquad (8.51)$$

The borrowing restriction at time 1 places a premium on funds at time 1 beyond that of the normal borrowing interest factor of 1.3. The nonzero value of β_1^* implies that we are borrowing the full amount and would like to borrow more. We can verify the right side of (8.51).

$$1.317 = (1.3)(1.0) + 0.017$$

What has happened in this example is as follows.

- Project 2, with the highest *IRR* of 31.26%, was accepted completely, exhausting the time 0 budget of \$1,000. The cheapest method of borrowing was with partial acceptance of project 6, which is equivalent to borrowing at 26%.
- Projects 3 and 5 had negative *PV*(20%) and would not justify borrowing at 26 or 30%.
- Projects 1 and 4 have similar *IRR*s, 29.1% and 28.9%, respectively, for the original cash flows. The *IRR*s are 28.7% and 28.1%, respectively, for the $a_{0j}, a_{1j}, a_{2j}, \hat{a}_j$ flows, which is what the LP program sees. However, project 1 requires twice as much investment at time 1 as at time 0, whereas the opposite is true for project 4. Since time 1 borrowing costs 30% and the time 0 borrowing costs 26% (via project 6), preference is given to project

4. Neither project justifies borrowing at 30% in both periods, so just enough of project 4 is accepted to reach the borrowing limit of $1,000 at time 1.

It should be noted that the pricing operation with Eq. 8.41 is still valid and yields results consistent with the solution in Table 8.7.

The concept of borrowing limit can be generalized to a series of limits, each applicable to a source of loan funds at a designated rate. For example, a firm may be able to borrow an amount, say 2,000, at 22%, an additional 1,000 at 25%, and a final 1,000 at 30%, as shown in Figure 8.1. This representation is called a sloping supply schedule for funds [20]. If we let w_{kn} represent the amount borrowed at the kth step at time n, the modification to the horizon model is straightforward, as shown in Table 8.10. By convention, we order the borrowing steps in increasing order of cost r_k; the LP algorithm will naturally start borrowing at the lowest cost and move to the next step as each limit is reached.

Analysis of the dual formulation is similar to that in Example 8.5. For each w_{kn} in the primal we have a dual constraint.

$$[w_{kn}] \qquad\qquad -\rho_n + (1 + r_{kn})\rho_{n+1} + \beta_{kn} \geq 0 \qquad\qquad (8.56)$$

The dual constraint of interest is the one corresponding to the last step k at time n. If we are at the limit on the last step, we can not say anything beyond Eq. 8.56 without the actual value of β_{kn}^* from the LP solution. If we are borrowing an amount below the limit on the last step, however, we have

$$\frac{\rho_n^*}{\rho_{n+1}^*} = 1 + r_{kn} \qquad\qquad (8.57)$$

Equation 8.57 illustrates the nature of the ρ_n^* as indicators of the marginal cost of funds.

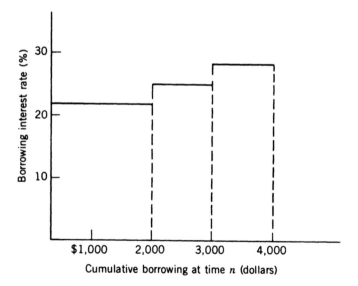

FIGURE 8.1. Sloping supply schedule of funds.

Table 8.10 *Primal Problem Formulation for Horizon Model with Sloping Supply Schedule for Funds*

$$\text{Max} \sum_j \hat{a}_j x_j + v_N - \sum_k w_{kN} \tag{8.52}$$

s.t.

$$[\rho_0] \quad -\sum_j a_{0j} x_j + v_0 - \sum_k w_{k0} \le M_0 \tag{8.53}$$

$$[\rho_n] \quad -\sum_j a_{nj} x_j - (1 + r_\ell)v_{n-1} + v_n + \sum_k (1 + r_k)w_{k,n-1}$$

$$\quad -\sum_k w_{kn} \le M_n, \qquad n = 1, 2, \ldots, N \tag{8.54}$$

$$[\beta_{kn}] \quad w_{kn} \le B_{kn}, \quad k = 1, \ldots, m; \quad n = 0, \ldots, N \tag{8.55}$$

$$[\mu_j] \quad x_j \le 1, \qquad j = 1, \ldots, j \tag{8.56}$$

all variables ≥ 0

where w_{kn} = amount borrowed at kth step at time n,
$\quad r_k$ = interest rate at kth step of borrowing,
$\quad B_{kn}$ = limit on kth step at time n.
Other terms are as previously described

8.5.4 Dual Analysis with Project Interdependencies

The presence of project interdependencies will affect the use of (8.33) in pricing out project activity vectors in a manner consistent with the LP solution.

Example 8.6

We add a contingency relationship that project 4 cannot be performed without project 5 in Example 8.3. Then we add to the primal the form 8.8, or

$$[\nu] \qquad\qquad x_4 - x_5 \le 0$$

and the dual constraints 8.33 would become

$$-\sum_n a_{n4}\rho_n + \mu_4 + \upsilon \ge \hat{a}_4$$

$$-\sum_n a_{n5}\rho_n + \mu_5 - \upsilon \ge \hat{a}_5$$

The pricing operation would reflect a penalty being applied to project 4 and a subsidy being applied to project 5. Since project 4 is so highly favorable, both 4 and 5 would be accepted. Using (8.41), we have

$$\text{Project 4:} \quad \mu_4^* = \$4,384 - (2,500)(1.44) - (1,300)(1.2)$$
$$+ (2,000)(1.0) - 360 = \$864$$

$$\text{Project 5:} \quad \mu_5^* = \$1,480 - (3,000)(1.44) + (900)(1.2)$$
$$+ (1,400)(1.0) + 360 = 0$$

The value of v is 360, just enough for project 5 to price out at zero, where it can be accepted. □

The mutual exclusivity constraints 8.7 would be handled in a similar manner. In practice, such constraints allow more projects to be fractionally accepted, and the typical end result is use of integer programming (Section 8.7).

8.6 BERNHARD'S GENERAL MODEL

All the features of the horizon model with borrowing constraints (Section 8.5.3) are retained in Bernhard's general model for capital budgeting [4]. Bernhard also includes dividends in a nonlinear objective function, with dividends constrained by a horizon posture restriction. In the following sections we will present the model and some general results. With few exceptions, the notation will follow Bernhard's, which is largely consistent with what we have been using. Appendix 8.A presents an application of the model to a dividend–terminal-wealth problem.

8.6.1 Model Formulation

The objective function is an unspecified function of dividends and terminal wealth.

$$\text{Max } f(D_1, D_2, \ldots, D_N, G) \tag{8.58}$$

where D_n = dividend paid at time n,
   G = time N terminal wealth, to be specified in more detail later.

It is assumed that $\partial f/\partial D_n \geq 0$ and $\partial f/\partial G \geq 0$, which imply that more dividends and terminal wealth, respectively, lead to greater utility values. Typically, f is defined to be concave.

The cash balance equations, or budget constraints, contain a liquidity requirement that reflects certain banking practices. The firm is required to maintain $C_n + c_n w_n$ in a bank account. The C_n is a constant representing basic

731

liquidity at time n, and the c_n ($0 \leq c_n < 1$) is a compensating balance fraction. The amount $C_n + c_n w_n$ earns interest at rate r_{ln}. The typical constraint is

$$[\rho_n] \qquad - \sum_j a_{nj} x_j - l_{n-1}(v_{n-1} + c_{n-1} w_{n-1} + C_{n-1})$$

$$+ (v_n + c_n w_n + C_n) + b_{n-1} w_{n-1} - w_n$$

$$+ D_n \leq M'_n, \qquad n = 0, 1, ..., N \qquad (8.59)$$

where M'_n = budget limit on externally supplied funds at time n,

l_n = lending interest rate factor at time n, $1 + r_{ln}$, and

b_n = borrowing interest rate factor at time n, $1 + r_{bn}$.

Equation 8.59 states that project outlays, minus previous-period lending, plus current lending, plus previous-period borrowing, minus current borrowing, plus current dividend cannot exceed the budget limit on externally supplied funds at time n. Regrouping terms gives

$$[\rho_n] \qquad - \sum_j a_{nj} x_j - l_{n-1} v_{n-1} + v_n + (b_{n-1} - l_{n-1} c_{n-1}) w_{n-1}$$

$$-(1 - c_n) w_n + D_n \leq M_n, \qquad n = 0, 1, ..., N \qquad (8.60)$$

where

$$M_n = M'_n + (l_{n-1} C_{n-1}) - C_n$$

Group payback restrictions state that at time n' the net outflows on the set of selected projects are recovered.

$$[\psi] \qquad - \sum_j \sum_{n=0}^{n'} a_{nj} x_j \leq 0 \qquad (8.61)$$

Scarce material restrictions are defined for a nonmonetary resource, which could be skilled personnel, special equipment, and so forth.

$$[\nu] \qquad \sum_j d_j x_j \leq d \qquad (8.62)$$

where d_n = amount of scarce resource consumed by project j,

d = total amount of scarce resource available.

The firm is prevented from paying excessive dividends and thus jeopardizing earning capability past the horizon. This is accomplished by a terminal-wealth horizon posture restriction. First it is necessary to define the terminal wealth. After the last dividend D_N at time N, the terminal wealth is

$$G = M' + \sum_j \hat{a}_j x_j + v_N + c_N w_N + C_N - w_N$$

where M' is the value at time N of posthorizon cash flows from other sources.

With the inclusion of M' and the liquidity requirement, the definition is the same as the objective function 8.29 of the horizon model. The definition is rewritten as

$$[\phi] \qquad -\sum_j \hat{a}_j x_j - v_N + (1 - c_N)w_N + G = M \qquad (8.63)$$

where M is $M' + C_N$.

The horizon posture restriction states that the terminal wealth must exceed some functional value of the dividends,

$$G \geqslant K + g(D_1, D_2, \ldots, D_N)$$

where K = a nonnegative constant,
g = a function, typically a convex one.

Rewriting, we have

$$[\theta] \qquad -G + g(D_1, D_2, \ldots, D_N) \leqslant -K \qquad (8.64)$$

Borrowing limits for $n = 0, 1, \ldots, N-1$, project upper bounds, and nonnegativity restrictions complete the model. Table 8.11 summarizes the objective function and constraints.

8.6.2 Major Results

With a concave objective function 8.58 and a convex constraint 8.64, the Kuhn–Tucker conditions are necessary and sufficient for optimality, and they enable us to make a number of statements about optimal solutions to the general model [17]. Table 8.12 presents the Kuhn–Tucker conditions. We present only the major results that can be obtained from them; derivations are in Bernard [4].

The pricing out of a project activity vector, analogous to (8.33), gives us

$$\mu_j^* \geqslant A_j^* = \sum_n a_{nj}\rho_n^* + \sum_{n=0}^{n'} a_{nj}\psi - d_j v^* + \hat{a}_j \rho_N^* \qquad (8.74)$$

where we have used the substitution $\phi^* = \rho_N^*$. The role of A_j^* in (8.74) is similar to that of PV in the horizon model.

Case 1: If $\qquad x_j^* = 1, \qquad \mu_j^* = A_j^* \geqslant 0$

Case 2: If $\qquad 0 < x_j^* < 1, \qquad \mu_j^* = A_j^* = 0 \qquad (8.75)$

Case 3: If $\qquad x_j^* = 0, \qquad \mu_j^* = 0 \geqslant A_j^*$

We should oberve that absent or nonbinding group payback and scarce material contraints imply ψ and v values of zero, and A_j^* reduces to $\sum_n a_{nj}\rho_n^* + \hat{a}_j\rho_N^*$.

Table 8.11 *Bernhard's General Model*

$$\text{Max } f(D_1, D_2, \ldots, D_N, G) \tag{8.58}$$

s.t.

$$[\rho_n] \quad -\sum_j a_{nj}x_j - l_{n-1}v_{n-1} + v_n + (b_{n-1} - l_{n-1}c_{n-1})w_{n-1} \tag{8.60}$$
$$- (1 - c_n)w_n + D_n \leq M_n, \quad n = 0, 1, \ldots, N$$

$$[\psi] \quad -\sum_j \sum_{n=0}^{n'} a_{nj}x_j \leq 0 \tag{8.61}$$

$$[\upsilon] \quad \sum_j d_j x_j \leq d \tag{8.62}$$

$$[\phi] \quad -\sum_j \hat{a}_j x_j - v_N + (1 - c_N)w_N + G = M \tag{8.63}$$

$$[\theta] \quad -G + g(D_1, D_2, \ldots, D_N) \leq -K \tag{8.64}$$

$$[\beta_n] \quad w_n \leq B_n, \quad n = 0, 1, \ldots, N - 1 \tag{8.65}$$

$$[\mu_j] \quad x_j \leq 1, \quad j = 1, \ldots, J \tag{8.5}$$

$$x_j, v_n, w_n, D_n \geq 0 \tag{8.66}$$

where x_j = project selection variable

v_n = lending amount from time n to $n + 1$,

w_n = borrowing amount from time n to $n + 1$

D_n = dividend paid at time n

a_{nj} = cash flow for project j at time n (inflows $+$)

$\hat{a}_j$ = horizon time value of cash flows beyond horizon

l_n = lending interest rate factor at time n, $1 + r_{ln}$

b_n = borrowing interest rate factor at time n, $1 + r_{bn}$

B_n = borrowing limit at time n

c_n = compensating balance fraction

M_n = budget limit on externally supplied funds at time n, adjusted for basic liquidity requirement

d_j = amount of scarce resource consumed by project j

d = total amount of scarce resource available

G = terminal wealth at time N, after paying w_N

M = value at time N of posthorizon cash flows from other sources, adjusted by basic liquidity requirement

K = nonnegative constant representing the minimum acceptable terminal wealth

$\rho_n, \psi, \upsilon, \phi, \theta, \beta_n, \mu_j$ are dual variables

Table 8.12 *Kuhn–Tucker Conditions for Bernhard's General Model*

$[v_n]$	$-\rho_n + l_n\rho_{n+1} \leq 0, \qquad n = 0,1, ..., N-1$	(8.67)
$[w_n]$	$(1 - c_n)\rho_n - (b_n - l_nc_n)\rho_{n+1} - \beta_n \leq 0, \qquad n = 0, 1, ..., N-1$	(8.68)
$[v_N]$	$-\rho_N + \phi \leq 0$	(8.69)
$[w_N]$	$(1 - c_N)\rho_N - (1 - c_N)\phi \leq 0$	(8.70)
$[x_j]$	$\displaystyle\sum_n a_{nj}\rho_n + \hat{a}_j\phi - d_j\upsilon + \sum_{n=0}^{n'} a_{nj}\psi - \mu_j \leq 0, \qquad j = 1, 2, ..., J$	(8.71)
$[D_n]$	$\left.\dfrac{\partial f}{\partial D_n}\right|_{D_n} - \rho_n - \theta\left.\dfrac{\partial g}{\partial D_n}\right|_{D_n} \leq 0, \qquad n = 0, 1, ..., N$	(8.72)
$[G]$	$\left.\dfrac{\partial f}{\partial G}\right|_G - \phi + \theta \leq 0$	(8.73)

SOURCE: Bernard [4].

Turning to the ρ_n^*, we let

$$\hat{b}_n = \frac{b_n - l_nc_n}{1 - c_n} \qquad (8.76)$$

This $\hat{b}_n$ is the effective borrowing rate. For example, if $b_n = 1.3$, $l_n = 1.2$, and $c_n = 0.2$, in order to borrow a usable \$100, we have to borrow \$125 at 30% and put $(0.2)(125) = 25$ back in the bank at 20%. Our true borrowing cost is

$$(\$125)(0.3) - (25)(0.2) = 32.5, \text{ or } 32.5\%$$

Equation 8.76 yields the equivalent factor of 1.325. In addition, let

$$\hat{\beta}_n^* = \beta_n^*/(1 - c_n) \qquad (8.77)$$

Then we can manipulate (8.67) and (8.68) to yield

$$l_n\rho_{n+1}^* \leq \rho_n^* \leq \hat{b}_n\rho_{n+1}^* + \hat{\beta}_n^*, \qquad n = 0, 1, ..., N-1 \qquad (8.78)$$

This equation is similar to (8.51), showing that compensating balance fractions do not necessarily complicate the model once we interpret them as higher effective borrowing rates.

If $v_n^* > 0$, complementary slackness indicates that the left side of (8.77) is satisfied as equality. In this case the ratio ρ_n^*/ρ_{n+1}^* equals the lending rate factor. If the company borrows, $w_n^* > 0$, and the right side is equality. Note that the ratio of dual variables is affected by the value of $\hat{\beta}_n^*$, the dual variable of the borrowing limit. If the borrowing constraint is absent or nonbinding, the $\hat{\beta}_n^*$ drops out and

(8.78) reduces to the analogous result 8.47 for the linear horizon model with time-varying rates.

The general model is a rather flexible framework for capital budgeting. Most of the results have been extended to the cases of linear mixed-integer programming and quadratic mixed-integer programming, respectively [18, 19]. A natural consequence of using any of these models is the need for a complete programming solution; simple acceptance criteria are possible only under very restrictive and simplistic assumptions.

8.7 DISCRETE CAPITAL BUDGETING

We have carefully avoided the issue of integer solutions until now, in order to present the concepts and theory of capital budgeting in the simpler LP framework. As we turn to discrete models, two issues face us. The first is practicality. Can we solve efficiently problems with integer restrictions? The second is the question of economic interpretation. Will the dual variables, particularly the ρ_n, play the same role in pricing out project opportunities?

8.7.1 Number of Fractional Projects in LP Solution

Before we delve into these issues, we briefly review the nature of the solutions to our example problems heretofore. Recall that in Example 8.1 we had a solution vector $\mathbf{x}^* = (0.22, 1, 0, 1, 0.16)$. Two of the five project selection variables had fractional values in the optimal LP solution. There are also two budget constraints in Example 8.1, and there are no project interdependencies. Weingartner [20] proved that in the LP formulation of the Lorie–Savage problem (the *PV* maximization in Table 8.2) the number of fractional projects in the optimal solution cannot exceed the number of budget constraints. An explanation of this fact is based on the following reasoning. If there is only one budget constraint, there need be at most one fractional project. All others would be either more preferable than the fractional one and accepted fully or less preferable and rejected completely. If there are two equally preferable fractional projects, we could adjust the investment amounts until one was completely accepted or rejected. If there are two budget constraints, it may be possible that one fractional project will exhaust the monies remaining after all fully accepted projects are funded, but more than likely two fractional projects will be needed. If there are three fractional projects in the presence of two budget constraints, one will be more (or equally) preferable, and its funding can be increased until it is accepted fully or one of the remaining two is rejected completely. The LP algorithm by nature seeks extreme points and avoids alternative optima with more variables than necessary. This type of inductive reasoning can be applied to three budget constraints and so forth.

Another way to regard the problem in Table 8.2 is as an upper-bounded LP problem [14]. A basic variable is then one whose value is allowed to be between its lower (0) and upper (1) bounds at some particular iteration. The projects' upper-bound constraints are deleted from the constraint matrix in the upper-bounded LP algorithm, and the rank of the constraint matrix is two for Example 8.1. Hence, there are at most two fractional projects in the optimal solution.

In the basic horizon model, in which the lending rate is equal to the borrowing rate for each time period and there are no borrowing limits and project interdependencies, as shown in Example 8.3, there is always an integer optimum solution. This fact is related to the equivalence between this model and the PV criterion. When the borrowing rate is greater than the lending rate, we can have fractional projects, as demonstrated by Example 8.4. The maximum number of fractional projects that are possible because the borrowing rate is greater is equal to the number of time periods with $r_l < r_b$, minus one. Moreover, the number of fractional projects may be increased by one for each project interdependency constraint and for each time period with a borrowing limit. The reasoning behind these last results is similar to that given for the PV maximization problem.

8.7.2 Branch-and-Bound Solution Procedure

Various algorithms have been developed for solving the mixed-integer linear programming problem [9]. It is beyond the scope of this text to deal with them, since many algorithms are designed for special problem structures and require a high level of mathematical sophistication on the part of the user. Instead, we will demonstrate the solution of a small problem with a branch-and-bound solution procedure which can be used by anyone with access to an LP code [17].

Example 8.7

Use Example 8.5 (Table 8.5) as a starting point and obtain an optimal integer solution. Table 8.7 shows the optimal LP solution vector $\mathbf{x}^* = (0, 1, 0, 0.15, 0, 0.58)$ and objective function value $z^* = \$9,210$. We will designate this as problem 1. The presence of two fractional project selection variables, x_4 and x_6, gives us a choice in the procedure. We will arbitrarily select x_4 and create two new problems.

Problem 2: Problem 1 with $x_4 = 0$ added as a constraint
Problem 3: Problem 1 with $x_4 = 1$ added as a constraint

We then proceed to solve problems 2 and 3 by using an LP algorithm.

Problem 2: $\mathbf{x}^* = (0.17, 1, 0, 0, 0, 0.37)$, $z^* = \$9,205$
Problem 3: $\mathbf{x}^* = (0, 0.89, 0, 1, 0, 1)$, $z^* = \$9,031$

The procedure so far has not eliminated all fractional x_i values but has, in fact, created others that did not appear in problem 1. The problem 2 solution has x_1 fractional, whereas x_1 was an integer in problem 1; the problem 3 solution has a fractional value for x_2, which was an integer in problem 1.

Undeterred, we proceed by taking problem 2 and creating from it two new problems.

Problem 4: Problem 2 with $x_1 = 0$ added
Problem 5: Problem 2 with $x_1 = 1$ added

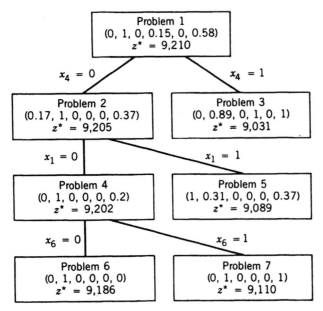

Figure 8.2. Branch-and-bound solution tree for Example 8.7. Numbers in parentheses are values of $\mathbf{x}^*$, the vector of project selection variables.

Figure 8.2 shows how the problems are derived from one another. The choice of problem 2 over problem 3 is based on the LP solution values, \$9,205 versus 9,031. We know that any integer solution derived from problem 3 (with added constraints such as $x_2 = 0$ or $x_2 = 1$) cannot exceed \$9,031, since the LP solution is always an upper bound on the integer solution. We think that a better integer solution is likely to be derived from problem 2. The LP solutions are

Problem 4: $\quad \mathbf{x}^* = (0, 1, 0, 0, 0, 0.2), \qquad z^* = \$9,202$

Problem 5: $\quad \mathbf{x}^* = (1, 0.31, 0, 0, 0, 0.37), \qquad z^* = \$9,089$

Because problem 4 has a better objective function value, we create from it two new problems.

Problem 6: Problem 4 with $x_6 = 0$ added

Problem 7: Problem 4 with $x_6 = 1$ added

The LP solutions are

Problem 6: $\quad \mathbf{x}^* = (0, 1, 0, 0, 0, 0), \qquad z^* = \$9,186$

Problem 7: $\quad \mathbf{x}^* = (0, 1, 0, 0, 0, 1), \qquad z^* = \$9,110$

At this point we have two integer solutions, and we can avoid further analysis of problems 6 and 7. We select the better of the two, that from problem 6 with $z^* = \$9,186$, and designate it as the incumbent (integer) solution.

Before we decide which of problems 3 and 5 to examine further, we check to see whether either can be ruled out by comparing its upper bound, or LP objective function value, with that of the incumbent. It happens that both have upper bounds less than \$9,186, and we do not examine them further. Problems

3 and 5 have been fathomed. There are no other candidate problems to examine, so we have finished and obtained the optimal solution $\mathbf{x}^* = (0, 1, 0, 0, 0, 0)$ with $z^* = \$9,186$. Figure 8.2 depicts the entire search process in tree form.   □

In Example 8.7 the optimal integer objective function value is not much below the LP optimum, about 0.3%. However, we cannot generalize such characteristics, because so much depends on the projects, interest rates, and so forth. Note that a typical rounding process applied to the LP solution would give $\mathbf{x} = (0, 1, 0, 0, 0, 1)$, as in problem 7, which is suboptimal. We could conjecture that if we had branched first on x_6 instead of x_4, we might have reached the integer optimum sooner. Again, it is beyond our scope here to deal with such issues [9]. Our purpose has been to demonstrate an easily available integer solution procedure on a small capital budgeting problem.

8.7.3 Duality Analysis for Integer Solutions

Two basic approaches to duality analysis for mixed-integer linear programming have been presented in the literature. We will briefly discuss the first, more difficult method and then concentrate on the second, more straightforward method and its variations.

Recomputed Dual Variables.   One method for solving mixed-integer linear programs is to use the cutting-plane procedure [9]. This approach begins with the LP optimum and successively adds constraints that delete portions of the feasible LP space but do not delete any integer solutions. Each time a constraint is added, the LP is solved again. The added constraints, called cutting planes, are derived from the current LP solution. When the current LP solution is an integer in the required variables, the procedure stops. At this point we have dual variables for both the original constraint set and the added constraints.

Gomory and Baumol [10] derived a technique for taking the dual variables for the added constraints and reapportioning them among the original constraint set. The purpose is to obtain a set of dual variables for the original problem only. (Dual variables for the cutting planes would be difficult to interpret in terms of the resources expressed by the original constraint set.) The disadvantage of this approach, apart from its complexity and the need to use the cutting-plane procedure, is that the recomputed duals are not always unique. Furthermore, the interpretation of the dual variables as measuring changes in the objective function value resulting from small changes in resource limits does not always apply in the integer case. Small changes in resource limits can cause jumps in the objective function value [20].

Penalties and Subsidies.   Let us assume we have reached the LP problem corresponding to the optimal integer solution in a branch-and-bound integer procedure. (In Example 8.7 this would be problem 6, with x_1, x_4, and x_6 constrained to be zero). The LP form of the problem will contain a number of constraints that force certain project selection variables to zero and other constraints that force some project selection variables to their upper bounds. To the primal formulation of the horizon model—whether it be the basic model in Table 8.6, the model with a sloping supply schedule of funds in Table 8.10, or a model with time-dependent interest rates and project interdependencies—we would thus add

$$x_j = 0, \quad j \text{ in } J_1$$
$$x_j = 1, \quad j \text{ in } J_2 \tag{8.79}$$

where J_1 = set of projects constrained to be zero in the optimal integer solution,

J_2 = set of projects constrained to be at upper bound in the optimal integer solution.

These additional constraints will have corresponding dual variables. At first glance, the dual variables appear to be unconstrained, since the primal constraints 8.79 are equalities. We can, however, reinterpret the constraints as

$$x_j \leq \epsilon, \quad j \text{ in } J_1$$
$$x_j \geq 1 - \epsilon \quad \text{or} \quad -x_j \leq -1 + \epsilon, \quad j \text{ in } J_2 \tag{8.80}$$

where ϵ is a very small positive number. (Some LP codes check for variables set at fixed values and delete the corresponding constraints during a preprocessing stage. If this is done, it is necessary to use (8.80) instead of (8.79) to obtain information about the dual variables. An ϵ value of 0.001 or 0.0001 usually does the trick.)

In the pricing operation of a project constrained to be zero in the optimal integer solution, we then modify (8.33) as follows (assuming no project interdependencies),

$$-\sum_n a_{nj} \rho_n + \mu_j + \gamma_j \geq \hat{a}_j \tag{8.81}$$

where γ_j is a dual variable, nonnegative. Rewriting, we have

$$\mu_j^* \geq \sum_n a_{nj} \rho_n^* + \hat{a}_j - \gamma_j^* \tag{8.82}$$

But since μ_j^* for a rejected project is zero, the γ_j^* acts as a penalty (without Eq. 8.79 the μ_j^* was positive) to force rejection of project j.

If the project was constrained to be at its upper bound, Eq. 8.41 becomes

$$0 \leq \mu_j^* = \hat{a}_j + \sum_n a_{nj} \rho_n^* + \gamma_j^* \tag{8.83}$$

In this instance the γ_j^* acts as a subsidy to enable acceptance of project j. These penalties and subsidies are a natural consequence of forcing the solution to satisfy the integrality requirements. They are known only through solving the mixed-integer programming problem. If we had solved the problem by some other method, such as the cutting-plane or enumeration method, we would still have to set up an LP model with the appropriate constraints of type 8.79 in order to extract the values of the penalties and subsidies.

We can apply these concepts to our integer solution for Example 8.5. The optimal dual variables for problem 6 are

$$\rho_0^* = 1.69 \quad \mu_1^* = 0 \quad \mu_4^* = 0 \quad \gamma_1^* = 0 \quad \beta_1^* = 0$$
$$\rho_1^* = 1.3 \quad \mu_2^* = 96 \quad \mu_5^* = 0 \quad \gamma_4^* = 0$$
$$\rho_2^* = 1.0 \quad \mu_3^* = 0 \quad \mu_6^* = 0 \quad \gamma_6^* = 80$$

The ratio analysis of ρ_n indicates borrowing at times 0 and 1, so projects 1 and 4 do not require penalties. Recall that project 4 was fractionally accepted in the LP optimum; project 1 was zero in the LP optimum but was introduced at an intermediate stage in the branch-and-bound procedure. We may verify the value of $\mu_6^* = 0$, which justifies rejection of project 6 (it was fractionally accepted in the LP optimum).

$$(\$1,000)(1.69) - (700)(1.3) - (700)(1.0) - 80 = 0$$

It is possible to reformulate the dual of the horizon model for an integer solution so that

- Projects forced into acceptance receive a subsidy, and projects forced into rejection receive no penalty, *or*
- Projects forced into rejection receive a penalty, but those forced into acceptance receive no subsidy.

The interested reader is referred to Weingartner [20] for further details of this method.

8.8 CAPITAL BUDGETING WITH MULTIPLE OBJECTIVES

In many situations it is not possible or desirable to evaluate different investment alternatives by one criterion, such as *PV* or terminal wealth. There are various techniques for dealing with multiple objectives, but most fall into one of three classes: goal programming, interactive multiple-criteria optimization, and nonlinear programming. In this section we provide an example of a goal-programming formulation, and we discuss the interactive approach.

Nonlinear programming can be applied if the decision maker can specify a utility function of the criteria, for example, dividends and terminal wealth. The major disadvantage of the approach seems to be the difficulty of specifying the utility function. Because each application depends so much on the utility function and on subsequent refinements in the solution algorithm, we will not discuss the approach in this section. Appendix 8.A provides an example of applying a quadratic programming algorithm to a problem involving dividends and terminal wealth.

8.8.1 Goal Programming

Goal programming is a technique that enables a decision maker to strive toward a number of objectives simultaneously. The first step consists of establishing a goal for each criterion. Next, an objective function is specified for each criterion with respect to this goal. Third, weighting factors are placed on deviations of the objective functions from their goals. Fourth, the separate objective functions are combined into one overall function to be optimized [13].

Example 8.8

Table 8.13 presents data for Example 8.8. The first-year after-tax profit and employment of specialized personnel are considered to be primary goals, and terminal wealth at time 2 is considered a secondary goal. Let us assume the goals are established, respectively, as

Goal 1, first-year after-tax profits: $2,500

Goal 2, specialized personnel needed: 700 person-hours

Goal 3, terminal wealth at time 2: $4,000

These imply

$$\$2,000x_1 + 3,000x_2 + 1,700x_3 - 500x_4 \geq \$2,500$$
$$100x_1 + 100x_2 + 300x_3 + 400x_4 = 700 \text{ person-hours}$$
$$v_2 - w_2 + \$800x_1 + 600x_2 + 3,000x_3 + 1,000x_4 \geq \$4,000$$

$$(8.84)$$

Table 8.13 *Goal Programming, Example 8.8*

	Project			
Coefficient Type	1	2	3	4
First-year after-tax profit	$2,000	$3,000	$1,700	−$500
Specialized personnel needed, person-hours	100	100	300	400
Cash flow at time				
0	−$1,000	−$800	−$2,000	−$200
1	300	200	1,000	100
2	400	200	1,000	200
$\hat{a}_j$	$800	$600	$3,000	$1,000

Budgets for external sources of funds: $n = 0, \$2,000; n = 1, -\$500; n = 2, -\$500$

The inequalities for profits and terminal wealth are typical of goals that can be exceeded without penalty. We now define auxiliary variables as follows.

$$y_1 = \$2,000x_1 + 3,000x_2 + 1,700x_3 - 500x_4 - 2,500$$

$$y_2 = 100x_1 + 100x_2 + 300x_3 + 400x_4 - 700 \text{ person-hours} \qquad (8.85)$$

$$y_3 = v_2 - w_2 + \$800x_1 + 600x_2 + 3,000x_3 + 1,000x_4 - 4,000$$

We are concerned with measuring positive and negative deviations, so we define components

$$\begin{aligned}
y_k^+ &= y_k \quad \text{if } y_k \geq 0 \\
y_k^- &= |y_k| \quad \text{if } y_k < 0
\end{aligned} \qquad k = 1, 2, 3 \qquad (8.86)$$

Our overall objective is to minimize some weighted sum of deviations,

$$\text{Min} \sum_k (c_k^+ y_k^+ + c_k^- y_k^-) \qquad (8.87)$$

where c_k^+ and c_k^- are weighting factors for the deviations. If a $100 profit deviation is deemed equivalent to a deviation of one specialized employee, we might set $c_1^- = 100$, $c_2^+ = 1$, and $c_2^- = 1$. Since terminal wealth is a secondary goal, set $c_3^- = 10$, an order of magnitude lower. The positive deviations for goals 1 and 3 have no adverse consequences, so $c_1^+ = 0$ and $c_3^+ = 0$. Thus, the objective function becomes

$$\text{Min } 100y_1^- + y_2^+ + y_2^- + 10y_3^- \qquad (8.88)$$

The constraints of the problem are of two types. The first type consists of goal constraints, obtained from (8.84).

$$\$2,000x_1 + 3,000x_2 + 1,700x_3 - 500x_4 - (y_1^+ - y_1^-) = \$2,500$$

$$100x_1 + 100x_2 + 300x_3 + 400x_4 - (y_2^+ - y_2^-) = 700 \text{ person-hours}$$

$$v_2 - w_2 + 800x_1 + 600x_2 + 3,000x_3 + 1,000x_4 - (y_3^+ - y_3^-) = \$4,000$$
$$\qquad (8.89)$$

The second type consists of the original set of constraints. In this example they would be cash balance equations for $n = 0$, 1, and 2, respectively; project upper bounds; and nonnegativity constraints. An LP solution of (8.88) subject to the two types of constraints yields values for the x_j, v_n, and w_n that result in the "best" set of deviations from the goals. Assuming that lending and borrowing occur at 10%, the solution is:

$x_1 = 0.483$	$v_0 = 0$	$w_0 = 494.2$	$y_1^+ = 1,825$	$y_1^- = 0$
$x_2 = 1.0$	$v_1 = 0$	$w_1 = 93.0$	$y_2^+ = 0$	$y_2^- = 0$
$x_3 = 0.51$	$v_2 = 496.5$	$w_2 = 0$	$y_3^+ = 0$	$y_3^- = 0$
$x_4 = 1.0$				

objective function value = 0

743

The solution indicates that the first-year after-tax profit will be \$4,325, or \$1,825 above the goal of \$2,500. Goal 2, specialized personnel needed, and goal 3, terminal wealth at time 2, are met exactly. Since there is no penalty for exceeding goal 1, the objective function value is 0. □

A number of variations of the goal-programming technique are suitable for particular circumstances [13]. In all of them care must be taken in formulating the goals and relative weights for deviations.

8.8.2 Interactive Multiple-Criteria Optimization

Another approach is to assume the operational setting of optimizing a nonlinear function of the decision variables, *without* knowing the explicit form of the trade-off (utility) function. Instead, we assume the decision maker is able to provide information about the gradient of the function. This information is then used to guide a search process over the domain of the function [6].

To illustrate the concept, let us take the three goals in Example 8.8, described in the previous section, and convert them into three criteria. We assume that we can measure each criterion by a function f_j and that we wish to maximize an overall utility function,

$$\underset{\mathbf{x}}{Max}\ U(f_1, f_2, f_3) \tag{8.90}$$

where $f_1(\mathbf{x})$ = criterion function for first-year after-tax profits,
$\quad\quad f_2(\mathbf{x})$ = criterion function for specialized personnel needed, and
$\quad\quad f_3(\mathbf{x})$ = criterion function for terminal wealth at time 2 (let $\mathbf{v}$ and $\mathbf{w}$ be included in an extended $\mathbf{x}$ vector).

We will be careful to specify the f_j as concave, differentiable functions and assume U is increasing in each f_j. Maximization of (8.90) by a steepest-ascent procedure will then lead to a global optimum [23].

The procedure begins with an initial feasible solution $\mathbf{x}^1$. At any iteration k the direction of the search is obtained from

$$\underset{\mathbf{y}^k}{Max}\ \nabla_{\mathbf{x}^k} U(f_1(\mathbf{x}^k), f_2(\mathbf{x}^k), f_3(\mathbf{x}^k)) \cdot \mathbf{y}^k \tag{8.91}$$

by letting the search direction be $\mathbf{d}^k = \mathbf{y}^k - \mathbf{x}^k$. But (8.91) can be replaced by

$$\underset{\mathbf{y}^k}{Max}\ \sum_j c_j^k \nabla_{\mathbf{x}^k} f_j(\mathbf{x}^k) \cdot \mathbf{y}^k \tag{8.92}$$

where

$$c_j^k = \frac{(\partial U / \partial f_j)^k}{(\partial U / \partial f_1)^k} \tag{8.93}$$

In many situations (8.92) is linear and can be solved by LP. In any case, if we can express f_j, we can express (8.92). What has happened is that the ratios of the partial derivatives of U with respect to f_j (which result from the breakdown of ∇U) have been replaced by trade-offs c_j^k. Each c_j^k measures the reduction in value of criterion function j that the decision maker would tolerate for one unit of increase in the value of criterion function 1, which is taken as a reference point. The trade-offs depend on the current solution and thus are indexed by the iteration counter k. They are obtained from the decision maker by an interactive procedure.

After the direction $\mathbf{d}^k$ is determined, the interactive procedure presents a number of solutions in the form of

$$f_1(\mathbf{x}^k + a\mathbf{y}^k), \quad f_2(\mathbf{x}^k + a\mathbf{y}^k), \quad f_3(\mathbf{x}^k + a\mathbf{y}^k)$$

where a is the step size, which is typically incremented by one-tenth of $\mathbf{d}^k$. The decision maker provides input again by selecting the preferred combination of f_1, f_2, f_3 values, without reference to the utility function U.

Given appropriate conditions on the f_j and U, the procedure will converge to a global maximum. The great advantage of the procedure is that no explicit form of the function U is required. The decision maker instead is required to provide information about trade-offs among f_j values and to indicate preferences for $f_1, \ldots, f_n$ combinations.

8.9 SUMMARY

In this chapter we have presented a number of techniques for capital budgeting under deterministic conditions. The methods are generally designed for selecting among many different investment alternatives (too many to enumerate explicitly) in the presence of budget limits, project interdependencies, and lending and borrowing opportunities. Linear programming is a major tool in the formulation, solution, and interpretation of many of the methods, either as the primary modeling technique or as a subroutine. The pricing of activity vectors is an important concept with direct economic interpretation, and we have devoted considerable space to illustrating the concept.

The models in this chapter may be grouped into three broad classifications. The first is the class of *PV* objective functions. This type suffers from some serious conceptual problems in the reconciliation of the discount rate used and the presence of budget constraints. The second class consists of horizon models; their objective is to maximize the end cash value or the terminal wealth at the end of some planning period. A number of desirable economic interpretations can be derived from such models. Moreover, models of this type are readily extended to include borrowing limits, a sloping supply schedule of funds, and integer restrictions.

The third class is characterized by objective functions containing different types of criterion variables. Bernhard's general model is the first of this type; it includes dividends and terminal wealth in the objective function. Other types discussed are the goal-programming approach and interactive multiple-criteria optimization. Appendix 8.A presents an application of Bernhard's approach to a problem which has dividends and terminal wealth to consider.

REFERENCES

1. ATKINS, D. R., and D. J. ASHTON, "Discount Rates in Capital Budgeting: A Re-examination of the Baumol & Quandt Paradox," *The Engineering Economist,* Vol. 21, No. 3, pp. 159–171, Spring 1976.

2. BALAS, E., *Duality in Discrete Programming,* Graduate School of Industrial Administration, Carnegie-Mellon University, Pittsburgh, December 1967.

3. BAUMOL, W. J., and R. E. QUANDT, "Investment and Discount Rates under Capital Rationing—A Programming Approach," *Economic Journal,* Vol. 75, No. 298, pp. 317–329, June 1965.

4. BERNHARD, R. H., "Mathematical Programming Models for Capital Budgeting—A Survey, Generalization, and Critique," *Journal of Financial and Quantitative Analysis,* Vol. 4, No. 2, pp. 111–158, 1969.

5. DANTZIG, G. B., *Linear Programming and Extensions,* Princeton University Press, Princeton, N.J., 1963. (See Chapter 12 for a discussion of economic interpretation of dual problem.)

6. DYER, J. S., "A Time-Sharing Computer Program for the Solution of the Multiple Criteria Problem," *Management Science,* Vol. 19, No. 12, pp. 1379–1383, August 1973.

7. FISHER, I., *The Theory of Interest,* Macmillan, New York, 1930 (reprinted by A. M. Kelley, New York, 1961).

8. FREELAND, J. R., and M. J. ROSENBLATT, "An Analysis of Linear Programming Formulations for the Capital Rationing Problem," *The Engineering Economist,* Vol. 24, No. 1, pp. 49–61, Fall 1978.

9. GARFINKEL, R. S., and G. L. NEMHAUSER, *Integer Programming,* Wiley, New York, 1972.

10. GOMORY, R. E., and W. J. BAUMOL, "Integer Programming and Pricing," *Econometrica,* Vol. 28, No. 3, pp. 551–560, 1960.

11. HAMILTON, W. F., and M. A. MOSES, "An Optimization Model for Corporate Financial Planning," *Operations Research,* Vol. 21, No. 3, pp. 677–691, 1973.

12. HAYES, J. W., "Discount Rates in Linear Programming Formulations of the Capital Budgeting Problem," *The Engineering Economist,* Vol. 29, No. 2, pp. 113–126, Winter 1984.

13. IGNIZIO, J. P., *Linear Programming in Single and Multiple Objective Systems,* Prentice-Hall, Englewood Cliffs, N.J., 1982.

14. LASDON, L., *Optimization Theory for Large Systems,* Macmillan, New York, 1970. (See Chapter 6 for upper-bounded algorithm.)

15. LORIE, J. H., and L. J. SAVAGE, "Three Problems in Rationing Capital," *Journal of Business,* Vol. 28, No. 4, pp. 229–239, October 1955; also reprinted in Solomon, E. (ed.), *The Management of Corporate Capital,* Free Press, New York, 1959.

16. MURGA, P., *Capital Budgeting Objective Functions That Consider Dividends and Terminal Wealth,* M.S. thesis, School of Industrial and Systems Engineering, Georgia Institute of Technology, Atlanta, 1978.

17. RAVINDRAN, A., D. T. PHILLIPS, AND J. J. SOLBERG *Operations Research: Principles and Practice,* Wiley, New York, 1987. (See Chapter 4 for branch-and-bound technique. See Chapter 11 for Kuhn–Tucker conditions.)

18. SHARP, G. P., *Extension of Bernhard's Capital Budgeting Model to the Quadratic and Nonlinear Case,* School of Industrial and Systems Engineering, Georgia Institute of Technology, Atlanta, 1983.

19. UNGER, V. E., "Duality Results for Discrete Capital Budgeting Models," *The Engineering Economist,* Vol. 19, No. 4, pp. 237–252, Summer 1974.

20. WEINGARTNER, H. M., *Mathematical Programming and the Analysis of Capital Budgeting Problems,* Prentice–Hall, Englewood Cliffs, N.J., 1963.

21. WEINGARTNER, H. M., "Capital Rationing: *n* Authors in Search of a Plot," *Journal of Finance,* Vol. 32, No. 5, pp. 1403–1431. December 1977.

22. WILKES, F. M., *Capital Budgeting Techniques,* John Wiley & Sons, New York, 1983.

23. ZANGWILL, W. I., *Nonlinear Programming: A Unified Approach,* Prentice–Hall, Englewood Cliffs, N.J., 1969.

PROBLEMS

8.1. You wish to include lending activities at 8% and borrowing activities at 12% in a *PV* LP model. The interest rate used for *PV* calculations is 10%. Define the activity vectors for lending and borrowing opportunities, and write a model formulation for a time horizon of 2 years and three budget constraints.

8.2. One of the criticisms of the typical capital budgeting LP model is that only short-term (one-year) lending and borrowing is represented. Can long-term lending and borrowing be included? If so, show how by defining variables and specifying coefficients in the objective function and constraints. Would long-term lending and borrowing be more appropriate in a *PV* LP model or a horizon LP model?

8.3. In many decision environments the total number of major projects to be considered is ten or fewer. Thus, enumeration of all combinations would be feasible, since there would be $2^{10} = 1,024$ or fewer combinations. In such a case, would it make sense to use a mathematical programming approach? What information would the mathematical programming approach give that is not available from enumeration?

8.4. Formulate a *PV* LP model for selecting among the three projects described below. *MARR* = 8%. There is a budget of $13,000 at time 0, and the projects are required to generate $3,500 at time 1 and $1,200 at time 2. The life of each project is 5 years. The projects are independent except that C cannot be selected unless A is also selected. What is the value of extra budget money at time 2?

Project	Investment	Annual Cash Flow
A	$5,000	$1,319
B	7,000	1,942
C	8,500	2,300

8.5. Formulate a *PV* LP model for selecting among the three projects described below. *MARR* = 15%. There is a budget of $16,000 at time 0, and the projects are required to generate $4,000 at time 1 and $1,300 at time 2. The life of each project is 10 years. The projects are independent except that A cannot be selected unless B is also selected. What is the value of extra budget money at time 2?

Project	Investment	Annual Cash Flow
A	$8,000	$1,900
B	5,000	1,400
C	10,000	2,500

8.6. Fromulate a horizon LP model for selecting among the three projects described below, with time 2 as the horizon. There is a budget of $2,000 at time 0, and the projects are required to generate $500 at time 1 and $500 at time 2. The life of each project is 20 years. The projects are independent except that C cannot be selected unless A is also selected. The lending rate is 15% and the borrowing rate is 20%, per year. Do you see any obvious difficulty with the application of the horizon model to this particular example?

Project	Investment	Annual Cash Flow
A	$1,000	$240
B	800	190
C	1,500	310

8.7. A horizon LP model was formulated and solved for five independent projects and four budget constraints. The lending rate is 18% and the borrowing rate 25%, per year. There are no posthorizon cash flows. The solution is:

Project selection variables $= (0.0, 1.0, 1.0, 0.5, 1.0)$

Budget dual variables $\quad = (1.7995, 1.475, 1.25, 1.0)$

Project dual variables $\quad = (10, 240, 310, 0, 110)$

a. Indicate whether borrowing or lending occurs in each period.
b. Do you see any difficulty in interpreting the solution of this example?
c. Suppose you wish to evaluate a new independent project.

Time	0	1	2	3
Cash flow	$-$1,000	$-1,000$	2,000	1,000

What would be your recommendation regarding acceptance?

8.8. A horizon LP model was formulated and solved for five independent projects and four budget constraints. The lending rate is 20% and the borrowing rate 25%, per year. There are no posthorizon cash flows. The solution is:

Project selection variables $= (1.0, 0.0, 0.4, 1.0, 0.0)$

Budget dual variables $\quad = (1.8, 1.44, 1.2, 1.0)$

Project dual variables $\quad = (560, 0, 0, 320, 0)$

a. Indicate whether borrowing or lending occurs in each period.
b. Suppose you wished to evaluate a new independent project.

Time	0	1	2	3
Cash flow	$-$1,000	$-1,000$	2,000	1,000

What would be your recommendation regarding acceptance?

8.9. A horizon LP model was formulated and solved for five independent projects and four budget constraints. The lending and borrowing rates are

Time 0 to 1: lend at 15%, borrow at 20%

Time 1 to 2: lend at 15%, borrow at 20%

Time 2 to 3: lend at 18%, borrow at 25%

There are no posthorizon cash flows. The solution is

Project selection variables $= (1.0, 0.0, 0.4, 1.0, 0.0)$

Budget dual variables $\quad = (1.628, 1.357, 1.18, 1.0)$

Project dual variables $\quad = (560, 0, 0, 320, 0)$

a. Indicate whether borrowing or lending occurs in each period.
b. Suppose you wish to evaluate a new independent project.

Time	0	1	2	3
Cash flow	$-\$1,500$	$-1,500$	$3,500$	800

What would be your recommendation regarding acceptance?
c. What does the first project contribute to the objective function?

8.10. Formulate and solve a horizon LP model for selecting among the five following projects. The lending rate is 13% and the borrowing rate 17%, per year. There are no posthorizon cash flows.

			Project			
n	A	B	C	D	E	Budget
0	$-\$10,000$	$-\$5,000$	$-\$7,500$	$-\$15,000$	$-\$20,000$	$\$30,000$
1	$-5,000$	$-12,000$	$-8,500$	$-3,000$	$-5,000$	$25,000$
2	$2,000$	$15,000$	$11,000$	$2,176$	$14,000$	$30,000$
3	$4,072$	$3,761$	$1,541$	$2,176$	$16,005$	$35,000$
4	$16,000$	$1,700$	$4,000$	$2,176$	$8,000$	$10,000$
5	$18,000$	$1,700$	$12,000$	$2,176$	$10,000$	$20,000$

Verify that projects with positive future worth are accepted and those with negative future worth rejected. Verify that the ratios of the budget dual variables indicate lending or borrowing.

8.11. Rework Problem 8.10 with the inclusion of borrowing limits of $2,000 at time 0 and $2,000 at time 1, at the 17% rate. Unlimited borrowing at 20% is available at times 0 and 1.

8.12. Formulate and solve a horizon LP model for selecting among the five projects below. The lending rate is 15% and the borrowing rate 20%, per year. There are no posthorizon cash flows.

			Project			
n	A	B	C	D	E	Budget
0	$-\$10,000$	$-\$20,000$	$-\$15,000$	$+\$5,000$	$-\$15,000$	$\$25,000$
1	$4,000$	$8,000$	$-2,000$	$-1,000$	$1,300$	$2,000$
2	$5,000$	$10,000$	$5,000$	$-1,000$	$1,700$	0
3	$4,400$	$3,000$	$7,300$	$-3,200$	$6,000$	$2,000$
4	$2,800$	$7,000$	$6,000$	$-1,150$	$4,000$	$1,000$
5	$1,000$	$6,000$	$7,100$	-800	$2,700$	0

Verify that projects with positive future worth are accepted and those with negative future worth rejected. Verify that the ratios of the budget dual variables indicate lending or borrowing.

8.13. Rework Problem 8.12 with the inclusion of another activity, project F, with cash flow

n	0	1	2	3	4	5
Cash Flow	−$25,000	10,000	8,000	8,000	8,000	7,000

8.14. Rework Problem 8.13 (six projects) with the inclusion of borrowing restrictions of $10,000 per year over the planning period (5 years).

8.15. Rework Problem 8.13 (six projects) with the inclusion of a sloping supply schedule of funds. During each year the first $5,000 of borrowing is at 20% and the next $2,500 at 25%, and unlimited borrowing is available at 30%.

8.16. A horizon LP model was formulated and solved for selecting among the five projects below. The lending rate is 10% and the borrowing rate 20%, per year. There are no posthorizon cash flows.

			Project			
n	A	B	C	D	E	Budget
0	−$1,000	−$1,200	−$900	−$1,000	$1,000	$1,000
1	400	900	300	500	−400	1,300
2	800	800	500	700	−400	1,500
3	135	700	250	700	−400	200

The optimal solution contains:

Project selection variables = (1.0, 1.0, 0, 1.0, 1.0)

Budget dual variables   = (1.452, 1.21, 1.1, 1.0)

a. Indicate whether lending or borrowing occurs during each time period.
b. Determine the project dual variable for project C and for Project E.
c. With a new set of budget amounts, the solution changes.

Budget amounts   = ($1,000, −1,000, 1,500, 200)

Project selection variables = (0, 1.0, 0, 1.0, 1.0)

Budget dual variables   = (1.584, 1.32, 1.1, 1.0)

Explain why project A is rejected here although it was accepted previously. Express your answer in LP terms, using specific numbers.
d. If you know nothing about the budget amounts, can you say *anything* specific about the acceptance or rejection of projects in this example?
e. Describe a method for determining the optimal value of the objective function for the original problem formulation, if you know the optimal values of the project selection variables and the budget dual variables.

8.17. Construct a horizon LP example with lending rate(s) less than borrowing rate(s). Demonstrate the relationships between lending or borrowing activities and the budget dual variables and the relationships between project dual variables and project future values.

8.18. Construct a horizon LP example where at least one of the projects is accepted fractionally. Explain why it is accepted fractionally by pricing out the project activity vector.

8.19. Construct a horizon LP example with a sloping supply schedule of funds. Validate the relationships between the budget dual variables and tightness of the borrowing constraints.

8.20. Construct a horizon integer programming example. Solve it by using a branch-and-bound algorithm. Determine the subsidies and penalties attached to projects that are fractionally accepted in the LP solution, in order to force them to be integer.

8.21. Solve the goal-programming example in Section 8.8.1.

8.22. Construct an example of Bernhard's general model, using a linear objective function and a linear terminal-wealth posture restriction. Use at least four time periods and different lending or borrowing rates. Try to construct the problem so that at least one project is accepted, at least one is rejected, and at least one borrowing constraint is tight.

8.23. The ABC Company has to determine its capital budget for the coming 3 years, for which data (in thousands of dollars) are given in the following table.

End of Year	Available Investment Capital	Investment Projects					
		1	2	3	4	5	6
0	300	−50	−100	−60	−50	−170	−16
1	100	−80	−50	−60	−100	−40	−25
2	200	20	−20	−60	−150	50	−40
Discounted future revenues		150	210	220	350	200	100

At the start of year 1 the company has $300,000 available for investment; in year 2 another $100,000 becomes available, and at the start of year 3 an additional $200,000 becomes available. Project 1 requires $50,000 at the start of year 1 and another $80,000 at the start of year 2; at the start of year 3, the project yields $20,000. The yield at the start of year 3 and the discounted yields for later years amount to $150,000. The company can borrow at most $50,000 plus 20% of the money invested so far in the various investment projects at an interest rate of 12% per year. If the company deposits money at the bank, the interest rate is 8%. The company has a bank debt of $10,000, on which it pays 11% interest and which may be repaid at the start of any year. Assume that the company may undertake 100% of each project or take a participation in each project of less than 100%.

a. Formulate the capital budgeting problem by using the horizon model.

b. Find the optimal capital allocations by using a linear programming package.

c. Find the optimal capital budget, assuming that no project can be undertaken partially.

8.24. The Micromegabyte Company is a small American manufacturer of microprocessors, which are vital components in many pieces of electronic equipment, including personal computers. In a recent meeting of the board of directors, the company was instructed to engage in the development of various types of software that would go with their microprocessor products. An ad hoc committee has been formed to come up with various proposals that can be initiated in the new fiscal period. The following six proposals were considered to be competitive in the market and to have good profit potentials. Because technology in this field advances rapidly, most software products will have a market life of about 3 years.

End of Period	Software Projects and Their Cash Flows*					
	1	2	3	4	5	6
0	−50	−100	−70	−130	−250	−300
1	−100	−50	−100	−50	−100	−60
2	50	100	90	−100	−60	150
3	100	50	150	260	300	200
4	50	30	100	250	150	100
5	30	30	30		100	

*All units in $1,000.

The company will have at the start of year 1 (end of period 0) $500,000 available for investment; in year 2 another $200,000 becomes available, and at the start of year 3 an additional $50,000 becomes available.

The company can borrow at most $200,000 over the planning horizon at an interest rate of 12% per year. The company has to repay an old loan of $50,000 over the planning horizon. No partial payment of this loan is allowed, but the company has to pay 13% interest at the end of each year until the loan is paid in full.

Projects 1 and 3 are considered to be mutually exclusive because both projects lead to the same software development but with application on different machines. The company does not have enough resources to support more than one type of operating system. Project 2 is contingent on project 1, and project 4 is contingent on project 3. Projects 2 and 4 are graphics softwares designed to run on the specific operating system.

The company has a total of 10,000 programming hours per year for the first 2 years that can be put into the development of these software projects. Annual programming hour requirements for the projects are estimated to be as follows.

Year	Project					
	1	2	3	4	5	6
First	2,000	3,000	3,000	5,000	4,000	4,000
Second	3,000	4,000	3,000	4,000	5,000	4,000

The company can always lend any unspent funds at an interest rate of 9%. Determine the firm's best course of action with a horizon time of 4 years.

8.25. The National Bank of Maine has $1 billion in total assets, which are offset on the balance sheet by demand deposits, time deposits, and capital accounts of $650 million, $250 million, and $100 million, respectively. The bank seeks your advice on how best to allocate its resources among the following list of assets.

Bank Assets and Their Expected Rates of Return

Asset	Expected Net Return (%)
Cash and cash equivalents	0
Loans	
Commercial loans	5.5
FHA and VA mortgages	5.0
Conventional mortgages	6.2
Other loans	6.9
Investments	
Short-term U.S. government securities	3.0
Long-term U.S. government securities	4.2

In allocating its resources, the bank is now constrained by the following legal and policy considerations.

Legal restrictions

- Cash items must equal or exceed 30% of demand deposits.

- Within the loan portfolio, conventional mortgages must not exceed 20% of time deposits.

Policy guidelines (goals)

- The management does not wish its total loans to exceed 65% of total assets. Each dollar of deviation from this target will carry a penalty of 3.5 cents per period.

- Within the loan portfolio "commercial loans" are not to exceed 45% or fall below 30% of total loans, and "other loans" are not to exceed the amount of total mortgages. Deviations of 1$ from these targets will carry uniform penalties of 0.8 cent per period.

- To ensure solvency, the management desires to limit its holdings of risk assets, defined as total assets less cash items less short-term U.S. government securities, to seven times the bank's capital accounts. Each dollar of deviation will carry a penalty of 4 cents per period.

- The management wishes to earn a target profit of $50 million. It places no premium on overattainment of this profit objective, but it places a penalty of $1 on each dollar of underattainment. Set up and solve a goal programming formulation for this problem.

Part IV: Additional Topics

- Lecture slides on deterministic capital budgeting

- Chapter 8 of "Advanced Engineering Economics" by Park and Sharp-Bette

- Lecture slides on utility theory

- Chapter 9 of "Advanced Engineering Economics" by Park and Sharp-Bette

Utility Theory

- **Consider the following game:**

  - ➢ A fair coin is tossed until the first time a head occurs. If it takes n tosses to obtain the first head, the payoff to the player is $\$2^n$

  - ➢ What is the expected payoff?

  - ➢ What is the maximum amount that you would be willing to pay to play this game?

Preference

- **Risk preference:**

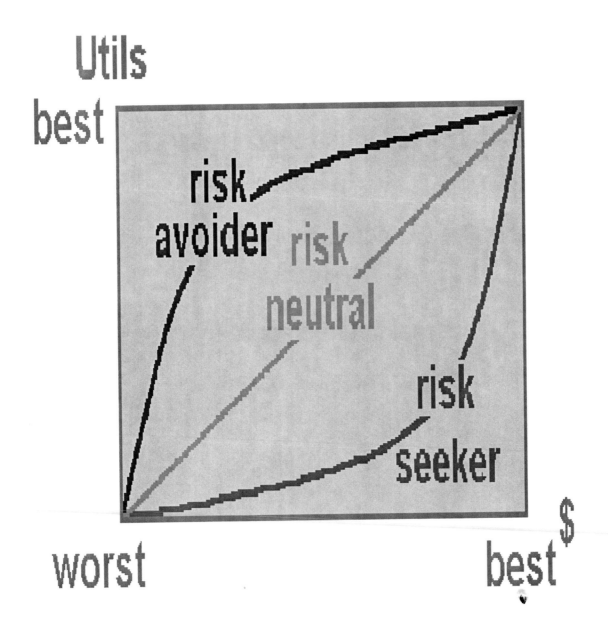

Utility Theory

- **Two famous economists: Von Neumann and Morgenstern**

    ➤ They developed a set of axioms of behavior that lead to the existence of a utility function

    ➤ Decision makers make decisions based on maximizing expected utility

Utility Theory

- **Risk averse investors have an *increasing* *concave* utility function**

  - $u(x) = \ln(x)$

  - $u(x) = x^{0.5}$

  - These are two examples of increasing concave

  - The increasing concavity reflects a decreasing incremental value from each incremental dollar of wealth

Utility Theory

- **Expected utility:**

  ➢ $E[u(X)]$

- **Jensen's inequality using concavity of u :**

  ➢ $E[u(X)] \leq u(E[X])$

  ➢ An individual with a concave utility function u (.) would prefer to have E [X] for certain, than face the random variable X

- **Certainty Equivalent:**

  ➤ An individual will take less than E [X] for
  certain, rather than facing the random variable X

  ➤ The exact amount that the individual will take is
  called the certainty equivalent: CE

  ➤ $u (CE) = E [u (X)]$

  ➤ Or: $CE = u^{-1}(E [u (X)])$

Outline

Part IV: Additional Topics

▪Lecture slides on deterministic capital budgeting

▪Chapter 8 of "Advanced Engineering Economics" by Park and Sharp-Bette

▪Lecture slides on utility theory

▪Chapter 9 of "Advanced Engineering Economics" by Park and Sharp-Bette

Utility Theory

9.1 INTRODUCTION

In the first two parts of this book we have assumed that decisions are made in a context of complete certainty. The decision makers are characterized as persons wishing to maximize cash flow, the present value of cash flow, or perhaps terminal cash wealth. Cash amounts at different points in time are converted to some common point in time, often time 0, by using an interest rate, and are then added to obtain *PV, FV,* and so forth.

In this third part of the book we relax these ideal assumptions in two important ways.

1. Project cash flow will no longer be regarded as certain. Instead, we will use probability concepts to describe project flows.
2. Decision makers will no longer be assumed to add (linearly) different cash flows at the same point in time or after conversion to the same point in time by use of an interest rate. Instead, small cash flows will usually be given more consideration per dollar than large cash flows.

In this chapter we give a brief introduction of the first concept, the probabilistic description of cash flows. We assume the reader is familiar with the fundamental concepts of probability theory. Probabilistic approaches to investment decisions are given extensive coverage in Chapters 10 to 13.

The principal emphasis in this chapter is on the second concept, namely the utility theory approach to combining and evaluating cash flows. Following the introduction of the concept in this section, the formal statement of utility theory is presented in Section 9.2. In Section 9.3 we discuss the properties of utility functions, followed by the procedures for assessing a utility function by empirical means in Section 9.4. An important operational method, mean–variance analysis, is shown in Section 9.5 to be based on the utility theory concept; mean–variance analysis is presented in depth in Chapters 10 and 11.

9.1.1 The Concept of Risk

We may introduce the concept of risk by asking why individual home-owners (with no outstanding mortgage or loan against their homes) would buy fire insurance. The possibility of damage from fire in a particular year is quite low, say 0.01. If the amount of damage caused by a fire is $60,000, we would say the *risk* of fire damage is a 0.01 chance (1% chance) of a $60,000 loss. If the fire insurance premium is $700 per year and the deductible amount on a loss (the amount the individual pays) is $250, then on an *expected monetary value (EMV)* basis an individual who buys insurance has the following yearly cost.

Event	Cost	Probability	Product
No fire occurs	$700	0.99	$693.00
Fire occurs	$700 + 250 = $950	0.01	9.50
		Expected annual cost	$702.50

Contrast this with the situation of an individual who decides *not* to buy fire insurance.

Event	Cost	Probability	Product
No fire occurs	0	0.99	0
Fire occurs	$60,000	0.01	$600.00
		Expected annual cost	$600.00

Most individual homeowners would clearly prefer to buy fire insurance in order to avoid the risk of a 0.01 chance of a $60,000 loss, even though the expected annual cost of $702.50 is greater than the expected annual cost of

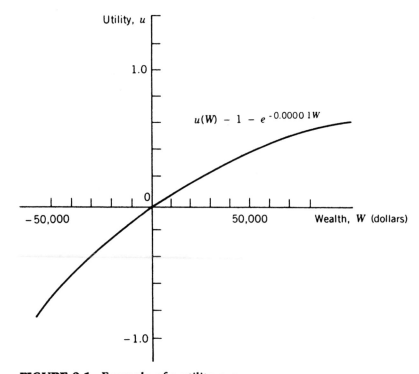

FIGURE 9.1. Example of a utility curve.

$600.00 without insurance. On the other hand, a large corporation with hundreds of retail outlets, facing similar risks and premiums at each outlet, might decide not to buy fire insurance. Such a corporation would become a *self-insurer*. The individual homeowner's way of evaluating the possible $60,000 loss is different from that of the large corporation, which can presumably make decisions regarding such amounts on an *EMV* basis. A $60,000 loss could be disastrous for an individual, whereas the large corporation would expect only one such loss per hundred retail outlets.

The individual's behavior, which is *not* based on an *EMV*, can be explained by the concept of *utility*. An example of a *utility function* for an individual, shown in Figure 9.1, has the following selected values. The function is

$$u(W) = 1 - e^{-0.00001W} \tag{9.1}$$

where W is the dollar amount of wealth.

Wealth, W	Utility Value
$100,000	0.63212
50,000	0.39347
10,000	0.09516
1,000	0.00995
0	0
−1,000	−0.01005
−10,000	−0.10517

The utility function in Figure 9.1 reflects a decreasing incremental value from each incremental dollar of wealth.

Following this line of argument, we can calculate an *expected utility* (*EU*) for our individual homeowner for the two decisions available: buy fire insurance or do not buy it. Let us assume the individual's total wealth, including the home, is $80,000. If the individual *buys* insurance, the *EU* of this decision for the next year is

Event	Resulting Wealth, W	Utility	Probability	Product
No fire occurs	$79,300	0.54751	0.99	0.54204
Fire occurs	$79,050	0.54638	0.01	0.00546

Expected utility $= E[u(W)] = 0.54750$

If the individual *does not buy* insurance, the *EU* of this decision for the next year is

Event	Resulting Wealth, W	Utility	Probability	Product
No fire occurs	$80,000	0.55067	0.99	0.54516
Fire occurs	$20,000	0.18127	0.01	0.00181

Expected utility $E[u(W)] = 0.54697$

Thus, on the basis of the *EU,* we can explain the decision of an individual homeowner to buy fire insurance even though the *expected annual cost* is higher. Large corporations also make decisions that do not result in the lowest expected annual costs, especially when potential losses are high. Such decisions can also be explained on the basis of *EU.* The difference is the scale of the cash flows; the corporation that is a self-insurer when losses are $60,000 per retail outlet might obtain insurance from an outside source when a single loss could be $25 million.

It is important to distinguish between *risk* and *uncertainty. Risk* applies to situations for which the outcomes are not known with certainty but about which we do have good probability information. Subsequent analysis could then be based on *EMV* or on *EU. Uncertainty* applies to situations about which we do not even have good probability information. In such situations other analysis techniques are appropriate, and the reader is referred to Luca and Raiffa [16].

9.1.2 *Role of Utility Theory*

In the preceding section we used utility theory to reconcile actual behavior with *EMV* decision making. This role of utility theory can be expanded to include behavior that is seemingly irrational because information is incomplete, because individuals have difficulties in establishing ordinal measurement scales, and because multiple-objective functions have been maximized [6]. Empirical behavior of individuals has prompted economists to construct some unusual utility functions. For example, an individual may buy insurance, normally an expected loss in a situation the individual feels offers no other choice. The same individual may buy lottery tickets, virtually always an expected loss in a situation in which the individual *does* have a choice. This type of observed behavior has led economists to hypothesize a compound-shaped utility function [7].

Utility theory can be used to justify the time value of money, as applied in Parts One and Two of this book. Furthermore, by including the effects of uncertainty in the future, we can argue for a discount rate *greater* than the equity rate or the weighted-average cost of capital presented in Chapter 5.

A very important role of utility theory is in the justification of the mean–variance method for analyzing risky cash flows. This is presented in Section 9.5.

It is important to remember that utility theory is both a *prescriptive* and a *descriptive* approach to decision making. The theory tells us how individuals and corporations *should* make decisions, as well as predicting how they *do* make decisions. The *hypothesis* aspect of utility theory should not be forgotten.

9.1.3 *Alternative Approaches to Decision Making*

Two related approaches other than utility theory, have been presented as constructs for decision making. They are based on principles other than expected value with a discount rate based on cost of capital. The first approach uses a risk-adjusted discount rate [2, 10]. Investment projects are assigned to risk classes, based on the uncertainty of the component cash flows. Investments in a "safe" risk class are evaluated by using an interest rate based on cost of capital, whereas investments with more uncertain cash flows are evaluated by using a higher interest rate.

The second approach is based on the concept of general states of wealth at different points in time and the implicit trade-offs an individual or corporation might make among these states [8, 14]. Although conceptually appealing, this choice–theoretic approach is difficult to implement.

9.2 PREFERENCE AND ORDERING RULES

In this section we present the formal definition of utility theory as it is commonly interpreted by economists. The theory consists of two parts: the hypothesis about maximizing expected utility and the axioms of behavior.

9.2.1 Bernoulli Hypothesis

The basic hypothesis of utility theory is that individuals make decisions with respect to investments in order to *maximize expected utility* [3]. This concept is demonstrated by the following example.

Example 9.1

An individual with a utility function $u(W) = 1 - e^{-0.0001W}$ is faced with a choice between two alternatives. Alternative 1 is represented by the following probability distribution.

Cash Amount	$-10,000	0	10,000	20,000	30,000
Probability	0.2	0.2	0.2	0.2	0.2

Alternative 2 is a certain cash amount of $5,000. The individual has an initial wealth of zero, and no investment is required for either alternative. Which alternative would the individual prefer?

For alternative 1 the expected utility is computed as follows.

Wealth, W	Utility	Probability	Product
$-$10,000	-1.7183	0.2	-0.3437
0	0	0.2	0
10,000	0.6321	0.2	0.1264
20,000	0.8647	0.2	0.1729
30,000	0.9502	0.2	0.1900

Expected utility $= E[u(W)] = 0.1456$

For alternative 2 the utility is 0.3935. As this amount is greater than that for alternative 1, the certain cash amount of $5,000 is preferred to the risky alternative 1, which has a higher expected value of $10,000.

We can begin with the utility value of 0.1456 and determine a certain cash amount that is exactly equivalent to alternative 1.

$$0.1456 = 1 - e^{-0.0001W}$$

$$e^{-0.0001W} = 0.8544$$

Taking natural logarithms of both sides, we obtain

$$-0.0001W = -0.1574$$

$$W = \$1,574$$

The amount \$1,574 is called the *certainty equivalent* (*CE*) of alternative 1. Our individual would prefer any larger certain cash amount to alternative 1, would prefer alternative 1 to any smaller certain cash amount, and would be indifferent about a certain cash amount of \$1,574 and alternative 1. ☐

Definition. A *certainty equivalent* (*CE*) is a certain cash amount that an individual values as being as desirable as a particular risky option.

9.2.2 Axioms of Utility Theory

Individuals are assumed to obey the following rules of behavior in decision making [13, 17, 20].

Orderability. We can establish distinct preferences between any two alternatives. For example, given alternatives A and B, an individual prefers A to B, shown by $A > B$; prefers B to A, shown by $A < B$—we read the symbol $<$ as "is less preferred than"; or is indifferent about choosing between the two, shown by $A \sim B$.

Transitivity. The preferences established by ordering are transitive. If A is preferred to B, and B is preferred to C, then A is preferred to C.

$$A > B \quad \text{and} \quad B > C \quad \text{imply } A > C$$

In addition,

$$A \sim B \quad \text{and} \quad B \sim C \quad \text{imply } A \sim C$$

Continuity. If A is preferred to B and B is preferred to C, there exists a probability p so that the individual is indifferent between receiving B for certain and obtaining A with chance p and C with chance $(1 - p)$. The second alternative is called a lottery involving A and C.

$$A > B > C$$

implies that there exists a p so that

$$B \sim \{(p, A), (1 - p, C)\}$$

Example 9.2

Consider the individual with utility function $u(W) = 1 - e^{-0.0001W}$. Find the probability p so that the individual is indifferent between receiving $20,000 for certain and entering a lottery with chance p of $30,000 and $(1 - p)$ of $10,000. The individual's wealth is $10,000, and there is no cost for either alternative. The comparison is between $30,000 (the initial $10,000 plus $20,000) for certain, a utility of 0.9502, and a chance p of $40,000 and chance $(1 - p)$ of $20,000.

$$u(\$40,000) = 0.9817$$

$$u(\$20,000) = 0.8647$$

$$0.9502 = (p)(0.9817) + (1 - p)(0.8647)$$

Solving for p gives 0.731. □

Monotonicity. If two lotteries involve the same two alternatives A and B, the individual prefers the lottery in which the preferred alternative has the greater probability of occurring.

$$A > B \quad \text{implies}$$

$$\{(p, A), (1 - p, B)\} > \{(p', A), (1 - p', B)\}$$

if and only if $p > p'$.

Decomposability. A risky option containing another risky option may be reduced to its more fundamental components. This axiom, often called the "no fun in gambling" axiom, is best explained by an example.

Example 9.3

Consider a two-stage lottery. In stage 1 there is a 0.5 chance of stopping and receiving nothing and a 0.5 chance of advancing to stage 2. In stage 2 there is a 0.5 chance of receiving $5,000 and a 0.5 chance of receiving nothing. This lottery may be reduced to its one-stage equivalent of

$$\$0: \quad (0.5) + (0.5)(0.5) = 0.75 \text{ chance}$$

$$\$5,000: \quad (0.5)(0.5) \qquad = 0.25 \text{ chance} \quad □$$

Independence. A risky option A is preferred to a risky option B if and only if a $[p, (1 - p)]$ chance of A or C, respectively, is preferred to a $[p, (1 - p)]$ chance of B or C, for arbitrary chance p and risky options A, B, and C.

$$A > B$$

if and only if

$$\{(p, A), (1 - p, C)\} > \{(p, B), (1 - p, C)\}$$

for any p, A, B, and C.

The foregoing axioms have been used to derive the Bernoulli hypothesis [17, 20]. There are several different versions of the axioms. Some authors define additional ones or declare that some are embodied in others and thus superfluous.

Psychologists and behaviorally oriented economists each year write numerous papers describing experiments in which individuals systematically violate one or more of these axioms. It is not uncommon for such authors to propose a modification or elaboration of the theory [1, 4, 5, 11, 18]. This point brings us back to the *hypothesis* aspect of utility theory. The theory is an elegant mathematical way to describe real behavior, but it will always be at variance, more or less, with observed behavior.

9.3 PROPERTIES OF UTILITY FUNCTIONS

Most economists agree that an individual prefers more wealth to less. Hence, a utility function should be an *increasing*, or at the very least a *nondecreasing*, function of wealth. Other desirable properties are continuity (actually guaranteed by the axioms) and differentiability. The major question is about *risk avoidance* versus *risk seeking*.

9.3.1 Risk Attitudes

In all the examples presented so far in this chapter, the individual has been willing to accept a certain cash amount that is *less* than the *EMV* of a risky option. This type of behavior is described as *risk-averse*, or *risk-avoiding* behavior. Risk-averse utility functions, such as the one in Figure 9.1, are *concave* functions of wealth.

It has been suggested that some individuals exhibit *risk-seeking* behavior, as demonstrated by the following example.

Example 9.4

An individual is observed to buy a $5.00 lottery ticket each week. The possible prizes are represented by random variable X, and the chances of winning them are represented by probability p as follows.

$X =$		$p = 0.98889$
	No prize	
	$100 prize	0.01000
	$1,000 prize	0.00100
	$10,000 prize	0.00010
	$100,000 prize	0.00001

Explain the behavior of the individual.

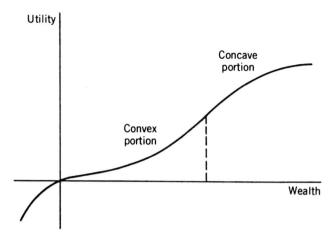

FIGURE 9.2. Utility function with a convex portion.

The *EMV* of such a lottery ticket is

$$E(X) = -5 + (0.98889)(0) + (0.01)(100) + (0.001)(1,000)$$
$$+ (0.0001)(10,000) + (0.00001)(100,000)$$
$$= -5 + 0 + 1 + 1 + 1 + 1$$
$$= -1$$

We may suggest two possible reasons for the individual to suffer the $1 expected loss each week. The first is that the purchase of a lottery ticket is a form of entertainment, similar to buying tickets to a sports event or a musical performance. The second, and more intriguing possibility, is suggested by the fact that poor people buy disproportionately more lottery tickets than middle-class and wealthy people, especially compared with other expenditures for entertainment. This fact has led many economists to suggest that the utility function for some persons may be *convex*, over a certain range of wealth, as shown in Figure 9.2. The rationale is that a poor person, in order to get out of his or her environment, is willing to take risks that a middle-class or wealthy person would not take [7]. □

We thus have a classification scheme for persons and their respective utility functions.

1. Risk-averse person: concave utility function.
2. Risk-neutral person: linear utility function.
3. Risk-seeking person: convex utility function.

Now let us reconsider the individual in Example 9.1 with utility function $u(W) = 1 - e^{-0.0001W}$. Assume that the individual has a starting wealth of $W_0 = \$20,000$ and is presented with the following lottery at no cost.

$$\{(0.5, \$10,000), (0.5, \$20,000)\}$$

773

The *CE* for the individual facing this lottery is obtained as follows.

Event, X	Resulting Wealth, W	Utility	Probability	Product
$10,000	$30,000	0.95021	0.5	0.47511
$20,000	$40,000	0.98168	0.5	0.49084

$$\text{Expected utility} = E[u(W)] = 0.96595$$

$$0.96595 = 1 - e^{-0.0001W}$$

$$e^{-0.0001W} = 0.03405$$

$$-0.0001W = -3.3798$$

$$CE = W = \$33,798$$

The difference between the *EMV* of $(0.5)(\$30,000) + (0.5)(\$40,000) = \$35,000$ and the *CE* of $33,798 is the *risk premium* (*RP*) the individual is willing to give up to avoid the risky option.

$$\text{Risk premium}, RP = \$35,000 - 33,798 = \$1,202$$

Definition [15].   A *risk premium* is an amount *RP* that solves Eq. 9.2.

$$E[u(W_0 + X)] = u[W_0 + E(X) - RP] \qquad (9.2)$$

where W_0 = the individual's wealth, a constant,

X = random variable representing the cash flow from a risky option,

RP = risk premium.

Here $W = W_0 + X$ is a random variable.

Let us recompute the *CE* for the previous lottery for an individual with the utility function of

$$u(W) = W - (0.00001)(W^2), \qquad 0 \leq W \leq 50,000 \qquad (9.3)$$

Event, X	Resulting Wealth, W	Utility	Probability	Product
$10,000	$30,000	21,000	0.5	10,500
$20,000	$40,000	24,000	0.5	12,000

$$\text{Expected utility} = E[u(W)] = 22,500$$

This corresponds to a *CE* of $34,190 (see Problem 9.7) and a corresponding *RP* of

$$RP = \$35,000 - 34,190 = \$810$$

The fact that the risk premium is different should not cause us much concern, since the utility functions for the two individuals are different. Let us recompute, however, the risk premiums for *both* individuals assuming an initial wealth of $W_0 = \$30,000$. For the individual with $u(W) = 1 - e^{-0.0001W}$, we have

Event, X	Resulting Wealth, W	Utility	Probability	Product
$10,000	$40,000	0.98168	0.5	0.49084
$20,000	$50,000	0.99326	0.5	0.49663

Expected utility = $E[u(W)] = 0.98747$

The *CE* is $43,796, which implies *RP* = $45,000 − $43,796 = $1,204. This amount is not much different from the previous $1,202. (It actually is the same.)

For the individual with the quadratic utility function, Eq. 9.3, and an initial wealth of $W_0 = \$30,000$, we obtain

Event, X	Resulting Wealth, W	Utility	Probability	Product
$10,000	$40,000	24,000	0.5	12,000
$20,000	$50,000	25,000	0.5	12,500

Expected utility = $E[u(W)] = 24,500$

The *CE* is $42,930, with a corresponding *RP* = $45,000 − $42,930 = $2,070.

The risk premium *increases* as the individual's wealth increases! In other words, the individual with the quadratic utility function is willing to give up *more* certain cash when faced with a risky option, as his or her wealth increases. Many economists argue that such behavior is not characteristic of intelligent investors. Instead, as their wealth increases, people should be willing to give up a *smaller* risk premium when faced with the same risky option.

9.3.2 Types of Utility Functions

Changes in the risk premium as a function of wealth are related to the behavior of the *risk aversion function* [21].

Definition. For a utility function u with first and second derivatives u' and u'', respectively, the *risk aversion function* is given by

$$r(W) = -u''(W)/u'(W) \qquad (9.4)$$

where W is wealth.

Specifically, if $r(W)$ is *decreasing* as a function of wealth, the risk premium (for a given risky option) decreases as a function of wealth. Similarly, an increasing $r(W)$ implies an increasing *RP*, and a constant $r(W)$ implies a constant *RP*.

A negative exponential function such as

$$u(W) = 1 - e^{-cW}, \qquad c > 0 \qquad (9.5)$$

has a constant risk aversion function, since

$$u'(W) = ce^{-cW} \qquad\qquad (9.5a)$$

$$u''(W) = -c^2 e^{-cW} \qquad\qquad (9.5b)$$

$$r(W) = c^2 e^{-cW}/(ce^{-cW}) \qquad\qquad (9.5c)$$

$$= c$$

This property makes the function appealing to analysts. One does not have to know the wealth of the decision maker to perform analysis regarding *CE*s and *RP*s.

A quadratic function such as

$$u(W) = W - aW^2, \qquad a > 0, \quad W \le 1/(2a) \qquad\qquad (9.6)$$

has an increasing risk aversion function, since

$$u'(W) = 1 - 2aW \qquad\qquad (9.6a)$$

$$u''(W) = -2a \qquad\qquad (9.6b)$$

$$r(W) = \frac{2a}{1 - 2aW} \qquad\qquad (9.6c)$$

and the denominator of Eq. 9.6c is less than 1.0.

In Section 9.3.1 we presented the classification of utility functions as follows.

1. Risk-averse person: concave utility function,

$$u''(W) < 0 \qquad\qquad (9.7a)$$

2. Risk-neutral person: linear utility function,

$$u''(W) = 0 \qquad\qquad (9.7b)$$

3. Risk-seeking person: convex utility function,

$$u''(W) > 0 \qquad\qquad (9.7c)$$

We can now add the subclassifications based on the risk aversion function, Eq. 9.4.

a. Decreasing risk aversion,

$$r'(W) < 0 \qquad\qquad (9.8a)$$

b. Constant risk aversion,

$$r'(W) = 0 \qquad\qquad (9.8b)$$

c. Increasing risk aversion,

$$r'(W) > 0 \qquad (9.8c)$$

An example of a risk-averse utility function with constant risk aversion is the negative exponential function given by Eq. 9.5. An example of a risk-averse utility function with increasing risk aversion is the quadratic function of Eq. 9.6. An example of a risk-averse function with decreasing risk aversion is the logarithmic function.

$$u(W) = \ln(W + d), \qquad d \geq 0 \qquad (9.9)$$

In addition, some utility functions have bounded functional values, and others are meaningful only over a bounded domain (range of wealth). Other characteristics are related to the *proportion* of wealth an individual would invest in a risky option [21].

Linear combinations of utility functions, where the weights are positive and all component utility functions have the same subclassification based on Eqs. 9.8a, b, and c, maintain that subclassification [21]. This property is useful when defining a utility function of present value. For example, we can define a utility function for cash F_n received in period n, when the utility is measured at time n.

$$u_n(F_n) = (F_n)^a, \qquad 0 < a < 1 \qquad (9.10)$$

A composite utility function for the vector of cash flows $(F_1, F_2, \ldots, F_n)$ can be expressed as

$$u(F_1, F_2, \ldots, F_n) = \sum_{n=1}^{N} \frac{(F_n)^a}{(1 + i)^n} \qquad (9.11)$$

Other functional forms are possible.

9.4 EMPIRICAL DETERMINATION OF UTILITY FUNCTIONS

9.4.1. General Procedure

The most popular way to determine a utility function is by the certainty equivalent method, whereby information from an individual is elicited by asking questions about lotteries [12]. Either a *numerical* or a *functional* approach can be followed. The numerical approach is presented first, for an individual with zero wealth.

The *numerical* approach requires two reference values for starting. Pick one as $0 with zero utility and one as $1,000 with utility 1.0.

$$u(0) = 0 \qquad (9.12a)$$

$$u(\$1,000) = 1.0 \qquad (9.12b)$$

Now present the individual with a lottery involving the nonzero reference point (there is no cost to play).

$$\{(p, \$1{,}000), (1 - p, -\$1{,}000)\} \tag{9.13}$$

The value p that makes the individual indifferent to the lottery results in the following relation.

$$(p)u(\$1{,}000) + (1 - p)u(-\$1{,}000) = u(0) = 0 \tag{9.14}$$

This is so because the individual values the lottery with p, the same as not playing, which is equivalent to the individual's current state of zero wealth. If, for example, a value of $p = 0.60$ makes the individual indifferent about playing, then substituting from Eq. 9.12, we have

$$(0.6)(1.0) + (0.4)u(-\$1{,}000) = 0$$
$$u(-\$1{,}000) = -1.5 \tag{9.15}$$

This gives us three value points, and we continue in a similar manner.

For example, we can present the individual with a choice between a certain cash amount of $1,000 and the following lottery.

$$\{(p, \$10{,}000), (1 - p, \$0)\} \tag{9.16}$$

The value p that causes the individual to be indifferent results in

$$(p)u(\$10{,}000) + (1 - p)u(0) = u(\$1{,}000) \tag{9.17}$$

If $p = 0.35$, for example, substituting and solving gives

$$(0.35)u(\$10{,}000) + (0.65)(0) = 1.0$$
$$u(\$10{,}000) = 2.86 \tag{9.18}$$

Continuing in this manner, we can develop a table as shown here and graphed in Figure 9.3.

Wealth (dollars)	Utility Value
$20,000	3.40
10,000	2.86
1,000	1.00
0	0
−1,000	−1.50
−2,000	−4.00

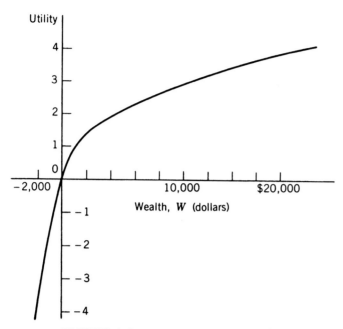

FIGURE 9.3. Typical empirically derived utility function.

The *functional* approach requires only one reference value for starting, most often $0 with zero utility. We also hypothesize the *functional* form. For example, assume the individual's utility function is Eq. 9.5,

$$u(W) = 1 - e^{-cW}, \quad c > 0 \tag{9.5}$$

Next, we present a lottery, such as Eq. 9.13, with no cost to play, and elicit the value p that makes the individual indifferent about playing. If the same value $p = 0.6$ is obtained, we have an equation with one unknown.

$$(0.6)[1 - e^{(-c)(1,000)}] + (0.4)[1 - e^{(-c)(-1,000)}] = 0$$

$$(0.6)(e^{-1,000c}) + (0.4)(e^{1,000c}) = 1 \tag{9.19}$$

This can be solved by trial and error for $c = 0.0004$. Thus, the specific form of Eq. 9.5 is

$$u(W) = 1 - e^{-0.0004W} \tag{9.20}$$

Determining utility functions must be done with extreme care, despite the apparent simplicity of these examples. Inconsistencies and irregular-shaped functions often result. Alternative forms of lotteries are recommended by some to reduce bias in the information-gathering process [19].

9.4.2 Sample Results

In this section we present empirical results for the bids in two lottery games.

Game 1: A number of individuals (more than 10) submit sealed bids for the right to play a lottery.

$$\{(0.5, \$50), (0.5, -\text{bid})\} \qquad (9.21)$$

The highest bidder *must* play the lottery.

Game 2: A number of individuals (more than 10) submit sealed bids for the right to play the St. Petersburg game [3]. The highest bidder *must* play. In the St. Petersburg game a coin is tossed repeatedly until it turns up "heads." The payoff is

$$\$(2)^{n-1} \qquad (9.22)$$

where n is the first time heads appears. This compound lottery is equivalent to the simple lottery of

$$\{(0.5, \$1), (0.25, \$2), (0.125, \$4), \ldots, [(0.5)^n, (2)^{n-1}], \ldots\} \qquad (9.23)$$

The lottery 9.23 has an infinite number of outcomes, and its *EMV* is infinity.

$$EMV = E(X) = (0.5)(1) + (0.25)(2) + (0.125)(4) + \cdots$$
$$= 0.5 + 0.5 + 0.5 + \cdots$$

Table 9.1 shows the results of the bids made by graduate engineering students during the early 1980s. The bidders are ordered by ascending game 1 bids and, for equal game 1 bids, by ascending game 2 bids. Some of the low bids clearly reflect the artificiality of a classroom situation, or perhaps the cash amount in the pocket of a student. Similar artificial distortions can exist in a corporate environment, however, where one may be trying to calibrate a utility function by posing lottery games.

Except for the very low bids of reluctant players, the game 1 bids jump in increments of $5 or more. The lack of bids in amounts of $17 and $22, for example, might lead us to question the continuity axiom. It is apparent that some game 1 bidders—those whose bids were at least $20 (bidders 25 to 31)—thought seriously about the possibility of playing the lottery. With the exception of the highest bidder (who was willing to accept an *EMV* of zero), all showed fairly strong risk aversion. This type of result was expected.

The game 2 bids are more interesting but not so much for the degree of risk aversion shown, which was also expected. Rather, it is interesting to compare the two bids made by the same individual. For example, bidder 27 bid $25 for game 1 and $0.5 for game 2. The $0.5 bid for game 2 is equal to the first payoff in *EMV* terms, so the individual either reflects an unusual utility function or has difficulties assessing probabilities and *EMV* and *EU*. Similar low bids for game 2 were made by bidders 25 and 26. Bidders 18 and 22 offered unusually large sums to play game 2—$12 and $20, respectively.

Such difficulties in assessing *EMV* and *EU,* with resulting inconsistencies, are likely to be experienced by most individuals in society. Recall that the bids

Table 9.1 *Results of Bids for Two Lottery Games*

Bidder	Game 1 Bid	Game 2 Bid
1–5	$1	$1
6	1	2
7	1.5	1
8	2	1
9, 10	2	2
11	5	1
12, 13	5	2
14–17	5	5
18	5	12
19	10	2
20	10	4
21	10	5
22	10	20
23	15	2
24	15	4
25, 26	20	1
27	25	0.5
28	25	2.5
29	25	4
30	40	3
31	50	4

were made by engineering students with some formal training in probability and statistics. Experiments conducted elsewhere show similar inconsistencies [11, 19]. Thus, the application of utility theory must be performed with great care and caution.

9.5 MEAN–VARIANCE ANALYSIS

The *EMV* and *EU* approaches are based on probabilistic expectation over the range of possible outcomes of a risky option. In this section we present arguments for methods that are operationally different but are still based on utility concepts. These operational methods are, in general, more popular and easier to use. Therefore, a theoretical justification is attractive from a modeling point of view. We outline the main arguments and refer the interested reader to detailed sources.

9.5.1 Indifference Curves

Take the view of an investor with a quadratic utility function, as in Eq. 9.3, facing a set of alternative lotteries,

$$\{(p, 0), (1 - p, \$X)\}$$

Table 9.2 *Lotteries Toward Which an Individual Might Be Indifferent*

p	$1 - p$	X	$E(X)$	$Var(X)$, 10^6
0	1.0	$10,000	$10,000	0
0.4375	0.5625	20,000	11,250	98.4
0.5714	0.4286	30,000	12,857	220.4
0.6250	0.3750	40,000	15,000	375.0
0.6400	0.3600	50,000	18,000	576.0

NOTES: 1. Lotteries are of type

$$\{(p, 0), (1 - p, \$X)\}$$

2. Utility function is

$$u(W) = W - (0.00001)W^2, \quad W \le 50,000$$

3. All lotteries have the same $CE = \$10,000$.

with X in the range $10,000 to $50,000. Table 9.2 shows the lotteries, along with $E(X)$ and $Var(X)$. The $Var(X)$ is the second moment about the mean. It is equal to $E(X^2) - [E(X)]^2$. (See Section 10.2.1 for a more detailed explanation.)

These $E(X)$ and $Var(X)$ values are plotted as curve U_1 in Figure 9.4. The lotteries in Table 9.2 have been constructed so that all have a CE of $10,000; each lottery has the same utility value, and the individual with utility $W - (0.00001)W^2$ would view them indifferently. Curve U_1 in Figure 9.4 can thus be interpreted as an indifference function relating $E(X)$ and $Var(X)$. Each combination of $E(X)$, $Var(X)$ on curve U_1 has the same utility value.

We could construct other sets of lotteries in which all in a set would have the same utility value. The result would be a family of curves $U_1, U_2, U_3, U_4, \ldots$, one curve corresponding to each set of lotteries. Higher curves represent higher utility values.

Points A and B on curve U_3 are valued the same by the individual. A point like C or D that is not on the same curve does not have the same utility as point A. Point C is considered less desirable than point A because it has the same $E(X)$ but a higher $Var(X)$. On the other hand, point D is preferred to point A because for the same $Var(X)$ it has a higher $E(X)$. Point B is preferred to point C because of higher $E(X)$ *and* lower $Var(X)$, but by the same reasoning point D is preferred to point B. These preference rules are specified in greater detail in Chapter 11. A formal analysis [22] along these lines shows that the mean–variance approach is justified when the investor's utility function is quadratic and the probability distributions of X can be characterized by only two parameters (e.g., normal, lognormal).

9.5.2 Coefficient of Risk Aversion

We may observe some characteristics of the utility curves in Figure 9.4. First, the intersection point of a curve with the vertical $E(X)$ axis represents the

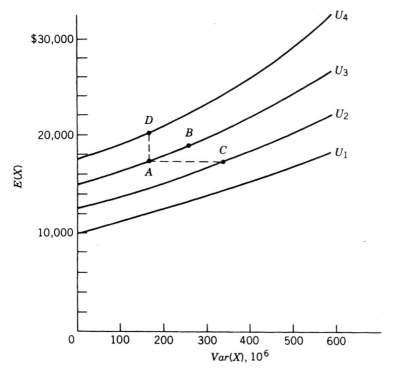

FIGURE 9.4. Utility indifference curves relating $E(X)$ and $Var(X)$.

certainty equivalent for all the points on that curve. Since such an intersection point has zero $Var(X)$, the cash outcome is certain. Second, the curves have positive slope. This reflects the fact that utility is an *increasing* function of $E(X)$ and a *decreasing* function of $Var(X)$. Third, the curves are concave. One way to explain the concavity of the indifference curves is that as risk increases, much larger increases in $E(X)$ are necessary to maintain the same level of utility for risk-averse individuals.

An approximation to the set of curves in Figure 9.4 might appear as in Figure 9.5. Here all the utility curves are linear and parallel. In Figure 9.5 we can obtain the CE of any point, such as Point D, as follows.

$$CE_D = E(D) - \lambda \, Var(D) \tag{9.24}$$

The value λ is called the *coefficient of risk aversion* (or sometimes the *risk aversion factor*). It measures the trade-off between $E(X)$ and $Var(X)$. This means that a CE is easier to calculate when λ is known.

Even if the linear approximation in Figure 9.5 is not appropriate, we can define λ as the *tangent* to a utility indifference curve in Figure 9.4. The value of the coefficient of risk aversion is then reasonably valid over a restricted interval. For known functional utility forms, expressions for λ as a function of the cash outcomes can be developed [9]. In practice, if we are not confident with assuming a single value of λ, then λ is varied parametrically (see Appendix 11A).

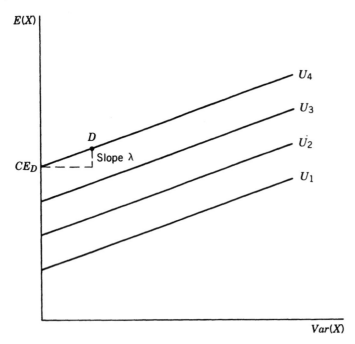

FIGURE 9.5. Approximation of indifference curves in Figure 9.4.

9.5.3 Justification of Certainty Equivalent Method

Applying Eq. 9.24 to a periodic cash flow F_n, which may be a random variable, we have

$$V_n = E(F_n) - \lambda\, Var(F_n) \tag{9.25}$$

For a series of cash flows from a project, we have in the simplest case, where λ is time-invariant and the F_n are independent random variables,

$$PV(i) = \sum_{n=0}^{N} \frac{V_n}{(1 + i)^n}$$

$$= \sum_{n=0}^{N} \frac{E(F_n) - \lambda\, Var(F_n)}{(1 + i)^n} \tag{9.26}$$

Here the interest rate i is a *risk-free* rate, which accounts for only the time value of money. This risk-free rate can be viewed as a rate at which the individual can always invest money in some risk-free projects (such as a short-term government bond). This is the amount forgone if the project is undertaken and a net income is received from the risk-free project. Thus, having a present value of the certainty equivalents greater than zero means that the project is acceptable to this investor.

Example 9.5

To illustrate the procedures involved in calculating the present value of certainty equivalents, let us examine a 5-year project with $E(F_n)$ and $Var(F_n)$ as shown in

784

the tabulation. We assume that the λ value is known to be 0.02 for this investor. Then the certainty equivalents for the periodic random cash flows F_n are

n	$E(F_n)$	$Var(F_n)$	V_n	$PV(10\%)$
0	-400	400	-408	-408.00
1	120	100	118	107.27
2	120	225	115.5	95.45
3	120	400	112	84.15
4	110	900	92	62.84
5	120	2500	70	43.46

$$\Sigma = -\$14.83$$

Since the total present value of the certainty equivalents is negative, the investor would reject the project. □

Returning to the general case, let us assume that the utility function for cash flows distributed over time is

$$u = \sum_{n=0}^{N} c_n u_n \tag{9.27}$$

where u_n is a utility function for the random cash flow F_n occurring at time n and c_n is a constant. This expression implies that contributions to total utility are additive over time, and periodic utility values are multiplied by the constant c_n to adjust for the time preference of the events F_n. The exact form of the periodic utility functions u_n is not specified. In fact, u_n could be different functions over time or, in the simplest case, time-invariant. For our discussion, let us assume that $u_n = u_1$ for all n. A Taylor expansion can be used to generate a reasonable approximation to an expected utility function [20].

$$E(u_n) = u_n[E(F_n)] + u_n^{(2)}[E(F_n)] \, Var(F_n)/2 \tag{9.28}$$

This expression is obtained by adopting "sufficient approximation" reasoning to justify ignoring the higher moments about the mean of the cash flow in the Taylor series. If the utility function is a quadratic, however, any term $u_n^{(n)}$ (nth derivative of u_n) with $n > 3$ will be zero. Thus Eq. 9.28 becomes the exact expression of the expected utility measure. Further, the term $u_n^{(2)}$ becomes a constant for the quadratic utility function. Thus, rewriting Eq. 9.28 gives us the expression

$$E(u_n) = u_n[E(F_n)] + A_n \, Var(F_n) \tag{9.29}$$

where

$$A_n = u_n^{(2)}[E(F_n)]/2 \tag{9.30}$$

Returning to the total utility function given in Eq. 9.27 and taking the expected value of each side of the equation, we obtain

$$E(u) = \sum_{n=0}^{N} c_n E(u_n) \tag{9.31}$$

Substituting Eq. 9.29 into Eq. 9.31 yields

$$E(u) = \sum_{n=0}^{N} c_n u_n [E(F_n)] + \sum_{n=0}^{N} c_n A_n \, Var(F_n) \tag{9.32}$$

If a certainty equivalent can be found for each time period so that

$$u_n(V_n) = u_n[E(F_n)] + A_n \, Var(F_n) \tag{9.33}$$

the present value of this set of certainty equivalents will be equal to the expected utility of the cash flows from the investment project by letting $c_n = 1/(1 + i)^n$ [20].

9.6 SUMMARY

Utility theory is a very important concept because it helps to reconcile real behavior with expected monetary value in decision making. The typical individual has a concave utility function, reflecting an aversion to risk, which is usually measured by the variance of the cash flow. The axioms of utility theory can be used to derive the Bernoulli hypothesis of expected utility maximization. Validation experiments reveal, however, that this hypothesis is not perfectly true.

Operationally, the utility indifference curves that relate $E(X)$ and $Var(X)$ provide the theoretical basis for the popular mean–variance analysis presented in Chapter 11. The coefficient of risk aversion, heavily used in portfolio analysis, is the slope of the indifference curve. Finally, the discounted sum of certainty equivalents is shown to be an approximation (exact for quadratic utility) to the expected utility of a random future cash flow stream. All these results will be used in later chapters.

REFERENCES

1. BECKER, J., and R. K. SARIN, "Lottery Dependent Utility," *Management Science,* Vol. 33, No. 11, pp. 1367–1382, 1987.

2. BERNHARD, R. H., "Risk-Adjusted Values, Timing of Uncertainty Resolution, and the Measurement of Project Worth," *Journal of Financial and Quantitative Analysis,* Vol. 19, No. 1, pp. 83–99, 1984.

3. BERNOULLI, D., "Exposition of a New Theory of the Measurement of Risk," *Econometrica,* Vol. 22, No. 1, pp. 23–36, 1954. (Accessible translation of "Specimen Theoriae Novae de Mensura Sortis," 1738.)

4. Brockett, P. L., and L. L. Golden, "A Class of Utility Functions Containing All the Common Utility Functions," *Management Science,* Vol. 33, No. 8, pp. 955–964, 1987.

5. Currim, I. S., and R. K. Sarin, "Prospect Versus Utility," *Management Science,* Vol. 35, No. 1, pp. 22–41, 1989.

6. Edwards, E., "The Theory of Decision Making," *Psychological Bulletin,* Vol. 51, No. 4, pp. 380–417, 1954.

7. Friedman, M., and L. J. Savage, "The Utility Analysis of Choices Involving Risk," *Journal of Political Economy,* Vol. 56, No. 4, pp. 279–304, 1948.

8. Hirshleifer, J., "Investment Decision under Uncertainty: Choice-Theoretic Approaches," *Quarterly Journal of Economics,* Vol. 79, No. 4, pp. 509–536, 1965.

9. Jean, W. H., *The Analytical Theory of Finance,* Holt, Rinehart and Winston, New York, 1970.

10. Johnson, W., *Capital Budgeting,* Wadsworth, Belmont, Calif., 1970, Ch. 5.

11. Kahneman, D., and A. Tversky, "Prospect Theory: An Analysis of Decision under Risk," *Econometrica,* Vol. 47, pp. 263–291, 1979.

12. Keeney, R. L., and H. Raiffa, *Decisions with Multiple Objectives; Preferences and Value Tradeoffs,* Wiley, New York, 1976.

13. Keller, L. R., "Testing of the 'Reduction of Compound Alternatives' Principle," *OMEGA, International Journal of Management Science,* Vol. 13, No. 4, pp. 349–358, 1985.

14. Lavalle, I. H., and P. C. Fishburn, "Decision Analysis under States-Additive SSB Preferences," *Operations Research,* Vol. 35, No. 5, pp. 722–735, 1987.

15. Levy, H., and M. Sarnat, *Portfolio and Investment Selection: Theory and Practice,* Prentice–Hall, Englewood Cliffs, N.J., 1984.

16. Luce, D. R., and H. Raiffa, *Games and Decisions: Introduction and Critical Survey,* Wiley, New York, 1957.

17. Machina, M. J., "A Stronger Characterization of Declining Risk Aversion," *Econometrica,* Vol. 50, No. 4, pp. 1069–1079, 1982.

18. Machina, M. J., "Decision-Making in the Presence of Risk," *Science,* Vol. 236, pp. 537–543, 1 May 1987.

19. McCord, M., and R. de Neufville, "'Lottery Equivalents' Reduction of the Certainty Effect Problem in Utility Assessment," *Management Science,* Vol. 32, No. 1, pp. 56–61, 1986.

20. Neumann, J. V., and O. Morgenstern, *Theory of Games and Economic Behavior,* 2nd edition, Princeton University Press, Princeton, N.J., 1947.

21. Pratt, J. W., "Risk Aversion in the Small and in the Large," *Econometrica,* Vol. 32, No. 1–2, pp. 122–136, 1964.

22. Tobin, J., "Liquidity Preference as Behavior toward Risk," *Review of Economic Studies,* No. 67, pp. 65–85, February 1958.

PROBLEMS

9.1. Consider the homeowner in Section 9.1.1 with the utility function given by Eq. 9.1. If the deductible amount on a loss is higher than $250, the homeowner might prefer not to buy fire insurance, on an *EU* basis. Using the data in Section 9.1.1 for other factors, determine the deductible amount that would make the homeowner *indifferent* about choosing between buying and not buying insurance, on an *EU* basis.

9.2. For an individual with zero initial wealth and a utility function

$$u(W) = 1 - e^{-0.0001W}$$

find the *CE* for each of the following alternatives (probabilities of the outcomes are given).

| | Cash Amount | | | | |
Alternative	-$10,000	0	$10,000	$20,000	$30,000
1	0.1	0.2	0.4	0.2	0.1
2	0.1	0.2	0.3	0.3	0.1
3	0	0.3	0.4	0	0.3
4	0	0.15	0.65	0	0.2
5	0.5	0	0	0	0.5

9.3. Solve Example 9.2 for the situation in which the individual's initial wealth is $20,000. Would you expect the probability to change as the initial wealth changes?

9.4. Consider a three-stage lottery. In the first stage there are a 0.2 chance of receiving $1,000 and a 0.8 chance of going on to stage 2. In stage 2 there are a 0.5 chance of receiving $2,000 and a 0.5 chance of going on to stage 3. In stage 3 there are a 0.2 chance of receiving $1,000, a 0.3 chance of receiving $2,000, and a 0.5 chance of receiving $5,000. Reduce this three-stage lottery to an equivalent one-stage lottery.

9.5. Construct a compound lottery and reduce it to its equivalent one-stage lottery.

9.6. Obtain information about a lottery. Calculate the *EMV* of the act of purchasing a ticket.

9.7. Derive the *CE* for an individual with initial wealth $20,000 and a quadratic utility function as given by Eq. 9.3, when facing the lottery {(0.5, $10,000), (0.5, $20,000)}. There is no cost for the lottery. Show all computations.

9.8. Can you specify a risk-seeking utility function with decreasing risk aversion? With constant risk aversion? With increasing risk aversion?

9.9. Conduct a lottery game of the type described in Section 9.4.2. Analyze the results for consistency.

9.10. Construct a set of lotteries, each with the same *CE* and similar to the ones in Table 9.2, to derive one of the higher utility curves in Figure 9.4.

9.11. Construct a set of lotteries, each with the same *CE* and similar to the ones in Table 9.2, but using the utility function given by Eq. 9.1. What is the shape of the indifference curve?

9.12. Using the worksheet provided, develop your utility function. In doing so, consider the following steps.

> **Step 1:** Find the certainty equivalent amount *B* for a given lottery (*A* or zero with 0.5 probability each). Once the amounts *A* and *B* are specified, find the certainty equivalent amount *C* for a new lottery (*B* or zero with 0.5 probability each). Continue this procedure for the remaining lotteries. You are likely to find some inconsistencies in the certainty equivalent amounts assessed. Resolve these inconsistencies by reassessing the certainty equivalent amounts.

> **Step 2:** Scale the certainty equivalent amounts (*A* through *J*) as a percentage of *A*. For example, if *A* = $1,000 and *B* = $300, then *A* = 100% of *A* and *B* = 30% of *A*.

Step 3: Plot the scaling preferences on the chart provided and smooth the curve when connecting the points plotted.

WORKSHEET FOR DETERMINING THE UTILITY FUNCTION

Certainty Equivalent

1	A _____ or zero	vs. B _____
2	B _____ or zero	vs. C _____
3	C _____ or zero	vs. D _____
4	A _____ or E _____	vs. zero
5	E _____ or zero	vs. F _____
6	F _____ or zero	vs. G _____
7	A _____ or F _____	vs. H _____
8	C _____ or E _____	vs. J _____

Scaling Preference

	Amount	%A	U
A			+8
B			+4
C			+2
D			+1
E			−8
F			−4
G			−2
H			+2
J			−3

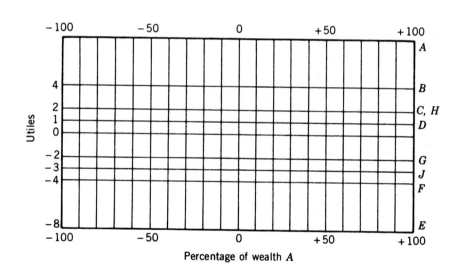

Index

Tables

9 780470 436196

ISBN 978-0-470-43619-6

90000>